AN INTRODUCTION TO AMERICAN GOVERNMENT

FIFTH
EDITION

AN INTRODUCTION TO AMERICAN GOVERNMENT

KENNETH PREWITT

Rockefeller Foundation

SIDNEY VERBA

Harvard University

ROBERT H. SALISBURY

Washington University

1817

HARPER & ROW, PUBLISHERS
New York

Cambridge   Philadelphia   San Francisco   Washington
London   Mexico City   São Paulo   Singapore   Sydney

Sponsoring Editor: Robert Miller
Project Editor: Jo-Ann Goldfarb
Text Design: Rafael H. Hernandez
Cover Design: Robert Bull/Design
Cover Photo: U.S. Capitol, Washington, D.C. © Rick Buettner 1986/Folio, Inc.
Text Art: Vantage Art, Inc.
Photo Research: Mira Schachne
Production: Willie Lane
Compositor: Arcata Graphics/Kingsport
Printer and Binder: Arcata Graphics/Kingsport

An Introduction to American Government, *Fifth Edition*

Library of Congress Cataloging-in-Publication Data
Prewitt, Kenneth.
    An introduction to American government.

    1. United States—Politics and government. I. Verba,
Sidney. II. Salisbury, Robert Holt, 1930–
III. Title.
JK274.P76 1986   320.973   86–18365
ISBN 0-06-045326-5

88 89 9 8 7 6 5 4 3 2

CONTENTS
IN BRIEF

CONTENTS

PREFACE

Politics and government are vivid and immediate to the citizen—at least to the citizen who pays attention to such matters. This is a world of current events, controversies, and crises found in the morning newspaper and on the evening television news. The president makes a speech on nuclear arms, meets with congressional leaders on the budget, leaves on a trip, or returns from one. Congressional leaders meet, speak, decide, or avoid decisions. The Supreme Court hands down a ruling on a major case. A governor takes one action; a city council takes another.

There is no shortage of information about politics. Attentive citizens can get more than they can absorb. What is in short supply is understanding: Why are things happening the way they are? Why are some decisions made and others avoided? Is the Supreme Court decision a new departure? What are its implications? Good journalism provides interpretation of the facts in the daily news; it tries to put things in perspective. But journalism sticks close to the immediate, with the goal of providing insight into the events of the day; the understanding sought is specific.

The political world of the scholar is different. The scholar seeks a more general understanding, abstracted from the specifics of a particular time and a particular place. There are many ways to seek such general knowledge: through studies with a broad historical sweep, through statistical studies of more current data, or through complex analyses using more or less formal frameworks and theories. Often this is very far from the day-to-day political world. The work of the scholar sometimes seems irrelevant to citizens or political practitioners, who want something that clarifies the real issues and situations they face. Yet is just such general scholarly understanding that can clarify the real world—indeed, its ultimate validation is in its ability to do so.

The task of an introductory textbook in American politics is to bridge the gap between scholarly studies of politics and the world of immediate political events. An introduction to American politics will fail the student if it merely repeats and elaborates on current events. The student may understand current events better but be ill prepared for the different events of tomorrow when the course has ended. On the other hand, the student is right to expect that a text will not remain at the abstract level of political science research. The material may derive from such a source, but it must be made relevant to the world of politics. We have taken that as our task.

We present neither a single political perspective nor a single scholarly perspective. Ours is not a "point-of-view" text, interpreting American politics from a political position on the left or the right. Nor do we argue a specific scholarly theory of politics. Rather, we think of politics itself as well as the scholarly study of politics as open matters. We stress in the text that there are many different political viewpoints in America and many alternative ways of interpreting politics. We try to provide structure and clarity, but we do not provide neat packages and solutions.

In preparing the fifth edition of our textbook, we have made a number of important changes. We have tried, of course, to bring the material up to date—to reflect recent developments in American politics and society and to incorporate recent research. More fundamentally, we have gone a step further along the path we began in our last edition by giving greater attention to the basic institutions of American government and by emphasizing the many ways in which the rules of the governmental process affect the public-policy results.

Part Four of this edition, "The System In Action," has been substantially rewritten in order to expand the treatment of the institutional arrangements of the national government. We have tried to show that these institutions are occupied by real people, whether politicians, public leaders, judges, or what have you. These people have values and commitments of their own and, at the same time, their actions in office respond to the demands, needs, interests, and pressures of groups throughout the nation. Although we must separate the chapters that deal with political participation, citizen beliefs, interest groups, political parties, elections, and the mass media from those that examine the policymaking process, we have tried to emphasize the interdependence between these two broad components of "the system."

The central theme of the first editions of this book was political economy—the interaction of the political system and the socioeconomic structures of society. It remains our basic concern. It should be apparent to any reader of the daily paper that budgets and taxes and economic regulations and subsidies constitute much of the agenda of the political system and that the actions (and inactions) of government are of massive shaping effect on the economy and the society. In going about the task of revision we have tried to illustrate this basic theme and to use it to present material so that its meaning would be less that of a general truth and more that of a daily politicoeconomic reality.

In this edition we have added a chapter on the mass media (Chapter 12) so as to present more information about them and invite discussion on their operations and the role they play in the political process. We have revised and relocated two chapters. The present Chapter 6, dealing with civil liberties, we have placed next to our treatment of equality and civil rights so as to give a more integrated treatment to those topics. The present Chapter 13, an introduction to the policymaking process, is a much-revised version of its "ancestor" chapter and has been placed in front of the chapters that treat the institutions of the national government rather than following them. The new chapter is designed to introduce and orient the student to the policy process and to emphasize that when the institutions are in action they are making policy—that is, deciding who will get what and other matters of great importance to each of us.

PEDAGOGICAL INNOVATIONS

In developing this edition we have introduced some new features. We have developed seven brief case studies of policymaking that we call "Institutions in Action." These are not intended to give the student a comprehensive grasp of the policy areas but to illustrate, in the context of a particular policy issue, the operation of some important elements of the institutional structures of government. We have also included a set of "Profiles," brief biographical sketches of some of the major figures, past and present, who have had especially important influences on the American polity. Finally, we have expanded our use of tables, graphs, and photographic illustrations to convey information that we think will be helpful to students seeking to understand how the American system works.

With the Fifth Edition we have made available manuals for further support for students and instructor. The *Study Guide* by Sandra L. Quinn and Freddy G. Musgrove, both of San Jacinto College, helps students to understand and review the text and provides practice tests in the form of short-answer, fill-in-the-blank, multiple choice, and essay questions. The new *Instructor's Manual* and *Test Bank* are both by Larry Elowitz of Georgia College. The *Instructor's Manual* includes chapter outlines, synopses, ideas for classroom activities, and teaching suggestions. The *Test Bank* includes true/false, multiple choice, completion, and essay questions.

ACKNOWLEDGMENTS

In preparing this edition our partnership has expanded to three. The new material reflects this expansion, but the total result is very much a collaborative effort. We want to thank the many people who have made contributions to the fifth edition of the book. Colleagues who have provided critical comment are as follows: F. Glenn Abney, Georgia State University; Danny Adkison, Oklahoma State University; Lewis Bowman, University of South Florida; John Cabe, Tri-County Community College; Babalola Cole, Howard University; Stephen Craig, University of Florida, Gainesville; James Eisenstein, Pennsylvania State University; Larry Elowitz, Georgia College; Michael Fuller, Miami University, Oxford; Terry Gilbreth, Ohio Northern University; Walter R. Giles, Georgetown University; Emily Gill, Bradley University; William Hall, Bradley University; Richard Hoffstetter, San Diego State University; Marianne Jameson, Texas Southern University; George Kacewicz, California State University, Long Beach; Fred Mabbutt, Santa Ana College; Tom McMichael, Oscar Rose Junior College; Roseanne Mirabella, Human Resources Administration, New York (formerly of Ohio University); Robert Monson, University of Arkansas; Jim Morrow, Tulsa Junior

College; Alana Northrup, California State University, Fullerton; Sandra Quinn, San Jacinto College South; Brian Radar, Northeastern State University; Gholan Razi, University of Houston; Richard K. Scher, University of Florida, Gainesville; Ofira Seliktar, University of Pennsylvania; Goldie Shabad, Ohio State University; William D. Spear, Eastern Oregon State College; William Thomas, Georgia State University; and Tinsley Yarbrough, East Carolina University. We also want to thank Marilyn Schad, who was immensely helpful in the process of manuscript preparation for this edition.

KENNETH PREWITT
SIDNEY VERBA
ROBERT H. SALISBURY

AN
INTRODUCTION
TO AMERICAN
GOVERNMENT

George Washington presiding over the Constitutional Convention, Philadelphia, 1787

THE BASIC SYSTEM

The 1985 Inauguration of President Reagan

Chapter 1

GOVERNMENT AND POLITICS IN A DEMOCRACY

W e start this textbook with some very basic and difficult questions. Why do societies find it necessary to have a government? Are not governments coercive, even tyrannical at times? Do they not capture in taxes some of the hard-earned income of a population? Are they not large and often clumsy bureaucracies? Given such a list of liabilities, why have a government?

If there is a reasonable answer to the first set of questions, and this text tries to provide one, why is there so much disagreement over what governments ought to do? In short, what causes politics? Politics is commonly defined as the struggle to control the allocation of benefits and costs brought about by government policies. Using the powers of government to make things happen will seldom benefit all citizens equally. Disagreement, then, exists over who is going to benefit and who is going to pay for those benefits.

How does democracy affect government and politics in the United States? All societies have governments, and all societies have political disagreements over what their governments should do, but some societies, like that of the United States, organize their governments according to the doctrine of democracy. This doctrine calls for the active participation of all citizens in the making of laws which affect them.

While this chapter cannot tell us all that we need to know about government, politics, and democracy, it will introduce some basic ideas. These ideas will be elaborated upon when we turn to the Constitution, Congress, elections, interest groups, and other topics.

A Parable for Our Times

In a small, midwestern town there is a busy downtown area that most elementary school children cross to get from their homes to the schoolyard. This town was proud that for 17 years there had not been a single car accident involving a schoolchild. Each May the school patrol was given a special award dinner in honor of another accident-free year. Only a few citizens, those particularly active in school affairs, understood that the school patrol was trained and supervised by a retired police officer, who was paid a small salary by the school board.

One year there was a "tax revolt" in the town, and legislation was passed to reduce the property taxes by 25 percent. School authorities, like administrators of other government programs in town, had to reduce their budget. Few people realized that one of the less costly items to be cut was the salary for the retired police officer who trained the school patrol each year.

The following year was the eighteenth accident-free year, and the annual school patrol dinner was held on schedule. Due to budget reductions, hot dogs were served instead of fried chicken, but the patrol enjoyed itself as much as always.

On a gray November day the following year, two 8-year-old boys, one of them in the school patrol, had a scuffle after school. Without anyone quite sure how it happened, a delivery truck backed out of a narrow alley and ran over one of the boys. He suffered serious back injuries that would probably cripple him for life.

For the next several weeks, the local newspaper printed letters to the editor from the town's citizens about the accident. One of the first things that became clear was how important the role of the retired police officer had been in training and supervising the school patrol. Here are two letters that the newspaper carried.

Dear Editor:

I am a parent, and I am furious. My son's best friend was needlessly crippled, and blame should be assigned where blame is due; on all those who didn't think about what would have to be cut from the school budget when they so happily voted for a tax reduction. These are the people who say, "Well, government cannot be responsible for everything and everyone." What do we have a government for, if not to protect its citizens, especially those too young to protect themselves? When citizens cannot easily provide for their own security, the government has a responsibility.

A Concerned Parent

Dear Editor:

The accident last week was a tragedy for the boy and his family. But who can say that it would not have happened however the school patrol had been supervised. We cannot afford a government that guards every street corner and watches over every schoolchild. Parents have to teach safety rules to their own children. Individual responsibility has to start somewhere.

A Taxpayer

Debates about the proper role of government, and the balance between individual responsibility and collective effort, are as old as organized society. These debates try to answer not only the question "Why have government?" but the more complicated question "What should governments do?" This political debate in a small, midwestern town about the government's responsibility for the safety of children walking home after school is echoed at all levels of our government where broader questions of national security, economic policy, and social welfare are debated.

WHAT IS A GOVERNMENT?

The dictionary definitions of the word *government* emphasize two elements. One is the idea of control or rule. Government involves the exercise of authority by some people (officials) over others (subjects or citizens). The second element is the concept of office or institution. Government consists of a set of institutions possessing the authority to rule. That means that if we are to understand how any particular government operates, we must study the governmental institutions and how they function. We will do so in later chapters of this book.

Also implied by our definition of government is the notion of coercion. Those who rule must, if necessary, be able to force compliance with their policies. Otherwise they would be regarded not as rulers or governors but only as advocates of some point of view trying to persuade others to agree with them. Genuine government is backed by force, and this immediately leads us to ask whether that force is justified. Why do people who occupy official positions in government have the right to tell the citizens what to do? This is an ancient and fundamental question; yet it is as fresh and vital as this year's tax bill or today's traffic ticket.

In the United States the most important answer to the question of what justifies governmental authority is *consent of the governed.* Numerous other arguments have been advanced through the many centuries of debate over political philosophy, including the divine right of kings, the alleged superior wisdom of a governing class, and the pragmatic test of the economic well-being of the people. For Americans, however, from the Mayflower Compact through the U.S. Constitution itself down to the latest referendum vote on a city charter, popular consent has been the basis for legitimate governmental authority.

Legitimacy

Efforts to understand the power of the state often start with a definition made famous by a German sociologist Max Weber: The state is the institution in society that has a *legitimate* monopoly over force. By legitimate we mean that people accept the exercise of force as right and proper. A parent spanking a child is exercising legitimate force. A stranger who attempts to punish the child for the same behavior is not acting legitimately.

When we speak of the legitimate powers of the state, we include the right of the state to hire and arm police, to build and fill prisons, and to punish wrongdoers by taking away their property or their rights. The idea of force or coercion is joined with the idea of appropriateness or legitimacy in our modern understanding of what constitutes the state.

The institution that comes closest to the state in this respect is the most private of all institutions in society: the family. A parent can punish a misbehaving child by taking away things valued by the child ("Just for that, you can't watch TV tonight."), by imprisonment ("Go to your room, and stay there until you can learn to behave yourself."), or by old-fashioned physical means ("Give me that hairbrush and bend over."). The only other nongovernmental institution that uses physical power in a systematic manner is organized crime, which is, in some respects, a "private state" within the state. Organized crime regularly punishes members who misbehave, even imposing the death penalty at times.

Americans have never liked being governed. America became a country through an act of political rebellion. The War for Independence started because early Americans did not like the way they were being ruled by the British Empire. Resistance to government has been part of American political culture ever since. For 200 years a favorite political saying has been "That government is best which governs least."

Nevertheless, we have in America a large and powerful government that reaches into every corner of life—collecting taxes every time you buy a book or put gasoline in your car, paying the teachers who assign the book, telling you how fast you can drive your car, regulating the labor practices of the company that publishes a book, and telling the automobile manufacturer what kind of pollution control device is required.

Our first task, therefore, is to answer the question "Why have a government?" There is a three-part answer: Government maintains social order, provides national security, and furnishes collective goods.

Maintaining Social Order

The first answer to "Why have a government?" stresses the role of government in maintaining social order. Government is the price citizens pay to lead a secure life. Several thousand years of history document that if people were allowed to live exactly as they pleased, life would include a great deal of conflict among them. The strong would be tempted to take from the weak. Thomas Hobbes, a seventeenth-century English philosopher, wrote perhaps the best-known sentence on this topic: "During the time men live without a common power to keep them all in awe, they

No community can survive without some machinery for settling disputes and keeping order.

are in that condition which is called war; and such a war is of every man, against every man." The common power to which Hobbes referred is, of course, government. The very term suggests law and order.

Hobbes urged the acceptance of a powerful sovereign in order to bring order and decency out of the chaos of the "natural" world. A few decades later another English philosopher, John Locke, constructed a somewhat different argument that came to be widely accepted by Americans. Locke asserted that people originally lived in a "state of nature," pursuing their private concerns without the need of regulation or social control. Inevitably, however, some people began to use force to threaten lives and steal property. Consequently, people came together and created a government, delegating to it only those powers necessary to protect life, liberty, and property. These Lockean concepts were translated almost verbatim into reality with the creation of the American republic, where limited government and consent of the governed were the twin pillars on which the Constitution rested. But the simplicity of Locke's formulation does not by any means fully describe the justifications of government's existence that we would offer today.

How we depend on law and order   In almost every area of life, government helps to provide the orderly conditions necessary for even the most mundane activities. Take, for instance, economic activities. Working for a salary, investing savings, and buying or producing products depend on contracts—contracts between worker and manager, lender and borrower, and seller and buyer. Some guarantee is needed to make sure people do not back out on their contracts—that the car buyer does not drive off and quit making payments, that the employer does not decide at the end of the month not to pay the workers, that the bank does not close its doors and keep the savings deposits.

One reason that such contracts, necessary for economic exchange, are usually honored is that they are backed up by the authority of the government; that is, people fulfill their contracts because the government makes sure they do and it may punish those who do not. Thus people comply with their obligations both out of fear of the consequences if they do not comply and out of respect for the government. In the area of social life and leisure activities, we depend on government to provide security for our lives and property. A person would be reluctant to ride a bicycle to work if he or she thought it would be stolen. Parents would not want their children to go to school if there were no traffic laws to make street crossings safe. A woman would refuse an invitation to a party if she risked assault by going across town at night.

It is easy to see why citizens might lose confidence in their government if law and order cannot be maintained. If you ask Americans today what worries them, a great number, especially those living in cities, will tell you that they fear crime. They have lost confidence in the ability of their local governments and police departments to provide basic protection. This contributes to a more general erosion of confidence in the institutions of government.

Law and order are not simply matters of physical protection, however.

We depend on a framework of law to set forth our rights and obligations in most aspects of our lives. Business transactions, marriage and divorce, housing arrangements, labor-management relations, and much else take place within a set of rules defining what we may do and assuring us that things will remain tomorrow more or less as they are today.

Providing National Security

The problems we define as "law and order" are mainly domestic issues. Government has a further and very substantial task of protecting American citizens from external threats, of providing for the national security of the United States.

It is commonly said that the United States has become a **national-security state.** The national government is expected to protect the national borders against the threat of foreign invasion and international outlaws. With nuclear weapons, international spy networks, worldwide business investments, multinational corporations, military treaties and trade agreements, international terrorism, and huge armies and navies deployed throughout the world, the task of providing national security becomes far broader than simply protecting national boundaries. For the past 40 years, the United States has increasingly interpreted the need to maintain social order at home as also requiring the maintenance of international order.

Indeed, American military might is spread around the world. Nearly 500,000 U.S. troops are presently stationed on foreign soil, even when the United States is not involved in any type of war or even in preparedness for war. In this day of nuclear missiles, stationing troops on foreign soil

The modern state invests huge sums in the equipment required for a believable defense of national security.

is not the major method of protecting national security. The key phrase is *nuclear deterrence,* the threat to launch nuclear missiles against any enemy that threatens the United States. The United States maintains a three-part nuclear force: land-based missiles, nuclear submarines, and bombers carrying nuclear weapons.

The strength of the U.S. military is considerable, but it is only part of national security arrangements. The United States also relies on a worldwide intelligence network to determine what other countries are planning and to discover if their activities can pose a threat to the United States. The United States also relies on its treaties and agreements with friendly countries. These agreements are part of what is generally called foreign policy.

Citizens expect their governments to protect the national borders against foreign invasion and, in this modern age, to protect their cities and farms, schools and businesses, and families and friends from bombs, missiles, and other destructive forces that can arrive unseen and unexpectedly. They also expect their government to protect U.S. citizens not living in the country, such as diplomats in the U.S. embassy in Beirut and around the world, American missionaries in Uganda, American business executives in Chile, and American students in China.

If a government is thought by citizens not to be providing national security, challengers to the existing leaders will strongly press this claim. For example, in 1960, John F. Kennedy charged that the United States, during eight years of President Dwight Eisenhower's leadership, had allowed a "missile gap" to grow between the United States and the Soviet Union. This theme was echoed during 1980, when the Republican party challenger, Ronald Reagan, claimed that the Democratic party, under President Jimmy Carter, was not investing adequately in defense. Reagan could take advantage of the frustration that many American voters felt because of the inability of the United States to protect the American embassy personnel in Iran who were taken hostage in 1979 by militant students. Reagan cited the Iranian situation as an example of American power and security being weakened by Carter's defense policies.

In summary, we have government to provide legal processes, police powers, and national security policies that establish the social order necessary for a civilized, peaceful life. However, there are other things that government does. It repaves an interstate highway in Nevada, supports a graduate student writing a dissertation on the tools used by prehistoric peoples in central Africa, raises the tax on gasoline to conserve energy, publishes a booklet naming the trees and plants along a trail in the Great Smoky Mountains, sends a monthly check to a blind pensioner in New York. What do these actions have to do with social order, police powers, and national security?

Obviously, we must look beyond the maintenance of social order, police powers, and the provision of national security to answer the question "Why have a government?" An important reason why we have a government and use its services continuously is the provision of what are called **collective goods.**

Providing Collective Goods

Governments often make binding decisions when individuals have goals that cannot be achieved without government intervention. A binding decision commits all citizens to a particular course of action. For example, all automobile drivers are interested in seeing that people drive on one side of the road or the other. It matters little which side is chosen as long as all drivers choose the same side. In such a case, all drivers benefit if they can turn over to the government the power to make a binding rule that all drivers must drive on a particular side.

Binding decisions are used to create what economists call collective goods. For example, air pollution caused by automobiles is a serious problem facing many communities. Reduction of air pollution benefits all residents, whether or not they did anything to help reduce it. Suppose a highly efficient pollution control device for cars is invented and costs $300. Every American would benefit from the reduction of pollution if such a device were installed on all cars. It is unlikely that the beneficial social goal of pure air would come about from citizens voluntarily installing devices on their cars.

The situation from the viewpoint of the individual citizen deciding whether to spend $300 is as follows: No citizen acting alone can have much impact on the overall pollution in a community. If only citizen *A* buys an antipollution device, the quality of the air in the city will not change very much. If citizen *A* does not buy an antipollution device, but all the other citizens in the community do, citizen *A* will benefit from the cleaner air and save $300.

Thus it is rational for individuals not to purchase such a device. If every individual acts in the way that is most rational, a situation is created in which all lose. This is why all citizens gain if there is some way of *coercing* everyone to buy the device. The most likely way to do this is by having a law requiring that all cars be equipped with the pollution-control device. Only when individual choice is taken away can the overall social goal be achieved.

This example illustrates two things about collective goods. First, they generally are too expensive for any individual to purchase. A clean Hudson River, a Grand Canyon national park, an interstate highway network, air control and weather prediction systems, and, of course, a national defense are simply beyond the economic reach of any one private citizen. Second, it is not easy to exclude people from using collective goods. A lighthouse will shine for anyone at sea. An air defense system protects all citizens. Anyone can breathe clean air or drink clean water. This nonexclusiveness creates the "free-rider problem." If a benefit cannot easily be reserved only for those who contribute to it, the rational thing for any individual to do is to let others do the work and then take advantage of their effort. This is getting a free ride off the work of other people.

Of course, many social goods could be made more exclusive. Public parks can and sometimes do charge user fees. Highways can be tollways. However, making a collective good available on a selective basis is often very inefficient, adding another large cost to providing the service in the first place. Try to imagine making the national defense system available only to those who contributed to it or providing clean air selectively.

Collective goods are generally expensive and nonexclusionary. These two facts help explain why binding decisions are needed to create public facilities. For any individual it makes a great deal of sense to wait until others have created a collective good, then to take advantage of it. In that case, however, many public facilities and services would never be created. Only a binding decision that makes all people contribute through taxes to certain public services can lead to a beneficial collective gain for all citizens. Governments exist, then, because in their absence a certain class of social services, those which are inefficient to provide on an exclusionary basis, would not be provided in a society. As we shall see below, which services are considered collective goods is a matter of great political controversy.

A Structure of Power

Government performs essential functions for the society, but we must recognize that it is at the same time a structure of power. The institutions of government have enormous resources under their control, and these may be used—inevitably will be used—to the advantage of some groups over others. For example, law and order is never a completely neutral concept. From Locke to the present it has meant, among other things, the protection of property and hence of the interests of those who own property against those who might wish to take it away. Further, in the production of such public goods as national defense, private benefits are also provided. For example, the contracts to build airplanes or tools are not distributed uniformly throughout the nation. Thus benefits go to specific corporations with plants in particular states and localities and are, accordingly, the subjects of much competition. In short, they involve politics.

WHAT CAUSES POLITICS?

Government would be simple indeed if all government decisions were like the decision that people must drive on the right-hand side of the road. For one thing, most drivers do not care whether they drive on the right-hand or the left-hand side, as long as everyone drives on the same side. Besides, this type of policy is cost free. No one loses money, because traffic laws require that everyone drive on the right. If government were simply a matter of using state authority to obtain goals that all citizens favor and from which all benefit equally, it would be a quite uncomplicated business.

Different Citizen Preferences

Government, however, is not always a matter of achieving goals that all citizens favor and that benefit all citizens equally. In fact, government decisions are usually sources of conflict. The reasons are clear. It is not easy to agree on what collective goods the government should provide, who should pay for them, and how much.

Not every group benefits equally from any public service, and not every group pays equally or even pays in proportion to its use of that service. Thus government involves a competitive struggle in which individuals and groups seek to maximize the benefits they receive from government while minimizing their costs.

We use the term *politics* to talk about the ways in which people try to pay the least possible for the best deal that they can get from government services.

Consider, for example, public highways. Certainly, they are a collective good in the sense that no individual could afford to build one. They are also a collective good in the sense that they are not reserved for particular groups but are open to any adult who is willing to obey the traffic laws. Yet the politics of highway construction can become very intense indeed. Downtown merchants may want an expressway to come directly into the central city; apartment dwellers about to lose their homes to the bulldozers will fiercely oppose such a plan. Truckers and automobile manufacturers will be on the side of more and faster expressways; conservationists insist that cities would be more livable if resources went to mass transit and public parks instead. Another group, favoring lower taxes, may not want the expressway at all and will oppose public transit and parks as well. Still another group, perhaps the largest, is indifferent to the whole issue.

Thus the first important point about politics and government is that individuals and groups have different preferences. A large, diverse nation like ours must include groups with different goals: labor and management, doctors and patients, whites and blacks, Catholics and Protestants, producers and consumers, landlords and tenants, and others. Doctors may want less government involvement in medical care; elderly citizens may want more complete care programs. Blacks may want the government to encourage integrated housing in suburbs; white suburbanites may want the government to stay out of this issue. Catholics may seek government aid for parochial schools; Protestants may oppose it.

The number of alternative preferences to be found in America is vast indeed. There are many issues, and on any single issue we are likely to find some citizens on one side, some on the other, and others who are indifferent. Different preferences of different groups lead of course to arguments over what collective goods the government should provide and who should pay the costs of those goods. It is these arguments that set in motion the struggle to control and influence government.

Differential Impact Leads to Different Levels of Involvement

If the political struggle begins with different preferences, it is spurred by a second fundamental point about government and society: Government decisions have differential impact. Any given policy is likely to benefit one group a lot, benefit another a little, and leave another unaffected. It may even hurt some people. The decision to build a highway next to my house benefits the highway builders and commuters a great deal, leaves most citizens unaffected, but may hurt me and a few of my neighbors substantially. The fact that government decisions have differential impact implies that on any particular issue we will find not only citizens with different preferences but citizens who hold these preferences with different levels of intensity.

The few citizens who have intense preferences, generally those who are most severely affected, will be concerned and active. Differences in intensity leads to different levels of political involvement. With regard to any particular policy, some individuals and groups will be more active and try harder to affect the outcome.

The Politics of Collective Goods

A continuous political debate goes on in the United States over the proper size of government. More correctly, the debate is over whether the government or the marketplace is the best way to provide the services and benefits citizens want. Though the debate sharpened wtih the election of President Reagan, it is as old as the government itself. Alexander Hamilton, for instance, wanted a more active and interventionist government than did Thomas Jefferson. More recently, during the 1920s, presidents Calvin Coolidge and Herbert Hoover deeply believed that minimal government and rugged individualism were the best foundation for a secure and economically healthy society. The government, Hoover felt, was an awkward and clumsy mechanism for delivering social services. A deep economic depression in the 1930s led to a revised view of the responsibility of government, a view that has generally prevailed since then. However, the fundamental debate between those who welcome an active role for the government and those who oppose it is not at all settled. It is a debate that will interest us at many points in the chapters to follow.

It might seem at first that there would be no conflict over whether government should provide collective goods. Nobody would want to oppose national security, clean air and water, or a highway system, but there is conflict. There is, in the first place, serious conflict over priorities. In what order and amounts should taxpayers' money be spent on building faster fighter planes, cleaning polluted rivers, or improving the highway system? Mathematicians and economists have demonstrated that there are no rules for determining the socially preferred ordering for a series of collective goods. There is no way of knowing which collective good is better than another. Calling things collective goods does not eliminate conflict because there remains a struggle over the priorities.

Some collective goods, such as national defense, have come to have a much higher priority in recent decades than in earlier days. Other social concerns, once regarded as matters for the private sector of society, are now treated as public concerns. One example is a clean environment, which has only in very recent years been considered a collective good and therefore a government responsibility. Another example is medical research. If cures for infectious diseases are found, every citizen will benefit, because everyone will be inoculated in order to prevent an infectious disease from getting started. A public highway system is considered a collective good; so are public parks and a stable economy.

Part of this expansion in the list of collective goods results from the growth of "collective bads." The evils of air and water pollution brought on by industrial growth and population density could not be escaped. Every-

Clean air is a collective good—everyone benefits but voluntary action seldom achieves it.

one suffered, and no one could contract privately for clean air. Moreover, the pollution in one state drifted with the breeze to its neighbors. Effective policy therefore required collective action and on a broad, nationwide basis.

The tendency to define benefits as collective goods expands the powers of government. Providing collective goods becomes the justification for government intervention in the economic sector, in social and family life, and in research and education. Creating a collective good such as national defense requires, laws, programs, and agencies. Government powers expand, and government grows.

The resulting growth in government alarmed the Republican party in 1980 and led to the nomination and subsequent election of Ronald Reagan. The administration of President Reagan has argued that too many social services and benefits are being defined as collective goods.

The Reagan administration charged that the tendency to call various services "collective goods" is really the result of a government bureaucracy trying to expand its powers. It is better to leave certain issues to the economic system. For example, although energy conservation is a worthwhile national goal, it need not be pursued through the cumbersome bureaucracy of the Department of Energy. It is better to let the marketplace price energy at a level that will force citizens to adopt measures to conserve energy.

One of Ronald Reagan's first recommendations was to dismantle the Department of Energy, which had been established to design a national energy policy just a few years prior to 1980.

Just what government should provide, and at what cost and to whom, will probably be the central political issues during the 1980s. Chapter 4, which discusses the economy and political life, will return to this theme and will review some of the broad economic theories that guide how the government and the economy interact.

The answer to "What causes politics?" has been straightforward. There is conflict over what government should do. Not all citizens agree about the scope of government, about whether government should provide benefits, such as medical care, or impose regulations, such as telling citizens to wear seat belts. Moreover, there are different views in society about how the costs and benefits of government programs should be allocated. Should the cost of providing medical care for the aged be spread equally across the population, taxing the old as well as the young, the poor as well as the rich; or should the cost be assigned to the groups that can best afford the higher taxes? Out of these different views about the proper role of government, and about who pays and who benefits, comes political conflict.

Our concept of politics does not refer simply to the existence of disagreement. Also included are the processes by which the contending forces seek to mobilize support in the society, compete for public office, and work their way through to decisions concerning what is to be done by government. Politics in this larger sense is an ongoing activity that takes place in many different institutional arenas.

WHAT IS A DEMOCRACY?

A society can have a government and can certainly have politics without being a democracy, but this is not supposed to be the case in the United States. Americans routinely put the word democracy together with the words government and politics; they speak of the United States as a democratic *government* and of democractic politics. To understand what is special about a government that calls itself democratic or a political process that claims to be democratic, we start with a simple definition of democracy.

Aristotle's Definition of Democracy

If you have read any political philosophy, you know that Aristotle, a famous Greek philosopher, classified governments as being either ruled by one, ruled by a few, or ruled by many. He used the term *democracy* to describe the third of these forms of government. For Aristotle, democracy was a technical term. It meant the gathering of *all* citizens in order to debate and decide the political issues of the day. The word itself means rule (*krateo*) by the people (*demos*). The city-state known to Aristotle was quite small, both in geographic area and in population. It was possible for all citizens—a group that excluded women, slaves, children, and people who did not own property—to meet in one place. Everyone could vote

Direct democracy remains an ideal, but even the New England town meeting is less and less able to cope with citizens' concerns.

directly on whether taxes should be raised to support the army or whether a new public building should be started. The closest that Americans have come to this **pure,** or **direct, democracy** is the New England town meeting, though the practice of all citizens of a New England town coming together face-to-face to govern themselves is now largely discarded.

Representative Democracy

We shall see in the next chapter that the leaders who fought in the War for Independence and who wrote the American Constitution were attracted to democracy as a form of government. They did not believe, however, that pure, or direct, democracy of the kind discussed by Aristotle was a practical possibility. Too many people, scattered across too great an area, lived in the 13 colonies which were to become the United States of America.

What emerged from this early period of American history is a greatly modified definition of democracy. It is one familiar to any American school-child. The key terms are **representation** and **majority rule.** If it is impracti-cal for all citizens to come together to debate and decide common issues, then special representatives can be selected to actually conduct the affairs of government. These special representatives can be selected by competi-tive elections, with the person getting the majority of votes being chosen. This is one of the basic principles of modern democratic nations. Those who govern the nation acquire their power in competition with each other for each person's vote. By this test it is said that America is a democracy. Major leaders reach their positions through electoral victory or by being appointed by those who have won elections. Officeholders are on "probation," as they are expected to hold office only as long as they satisfy a majority of the electorate.

Democratic Principles

Without competitive elections to choose public officials there cannot be what we commonly understand as democratic politics. But there is more to democracy. Some of the other key democratic principles are political equality, governmental reponsiveness, individual liberty, and limited government.

Political equality   In a representative democracy one of the first issues to be faced is what or who shall be represented. There are many possible bases of representation, including social class, occupational group, and geographical units such as counties or states. What has come to be the main basis of representation in the United States, and not without considerable struggle through the years, is the individual citizen. Each citizen is entitled to an equal voice in selecting officials. Each is equal before the law and each has a claim to equal economic and social opportunity. None of these claims has been easy to realize in practice, as we will see in greater detail in Chapter 5. They do, however, form the core of democratic commitment.

Political equality is also at the basis of our modern understanding of majority rule. The first question raised by the majority-rule principle is, "A majority of what?" The democratic answer follows logically from the principle of equality: "A majority of the people, with each person counted as one."

Governmental responsiveness   Democracy requires more than simply the election of officials by popular majorities. There is the further expectation that those officials will be responsive in their actions to the desires of those who chose them. This is never easy to achieve because many citizens will know or care little about a large share of the matters with which government deals. Moreover, there is seldom much assurance that popular preferences constitute effective solutions to problems. This ancient dilemma is one that American democracy must face all the time. Some urge that we restrict democracy in order to improve efficiency: elect fewer officials, and do not insist that they reflect public opinion so faithfully. Others reply that such cures are worse than the disease—that the way to make democracy more efficient is to improve the understanding and increase the active participation of the citizens. The debate continues.

Individual liberty   For American democratic theorists the ultimate criterion of value has always been the individual citizen. In particular, drawing on the philosophy of Locke and others, the premier objective of the political system is to enhance the liberty of individuals to make their own way with a minimum of interference, either by government or any other social force. Government is expected to clear the path for individual initiative and talent and provide the conditions of equal opportunity. In several periods of our history this commitment has meant that government was expected to play quite an active role, providing a "safety net" for the weak, breaking up private concentrations of economic power, or underwriting the development of particular industries or regions of the country. But the main justification of this involvement has remained the liberty of individuals to make their own choices, not the aggregate growth of the whole society or the equitable distribution of its wealth.

Limited government Americans have a commitment to individual liberty. They subscribe to a philosophy that justifies the power of government by resting that power on the consent of the governed and on government's continued responsiveness to public opinion. It follows from these convictions that the power of government must be limited. As we shall see in Chapter 2, the United States was founded with explicit principles in mind. Those who established the United States feared political tyranny. Thus they founded a government based on the principle of limits. Usually we think of a government in terms of what it can do, but the U.S. Constitution also speaks to what the government *cannot* do.

To limit government and prevent tyranny, the founders adopted the idea of divided powers. They wanted no single group of leaders to have all the powers of the government. This division, or fragmentation, of powers was accomplished through four devices:

1. *Federalism.* Some powers of government were assigned to the national government; other powers were reserved for the state governments. Still others, such as taxation, could be exercised by both. On many important issues, the national government was to be unable to act unless the various states cooperated. On other issues, such as education, the states would have the main authority. By this layering of government the founders intended to limit the powers of the national government.

2. *Separation of powers.* The national government was further divided into three separate branches: the executive branch, or the presidency; the legislative branch, or the Congress; and the judicial branch, or the court system. State governments adopted similar arrangements. Each branch of government would have to cooperate with other branches in order to exercise its powers fully, a cooperation assured by the third device.

3. *Checks and balances.* The powers of one branch were to be checked by another in the sense that for one branch to do its work it needed the cooperation of the others. Congress was checked by the Court, the Court by the president, the president by Congress, and so forth until every part of government was checked by every other part. This may not be the most efficient way to arrange government power, but it has had the result intended by the writers of the Constitution. No single branch of government can exercise all the powers of government and thereby be in a position to enlarge its authority so much as to endanger our liberty.

4. *Bill of Rights.* The basic political rights of citizens, such as freedom of speech, freedom of the press, and the right to form political associations, were protected in a series of 10 amendments to the Constitution known as the **Bill of Rights.** These rights, along with competitive elections, were to create a balance of power between the leaders and the citizens, further insuring that the government would have limited rather than unlimited powers.

Democratic Dilemmas

It is easier for a society to announce its commitment to democratic principles than to work them out in practice. Principles often conflict with each other, requiring the kind of political compromises that adjust one principle with another.

Limited government and equality   The principle of limited government and the principle of equality are difficult to honor at the same time. The list of groups in American society which at one time or another have been denied equal treatment and equality of opportunity is long indeed: blacks, Native Americans, Irish, Italians, Eastern Europeans, Spanish-speaking Americans, women, the poor, the elderly, and the physically disabled.

When government acts to correct inequality—by protecting the voting rights of black citizens, providing equal educational opportunities for Hispanic Americans, or prohibiting sex discrimination—it is difficult for the programs of government not to expand. Chapter 5 will take up this theme in more detail.

Equality and individual liberty   Protecting the equality of one group can easily hamper the freedom of another. Busing children to schools might increase equality of educational opportunity; it might also decrease the freedom of parents to choose the kind of school they want for their children. Programs designed to provide equal rights for women are viewed by some people as destroying the traditional freedom of institutions to run their own affairs.

Limited government and democratic responsiveness   The Constitution, in part, defined the government in terms of what it cannot do. This was because the nation's founders greatly feared political tyranny and greatly loved individual liberty. To avoid tyranny and to preserve liberty, they wanted to put restraints on government powers.

Yet the government is supposed to respond to the wishes of a very diversified population, made up of groups wanting many different services and programs. In a complex and often hostile international environment, national security cannot easily be furnished by a small, limited government. A limited government also cannot effectively coordinate and manage the economy, as we will see in Chapter 4. Providing for individual security against illness, unemployment, and old age has been a responsibility assumed by government since the 1930s. Then there are the issues of pollution and consumer protection. These programs have been fashioned in response to democratic pressures. Democratic pressures, then, can push for government expansion and activism despite the constitutional doctrine of limited government.

This perhaps is the deepest dilemma of all: How can a government be kept in its place, as the founders wished, yet respond to the full range of complicated domestic and international issues that confront the United States in the closing years of the twentieth century? As we turn our attention in the chapters that follow to the institutional design of American government we will wish to keep this question before us.

PROFILE ■

JOHN LOCKE (1632–1704)
English Philosopher

The most important English philosopher for Americans in the latter eighteenth century, <u>Locke argued that people began in a state of nature, that the rights to life, liberty, and property were "natural," and that people consented to establish government in order to protect those rights.</u> These ideas were at the core of the Declaration of Independence and the Constitution. Locke's individualistic starting place and emphasis on limiting the scope of government, which he

portrayed as necessary but unfortunate, have continued as the widely accepted assumptions of American political ideas.

Locke wrote extensively on other aspects of philosophy. The *Essay Concerning Human Understanding* (1690), denying that people had innate ideas and emphasizing the experimental or empirical basis of all knowledge, was an important contribution to the Enlightenment. He explored the implications of these ideas for education. Unlike many philosophers of his time, Locke was not a clergyman, but he did write an important book dealing with religion called *The Reasonableness of Christianity* (1695). His *Two Treatises on Government* (1690) contain his most explicitly political ideas, but his *Essay Concerning Human Understanding* is his most fundamental work.

Locke was actively engaged in the politics of his time. He worked closely with Lord Shaftesbury, an important political leader during the reign of Charles II, but when James II came to the throne in 1683, Locke and Shaftesbury went into exile in Holland. Much of his major writing was completed during this period and published after William of Orange, from Holland, took the English throne as William III. Locke's political theories were welcomed as justifications for the Glorious Revolution of 1688, by which James had been deposed and William brought in, but to a government of more restricted authority. When political discontent began to build up in the American colonies, Locke's ideas were once again congenial justifications for a program of action leading toward independence and limited government. They still are.

CHAPTER HIGHLIGHTS ■

1. Governments exist to maintain order, which involves the police powers of the state, which are supposed to seek out and restrict illegal or criminal ("antisocial") behavior, and civil arrangements, such as laws that insure contracts are honored.

2. Governments exist to provide national security, which involves protecting the national borders against invasion or attack as well as protecting one's own citizens who live and work abroad.

PROFILE ■

ARISTOTLE (384–322 B.C.)
Greek Philosopher

Along with Plato the source of many of the philosophical conceptions that make ancient Greece such a rich and fascinating study, he was for 20 years a member of Plato's academy and then became tutor to Alexander the Great. He later founded his own school, the Lyceum, where he lectured, organized research projects, and collected many kinds of materials for study and exhibition. Most of these have long since been lost, but his lectures, perhaps in the form of notes taken by his students, on logic, physics, ethics, rhetoric, poetics, and politics survive.

Aristotle contrasts sharply with his mentor, Plato. Where Plato held that there were pure ideas that had an abstract existence of which our ideas and observations were imperfect reflections, Aristotle built his theories from observables. He was empirical in both method and conception. Much of his political analysis was developed on the basis of evidence gathered from his extensive collection of over one hundred constitutions of the Greek city-states. Where Plato's *Republic* was an effort to construct an ideal political community, Aristotle's *Politics* is primarily a treatise on political institutions and behavior in real situations.

One of Aristotle's central ideas was that people cannot have a truly meaningful existence apart from the political community. For him that was the city-state, a relatively small, intimate community that depended substantially on slave labor in order to allow the citizens (male only) to devote their time to public affairs. Aristotle insisted that citizens had to participate actively in order to be fully human. Self-interested individualism was not enough either to sustain a community or to fulfill the individual's potential.

Aristotle was convinced from his study of Greek political experience that a "mixed constitution," representing several social classes and giving special weight to the middle class, was the most likely to be both lasting and just. He thought pure democracy was unstable, likely to succumb to demagogues and turn into tyranny. Better to seek the "golden mean" in all things. The balance and moderation that permeate Aristotle's thinking were prominent values as well in the minds of the Founding Fathers.

3. Governments exist to provide collective goods, those public services and public benefits—such as clean air and water, fire protection, and a highway system—which are likely to be provided only by making a binding decision that requires the general contribution by all citizens.

4. Politics occurs, because citizens have different preferences about what they want the government to provide and how the costs should be assigned. Politics can be understood as the effort by different groups in society to maximize their benefits while minimizing their costs. Understood at its

broadest level, contemporary politics in the United States is concerned with the proper scope and role of government.

5. Democracy is a form of government in which those who govern are selected in competitive, open elections. Officeholders are constantly on probation; if their performance is less than what the citizens expect, they lose their position.

6. The principle of limited government is the idea that a government must be defined in terms of what it cannot do as well as in terms of what it is able and expected to do. The four major features of American government that establish limits are federalism, separation of powers, checks and balances, and the Bill of Rights.

7. Individual liberty is the basic political principle that every citizen should meet with as little interference by government as possible given the job that government is supposed to do.

8. Equality is the principle that no arbitrary distinctions, such as race, social class, gender, and religion, should be used to assign political rights or economic opportunities.

9. Democratic dilemmas occur, because these principles quite often conflict with each other. Politics becomes working out the compromises that attempt to honor as much of each principle as is possible. The following chapters will identify notable successes, as well as failures, as the United States has struggled to honor such principles as liberty and equality.

SUGGESTED READINGS ■

The nature and forms of government and politics have attracted the most profound efforts of philosophers and scholars for more than 2000 years.

Classics include Aristotle, *Politics;* John Locke, *Two Treatises of Government* (1690); Thomas Hobbes, *The Leviathan* (1651); Max Weber, *From Max Weber: Essays in Sociology,* translated and edited by Hans Gerth and C. Wright Mills (1947).

Modern commentaries include Karl Deutsch, *The Nerves of Government* (1963); Robert Dahl, *A Preface to Democratic Theory* (1956); Harold Lasswell, *Politics: Who Gets What, When and How* (1936); Joseph A. Schumpeter, *Capitalism, Socialism and Democracy* (1942).

Independence Hall, Philadelphia

Chapter **2**

THE CONSTITUTIONAL FRAMEWORK

The Constitution of the United States was written during the hot summer of 1787 in Philadelphia and has been argued about ever since. A constitution normally accomplishes two things. It states the aims that the people bound by the constitution are supposed to share. However, those who write constitutions know that different interests will not always see these aims in the same way or agree about how best to achieve them. Therefore, constitutions, if they are to be effective, will state rules and procedures that guide how the political process will settle disputes. We start this chapter with some brief political history, because the broad aims and the rules for settling political arguments we find in the U.S. Constitution are in large measure the product of early political history.

We then turn to the theory of democracy, which guided the drafting of the Constitution. The writers of the Constitution faced a monumental task. They wanted to design a constitution that would establish a democratic and effective national government, that would be responsive to difficult social and economic problems while respectful of individual liberties. On the one hand, they knew that strong governments could be oppressive. On the other hand, they knew that weak governments endangered order and liberty. Was it possible to create a proper balance between governmental power and individual liberty?

The writers created a constitution that not only secured adoption but has endured to the present day. How the U.S. Constitution has endured so long and accommodated itself to a society that has changed so much is the third topic reviewed.

Constitutional Theory in Practice

During 1979 the federal government authorized up to $1.5 billion in loan guarantees to the Chrysler Corporation in order to prevent the giant corporation from going bankrupt.

On November 4, 1980, more than 83 million American citizens voted in the presidential election that sent Jimmy Carter back to Plains, Georgia, and brought Ronald Reagan to the White House.

Local officials in Missoula, Montana, passed an ordinance prohibiting the transport of radioactive waste materials on local city streets.

While the Vietnam War was still going on, two newspapers published sections of secret, classified government documents, called the Pentagon Papers, which gave an account of how presidents Kennedy and Johnson had misled the public as well as Congress about the extent of American involvement in the early years of the Vietnam War.

In order to protect black children who were about to attend a previously all-white school, President Dwight Eisenhower sent federal troops to Little Rock, Arkansas.

On two occasions, the nominees of President Nixon to the Supreme Court were rejected by the Senate and did not become Supreme Court justices.

In 1920, after many years of protest activity, the Nineteenth Amendment to the Constitution was passed, assuring that people could not be denied the right to vote on account of sex.

In 1973 Congress, overriding a presidential veto, passed the War Powers Act, which limits to 60 days the period that a president can commit American troops in overseas combat without specific congressional approval.

The Reagan administration, shortly after taking office in 1981, announced that it would reduce by about 60,000 persons the number of employees in the executive branch of the federal government, with particularly deep reductions in the regulatory agencies established under preceding Democratic administrations.

Not a single one of these facts, all of which appear in subsequent chapters in the textbook, can be fully understood without some prior knowledge of the constitutional system on which American politics and government rest. The Constitution embodies a theory of politics which, among other things, insists on the separation of powers, provides a system of checks and balances, protects the freedoms of political association and the press, provides for contested elections for political office, and assigns specific powers to different branches and units of government. These are among the deeper principles of American government, which help us to understand the interconnections among seemingly disjointed political events. This chapter, as well as chapters 3 (on federalism), 6 (on individual liberty), and 17 (on the Supreme Court), will examine these deeper principles.

THE POLITICS OF NATION BUILDING

In the span of 15 years, America was tranformed from a group of separate colonies to a united nation. The process of building a new nation, in America or any other country, involves two stages. During the first stage, dissatisfaction with colonial oppression leads to the overthrow of the colonial rulers. Just as the American colonies gained their independence from Great Britain, so Kenya gained independence from Great Britain, Indonesia from Holland, and Algeria from France. Simply gaining independence, however, does not mean that a revolution has succeeded.

During the next stage of building a nation, new nations confront two difficult problems. First, the new government must maintain its authority against the forces inside the country which threaten to fragment and divide the nation. In America this involved checking the tendency for all power to flow into the hands of the states. The Articles of Confederation failed to do this, leading to the adoption of the present Constitution. Second, the new government must allow the citizens to enjoy the better life for which they fought. In many revolutions, nations have merely exchanged one form of tyranny for another. This second stage of successful nation building—consolidating authority without sacrificing the aims of the revolution—requires unusual statesmanship.

Table 2.1 lists some of the major events in the building of the American nation.

The First Stage: Gaining Independence

Although economic interests were important in producing support for the Revolution, the basic issues dividing the colonies and Great Britain were political. After the French and Indian War (1754–1763), the British government attempted to exert greater control over the colonies. The colonists resisted these efforts to change their relationship to the mother country, arguing that it violated their rights as Englishmen. The British government had been unsympathetic to these claims, and many colonists concluded that individual oppressive measures were part of a grand design to deprive them of their liberties. Rather than passively awaiting the success of the design, the colonists revolted.

The principles underlying the Revolution are spelled out in the Declaration of Independence (see Figure 2.1). All persons, Jefferson wrote, possess "certain unalienable rights," among them "Life, Liberty, and the pursuit of Happiness." Since people establish governments to protect these rights, government cannot infringe on them. If a government threatens those rights or fails to safeguard them adequately, the people, who instituted the government, may change it or institute a new government. By infringing on the rights of Americans, the British government forfeited its claim to rule. Thus the basic principle of the Revolution was the protection of individual liberties.

The Second Stage: Forging a New Nation

The **Articles of Confederation,** ratified in 1781, were the first attempt to establish a national political authority. Framed in the spirit of the War of Independence, they reflected the revolutionaries' fear of centralized political power. They also reflected the prevailing view that local self-rule could best preserve individual liberties. The national government was given

TABLE 2.1

BUILDING OF THE AMERICAN NATION

1774	The First Continental Congress, formed extralegally. Fifty-six delegates from 12 colonies meet in Philadelphia to discuss problems common to all of the colonies.
1775	Military action between Britain and the colonies becomes stronger. The famous ride of Paul Revere; the British expedition against the Concord Minutemen; the Battle of Bunker Hill.
1776	Thomas Paine publishes "Common Sense," a radical call to break all ties with Great Britain. Signing of the Declaration of Independence.
1777	The Articles of Confederation are drafted. They link the 13 states in a loose "League of Friendship" and are finally adopted in 1781.
1782	The War for Independence comes to an and. Peace talks begin in Paris, and the treaty is ratified the following year.
1786	Shays's Rebellion in Massachusetts, an attack by debtors on their creditors.
1787	An assembly to draft a constitution meets in Philadelphia.
1788	Enough states ratify the new Constitution so it can be put into effect.
1789	George Washington is elected first president of the United States.
1791	Bill of Rights added to the Constitution.

FIGURE 2.1

Political Theory of the Revolution: The Declaration of Independence

We hold these truths to be self-evident, that all men are created equal, that they are endowed by their Creator with certain unalienable Rights, that among these are Life, Liberty, and the pursuit of Happiness. That to secure these rights, Governments are instituted among Men, deriving their just powers from the consent of the governed. That whenever any Form of Government becomes destructive of these ends, it is the Right of the People to alter or to abolish it, and to institute new Government, laying its foundations on such principles and organizing its powers in such form, as to them shall seem most likely to effect their Safety and Happiness. Prudence, indeed, will dictate that Governments long established should not be changed for light and transient causes; and accordingly all experience hath shown, that mankind are more disposed to suffer, while evils are sufferable, than to right themselves by abolishing the forms to which they are accustomed. But when a long train of abuses and usurpations, pursuing invariably the same Object evinces a design to reduce them under absolute Despotism, it is their right, it is their duty, to throw off such Government, and to produce new Guards for the future security. Such has been the patient sufferance of these Colonies and such is now the necessity which constrains them to alter their former Systems of Government.

very limited powers and ultimately had to rely upon the states to implement its mandates. Not surprisingly, the Articles failed to achieve the purposes of union and were replaced in less than a decade. Nevertheless, the Founders' experience under the Articles strongly influenced the type of constitution that was eventually proposed.

Weak Government Under the Articles of Confederation

The structural defects of the Articles of Confederation are detailed in Table 2.2. The effects of these deficiencies were felt throughout the nation. In the area of national defense, the revolution had conclusively demonstrated that the national government was poorly constructed for dealing with the exigencies of armed conflict. A strong, independent executive branch seemed to be required. In foreign affairs the United States spoke with 13 voices as often as with one. Some states actually conducted formal negotiations with European powers. All states retained the authority to set their own duties on the imported goods, thus making it virtually impossible for Congress to enter into general commercial treaties with other nations. As a result, Congress under the Articles simply could not exercise the collective strength of the new nation in bargaining for commercial and military advantages. To many, however, the most serious defect of the confederation was its impact on domestic commerce. Because Congress was denied the power to regulate domestic commerce, this was left entirely to the 13 separate states. But state-imposed tariffs often crippled small industries in neighboring states and generally inhibited the free flow of goods among the states. The various restrictions on interstate trade slowed the growth of a vigorous, integrated national economy.

TABLE 2.2

THE ARTICLES OF CONFEDERATION AND THE CONSTITUTION: A COMPARISON

	Articles of Confederation	Result	Constitution
Structure of government	One-house Congress, no executive branch	Inefficient administration: Congress had to entrust execution of its policies to committees, ad hoc panels, and individuals	Two-house Congress, independent executive
Mode of representation	Delegates selected by state legislatures and subject to immediate recall; one vote per state delegation	Delegates excessively tied to parochial state views	Fixed and extended terms for members of Congress; each member votes individually
Passage of legislation	Nine of 13 votes needed for all major legislation: unanimous vote needed to amend Articles	Deadlock on legislation and Congress unable to address fundamental defects of Articles	Majority rule in Congress; no unanimity for amendment
Limits on powers	No direct national power over individuals, i.e., Congress depended on states to enforce its laws	The "great and radical vice" of the Articles, leading to nonenforcement of many laws	National government given direct control over individual citizens
	No national taxing power, forcing reliance on state contributions	Lack of state contributions, leading to perpetual threat of bankruptcy	National government given taxing power
	No national power to regulate commerce or impose tariffs	Trade wars between the states and a general decline in commerce	National government given power over foreign commerce and commerce among the states

It is obvious, then, that the merchant and commercial interests, small though they may have been, were suffering under the Articles of Confederation. But these were not the only economic groups hurt by the weaknesses of the Articles. In addition, those who had lent money for the war effort would lose everything if the government went bankrupt. People like Hamilton were aware that if the government defaulted on its debts, it would be hard to raise money in the future. Also, those who wished to open the vast areas west of the Appalachians to settlement and trade felt that their interests were hurt by the weaknesses of the Articles. The inability of the central government to protect settlers from Indians and to dislodge the British from their trading posts severely hurt land speculators.

In short, many economic interests were severely hampered by the inability of the central government to maintain a standing army, to tax citizens in order to pay its debts, to regulate commerce among the states, to impose tariffs on foreign goods, and to protect economic investments.

But some groups—particularly debtors—were not hurt, at least in the short run, by the weakness of the central government under the Articles. Many farmers who were in debt benefited from the cheap paper money being issued by state governments. Using their influence in state legislatures, they were able to pass laws delaying the collection of debts.

Debtors benefited not only from some of the economic conditions but also from the central government's lack of an effective police power. Incidents of open rebellion against creditors, the most famous of which was led by Daniel Shays in Massachusetts, were fairly common. Although the rebellion was put down by a mercenary army, the lesson of Shays's Rebellion was not lost on citizens who were concerned about protecting property. Many citizens felt that the central government was too weak.

The Constitutional Convention

By the mid-1780s there was widespread agreement that something had to be done. There was less agreement as to what specific reforms were required. Seizing upon this general dissatisfaction, a group of respected political figures, including James Madison and George Washington, persuaded Congress to call a convention "for the sole purpose of revising the Articles of Confederation." These political figures also dominated the memberships of delegations that were sent to Philadelphia by the states. Once assembled, those attending the convention quickly concluded that the Articles were so inadequate that an entirely new constitution was needed. Meeting in strict secrecy throughout the hot summer of 1787, they devised and submitted for ratification the constitution that governs us today.

Writing a constitution is a difficult business. Political leaders are often strong willed, and if they differ in their views of the social order, in their personal interests, and in the people they represent, they are unlikely to write a document agreeable to all. The delegates to the Philadelphia Constitutional Convention, however, were able to agree because they shared so much in common.

First, the delegates shared a common background in political theory and law, which assisted them in their deliberations. John Locke's *Two Treatises on Government,* James Harrington's *Commonwealth of Oceana,* both seventeenth-century writings, and Montesquieu's *Spirit of the Laws,* written 40 years before the convention, were familiar to all the delegates. In these writings were many of the basic ideas that found their way into the Constitution. Most of the delegates could reach back still further. They were well read in the Greek and Roman philosophers of antiquity. In addition, more than half the delegates were trained in law and had read some of the great commentaries on English common law, a system that remains the basis of our own legal system.

Of even greater importance was the delegates' shared view, obtained through firsthand experience, of the deficiencies of the Articles of Confederation and the state governments. Twenty delegates had had prior experience writing state constitutions, and in many respects the federal Constitution was an extension of the basic rules that had proven effective in the different states. Thirty of the delegates were serving in state legislatures at the time of the convention; thus they were familiar with the weaknesses of some of the existing state constitutions and were able to avoid certain mistakes. More than three-fourths had been members of the national congress established by the Articles. Their disappointment with that institution also played a large part in shaping the decisions made at the Philadelphia Convention.

In addition, the vast majority of the delegates shared a strong commitment to the idea of an American nation. Whereas many political leaders in the states had reached political maturity during the colonial period and retained strong state loyalties, most of the delegates were part of the Revolutionary generation. For them the decisive political event was the War for Independence, which had shown the importance of American unity. This was reinforced by the disappointments of the Articles of Confederation. Thus they came to the convention convinced of the importance of a unified nation.

The men who dominated the convention shared a desire to promote economic growth, which seemed to be jeopardized by state debtor legislation and the weaknesses of the Confederation. A number of writers have argued that these shared economic concerns were the driving force of the convention. Yet, although the delegates clearly sought to protect property interests and curb the excesses of democracy, they were also committed to the experiment in self-government. They deeply believed in the value of active public service and responsible citizenship for everyone.

Finally, the Founders had had a common set of experiences with the failure of the Confederation and had a generally shared sense of how the institutional arrangements of a democratic republic ought to be designed. For this is what they did in Philadelphia; they designed a set of institutions and procedures for making authoritative, binding decisions for an entirely new nation, the United States of America.

In sum, the writing of the Constitution was left largely to men of influence with basically similar political philosophies. Others either chose to ignore the convention or were not sent as delegates. Perhaps for this reason, the most difficult battles over the Constitution occurred not in Philadelphia but over whether to ratify the new system in the various state legislatures. For instance, the Founders completely ignored the question of a bill of rights and were able to win ratification in several states only when the first ten amendments were promised.

Despite these bases for agreement, at several points during the convention the delegates came close to disbanding. Some issues deeply divided them, and the only solution was compromise. One major source of disagreement was the issue of slavery. Many delegates recognized that slavery was inconsistent with a government proclaiming individual liberty. A Virginia delegate, George Mason, attacked the slave trade as "infernal traffic" and warned that slavery "would bring the judgment of heaven on a country."

Other delegates, however, said that their states would not join in the union if the Constitution banned slavery. The compromise, included in Article I, prevented Congress from banning the slave trade until 1808, the year in which Congress did outlaw the slave trade, though not slavery itself. (However, the southern states continued illegally to import some slaves until the beginning of the Civil War.)

The most famous compromise was in the makeup of Congress. The question was whether the individual states should be represented in Congress in proportion to their population, giving an advantage to larger states, or on an equal basis, giving an advantage to smaller states. The latter arrangement prevailed under the Articles of Confederation and was considered unworkable by representatives from the more populous states. They argued that since the new government was to be the instrument of the people themselves, not of 13 equal sovereign states, it should be based on a broad foundation of popular representation. But delegates from small states such as Maryland and New Jersey were strongly opposed to assigning seats in Congress on the basis of population. A few large states could easily outvote all the smaller states.

In what is known as the **Connecticut Compromise,** the Constitution established Congress in the form that is familiar today. There would be a House of Representatives in which seats would be granted depending on the population of the state. In the Senate, or upper house, each state, no matter how small, would have two seats. Because most important legislation must be passed by both the House and the Senate, this compromise allowed the smaller states to check the larger ones.

In sum, the Constitution, like any product of the political process, required compromise. However, only by compromising on the issue of slavery did the delegates depart from their political principles. With this single important exception, then, the Constitution is based on a coherent view of government and political behavior.

Ratification: Federalists Versus Anti-Federalists

The new Constitution was completed during September 1787 and presented to the nation for ratification. Special conventions for considering the Constitution were elected in each state. A positive vote by nine of those conventions was necessary to bring the new government into existence.

People opposed to the Constitution, called the **Anti-Federalists,** maintained that the delegates at Philadelphia had gone too far. They conceded that reform was needed. They feared, however, that the new government, with all its awesome powers, would soon eclipse the state governments, the true homes of democracy, and thereby threaten the very liberties fought for in the Revolution. In addition, various features of the Constitution, such as a strong independent executive and lengthy terms for members of Congress, were incompatible with democratic government. Finally, they noted, the Constitution did not have a bill of rights. They urged that a new convention be called to devise a better constitution.

The Federalists, on the other hand, denied that the states had been effective in securing the rights set forth in the Declaration of Independence.

They criticized the states for their democratic excesses, especially for the "multiplicity," "mutability," and "injustice" of state laws. Only a strong and effective union would truly secure the rights they had fought for. The national government must be made competent to accomplish its proper tasks, and at the same time it must be structured so as to be safe. The Constitution of 1787, the Federalists maintained, would provide the competent and safe republican government America needed. The arguments of the Federalists prevailed, and in 1789 the new government went into effect.

The delegates who gathered at the Constitutional Convention were anxious to create a strong and effective government without repeating the mistakes of the Articles. They were able to handle the difficult task of writing such a constitution, because they agreed on the basic issues, and because they were willing to compromise on divisive issues. Yet, to understand the Constitution fully, one must understand not only the politics of its creation but the theory of government it incorporates.

THE POLITICAL THEORY OF THE CONSTITUTION

Two views of the Founders and their work have competed for acceptance throughout our history. According to one view, the Founders were far-sighted statesmen, dedicated to the common good, who designed a constitution that would serve that end. According to the opposing view, the Founders were members of a single economic class, who designed a constitution that safeguarded their own interests and the interests of their class. It is difficult to disprove either of these views. Politicians may promote the public interest while pursuing their own interests and, conversely, may promote their own interests while pursuing the common good. However, those who see the Founders as a self-interested elite maintain that they were hostile to democratic government. By considering the Founders' view of democratic government we can understand the system they created.

The Problem of Democratic Government

The Founders had been hopeful that, freed from the corrupting influences of Europe, Americans would exhibit sufficient civic virtue to enable popular government to work. Very quickly, however, the experience of the Revolutionary period raised grave doubts concerning how virtuous Americans would be. In this regard, John Adams wrote to his cousin Samuel Adams:

> Human appetites, passions, prejudices and self-love will never be conquered by benevolence and knowledge alone. . . . "The love of liberty," you say, "is interwoven in the soul of man." So it is (also) in that of a wolf; and I doubt whether it be much more rational, generous, or social in one than in the other. . . . We must not, then, depend upon the love of liberty in the soul of man for its preservation. Some political institutions must be prepared, to assist this love against its enemies.

In other words, Adams was saying that without institutional restraints, people could not to be trusted. They would break contracts. Their passions and ambitions would dominate their reason and self-restraint. This may seem to suggest the need for an authoritarian government. However, the Founders recognized that this would not solve the problem. The unchecked ambitions of leaders are just as dangerous as the excesses of the people. The problem, as James Madison observed, is that: "You must first enable the government to control the governed; and in the next place oblige it to control itself."

The Founders faced a real problem: Could democratic government do the job? Certainly the fact that a government was democratic did not guarantee that it would be a good government. The Founders knew that previous democratic governments had usually been short-lived, wracked by internal conflicts that often led to civil war. Some of the harshest language in the Convention was reserved for the evils of democracy, but this language must be read in context. The Founders were concerned about the evils of popular government because they wanted to create a democratic government that would avoid those evils.

The solution the Founders proposed was a new theory of democratic government. Government must have sufficient power to govern effectively. Thus the Constitution created a strong national government—but how could the government be obliged to control itself? No reliance could be placed on man's natural goodness because people were basically self-interested. This very self-interest, however, could be used to safeguard liberty. As Madison put it, "Ambition must be made to counteract ambition." Put differently, the Founders sought to design the government in such a way that its several parts would check one another and prevent any part of the system from gaining domination over the others. Then, and only then, could government be entrusted with extensive power. Three aspects of the Founders' plan deserve special attention. They are representation, the extended republic, and the fragmentation of power.

A representative form of government   First and foremost, the Founders created a government based on the consent of the governed. This found its most concrete expression in regular elections. Of course, **suffrage,** or the right to vote, extended only so far. Individual states were allowed to legislate their own voting regulations. Moreover, only members of the House of Representatives were directly elected by citizens. Senators, who were expected to be members of a more "aristocratic" house, were indirectly elected, being nominated and chosen by the state legislatures. (Indirect election of senators was changed to popular election in 1913, when the Seventeenth Amendment was ratified.) The president and vice-president were even further removed from popular election; they were chosen by an electoral college, whose composition was determined by the state legislatures. Judicial posts were filled by presidential appointment.

Despite these qualifications, two points stand out. First, all governmental officials under the Constitution owe their positions to the people, either directly or indirectly. The Constitution recognizes no claim to office other than popular consent. Even Supreme Court justices are appointed by the president, who is indirectly elected by the people, and may be impeached by the Congress, an elected assembly. Second, the Constitution does not impose excessive barriers to officeholding or voting. Although the Founders hoped that voters would choose unusually qualified people to represent them, they left the voters free to choose. It was the states, however, that were given the power to determine who could vote in both state and national elections. Consequently, when efforts were made to extend the franchise to blacks, women, and other groups, it was state laws that had to be changed. There were no constitutional barriers to voting in the U.S. Constitution.

Elections are a major prop supporting popular control over government. Periodic elections mean officeholding is probationary. Leaders serve limited terms, at the end of which they face the electorate (or other agencies) that granted them power in the first place. As stated in *The Federalist* (*No. 57*), elections are held to create in political leadership a "habitual recollection of their dependence on the people." In a manner recalling the Founders' belief, shared with Lord Acton, that "power tends to corrupt," this passage continues:

> Before the sentiments impressed on their minds by the mode of their elevation can be effaced by the exercise of power, they will be compelled to anticipate the moment when their power is to cease, when their exercise of it is to be reviewed, and when they must descend to the level from which they were raised; there forever to remain unless a faithful discharge of their trust shall have established a title to a renewal of it.

This passage contains much that is relevant to an understanding of representative government. Being elected to political office is to be "elevated," and being evicted from that office is to be "punished." Officeholders, therefore, use power in a manner "faithful" to the trust placed in them by the electorate. In sum, representative government intends to secure popular control over government. Yet this is not its only virtue. Today we think of representative government as a compromise between the principle of "perfect" democracy, direct popular participation in making the laws that govern the people, and the realities of a huge and complex nation. Because there is no way for the people to assemble, debate, and decide, we compromise our commitment to these principles and institute representative government, in which a select group of people meet and decide on the issues of the day but are always aware of the wishes of those who sent them. We can diagram the logic of this position, as shown in Figure 2.2.

For the Founders, however, representative government was not an expedient imposed by the size of the nation but a key to good government. Both representative government and direct democracy could prevent a minority from dominating. Only representative government, however, could ensure popular control while protecting individual rights. This would occur for two reasons. First, representatives drawn from large constituencies would generally possess the moral and intellectual qualities necessary for political leadership. Often they would be wiser and more cautious of the social order than the general citizenry. As Madison put it, representative government would ". . . refine and enlarge the public views by passing them through the medium of a chosen body of citizens."

In addition, representatives would temper sudden popular enthusiasms

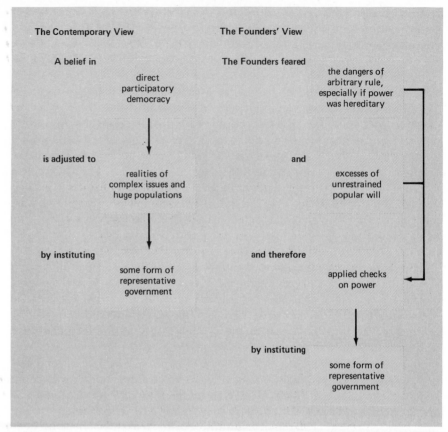

FIGURE 2.2

Two Conceptions of Representative Government

for unwise or unjust policies. If all citizens participated directly in legislation, there would be nothing to retard the enactment of ill-considered measures. Representatives, however, would not be immediately answerable if they failed to enact such measures, since they served fixed terms of office. On the other hand, they would eventually face the prospect of electoral defeat if the measures they adopted did not benefit their constituents. Even if the members of Congress acted merely in their self-interest, they would retard the enactment of unwise measures and support only those measures that were consistent with "the cool and deliberate sense of the community."

The extended Republic By instituting a representative government based on the consent of the governed, the Founders had addressed the problem of oppression by a minority of the citizenry. However, democratic governments in the past had also been prone to oppressive action by political majorities. A majority of citizens, sharing a common interest or common beliefs, might obtain control of the government. Once they did, they might use this power to pursue their own ends at the expense of other groups and of the public good. The result would be a tyranny of the majority.

For the Founders the difficulties of combating this evil were substantial. They could not restrain majority tyranny by depriving majorities of the opportunity to govern. To do so would violate their commitment to popular government. They could not rely on a community of interests in the society; nor could they rely on the natural goodness of man, since they saw man as essentially self-interested and self-seeking. Rather, they recognized that conflict was inevitable in political society. Nonetheless, the problem of majority tyranny could be overcome through the extended republic.

James Madison explained the Founders' solution for the problem of majority tyranny, or "majority faction," in *The Federalist (No. 10)*, which continues to be among the most important analyses of American politics. The problem with previous democratic governments, Madison suggested, was that the societies they governed were too small and not diverse enough. In such societies there are fewer different interests competing for political power, so it was more likely that a majority of citizens would share a common interest. Thus the potential for *majority faction* was particularly great in less diverse societies.

The Founders had reduced the likelihood of majority faction, however, by transferring governmental power to the national government, because in a large republic like the United States there was greater diversity—a wide variety of economic, religious, social, and other interests all seeking political power. This, in turn, reduced the possibility of majority faction:

> Extend the sphere, and you take in a greater variety of parties and interests; you make it less probable that a majority of the whole will have a common motive to invade the rights of other citizens; or if such a common motive exists, it will be more difficult for all who feel it to discover their own strength, and to act in unison with each other.

The transformation of economic conflict in the extended republic illustrates the effectiveness of Madison's solution. Although majority factions might form on a variety of bases, such as race, religion, or social position, Madison recognized that "the most common and durable source of factions has been the various and unequal distribution of property." In previous small republics, which had relatively simple economies, economic divisions had tended to occur along class lines, pitting rich against poor. The resulting class conflicts often made democratic government impossible. However, an extended republic tends to contain a more diverse economy, including a wider variety of distinct economic groups. Economic divisions cut across class lines, pitting different types of economic enterprises against each other. Since no sector of the economy includes a majority of the citizens, no majority faction can develop on the basis of this economic conflict. The fragmenting of the population, which occurs in an extended republic, provides a secure check against the peril of majority faction. It lessens the chances of a tyranny of the majority, which Madison realized could prey upon the democratic form of government. Madison was not trying to describe the best form of government possible. He was seeking a way to avoid the worst. This led him in the direction of democracy, but a democracy which had to be protected from its own weakness.

Fragmentation of powers   In their search for the delicate balance between authority, or ability to rule, and liberty, or protection from unjust rule, the Founders relied on a variety of external checks: elections, a system of representation, and the extended commercial republic. However, these precautions were not enough. As Madison noted in *The Federalist (No. 51)*, "a dependence upon the people is, no doubt, the primary control on the government; but experience has taught mankind the necessity of auxiliary precautions." These extra precautions were to be found in the **fragmentation of powers** within the government through federalism and the separation of powers.

Federalism.   Some powers went to the national government; some were reserved to the individual states. This is fragmentation of powers across the layers of government. It was a great act of political engineering, for it served two seemingly contradictory ends. The first goal was to establish a strong, effective central government. Nothing short of this would guarantee social order, pay the public debt, provide a monetary system, and make possible the development of the country's resources. It was also necessary to preserve the independence of the state governments, for this would check the concentration of powers in the federal government. Out of the tension between these two goals grew the federal system. Federalism is reviewed in detail in the next chapter.

Separation of powers.   The writers of the Constitution were not content with federalism. They also divided powers across three different branches of government, giving different powers and resources to the legislative, executive, and judicial branches. This served as protection against political tyranny, defined in *The Federalist (No. 47)* as ". . . the accumulation of all powers, legislative, executive, and judiciary, in the same hands." It was not enough to have popular control over government. It was not enough to have two layers of government. Beyond these controls was the need to fragment further the powers of government.

The separation of the federal government into legislative, executive, and judicial branches was, according to *The Federalist,* to accomplish three goals. First, the powers of government were to be fragmented. The federal form of government was complemented by the **separation of powers.** The argument is stated clearly in *The Federalist (No. 51):*

> In the compound Republic of America, the power surrendered by the people is first divided between two distinct governments (Federal government and the States), and then the portion allotted to each subdivided among distinct and separate departments. Hence, a double security rises to the rights of the people. The different governments will control each other, at the same time that each will be controlled by itself.

Second, through a system of **checks and balances,** each branch of government could check the activities of the others. There are many examples. Congress legislates, but the president can veto a bill of Congress before it becomes law; however, Congress can override the veto, though

TABLE 2.3
USE OF CHECKS AND BALANCES, 1789–1984

There were 2425 presidential vetoes of congressional acts.

Congress subsequently overruled 98 of those vetoes.

The Supreme Court ruled congressional acts or parts of acts unconstitutional on 113 occasions.

The Senate refused to confirm 27 nominees to the Supreme Court out of a total of 140 nominees.

Congress impeached 9 federal judges; of these, 4 were convicted.

The Senate rejected 8 cabinet nominations.

SOURCES: *Guide to Congress*, 2d ed. (Washington, D.C.: Congressional Quarterly, 1976); *Guide to the U.S. Supreme Court* (Washington, D.C.: Congressional Quarterly, 1979); *Congress and the Nation*, vol. 6, 1981–1984 (Washington, D.C.: Congressional Quarterly, 1985).

it takes a two-thirds vote. The president appoints judges, but they must be confirmed by the Senate. The judges are appointed for life unless impeachment proceedings begun in Congress are successful. So it goes throughout the federal government, and every state government as well. There are a multitude of cross-checking restraints on authority. Table 2.3 shows how often some of these restraints have been used.

Third, the kinds of checks and balances just described mean that various units of government must cooperate with one another to reach common goals. A wider range of interests is thereby reflected in government policy. Each branch has its own particular configuration of interests. If these different perspectives were blended together, it would mean that a broad consensus had been achieved in the society. If consensus was not reached, however, the ability of interest groups to use one part of the institutional machinery or another to defend its values would force competing groups to compromise. The system of separated functions requires a greater effort at communication among various groups. This may or may not produce a true "national interest," but it is designed to prevent the domination by a single social group over the rest of society.

It cannot be said that each of these goals has always been achieved in American political history. The separation of powers has often worked out differently than the Founders thought it would. Yet the fragmentation of authority and the need for cooperation remain basic features of American government, and over the years the goals of the Founders have been served remarkably well.

Limited Government and the Protection of Rights

As we have seen, the problem the Founders faced was to establish a government with enough power to govern effectively, but one which would not jeopardize individual freedom. The Constitution created a strong national government. Yet in granting broad powers to the national government, the Constitution also limited it; for since the national government derives its powers from the Constitution, it is limited to the powers the Constitution grants. The Constitution supplies a standard for measuring the validity of all lesser laws. The principle of limited government, a government of laws and not of persons, is rooted in this idea of *constitutionalism*.

The Federalists believed that the constitutional limits on government, its dependence on the consent of the governed, and its internal safeguards ensured that it would not violate individual rights. Many of the delegates to the state ratifying conventions, however, were not so sure. They conditioned their acceptance of the Constitution on a promise that the First Congress would consider amendments designed to protect individual rights.

Madison led the fight for the Bill of Rights during the First Congress. The ten amendments adopted do not withdraw powers from the national government. However, they do specify certain things government cannot do. It may not, for example, deny citizens the right to practice their religion, the right to say and write what they please, the right to assemble for political purposes, or the right to bear arms. Moreover, it cannot deprive anyone of life, liberty, or property without **due process of law,** which includes the right to a speedy, public, and fair trial and to a trial by a jury of peers.

The complications of applying such principles in concrete cases are discussed in Chapter 6. Throughout the book there are examples showing that the protections promised by the Bill of Rights have had a checkered political history. Nevertheless, these amendments provide an important additional check on government illegality.

The court system   The court system in the United States provides the means for testing the constitutionality of government actions. A citizen who has been hurt by an act of the government can challenge that action in the courts. If the courts accept jurisdiction, the government must show that its action was based on an authorizing law. A police officer cannot simply arrest any citizen; the citizen must be charged with violating a specified statute, and the officer must be able to show the legal basis for the arrest. Welfare officials cannot simply issue checks to friends or refuse to pay those whose hairstyles they dislike. In each instance they must be prepared to show in court that their decision was controlled by whether or not the applicant for welfare was in one of the welfare categories authorized by law. In principle, if not always in practice, courts offer the citizen the means to check arbitrary government power.

But the courts play an even more important role in American politics. Even if a government official can show that his or her act was in accordance with a local, state, or national law, that act can still be reversed if it can be shown in court that the *law itself* is contrary to the Constitution. The American system of government thus allows courts to limit what the popularly elected branches of government may authorize the government to do. Only a constitutional amendment—a cumbersome, time-consuming, politically awkward expedient—can reverse the United States Supreme Court's interpretation of the Constitution. (Of course the Court itself can always reverse its earlier decisions.)

Like the Bill of Rights, the idea of a "government of laws" has had a checkered history. Secrecy, duplicity, and lawlessness are not unknown in the highest government circles. The law can be bent, and often is, for those with power and money. Some examples appear in the chapter on the Supreme Court (Chapter 17) and throughout the book. But however misshaped by political pressures, the principle of constitutionalism remains a constant check on arbitrary government.

CONSTITUTIONAL CONTINUITY AND POLITICAL CHANGE

Speaking for the United States Supreme Court in the case of *McCulloch* v. *Maryland (1819)*, Chief Justice John Marshall observed that the Founders created a "Constitution intended to endure for ages to come and, consequently, to be adapted to the various crises of human affairs." Yet no group of political thinkers, no matter how brilliant, could possibly anticipate and resolve all the political-legal issues that would emerge as the nation developed and changed. Nor did the Founders attempt to do so. Instead, they attempted to design a Constitution with sufficient flexibility to retain its basic character while serving the changing needs of new generations. Three factors in particular have contributed to the Constitution's flexibility: the formal amendment process, constitutional silences, and constitutional generalities.

The Amendment Process

The Founders recognized that changes in opinions and conditions might suggest the need for constitutional changes, so they provided for a formal amendment process. It is a two-step process: proposing an amendment and then ratifying it. Under the federal mode, Congress proposes an amendment by a two-thirds vote of each house. Under the convention mode, Congress calls a special national convention for proposing amendments when requested to do so by two-thirds of the state legislatures. This method has never yet been used, but by 1986 nearly two-thirds of the states had asked for a convention to consider an amendment requiring a balanced federal budget. Under either mode, three-fourths of the states must ratify proposed amendments, either by vote in the state legislatures or, if Congress so designates, by special conventions in each of the states. The procedures for constitutional amendment are shown in Figure 2.3.

The formal amendment process has been used infrequently (apart from the Bill of Rights, only 16 times), sometimes for minor changes in the mechanics of government. Most of the amendments, however, have been significant in adapting government to new social conditions. The famous "Civil War Amendments" (the Thirteenth, Fourteenth, and Fifteenth Amendments) outlawed slavery, defined the privileges and immunities of national citizenship, set limits on state interference with equal protection and due process, and gave the right to vote to all men without regard to race, color, or prior servitude. Other amendments have broadened the democratic meaning of the Constitution, providing for direct election of senators, women's suffrage, repeal of the poll tax, and a voting age of 18. One of the most important amendments, the Sixteenth, ratified in 1913, authorized the income tax.

The "Noble Experiment" of Prohibition was widely scorned, and repeal, by the Twenty-first Amendment, was cause for celebration.

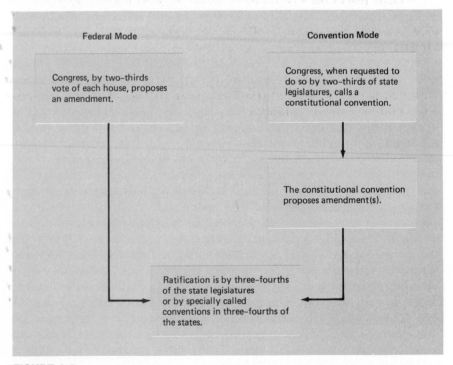

Federal Mode

Congress, by two–thirds vote of each house, proposes an amendment.

Convention Mode

Congress, when requested to do so by two–thirds of state legislatures, calls a constitutional convention.

The constitutional convention proposes amendment(s).

Ratification is by three–fourths of the state legislatures or by specially called conventions in three–fourths of the states.

FIGURE 2.3

Amending the Constitution

The rather cumbersome amendment process was designed to ensure that constitutional changes had strong support throughout the country. The recent failure to ratify the proposed Equal Rights Amendment, which would have required equal treatment of men and women, suggests that even changes enjoying broad support may not gain adoption. The most important changes in the scope of national governmental power have occurred without constitutional amendment.

Constitutional Silences

The Constitution promotes political flexibility by its silences as well as by its provisions. By failing to regulate matters it allows them to be decided through political action. A prime example is the development of political parties. The political-party system is entirely extraconstitutional. Yet, who could imagine twentieth-century politics in the United States without political parties of some sort? All major elected officials, and most appointed ones, take office under the banner of a political party (Chapter 10). Also, political parties largely organize and manage the elections (Chapter 11). All of this takes place outside the framework of the Constitution and, indeed, largely outside of any type of federal law at all.

By leaving matters for future generations to resolve, the Founders enabled political institutions and the formal government to adapt themselves to the requirements of twentieth-century politics.

Constitutional Generalities

In many places the Constitution speaks in general terms. Perhaps this broad language was useful in winning the approval of various factions. In any case, it has permitted necessary flexibility in our governmental system.

Expanding responsibilities under the Constitution By defining governmental powers in general terms, the Constitution allows government to respond to changing conditions. Government's expanding control over economic activity is a prime example. Because the Founders recognized that state regulations might impede the nation's commercial development, they gave Congress the power "to regulate commerce among the several states." For over a century, since most firms were small and most commerce localized, Congress rarely exercised this power, and state regulations predominated. With the development of large corporations and national markets, Congress assumed a much more active role. Today, when transactions in one section of the country may affect all other sections, Congress's regulatory authority has expanded to encompass virtually all economic activity.

New meanings for old words Using a general language allows new meanings to be given to old words. Consider the example of "unreasonable searches." The Founders disliked the way colonial officers searched private homes at will, so in the Fourth Amendment they declared that "the right of the people to be secure in their persons, houses, papers, and effects, against unreasonable searches and seizures, shall not be violated." This expresses a clear principle in such general language that it can still be applied today, despite an entirely different technology of search and seizure. Today, the right of government agents to use electronic surveillance techniques—telescopic cameras, wiretaps, and hidden microphones—is challenged according to the principle and with the language of the Fourth Amendment as adopted in 1791. A new technology, yes, but an old argument that places individual rights above the government's right to know.

The Supreme Court, as we will see in Chapter 17, has been the most prominent governmental interpreter of the constitutional language. Much of the Court's role in the political system revolves around its efforts to define, apply, and clarify the meanings of those important words. But in a larger sense the entire political system and, indeed, the whole society are constantly involved in defining, redefining, and adapting the legitimizing language of the Constitution. For that is what the Constitution does. It states the extent and limits of legitimate governmental authority in the United States, and it stipulates how that authority may properly be exercised. The world of the 1980s is dramatically different from that of two centuries ago, and yet most of the constitutional language is still intact. To understand American politics we must see how that language has evolved to meet new circumstances.

The Dynamics of Constitutional Change

Saying that the Constitution is flexible is another way of saying that it does not seek to provide ready-made answers for new political questions and social issues. We have identified aspects of the Constitution that give it flexibility, but we have not yet accounted for specific examples of major constitutional change.

No general formula can account for each major change and reshaping of the Constitution, but it would help to keep in mind that a document that divides power among political institutions is bound to produce disputes when the interests of those institutions conflict. The clashes leading to constitutional crises have been of four general sorts: (1) clashes between the federal and state governments, (2) clashes over the authority of a particular branch of government, (3) clashes over the separation-of-powers doctrine, and (4) clashes over the extension of citizen rights.

Federalism   In Chapter 3 we will learn how easy it is for conflicts to occur over what each level of government is responsible for and authorized to do. The Civil War was fought to establish the supremacy of the national government, a supremacy that was ratified by the adoption of the Thirteenth, Fourteenth, and Fifteenth Amendments. The war did not end disputes among the levels of government, however, and the principle of federalism is constantly being tested.

Scope of authority   Many of the new social conditions that government has had to deal with over the past two centuries have been handled within the guidelines set by the Constitution. However, some conditions have presented such complicated problems that government has had to undertake major new responsiblities. Often these new responsibilities have

The Nineteenth Amendment to the U.S. Constitution was adopted only after decades of struggle by "militant" women, willing even to go to jail to dramatize their case. Here Alice Paul, leader of the National Women's Party, receives congratulations on the passage of the amendment.

required a reinterpretation of congressional or presidential power. As we shall see in later chapters, sometimes the courts have resisted the process of constitutional adaptation. For example, the Great Depression of the 1930s seemed to many to require broad new governmental authority and programs. Nevertheless, the Supreme Court declared important new legislation unconstitutional, claiming that Congress and the president were exceeding their constitutional authority. Only after heavy political pressure from the Roosevelt administration did the Court reverse itself. During other periods the Court itself has stimulated constitutional adaptation. Citizenship rights and liberties were greatly enlarged in a series of decisions by the Warren Court (so called because the Chief Justice was Earl Warren) in the 1950s and 1960s.

Separation of powers   We have noted that the writers of the Constitution feared a government in which all powers were centered in only one institution, and that they therefore devised a system in which each branch would have the means and the incentive to keep the others in their proper place. This situation has led to many disputes and conflicts between the presidency and Congress, between Congress and the courts, and between the courts and the presidency. Most of these disputes have been settled without major constitutional revision, but during the 1970s the nation went through a separation-of-powers conflict with broad implications for constitutional government. This conflict, the Watergate affair, and the resignation of Richard Nixon from the presidency, will be discussed in the chapter on the presidency (Chapter 15).

The meaning of citizenship   American history has put the Constitution to many severe tests, but probably none has been as severe as the problem of defining the principle and the practice of equal citizenship. In Chapter 5 we review the gradual transformation of the principle of equal citizenship. The elimination of barriers to citizenship rights has been a long and politically painful process. Some of the most recent issues have been those associated with the policies and programs of affirmative action.

The federal constitution is a document of a few thousand words, written 200 years ago. Yet these few thousand words still operate as the standard against which to measure the fairness and appropriateness of government policy. Thomas Jefferson, speaking of the Constitution, said that ". . . as new discoveries are made, new truths disclosed, and manner and opinions changed . . . institutions must advance also, and keep pace with the times."

In some quite important ways the Constitution has been formally amended. But also it was adaptable to changing times by not trying to say everything and to settle every political issue. It left ample room for the political process—usually peaceful, but not always so, in American political history—to sort out the difficult questions of citizenship, federalism, separation of powers, and the scope of government authority. The chief reason for the durability of the Constitution, however, is in the broad principles it reflects, which are as attractive to American citizens today as they were two centuries ago.

CHAPTER HIGHLIGHTS ■

1. The writers of the U.S. Constitution drafted a document that was to stand as the basic law of the land. It has become the principle against which other laws are measured. The Constitution states those rights in the society which are nonnegotiable. All citizens, by virtue of being citizens, can claim these basic rights.

2. There were two major political aspects which influenced the Constitution: The War for Independence emphasized the principle of liberty and freedom from a centralized and possibly coercive government; and the problems of governing under the loose arrangements of the Articles of Confederation established the need for some central coordination by a government with sufficient authority to command obedience to its rules.

PROFILE ■

JAMES MADISON (1751–1836)
**Fourth President of the United States
and Secretary of State
Under Thomas Jefferson**

Madison was one of the several important Founding Fathers from Virginia, where during the 1780s he was a leading figure in the state legislature. He was a delegate to the Philadelphia Convention where he played a leading role in two respects: one, as an active participant in debate and, two, as a careful taker of notes on the proceedings. We owe to Madison much of our knowledge of the Convention and of how the constitutional design was developed.

Of even greater importance, we owe to Madison some of the most profound theoretical discussion and analysis of the American political system. Along with Alexander Hamilton and John Jay, he wrote the *Federalist* papers in 1787–1788 as part of the campaign to secure ratification of the Constitution in New York. *Federalist No. 10* is still a brilliant statement of how Madison hoped Americans under the Constitution could reconcile majority rule with the protection of minority rights and individual liberty.

Madison was elected to the first U.S. House of Representatives, where drawing on his earlier experience with such issues in Virginia, he drafted and led the legislative maneuvering to pass the first ten amendments to the Constitution: the Bill of Rights. Later, when John Adams became president, Madison joined Jefferson, under whom he served as secretary of state, in increasingly embittered opposition to the Federalist. With Jefferson, Madison conducted extensive correspondence throughout the young nation to build what in the election of 1800 became the Democratic-Republican party. Madison's own presidency (1809–1817) was a disappointment, marked by conflict within his party and eventually by the War of 1812 and the burning of Washington. His contributions had been made in other ways, however. He stands (all 5 ft. 4 in. of him) as one of the most important members of the founding generation of American political leaders.

The Constitution was therefore a political document that attempted to compromise between the population's fear of arbitrary government and the equally strong fear that disorder and economic disarray would prevail in the absence of a central government.

3. The political theory of the Constitution rests on the assumption that the government must be able to control the governed, but that there must also be ways to control the government itself. Four features of the Constitution establish the control *of* government:

    a. Representative government: Those who make the rules are elected by the larger population and serve at the pleasure of the voting population.

PROFILE ■

ALEXANDER HAMILTON (1755–1804)
Federalist and Founding Father

A powerful figure in the early days of the Republic, he was born in the West Indies and in his twenties played an important role as aide to Washington during the Revolution. He became a lawyer in New York City and an active participant in the Constitutional Convention, advocating a strong central government. He wrote more than half the *Federalist* papers and managed over strong opposition to persuade the New York convention to ratify the Constitution. Hamilton was the first secretary of the treasury, initiating the country's fiscal and monetary policies. He wrote a *Report on Manufactures* advocating tariffs to encourage the development of industry and an extensive program of internal improvements by the national government.

Hamiltonian policies, involving an active role in economic development for the national government, came to be a major basis of conflict between the Federalist and the Jeffersonian Democratic-Republicans. Hamilton himself went back to New York. Although still a Federalist, he opposed John Adams, and in 1800 he supported his old rival, Jefferson. His last years, politically, were dominated by his intense rivalry with another New York City lawyer, Aaron Burr. After a particularly bitter exchange, Burr challenged Hamilton to a duel and killed him.

   b. The extended republic: A sufficiently large republic ensures the presence of many conflicting interests, so that no single interest is able to bend the powers of government solely to its wishes.
   c. Fragmentation of powers: The powers of government are split into different branches (separation of powers) and different layers (federalism), and the various branches and layers can check excesses in the use of power.
   d. Limited government: The Constitution establishes certain citizen rights (especially in the first 10 amendments of the Constitution, or the Bill of Rights) that are beyond the reach of government power, and those rights are protected by a judicial system that is as far removed from current political moods and majority opinions as possible.
   4. A document written 200 years ago will, of course, have to be adapted as the times change. Several factors contributed to the adaptability of the Constitution. There is, of course, a formal amendment process, which was initially used to add the Bill of Rights and has been used 16 additional times. The Constitution's adaptability has also derived from the way in

PROFILE ■

JOHN MARSHALL (1755–1835)
Third Chief Justice of the United States

In many respects the most important figure in Supreme Court history, Marshall was another of the notable Virginia leaders of the founding generation. He served in Congress and was secretary of state for a brief time under John Adams, who appointed him chief justice just before leaving office. A staunch Federalist, Marshall was at odds with the Jeffersonians. His insistence that the Constitution had established a strong national government, supreme over the states, and that the Supreme Court had a powerful independent role to play angered many Democratic-Republicans committed to a states' rights view. Late in life his opinions were opposed also by Andrew Jackson.

Marshall was the author of over 500 opinions of the Supreme Court during his 34 years as chief justice (1801–1835). He was not much inclined to load his opinions with references to legal precedents. His great talent was in combining persuasive logical argument with eloquently expressed broad principles of interpretation. We still read his opinions in *Marbury* v. *Madison* (1803), *Fletcher* v. *Peck* (1810), *McCulloch* v. *Maryland* (1819), *Gibbons* v. *Ogden* (1824), and other cases, partly because they established important precedents that guided the Court for generations thereafter, and partly because Marshall stated the important constitutional points so well.

Language is perhaps the most effective weapon the Supreme Court has to persuade Americans to accept its decisions. No member of the Court has ever used the language with as much lasting effect as John Marshall.

which its basic provisions were stated. Broad principles were stated, leaving to the political process of subsequent generations the decisions about how to translate those principles into practices.

5. The very adaptability of the Constitution, whether through formal amendment or new interpretations of old principles, places it in the middle of ongoing political struggles, especially over the meaning of federalism, the proper scope of government authority, the rightful powers of different branches of government, and the never ending effort to work out the full implications of equal citizenship.

SUGGESTED READINGS ■

The framing of the U.S. Constitution was an extraordinary political process, and it has been the object of extensive analysis and commentary.

Classics include *The Federalist Papers*; Max Farrand, *The Framing of the Constitution of the United States* (1913); Charles Beard, *An Economic Interpretation of the Constitution of the United States* (1965).

Modern commentaries include Bernard Bailyn, *The Ideological Origins of the American Revolution* (1967); Gordon S. Wood, *The Creation of the American Republic* (1969); Clinton Rossiter, *1787: The Grand Convention* (1966); Louis Hartz, *The Liberal Tradition in America* (1955); Robert A. Goldwin and William A. Schambra, eds., *How Democratic Is the Constitution?* (1980); Forrest McDonald, *Novus Ordo Seclorum* (1985); Herbert Storing, *What the Anti-Federalists Were For* (1981).

Iowa State Capitol, Des Moines

FEDERALISM

P erhaps the most novel invention of the Constitutional Convention of 1787 was what we have come to call federalism. The Founders realized that they had to preserve the states as important components of the Union with substantial authority that could not be taken away by the central government. To do that and at the same time to establish effective national institutions required creative political engineering. The result was a complex mixture that fit none of the established formulas or labels. To capture the essential meaning of how American federalism distributes governmental power, one political scientist said it is like a marble cake, not a layer cake; functions and powers are too mixed and shared for easy description. Another metaphor is that of a picket fence, with authority running up and down between federal and state levels as well as "horizontally" in those policy areas each level controls more or less exclusively. Whatever the image employed, however, it is clear that the American federal system is immensely complicated, and in this chapter we will explore those complexities. Federalism is also full of uncertainties. Consider the case of the Concorde.

Paris to New York by Supersonic Jet: Who Gets to Decide?

The Concorde was the first supersonic commercial jet. It was a boon to hurried travelers who can afford the stiff surcharge. The plane was also meant to be a boon to the ailing French and British aircraft industries that jointly built it at a cost of $3 billion. To be a commercial success, however, the Concorde had to fly the most lucrative international routes. The best of such routes was that between Paris and New York.

The Concorde may be sleek and supersonic in the air, but on the ground it is just another noisy jet—much noisier during takeoff and landing, its critics claim, than ordinary subsonic jets. In France this fact caused no problem for Concorde flights. The national government in Paris backed the plane and had control of where the plane could land and take off. Concorde flights were scheduled from DeGaulle Airport, just north of Paris, even though some local residents were unhappy.

In the United States, things were much more complicated. John F. Kennedy Airport in New York is not under the control of the federal government in Washington. It is run by the Port Authority of New York and New Jersey, an interstate agency operated by New York and New Jersey. Hugh Carey, governor of New York during the 1970s, was sensitive to the complaints of those who lived near Kennedy Airport and did not want to give the Concorde landing rights.

International diplomatic contacts took place at the highest level. French President Valery Giscard d'Estaing called President Jimmy Carter to suggest that France's commitment to the North Atlantic Treaty Organization (NATO) might be weakened if the Concorde could not land in New York. British Prime Minister James Callaghan flew here to protest. (He flew on a Concorde, landing at Washington's Dulles Airport because he could not land at Kennedy.) Despite these high-level contacts, President Carter continued to claim that the decision should be made by the state of New York.

Air France and British Airways also went into the federal court. They

The supersonic Concorde has reduced the time required for transatlantic flights, but its noise level made it highly unpopular in many local jurisdictions.

claimed that the state of New York was meddling in foreign policy, which was a matter for the federal government. *New York Times* columnist Russell Baker wrote a column, "C'est la Guerre," describing a war between France and New York City: ". . . Mayor Beame [of New York] conferred with his advisors. . . . They knew they could expect no help from the U.S."

Ultimately, the U.S. Supreme Court overrode the Port Authority's ban on the Concorde on technical grounds. The plane was allowed to land in New York on a trial basis until tests could be taken to see how much noise it in fact made. It turned out to be less noisy than predicted, and it has been flying the Paris-New York route ever since.

The delay and complex dispute must have been frustrating and puzzling to the French. In France the central government determined when and where the Concorde could land. In the United States many government units were involved—the states of New York and New Jersey, the federal government in Washington, the Port Authority, and even the town of Hempstead, New York. It was never quite clear who could decide. The president of France might warn the president of the United States about the NATO treaty, but the governor of New York was listening to the complaints of the voters who lived near Kennedy Airport.

By the time the incident was over, though, the French government must surely have learned a major fact about American government: we

TABLE 3.1

NUMBER OF LOCAL UNITS OF GOVERNMENT, BY TYPE, 1972, 1977, AND 1982

Type	1972	1977	1982	% Change 1972–1982
Counties	3,044	3,042	3,041	a
Municipalities	18,517	18,862	19,076	+3.0%
Townships	16,991	16,822	16,734	−1.6
School districts	15,781	15,174	14,851	−5.9
Special districts	23,885	25,962	28,588	+19.1
Total	78,218	79,862	82,341	+5.3

a less than 0.05%

SOURCE: U.S. Bureau of the Census, Census of Governments, *Governmental Organization* (Washington, D.C.: U.S. Government Printing Office, 1983), p. vi.

have a federal system where governmental power is shared among many governmental units (see Table 3.1).

THE MEANINGS OF FEDERALISM

The men who wrote the Constitution had to solve two problems. On the one hand, they were convinced that the United States required a stronger central government if it was ever to overcome the chaotic economic conditions that had developed under the Articles of Confederation. Under the Articles nearly all authority was in the hands of the individual states, and as each state proceeded to enact its own regulations, trade among the states became more and more cumbersome. Moreover, a weak national government had grave difficulty dealing effectively with foreign governments. The inability to force the states to contribute troops and money to support General Washington's army had very nearly caused the Revolution itself to founder. There were substantial elements in the states which opposed a strong central government—these became known as the Anti-Federalists—but the men at Philadelphia agreed that greater centralization of governmental authority was essential.

At the same time, the Founders were equally convinced that a powerful government was dangerous. As we have seen in Chapters 1 and 2, the Founders shared the philosophy that government was instituted only out of necessity and should have only those powers necessary to deal with the greater evils of foreign attack, domestic crime, and economic chaos. In designing a stronger national government, therefore, it was vitally important to build in elements that would limit its power and prevent it from degenerating into tyranny. In Chapter 2 we identified the basic strategies of constitutional design chosen by the Founders: separation of powers, checks and balances, federalism, and the Bill of Rights.

The amendments known as the Bill of Rights limit the ways in which the national government may exercise the powers granted it by the Constitution. As the Supreme Court has interpreted the language of the Fourteenth Amendment nearly all of these same restrictions apply to state and local governments as well. We will explore these limits in detail in Chapters 5 and 6.

The separation of powers created a unique governmental structure in which three largely autonomous institutions—Congress, the president, and the Supreme Court—shared the powers of government and checked and balanced one another so as to prevent any one branch from dominating. We will examine the complex workings of this system in Chapters 13 through 18.

In this chapter we look at the third component in this complicated piece of political engineering: federalism. By dividing governmental power both horizontally among three branches of the national government and vertically between the national government and the states, a double protection against excessive governmental power was achieved.

As we examine how American federalism works, we must try to keep in mind that there are three distinct levels of meaning to the concept. First, federalism is a matter of constitutional design and legal interpretation. Questions of where the boundaries are to be drawn between what the national government may do and what is left to the states are legal disputes largely determined by the Supreme Court. Second, however, there is an ideological component involved. Regardless of what the Court says, some Americans have argued that important areas of public concern should be left to the states; others have urged increased action on a national basis. Disputes over states' rights and centralization versus decentralization often invoke broad moral justifications that go far beyond the merely legal issues of constitutional interpretation.

Third, ideological debates over centralized government and legal disputes over constitutional interpretation are never entirely separate from political conflicts among contending group interests. In one case, the strongest advocates of states' rights may be the state governors, seeking to bolster their power. In another instance, business interests, hoping to have greater impact on state legislatures than on Congress, may espouse states' rights. Over the years the combinations of interest groups, constitutional interpretation, and ideological doctrine have shifted, but in any particular case, now as in the past, we should be alert to the ways these three levels of meaning interact.

Definitions

When the Constitution was written, there were, in essence, two models to choose from in deciding how to design the relationships between the central government and its constituent units. The most common was **unitary government** in which all the smaller components—cities, countries, provinces, states, or whatever—are entirely subordinate to the central authority. The latter creates the constituent units; it grants them whatever authority they possess; it can merge them, reorganize them, or even abolish them. The large majority of nations are unitary states. Indeed, the American states themselves are unitary systems with respect to the local governments within their borders. Counties, cities, and school districts and other local units are entirely the legal creations of the state and have only those powers the state permits.

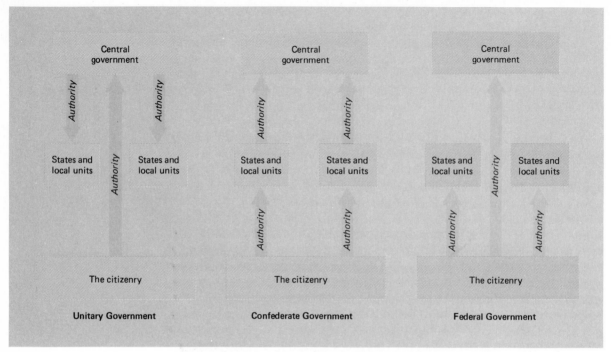

FIGURE 3.1

The Flow of Authority in Three Forms of Government

At the other end of the spectrum is the **confederation.** In a confederate system it is the constituent units that create the central government and endow it with whatever authority it may possess. The Founders knew about numerous attempts at confederation in the ancient past and had had direct experience with this form under the Articles of Confederation. In every instance of confederation the central government was weak, dependent on the cooperation of the constituent governments with little or no direct power of its own over individual citizens. Confederations were tried when the need for cooperation was great but the cooperating units were unwilling to give up their freedom of action.

The federal form of government is a hybrid. When the Constitution was written, there was no example to be found, and though the term *federal* was familiar, it meant something quite different at that time. Federalism as we know it was a political invention of the Founders. In it both the central government and the constituent units, the states in our case, derive their authority directly from the people. Neither is legally the creature of the other nor can abolish the other. Neither can prevent the other from acting within its own sphere of authority. Both the national government and the states have authority directly over their respective citizens, which means among other things that each may levy taxes and raise money without depending on the other. Figure 3.1 shows the differences among the unitary, confederate, and federal forms of government.

Even though neither the national government (confusingly, we often refer to it as the federal government) nor the states can eliminate the other (nor, as the Civil War demonstrated, can states withdraw from the union), the two levels of government are not equal. The Constitution itself provides for supremacy of the national government:

> This Constitution, and the Laws of the United States which shall be made in Pursuance thereof; and all Treaties made, or which shall be made under the authority of the United States, shall be the supreme Law of the land; and the Judges in every state shall be bound thereby, anything in the Constitution or Laws of any state to the contrary notwithstanding.
>
> *Article 6, paragraph 2*

Apart from the clear legal supremacy of the central government, however, there have been many uncertainties regarding just exactly which level of government may do what. Some of these disputes have required judicial determination. All of them have involved conflicts among various groups seeking to advance or to block particular policy interests. Let us look at the evolution of American federalism, keeping in mind its legal, ideological, and political dimensions.

THE EVOLUTION OF FEDERALISM

Why the Delegates Gave Up the Power of the States

Why were the delegates to the Constitutional Convention from the various states willing to give up power? Giving up power is dangerous: it may be hard to get back; it may be used against you. For generations people have talked of a world federation, of a federation of Europe, of a federation of African states—new, centralized governments that would replace the individual nations. Yet except for unions created by force of arms, in which the various parts do not *give up* their independence but have it *taken away* from them, there are few successful federations. Why were the states willing to give up their power in 1787? There are several answers.

The states gained from union The first answer has already been suggested. There was something to be gained from union. Our review of early American history showed that there had been commercial and administrative chaos under the Articles. Trade among the states was hampered. Trade with other nations was difficult without a central, treaty-making power. The rich new territories on which the states bordered could not be developed without some central authority. Moreover, there were very serious threats from foreign governments. England was still a powerful antagonist and France an uncertain ally. At home, business affairs were not going very well. A stronger central government would improve things.

The society was homogeneous As important as the gains that would come from union was the question of what losses might be suffered. No group is likely to give up power to another, be it an opposition party or a central government, if it feels that its *vital* interests will suffer. One thing that has prevented the union of nations throughout history is that they have different basic cultures: they speak different languages, follow different religions, and have different ways of life. An independent political unit is unlikely to give up its independence to a larger unit if it feels that the latter will not respect these vital interests. If an independent unit has such interests, it will join a larger union only if it can be guaranteed that its interests will be protected, usually by limitations on the power of the new central government to legislate on such matters. The more extensive and diverse such interests are, the more limited the central government and the less meaningful the union will be.

The answer to why the states were willing to join a new central government becomes obvious. They had a common language and a relatively common culture. They were not sharply divided on religion. In short, union was based on a relatively homogeneous society. The individual states had few special interests to protect.

The states' vital interests were protected   In areas in which there was potential conflict over interests that were seen by the states to be vital, they hedged the Constitution to protect those interests.

For one thing, the Constitution did not destroy the states—quite the contrary. Although the Founders knew that power was being shifted from the state level to the national level, they also saw the Constitution as preserving the independence of the states in many important matters. The states had, after all, existed before union.

Small states also feared that their vital interests would suffer in a union dominated by a few of the larger, more powerful states. That is why they pushed for a Senate in which each state, no matter what its size, would have equal representation. The convention spent a lot of time worrying about the large-versus-small-state issue, though this never thereafter became a major conflict in America.

The South's interests were protected   The deepest conflict of interest was between the economies and social systems of the North and the South. The North had a growing economy based on manufacturing. The South had an economy solidly based on the cultivation and export of cotton and organized around plantation slavery. The South (the southern delegates representing the white population) had a vital interest that they feared might be hurt by a government dominated by northern states.

To protect these interests, certain clauses were included in the Constitution. One barred the national government from taxing exports, of advantage to the South which depended on finding foreign markets for its tobacco, rice, and cotton. Another clause increased the representation of southern states in the House of Representatives by including slaves at three-fifths of their number for purposes of determining the number of representatives apportioned to each state. In addition, the Constitution barred Congress from interfering with the slave trade until 1808. This point is a good illustration of what a group may consider a vital interest.

The southern delegates would not have compromised on slavery itself; this they considered vital. The compromise that allowed future limitations on the slave trade was less vital, since the southern states could breed slaves.

The issue of North versus South and the related issue of slavery make it quite clear that the Constitution only temporarily settled the question of the relationship between the states and the nation. During the first several decades of the Republic, southerners argued strenuously for states' rights, and in 1861, following the ultimate logic of their position, tried to withdraw from the union. But the northern victory in the Civil War did not finally settle the matter either.

Constitutional doctrines Some of the main lines of legal argument over the meaning of American federalism were laid out by Chief Justice John Marshall in 1819. Marshall's decision, in the case of *McCulloch* v. *Maryland*, held that the state of Maryland could not levy a tax on the Bank of the United States, which had been established by Congress. Marshall's reasoning had two components. First, he said that although the Constitution did not specifically grant Congress the authority to establish a national bank, the authority to do so could be fairly implied as "necessary and proper" to carry out Congress's explicitly delegated powers. This **implied-powers doctrine** greatly enlarged the potential scope of national authority and paved the constitutional way for the later expansion of the central government.

The second element of Marshall's argument was that the state of Maryland could not interfere with the exercise of legitimate authority by the national government. Maryland certainly had the power to tax, but since Marshall held that "the power to tax was the power to destroy," Maryland could not tax and thereby injure an instrumentality of the national government.

Later court decisions made it clear that Marshall's principle worked both ways. The federal government could not tax instrumentalities of the states either—which is why, for example, state and local government bonds are exempt from federal income tax. Nor could the central government *require* states or local governments to adopt particular labor, education, or welfare policies. Washington might well persuade them to go along, and as we will see that has often happened. But the constitutional balance, though tipped toward the national government, retains a position of considerable legal autonomy for the states.

For a time, roughly from the 1890s until the late 1930s, the Supreme Court made use of another doctrine that made the authority of the states into a limitation on the power of the national government. This doctrine, called **dual federalism,** hinged on interpretation of the language of the Tenth Amendment, which reserves all powers not delegated to the national government to the state or to the people. The Court held this to mean that policy areas such as agriculture or education, traditionally within the jurisdiction of the states, could not therefore be regulated by the national government. The result of this legal doctrine was that regulation of business and assistance to disadvantaged social groups was often impossible. Action at the state level was ineffective in dealing with economic problems that were national or international in scope. In any case, because of the influence of business interests many of the states would not enact such legislation even if they had the legal authority to do so. Now the Court was saying the national government *could* not act either.

The constitutional disputes were, of course, always political disputes as well. Arguments about the meaning of federalism have grown out of the fact that in most cases the combinations of interests that were powerful in the national government were quite different from those that dominated many of the states. The most obvious example throughout much of our recent history was the differential position of racial minorities. During the 1950s and 1960s blacks were able to gain a considerably more sympathetic hearing in Washington than in the southern states. So were those groups seeking increased spending for welfare, education, and housing. Labor unions fared better in Washington than in most state capitals, and so did big city mayors. For many business corporations it was the other way around. We will return to this point later in the chapter.

The American states are not all the same, of course, and to advance the doctrines of states' rights and decentralization may have quite diverse effects. For example, if the states are held to be the proper focus for decisions about pollution regulations, then California can enact, as it has, far more stringent rules regarding automobile discharges than Nevada or Wyoming. And since the California market for automobiles is so large, its regulations will have a major impact on what manufacturers do, regardless of whether there is national legislation or not.

If Michigan allows union shop contracts, whereby labor union membership is required of all workers in a plant that has accepted union representation, while North Carolina does not, firms may prefer to locate in North Carolina rather than Michigan in hope of holding down labor costs. (Unions are strong in Michigan politics and weak in North Carolina.) Between 1935 and 1947 there was a national law permitting union shop agreements, so that the different levels of union strength among the states did not matter. In 1947, however, Congress passed the Taft-Hartley Act, specifically allowing the states to enact so-called right-to-work statutes, and those states where labor was relatively weak politically did so. Labor unions have remained weak in those states.

The Federal Balance of Power Today

In recent years the Supreme Court has played a relatively minor role in determining how the powers of government will be divided between the states and the national government. In most functional areas of governmental activity both levels are active to some extent, and the degree to which one or the other is dominant changes with the shifting balance of political forces. States may not constitutionally act so as to burden unduly the flow of economic activity among the states, but neither can the Congress require states to recognize public-employee unions. The states still have exclusive jurisdiction over marriage and divorce, and the national government alone controls foreign policy. Much of what the national government does has important effects on the states, and numerous federal statutory regulations govern state actions, as Table 3.2 indicates.

There has been a significant impact of constitutional doctrines on the contemporary federal balance as a result of court decisions that impose requirements on state and local governments under the terms of the U.S. Constitution. For example, there have been several decisions holding that state prisons and mental hospitals must be brought up to a more humane standard or else be shut down entirely as violating the equal protection clause of the Fourteenth Amendment. Other decisions have forced reorganization of local school systems to overcome racial discrimination. Local governments have been held by the Supreme Court to be subject to suit for damages when civil rights or antitrust violations occur. In these and other ways the federal system continues to be shaped by constitutional interpretation. Nevertheless, much the largest factor affecting the federal balance is the flow of grants. Taxes, grants, and other expenditure patterns are the central focus of American federalism today.

Fiscal Federalism

There is nothing new about the idea of a national government providing grants of funds to the states. Early in the nineteenth century, for example, some of the money from the sale of public lands was turned over to the states to help them develop institutions of higher education. The Morrill Act of 1862 revived this program on a permanent basis, and subsequently numerous other grants-in-aid programs were adopted to assist the states in such diverse fields as vocational education, agricultural extension, and highway construction.

With the coming of the New Deal, the use of grants-in-aid to the states was greatly expanded. Rather than require the states to establish programs of aid to the disadvantaged, for example, they were encouraged to do so by offering a federal subsidy to pay part of the costs. A state that refused to participate would lose the federal revenue to which, of course, its own taxpayers had contributed. In due course all the states fell into line, adopting numerous programs of aid to various groups—the indigent, the unemployed, the blind, dependent children, and many others. Table 3.3 presents some recent data on the magnitude of federal grants-in-aid programs.

Federal grants to state and local governments have seldom been without strings attached, however. The original money "carrot" encouraged states and cities to create programs. As the years went on, demands built up in Congress to push for additional policy objectives by linking them as conditions to the grants. Requirements prohibiting discrimination on the basis of race, color, sex, or handicapped status were imposed, as were rules regarding treatment of human subjects, historic preservation, and many others. Individual grant programs often had, in addition, their own specific requirements that states or local governments had to meet in order to qualify for the funds. (Many of these same restrictions applied as well to private grant recipients such as corporations or universities, but they are not our concern here.)

The burden of these federal requirements was felt by the grantees in several ways. For one thing it was often quite expensive and time-consuming to comply with the federal regulations. In addition, the regulations applied to the entire country might not fit the particular conditions of a given state or city. Quite often the federal regulations conflicted with the interests

TABLE 3.2

MAJOR FEDERAL STATUTES REGULATING STATE AND LOCAL GOVERNMENTS

Title	Objective	Public Law
Age Discrimination in Employment Act (1974)[a]	Prevent discrimination on the basis of age in state and local government employment.	93–259 90–202
Architectural Barriers Act of 1968	Make federally occupied and funded buildings, facilities, and public conveyances accessible to the physically handicapped.	90–480
Civil Rights Act of 1964 (Title VI)	Prevent discrimination on the basis of race, color, or national origin in federally assisted programs.	88–352
Civil Rights Act of 1968 (Title VIII)	Prevent discrimination on the basis of race, color, religion, sex, or national origin in the sale or rental of federally assisted housing.	90–284
Clean Air Act Amendments of 1970	Establish national air quality and emissions standards.	91–604
Coastal Zone Management Act of 1972	Assure that federally assisted activities are consistent with federally approved state coastal-zone management programs.	94–370
Davis-Bacon Act (1931)[b]	Assure that locally prevailing wages are paid to construction workers employed under federal contracts and financial assistance programs.	74–403
Education Amendments of 1972 (Title IX)	Prevent discrimination on the basis of sex in federally assisted education programs.	92–318
Education for All Handicapped Children Act (1975)	Provide a free appropriate public education to all handicapped children.	94–142
Equal Employment Opportunity Act of 1972	Prevent discrimination on the basis of race, color, religion, sex, or national origin in state and local government employment.	92–261
Fair Labor Standards Act Amendments of 1974	Extend federal minimum wage and overtime pay protection to state and local government employees.[c]	93–259
Family Educational Rights and Privacy Act of 1974	Provide student and parental access to educational records while restricting access by others.	93–380

[a] Coverage of the act, originally adopted in 1967, was extended to state and local government employees in 1974.

[b] Although the act initially applied only to direct federal construction, it has since been extended to some 77 federal assistance programs.

[c] Application was restricted by the Supreme Court in *National League of Cities* v. *Usery*, 426 U.S. 833 (1976).

SOURCE: Advisory Commission on Intergovernmental Relations, *Regulatory Federalism: Policy, Process, Impact and Reform,* Washington, D.C., February 1984.

TABLE 3.2 (*Continued*) 63

Title	Objective	Public Law
Federal Insecticide, Fungicide, and Rodenticide Act (1972)	Control the use of pesticides that may be harmful to the environment.	92–516
Federal Water Pollution Control Act Amendments of 1972	Establish federal effluent limitations to control the discharge of pollutants.	92–500
Flood Disaster Protection Act of 1973	Expand coverage of the national flood insurance program.	93–234
Highway Beautification Act of 1965	Control and remove outdoor advertising signs along major highways.	89–285
Marine Protection Research and Sanctuaries Act Amendments of 1977	Prohibit ocean dumping of municipal sludge.	95–153
National Energy Conservation Policy Act (1978)	Establish residential energy conservation plans.	95–619
National Environmental Policy Act of 1969	Assure consideration of the environmental impact of major federal actions.	91–190
National Health Planning and Resources Development Act of 1974	Establish state and local health planning agencies and procedures.	93–64
National Historic Preservation Act of 1966	Protect properties of historical, architectural, archeological and cultural significance.	89–665
Occupational Safety and Health Act (1970)	Eliminate unsafe and unhealthy working conditions.	91–596
Public Utilities Regulatory Policies Act of 1978	Require consideration of federal standards for the pricing of electricity and natural gas.	95–617
Rehabilitation Act of 1973 (Section 504)	Prevent discrimination against otherwise qualified individuals on the basis of physical or mental handicap in federally assisted programs.	93–112
Resource Conservation and Recovery Act of 1976	Establish standards for the control of hazardous wastes.	94–580
Safe Drinking Water Act of 1974	Assure drinking water purity.	93–523
Surface Mining Control and Reclamation Act of 1977	Establish federal standards for the control of surface mining.	95–87
Water Quality Act (1965)	Establish federal water quality standards for interstate waters.	88–668
Wholesome Poultry Products Act of 1968	Establish systems for the inspection of poultry sold in intrastate commerce.	90–492

TABLE 3.3

NATIONAL GRANTS-IN-AID, EXPENDITURES BY FUNCTION, SELECTED YEARS, 1902–1983 (MILLIONS OF DOLLARS)

Calendar Year	Total	Transportation	Education	Public Welfare	Housing and Urban Development	Other
1983	$88,539	$8,851	$12,528	$36,282	$5,583	$25,295
1980	90,836	9,457	12,889	28,494	6,093	33,903
1976	69,057	6,243	9,254	17,225	2,820	33,515
1972	33,178	4,741	6,250	13,251	1,981	6,955
1968	17,216	4,313	2,498	7,480	787	2,138
1964	9,969	3,978	479	3,875	564	1,073
1960	6,889	2,999	358	2,612	226	694
1956	3,642	746	208	1,879	125	684
1952	2,393	448	122	1,476	106	241
1948	1,629	334	37	892	69	287
1944	1,009	153	25	506	206	118
1940	2,401	167	24	1,990	37	193
1936	2,318	230	13	2,042	—	33
1932	229	132	11	60	—	26
1925	123	95	8	2	—	18
1920	43	20	5	3	—	15
1912	11	—	3	1	—	7
1902	7	—	1	1	—	5

SOURCES: U.S. Bureau of the Census, *Governmental Finances in 1982–83* (Washington, D.C.: U.S. Government Printing Office, 1984), p. 18; Advisory Commission on Intergovernmental Relations, *Periodic Congressional Reassessment of Federal Grants-In-Aid to State and Local Governments* (Washington, D.C.: U.S. Government Printing Office, 1967), pp. 16–33; Advisory Commission on Intergovernmental Relations, *Significant Features of Fiscal Federalism, 1982–83 Edition* (Washington, D.C.: U.S. Government Printing Office, 1984), p. 122; and U.S. Bureau of the Census, *Historical Statistics on Governmental Finances and Employment* (Washington, D.C.: U.S. Government Printing Office, 1969), pp. 37, 38.

dominant in the statehouse or city hall. For all these reasons methods were sought to reduce the restrictiveness of federal regulations while maintaining the flow of funds.

Until the 1960s most federal grant programs were what are known as **categorical grants,** which provided for specific purposes such as school lunches or highway construction. In most cases these were allocated to states and cities according to some formula that minimized administrative discretion in handing out the money. Some programs utilized *project* grants. Urban renewal money, for instance, was granted by Washington to local governments for specific projects of slum clearance and reconstruction. The Nixon administration instituted the concept of **block grants,** whereby funds for a wide range of categorical programs in health or education were lumped together in a single grant, and state and local authorities had much greater discretion in allocating the money among specific programs. Another Nixon initiative, *revenue sharing,* took this a sizable step further. This program allocated several billion dollars a year to state and local governments with few limitations on how the money could be spent.

The American highway network is both extensive and expensive. National, state, and local governments have collaborated to finance and build our roads.

The politics of fiscal federalism involves not only the form of the grants, however. Always at issue is the amount of money that will be transferred from Washington to the states and cities and the criteria by which the money will be divided among them. The efforts to consolidate categorical programs into block grants, undertaken by both the Nixon and Reagan administrations, were intended not only to reduce red tape and improve efficiency but also to hold down the total level of federal spending. The reasoning was that the state and local interests—bureaucrats, recipient groups, and so on—would turn their political attention to the state or local arena in pursuit of their share of a relatively large but fixed pie rather than press Congress to increase the categorical grants, each of which might be rather small, but which taken together added up rapidly.

Federal grants to states and cities began and grew rapidly in a period when many state and local treasuries were bare. During the 1960s and 1970s a good many of the older, less affluent communities became quite dependent on federal funds to provide basic local services. In recent years, however, most states and some, though by no means all, local governments have found themselves in much improved fiscal condition, while the national government has been incurring massive deficits. This fact, combined with the Reagan administration's opposition to an active governmental role in many program areas, has resulted in significant reductions in federal grants. Revenue sharing is being phased out of existence, and many other grant programs have been substantially reduced.

Whether this trend will continue will depend, as in the past, on the political balance of forces. Most of the groups benefiting from grant pro-

The large cities of the United States display the pluralism of American politics as ethnic and racial minorities gradually achieve enough local political strength to elect ''their own.'' Chicago's black mayor Harold Washington joins New York's Jewish mayor Ed Koch (top). San Francisco is led by two-termer Dianne Feinstein (above), and Henry Cisneros, of Hispanic origin, is San Antonio's mayor (right).

grams—the urban poor in particular—have lost political strength in recent years. But there are other beneficiary groups—senior citizens, for example—which are growing in size and political impact. In 1985 President Reagan, in his effort to reduce the deficit, tried to persuade Congress to eliminate grant programs for urban renewal; congressional majorities chose instead to keep them going. Once in place, most grant programs quickly acquire supportive constituencies that lobby to maintain the activity; and in a democratic society supportive constituencies are generally defeated only by larger groups in opposition.

The Dynamics of Federalism

We have examined the development of two important aspects of American federalism: the *constitutional doctrines* that justify and limit the exercise of governmental authority, and the *fiscal relationships* between the national government and state and local authorities. Over the two centuries of our existence both the states and the national government have enormously expanded the scope of their activities. Indeed, in recent years, states and local governments have increased their expenditures and employment more rapidly than has the federal government. This would not have been possible, however, without their use of large amounts of federal money, and it is clear that the national government has gained much the greater power in the federal relationship. Why?

An industrial economy The first factor has been the growth of a highly sophisticated industrial economy composed of many interdependent firms that operate in national and, increasingly, international markets. The goods in a local shop come from all over the country. An energy crisis triggered by Middle East politics touches all parts of America. Unemployment in Detroit may follow from a shift in the tastes of Californians toward smaller cars. The price of corn in Iowa results from the interaction of supply and demand throughout the world. Individual states can and do try to respond to the concerns of their own citizens over jobs and prices, but often there is little they can do. They lack the authority to control events beyond their borders. National problems, as well as those like energy and trade that are greatly affected by international forces, can only be approached effectively by a government with the authority to act across a broad front. The national government can regulate labor relations and farm prices across state lines, and it can impose tariff barriers and quotas against imports. The states cannot. The more interdependent we have become economically, the larger the role of the national government has become.

Also closely related to industrial growth is the increase in "spillover" effects whereby what is done in one state spills over to affect its neighbors. Coal-burning industry in Indiana may thus generate pollution in the form of acid rain that blights the forests of New York. Once upon a time it made little difference whether raw sewage was dumped in a river, but population growth means that today the toxic effects of such pollution will not only be dangerous but will be felt far downstream in neighboring states.

Interstate competition   Even if the states had jurisdiction adequate to solve the problems generated by industrial development, they would be greatly handicapped by the fact that they are in competition with one another to attract business. Each hopes to stimulate economic growth for the benefit of its citizens, and to do so each must be careful not to impose too heavy burdens of taxation or regulation, lest business firms move elsewhere. Yet, if each state keeps taxes low in order to attract investment, how can welfare or education programs be funded? No state will have enough tax revenues. If the federal government levies the necessary taxes, on the other hand, they will fall upon the whole country and there will be less advantage in attracting business to the low-tax states. To overcome the tendency for interstate competition to hold down the level of spending, the groups that want increased public education or welfare have looked to Washington for the money.

Taxing authority   The passage of the Sixteenth Amendment in 1913 made it possible for the federal government to levy a tax on personal and corporate incomes. With that authority the potential tax resources available to Washington increased far beyond what the states or cities could hope to raise. States have the legal authority to impose income taxes, and most of them do, but because of the competitive situation we have just described, there are severe limits to the amount of revenue that can be raised by this means. Moreover, most states and local governments are restricted by their own constitutions and charters with regard to borrowing. The U.S. Government is not. Thus, when the demand for more extensive public spending grew insistent during the 1930s, only the national government had the fiscal resources to meet that demand. It had broad taxing power and full authority to borrow and hence to engage in deficit spending.

In recent years there has been a vigorous campaign on behalf of a constitutional amendment to limit federal deficit spending by requiring some form of a balanced budget. At the same time there have been reductions in federal tax rates and strong efforts to reduce them further. By the mid-1980s the net result of these attempts had already been to shrink the funds available for distribution to the states, and the pot was expected to be reduced considerably more in the near future. As that happens the federal balance of power will also shift, with more control back in the hands of the individual states but, in most parts of the country, less money to spend for public purposes.

National government growth through national defense   The balance of power in American federalism has been greatly affected by the increased salience of foreign affairs. Two world wars and the unending tensions and conflicts since 1945 have led to huge expenditures on national defense. Permanent world crisis has generated or strengthened many other areas of national government activity as well. Military preparedness requires good roads, and the primacy of national defense has helped a good deal in securing federally funded highways. Federal money for local schools came first through the "Impacted Areas" program, which provided funds to areas with large federal installations (and consequently numerous school-age children), most of them defense-related. Later, money was funneled to universities to aid science and language training, again in the name of national defense. The space program was also begun in response to the Soviet challenge. In each case, of course, it was the national government that acted, not the state or local governments.

The quest for equal treatment   A further factor leading to expanded national activity has been the pressure brought by various groups that have been unable to secure their demands within local or state arenas and have turned hopefully to Washington. For example, for many years prior to the 1960s most state legislatures were dominated by rural interests and inhospitable to requests for assistance from the large cities. In 1933 the latter organized themselves into the United States Conference of Mayors and began to lobby for financial aid for housing, urban renewal, and related purposes. During the 1960s a comparable effort by inner-city groups provided support for the federally funded War on Poverty (see Table 3.3).

The most dramatic and long lasting struggle for equal treatment across the federal system has been that of black Americans. Indeed, political scientist William Riker has claimed that "in the United States the main effect of federalism since the Civil War has been to perpetuate racism."[1] Denied equal treatment within the states and communities of the South, blacks sought redress from the national government. There too, however, they faced long periods of frustration. Southern white interests were powerful in Congress and often quite influential in the executive branch as well. The Supreme Court was more receptive, however, and beginning as early as 1915 gradually enlarged the area of equal treatment for racial minorities. The executive branch gave active support to civil rights in 1941 and after, but not until 1957 did Congress pass a civil rights act. Once blacks achieved full legal equality they could win political power in parts of the South and in many of the big cities. As this happened, they sometimes have taken a different view of the question of how much control should be in the hands of the national government and how much should be left to the states and localities.

In several areas of public policy a nationalization of standards of treatment has been brought about in recent years. Police practices and criminal trial procedures have been made more uniform by means of Supreme Court decisions imposing equal protection of the laws under the terms of the Fourteenth Amendment. State variations in the rules regarding voting have been greatly reduced in the effort to end discrimination against blacks. Affirmative-action programs and attention to the needs of the handicapped have been extended to both public and private agencies throughout the nation as requirements attached to federal funds.

Not every group has won acceptance of its particular version of equality of treatment, and the search for advantage between federal and state levels

---

[1] William Riker, *Federalism: Origin, Operation, Significance* (Boston: Little, Brown, 1964), p 153.

of authority continues. Nevertheless, the trend toward national uniformity of legal standards has been strong, as have the pressures, generated by economic interdependence, for economic policy to be shaped on a nationwide basis. In view of these developments we may ask why it is that the states still exist. What preserves these "old-fashioned" subdivisions, as well as local governments, against pressures to reorganize them into more "efficient" units? The answer lies in the fact that American federalism continues to have strong political vitality.

CONTINUED VITALITY OF THE STATES

In many respects the American states are historical accidents. No grand design or coherent plan guided their creation. They vary greatly in size and population and in their economic and social composition. A few are relatively homogeneous, but many contain enormously diverse elements. Yet no state has ever been merged, abolished, or reorganized. The Constitution forbids dividing a state without its consent, but the real explanation is political. Each state has a set of elected officials whose concern it is to secure what policy benefits they can for their constituents. Among these elected officials are the members of the U.S. Senate and House of Representatives, and each state's congressional delegation tries to make sure that in passing federal legislation their particular state's interests are protected. In each state and city there are bureaucrats likewise trying to protect their funding, jurisdiction, and as much freedom of action as possible.

The American party system, as we shall see in later chapters, is highly decentralized. No national party leaders can determine who will be elected within any particular state. Not even the president can control local elections. Those officials derive their power from the support they receive within their respective constituencies, and they generally approach the policy issues of national government with the desire to preserve their state or local power bases.

A striking example of the power of local political interests over federal programs was provided, in 1965, by the federal Office of Economic Opportunity's attempt to cut off aid to the Chicago school system. The OEO decided that the city of Chicago was not following federal guidelines on school desegration. Federal aid to the Chicago school system was needed to keep the system running; however, in this case federal involvement in local school matters could mean federal control of local school operations. The OEO did cut off school aid to Chicago, but within a few weeks it backed down. In the process it suffered a major blow to its prestige and authority within the government.

Why did this happen? The OEO did not go beyond its legal powers. It would probably have been backed up by the courts, which were pushing in the same direction. It had the resources to back up its demand; the school district could not have functioned without federal aid. These two forces, the absence of court or constitutional limits on government power and its control over revenue sources, are what make the federal government so powerful.

Federalism has encouraged states to experiment. Women were able to vote in Wyoming as early as 1888. The nation did not collapse, and eventually other states followed Wyoming's example.

The one factor the OEO did not reckon with was the political power of the Chicago Democratic organization and its leader, Mayor Richard J. Daley. The Chicago political machine, one of the most effective such organizations in the country at that time, controlled a number of important resources, such as the Democratic votes of a major state, numerous members of Congress, and an important block of delegates at presidential nominating conventions. On the basis of such real political power, local government can thrive.

Of course, not all localities are as large as the city of Chicago, nor is power a matter of size alone. Few other cities have local governments as powerful as Chicago's at the time. Yet the localities, even small ones, have some influence over the federal government because of their political independence and because their representatives in Congress will defend that independence.

An additional factor that helps sustain the pattern of state and local governments in the United States is the fact that during most of our history they have been regarded with greater trust and confidence than the national government. The concept that government is better when it is "close to the people" has deep roots in American experience. Local government in particular is regarded as more within reach of citizen action, so that even if it is not always efficient, it is at least thought to be responsive to popular concerns. Reinforced by the self-interest of local officials and others happy with the status quo, this attitude has effectively resisted the plea for more logical organizational arrangements at state and local levels.

Moreover, states and cities have quite often worked out effective solutions to the problems peculiar to a particular area. These results might have been far more difficult to attain if they all had to be decided in Washington. The states have often functioned as experimental laboratories of public policy. Reforms such as the direct primary or the initiative and referendum, teacher competence testing and incentive pay, antilittering laws, tax and expenditure limitations like Proposition 13 in California, and a host of others—all could be adopted by one or two states and watched by others to see how they worked. Even some policies that eventually became national policies had their start at the state level. The Social Security system, for instance, was introduced in the United States as a program of old-age assistance in Wisconsin. In any case, state and local governments provide major services for all of us (see Table 3.4).

Policy experimentation by states and local governments is more effective today because of the structures of cooperative action and information

TABLE 3.4

STATE AND LOCAL GOVERNMENT SPENDING, 1981

Function	Spending Total (billions)	% of Total
Education	$145.8	35.9
Higher education	38.1	
Elementary and secondary	100.5	
Highways	34.6	8.5
Welfare	52.2	12.8
Health and hospitals	36.1	8.9
All other	136.9	33.7
Total	$405.6	99.8

SOURCE: *Statistical Abstract of the United States, 1984* (Washington, D.C.: U.S. Department of Commerce), p. 285.

State and local public officials are often influential advocates of national programs they believe important to their areas. Here Governors Mario Cuomo of New York and George Nigh of Oklahoma participate in a meeting of the National Governors' Association.

exchange that have been developed and strengthened in recent years. The National Governors Conference, the National Association of State Legislatures, the Council of State Governments, the National Association of Counties, the National League of Cities, the U.S. Conference of Mayors, and numerous other bodies provide the basis for research and interaction that have greatly enhanced the competence of state and local officials. At the same time, these organizations act as lobbying groups vis-à-vis Washington to preserve and perhaps expand the role of state and local governments in the American federal system.

Federalism and the Democratic Dilemma

We conclude our discussion of federalism by examining it in light of some of the fundamental tenets of democracy discussed in Chapter 1. In particular there is the problem of majority rule. In a unitary system where every citizen has one vote it is relatively easy to discover the majority's preference. But in our federal system the majority in Minnesota will often take a very different position from that preferred by the majority in Texas.

PROFILE ■

JOSHUA, COMMANDING THE SUN TO STAND STILL.

JOHN C. CALHOUN (1782–1850)
Political Leader for States' Rights

A public man for 40 years, and one of the most interesting political philosophers in American history. Calhoun was a member of the U.S. House of Representatives from South Carolina and a leading "war hawk," urging armed resistance to the British in 1812. Subsequently he served as secretary of war under President Monroe, vice-president under both John Quincy Adams and Andrew Jackson, a senator for 12 years, secretary of state under Tyler, and finally senator again.

Calhoun articulated South Carolina's opposition to the tariff of 1828 and in doing so developed the concept of state nullification of national action. Earlier he had supported strong measures by the central government, but as the sectional conflict between North and South grew more severe, Calhoun became a leading spokesman for states' rights in general and southern rights in particular.

In his last days Calhoun sought desperately for some way to reconcile southern autonomy and the protection of slavery with the continued viability of the Union. As he was dying, he wrote his *Disquisition on Government,* in which he developed the idea of concurrent majorities, whereby intensely held interests, like those in the south, could be protected against majority tyranny by requiring that on such questions a majority support be obtained in each major group or section concurrently.

Calhoun's arguments in politics and on paper were often brilliantly developed, but he was on the side that ultimately lost the political argument.

What does democratic theory tell us should be done in such cases? In a highly decentralized federalism we can allow each state to determine its own course of action, but that may allow some states to adopt policies that are strongly opposed by a large majority of the total population in the country. That is what happened, of course, with regard to slavery and, later, racial segregation in the South.

We do not escape from this dilemma by turning to centralized national decision making, however, for then the national majority may override the strong preferences of locally dominant points of view and impose the national view within the state or locality where it is extremely unpopular. Democratic theory does not give us clear guidance on the question of which majority ought to govern. A federal system in effect creates multiple arenas of governmental action with a different majority in each.

In the pre-Civil War era the distinguished political leader from South Carolina, John C. Calhoun, proposed the idea of **concurrent majorities.**

He argued that before a policy was adopted in the United States it should have majority support from each of the major sections of the country. Calhoun, of course, was attempting to defend slavery in the South, and the effect of his principle would have been to give the South a veto over national policies that offended their core values.

Veto group politics, though never officially incorporated into the constitutional rules of American government, has often been practiced in actuality. When there are several distinct interests in the country, each in disagreement with the others and relatively intense in its convictions, a majority will be hard to assemble. Even if one can be formed, however, it may be unable to persuade the rest of the country to accept its program without protracted conflict and resistance. In a democracy should each majority be able to impose its will on the rest? Or should there be some sort of veto, some form of concurrent majority principle, or some other way to protect the vital concerns of minorities? Federalism has provided one type of solution to this dilemma by decentralizing some of the decisions of government to the state level and letting state majorities determine the course of events within their own borders. But which issues should be left to the states? Which minorities should receive protection from majorities within a state or in the nation as a whole? We will return to these questions in Chapters 5 and 6 when we consider some of the issues of equality and human rights.

INSTITUTIONS IN ACTION ■

THE RISE AND FALL OF REVENUE SHARING

The story of relationships between the national government, on the one hand, and state and local governments, on the other, has a plot that is largely characterized by expansion—expansion in the dollars involved, in the substantive policy areas affected, and in the complexity of the connections that have evolved among the several levels of government. Federal grants-in-aid to state and local governments have been used for many years, of course, especially for programs in the areas of welfare and highway construction. As recently as 1960, however, less than $7 billion was spent in this fashion. More than 90 percent of this total went to the states, and the funds were disbursed under one or another of 132 different categorical grant programs. That seemed like a great many at the time, and during the 1940s and 1950s several different advisory commissions studied the problem, searching for simpler and more effective ways of addressing the nation's policy needs within the framework of a federal division of authority.

The 1960s transformed the intergovernmental system. By 1968, the end of the Johnson administration, the number of grant programs had tripled, to 387. Expenditures had risen to more than $18 billion with major increases in the fields of health (Medicaid), education, and welfare. Many of the new grant programs sent money directly to local governments, bypassing the states. Some bypassed city halls as well, and considerable tension resulted between mayors, governors, and other elected officials versus program bureaucrats and beneficiary groups. Also, many of the new grant programs were attached to expanded regulatory "strings," with requirements involving civil rights, environmental protection, and historic preservation, as well as a host of others.

The expanded federal role vis-à-vis state and local governments was largely the result of three facts. First, in the years following World War II states and especially cities found themselves facing rapidly growing needs for services and physical reconstruction. Second, state and local governments faced great difficulty in raising money to finance those needs. In part, this was because traditional revenue sources such as the property tax were not as flexible or responsive to economic growth as the federal income tax. Also, cities and states could not raise their tax rates without fearing that industry and residents would move to lower-tax communities. Third, the rural interests that dominated many of the malapportioned state legislatures of those years were often indifferent to the fiscal plight of the big cities, although the latter had somewhat greater political leverage with Congress and the president.

In 1969, when Richard Nixon took office as president, one of his early proposals to alter the policy course set by President Kennedy's New Frontier and President Johnson's Great Society was called New Federalism. There were several components to this initiative. One major effort was the consolidation of various categorical grant programs into a small number of block grants that would allow states and localities greater flexibility to set priorities and allocate moneys without so much detailed federal interference. Some block grants were developed—most notably in the areas of job training and community development—but the categorical programs continued to grow also, until the beginning of the Reagan administration, when both the number of grants and the dollar amounts began to decline.

A second thrust of the Nixon New Federalism was to rearrange certain program responsibilities. Specifically, he sought to make funding of Medicaid, Aid to Dependent Children (ADC), and various supplements to Social Security payments the exclusive responsibility of the national government, both as to standards of eligibility and amounts of money. A part of this was enacted, but Medicaid and ADC continued to be financed in part by the states, which vary in their levels of support. The Reagan administration also proposed to consolidate programs into block grants and to "nationalize" Medicaid, in return for which the states would take over ADC and food stamps. For the most part these proposals for realizing program responsibilities have not gained much support. What has turned out to be far more subject to political action, pro and con, is money.

In 1969, at the beginning of the Nixon administration, the prospects for federal revenue were optimistic. It was widely believed that the Vietnam War would soon come to a close, and that when it did there would be a large "dividend" of money that had been used for military purposes and could be reallocated among worthy domestic purposes. Moreover, many state and local governments were controlled by fiscally conservative Republicans whereas the more liberal Democrats had held Congress almost without interruption since 1933. If, as it seemed to many, the national government was very efficient at raising revenue but bureaucratically clumsy about operating programs, then it made sense to raise the money centrally and distribute it without any strings or requirements to the states and local governments. With these thoughts in mind *general revenue sharing,* as it was termed, was enacted in 1972.

For the first several years the program distributed about $6 billion per year among recipient governments according to a complicated formula in which population played the largest part. Two-thirds of each state's share was passed through to local levels, and after 1980, as state revenue prospects brightened, the state government share was eliminated. Different cities, counties, and states did different things with their revenue-share money, which, of course, was the main idea behind the program. Some invested in ice rinks and golf courses, while others folded the money into their regular budgets and thereby managed to avoid increases in local taxes. Most local governments were wary, however, of becoming fiscally dependent on a revenue source that might be taken away, and so there was a tendency to use the money for special projects, especially those expected to stimulate local economic investment and growth.

The political support for revenue sharing was always rather fragile. In Congress there were many members who felt that it was the height of political irresponsibility to turn billions of dollars over to states and cities without any control over the purposes of their spending. Others were worried about the growing proportion of state and local resources coming from the federal government, and they feared that such fiscal dependency might fatally undermine the autonomy of the states and cities. Still others were dubious about many of the program purposes for which revenue sharing and other federal grant money was being spent, and as part of a general effort to cut back the scale of government they hoped to trim large amounts from these intergovernmental transfers.

During the late 1970s the political and fiscal contexts of revenue sharing changed substantially from what its original sponsors had expected. For one thing, there was no fiscal dividend when the Vietnam War finally ended. Defense budgets remained high, and after the Reagan Administration took office in 1981, defense spending claimed still more of the revenue available to the federal government. Furthermore, spending for key domestic programs such as Social Security, Medicare, and Medicaid increased dramatically as costs went up and benefit levels were increased. Beginning in 1974 the oil crisis intensified inflationary pressures that drove up interest payments on the federal debt. In addition, inflation pushed personal incomes up into higher tax brackets, so that people found themselves paying significantly increased federal taxes and were complaining vociferously about it.

The first great push of the Reagan presidency in 1981 was to reduce federal taxes in the hope of stimulating economic growth. There is disagreement over how effective the tax cut was, as well as what may have been the impact of the 1982 increase in federal tax rates. In any case, it was clear that the federal deficit was growing rapidly, reaching proportions that alarmed nearly everyone in public life. Meanwhile, many state governments had entered a relatively prosperous phase. An important part of their revenues came from income tax, too, but state income tax rates were seldom very progressive, so that inflation did not push people as rapidly into higher brackets. Moreover, states drew more and more of their income from such sources as lotteries and from the sales tax, which responded to economic growth but did not seem to generate so much

protest from fiscal conservatives. Local governments, too, were finding methods of escaping some of the limitations of the property tax. The state of Michigan, New York City, and Cleveland had well-publicized budget crises in the 1970s, but, in general, state and local finances appeared by the mid-1980s to be in better shape than they had been, perhaps better than the financial state of the federal government.

All of this meant that programs of federal assistance to state and local governments were prime targets for severe budget cutting. In 1980, as we noted, the states were dropped as recipients of revenue-sharing funds. The program was reauthorized in 1983 for another three years, but President Reagan proposed its complete elimination thereafter, and inasmuch as there seemed little chance it would survive the deficit-reduction pressures, local governments began to plan ways to adjust to the reduction in their income. In the 14 years of its existence, revenue sharing shuffled $78 billion to states and to some 39,000 local governments. When the fiscal crunch came and federal spending had to be cut, however, it was this "no strings" revenue sharing that was the most vulnerable. No distinct constituencies existed for revenue sharing, unless it was the mayors and other local officials, in the way that they did for highway programs or Medicare or agricultural extension work. When President Reagan proposed a 60 percent reduction in agricultural extension for 1987, a vociferous aggregation of bureaucrats, farm interests, agriculture school officials, and others sprang to action. Revenue sharing served many groups, but its funds were never earmarked, and the beneficiaries differed considerably from year to year and place to place. The very flexibility of revenue-sharing money—that it could be used according to the priorities of each recipient government and reallocated according to shifting local need—prevented the emergence of a strong constituency that could defend the program when the federal fiscal stream began to run dry. Thus the story of revenue sharing is full of important lessons about how politics work in the United States. It is one of the few examples of a widely popular governmental program that could not survive serious budget competition.

CHAPTER HIGHLIGHTS ◼

1. Governmental power may be divided several different ways. In the United States the *federal* system is a hybrid form that preserves the states' rights while creating a strong national government.

2. Tensions between state-centered interests and those seeking a stronger, more centralized national political system have been continuous. They have been expressed in important constitutional cases as well as in other forms of political conflict.

3. Federal power over the states has grown, partly through increased regulation of state and local activity, but mainly because substantial federal money has been provided through various programs or grants.

4. Until recently the federal government had superior tax resources, and pro-spending interests had greater leverage there than at the state level. Thus pressures were strong to increase the level of federal aid to states and cities. Many, though by no means all, of the latter now are in better fiscal condition, while the federal government faces a huge deficit. The pressures for program growth have therefore changed.

5. State and local governments continue to be important political forces. Their officials are often effective lobbyists, and they display vitality in developing new ways to solve governmental problems.

SUGGESTED READINGS ◼

The development of American federalism is highly dynamic, for it involves the politics of 50 states and thousands of local governments as well as the national institutions.

Modern commentaries include William Riker, *Federalism: Origin, Operation, Significance* (1964); Morton Grodzins, *The American System* (1962); Daniel Elazar, *American Federalism: The View From the States* (3d ed., 1981); Robert Jay Dilger, ed., *American Intergovernmental Relations Today* (1985); George F. Hale and Marian Lief Palley, *The Politics of Federal Grants* (1981); David B. Walker, *Toward a Functioning Federalism* (1981).

Justice: Myth and Reality

LIBERTY, EQUALITY, AND JUSTICE

Federal Reserve Building, Washington, D.C.

Chapter 4

THE ECONOMY AND POLITICAL LIFE

A political democracy cannot be isolated from the economic environment in which it operates. Nor, for that matter, can economic activity be undertaken without reference to the framework of law and regulation that make it possible to conduct private business in an orderly way. From the time the Constitution was written, governments at every level have been involved in various economic activities: subsidies, protection, purchases, regulation, and sometimes even direct ownership. All of these manifold relationships are called the political economy. In this chapter we examine the principal elements of the American political economy.

We must keep in mind that there are deep differences of opinion about what is proper and what is effective in government-economy relationships: tax rates, monetary policy, bankruptcy laws, tariffs and import quotas—the list can go on and on. Moreover, these issues have been with us in one form or another since Alexander Hamilton, as President Washington's secretary of the treasury, proposed his broad program to promote the development of American manufacturers and was vehemently opposed by the secretary of state, Thomas Jefferson. Conflicts over the political economy raise fundamental questions about the ties between democracy and capitalism. As we examine these questions we will see some of the ways that each of these two sets of institutions and values imposes limits upon the other. The resulting tensions produce a great deal of what our political debates are about.

Economic and Political Ties

Each day, the *New York Times* includes an index to its special business section. One part of the index appears under the heading, The Economy. Here is a reproduction of that part of the index for one day in the fall of 1981. It is typical of the kind of news stories that this newspaper reports on the economy.

The Economy

The Government will institute a trade action for the first time next week accusing foreign governments of unfairly subsidizing steel exports to this country, Commerce Secretary Malcolm Baldrige announced. The move was viewed as increasing the dangers of a trade war. The countries that are expected to be cited are France, Belgium, Luxembourg, Rumania and South Africa. [A1.]

President Reagan is inclined to maintain his economic package unchanged, despite advice from aides and Republicans in Congress that he raise taxes to balance the budget. The debate within the Administration on the course of economic policy was said to be growing increasingly bitter. [D1.]

The prime lending rate was cut by the Chemical Bank for the second time this week. The new rate, down half a percentage point to 17 percent, matched the lowest rate of the year, set in March, but no other major banks followed Chemical's lead. Some economists predicted an industrywide move to the lower rate within days. [D1.]

The F.C.C. moved toward dropping its ban on ownership of cable TV stations by broadcasters and major television networks. It approved publication of a staff report supporting that view, and after 30 days is likely to propose the new policy formally. [D1.]

Most retail chain stores reported October sales gains were modest at best compared with the same month last year. Two retailers—Woolworth and Montgomery Ward—said sales for the month slipped from October 1980. Analyst warned that the Christmas season, when 40 percent of general merchandise is sold, could be bleak. [D2.]

The White House issued its list of Federal loan guarantee cuts. The main item in the $20.3 billion reduction will be $16 billion cut from Federal support for home-purchase loans. Also included will be cuts for small business, rural development and trade adjustment. [D3.]

Sugar prices support loans that would increase sugar users' prices at least 2 cents a pound this year were accepted by a House-Senate conference committee working. The current market price for raw sugar delivered in New York is about 16 cents a pound. [A19.][1]

What is striking about this list of news stories? Five of the seven stories are as much about the government as they are about the economy. One story is about the possibility of a trade war, set off by an action of the federal government. There is a story about President Reagan's tax and budget policies as they may affect the economy. The Federal Communication Commission (FCC) is considering a new policy that will affect the television industry. Another story reports that the federal loan program for home-purchases, small businesses, rural development, and trade adjustments is to be substantially reduced. Finally, there is a story about Congress-set sugar price support loans. In only two of the "economy" stories is there no reference to the government: a news item about commercial bank lending rates and another about levels of retail sales.

Fifty or a hundred years ago, a similar list of leading stories about the economy would not reveal such a close and constant relation between government and economy. The economy was more "independent" of government, though never completely independent. From the beginnings of the United States, there have been important mutual supports between actions taken in the economy, by so-called economic actors, such as banks, businesses, farmers, or workers, and actions taken in the polity, by so-called political actors, such as courts, executive agencies, voters, or lobbyists.

The thickening of the links between economy and government has accelerated during the twentieth century, especially during the last 50 years. Therefore, today, an analysis of the economic news is in large part an analysis of the political news as well, and vice versa—not many important political events can be described without reference to their economic causes and consequences.

This chapter provides a general introduction to the political economy of the United States. Subsequent chapters of the text provide examples and analysis to show the political economy at work.

---

[1] *New York Times,* November 6, 1981. Copyright 1981 by the New York Times Company. Reprinted by permission.

ECONOMIC ACTS IN THE POLITICAL SYSTEM

When we think about politics, we think about power and authority. The government, as was noted in Chapter 1, can force citizens to obey the laws, to contribute to government programs, and even to fight on behalf of a cause if the government declares war against another nation. Although the word *coercion* is harsh, it does in fact describe a great deal of the relationship between citizens and their government. Of course, citizens also enjoy rights and privileges, because they obey government laws. However, citizenship is, finally, an involuntary status. It is not really possible to live outside the boundaries of a nation-state, and all the laws and obligations associated with a nation-state.

Economic life, in contrast, supposedly provides a great deal of free choice, at least in the kind of economic system enjoyed by Americans. When we think about the economy, we think about the voluntary exchange of money and goods and labor. A consumer faces a large array of products and can choose whether to spend money on leisure activities, housing, or groceries. The consumer can also decide to keep consumption to a minimum, and invest in the future instead. Education is an investment in the future. It is spending money to improve skills so that a better lifestyle will be available at a later time. The economy offers a wide range of jobs, in many different locations. What skills people acquire and to whom they sell their labor are matters of choice.

Are economic choices free of constraints? Is it really accurate to see economic exchanges as completely voluntary, matters only of individual choice? A simple situation, one familiar to most Americans, suggests otherwise: buying a car. There is an economic choice at work here that appears to involve free decisions (a "market") by buyers and sellers. First, as consumers reveal their increased demand for smaller cars by buying more small cars, the industry responds by maintaining the supply: it builds more compacts and subcompacts. Because of the demand, the industry may raise prices on its current small-car models. Second, the decision to buy a car is a voluntary exchange, since no one is forced to buy or sell a car. The transaction will occur only when both sides are satisfied with the purchase contract.

There is something else at work here besides the market. The transaction between the buyer and seller is heavily influenced by factors not entirely within the control of the automobile dealers, manufacturers, or purchasers. Government policies have affected the interest rate that must be borne by the buyer if an installment loan is needed. Import quotas protect the American auto industry by limiting the flow of foreign-made cars into the United States, but they have reduced the number of less expensive foreign cars that are available. Safety and environmental regulations have forced impact-resistant bumpers and pollution control devices into the purchase. The list could go on.

However, at the same time that government seems to be complicating this otherwise voluntary economic decision, it is also taking actions that make the purchase feasible in the first place. For example, largely due to the influence of automobile and petroleum industries, public highways have been built and maintained by government so that we have somewhere to drive. Tax breaks have recently been offered to corporations that explore for oil so that we will have a continuous supply of fuel. Business has had much to say, some would argue too much, about those import quotas and regulations that can either help or cost the American automobile industry.

It would be easy to keep listing examples of how political life and economic life interact, how the government makes economic policies, and how economic events and trends affect the government. We need more than examples. We need some general perspectives on what can be called the **political economy** of the United States.

The Political Economy Question

Economics is the study of how society chooses to use **scarce resources**—labor, minerals, land, water, capital, knowledge—to produce various goods and to distribute those goods, now and in the years ahead, among different groups and people in society.

This definition of economics poses interesting questions. For what purposes should scarce resources be used? Difficult decisions have to be made, such as whether limited oil supplies should be used to heat homes or to keep gasoline prices down or to maintain the military at full strength. How much should go to satisfying current needs and how much to investing in long-range goals? Again these are difficult decisions, such as whether to close down a factory in Gary, Indiana, and throw some breadwinners out of work, or keep the factory operating even though it is contributing to the pollution of Lake Michigan. How should the goods in society be distributed among many competing groups? More difficult decisions: for example, providing free medical care for the elderly may mean reducing research on children's diseases.

Underlying all of these difficult questions is the most difficult question of all: Who in society will make the decisions about the use of scarce resources, the balance between present needs and long-term goals, and the distribution of goods among many groups? Should these decisions be made by the government? Stated most broadly, what is the proper relation between politics and economics?

This question has vexed many philosophers and social thinkers. Two of these thinkers have been especially influential: Adam Smith and Karl Marx. They provided the broad frameworks for the two grand economic schemes that exist and compete in the world today. We associate the term **capitalism** with Adam Smith and the term **communism** with Karl Marx. Both terms and the arguments they involve attempt to set out the proper relation between politics and economics.

Adam Smith   Two profound revolutions occurred in 1776. One was the rebellion of the American colonies against the English monarchy. The other was much more quiet. A Scotsman named Adam Smith published *The Wealth of Nations,* one of the most complete analyses ever done of human economic behavior and its proper effect on, and control by, the state.

Smith's book presented a compelling argument about the importance of individual initiative in an economic system. His thoughts had two major focal points: the individual himself and how a society composed of so many independent parts could hold together. In particular, Smith argued that a society of self-interested people, each person free to pursue his or her own wants in a competitive environment, will produce the correct amount of goods, and at the correct prices. The key to the market system was individual independence more than self-interest. Supply and demand, if left alone, would find a mutual balance at a suitable price, and from this, all would benefit. An individual, Smith said, "neither intends to promote the public interest, nor knows how much he is promoting it . . . he intends only his own gain; and he is in this, as in many other cases, led by an invisible hand to promote an end which was no part of his intention."[2] The *invisible hand,* perhaps the most famous phrase from Adam Smith, refers to the natural and unintended outcome of a free-market system: the efficient and automatic matching of consumer demand to economic production.

While Smith praises the market and is generally suspicious of government's effectiveness in helping the invisible hand, he saw some distinct flaws in the market that government might correct. For example, he believed that economic monopolies were inherently noncompetitive and should be dissolved. He promoted public education and worried about the effects of mass production techniques on the workers. Smith even tolerated the redistribution of wealth: "When the toll upon carriages of luxury . . . is made somewhat higher in proportion to their weight, than upon carriages of necessary use . . . the indolence and vanity of the rich is made to contribute in a very easy manner to the relief of the poor."[3]

We cannot overestimate the impact of *The Wealth of Nations.* Perhaps its impact was aided by the coincidence of its publication date: many have incorrectly assumed that it became an economic bible for the founders of the American republic as they tried to remove the burdens of government from their personal and economic lives. In any case, on its own merits, Smith's book stands in importance as a political-economic partner to the American Declaration of Independence.

Karl Marx   Many more persons in the world, even in the United States, are familiar with the name Karl Marx than with the name of Adam Smith. It is safe to say that there are many more people living under Marxist systems than under market systems. Karl Marx was the German social theorist who outlined the stages by which advanced capitalist countries would eventually become communistic. Though Marx was in many ways wrong in his predictions, his ideas about the most just way to organize the political economy have been enormously influential.

Karl Marx and Adam Smith actually had some similar assumptions

---

[2] Adam Smith. *The Wealth of Nations* (New York: Modern Library, 1937), book 4, p. 423.

[3] Ibid., book 5, p. 683.

about human economic behavior. They both believed that economic incentives were strongly motivating factors, indeed, that economic self-interest is more powerful as a motive than moralistic altruism. They both believed in the free will and self-interest of human beings. For Smith, such qualities were necessary for the invisible hand to operate in a capitalistic economy, while for Marx, such qualities would lead the working class to revolt against the exploitation by the ruling class.

Both theorists believed that the *proper price,* or the value, of a commodity, such as a bag of potatoes or a coat, is the amount of labor that was required to produce it. In addition, they both understood that capitalism is a form of organizing labor in order to produce "social surplus." A certain amount of material wealth is necessary if the people living in a society are to maintain their standard of living at its present level. If more wealth is produced than is necessary for this maintenance, it is called surplus wealth. The surplus can be used to create new wealth. It can be invested in research to produce new products, in machinery and equipment to increase the productivity of labor, in education to expand the talent and skills of the population, and so forth.

In a capitalist economy, this surplus is gathered through the system of wage labor. Workers are paid to work. Their time is bought, not the thing that they produce. Wage labor separates the worker from the product of his or her effort. Workers do not *own* the cars, the TV sets, or the garden tools that come off the assembly line. These things are owned by the company that owns the assembly line. Thus it is the company that accumulates the surplus wealth. It does so by selling the car or the TV set at a profit, the amount something can be sold for over the amount it costs to produce it.

Adam Smith argued that capital accumulation—the growth of the surplus wealth—would be beneficial to society if capitalists were left alone to invest their money in new enterprises. This is called *working capital.* It would buy new machinery and start new factories that would increase the demand, and the wages, of workers. All would benefit.

Karl Marx took a different view. The owners of capital not only would acquire wealth, some of which they would spend on luxury goods for themselves and their children rather than on new economic investments, they would also acquire power over the workers. They would force the workers to labor for the lowest wage possible in order to earn the greatest profits. Moreover, said Marx, the government would become an agency for the capitalist class. In Marxist theory, political power is merely the organized expression of one economic class, the owners or capitalists, oppressing another economic class, the working class. The solution was to abolish private ownership, to "socialize" the means of production. Those who labored should own the farms, the factories, and the mines. Class distinctions would disappear, and all citizens would benefit equally from the productive effort of society.

The United States, of course, has patterned its economy much more after Adam Smith than after Karl Marx. Yet the arguments of Marx have not been without influence. The political economy of the United States is not the pure capitalism envisioned by Smith.

DEVELOPMENT OF THE U.S. POLITICAL ECONOMY

Is the United States a capitalist society? Most citizens would probably agree when thinking about their right to own property or buy shares of stock in corporations. However, in its pure form, a capitalist market system cannot tolerate more than the very slightest role for government in making economic decisions. As we have already begun to realize, the American government plays a very significant part in economic matters, ranging from broad monetary policies that affect the number of dollars in circulation, to specific regulatory policies that determine the cost of automobile bumpers. American citizens have always seen a need for the state to support or direct some economic activities. After reviewing the evolution of economic policy, we will summarize the tools and approaches of contemporary American government as we struggle with the problems of the 1980s.

Politics and Economics in the New Republic

Many settlers came to the New World seeking economic freedom as well as political freedom. One cause of the American Revolution was resentment about the connection between England's economic policies toward the colonies (taxation) and its political policies (lack of political representation). Considering the history of the colonies and the issues of their time, it is not surprising that the writers of the Constitution of the United States were explicitly concerned with political economy.

One indication of that concern was the early American perspective on the proper role of government, with limited and divided powers that prohibited many forms of government intervention in economic matters. Yet the Founders did not always draw a distinct line between economic and political matters. During 1792, James Madison wrote that "government is instituted to protect property of every sort," and he was careful to distinguish between two kinds of property. First, he wrote, "a man's land, or merchandise, or money is called his property"; but also, "a man has property in his opinions and the free communication of them," that is, in certain political rights.

The early American Republic was quickly implicated in disputes about economic issues. Among the first major problems for the United States were the disposition of debts accumulated by the state governments to fight the Revolutionary War, the creation of a national bank to administer the government's taxing, borrowing, and currency powers, and an import tariff to protect fledgling American industries. All of these policies were politically controversial, with some factions arguing that these government activities were crucial for the new nation's survival, and with other groups insisting that these interventions were discriminatory abuses of national power. Nevertheless, by 1820, the leaders of the Republic had, for the most part, accepted a wider role for the federal government in economic matters than the Constitution had specifically prescribed.

The flexibility in the political-economic relationship that quickly emerged during the 1790s indicated several important features of the new American system. First, the response of the Founders to emerging crises (for example, the need to resolve the war debt, and the threat of cheap foreign imports to young American industries) showed that the American people would depend upon a government-business relationship that would not be fixed and unchanging, but would adjust to the needs of the times. That flexibility has allowed rapid and enormous expansions of the degree of government interference in the private sector (and perhaps some contraction in the 1980s). American business and political leaders have often shown more pragmatism than idealism.

Second, it became clear during the first 30 years of the United States that government was *required* to do some things to support the economy. The United States would need a stable currency and similar economic rules for all states. It would need a judicial system that would uphold the rights of individuals to enter into voluntary contracts and their rights to have those contracts upheld by law. It would flourish only if the individual enterprise of people could be rewarded with an improvement of their condition and social status. To avoid the growth of an America equivalent to the despised European aristocracy, class privileges would need to be abolished, or at least earned. All would need equal protection under the law. Economic and political freedom were necessary for each other.

Economic freedom in the United States, however, was not to be purely **laissez faire.**[4] Not only did the federal government support the economy with a legal framework of contracts and uniform currency and measures, but it also provided subsidies for private enterprise with public money. When Alexander Hamilton championed the National Bank (a public bank that would serve as an agent of the Treasury Department by taxing, borrowing, and controlling the currency), he was promoting a scheme that envisioned the federal government as an active participant in economic enterprises—eventually providing assistance in the form of subsidies, bounties, and tariffs. Only during the middle of the nineteenth century did Congress come close to rejecting Hamilton's vision, when, under the influence of southern cotton interests, it abandoned ship subsidies and talked seriously of genuinely free trade. The Civil War brought about an end to those discussions. Even today, presidents who speak of ending the government's involvement in the private sector seldom propose ending or even significantly reducing most forms of direct government support for various private interests.

Subsidies Today the federal government provides direct support of private enterprise in a variety of ways. One general category of support is the **subsidy,** which occurs in four principal forms. *Cash payments* can occur directly or indirectly and include various agricultural, medical, housing, and transportation programs. Recipients often prefer the less obvious (and thus less politically vulnerable) indirect payments. *Tax subsidies,* or tax expenditures as they are often called, are government policies that favor particular individuals or corporations by exempting some, or sometimes all, of their income from taxes. Most tax subsidies are designed to

---

[4] From the French "let alone," referring to an economic doctrine of keeping government intervention in the economy to a minimum. Sometimes used to refer to a free-market economy.

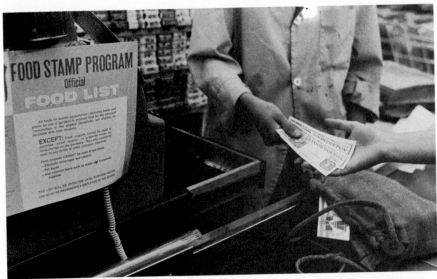

Food stamps are a form of government subsidy intended to assure an adequate diet for low-income people and, at the same time, help get rid of agricultural surpluses.

encourage investment, such as in mineral exploration or new residential housing (see Table 4.1). *Credit subsidies* involve the government absorbing the risk for loans. Many college students have benefited from federally guaranteed loans, but the largest credit subsidies have been in agriculture, housing, and foreign trade. Finally, the federal government provides *benefit-in-kind programs* that provide goods or services directly to citizens at public expense. Most of these programs have been in food, medicine, transportation, and postal service.

TABLE 4.1

TAX EXPENDITURES OF THE FEDERAL GOVERNMENT FOR HOUSING (BILLIONS OF DOLLARS)

	1983 (Actual)	1984 (Estimate)	1985 (Estimate)
Deductions on owner-occupied homes			
Mortgage interest	25.1	27.9	30.1
Property taxes	8.8	9.5	10.5
Deferral of capital gains	0.8	1.1	1.3
Exclusion of capital gains for owners over 55	1.3	1.6	1.9
Total	36.0	40.1	43.8
Exclusion of state and local bond interest	1.6	1.7	1.7
Tax breaks for mortgage lenders	2.7	1.1	0.8
Tax breaks for rental properties	1.4	1.8	1.9
Grand Total	41.7	44.7	48.2

SOURCE: U.S. Congressional Budget Office, *Tax Expenditures: Current Issues and Five-Year Budget Projections for Fiscal Years 1984–88* (Washington, D.C.: U.S. Government Printing Office, 1983), table A4.

The federal government began supporting industries through subsidies as soon as the Republic was founded. Public money was used to assist the dredging of rivers and lakes for navigation during the early 1800s. However, the majority of subsidy programs are no more than 50 years old. The largest programs date back to the 1930s, when agricultural price supports and merchant marine subsidies began, and to the 1960s, when "social" subsidies such as food stamps and medical care assistance were begun. Today all subsidy programs account for more than 25 percent of the total federal budget.

Purchases The **gross national product (GNP)** is the dollar figure obtained by adding together all the consumption goods, services, and investments produced by society. GNP is the yardstick that tells a society how well it is doing. When more goods are produced, more services are available, and more investments are being made, so the GNP increases. When there is an economic slowdown, the GNP drops.

The importance of government to the private economy can be seen in the percent of GNP accounted for by government expenditures. The federal government alone accounts for more than one-fifth of the GNP. Some of the federal budget is allocated for salaries for the 3 million civilian employees and the 2 million members of the armed forces. However, only about 15 percent of federal expenditures is used to pay the civilian workers, and about one-third of the defense budget is allocated to salaries and pensions. Much of the rest of government expenditure is on goods and services.

Since World War II, the U.S. government has been the largest single

President Reagan's expanded defense budget has meant, among other things, a great increase in contracts and jobs in defense industries.

customer for American industrial products and services. Were government purchases to stop, huge gaps would be left in the economy. This is especially true of the industries that supply the military. For example, the federal bailout of Chrysler during 1979 (with $1.5 billion of loan guarantees) would not have been sufficient without the Defense Department's multibillion-dollar purchase contract for new MX-1 tanks. Many of America's largest corporations depend on government contracts for most of their business.

Government purchase policies often have enormous impacts on particular industries. Strategic stockpiling of scarce materials such as zinc and titanium (used, for example, in the construction of fighter planes and the space shuttle) has cost the federal government billions of dollars, while higher prices are maintained for private buyers and sellers. It is estimated that one-fourth of American Telephone and Telegraph's revenues (over $20 billion in 1978) result from the government's use of telephones and other communications, and its function is so intertwined with that of the Defense Department that the military argued (unsuccessfully) that a federal breakup of the company would not be in the interest of national security. More generally, the space program's billions of federal dollars provided the research and development costs for today's growth in the telecommunications and computer industries.

Regulation   Government economic regulation dates back to the latter part of the nineteenth century, when a nation of farmers and traders was slowly being transformed into one of factory workers and industrialists. It was during the post-Civil War era that the United States was crisscrossed with railroads. Canals and harbors were opened up for shipping. Natural resources, especially coal, lumber, and oil, were being put to industrial use. Factories were mass producing consumer goods, telegraphs and telephones were spreading, and electricity was being introduced into at least city homes. By 1880 industry had replaced agriculture as the most important productive sector of the economy; the urban middle class quintupled between 1870 and 1910; and between 1860 and 1920, the number of people employed in agriculture fell from 59 percent to 27 percent. As America's economy was transformed from a largely agricultural system to a complex conglomeration of industries and corporations, new challenges were presented to the political system.

Recognition of a need for government regulation of some business activities grew slowly during the 1800s. For example, many states had tried regulating the railroads (primarily by limiting the rates that shippers could be charged), but interstate carriers were able to avoid many of those rules. Attempts by the industry to regulate itself always failed. The result was chaos, with continually changing shipping rates and railroads offering kickbacks to customers. By 1887, when the Interstate Commerce Commission was formed, many, but certainly not all, businesses and most consumers were willing to experiment with a new type of government intervention in the private sector.

Some historians have argued that since many railroads supported the idea of some regulation, the ICC must have been formed under their influence to serve them. The growth and direction of the ICC was heavily influenced by the railroads during its early years, but the beginning of economic regulation was not a total victory for big business. The Interstate Commerce Act specifically forbade some business practices, such as discriminating against shippers or combining railroads' earnings into a common "pool," and it established a federal regulatory commission with the authority to discourage "destructive competition" and investigate charges of railroad discrimination or extortion of small businesses.

The problems of small businesses were particularly important in the late nineteenth century. **Monopolies** and *trusts* were replacing the small entrepreneur as the moving force behind economic expansion—and as the most powerful segment of the political economy. The early "captains of industry" are remembered for the industrial empires they established: Rockefeller (oil), Carnegie (steel). Armour and Swift (meat packing), Pillsbury (milling), Vanderbilt and Stanford (railroads), and Morgan (banking).

The new way of doing business sometimes gave rise to monopolies, as when a single firm (say, Standard Oil of New Jersey) could so monopolize an industrial sector (mining, refining, and distribution of oil) that it could set prices at will. No other firm would be big enough to provide serious competition.

These conditions were considered the very root of the economic evils so distressing to the late-nineteenth-century reformers. The reformers wanted to break up the enormous concentration of economic power. "Trustbusting" became a popular political slogan. Supreme Court Justice Louis D. Brandeis, speaking of "industrial absolutism," warned of the danger to democracy when "there develops within the State a state so powerful that the ordinary social and industrial forces existing are insufficient to cope with it." Regulatory legislation was passed, such as the Sherman Antitrust Act of 1890, which prohibits monopolistic activities in restraint of trade, and the Federal Trade Commission Act of 1914, which prohibits unfair competition.

In the early decades of the twentieth century, the federal government began to establish regulations on working conditions and hours of work, especially for children and women. Consumer safety laws had begun with the Pure Food and Drug Act of 1906. Clearly, the American political-economic system had moved beyond laissez faire and mere support to direct government involvement in corporate and individual welfare.

Two more waves of regulatory growth have followed. The Great Depression of the 1930s sparked government intrusions in the securities industry (the Securities and Exchange Commission) and in worker-employer bargaining (the National Labor Relations Board). Regulatory agencies were also established in aviation (the Federal Aviation Administration) and in communications (the Federal Communications Commission). During the 1960s and early 1970s, a burst of reform attempts gave us the Environmental Protection Agency, the National Highway Traffic Safety Administration, the Occupational Safety and Health Administration, and other new regulatory agencies. Figure 4.1 shows that the decade of the 1970s had the highest number of new regulatory agencies in this century. The figure also indicates how for 80 years the government has intruded further and further into the economic system. The Republican administration elected in 1980 ex-

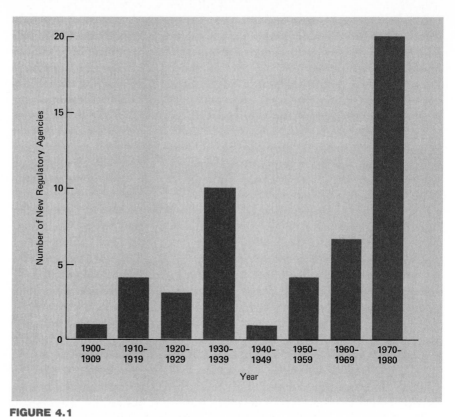

FIGURE 4.1

The Recent Acceleration of Regulatory Growth, According to the Center for the Study of American Business, Washington University, St. Louis

SOURCE: The *New York Times,* Feb. 15, 1981. Copyright 1981 by the New York Times Company. Reprinted by permission.

pressed great concern about this intrusion, and has attempted to slow down or even reverse the trend of government regulation.

Whether the cost to economic and individual freedom of government regulation has been worthwhile is very difficult to answer. How do we measure and compare the value of clean rivers versus employment opportunities from new factories? Is it justifiable to keep a dozen potentially useful drugs off the market in order to catch one cancer-causing chemical? Who has benefited the most? In spite of antitrust regulation, the United States still contains monopolies and oligopolies (only a few corporations control a particular part of the economy, such as in automobile manufacturing). Have the rich and powerful manipulated the government into providing regulations that limit the number of new competitors to existing firms, and guarantee their profits? These and related questions about the regulatory role of government will be discussed at several points in subsequent chapters, especially in Chapter 13 on public policy and Chapter 16 on the bureaucracy.

Public ownership   As we saw earlier in this chapter, the Founders of the American Republic recognized the importance of private property in our political and economic systems. That commitment has not diminished over the last 200 years. As the eighteenth-century America of farmers and small tradesmen was transformed into a modern industrial nation, forms of property other than land became increasingly important. Yet nearly all natural resources, productive processes, patents, and related components of an industrial economy remain privately owned. In this sense, the economy is still very much a capitalist one: private individuals, not the public or the state, own and reap the profits of the economy.

In this way, the United States is unusual among industrial nations. Of course, we expect that in socialist nations, such as the Soviet Union or East Germany, much of the economy is state-owned. These nations are greatly influenced by the writings of Karl Marx. However, it is easy to overlook the fact that there is much public ownership of economic enterprises even in Western democracies such as France or Great Britain. The United States is an exception, for there is very little government ownership and operation of natural resources, factories, transportation and communication systems, and basic social services.

Figure 4.2 makes this very clear. Variations in the scope of public enterprise are compared for selected countries. It is striking that only in the United States are most industrial sectors still in private hands. Of course, most of those privately owned industries are closely *regulated* or *supported,* so the American government does play a role in major businesses, but the state has been allowed only a small function as an owner.

The few exceptions to the American policy of private ownership offer

Industrial Sectors

(Privately owned: ○)   Proportion of public ownership: ◔ 25%   ◑ 50%   ◕ 75%   ● All or nearly all)

Country	Posts	Telecommunications	Electricity	Railroads	Gas	Coal	Airlines	Automobile Industry	Steel	Shipbuilding
United States	●	○	◔	○	◔	○	○	○	○	○
Belgium	●	●	◔	◔	●	○	●	○	○	○
Switzerland	●	●	●	●	●	n.a.	○	○	○	n.a.
Spain	●	◔	○	◕	●	◑	●	○	◕	◕
Germany	●	●	◕	◑	●	◑	●	◕	◕	◕
France	●	●	●	●	●	●	◕	◑	○	○
Britain	●	●	●	●	●	●	◕	◑	◕	○
Austria	●	●	●	●	●	●	●	●	◕	n.a.
Yugoslavia	●	●	●	●	●	●	●	●	●	●

The proportions shown are often approximate.

FIGURE 4.2

Share of Public Ownership in Selected Sectors in Selected Countries, 1978

SOURCE: Adapted from *The Economist,* March 4, 1978, p. 93.

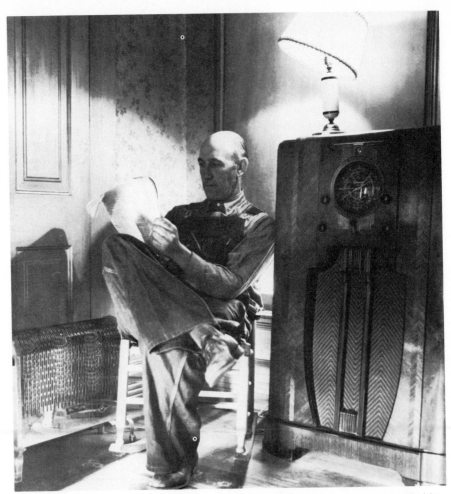

The TVA program built hydroelectric power plants in the Tennessee region, and its residents soon came to enjoy the results—electric lights, radio, and other modern conveniences.

some interesting illustrations of the occasional confusion over the proper role of government in the economy. At the local level, services such as electricity, water, sewage, and garbage disposal are provided by many but not all cities and counties. These utilities are characterized as "natural monopolies," where competition would be illogical. Sixteen states provide liquor retailing, two are involved in electric utilities, and most operate parks, toll roads, and bridges. In general, however, state governments are not directly involved in furnishing goods or services directly to individuals.

At the federal level, public enterprises are few but large. The Postal Service has a legally guaranteed monopoly on mail delivery, and costs taxpayers nearly $1 billion each year in federal subsidies. The Tennessee Valley Authority (TVA) was established in 1933 by President Franklin D. Roosevelt's New Deal policies with the intent of providing electric power to the impoverished Appalachian region. (The TVA is actually a government-owned corporation with private management which must charge electric rates that are competitive with private utilities; it is best described as a mix between the public and private sectors.) The Communication Satellite Corporation (Comsat) is another government corporation, as is the Consolidated Rail Corporation (Conrail), which was established during 1973 to provide a channel for public funds into the failing railroad industry in the northeastern and midwestern states.

In general, governments in the United States have been reluctant to enter the realm of business ownership. The local, state, and federal governments became owners or operators of businesses because of social pressures (such as the Progressive movement of the late 1800s that encouraged public ownership of utilities) or economic crises (such as TVA's origin during the Great Depression or the collapse of the Penn Central rail system during the late 1960s). Only a few public activities (postal, Comsat, roads) have emerged from a belief that the public sector could provide a service more effectively than the private sector. The Reagan administration has actively attempted to sell federal assets, such as Conrail. Among Western democracies, the United States is striking in its devotion to private enterprises.

Management We have seen that the federal government regulates some economic activities, subsidizes others, and owns a few. However, these functions should not be confused with management of the economy. The policies we have described are piecemeal; they attempt to correct particular flaws in the economic system. The flaw might be deceptive advertising: The government steps in to protect the consumer from being misinformed. The flaw might be something as substantial as monopoly control: The government steps in to break up the monopoly. However, regulation, subsidy, and public ownership have never been intended to manage the economy. It was not until the Great Depression of the 1930s that the government turned its attention to management questions.

During the period of industrial growth between the Civil War and the Great Depression, it was believed that a capitalist economy was self-adjusting. Full employment and price stability could occur if workers freely traded their labor for pay, if supply and demand regulated production and prices, and if profits guided the rate of growth and investment. Management of the economy was seen as unnecessary, in spite of occasional economic recessions, which are characterized by inflation and unemployment.

The *Great Depression,* which began with the stock market crash in 1929, altered many opinions about the relationship between government and business. Bankers and brokers had clearly failed to rescue financial institutions from the consequences of some ill-conceived business practices; so as unemployment climbed, factories closed, and banks failed, government leaders began to reject the old concept of a self-correcting capitalist economy.

Keynesian economics. The source of the new approach to government management of the economic system was a British economist, John Maynard Keynes, who argued that the government could stop the dangerous cycles of "boom-bust," in which periods of economic growth are followed by periods of recession. The tools of intervention, according to Keynes, would be tax adjustments, the level of government spending, and controls on the supply of money and credit. To stimulate employment and increase demand for goods and services, government should increase its expenditures—even spend more than it takes in from taxes (**deficit spending**). This fiscal policy would be accomplished by instituting public works programs such as the Public Works Administration (PWA): Between 1933 and 1939, the PWA built courthouses, hospitals, schools, the Key West causeway, aircraft carriers, combat planes, and many other projects that infused large amounts of federal money into a sluggish economy.

Today the government's economic policy is a major force in the free-enterprise system. The radical attempts during the 1930s to lift the nation out of its worst economic crisis led to programs and policies that are largely unquestioned today (see Table 4.2). The responsibility of the government for the health of the privately owned economic sector was established by the Employment Act of 1946, which declared that "it is the continuing policy and responsibility of the federal government . . . to promote maximum employment, production, and purchasing power." The intent of that sweeping policy has never been seriously challenged by political leaders, even those who claim to favor a greatly reduced role for government. In 1969, Richard Nixon could say, "We are all Keynesians now."

TABLE 4.2

GOVERNMENT EXPENDITURES BY FUNCTION LEVEL, 1981 (BILLIONS OF CURRENT DOLLARS)

Function	Federal Government			State Governments			Local Governments	
	Purchases	Transfer, Interest, Subsidy	Grants	Purchases	Transfer, Interest, Subsidy	Grants	Purchases	Transfer, Interest, Subsidy
Defense and veterans	$169.3	$ 20.2	$ 1.4	—	—	$ 0.6	$ 21.7	—
Civilian safety	2.1	—	0.2	$ 7.1	—	62.2	116.8	—
Education	1.4	6.0	7.9	33.8	$ 2.5	2.2	19.3	—
Health and hospitals	5.9	0.7	3.4	18.5	0.1	10.8	7.3	$9.0
Income support	5.2	258.2	39.9	32.4	11.1	0.8	13.3	-3.5
Housing and community service	0.4	6.4	8.2	0.9	0.4	0.8	5.5	—
Recreation and culture	1.2	0.4	0.3	1.2	—	—	2.6	-2.5
Energy and utilities	11.1	-1.4	1.1	0.4	-0.2	—	—	—
Agriculture	6.7	4.9	0.8	2.0	—	0.7	1.3	—
Natural resources	4.9	—	1.1	2.0	—	—	15.1	0.2
Transportation	6.5	2.3	11.7	17.7	0.9	4.6	—	—
Post office	0.5	0.9	—	—	—	—	1.0	—
Economic development	1.7	-0.1	0.9	1.9	—	—	—	1.0
Labor training	1.6	0.6	5.9	3.0	0.6	—	0.1	0.2
Commercial activities	—	—	—	—	-1.9	—	—	—
General purpose	10.5	73.1	5.0	17.0	-2.2	11.5	25.8	1.5
Total	229.2	372.2	87.9	138.0	11.2	93.4	230.0	5.9

SOURCE: Edward M. Gramlich, "Reforming U.S. Federal Fiscal Arrangements," in John M. Quigley and Daniel L. Rubinfeld, *American Domestic Priorities* (Berkeley, University of California Press, 1985), p. 38.

Monetarism. Not quite. During the late 1960s, another school of economic thought became important for the debate over economic policy. **Monetarism** challenged the Keynesian view as the era of low inflation and government budget surpluses ended. Keynes saw instability in private investment as a major cause of economic stagnation, and that government spending could be corrective. The monetarists, led by economist Milton Friedman, focused instead on instability of the money supply.

Beginning in 1913, with the formation of the Federal Reserve System (led by a rather independent Board of Governors), the government has attempted to manipulate the economy by changing the amount of money in circulation. The Federal Reserve Board can require its many member banks, 6000 in all, to hold more money in reserve and to lend or invest less. It can indirectly affect interest rates on loans to businesses and individuals by changing the interest rates that banks must pay. It can also alter the money supply by buying and selling government securities, thereby releasing or absorbing money.

Monetarists claim that the Federal Reserve Board (FRB), which is often immune to presidential or congressional pressure, has actually contributed to depressions, recessions, and **inflation.** Because FRB policies have a much quicker impact on the economy than most presidential or congressional policies (which are mainly fiscal policies since they usually involve tax adjustments or budget changes), monetarists believe that the unevenness of monetary policy is the primary villain in our economic troubles. In addition, because the FRB may be trying to control inflation by restricting the money supply at the same time that elected politicians are increasing the money supply through tax reductions or increases in federal spending, our national economic policies may sometimes conflict and cancel each other.

Both Keynesian and monetarist approaches are based on some very important assumptions about economic mechanisms, for example, why we have inflation and unemployment and how the two are related. One point of view was particularly important in economic policy during the 1960s. An English economist. A. W. Phillips, published an influential paper during 1958 that led to a belief that a negative relationship existed between inflation and unemployment. When the rate of unemployment is high, the rate of inflation is low, and vice versa.

Thus during the 1960s, many economists believed that a Phillips curve trade-off existed and that lower unemployment could be obtained if higher inflation were tolerated. Unfortunately, *both* inflation and unemployment rose during the recession of 1970. During 1971, Richard Nixon took the very strong step of imposing the first peacetime wage and price controls in American history. With few exceptions, employers were forbidden by the federal government to raise workers' salaries, and sellers were prevented from raising their prices. Inflation did decline during the 18 months of the wage-price freeze (from 4.5 percent to about 3.3 percent), but prices skyrocketed when the constraints were lifted. The combination of inflation and unemployment, sometimes called "stagflation," continued into the 1980s.

Supply-side economics. Still another approach to management of the economy emerged during the late 1970s and became a political issue during

Modern business corporations are enterprises of enormous scope, often with worldwide interests, huge capital investment and thousands of employees, and substantial power.

the 1980 presidential campaign. It is called **supply-side economics,** because it stresses the supply of money for new economic activities. The supply-side model emphasizes the incentives that encourage consumers to buy, savers to invest, and individuals to work. If government reduces taxes, argues the supply-side model, then citizens keep more of each dollar they earn, and they will have a large incentive to work, save, and invest. Only by increasing the output of the American economy can we expand our real income, cut inflation, and create new jobs.

The supply-siders base their arguments partly on a concept called the Laffer curve. At a zero tax rate there will be no tax revenues, and at a

100 percent tax rate no one will bother to work (since they would lose everything to the Internal Revenue Service). There should be some tax rate between zero and 100 percent that maximizes tax revenues. Because a tax cut will stimulate the efforts of individuals and corporations to produce more, tax revenues should increase (as people and businesses have more income to tax).

Supply-siders also point to some evidence they think supports their concept of economic policy. A tax cut during 1964 reduced individual tax rates by about 20 percent, and corporate taxes by about 8 percent, yet the federal government appears to have taken in more tax revenues during the following three years. Some economists, including the architect of the 1964 tax cut, find different explanations for its success, and they worry that a massive tax cut at a time of high inflation would simply enlarge the federal deficit and increase inflation even more. The fact is that no one really knows for certain what the precise effects of tax cuts are on tax revenues and inflation (that is, where the rightmost point of the Laffer curve is).

The Reagan administration was elected during 1980 largely on the basis of its plan to cut inflation by cutting taxes, a policy that is attractive to politicians and taxpayers alike. It quickly became clear, however, that because the potential benefits of supply-side economic policy (increased tax revenues) would require some time to be realized (since the incentives from lower tax rates would only gradually produce more taxable "supply"), the administration and Congress needed to make some painful decisions on budget cuts in order to avoid even more enormous federal deficits— and inflation. The need to reduce the federal budget conflicted with Reagan's determination to increase military spending, and by 1982 the government was announcing very large federal deficits—spending approximately $100 million more than it took in revenues. The economy was not responding to the Reagan economic policy. There was widespread concern that the tax cuts would not lead to economic growth. By the middle of 1982 Reagan was being forced to compromise on the supply-side economic policy initiated only a year earlier, and he reluctantly agreed to a tax increase.

By 1983, however, the economy began to surge forward. Unemployment dropped and inflation nearly disappeared. The Reagan administration insisted that this success was due to its efforts to reduce the federal government's economic role. In the 1984 election it was apparent that many voters agreed. Nevertheless, the deficit continued to grow, approaching the $200 billion level by 1986 (see Figure 4.3). The central issue of domestic politics had become how best to gain control of the deficit.

AMERICAN CAPITALISM AND DEMOCRACY

Two facts are now clear. First, the government is heavily involved in economic affairs. This is shown by the importance to society of the annual government budget, possibly the single most critical document produced by the government. It is apparent in the structure of the government.

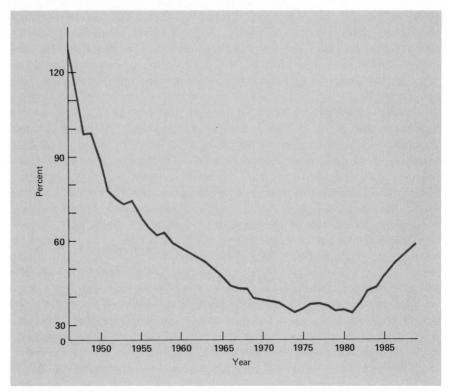

FIGURE 4.3

Gross Federal Debt As Percentage of Gross National Product, Fiscal Years 1946–1989

SOURCE: Paul E. Peterson, "The New Politics of Federalism," in John E. Chubb and Paul E. Peterson, eds. *The New Direction in American Politics* (Washington, D.C.: Brookings Institution, 1985), p. 369.

The president's cabinet includes secretaries of commerce, agriculture, labor, the treasury, and transportation; important executive agencies include the Federal Trade Commission, the Interstate Commerce Commission, and the Securities and Exchange Commission; and the most powerful committees in Congress are those that deal with taxation, budget review, and appropriations (see Chapter 14). Through its involvement in the economy, the government supports private enterprise, regulates economic activities, and attempts to manage general economic conditions.

The second fact, however, balances this picture of government involvement. Major features of capitalism remain. Private individuals own the mines, the trucks, the chemicals, the factories, the grocery stores, and the land of America. These private individuals are very often organized as corporations, and the amount of resources and wealth controlled by the larger corporations is great indeed. Because the economy is privately owned, it is run in order to make profits for the owners. Thus private ownership and unplanned and uncoordinated economic exchanges remain important features of economic life in the United States. They distinguish the American capitalist economy from, say, the economy of the Soviet Union or China. In the Soviet Union, greater emphasis is put on centralized authority to direct behavior in socially productive ways. In China there is more emphasis on the techniques of education and propaganda to instill appropriate social values in the population. The United States relies more on the marketplace, the incentives, the temptations, and the coercive nature of economic reward.

The "free market" is a concept that is derived from individual self-interest and the attraction of rewards. People work, consume, produce, invest, and save, because they expect to be compensated for their efforts. In other words, the free-market system offers *incentives* for individuals to participate in the economy. To some degree, that system operates in the United States: business magazines commonly carry stories about entrepreneurs with clever ideas who have made their fortunes by exploiting the demands and opportunities of the market. Of course, the market system also offers *disincentives* (sticks, as opposed to carrots) to those who fail, or who do not take advantage of their opportunities. Those same magazines also report on new business ventures that have collapsed. Although the incentive system has been softened somewhat by "safety nets" (for example, unemployment insurance, bankruptcy reorganization laws, and federal subsidies), it is still possible to win or lose in the American economy.

There seems to be little debate in the United States about the rules of the game, at least as far as the winners are concerned. It is accepted, both as faith and as common sense, that people work more when they are rewarded, and work less—or not at all—when they are not rewarded.

As we have seen, however, the United States does not have a completely

Much American economic activity operates through a highly competitive market, but the "mom and pop" store may seldom be able to survive the demand for efficient performance.

free-market economy. As Adam Smith predicted, there is a tendency in a capitalist system for economic power to aggregate into a few (oligopolies) or single (monopoly) corporations. Entrepreneurs who attempt to enter the market with hard work and clever ideas can find themselves blocked, co-opted, or bought out by giant companies acting alone or in cooperation with each other (cartels).

The inventor or business executive who follows the free-market incentives to seek rewards for his or her efforts may run into other obstacles in the American economic system. Existing corporations may be able to deflect such challenges by cooperating with the government in devising "market entry" regulations that restrict new companies from competing with existing ones, or by exploiting their federal contracts, subsidies, or loan guarantees to boost their market strength. The government also continually changes many of the rules for success by altering its economic policies. For example, new enterprises can find it very difficult to raise the funds to build new plants or buy equipment if federal policies have raised interest rates on business loans.

Of course, the effects of government intervention in the economy are not all opposed to entrepreneurs. Many government policies are intended to improve the overall business environment. Economist John Kenneth Galbraith, in *The New Industrial State,* spells out the chief goals of the state: "The state is strongly concerned with the stability of the economy. And with its expansion or growth. And with education. And with technical and scientific advance. And, most notably, with the national defense,"[5] stability is necessary to long-term corporate planning. Economic growth brings profits, promotions, and prestige. Trained manpower, scientific research, and technical development are necessary to a modern industrial system. Defense spending directly supports, through government contracts, a large part of the economy. In addition, there are many government programs, for example, Small Business Administration loans, that are designed specifically to encourage or support new businesses.

Critics of Contemporary Capitalism

Although most observers agree on the facts of the relation between the economy and the government, not all feel comfortable with these facts. The critics note that the growth of concentrated economic and political power, and especially the joint operation of these powers, makes it more and more difficult for citizens to control their own lives.

Milton Friedman is one such critic. Freedom, he writes, "is a rare and delicate plant." Great care is necessary to protect it. "Our minds tell us, and history confirms, that the great threat to freedom is the concentration of power." Friedman is especially concerned about concentration of power in the government. Although government is necessary to preserve freedom, it can also threaten freedom. The truly free person will ask, "How

---

[5] John Kenneth Galbraith, *The New Industrial State* (Boston: Houghton Mifflin, 1967), p. 304.

can we keep the government from becoming a Frankenstein that will destroy the very freedom we establish it to protect?"[6]

In this analysis it is the concentration of power in the government that is to be avoided. The government has grown huge because it is so involved in the economy. If it allowed the economy to take care of itself, the need for large government bureaucracies and budgets would be less. And there would be less risk that the government would restrict individual freedom.

Other critics give more attention to the dangers of concentrated economic power. This criticism takes note of the ease with which great wealth in the hands of a small group can be converted into political control. If there are great inequalities of control over economic resources, the argument goes, it is hard to see how the equal political influence promised by a democracy is possible.

Paul Baran and Paul Sweezy, noted Marxist economists, claim that "the incessant repetition that the political regime in the United States today is a democracy" is a falsehood "devoid of all descriptive or explanatory validity." In the United States, they continue, "the propertyless masses have never been in a position to determine the conditions of their lives or the policies of the nation's government." A tiny group "resting on vast economic power and in full control of society's political and cultural apparatus makes all the important political decisions. Clearly to claim that such a society is democratic serves to conceal, not to reveal, the truth."[7]

Whether they express fear of government power or fear of corporate power, the critics share a concern that the political-economic partnership in the United States is a threat to individual liberty and democratic values, a fear that is somewhat confirmed in this book. Friedman's concern over the erosion of individual liberty, for instance, seems to be well founded when we begin to review the enormous government bureaucracy and the range of government regulations that impinge on individual citizens. And the strong language of Baran and Sweezy, who claim that the wealthy class of owners and managers is not subjected to democratic controls, is supported by evidence of how economic inequality affects political participation (Chapter 7) and by data on the strong role of interest groups (Chapter 9) and the weaker role of political parties (Chapter 10).

Politics and Economics: Mutual Dependence

Despite the fears of concentrated powers, most observers recognize the necessary ties and tension between capitalism and democracy. An analysis has been provided by Charles Lindblom, a political scientist.[8] He described American (and Western European) societies as being composed of two major leadership groups: government officials, who (more or less) express the wishes of the voters, and business executives, who bear the

---

[6] Milton Friedman, *Capitalism and Freedom* (University of Chicago Press, 1962), p. 2.

[7] Paul A. Baran and Paul M. Sweezy, *Monopoly Capital: An Essay on the American Economic and Social Order* (London: Pelican, 1968), p. 327.

[8] Charles E. Lindblom, *Politics and Markets* (New York: Basic Books, 1977).

major burden in organizing the most important functions of modern society, namely, producing, putting people to work, and distributing income.

In systems such as ours, business executives usually cannot be forced to perform these functions. Only in national emergencies such as war or economic crisis can governments legitimately command businesses. During normal times, the government must provide support and incentives to induce businesses to provide a satisfactory economic network of goods, services, and jobs. This, according to Lindblom, is the most important task for government, since a failure in such policies would lead to economic stagnation and unemployment—and defeat for those in elected offices.

Capitalist democracies, therefore, consist of two major sources of influence. Voters can control governments with the rather blunt instrument of the ballot, and democratic governments *are* ultimately responsible to them. However, businesses have a privileged position, because government often must work through businesses (that is, their prices and wages) in order to gain that electoral support. Consequently, the economic controls of business executives (exercised by their financial and organizational advantages in influencing elections) are always a potential threat to the democratic controls of voters.

The outcome of these stresses need not be disastrous. After all, most people, citizens and business leaders alike, basically share the same desires for financial and personal success and security. When a business is successful, with or without government help, it does create more jobs and offer new goods and services for consumers. Yet in this chapter we have seen that dislocations occur along the way to those ultimate goals. A new product may make an old one obsolete, leading to layoffs for the producers of animal harnesses or slide rules. Corporations can form cartels that deny equal opportunities for success to entrepreneurs. Past inequalities in income can cascade down the generations as the descendants of the poor are denied the opportunity to learn new skills.

All of these problems are rooted in the characteristics of our economic and political systems. Whether they can be resolved or tolerated is an issue for every generation of Americans. In Chapter 5 we will examine the nature and causes of these tensions.

Indeed, the picture of the American economy and government that emerges from this chapter is in large part the context within which many aspects of politics must be examined. In the next chapter, for example, we look more closely at the tension between citizenship equalities, on the one hand, and economic inequalities, on the other. In later chapters we review how citizens' political participation and choice of leaders are affected by the distribution of wealth.

The economy also sets the context within which many political conflicts take place. For example, interest groups compete to attract federal moneys to the causes they represent, as when a truckers' association wants more money spent on the federal highway program and a citizen action group wants that money spent on mass transportation. Because so many of the issues of American politics are derived from contemporary capitalism, the formulation of public policies in the legislative, executive, and judicial branches of government is closely linked with the political economy. As briefly noted earlier, the organization of the government reflects concern with the economy. There are government programs that fund research and train personnel; there are government bureaucracies that regulate economic activities; there is the taxing and spending power of government, which is used to influence prices, employment, and private investment.

As we turn to the actual working of the national, state, and local governments in the United States, we will be constantly reminded that there are political-economic conditions that loom large in the who, what, how, and why of American politics.

CONCLUDING THOUGHTS

We have seen that no tidy or constant boundary separates the government and the economy. Rival theories and competing interests abound, each seeking to persuade the public that its program or formula will be more effective in promoting economic growth and providing jobs. No political leader in the United States, or elsewhere, can disavow responsibility for making the economy work. The political economy involves more than generating a large Gross National Product. It also raises questions of fairness and justice. As political leaders stimulate growth, how much attention should they pay to those whose jobs are lost to new technologies? How much help (i.e., subsidy) should be given to aid the less efficient automobile producer or the farmer who produces more than consumers want? In a democratic society a fair distribution of economic rewards may be as important as the overall size of the economic pie. And what is fair?

We have seen that a very difficult economic dilemma grows out of the fact that large business corporations possess substantial power over their employees, over the communities in which they are located, and sometimes over the institutions of government themselves. Concentrations of power were feared by the Founders because they realized that power, whether political or economic, could be abused, and that is still true today. Moreover, political or economic power fosters inequality. Indeed, it tends to multiply inequalities as money, social position, and political influence accumulate in the hands of some citizens and elude the grasp of others. In the next chapter we examine the issues of equality in the United States.

CHAPTER HIGHLIGHTS ■

1. No tidy boundary separates the government and the economy. This fact raises questions about the proper relations between the two.

2. Adam Smith provided one answer: The government's role should be kept to a minimum, allowing as much free choice and exchange as possible in the economy. This would promote economic growth and the well-being of all citizens. Karl Marx came to different conclusions: The free market promotes the accumulation of wealth, which in turn gives excessive powers to the owners of the means of production. This will damage, not further, democracy. The political economy of the United States has developed in several stages and is much more influenced by Smith than by Marx.

PROFILE ■

ADAM SMITH (1723–1790)
Scottish Philosopher

His *Wealth of Nations* (1776) was a wide-ranging examination of the economic order and a brilliantly persuasive argument on behalf of a free economy over one that was state directed. Widely regarded as the intellectual godfather of modern capitalism, Smith acknowledged that most people would seek their own interests without regard for larger public needs, but he contended that the aggregate social outcome of unfettered individual enterprise would be enhanced well-being for the whole society. His

famous "invisible hand" would produce the greatest good for the greatest number out of the apparently uncoordinated efforts of countless individual entrepreneurs.

Smith did not depend entirely on the invisible hand for desirable social results. In his *Theory of Moral Sentiments* (1759) he stressed the importance of a sympathetic concern among people for one another as a natural part of a cohesive society. Individuals should not be thought of as isolated from each other or lacking in social concern. The free workings of a market economy would encourage specialization and division of labor and increase the efficiency of production and trade. Mercantilism, the prevailing style of governmental economic policy in Smith's era, whereby the state directed much of economic life and tried to protect domestic enterprise against foreign competition, was bad because it deprived the society of the advantages stemming from improvements in productivity. Smith favored free trade and was an opponent of monopoly. But he also spoke about the importance of virtue and sympathy as necessary elements of the human situation. For Adam Smith the invisible hand of individualistic capitalist enterprise played a big part in his theory, but it was only a part.

3. The early period established the principle of flexibility in the political economy. The federal government supported the economy with a legal framework of contracts and uniform currency and measures. It also allowed the introduction of government subsidies for certain desired economic activities.

4. Early subsidies included funds to dredge rivers, and land to build railroads. More recent subsidies include price supports for agriculture, special cash payments, tax credits, and programs that provide services to citizens at public expense.

5. Government also supports the economy through its purchases, and it now accounts for about 20 percent of the total Gross National Product.

6. Starting around the turn of the century and continuing through the 1970s, the government has been actively engaged in economic regulation especially intended to minimize some of the damage caused by capitalist activity.

7. Public ownership has been minimal in the U.S. economy, but not totally absent. There is public ownership of the postal services, and of some transportation systems and utilities.

PROFILE ■

KARL MARX (1818–1883)
German-born Philosopher
and Social Theorist

Marx's writings, which were prodigious in both quantity and complexity of argument, have formed the basis of even more prodigious amounts of commentary, elaboration, and analysis. Marx started along the path to a normal academic career, but his political and social views soon got him in trouble, and he moved into radical journalism, first in Germany and then in Paris, Brussels, and, from 1849, England. Marx was active in organizing radical parties of workers and intellectuals—generally called socialist of some sort or communist—and in constructing international linkages among them.

The *Communist Manifesto,* written in 1848 with his friend and principal financial supporter, Friedrich Engels, was Marx's most eloquent (and shortest) version of his basic assumptions and arguments about the nature of industrial capitalism and the possibilities of revolutionary action. The next year, however, Marx was forced to leave continental Europe and take up residence in the much freer atmosphere of England. There he began to work in the British Museum and to produce the complex analyses of economic and social history and theory that culminated in the three volumes of *Capital.*

Marx wrote so much and on so many topics, and his theories were on such a grand scale, it is no wonder that his writings have spawned a vast array of commentary and interpretation. What Marx really meant is the theme of whole libraries of work by scholars and political activists throughout the world. Some of that work is hostile, but for many intellectuals Marx represents the foundation of any radical critique of modern society. To oppose industrial capitalism is to be Marxist—to find one's arguments and analytic perspectives somewhere in Marx's writing. Marxism has thus become a kind of secular faith of the political left, a set of beliefs and commitments and not just an analytic orientation. Marx himself helped found the Socialist International, and socialists ever since, in all their rich variety of perspective and interpretation, claim intellectual descent from Marx. Different "brands" of socialists and communists often oppose one another bitterly but share a professed reverence for Marx.

Marx was buried in Highgate cemetery in North London. After a time his admirers had a grave marker constructed. It consisted of a large marble block with a massive sculpture of Marx's head on top. It was a fitting memorial to a man whose thinking has been the basis of so much of the modern agenda of political action.

8. Economic management was first tried in the 1930s, using the doctrines of Keynesianism. More recently, there have been economists advocating monetarism and supply-side economics. The intent is to manipulate government spending, taxes, money supply, and budget deficits in order to sustain economic growth at low levels of unemployment and inflation.

9. There are tensions in the relation between capitalism and democracy. Some observers worry about the damage to democracy if government is too involved in the economy, and therefore accumulates too much control over the citizens. Other observers worry about the damage to democracy if business is unregulated and uncontrolled, and therefore becomes a social power in its own terms.

10. Our political economy has evolved to the point where political leaders and business leaders are linked through a complex network of mutual dependence. An economy in trouble creates difficulties for both sets of leaders.

SUGGESTED READINGS ■

Economists and social theorists have generated a vast literature assessing political economies, past and present, and prescribing what they believe could be desirable reforms.

Classics include Adam Smith, *The Wealth of Nations* (1776); Karl Marx, *Das Kapital* (3 vols., 1867–1894). Modern commentaries include Paul Baran and Paul Sweezy, *Monopoly Capital: An Essay in the American Economic and Social Order* (1968); Albert Szymanski, *The Capitalist State and the Politics of Class* (1978); John Kenneth Galbraith, *The New Industrial State* (1967); Irving Kristol, *Two Cheers for Capitalism* (1978); James Alt and Alec Chrystal, *Political Economics* (1983); Herbert McClosky and John Zaller, *The American Ethos: Public Attitudes Toward Capitalism and Democracy* (1984); Charles Lindblom, *Politics and Markets* (1978).

A Polling Place

Chapter 5

CITIZENSHIP: EQUALITIES AND INEQUALITIES

We hold these truths to be self-evident that all men are created equal.

Declaration of Independence

No State shall "deny to any person within its jurisdiction the equal protection of the laws." [U.S. Constitution, Amendment XIV, Sec. 2]

Civil Rights Act of 1964, Title VII

W ith these statements Americans have affirmed a basic commitment to equality. No person is to be burdened with an inferior legal status. Everyone is entitled to evenhanded treatment. But what exactly do those noble phrases mean in actual practice?

When I Grow Up

In 1940, a 15-year-old black youth named Malcolm Little had a conversation with a teacher about what he should become when he grew up—hardly an unusual or remarkable event. What was unusual was that this particular youth wrote that conversation down 25 years later in a book he wrote about his life, under the title *The Autobiography of Malcolm X.*

Somehow, I happened to be alone in the classroom with Mr. Ostrowski, my English teacher. He was a tall, rather reddish white man and he had a thick mustache. I had gotten some of my best marks under him, and he had always made me feel that he liked me. He was, as I have mentioned, a natural-born "adviser," about what you ought to read, to do, or think—about any and everything. We used to make unkind jokes about him: why was he teaching in Mason instead of somewhere else, getting for himself some of the "success in life" that he kept telling us how to get?

I know that he probably meant well in what he happened to advise me that day. I doubt that he meant any harm. It was just in his nature as an American white man. I was one of his top students, one of the school's top students—but all he could see for me was the kind of future "in your place" that almost all white people see for black people.

He told me, "Malcolm, you ought to be thinking about a career. Have you been giving it thought?"

The truth is, I hadn't, I never have figured out why I told him, "Well, yes, sir, I've been thinking I'd like to be a lawyer." Lansing certainly had no Negro lawyers—or doctors either—in those days, to hold up an image I might have aspired to. All I really knew for certain was that a lawyer didn't wash dishes, as I was doing.

Mr. Ostrowski looked surprised, I remember, and leaned back in his chair and clasped his hands behind his head. He kind of half-smiled and said, "Malcolm, one of life's first needs is for us to be realistic. Don't misunderstand me, now. We all here like you, you know that. But you've got to be realistic about being a nigger. A lawyer—that's no realistic goal for a nigger. You need to think about something you can be. You're good with your hands—

Malcolm X, a strong advocate of black power, moved people when he spoke at this Harlem rally.

making things. Everybody admires your carpentry shop work. Why don't you plan on carpentry? People like you as a person—you'd get all kinds of work."[1]

Malcolm Little did not become a dishwasher or even a carpenter. He became a minister in the Black Muslim Church, and he took a new name, Malcolm X. He also became one of the most learned, articulate, and forceful leaders in American society. Until his death by an assassin's bullet in 1965, Malcolm X, by force of intellect and force of personality, worked with a small handful of men and women who revolutionized race relations in America.

The message delivered by Mr. Ostrowski in 1940 was not particularly unusual. The promises of citizenship aside, various racial, ethnic, and religious groups, as well as women, have been told, at different times in our political history, to "keep in their place" or, more gently, "to have realistic goals."

But keeping people in their place is exactly what American citizenship is not. Citizenship in the American democratic tradition is the assertion that all members of society—without regard to race or national origin or sex—have certain equal rights. Bringing these rights to all citizens has proved to be a slow and painful, at times even violent, process. Substantial progress, however, has been made. Forty years after Malcolm Little was told, "A lawyer—that's no realistic goal for a nigger," American law schools are actively recruiting black students, as they are women and other groups

[1] Malcolm X, with the assistance of Alex Haley, *The Autobiography of Malcolm X* (New York: Grove Press, 1965), pp. 36–37. Reprinted by permission of Random House, Inc.

previously discriminated against. This chapter talks about the role of citizenship in trying to achieve a society without discrimination and injustice.

CITIZENSHIP AND EQUALITY

When Thomas Jefferson drafted the Declaration, he knew, of course, that all people were not "created equal." Individual differences in ability, intelligence, ambition, and talent can hardly be denied. Yet Jefferson and those who signed the Declaration with him were not just spouting empty political slogans. The signers wanted to go on record against a political order in which members of society were *legally* unequal.

In this regard, the nation's Founders were being boldly innovative. They were deliberately breaking with English traditions, in which members of society were assigned to different legal classes. In those traditions, certain privileges and rights would be allowed to one class of citizens but denied to others. For instance, to be allowed to participate in the exercise of public authority, one had to belong to the gentry. The commoners or serfs were legally inferior. They were subordinate to the law that was fashioned by the nobility.

A term often used in discussion of first- and second-class citizenship is *aristocracy*—rule by the "best," which usually meant the wealthy and the privileged. The aristocratic justification of different classes of citizenship is well summarized in the following passage:

> The lot of the poor, in all things which affect them collectively, should be regulated for them, not by them. They should not be required or encouraged to think for themselves, or give to their own reflection or fore-cast an influential voice in determination of the destiny. It is the duty of the higher classes to think for them, and to take responsibility for their lot. . . . The rich should be (like parents) to the poor, guiding and restraining them like children.[2]

Democratic thought contrasts sharply with this point of view. It rejects the idea that people who are richer, more accomplished, more intelligent, or of nobler birth than others are somehow "better." It is no accident that the principle of equal worth developed at the same time as radical religious movements. The idea that all people are equal in the eyes of God gave rise to the idea that all people are equal in the eyes of the state.

It is true, of course, that the principle of equal worth is not completely accepted and probably never will be. Nevertheless, it is deeply rooted in Western political systems. Justifications for special statute or hereditary rights have been undermined, and this in itself is a major achievement. This does not mean that privileges and special rights no longer exist, but it does mean they no longer have the open protection of the state.

---

[2] John Stuart Mill, *Principles of Political Economy, II* (Boston: Little, Brown, 1848), pp. 319–320. Here Mill is summarizing the aristocratic viewpoint, not endorsing it.

Types of Citizenship

The constitutional guarantees of citizenship are supposed to bring about the equality promised by the Declaration of Independence. The two major types of citizenship protected by the Constitution are **legal citizenship** and **political citizenship.** We will discuss these two types of citizenship and then turn to a third type, often called **social citizenship.** Social citizenship is a product of twentieth-century politics, especially in the last 40 or 50 years of American political history.

Legal citizenship Early American political history was dominated by legal-constitutional issues. The problems to be solved included the definition of citizenship rights and the extension of these rights to the entire population. Legal citizenship, or what we today call civil rights, includes the basic freedoms of speech, worship, and assembly. It also includes economic rights, especially the right to acquire and dispose of property, the right to choose one's place and type of work, and the right to enter into valid contracts knowing that they will be upheld in courts of law.

The first 10 amendments to the Constitution, usually called the Bill of Rights, were discussed in Chapter 2. It is these amendments that generally give constitutional status to legal citizenship. They were designed to protect citizens against the power of the national government, and the Fourteenth Amendment extends these protections to state and local governments. This is one of the essential ideas of democracy. The Founders knew that it is easy for government, with its power to imprison, to take away individual rights or private property. How does one isolated individual stand against all the resources of government?

Think of the Bill of Rights as laws *against* the government. They are intended to keep the government in its place when it comes to the right of citizens to criticize government (free press, free speech, freedom of assembly) and to hold private property. And if a citizen is accused of a crime, they guarantee that the government cannot prosecute in an arbitrary manner, but must follow standard and open procedures. The Bill of Rights is designed to protect citizens from their own government.

The institutions that are central to legal citizenship are the courts, and here the basic citizenship principle is called due process of law. Under this principle every person is entitled to fair treatment, to what is *due.* Obviously, people can and do disagree about what "fair" means in particular cases, but the Bill of Rights spells out many of the basic elements. A citizen is presumed innocent until proven guilty. A citizen has the right to be tried by a jury of fellow citizens. No one can be kept in jail unless there is reasonable evidence that he or she is guilty of a crime. Due process of law also includes the right to legal counsel, protection against self-incrimination (no one can be forced to testify against himself or herself), the right to face and to question witnesses, and protection from unreasonable searches, such as telephone taps.

In Chapter 6 we will review the basic freedoms in detail. We will see that the translation of citizenship principles into specific laws and their application to particular cases have been an ongoing process throughout American history.

Political citizenship   The second major form of citizenship is political participation. Democratic theory states that government should be based on the consent of the people. Because all members of society are governed, they should all have an equal right to choose the governors. The principle of equal political citizenship is clearly stated in *The Federalist* (*No. 57*):

> Who are the electors of the federal representatives? Not the rich, more than the poor; not the learned, more than the ignorant; not the haughty heirs of distinguished names, more than the humble sons of obscurity and unpropitious fortune. The electors are to be the great body of the people of the United States.

Despite the ringing promise of *The Federalist*, the Constitution did not really give the vote to all the people of the United States. It has taken 200 years of political pressure, including violent political action, and no less than four constitutional amendments to extend the vote to all adult citizens of the United States.

Initially, the Constitution left voting laws to the states; if a person could not vote in a state election, he could not vote in a federal election. Generally, states restricted the vote to white male property owners. In some states, as few as 10 percent of the white males could vote. By the time of the presidency of Andrew Jackson (1829–1837), however, most property standards had been dropped, and universal (white) manhood suffrage became the rule. America was hailed as a model for the democratic world. It was 50 years before Britain reached the same level of voting rights.

Still, as Figure 5.1 shows, less than 40 percent of the adult population could vote at the time of the Civil War. Blacks, of course, were forbidden to vote in the South, and with few exceptions they were also unable to vote in the North. After the Civil War, the Fifteenth Amendment established that "the right of citizens of the United States to vote shall not be denied or abridged by the United States or by any State on account of race, color, or previous condition of servitude." In the South, however, the reality of blacks voting faded with the end of Reconstruction in 1877. When white southerners got back in control of their state governments, they moved to undermine the Fifteenth Amendment through such means as the poll tax (one had to pay to vote), phony literacy tests, and the all-white primary, as well as intimidation and violence. By the 1890s few southern blacks could any longer participate in politics.

Throughout the late nineteenth century the electorate continued to grow as new states were added and large numbers of immigrants arrived. However, although some blacks could vote in some areas, and although women were gaining the right to vote a little at a time, during the early twentieth century the electorate was mainly white and male.

The next major expansion of the electorate was the addition of women. In 1869, Wyoming became the first state to grant voting rights to women; it was followed by several other states, chiefly in the West. The drive for women's rights—the suffragist movement—was led by, among others, Susan B. Anthony and Elizabeth Cady Stanton. Beginning in 1917, the suffragettes began marching in front of the White House, only to be arrested and jailed. Their cause triumphed in 1920 with the adoption of the Nine-

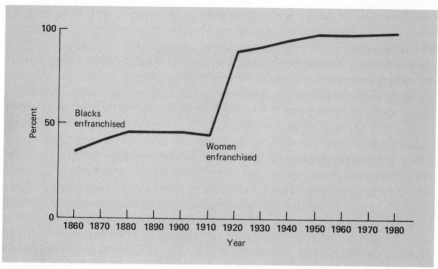

FIGURE 5.1

Proportion of the Adult Population Eligible to Register to Vote, 1860–1980

SOURCE: Robert Lane, *Political Life* (New York: Free Press, 1959), p. 21; *Statistical Abstract of the United States, 1969* (Washington, D.C., U.S. Department of Commerce, 1969), p. 369.

teenth Amendment, which states that the right to vote cannot be denied on account of sex.

In recent years a number of actions taken at the federal level have helped to remove other barriers set up by certain states and localities. The Twenty-fourth Amendment, adopted in 1964, banned the use of the poll tax in federal elections, and the Voting Rights Act of 1965 extended the ban to cover state elections. However, the real significance of the Voting Rights Act was to put federal authority behind the drive to enable southern blacks to vote: federal examiners were given the power to register voters. The effect of this legislation was dramatic. Between 1964 and 1968, black registration in the 11 southern states increased by over 50 percent (see Table 5.1). In 1970, Congress extended and broadened the Voting Rights Act to suspend the use of literacy and character tests in all states and to establish uniform residency requirements (30 days) for voting in federal elections.

TABLE 5.1

REGISTERED VOTERS AS PERCENTAGE OF ELIGIBLE POPULATION IN ELEVEN SOUTHERN STATES, 1960–1982

	White Voters	Black Voters
1960	61.1%	29.1%
1970	69.2	62.0
1980	71.9	55.8
1982	65.8	56.5

SOURCE: *Statistical Abstract of the United States* (Washington, D.C.: U.S. Department of Commerce, 1984), p. 261.

The suffrage was extended again in 1971 with the Twenty-sixth Amendment, which lowered the voting age to 18. About 10.5 million people were thus added to the electorate.

The history of citizenship rights started with the principle that all citizens are to be treated equally. There was to be no such thing as first- and second-class citizenship, with one group having rights and privileges that were denied to others. We have begun to see that actual practice has often failed to live up to this principle. In particular, black Americans and other minorities, as well as women of all races, have found their legal and political rights to be less than those of white males.

Social citizenship   President Roosevelt's twelfth State of the Union Address, delivered in 1944, contained a surprising departure from earlier definitions of citizenship. In 1941, as a kind of platform for World War II FDR had proclaimed Four Freedoms: freedom from want and fear to accompany freedom of worship and speech. His later speech expanded the platform. "The Republic," he said, "had its beginning and grew to its present strength, under the protection of certain unalienable political rights—among them the right of free speech, free press, free worship, trial by jury, freedom from unreasonable searches and seizures. They were our rights of life and liberty." As he continued, however, he spoke of America's failure to provide for its citizens and stated the principle behind a whole new area of citizens' rights. He said that the legal and political rights set forth in the Constitution were not enough and that citizenship must include social well-being and security against economic injustices.

> As our Nation has grown strong in size and stature, however—as our industrial economy has expanded—these political rights proved inadequate to assure us equality in the pursuit of happiness. . . . We have come to a clear realization of the fact that true individual freedom cannot exist without economic security and independence.

Roosevelt also mentioned areas in which the rights of social citizenship should apply:

> We have accepted, so to speak, a second Bill of Rights under which a new basis of security and prosperity can be established for all—regardless of station, race, or creed.

Among these rights are:

> The right to a useful and remunerative job in the industries or shops or farms or mines of the Nation.
> The right of every farmer to raise and sell his products at a return which will give him and his family a decent living.
> The right to earn enough to provide adequate food and clothing and recreation.
> The right of every businessman, large and small, to trade in an atmosphere of freedom from unfair competition and domination by monopolies at home or abroad.

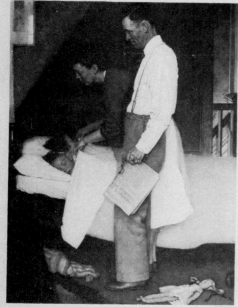

OURS...to fight for

FREEDOM FROM FEAR

OURS...to fight for

FREEDOM FROM WANT

SAVE FREEDOM OF WORSHIP

EACH ACCORDING TO THE DICTATES
OF HIS OWN CONSCIENCE

NORMAN ROCKWELL

BUY WAR BONDS

SAVE FREEDOM OF SPEECH

BUY WAR BONDS

These four posters by Norman Rockwell were popular expressions of President Roosevelt's call for Four Freedoms.

The right of every family to a decent home.

The right to adequate medical care and the opportunity to achieve and enjoy good health.

The right to adequate protection from the economic fears of old age, sickness, accident, and unemployment.

The right to a good education.

When Roosevelt used the word *right,* he was describing a new concept of citizenship, a citizenship enlarged far beyond what was included under the original concept of due process of law.

The social-welfare state   The idea of social rights was an outgrowth of the New Deal that President Roosevelt promised to America from the mid-1930s. Since Roosevelt's first term as president (1933–1937), the government has been actively involved in establishing a **social-welfare state.** This is a general term that describes a large number of government programs and laws that together provide the kind of social rights listed by President Roosevelt—a useful job, decent housing, an adequate diet, education, and economic security against the threats of sickness, unemployment, and old age.

The government programs most central to social citizenship include Social Security and unemployment insurance. Social Security taxes the workers of one generation to pay for the retirement of an older generation of workers. Unemployment insurance provides government payments to persons thrown out of work through no fault of their own, as when a factory closes down because no one is buying the cars it is manufacturing. These basic programs to protect citizens against economic insecurity were established during the 1930s. Since then, a large number of new programs have been added. These include food stamps for the poor, special job training for those who cannot find work, aid to mothers who have dependent children and no means of supporting them, and Medicare and Medicaid, which provide health care for the elderly and the poor.

These programs have given rise to great public controversy, and in general, the Republican party has been less favorable to them than the Democratic party. In 1935, for example, a key congressional vote on establishing Social Security received support from 85 percent of the Democratic members and only 1 percent of the Republican members. Thirty years later, in 1965, there was a key vote on Medicare in Congress, in which Medicare received the support of 80 percent of the Democrats but only 7 percent of the Republicans. (See Chapter 10 for fuller discussion of policy differences between the parties.)

The argument between Democrats and Republicans or, more generally, between liberals and conservatives is *not* over the importance of a decent job or good health care or economic security. The argument is over whether the social-welfare state is a very effective way to create these citizens rights.

Conservatives fear that the public cost of maintaining the social-welfare state will take so much money out of the private sector that the health of our market economy will be threatened. They note that in only 25 years, from 1950 to 1975, the federal expenditures on social welfare went

TABLE 5.2

SOCIAL WELFARE EXPENDITURES FOR NATIONAL, STATE, AND
LOCAL GOVERNMENTS IN THE UNITED STATES, 1950–1980
(BILLIONS OF DOLLARS)

	1950	1960	1970	1980
Social insurance	$ 4.9	$19.3	$ 54.7	$229.6
Public Aid	2.5	4.1	16.5	72.4
Health and medical	2.1	4.5	9.9	28.1
Veterans	6.9	5.5	9.1	21.5
Education	6.7	17.6	50.8	120.6
Housing	0.02	0.2	1.0	7.2
Other	0.4	1.4	4.1	14.0
Total	23.5	52.3	145.9	493.4

SOURCE: *Statistical Abstract of the United States* (Washington, D.C.: U.S. Department of Commerce, 1984), p. 367.

from 26 percent of the total budget to 56 percent. Social-welfare costs now account for 12 percent of the total gross national product of the United States (see Table 5.2).

Conservatives also feel that the welfare system allows no dignity for the poor. It violates fundamental American values of self-reliance and individual effort. The conservatives believe that if government leaves the economy alone, the hard work and imaginativeness of Americans will create enough jobs and enough economic well-being that costly federal programs will not be necessary.

Liberals do not believe that individual well-being can be automatically provided by the workings of a competitive market economy. They believe that without government programs, the inequalities in society will reproduce themselves from one generation to the next. The unemployed and the poor will not be able to provide the kind of education or help that will allow their children to find decent jobs. Liberals also emphasize the discrimination that operates in the market economy—discrimination against racial groups, against women, against the elderly. Only government action can reverse years of prejudice and discrimination. From the liberal viewpoint, the market economy has to be supplemented with government assistance programs such as Social Security, unemployment insurance, and medical care.

The victory of President Reagan in the 1980 presidential campaign was widely interpreted as a victory for the conservative viewpoint on the social-welfare state. Many of the early budget reductions proposed by Reagan and his advisors were directed toward social-welfare programs. In the proposed budget for 1982, for example, the Reagan administration recommended a 13 percent cut in aid to families of dependent children, a 37 percent cut in child nutrition programs, a 92 percent cut in a program that provides legal services to the poor, and the total elimination of Headstart, a program to give children from disadvantaged homes special care in the early years of education.

The Reagan proposals of that year and similar efforts since have been vigorously resisted in Congress, however, and although nearly all have been reduced in scope, the programs of social assistance have remained in operation. In his 1986 State of the Union message the President once again urged restructuring of welfare programs with the goal of greatly reducing their ultimate scope and cost.

These proposed budget reductions challenged some of the underlying principles of the social-welfare state. David Stockman, director of the Office of Management and Budget from 1981 to 1985, spoke on this issue. He said that the idea established in our society "that almost every service that someone might need in life ought to be provided, financed by government as a matter of basic rights, is wrong. We challenge that. We reject that notion."[3] Stockman was stating a conservative Republican answer to the liberal Democratic claim that the government is responsible for providing social-citizenship rights.

Stockman's observation touches upon a very difficult issue for a democracy. What happens when not all citizens have the money to take advantage of those rights guaranteed by the Constitution to all citizens? The Constitution, for instance, guarantees due process of law—but in the complicated legal environment of the 1980s a person who goes into a courtroom without a lawyer is at a very great disadvantage. The Supreme Court has ruled, therefore, that if a person accused of a crime is too poor to afford a lawyer, one should be provided at government expense. However, many citizenship rights, not just due process of law, are more available to people with money than to people without. The Constitution guarantees freedom of speech and press so that any citizen can try to persuade fellow citizens about the merits of one or another political view. Obviously, a person who owns a newspaper is in a better position to exercise this right than the poor or the uneducated. Yet we do not expect the government to provide free mimeograph services so that every citizen can exercise freedom of the press.

Let us summarize our discussion of the three different types of citizenship:

1. *Legal citizenship* is the right of all citizens to free speech, freedom of assembly, and the like; and the right of all citizens to due process, such as a fair trial and protection from unreasonable searches. Many of these basic rights were included in the Bill of Rights and were intended to protect the citizens from the government itself.
2. *Political citizenship* is the basic right to participate in politics, especially through the vote. The principle of citizenship underlies the democratic concept of self-government and the idea that the government is supervised by the people themselves.
3. *Social citizenship* is the right of citizens to participate in the material benefits of society, such as decent housing and adequate food and a job.

---

[3] Quoted in the *New York Times*, March 24, 1981.

Some of the ways in which these citizenship rights are provided have been discussed, and just how the American society puts into practice the principles of citizenship is a topic to which we will return again and again. Next, however, we examine a major set of citizenship issues, those involving discrimination against large disadvantaged groups.

DISCRIMINATION

The struggle to provide equal citizenship rights to all citizens has had to deal with many forms of racial and social discrimination. Sometimes this discrimination has been backed by the authority of government. Native American Indians, for example, were forcibly removed from their homelands in order to make way for settlers and pioneers moving from the eastern seaboard into the rich farmland of the Ohio Valley and the Midwest. Japanese-American citizens living along the west coast at the start of the war with Japan in the 1940s were labeled an "alien minority" and were removed from their homes and businesses and placed in detention camps. No persons of Jewish origin became members of the Supreme Court until 1916. As we have already noted, women and blacks were denied the right to vote for more than half of American political history.

Of course, many laws discriminate by identifying categories of people to receive certain services. Price supports for farm crops discriminate in favor of farmers. Grants to small businesses discriminate in favor of persons wanting to set up in business. Disaster insurance discriminates in favor of homeowners who live in flood plains or in earthquake-prone areas. Other laws discriminate in terms of who owes what to government. Wealthy people pay a higher percentage of their income in taxes than poorer people. Historically, men, not women, could be drafted into the armed forces.

The issue is not that law sometimes discriminates in favor of or against certain social groups. The issue is whether the discrimination is *reasonable.* If classifying people into different groups serves some acceptable public purpose—such as delivering services to those who need them, raising money for the government, or supporting the army and navy—then we say that the discrimination is reasonable. It is not in conflict with the rights of citizenship. What is in conflict with the rights of citizenship is classifying people in terms of their skin color or their religion or their ethnicity or their sex, though in each of these instances, both history and present practice have often allowed serious discrimination. The two instances that have received the most political attention have been discrimination against blacks and against women, though there has also been serious discrimination at various times in political history against Chinese and Japanese; Catholics, Jews, and Mormons; and Indians, Irish, and Hispanic Americans.

Discrimination Against Women

Two centuries after the Declaration of Independence and the Constitution were written, women are trying to gain the same rights in society as men. Many women have felt that an amendment to the Constitution would be the best way to secure these rights. They supported the Equal Rights

Amendment: "Equality of rights under the law shall not be denied or abridged by the United States or by any state on account of sex." After many years of delay Congress passed the ERA, and so did 35 of the 38 states needed to ratify it. In the late 1970s, however, a campaign of opposition, led by conservative women, blunted the drive, and in 1982 the deadline for passage expired.

Women have long been second-class citizens. Except in some state and local elections, women were not allowed to vote until 1920. Certain government jobs, especially in the military, have until recently been reserved for men. Many states have laws that discriminate against women in property ownership, in employment and salaries, and in the terms of marriage and divorce. Women find it hard to get loans, because credit agencies see them as "bad risks."

In addition to legal and political discrimination, there are many informal barriers to full women's rights. Women are paid less than men, even for doing the same work. On the average, women receive about $0.60 for every $1.00 earned by men. For example, male administrators in elementary and secondary schools earned a weekly average of $520 in 1981; women in similar positions earned an average of $363. Even women teachers earned about $68 a week less than male teachers. In addition, women have had a difficult time reaching high positions. There are very few women among the directors and officers of the largest corporations in America. There are 300,000 doctors in the United States; fewer than 10 percent are women. The number of women in political office is small: there are at present 2 women in the Senate, only 19 (out of 435) women in the House of Representatives.

The Equal Rights Amendment to the Constitution was but one of many legal and political challenges to second-class citizenship for women. In a single year more than a hundred bills and resolutions were introduced which, if passed, would have affected women's rights. For example, a proposed Pregnancy Disability Act would prohibit sex discrimination on the basis of pregnancy. Employers would have to cover pregnant workers under standard health insurance programs and under temporary disability plans so that a woman who became pregnant would not risk losing her job. Related to the questions of employment were dozens of other bills that would authorize more flexible working hours for mothers with small children. There were also proposals for increasing and improving day-care facilities. Protection of rape victims is another issue that has come before legislators and judges. A provision of one bill would protect rape victims from being cross-examined on their sexual histories in federal courts.

Introducing bills is much easier than enacting them, however. Some legal battles have been won, both in courts and in legislatures and on both national and state levels. Many barriers to equality for women have been partially overcome, in significant part because women have become more aware of their rights and have organized themselves to exert political and social pressure. Gradually, too, more women have come to hold public office and other positions of leadership in American society. But progress is slow.

Abortion   One of the most hotly debated issues in the area of women's rights is abortion. For many decades abortion was generally illegal (though scarcely unknown). The **feminist** movement argued that women should have the right to decide whether to give birth or not. During the 1970s their views finally prevailed. Following the Supreme Court decision in *Roe* v. *Wade* (410 U.S. 113, 1973) forbidding interference with a woman's freedom to choose to have an abortion during the first three months of pregnancy, restrictions on abortions were reduced, and by the end of the decade the legal barriers were practically nonexistent. The legalization of abortion has been strongly resisted by "right-to-life" groups. These groups claim that abortion is a form of murder and should be punished by the state in the same manner that other murders are punished. They argue that the fetus is a citizen. Some political leaders have tried to pass a constitutional amendment that would, in effect, deny the Supreme Court the right to rule on abortions.

Even though most legal barriers to abortion have been struck down, certain economic barriers remain. During the mid-1970s, as many as 300,000 women a year, mostly poor women, were having abortions that were paid for out of government-supported medical-care programs. Under pressure from right-to-life groups, Congress cut off federal funding for abortions, and the Supreme Court ruled that neither the Constitution nor federal law requires states to use federal funds for elective abortions. Moreover, public hospitals are not required under the Constitution to provide or even to permit elective abortions.

The majority view of the Court was stated by Justice Potter Stewart:

> It simply does not follow that a woman's freedom of choice carries with it a constitutional entitlement to the financial resources to avail herself of the full range of protected choice (*Harris* v. *McRae*, 488 U.S. 297 1980).

Dissenting from this view was Justice William J. Brennan, who argued that the law upheld by the Court

> imposes the political majority's judgment . . . upon that segment of our society which, because of its . . . political powerlessness . . . is least able to defend its privacy rights.

Brennan was taking the position that poor women are being denied their citizen right to privacy if they are prevented by their own poverty from having an abortion they otherwise want, just as a poor defendant would be denied due process of law if he was prevented by poverty from having a lawyer represent him in court.

Abortion is one of the most divisive questions in American society today. It lines up on one side those who believe that the government has no right to infringe upon a woman's privacy in deciding whether or not to bear a child. It lines up against this view those who believe that family values and moral standards are undermined by abortion on demand. It is an issue that threatens to slow down or even reverse the advances

The abortion issue has generated strong opinions and protest action on both sides.

made by the women's movement in the last 20 years. The issue divides women as well as men. Both Catholics and Protestants disagree among themselves, as do political liberals and conservatives.

It has been conservative political groups, however, which have pushed most vigorously to overturn the Court's ruling in *Roe* v. *Wade.* Their special target has been the Supreme Court itself. If they can influence the selection of the next appointees to the Court, they believe they can persuade the Court to reverse its earlier decision. Thus the issues of equality are very much tied in to the politics of judicial selection (see Chapter 17).

Discrimination Against Blacks

Racial discrimination has a long history in our society. Its most persistent expression has been directed against blacks, but even before the first blacks arrived as slaves, white settlers treated the Native Americans as racially inferior. The settlers did not hesitate to push them from their own homelands, and in the process to destroy their culture and their means of making a living. This was justified in terms of the "superiority" of European civilization. The same justification was used in the establishment of slavery.

Slavery   The essence of slavery is the denial of citizenship. Slavery was protected by law in the United States until after the Civil War, and of course in the eighteenth century most American blacks were slaves. Slaves could not say what they wanted to say, be with the people they wanted to be with, offer their labor to the highest bidder, or enter into binding contracts. American citizenship gave people the right to the product of their labor; slavery forbade this right. Despite the promises of the Declaration of Independence, the Constitution allowed a double standard: one class of people had rights and privileges that were denied to another class.

At first, this double standard was not a racist doctrine. It separated free people and slaves, but it did not separate whites and blacks. There were free blacks. Nearly 100,000 had escaped slavery; they had bought their freedom or had been given it by their owners and lived in the North and West much like other citizens. They paid taxes, voted, and in a few cases they held political office. However, in 1857 this changed when the Supreme Court, in the infamous Dred Scott case, held, in effect, that blacks, free or slave, "had no rights which the white man was bound to respect."

Racial segregation   Dual citizenship based on race continued long after the Civil War had officially ended slavery. The clear language of the Fourteenth Amendment—"all persons born or naturalized in the United States, and subject to the jurisdiction thereof, are citizens of the United States. . . . No state shall make or enforce any law which shall abridge the privileges or immunities of citizens"—was modified by later court decisions and blocked by the establishment of what came to be known as the "Jim Crow" society.

Special laws, often called Jim Crow laws, allowed nearly total segregation of blacks into separate and inferior institutions. As described by the Commission on Civil Rights (1963), Jim Crow laws applied to "waiting rooms, theaters, boardinghouses, water fountains, ticket windows, streetcars, penitentiaries, county jails, convict camps, institutions for the blind and deaf, and hospitals for the insane." This is just a partial list. Laws allowing or establishing racial segregation affected schools, businesses, clubs, churches, and the armed forces. Facilities reserved for blacks were always inferior, though equal prices had to be paid for unequal services.

Racist ideologies received the backing of the Supreme Court. As Justice Brown remarked in *Plessy* v. *Ferguson* (163 U.S. 537, 1896), the case that established the "separate but equal doctrine," which remained in force until 1954: "If one race be inferior to another socially, the Constitution of the United States cannot put them upon the same plane." So much for the Fourteenth Amendment, and so much for the idea that citizenship placed everyone on an equal footing before the law.

Racial integration   During the last four decades, the black civil rights movement and other political actions have gradually transformed our gov-

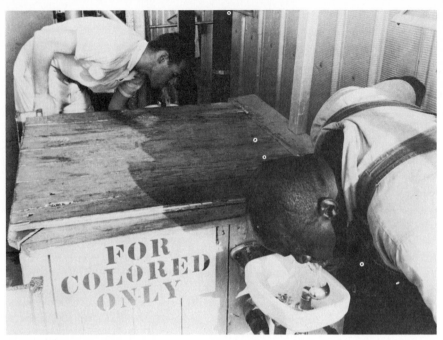

Segregated "Jim Crow" facilities persisted in some areas until the passage of civil rights legislation in the 1960s.

ernment from one that promoted racial inequality to one that opposes discrimination and promotes equality for blacks. We can trace the roots of this change by quickly summarizing the recent history of racial attitudes and policies in American society.

A "colorblind" government.   The initial breakthrough in racial values occurred during and after World War II and is best illustrated by the Supreme Court's decision in *Brown* v. *Board of Education* (347 U.S. 483, 1954). This decision ruled that segregated public schools were illegal. More broadly, the implication was that the government could take no action that discriminated against or treated separately people of different races; that is, correct legal discrimination by ending it.

A "colorblind" society.   Gradually, society followed the lead of government. Professional sports, television programs, colleges and universities, corporations, and dozens of other sectors of the society paid less and less attention to race. Public opinion also shifted. Fewer and fewer whites thought that blacks should be kept out of their neighborhoods or away from "white" colleges. The traditional commitment of Americans to equal treatment based on merit began to wash away racist attitudes.

Private action to encourage black achievement.   It did not take long for people to realize that ending discrimination would not necessarily promote the interests of the black population. Many private institutions, especially in the educational sector but also to some extent in business and the professions, actively began to seek out qualified blacks. Often special training programs or fellowship money was provided as a way to compensate for past educational disadvantages or family poverty. It was the logic of Headstart, a program in which groups that had been discriminated against in the past would now be given a chance to catch up and compete on an equal footing.

Linda Carol Brown was plaintiff in the historic case that declared racial segregation in the schools unconstitutional.

The 1963 civil rights march in Selma, Alabama, was led by the Reverend Martin Luther King, Jr. (fourth from right).

Affirmative Action

During the 1970s the United States experienced a new debate about citizenship. Like so many debates that preceded it, this one was about equality. The catch phrase **affirmative action** was at the center of the debate. Crudely stated, affirmative action was thought to be reverse discrimination—that is, intended to discriminate on behalf of those who have been discriminated against in the past.

We can best understand the dynamics of affirmative action by concentrating on racial equality, though the logic of affirmative action is also applicable to sex discrimination, age discrimination, or any other form of discrimination.

Affirmative action emerged during the 1970s, following a decade in which civil rights activity had lessened some forms of racial discrimination. Blacks and other minorities were no longer systematically excluded from the rights of citizenship, such as voting or holding office, and they were no longer legally excluded from jobs, housing, good schools, restaurants, and baseball teams.

This social transformation failed to end segregation, however. In 1984 the public schools of Detroit were 91 percent nonwhite; in Baltimore the figure was 81 percent; in Newark, 76 percent; and in Washington D.C., 99 percent. Persistent segregation is accompanied by persistent economic inequality. The 1970 census was taken at the end of a decade that gave a lot of attention to racial justice—more books were written, more meetings held, more marches organized, more legislation passed, more programs started, more commissions formed, and more money spent on solving "the American dilemma" than in any other period of our history. At the end of that decade, the median income of white families was $9,961, whereas for black families it was $6,067. A decade later the ratio was slightly worse, $21,904 to $12,674.

It was out of frustration with the persistence of segregation and inequality that the drive for affirmative action arose. Ending discrimination did not correct the lingering effects of past discrimination: inferior schools, urban ghetto living, poverty, and broken homes. Moreover, initiatives in the private sector produced little more than tokenism.

At this point, the actions of government began to force society to abandon the principle of colorblindness. The civil rights movement of the 1960s sought to make the law colorblind, to rid the law and society of a tradition of discrimination. The affirmative-action movement of the 1970s sought to make the law again take race into account. The principles

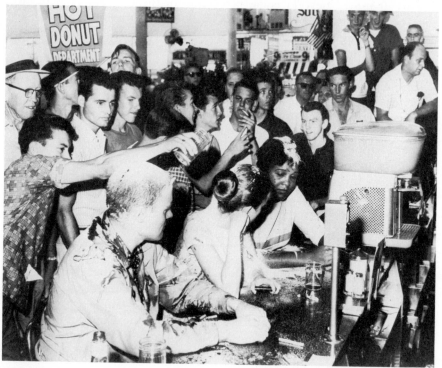

Civil rights sit-ins and protests required great self-discipline and determination so as not to react with violence to hostile treatment.

of affirmative action were also applied in order to compensate for sex discrimination. According to the idea of reverse discrimination, it is the "haves" who will be inconvenienced, and even discriminated against, so that the "have-nots," especially blacks, Native Americans, Mexican Americans, and Puerto Ricans, can have a better chance at the good schools and the good jobs that will produce economic equality with whites. Similar efforts have been made to improve the status of women.

The language of affirmative action has been that of "targets," "goals," or "quotas." If the outcome of college admission procedures or employment and promotion practices was not proportional to the representation of racial minorities in the population, this was taken as evidence of lingering discrimination. Guidelines were then suggested for the college or business, with the threat that federal moneys might be withdrawn or other penalties imposed if the target figure was not reached.

Implicit in affirmative-action programs was the idea that nominal equality of opportunity meant very little when one group had been the victim of long years of discriminatory treatment. The success of a college admissions program is measured not by whether it gives everyone an equal chance at admission but whether it achieves a certain outcome. Given past discrimination, a colorblind admissions program will probably result in very few blacks being qualified for college entrance. Only if the college takes color into account and attempts to meet some quota is it likely to enroll a large number of blacks.

Affirmative action as government policy is deeply troubling to many citizens. It moves beyond equal protection of the law and even beyond equal opportunity to a new concept of citizen rights: the right to be treated unequally, though favorably, in compensation for previous unequal and unfavorable treatment.

In a number of recent decisions, most noticeably in the case of *Regents of the University of California* v. *Bakke* (438 U.S. 265, 1978), the Supreme Court has refused to incorporate this new concept into the meaning of equal protection or due process of law. In addition, the Reagan administration has drawn back from affirmative-action enforcement, returning instead to the doctrine of equal, colorblind treatment of all groups. Most black Americans, accordingly, opposed Reagan's reelection in 1984, but many other voters, including some minority citizens, clearly preferred the Reagan administration's view.

ECONOMIC INEQUALITIES

Citizenship promises equal standing before the law, the equal right to participate in political life, and to some degree, as yet unclear, equal access to the material benefits of society. It does not, of course, promise that all citizens will be equal in all respects. Indeed, the Constitution, which promotes the principles of citizenship, also promotes an economic system compatible with capitalism. Capitalism, in turn, includes the principle of unequal rewards for different tasks.

Under capitalism, men and women sell their labor power to the highest bidder. The more valuable their labor power, the higher the wages they can command. Unequal economic rewards are viewed as "fair": More talented and harder-working people should receive greater rewards than the less talented and the lazy. Unequal economic rewards are also viewed as "practical": society should have an incentive system to ensure that the most important positions are filled by the people who are most able to perform well in them. Unequal economic rewards, in the doctrine of capitalism, operate like a grading system. To the most deserving go the A's, to the least deserving the F's, and to those somewhere in between the B's, the C's, and the D's.

Inequality of Income

Income is the money that people receive from various sources. Most of the income people receive comes from wages and salaries. Some people also have investments, such as stocks and bonds, which produce income in the form of dividends or capital gains. Rent received by owners of rental property is also income. Income is what people report on their income tax return each year.

None of us needs reminding that people make very different incomes. At the high end of the scale are corporate executives, baseball players, movie stars, rock'n'roll singers, and TV personalities. Salaries in excess of a million dollars a year are not uncommon. For example, income tax returns for 1978 showed that more than 2000 citizens earned more than a million dollars that year, and most of this group earned quite a bit more than a million. Of course, even 2000 people is a small number when you realize that the total number of tax returns filed in the United States is about 90 million.

Many more people earn salaries at the bottom end of the scale, such as the migrant workers who pick fruit in California or Texas, the housekeepers who clean the homes of persons who can afford domestic help, the illegal immigrants who work in sweatshops in New York or Chicago, and the uneducated and unskilled who do odd jobs such as shining shoes or picking up garbage in public parks. The most recent population and income data (from 1983) indicate that about 35 million Americans live below the official poverty line, which varies from about $5000 to over $20,000 depending on family size and where one lives.

This is quite a spread, the highest incomes being 200 times greater than the lowest income. For every citizen making a million dollars a year, there are about 12,000 citizens who live at or below the poverty line.

Although there are many, sometimes contradictory, measures of income distribution, a useful method of determining inequality is to divide the entire population into five equal groups by income range, from the highest to the lowest. We can then find the average income of the highest-paid 20 percent of the population and so forth, until we see the average income of the least-well-paid 20 percent. These groups are often called *quintiles.*

If there were perfect income equality in the nation, each quintile would account for 20 percent of the total income in the society. This distribution is shown in the left-hand column of Table 5.3. The right-hand part of Table 5.3 shows the actual distribution at intervals, starting with 1929.

Even when the economy is booming, large numbers of Americans are without jobs.

TABLE 5.3
INCOME INEQUALITY: 1929–1982

	Perfect Equality	Population Ranked by Quintiles			
		Actual Distribution of Family Personal Income by Quintiles			
		1929	*1950*	*1970*	*1982*
Highest	20%	54.4%	42.6%	41.6%	42.7%
Next highest	20	19.3	23.5	23.5	24.5
Middle	20	13.8	17.4	17.4	17.1
Next lowest	20	9.0	12.0	12.0	11.2
Lowest	20	3.5	4.5	5.5	4.7

SOURCES: For 1929, Edward C. Budd, ed., "An Introduction to a Current Issue of Public Policy," in *Inequality and Poverty* (New York: Norton, 1977), pp. x–xix; U.S. Bureau of the Census, *Current Population Reports,* Series P-60, no. 80 (October, 1971); *Statistical Abstract of the United States,* 1984 (Washington, D.C.: U.S. Department of Commerce), p. 465.

This table tells us three important things about income inequality:

1. The richest 20 percent of the families in the United States receive about 8 to 10 times as much income as the poorest 20 percent.
2. The first interval from 1929 to 1950 includes the social-welfare legislation of the 1930s and the economic changes brought about by World War II during the 1940s. Substantial income redistribution took place during these years. The percentage of income received by the richest families dropped from 54 percent to 42 percent. All other income groups were doing better at the end than at the beginning of that period.
3. During the next two intervals, 1950–1982, there was almost no change. Income redistribution, as measured in Table 5.3, stopped about 30 years ago.

Income is one way to measure economic inequality; wealth is another. The distribution of wealth is more unequal than the distribution of income.

Inequality of Wealth

Wealth is the value of the possessions and property that people own. A house, furniture, and an automobile are part of a person's or family's wealth. Included in wealth would be the market value of the stocks and bonds owned by the family. A farmer's wealth would include not only land but also livestock and farming equipment. The simplest way to think about wealth is to ask how much cash your family would have if all the things it owned were sold. About income, we ask, "How much did I make?"; about wealth, we ask, "What am I worth?"

The distribution of wealth in the United States is much more unequal than the distribution of income. Wealth is an estimate of who has what, and though available measures are far from complete, it is certain that a very large share of the personal wealth in the United States is owned by a very small percentage of the population. Table 5.4 shows that since the founding of the United States, the wealthiest 1 percent of the population has owned between 20 and 30 percent of all privately-owned wealth. In one study, carried out in 1962, it was estimated that the richest one-fifth of the families owned 77 percent of the wealth, while the poorest one-fifth of the families owned less than 0.5 percent.[4]

Of course, even this fact fails to take into account the different forms of wealth. The most common forms of wealth are personal possessions, for example, a house, a car, a stereo set, and appliances. Personal possessions of this sort produce pleasure for their owners, but such wealth is not influential. Influential wealth is wealth that produces more wealth in the form of income for its owners, such as rental property, stocks and bonds, patent rights, and royalty rights. Close to 100 percent of this income-

---

[4] Robert J. Lampman, *The Share of Top Wealth-Holders in National Wealth, 1922–1956* (Princeton, N.J.: Princeton University Press, 1962).

TABLE 5.4

INEQUALITY OF WEALTH, 1810–1972:

SHARE CONTROLLED BY THE TOP ONE PERCENT[a]

1810	21.0%
1860	24.0
1900	31.0
1922	31.6
1939	30.6
1948	20.8
1956	26.0
1962	22.0
1972	20.7

[a] Figures for the first three years are for families; thereafter the figures are for individuals.

SOURCE: Figures for 1810–1900 are from Robert Gallman, *Six Papers on Size Distribution of Wealth and Income,* ed. L. Soltow (New York: National Bureau of Economic Research, 1969), 23:6. For 1922–1956, see Robert Lampman, *Changes in Share of Wealth Held By Top Wealth-Holders, 1922–1956* (New York: National Bureau of Economic Research, 1960), p. 21. Later data are from *Statistical Abstract of the United States* (Washington, D.C.: U.S. Department of Commerce, 1984), p. 481.

producing wealth is controlled by the richest 20 percent of the families. Indeed, most of this form of wealth is owned by a very small number of families. For instance, the top 1 percent of wealth owners in the United States control approximately one-fourth of all notes and mortgages, one-half of all bonds, and three-fourths of all corporate stocks.

Thus we see that there are two forms of economic inequality in our system: income inequality, which measures how much people receive each year in wages, salaries, profits, and other sources of income; and wealth inequality, which measures how much people own, and especially whether what they own can produce additional wealth. How are these features of the economic order affected by the political system in which each individual has a single vote, and voting majorities elect people to public office?

POLITICAL CHALLENGES TO ECONOMIC INEQUALITY

Despite the expansion of legal, political, and even social citizenship, there has not been a major redistribution of wealth in the United States. This fact confounds the fears of conservative political thinkers, who have long felt that equal political rights would eventually be translated into an equal economic condition, a leveling of society.

When equal political rights were first proposed, many opposed the idea. They feared that those who lacked money would use their voting power to tax away the profits and savings of the talented and hardworking citizens. More correctly, they feared that the rights of property would be threatened by, as they put it, "too much democracy." In 1821, political leaders in New York were debating the merits of extending the vote to all white males. An active opponent was Chancellor James Kent, the highest official in the state. He felt

> . . . that extreme democratic principle, universal suffrage, has been productive of corruption, injustice, violence, and tyranny. . . . The apprehended danger from the experiment of universal suffrage applied to the whole legislative department, is no dream of the imagination. It is too mighty an excitement for the moral constitution of men to endure. The tendency of universal suffrage is to jeopardize the rights of property and the principles of liberty. There is a constant tendency in human society, and the history of every age proves it; there is a tendency in the poor to covet and to share in the plunder of the rich—in the debtor to relax or avoid the obligation of contracts—in the indolent and profligate to cast the whole burdens of society upon the industrious and the virtuous.[5]

Echoes of this sentiment can be heard today. During the spring of 1977, for instance, there was widespread discussion of universal voter registration, a program designed to increase the number of Americans who go to the polls. The supporters of this program viewed it as one more step toward universal suffrage and citizenship equality. However, the opponents believed that the nonvoters include too many poor people who, with voting made more easy, would support political programs that would radically redistribute wealth in the United States. One of the most forceful statements appeared in a nationally published newspaper column by the political writer, later aide to President Reagan, Patrick J. Buchanan:

> Universal registration . . . may be the method through which the nation's tax-consumers and nonproducers set about the systematic plunder of the tax-paying and producing majority. . . . [Members of the welfare class are] parasitic slugs who pay no taxes, who show such disinterest in the political process that they will not get off their duffs to register, have no business at the ballot box election day, casting a vote in ignorance and canceling out the ballot of some conscientious citizen.[6]

This argument faces the same difficulties that it did when used by Chancellor Kent in 1821, since universal suffrage has not brought about a radical redistribution of wealth.

To understand why there has not been a radical redistribution of wealth, we will look at two important activities of the U.S. government. One activity has already been mentioned: the social-welfare programs, which were intended to promote the rights of social citizenship. We will ask how much these programs have led to a redistribution of income or wealth in the United States. The second major activity is the use of the government's power to tax. Do taxes, especially the progressive income tax, increase economic equality?

---

[5] Quoted in Alpheus T. Mason, ed., *Free Government in the Making*, 2d ed. (New York: Oxford University Press, 1956), p. 399.

[6] "Reform Aids Welfare Class," *Chicago Tribune*, March 3, 1977.

Equality and the Social-Welfare State

The major social-welfare programs are Social Security, unemployment compensation, aid to the blind and disabled, aid to families with dependent children, Medicare and Medicaid, and food stamps. A strong case can be made that these programs have made citizens more equal, but the relationship is complicated. First, we must describe two different types of inequality: inequality of distance and inequality of scope.

Inequality of distance refers to the size of the gap between the richest and poorest or between any two points along the income distribution scale. In a society where the richest group earns 20 times as much as the poorest group, the inequality of distance is great. In a society where the richest group earns only 5 times as much as the poorest group, inequality of distance has been reduced. The kinds of social-service programs that provide a cushion for the sick, the old, and the unemployed—what President Reagan has called the "safety net"—do not greatly reduce the distance between rich and poor. The major social-service programs are simply government-managed insurance plans to which workers contribute during their working years. For instance, 9 out of 10 working people in America now contribute to Social Security. Other social-service programs, such as Medicare, help a citizen out in times of financial need, in this case older citizens who cannot afford high medical costs. However, these programs do not "level" society in the sense of cutting heavily into the wealth of the rich and increasing that of the poor.

Does this mean that social-service programs are unrelated to equality in America? Not at all, but now we must speak of **inequality of scope.** This term refers to the number of ways in which the rich are better off than the poor.

Assume the following extreme case. *Every* social benefit is available only through the private sector at market prices. The wealthy, having more money, can purchase far more of these services than the poor. Education, medical care, insurance, recreation, transportation, communication services, and even security against personal attack are available in unequal amounts and unequal quality. The less wealth you have, the less of any of these services you can get, until we get to the bottom of the scale, where none are available—no education, no medical care, no parks, no insurance, no transportation or communication systems, except those used by the wealthy, and not even a police force. Under such conditions, inequalities of scope would be enormous. Every social value would be more available, and in a better form, to the wealthy than to the poor.

Now assume the opposite case. *No* social benefit is priced. Lack of income is no barrier. All are equally available to every citizen. Public schools are excellent, and education attainment is based on intelligence; health and insurance programs protect all citizens equally against illness, accident, and disability; there are many public parks, and entertainment is widely available; transportation is cheap, as are telephone and mail services; and the standing army and police force protect everyone's possessions. Under such conditions, inequalities of scope are greatly narrowed. There are still rich and poor, and the rich can afford luxuries that are denied to the poor. However, the rich cannot buy superior social services. The advantage of wealth is limited to certain areas of consumption.

The difficult question of whether basic social services should be available to all citizens equally or only to those who can afford them was posed to President Jimmy Carter. Carter had spoken against using federal funds to support abortions. A reporter asked

> Q. Well then, how fair do you believe it is that women who can afford to get an abortion can go ahead and have one and women who cannot afford to are precluded from this?

and Carter replied,

> A. Well, as you know there are many things in life that are not fair, that wealthy people can afford and poor people can't. But I don't believe that the federal government should take action to try to make these opportunities exactly equal, particularly when there is a moral factor involved.

The question of what is fair is exactly the issue of whether government programs should reduce the benefits of wealth by making social services available to the poor and the rich alike. Whereas the phrase "inequality of distance" describes *how much* better off the rich are, the phrase "inequality of scope" describes in *how many ways* they are better off.

Welfare policies are egalitarian in the sense that they increase the number of services for which wealth is unnecessary. Inequality is reduced by providing social services that are available to all, regardless of income.

If citizenship reduces inequalities of scope, it has made a major contribution to equality. This has happened, but less than either supporters or critics of the social-service state admit. For one thing, the benefits of social programs are not always directed toward the poorer groups in society. Free higher education, for instance, has serviced the middle class and to a lesser extent the working class, but it has not done much for really poor families whose children much less often seek to attend college at all.

Even the programs generally designed to help the poorest families do not go only to the poor. The Census Bureau has studied who gets help from such federal benefit programs as Medicare, Medicaid, food stamps, school lunches, and subsidized housing. In recent years these programs have reached one out of every three American households. That such a large number of citizens are helped indicates that the assistance reaches more than the poor. The major criteria for Medicare, for instance, are age and disability, not income.

The results of social-rights citizenship have been less egalitarian than some hoped and others feared. Nevertheless, if decent social services are provided by the government, either free or at minimal cost, then inequalities of scope are reduced. The rich can still support private universities and send their children to them, but excellent public universities reduce this educational advantage. Government programs therefore equalize somewhat the opportunities to compete for the benefit of quality education.

Of course, government sponsored social-service programs must be paid for. If these programs primarily benefit poorer citizens but are paid for with taxes from richer citizens, then there has been some important income redistribution in society. We should take a look at how the progressive income tax works in this society.

The Progressive Income Tax

The principle of the progressive income tax is simple enough: the more money a person earns, the higher the portion he or she pays in taxes. The progressive income tax would be one of the easiest ways in which the poorer citizens might bring about a redistribution of wealth. The poorer citizens would vote for sharply graduated taxes, taking a very high percent from the richer classes. This would be the method by which political equality (one person, one vote) would lead to economic equality (one person, one dollar).

In practice, nothing like this has happened. The income tax was authorized by the Sixteenth Amendment to the Constitution, passed in 1913. Congress can set whatever tax rate it chooses, and indeed the official tax rates are graduated. The families with the least income may pay nothing. Rates begin at 11 percent and rise to a top rate of 50 percent. During and after World War II the highest rate of income tax was 91 percent, but in actual practice very few people ever had to pay income tax at such sharply progressive rates.

Tax Loopholes

The reason for this is suggested by the term *tax loophole.* The primary purpose of taxes is to raise revenue for government programs; however, in the act of raising money through taxes, the government has a hard time resisting other goals as well. The tax law can be written to encourage certain kinds of activities and to discourage others. If the government does not tax gifts to charities, this will encourage people to give to the charities of their choice rather than give the money up in taxes anyway. If the government wants Americans to work abroad, it can decide not to tax them on the salaries they earn outside the United States. If the government wants people to invest in stocks and bonds to provide working capital for American business and manufacturing, it can lower the tax rate on interest and dividends earned from such investments. If the government wants people to buy homes, to stay married, or to send their children to college, it can alter the tax laws to encourage home ownership, marriage, and education.

Technically, we refer to these arrangements as tax deductions. Tax deductions have allowed upper-income groups in the United States to reduce their actual tax to about half the official rate. Another term applied to these deductions is *tax expenditures,* so called because in theory the U.S. Treasury is giving up revenue it might otherwise have received had the deduction/expenditure not been available. Thus the huge aggregate amount deducted each year for home mortgage interest is essentially the same as though home buyers, mostly middle class, had received a check from the government.

The Sixteenth Amendment, authorizing the income tax, allows Congress to tax income "from whatever sources derived," but tax legislation has played havoc with this principle. Dollars earned from some sources, though worth just as much in consumer goods, leisure, or the like, are not taxed at the same rate as dollars earned from other sources. The dollars that are most heavily taxed are earned as wages and salaries; those least heavily taxed are earned from various types of investments: long-term capital gains, real estate, stock options, oil, and state and local bonds.

Thus people who gain their income by working pay a greater share of it in taxes than those who gain it by investing. Furthermore, since the income of the wealthy is derived primarily from nonwage sources, it is the wealthy, not the low- and middle-income wage earners, who benefit from these different rates of taxation.

The progressive income tax does flatten out the income distribution at the lower end of the scale. For example, the income tax brings the family with an income of $35,000 closer to the family with an income of $25,000. But its impact on the top of the income scale is much less. Before taxes, the average income of the richest 20 percent in the country is about 10 times that of the poorest 20 percent; the effect of the income tax is to reduce this only to 9 times as much. In general, under present laws the income tax is not nearly as progressive as is often thought; it does not greatly reduce the distance between the wealthy and the poor.

Other types of taxes are even less progressive. The sales tax, for instance, takes a much larger share of the income of the poor than of the rich. Say, for example, a family earns $10,000 and pays a 5-percent sales tax on the $8,000 it spends on consumer goods and basic necessities. This family would pay $400, or 4 percent of its total income, in sales taxes. A family that earned $50,000 and spends $16,000 on items bearing the 5-percent sales tax would spend $800, or 1.6 percent of its total income, in sales tax. Thus the poorer family is being taxed at a higher rate.

Scholars who have tried to assess the total effect of all U.S. taxes—sales tax, income tax, property tax, payroll tax—have come to the conclusion that there is very little progressiveness. The extent of economic inequality in the United States has not been very much affected by the various taxes that the government uses to pay for its programs.

In recent years, Republican political leaders, including President Reagan, have contended that taxes are a bad way to increase equality. Rather, they argue, tax rates should be reduced so that the wealthy will save and invest in productive enterprise and the less well-to-do will be able to decide for themselves what services they want and what they are willing to pay for them. The overall result, it is claimed, would be a more prosperous society for all, rich and poor, with less need for a tax-supported "safety net." In this view, taxes, especially at progressive rates, are seen more as barriers to economic growth than as mechanisms for reducing either the scope or the distance of inequality.

Critics of this supply-side argument are numerous and strong in their belief that tax reduction would increase inequality. Nevertheless, tax reform has become very popular politically, and leading Democrats have also sought to fashion a less steeply progressive and simpler federal tax code. In 1985 the Democratic-controlled House of Representatives passed a bill that would lower the top individual rate to 37 percent and eliminate or reduce many existing tax loopholes. In 1986 it appeared that the Senate would move in a similar direction.

Relative Contribution of Different Tax Groups

It is surely misleading to conclude that taxes have no effect on economic inequality. The large share of dollars that are needed to support the social-service programs, which generally benefit the poorer citizens, is paid by the better-off citizens. That is, despite tax deductions and loopholes, the richest half of the nation supports federal programs.

How much of the federal budget is supported by those in the top half, and how much is supported by those in the bottom half? About 95 percent of all income tax dollars are collected from the top half. About 5 percent, then, are collected from the bottom half. Obviously, not all of the tax dollars go to support programs for poorer citizens. Tax dollars support national defense and scientific research, build highways and airports, and provide benefits to veterans and the elderly. Many citizens benefit from such programs.

Still, those programs that do primarily benefit the poorer citizens are largely paid for from taxes collected from the better-off citizens. In this important way, income taxes do create more equality in the society. They provide programs that reduce the inequality of scope, even if they do not reduce inequality of distance.

THE "ASTOUNDING POLITICAL CONTRADICTION" OF DEMOCRACY

We have seen that "one person, one vote" has not led to "one person, one dollar." The democratic commitment to political equality has not been translated into economic equality. Charles A. Beard, in his famous book, *The Economic Basis of Politics*, saw this as a major paradox:

> Modern equalitarian democracy, which reckons all heads as equal and alike, cuts sharply athwart the philosophy and practice of the past centuries. Nevertheless, the democratic device of universal suffrage does not destroy economic classes or economic inequalities. It ignores them. Herein lies the paradox, the most astounding political contradiction that the world has ever witnessed.[7]

American Values of Equality

More than 150 years ago, a very intelligent visitor from France came to the United States. He was Alexis de Tocqueville, and he wrote a book about democracy in America based on his travels and observations. He wrote that Americans care deeply about egalitarianism. All citizens are equally deserving of respect. No citizen should have to bend his view to that of another citizen who happens to have more wealth or a better job. Most important, for people to be truly equal, they have to have an equal opportunity to succeed. Discrimination which gets in the way of equal opportunity is, therefore, profoundly un-American. People should be judged in terms of what they do, not who they are. No accident of birth,

---

[7] (New York: Vintage, 1960), p. 69.

race, or sex should prevent people from becoming what their talents and ambitions can make of them. Tocqueville's observations of 150 years ago were remarkably accurate. In important ways, they describe American values in the 1980s as accurately as they did in the 1830s.

If Americans care so much about equality, why have the social and economic inequalities persisted so long? What explains this "astounding political contradiction"? The simple and most correct answer is that there is no political contradiction, at least not in the values that most Americans share.

American Values of Achievement and Mobility

The emphasis on equality is not on **equality of condition** or of wealth; it is on **equality of opportunity**. Every citizen should have a right to achieve, and if some achieve more than others, then there will naturally be inequality. This inequality is not considered wrong in itself, but it is wrong when based on discrimination or unfair advantage. If people get ahead by hard work and ability, then getting ahead is a good thing, not a social wrong. Americans attach every bit as much importance to competition and achievement as they do to egalitarianism.

Scholars have given a great deal of attention to whether achievement is really possible in the United States. They have studied particularly whether the position of men and women in the social and economic hierarchies is fixed by the position of their parents. Although these are complicated studies and can be interpreted in several different ways, scholars generally conclude that social status and economic accomplishment are not inherited.

One study reported that at the turn of the century about 45 percent of big business executives came from wealthy families. This percentage had dropped to 36 percent in 1950 and all the way down to 10 percent by the mid-1960s. Many persons from poor backgrounds were entering top positions in American business and government by the 1970s.[8] Of course, these studies do not deny that privileged family and class background can be great advantages. But class background cannot totally determine who will be successful and who will not; there is downward mobility as well as upward mobility from one generation to the next.

Not all groups benefit equally from economic opportunities in the United States. We have already emphasized that discrimination against women and racial groups has denied many citizens the promise of equal opportunity. Here is what one study concluded about opportunities for blacks prior to the mid-1960s:

> Negroes are handicapped at every step in their attempt to achieve economic success, and these cumulative disadvantages are what produce the great inequalities of opportunities under which the Negro American suffers.

---

[8] See *The Business Executive 1964: A Study of His Social and Educational Background,* a study sponsored by *Scientific American*, conducted by Market Statistics, Inc., of New York City in collaboration with Dr. Mabel Newcomer.

The sustained attack on racial discrimination during the last decade changed this situation somewhat. As blacks have had greater opportunities to improve their education, they have improved their position in the economy. However, the effects of discrimination take a very long time to eliminate.

Scarcity: Challenge to American Values

The period from the end of World War II in 1945 until the early 1970s convinced many Americans that ours was a society of abundance. There was an enormous increase in educational opportunities, and literally hundreds of new colleges and universities were started. There was a substantial increase in the purchasing power of many Americans, and there were nice things to buy. American technology mass produced such important labor-saving devices as automatic washing machines and dishwashers. It also produced entertainment through television and movies. Even work seemed to be easier. Shorter working hours and longer paid vacations became the custom. There was also an increase in the number of "high-status" jobs as professional and technical positions became available in government, education, and new industries. Memories of the Great Depression faded. The result of all this was a growing and largely satisfied middle class.

Few Americans noticed that this abundance was based on fragile conditions. The "American way of life" was based in part on cheap labor, some provided in this country by the rural poor and the underpaid blacks; the remainder was provided by cheap labor abroad. The minerals needed by American industry were in part mined by poorly paid workers in South America and parts of Africa. The fresh fruit enjoyed by Americans was picked by migrant workers in California or local workers in Honduras.

Even less noticed by Americans was the importance of a constant supply of cheap energy, energy that filtered swimming pools and illuminated theater marquees, that heated glass-walled skyscrapers in the winter and air-conditioned them in the summer, that drove motor boats and campers, that brought big-time sports into everyone's living room. The source of this cheap energy was cheap oil.

In the 1970s the price of oil went up dramatically, and so did the cost of the labor that provided many of the services and products enjoyed by middle-class America during the 1950s and 1960s. Oil prices came down again in the mid-1980s, but by then it had become clear that the world does not have an unending supply of resources and labor available to support the way of life many Americans have become used to.

Thus we enter a period in which abundance may become scarcity. We can no longer assume a constantly rising standard of living. Workers in many industries have had to accept wage cuts. Children born during the 1930s and 1940s were confident that their lives would be better than those of their parents. For children born during the 1960s and 1970s this upward progress is more doubtful. If it turns out that large numbers of people experience "downward mobility" when they had been raised to expect "upward mobility," the delicate balance between the values of achievement and egalitarianism will be placed under severe strain.

Finally, we should note that changing world conditions have affected the patterns of inequality and the political responses to it in the United States. In the years following World War II the assumption was widely held that this was the "American Century," and that the United States would continue indefinitely to be the most powerful and productive nation in the world. It has been with considerable dismay that Americans have come to realize that there are numerous potent competitors in both Europe and Asia. Japan is a powerful economic rival. Income per capita is higher in Switzerland and Sweden, among others. In 1985, for the first time since before World War I, the United States became a debtor nation, with Americans owing more to foreign investors than they in turn were owed.

The effects of this new world situation include severe and painful damage to the economic conditions and prospects of large areas of the nation. Parts of the industrial heartland languish, and the people living in this so-called Rust Belt look with envy at the prosperity and growth of the Southwest or at California's Silicon Valley with its booming computer industry. That industry itself has felt the effects of competition from abroad, however, and oil-dependent cities like Houston have found that a drop in oil prices leaves them with empty office buildings and rising unemployment. The regions of economic hardship seek redress through political action, just as women and racial minorities have done, and as they still do. Their efforts give additional meaning to the arguments about how much and what kind of equality and fairness Americans deserve.

CHAPTER HIGHLIGHTS ■

1. There are three types of citizenship rights:
   a. legal citizenship, which primarily refers to the rights that citizens enjoy against the awesome powers of a government; namely, freedoms of speech, worship, the press, assembly, and the right to a fair trial and due process of law.
   b. political citizenship, which primarily refers to the arrangements that guarantee and make political participation meaningful: voting, standing for election, forming political parties, expressing political views, and so forth.
   c. social citizenship, which primarily refers to employment, housing, economic security, education, and health care.
2. Discrimination, especially racial, religious, and sexual discrimination, has prevented some citizens from fully enjoying their equal rights as citizens. There has been throughout American political history a series of political battles to eliminate discriminatory laws and practices. Substantial progress has been made, especially since the black power and feminist movements of the 1960s. At present, the society is struggling with the very complex issue of whether there should be some form of compensation, even reverse discrimination, to accelerate the achievement of full racial and sexual equality.

5. Whether government-provided social benefits and government taxation policy should help redistribute wealth in the society is an issue of considerable political discussion at present, as it has been in the past. One position holds that the government should go no further than providing for equality of opportunity. Another position holds that simply providing equality of opportunity for citizens already vastly unequal in economic resources will perpetuate unfair inequalities. The first view puts emphasis on the American values of achievement and upward mobility. The second view puts more emphasis on citizenship equalities and redistribution.

6. As we near the end of the twentieth century, it has become apparent that American resources are limited. Scarcity has revived social tensions, and raised anew the dilemmas of our commitment to equality.

SUGGESTED READINGS ■

Equality involves legal, philosophical, political, and economic dimensions, and relevant literature can be found in each of these fields.

Classics include Alexis de Tocqueville, *Democracy in America*, 2 vols. (1835–1840); T. H. Marshall, *Class, Citizenship, and Social Development* (1964); Gunnar Myrdal, *The American Dilemma* (1944).

Modern commentaries include Sidney Verba and Gary Orren, *Equality in America* (1985); Jennifer Hochschild, *What's Fair? (1981)*; Benjamin Page, *Who Gets What from Government* (1983); Paul M. Sniderman with Michael Gray Hagen, *Race and Inequality, A Study in American Values* (1985); Barbara Sinclair, *The Women's Movement* (2d ed., 1979); Charles Murray, *Losing Ground* (1985); David W. O'Brien, *Privacy, Law and Public Policy* (1979).

National Archives Building, Washington, D.C.

Chapter 6

THE STATE, THE INDIVIDUAL, AND LIBERTY

T he Founders of the Republic were concerned about tyranny—not only the tyranny of a minority over the American people, but also about the possibility of tyranny by the majority over minorities. How do we protect the rights and freedoms of individuals and groups in America, especially unpopular individuals and groups that the majority might want to suppress? The Bill of Rights, particularly the First Amendment, was meant to protect those rights and freedoms, but the protection of freedom is rarely simple.

It is easy to protect the freedom of speech of those who speak out in favor of the American way of life. Their freedom does not even need defending, for who would challenge it? The serious issues involve the free speech of those who attack the American way of life, who say things that are offensive to many or whose words are damaging to individuals or harmful to national security. In these cases, freedoms have had to be balanced against other values. This chapter will look at the way in which that balance has been drawn in relation to freedom of speech and the press, freedom of religion, and freedom to use one's property as one wants.

Freedom to Protest

November 14, 1969, was Vietnam "Moratorium" day. Opponents of American involvement in the war in Vietnam organized protests across the country, including teach-ins and silent vigils. Anti-Vietnam protestors decided to wear black armbands on that day to demonstrate their opposition to the war. Charles James was a high school teacher in Addison, New York, a small town in rural New York State. He was a Quaker and opposed to the war. On that day he wore a small black armband to school.

The school principal ordered him to remove the armband. He refused, arguing that he had a right to express his conscience. James was suspended from teaching, and shortly thereafter he was fired from his job. James called the American Civil Liberties Union (ACLU), an organization that defends those who feel their freedom of speech has been violated. In its opinion the school board had violated his rights.

A long series of appeals to get James reinstated began. The ACLU gave him legal assistance. The case went through the administrative boards of the New York State school system, the New York State court system, and finally into the federal court system. The Addison School Board claimed that James had been disruptive by wearing a black armband to school and insubordinate in refusing to remove it. James and his lawyers claimed that his action had not disrupted the school, that it merely represented his attempt to express his views on a major political issue, and that his freedom of speech under the First Amendment had been violated. The position of the school board was supported by the New York State school system, by the New York Supreme Court, and by the U.S. District Court. However, James and the ACLU continued to appeal, and the U.S. Court of Appeals finally supported his position, ordering the school board to reinstate him with back pay.[1]

---

[1] This account is based on Richard Harris, *Freedom Spent* (Boston: Little, Brown, 1974), pp. 7–122.

152

In the end it was a victory for free speech and the First Amendment, but the end was a long way from the beginning. Even after the Court of Appeals ruled in favor of James, the local school board dismissed him again and refused to pay his back salary. He had to take them to court again. Indeed, it was not until the end of May 1975, that the case was finally settled and James received the back pay owed him.

Five and a half years is a long time to wait for vindication, and those years were particularly long for someone with a young family and no job. The appeal was expensive and would never have been pressed if it had not been for the support of the ACLU. James's family lived on welfare a good deal of the time. When he finally received his job back and a financial settlement from the school board, he had long since lost interest in teaching, and much of the money had to go to pay the debts he had accumulated. In the end, Charles James commented. "If I hadn't fought on I never would have felt free again." His wife, however, said, "I feel a kind of despair. . . . All I have left is the hope that we can finally find a way to live simply and self-sufficiently, and stay out of it."

Free speech is fundamental to democracy. In America, we turn to the courts to defend us against those who would violate our free speech. But Charles James's case shows it is not all that simple. Those who would limit speech usually point to some other important value they are defending. The Addison School Board claimed it was defending the school from disruption and defending the pupils from being exposed to one-sided political propaganda—certainly serious values worth defending. Their argument was convincing to the state courts and the U.S. District Court, though it was not to the U.S. Court of Appeals. When courts look at questions of free speech, they usually find themselves balancing the claims of liberty against other important claims. The balance does not always come out on the side of liberty. Furthermore, as the case of Charles James shows us, the process of appeal to the courts can be long and agonizing. In this chapter we will look at liberty in America to see who defends it and how it is defended.

MAJORITY RULE VERSUS INDIVIDUAL AND MINORITY RIGHTS

What is a democracy? A democracy is a government that allows individual freedom: Citizens in a democracy are free to speak as they wish and to worship as they wish; they cannot be arbitrarily put in jail for unpopular acts.

What is democracy? A democracy is a government in which the majority rules: Laws and regulations are determined by the will of the majority.

Most citizens would agree that these two answers describe basic democratic principles, individual freedom, and majority rule. Yet these two principles are often in conflict. If we fully achieve either principle, we will wind up violating the other.

The Tyranny of the Majority

Many writers have warned of democratic tyranny—the so-called **tyranny of the majority.** In some respects, such tyranny is more to be feared than the tyranny of a smaller group. Many foreign observers of life in America have commented on the power of public opinion, particularly over unpopular ideas and behavior. They have said that Americans conform too easily to the popular view and are intolerant toward dissenters. But public opinion, however intolerant it may be, is not as much to be feared as the power of government. When the state carries out the intolerant will of the majority, it becomes a force that a deviant minority cannot easily resist.

The writers of the Constitution were concerned with this problem. They designed a government that would curb the power of the majority in many ways. Federalism, checks and balances, and the Bill of Rights all help prevent the concentration of power in the hands of any one group, including the majority. In this, the Supreme Court has played a major role in defining and enforcing the protection available to those who would vocally express or write unpopular ideas in America. It symbolizes the limitations on the majority that are built into the constitutional framework. In this chapter we look at the role of the Supreme Court and the Constitution in relation to majority rule and the rights of minorities, including those consisting of a single individual, to speak, write, publish, and worship as they please without being coerced by any government authority.

Reconciliation of Majority Rule with Minority Rights

The reconciliation of majority rule with minority rights is one of the great dilemmas of democracy. If majority rule is not an easily acceptable absolute principle, neither is minority rights. Give all rights to all minorities—that is, give all minority groups in society the right to disobey the government—and one no longer has a society; rather, one has a war of all against all. Each of us, after all, is a minority of one. Also, sometimes speech can be dangerous, threatening to incite riot or treason, to undermine a war effort or weaken confidence in our very system of government.

Where then does one draw the line? When are minorities to be respected and how far may they go? Much of the debate on the nature of democracy centers on this question. What rights are so important that they should be protected from the ordinary procedures of democracy so that the wish of the larger number is not allowed to become the rule for all? Historically, several kinds of rights have been singled out for protection from the wishes of the majority; they are what we call civil liberties:

1. The right to freedom of speech, a free press, and freedom of assembly.
2. The right to freedom of religion.
3. The right to have one's property protected from arbitrary acts of the government.
4. The right to have one's person protected from arbitrary acts of the government.

Each of these rights is a right against the government, but each has a somewhat different justification in democratic theory, and each has had an uneven history in the United States.

FREEDOM OF SPEECH, THE PRESS, AND ASSEMBLY

Many people believe the right to argue is absolutely essential and must be protected from the majority if democracy is to survive. These First Amendment freedoms are central to a democratic system for several reasons. For one thing, effective majority rule depends on knowledge of alternatives. Only if there is freedom to present all sides of an issue can there be a real choice. Therefore, minorities must be allowed to put forward their ideas. The guarantees of freedom of speech, the press, and assembly give each minority a chance to convince others to join with it, thereby forming a new majority. Today's minority can become the basis of tomorrow's majority.

Some have seen in this process the best road to truth. Justice Oliver Wendell Holmes said that the best test of the truth of an idea was its ability to win acceptance in a free marketplace of ideas. This faith that free competition will lead to truth may seem overly optimistic at times, but even if truth does not always win out, a really free society may need to let people talk and talk, regardless of how it comes out.

One other consideration involved in free speech involves the individual's right to express ideas and beliefs as a fundamental element of personal expression and self-development. From this perspective, the ultimate standard in a democracy is not the good of society, but the moral and intellectual growth of each individual.

Considerations like these have given the First Amendment freedoms a special place in democratic thought. Some claim that they are absolute rights that must never be limited by the majority. Most Americans, however, have regarded the First Amendment freedoms as relative, to be weighed in relation to other values with which the rights of individual expression may conflict. These conflicts of values take many forms.

First, there is the freedom of the individual versus the security of the state. Democracy depends upon the right of individuals to speak out against the government, to criticize it, and call for changes. But does not the state have the right to protect itself against those who would overthrow it by fomenting revolution or who would harm national security by giving away state secrets? Out of this conflict of values have grown many cases dealing with free speech versus loyalty and national security.

Second, there is freedom of speech for the individual versus the right of the majority to have the kind of society it wants: the rights of individuals to say what they please when that runs counter to the norms and desires of society. Does the individual have the right to free expression even if it is fundamentally offensive to many or most other people? Or does society have the right to limit free expression if it believes that it is fundamentally offensive or damaging to morality? This issue comes up in many cases dealing with obscenity. Similar issues come up in connection with public order and safety. Is my freedom to speak protected even if it might lead to violence or a riot? Or can the government block such speech?

The issue also comes up in a somewhat different form in many cases dealing with freedom of religion. How far can the community go in estab-

The March on Washington in August 1963, organized to support civil rights legislation, provided the occasion for Martin Luther King, Jr., to deliver his famous "I Have a Dream" speech.

lishing standards of behavior of a religious sort? Can the community, for instance, provide prayers in the public schools? Most Americans favor such prayers; some religious groups consider it a violation of their freedom of religion to have such observances in the public schools. In cases of this sort, the rights of minorities—those who would publish or purchase obscene magazines, those who oppose school prayers, those who would make speeches offensive to the community—are pitted against the wishes of the majority. What is the democratic thing to do? Protect the minority or follow the wishes of the majority?

And, finally, there is the individual's right to free speech versus the rights of other individuals. The first two dilemmas of free speech involved a clash of individual rights versus the rights of the community. Sometimes, however, an individual's right clashes with the right of some other individual. How far can an individual use the right of free speech to violate the privacy or damage the reputation of other individuals? Much court litigation having to do with the law of libel deals with this issue.

We will look at each of these clashes of values and at how the courts have dealt with them. First, let us consider the origin of the First Amendment.

There was fairly widespread agreement among those at the Constitutional Convention that citizens should have guaranteed rights such as free press and speech, freedom of religion, and the right to a fair trial. But there was debate on whether an explicit guarantee of those rights was needed. The Federalists said that a specific bill of rights would be superfluous. The national government had been given delegated powers—over commerce and the like—but had been given no power to curb the press or to limit free speech or control religion. There was therefore no need to guarantee these rights; the government did not have the power to take them away.

As we have seen, the anti-Federalists at the Constitutional Convention and many people in the individual states were adamant. They did not feel adequately protected unless more explicit provisions were put into the Constitution. In the end, those who wanted the Bill of Rights won, and the first 10 amendments were added to the Constitution.

The First Amendment is the most important of these. Its language is striking: "Congress shall make no law respecting an establishment of religion, or prohibiting the free exercise thereof; or abridging the freedom of speech, or of the press; or the right of the people peaceably to assemble, and to petition the government for a redress of grievances."

Several things stand out when one looks at the First Amendment. To begin with, it is negative. It says what Congress *cannot* do. It protects people *against* the use of governmental authority. This fact helps explain why so much of the history of the First Amendment takes place in the federal courts. In order for the government to restrict free speech or a free press they must arrest and prosecute the individual they believe is committing some offense against public order with what is said or published. The matter then goes to court, so that it is to the courts that citizens turn if they believe the government is limiting their rights under the First Amendment.

A second point one should notice is the strong language: "Congress shall make *no* law. . . ." The amendment does not say that Congress shall make no "unreasonable" law (as the Fourth Amendment protects citizens from "unreasonable searches and seizures"). Clearly the amendment was meant to leave Congress with little scope to limit freedom.

Last, note who it is that the First Amendment limits. It says that "*Congress* shall make no law. . . ." The Bill of Rights, as originally written, applied only to actions of the federal government, not to actions of the state legislatures. The amendment refers to Congress, not the executive branch. However, the latter can only act if there is a law of Congress, so that the amendment was designed to protect against action of either branch of the federal government. In fact, the First Amendment and the other amendments of the Bill of Rights were not applied to state and local governments until the twentieth century. It was not until the case of *Gitlow* v. *New York* (268 U.S. 652) in 1925 that the Supreme Court held the First Amendment to apply to actions of state governments. The Court based its ruling in the Gitlow case on the Fourteenth Amendment, which was passed after the Civil War. That amendment applied to state governments and said that no state shall "deprive any person of life, liberty, or property, without due process of law." The justices ruled that the liberty mentioned in the Fourteenth Amendment included the freedoms of the First Amendment.

Over time, the Supreme Court has held that the other liberties, rights, and freedoms specified in the amendments of the Bill of Rights are also "incorporated" in the "liberty" of the Fourteenth Amendment. Neither state or local governments nor Congress can infringe them.

The Supreme Court has made it clear that the First Amendment applies to action of individual states and their subdivisions as well as to the federal government. In other respects, however, the First Amendment is not as clear as might at first seem to be the case. The language seems absolute— "Congress shall make *no* law . . ."—but the issues are not nearly that clear. Congress may do many other things that may, in some circumstances, limit the freedom to speak or write. One of the few clear principles associated with First Amendment freedoms is that they have never been absolute. Important, yes, but not absolute. Under some circumstances, free speech or free press may legitimately be curbed by the government. What are those circumstances?

Free Speech: The Early Years

The First Amendment, as well as the other amendments of the Bill of Rights, became part of the supreme law of the land shortly after the Constitutional Convention in 1787. But the First Amendment was little used or noticed for over a century. Shortly after the establishment of the new government under the Constitution, Congress passed a law that seriously challenged free speech and press—the Alien and Sedition Act of 1798. Under the act, people who made "false, scandalous and malicious" statements about government officials in such a way as to create "public contempt" for those officials could be punished by up to two years in jail and a fine of $2000. The law was passed by the Federalist majority in Congress. It represented an attempt to silence their Republican opponents and to curb the freedoms of those who would defend the alien ideas of the French Revolution. If the law had been allowed to stand and had been successfully applied, the development of a democratic government in the United States might have been stopped right then.

There was great public opposition to the law and its abuses—opposition that led to the weakening of the Federalist Party. In 1801, shortly after Thomas Jefferson took office as president, the Alien and Sedition Act expired, and it was not renewed by Congress. The law had been passed by Congress and was allowed to expire by Congress. The opposition to the law had come from the public and from Jefferson's Republican party, which had been its target. The Supreme Court did not rule on the constitutionality of the law, and the First Amendment played little role in defeating it.

Issues of free speech and press did not often appear before the Supreme Court during the nineteenth century. The Supreme Court was much more concerned with defining the power of the government to regulate business and in the power of the national government versus that of the states. There were many instances of suppression of unpopular speakers and government interference with the freedom to speak, publish, or worship. Most of these involved state or local authorities, however, and cases did not reach the federal courts for resolution. Not until World War I, and the emergence of conflicts between the freedom to speak and the war effort, did First Amendment cases begin to come before the Supreme Court.

Freedom of Speech and Subversion

The major area of conflict over freedom of speech—and the most important one from the point of view of democratic politics—is the conflict between freedom of speech and national security. Freedom of speech is particularly important when it protects people with unpopular political opinions, especially opinions that are severely critical of government. But the right to express unpopular political opinions may conflict with another right—the right of a democratic government to protect itself against subversion.

It is easier to state these principles than to apply them. For instance, the First Amendment guarantee of freedom of speech does not give the citizen the right to commit sabotage or to use violence against government officials, and Congress can pass (and has passed) laws punishing those who commit or try to commit such acts. This principle should be easy to apply, but the boundary between speech and action is by no means clear. Speech, some have argued, can itself be violent, and there is no doubt that speech can be used to incite violent action.

Consider sabotage. The government can arrest and prosecute those who commit or try to commit sabotage. But:

1. What if I plan an act of sabotage with someone else? I tell my partner where to plant the bomb and when to do it. I only "speak." My partner does the actual bombing. Is my "speech" protected by the First Amendment?
2. What if I make a speech at a public meeting saying that people should sabotage government operations? After the meeting, some of those who heard me speak go out and plant bombs in government buildings. Is my "speech" protected?
3. What if I make a speech like the one described in example 2, but no one acts? Is my "speech" protected?
4. What if I make a speech that merely says that "there are times when it would be justifiable to sabotage the government"? (That is, I do not directly advocate such sabotage.) Suppose someone hears the speech, decides that the current circumstances justify sabotage, and attempts it. Is my "speech" protected?
5. Suppose I write a book on the history of sabotage and treat some famous saboteurs sympathetically? Is my "speech" protected?

It should be clear from these examples that the clash between the principle of freedom of speech and the principle that the government can punish actions directed against it can arise in many circumstances. Furthermore, at times it is unclear whether one is dealing with speech or action. For one thing, it is hard to determine when speech directly advocates action and when it does not. In example 1 it would seem clear that it does, and perhaps in example 2 as well. But what if one says, as in example 4, that there are times when one must act? Is that person advocating action?

It is hard to tell whether speech in fact leads to action. Again it would seem clear that it does in example 1. But can we be sure in example 2 that the speech led to the action? (What if the action comes a month later?) In example 1 the "speech" involved would probably not be protected by the First Amendment. It is clearly part of a criminal action and punishable without violating the Constitution.

Example 5 is a fairly clear case of "speech" that is protected under the First Amendment (even though it is possible that someone would read such a book and be motivated to imitate a saboteur).

Examples 2, 3, and 4 lie in between, and it is not clear whether the courts would consider the behavior involved to be *speech* protected by the Constitution or *activity* punishable as subversive.

Government Actions Against Conspiracy and Subversion

First Amendment problems arise only when government officials proceed against a person or group for some action that is claimed to be protected. Both the prosecution and the "offending action" occur in a broader social context, however. Drawing the line between civil liberties and the right of the government to protect itself is made difficult by the fact that attempts to limit these liberties usually take place during times of national emergency—in particular, in time of war. At such times, the dangers of sabotage and subversion loom large in the eyes of the government and the public. Civil liberties usually suffer. During the Civil War, for instance, President Lincoln suspended the writ of habeas corpus (a fundamental right guaranteed in the Constitution, under which citizens cannot be held in jail without being brought into court or to trial). During and after World War I, the government cracked down on radical political activity. A number of raids were carried out by Attorney General Palmer on so-called subversive organizations. In World War II, all Americans of Japanese ancestry, whether there was evidence of subversive activity or not, were moved from the West Coast to relocation centers in the Midwest, where they were kept until the war was over.

After World War II, there was a long period of acute national anxiety over communism at home and abroad. Under President Truman the federal government set up a loyalty and security program to eliminate "subversives" from the government.

Perhaps the most important figure of the era was Senator Joseph McCarthy (R–Wis.). He gave his name to the American postwar period, which has been known ever since as the McCarthy era. He was elected senator in 1946. In 1950—a time of national fear about foreign policy, when America worried about a Communist takeover in Eastern Europe and China and when Russia had just gotten the atomic bomb—McCarthy became the voice of anticommunism. He announced that there were 205 Communists in the State Department. That and other such announcements raised him to national prominence. In 1953 he became chairman of the Senate Committee on Government Operations and of its Permanent Investigations Subcommittee. His investigations of "subversives"—a term never clearly defined by him, but sometimes seeming to include all who held liberal and radical opinions with which the senator disagreed—were felt by many to be a threat to free speech. The McCarthy charges did not reach court. They, and others like them, were mainly political in the sense that they were intended to arouse and shape public opinion. Eventually the Senator turned against fellow senators and other formidable opponents. Ultimately, he was censured by the Senate, and his power faded.

Senator Joseph McCarthy was so reckless in his attacks on alleged Communists in the government that his very name came to signify an atmosphere threatening to free speech.

To understand why issues of free speech become so important, one has to understand the kind of appeal made by people like Senator McCarthy. The appeal was moral: He argued for defense of the American way of life. The appeal was against an enemy: He denounced Communists at home and abroad. The appeal was to an anxious America: He would protect it from a conspiracy of evil forces. Such an appeal can capture much emotional support. At such times, when the country is uneasy and uncertain, the threat to free speech can become quite real. Many Americans at the time questioned McCarthy's methods and felt he was overly zealous but nevertheless applauded him for contributing to what they took to be a higher goal, the protection of the nation against subversion.

Freedom and Restraint: Finding a Standard

The Smith Act of 1940 In the three decades since World War II, the judicial determination of issues of civil liberties versus national security has centered on a series of laws aimed at blocking conspiracy and subversion. The Smith Act, passed in 1940, made it a crime to teach or advocate the violent overthrow of the U.S. government. In 1951, the Supreme Court upheld the conviction of Eugene Dennis, head of the U.S. Communist party, under the Smith Act (*Dennis et al.* v. *United States*, 341 U.S. 494). Critics of this decision (including the dissenting justices) argued that the defendants were convicted for speech, not action (for "teaching and advocating"), but the Supreme Court majority held that the government had the right to protect itself against the *actions* that the defendants taught and advocated. These actions, the overthrow of the government, were so dreadful that, even though they were not likely to occur, the advocates of the action could be punished.

In later cases, the Supreme Court backed away from this view. In 1957, a majority of the justices held that the "mere advocacy" of doctrine could not be restricted (*Yates* v. *United States*, 354 U.S. 298). There had to be actual incitement to action.

Clear and present danger test   What the Dennis and Yates cases illustrate is that as the Supreme Court attempts to resolve free-speech cases, balancing the value of speech against other public concerns, it looks for verbal formulas that explain and justify the decision reached. These formulas are attempts to articulate a general rule or standard that will guide decisions by the courts, and other public officials as well, in dealing with conflicts between First Amendment concerns and other social values. Some of these verbal standards are more persuasive than others. In addition, as the Court's personnel changes, the values the Justices hold to be most important may also change. New Court majorities may look for new constitutional doctrines.

The **clear and present danger** test is perhaps the best-known free-speech standard set down by the Supreme Court. In fact, it is a standard that is very difficult to apply in practice and has rarely been used. It was first expressed by Justice Oliver Wendell Holmes in the 1919 case of *Schenck v. the United States* (249 U.S. 47). Schenck was secretary of the Socialist party. During World War I, he had printed and distributed 15,000 pamphlets denouncing the draft and trying to persuade people to resist it. Some of the pamphlets were sent to draftees. Was this free speech to be protected or was this dangerous subversion?

Justice Holmes wrote the majority decision in the case. He argued that a person's statements could be limited by law only if two circumstances held. In the first place, the "evil effects" of the statement had to follow immediately after it was made, with no chance for others to answer it or for those who heard it to reflect on its meaning. The danger had to be clear and present, not something that might happen in the distant future. Secondly, the evil effects had to be something that Congress had the right to prevent. If your speech leads immediately to a riot, to the robbing of a bank, to the sabotaging of a train, or to some other clearly illegal act, your speech can be punished under this doctrine. But if your speech merely leads to someone's becoming angry, it is protected under the First Amendment, since it is not a criminal offense to anger other people.

In the Schenck case, the Court decided that Schenck could be punished for the pamphlets he circulated. The Court reasoned that because the nation was at war, any speech or writing that might lead people to disobey the draft law represented a clear and present danger.

The clear and present danger doctrine is, at first glance, attractive. If there is time for one speech to be answered by another—say, for your argument opposing the draft to be answered by mine supporting it—we are dealing in the marketplace of ideas, where opposing views should be allowed freedom to flow back and forth. But if someone's speech leads immediately to some criminal act, with no time for intervening discussion, then the speech is not protected by the First Amendment. The standard is often difficult to apply in practice. It is hard to know precisely what the consequences of a speech will be and how swiftly those consequences will come about. For the justices on the Court to determine that an act of speech represented a clear and present danger, they must study very closely the events surrounding the speech. This standard clearly favors protecting speech against government interference, however, and not every Court majority has accepted this priority; so other formulas are offered.

Bad tendency This doctrine is much more restrictive of free speech than is the clear and present danger doctrine. It was first clearly enunciated in 1925, in *Gitlow* v. *New York* (268 U.S. 652). This is the case, mentioned earlier, in which the Supreme Court ruled that the First Amendment's prohibition against limiting freedom of speech applied to state governments as well as to Congress. The expansion of the First Amendment to cover the states was a great victory for free speech. But in the rest of the case, free speech (and Gitlow) did not do so well.

Benjamin Gitlow represented the left wing of the Socialist movement in the United States. He published leaflets calling on citizens to join together to overthrow the bourgeois government. The Court ruled that Gitlow could be punished for his statements. Furthermore, the Court said that it was not necessary that his statements present a clear and present danger. When it came to something as serious as the overthrow of the government, the Court argued, one could not expect that government to wait until the very last minute and act when the danger was already upon it. The "revolutionary spark" should be extinguished early even if the real danger of revolution was far in the future.

This standard looks for **bad tendencies**—the dangers deriving from the statement may not appear immediately, but they may appear in the future. The standard is close to the one used by the Court to convict the leaders of the American Communist party under the Smith Act in 1951. The majority of the Supreme Court agreed that there was no immediate danger of the overthrow of the U.S. government from the writing and teaching of the Communist leaders. But they argued that the evil that Congress was trying to avoid—the overthrow of the government—was of such a magnitude that Congress had the right to make "teaching and advocating" it a crime even in the absence of a clear and present danger.

The bad tendency test allows much more restriction of free speech. One has merely to show that the speech might lead, in the long run, to some illegal consequence. The doctrine means that the Court gives much more leeway to the legislature—to state legislatures or Congress—in defining what speech should be allowed and what should be barred. Under the bad tendency doctrine, the Court is not an active advocate of free speech.

Preferred position Many justices of the Supreme Court have argued that free speech and a free press deserve stronger protection than they receive under the clear and present danger standard or the bad tendency standard. They believe that these rights should have a special and **preferred position** in the American scheme of things. Free speech and press, they argue, are more basic to our democratic government than are economic or property rights. The logic for this preferred position is straightforward. If Congress limits the economic liberties of individuals—by regulating the way in which they run their business or by raising their taxes—those who oppose such limitations can argue against the law, can lobby in Washington for a change in the law, and can work to elect candidates who are sympathetic with their position. In other words, Congress may have passed a law on a particular subject, but the political process remains open so that those who oppose the law can work for change.

Laws that limit freedom of speech or of the press are quite different. They close the very process that would allow for the revision of such laws. Thus, to preserve democracy, freedom of speech and of the press must be given special protection.

Before the 1930s the Court did not give First Amendment freedoms a preferred position. Economic rights were more fully protected. But since the late 1930s the Court has tended to treat government actions restricting free speech and press with much less sympathy than it treats laws regulating the economy. When Congress or a state legislature passes a law on an economic matter, the Supreme Court generally assumes that there is a reasonable basis for such a law and lets the law stand. It defers to the judgment of the legislature and seems to say, "If the legislature wanted to pass this law, it must be all right." When it comes to laws dealing with freedom of speech or of the press, the Court applies a much stricter standard. There must be some compelling reason for the limitation of freedom if the law is to be allowed to stand. The justices do not say, "If the legislature wants it it must be all right"; they look with much greater suspicion upon laws that touch the First Amendment.

The current positions: balancing freedom and restraint   In recent years the Supreme Court appears to have moved away from the more restrictive bad tendency test and to have given the First Amendment freedoms a preferred position. That position, however, is by no means absolute. The Court has allowed some limitation on free speech and press. The position of these freedoms is "preferred" in that the Court looks very closely at laws that seem to limit these freedoms. It will not accept vague laws or very broad laws. To restrict freedom of speech or of the press, a law must have a very serious purpose, such as protecting national security secrets or avoiding violence. The law must also be very precisely written so that there is no danger that it will be used to block more than the specific kind of speech at which it is aimed. The Court allows the government to pass very broad and general laws regulating the economy, but laws regulating speech will be ruled unconstitutional if they are broad or imprecise.

The Court has defined its basic task as balancing one value against another—the value of free speech against some other value that people consider important. In this balancing process the freedom to speak, write, and publish will be given special weight, but the Court has tended to avoid coining new phrases of broad application. A majority of the justices appear to prefer examining each case and its circumstances, judging each on its own terms. In the absence of a more precise doctrine, it is difficult to know how a particular free speech case will come out. But Congress and the state legislatures know that any law affecting the First Amendment freedoms will be looked at very closely and with great skepticism by the Supreme Court.

One result of the Court's position of skepticism toward laws that restrict freedom of speech is that the prosecution for expressing or teaching unpopular or "dangerous" political doctrines—prosecutions such as those of Schenck or Gitlow after World War I and of Dennis and the leaders of the Communist party after World War II—disappeared by the 1970s. Cases remain, however, referring to public order, military secrets, obscenity, and libel. Of course, the climate of opinion may change, and so may the views of the Supreme Court. We cannot be sure that cases involving political speech may not appear again.

BALANCING FREE SPEECH AND OTHER VALUES

Free Speech and Public Order

We have seen that the Court has often tried to balance free speech against threats to national security. At times, however, free speech must be balanced against more local threats to public safety. Indeed, there are many more cases in which the Court balances the right of an individual to speak against the right of the public to peace, safety, and tranquility in the community. A soapbox orator may stand on the street corner denouncing racketeers in government, greedy business executives, Catholics, Jews, blacks, or whites. What if his words incite others to violence, either because they agree with his attacks or—as is more often the case—because they disagree and want to silence him? What if the crowd he gathers blocks traffic? What if he uses a powerful loudspeaker, so that even if what he says is not offensive, the noise level is a public nuisance?

The Court deals with many cases of this sort. It has not developed a very precise doctrine but takes each incident on a case by case basis, trying to balance the right of free speech with the public's right to safety and order. The Court follows some general guidelines, however. It looks closely at attempts to regulate free speech in the name of public safety, to make sure that there is a real safety issue involved.

The Court has insisted that the laws be narrowly and precisely drawn and applied so as not to give government officials an opportunity to bar speech that they regard as merely inconvenient or unpopular. It tries to make sure that any limitations on speech are carried out in a nondiscriminatory manner, allowing the government to control in a reasonable way public order. Restrictions on public demonstrations such as parades or mass meetings, which have a greater potentiality of disrupting public order, have been permitted. Cities and towns may control the "time, place, and manner" of parades and demonstrations. The Court is careful, however, to see that this is not done in a way that discriminates against some particular group or point of view.

The balance between freedom and restraint that the courts must find in cases involving public order is no less important and no less difficult than the balance they seek between free speech and the right of the government to resist being overthrown. Compare the views of two leading Supreme Court justices in a case involving public order. The case was of a man named Terminiello, who spoke at a meeting in Chicago in 1946, denouncing in the strongest and vilest terms Jews, blacks, and the Roosevelt administration. Many hundreds gathered outside the meeting hall tried to break in to disrupt the speech. The police arrested Terminiello for disturbing the peace, claiming his speech had incited the angry mob.

When the courts try to balance free speech and public order they often must uphold the rights of "not very nice" people, such as the American Nazis.

The Supreme Court overruled his conviction, claiming that free speech should not be curtailed even if it might bring about unrest or create a disturbance. In *Terminiello* v. *Chicago* (337 U.S. 1, 1947), Justice William O. Douglas, a staunch defender of First Amendment freedoms, wrote as follows in the Court majority opinon: ". . . free speech under our system of government [invites] dispute. It may indeed best serve its high purpose when it induces a condition of unrest, creates dissatisfaction with conditions as they are, or even stirs people to anger. Speech . . . may . . . have profound unsettling effects." Such speech, he went on to say, must be protected despite the unrest it causes, ". . . for the alternative would lead to standardization of ideas either by legislatures, courts, or dominant political or community groups." A majority of five justices agreed with him.

Four justices dissented, and Justice Robert H. Jackson wrote the dissent. He was more concerned about the danger to public order that could grow out of a speech like that made by Terminiello. Unless the government were empowered to preserve order, total disorder might follow; ". . . the choice is not between order and liberty. It is between liberty with order and anarchy without either. There is danger that if the Court does not temper its doctrinaire logic with a little practical wisdom, it will convert the constitutional Bill of Rights into a suicide pact."

The reconciliation of the two values—free speech and public order— is rarely easy, as the confrontation of Justice Douglas's and Justice Jackson's positions shows. In a more recent case the Court ruled, again 5–4, that the National Socialist Party of America must be allowed to defend in court its right to march in a heavily Jewish suburb of Chicago (*National Socialist Party of America* v. *Skokie*, 432 U.S. 43, 1977). The case of the American

Nazis, like Terminiello, illustrates that free speech cases often involve extremely unattractive minorities. Under the terms of the First Amendment, however, even these are entitled to consideration.

In the Terminiello case, the Court, by a narrow margin, supported free speech over public order. At times, it has come out on the side of public order. Some criticize the Court for not having a firm and unambiguous position on one side or the other. But given that the values of free speech and public order are both important, there may be no better alternative than to try to balance these values in each individual case.

Obscenity and Free Speech

Obscenity is another field in which the Supreme Court tries to balance conflicting interests. On one side is the right to publish what one wants (a First Amendment right). On the other side is the right of citizens to protect their children from exposure to material that they think will be harmful or to protect themselves from speech that they find offensive. On the one hand is the principle that free speech should be limited when it becomes pornographic; that is, all literature and movies ought to be allowed except those that appeal solely to "base or prurient" interests and have no "redeeming social value" or literary qualities. On the other hand is the principle that all writings and movies should be allowed, regardless of their content.

Most states have some laws banning pornography, but it is hard to define what books and movies fall beyond the line of acceptability. Some people consider many great literary works so damaging to morals that they ought to be barred. In this difficult area, the burden falls on the courts to draw the lines.

The Supreme Court has tried for a long time to define what may be barred by state and local pornography laws and what is protected by the First Amendment. At one time, a work could be banned if it had "no redeeming social value." Material that appealed primarily to "prurient interest" could also be suppressed. Then the Court proposed that a work that might otherwise be censored as obscene would be saved if it had "serious literary artistic, political, or scientific value." The problem is that none of these terms has a clear meaning, and the Court found itself deciding what is obscene on a case by case basis. In a well-known comment Justice Potter Stewart observed that while he could not define pornography, he knew it when he saw it.

In 1973 the Supreme Court took a new approach to the definition of pornography in *Miller* v. *California* (413 U.S. 15). It ruled that individual communities should have the right to decide for themselves what constitutes pornography and obscenity. Communities, according to this ruling, could decide whether they wanted *Hustler* magazine sold or the movie *Deep Throat* shown. The new approach was aimed at creating diversity—a value that, as we saw in the chapter on federalism (Chapter 3), is often associated with local control. What the public in New York or San Francisco might accept would be unacceptable in more conservative communities.

This decision has by no means settled the matter. There are still no clear guidelines as to how one determines what community standards are.

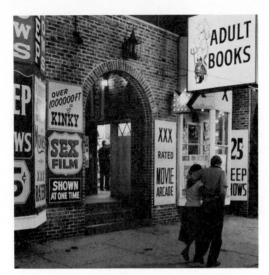

Does the constitutional guarantee of free speech account for the public availability of pornography shops?

Furthermore, there have been several controversial convictions of publishers of nationally circulated magazines. They have been prosecuted in conservative communities, despite the fact that the circulation of the magazine in that community was very limited. The publisher of *Hustler* magazine was convicted for selling an obscene publication in Cincinnati, Ohio, even though the magazine is not published there, and the publisher of *Screw* was convicted on charges of distributing obscene material in Wichita, Kansas, although *Screw* had only a few subscribers in Wichita. Opponents of the obscenity laws claim that the new rule established by the Court does not protect the autonomy of local communities to set their own standards; rather, it allows zealous prosecutors to choose the locality where they can most easily convict those who are accused of obscenity. In this way, any community can be used to set standards for the nation.

This complex issue is still unresolved. The law on pornography and obscenity is still vague. The Court continues to try to define the boundary between the competing claims of those who would limit pornography and those who claim the right of freedom of speech under the First Amendment.

FREEDOM OF RELIGION

The same constitutional amendment that guarantees freedom of speech contains the equally basic guarantee of freedom of religion: "Congress shall make no law respecting an establishment of religion, or prohibiting the free exercise thereof." Two provisions concerning religion are contained in these famous words of the First Amendment. The first, the "non-establishment" clause, forbids the government to support any particular religious establishment. The second, the "free exercise" clause, bars the government from interfering with the freedom of Americans to worship as they wish. These provisions are related. If the government were to favor one religion over another, it would be reducing the freedom of some Americans to exercise their faith. This may be one of the cornerstones of civil peace in America. In a society with many religions, severe conflict may arise if the government favors one over another. The First Amendment reduces this possibility.

Yet, as with freedom of speech, the wording of the First Amendment does not settle the issue. The words of the First Amendment are striking but ambiguous. The amendment was meant to bar a state-supported religion and permanently to separate church and state. But how wide that separation was supposed to be remains unclear.

The government cannot establish a church. But does this mean that it cannot give aid to parochial schools? Does it mean that it cannot provide buses for children going to such schools? What about police officers who direct traffic outside such schools? Can public schools put on Christmas pageants?

The government cannot prohibit individuals from practicing their religion. What if that religion involves polygamy or snake handling? Or forbids its members to pay taxes, serve in the armed forces, or salute the flag? Are all activities justified if they represent "exercises of religion"? If not, has freedom of religion been limited?

As with freedom of speech, it can be seen that the Constitution leaves some questions unanswered. The result is a mixed, inconsistent system under which the government respects the separation of church and state in general, but does not draw the boundaries of separation with complete clarity. Disputes arise over who has the right to do what. Since the Supreme Court is the main agency responsible for determining questions of rights, it is drawn into these disputes. Thus the Court has not permitted aid to be given to parochial schools. But it has allowed the states to provide bus transportation for children who go to such schools. Chapel attendance was required at the nation's military academies—West Point, Annapolis, and the Air Force Academy—until 1972, when the Supreme Court ruled it unconstitutional. But the federal government still supports chaplains in the armed forces, and the sessions of Congress open with prayer. Those who object for religious reasons can refuse to salute the flag, but citizens cannot refuse to pay taxes for religious reasons.

All of these seeming inconsistencies stem from the same general problem—the need to balance one value with other values. Consider the following aspects of church-state relations.

The Right to Worship as One Sees Fit

Freedom of religion is clearly guaranteed in the First Amendment. The government can neither prohibit nor enforce any particular religion. Yet the boundaries of the free exercise of religion become controversial when a religious practice would violate some other principle. In the nineteenth century the Supreme Court upheld the government's prohibition of polygamy, even though this was a fundamental practice of the Mormon religion (*Reynolds* v. *United States*, 98 U.S. 145, 1879). The Court reasoned that polygamy was so contrary to the American moral code that even though it was a matter of religious faith, it could not be allowed to continue. One wonders what decision the Court would reach today, when views about the nature of marriage have loosened somewhat. But even if the Court decided that polygamy is no longer as shocking as it once was, there are certainly many other practices—such as public nudity—that, though claimed by some as expressions of religious belief, would still be prohibited.

What about Sabbath observance? Do Sunday closing laws unfairly punish Jewish merchants who also close on Saturday, their Sabbath? (No, according to *Brunfeld* v. *Brown,* 366 U.S. 617, 1961.) And what of the Seventh-Day Adventist who had been denied unemployment benefits after she had been fired for refusing to work on Saturdays? (The employee is entitled to benefits, according to *Sherbert* v. *Verner,* 374 U.S. 398, 1963.) The immense diversity of religious belief and practice in the United States has generated an increasing number of cases in which religion-based claims come into conflict with other values or policies endorsed by local, state, or national authorities. The Supreme Court has been attempting to steer a careful course among these competing positions, and clearly it has not discovered any easy or quick solution.

Freedom of Religion in the Field of Education

The field of education offers many examples of the delicate balance between freedom of religion and the requirements of the state. The Supreme Court has limited the application of compulsory-education laws for members of religious groups that are opposed to formal education, such as the Amish (*Wisconsin* v. *Yoder,* 406 U.S. 205, 1972). It has allowed parents to choose religious schools for their children as long as those schools meet state educational standards (*Pierce* v. *Society of Sisters,* 268 U.S. 510, 1935). Religious schools are not able to get government support, however.

The flag salute cases   The attempt to balance the rights of minority religious practices against obedience to general laws is found in the so-called flag salute cases. The Jehovah's Witnesses—whose firm rejection of secular authority has led to many run-ins with the law and to numerous court cases—oppose the worship of images. They do not allow their children to salute the flag. But many state laws have required a flag salute ceremony at the beginning of the school day, the justification of such laws being that the state had the right to teach children respect for national symbols.

In 1940 the Supreme Court upheld such a law, saying that Jehovah's Witnesses could be required to salute the flag (*Minersville School District* v. *Gobitis,* 310 U.S. 586, 1940). Three years later the Court reversed itself, with four justices who had supported the right of the state to require a flag salute now supporting the right of the minority group to refuse to do so (*West Virginia State Board of Education* v. *Barnette,* 319, U.S. 624, 1943). The new reasoning of the Court was that the state's interest in a flag salute was not important enough to override the right of the minority to follow its religious convictions.

The 1943 flag salute case was a landmark in the attempt by the Supreme Court to locate the proper boundary between individual freedom of conscience and the right of the government to demand respect for its institutions. But open issues remain in drawing this boundary. Under a New Jersey law, public school students who did not wish to take part in the daily pledge of allegiance were required to stand at attention during the ceremony. In 1977 a federal court overturned the law as unconstitutional. The court ruled that students could remain seated as long as they were not unruly. This case illustrates the subtle distinctions that courts are called upon to make in drawing the line between the rights of individuals and the power of the state.

Freedom of Religion for Nonbelievers

The provisions of the First Amendment were intended to prevent the government from favoring a particular religion over another. But might not the government favor those who were religious over those who were not? In many ways, government policy seemed to do this, but in recent years the Court has curtailed such practices. We have mentioned the abolition of compulsory chapel attendance at the military academies. In addition, the Supreme Court struck down a long-standing provision of the Maryland constitution requiring that public officeholders say that they believe in God.

Conscientious-objector status   The Court has extended the right to refuse to do military service to those who neither belong to an established religion nor say they believe in God. Before this ruling, those who claimed conscientious-objector status had to prove their right to such status on religious grounds—usually membership in a recognized religious group, such as the Quakers, which traditionally opposed military service. But in 1965 the Court decided that this discriminated in favor of particular religions, and extended the right of conscientious-objector status to those who oppose war on ethical grounds (*United States* v. *Seeger*, 380 U.S. 163).

School prayers   Perhaps the most controversial recent problem of religious freedom is in the area of school prayers. Does it violate the freedom of nonbelievers if the government sponsors prayers in the public schools, even if the prayers are nonsectarian and not compulsory?

Many school systems around the country traditionally opened the school day with some prayer. In 1962 the Supreme Court barred such prayers (*Engel* v. *Vitale*, 370 U.S. 421). It ruled that a school district in New York State violated the Constitution by requiring that classes be started with a nonsectarian prayer composed by the New York Board of Regents. The school board had specifically indicated that pupils could be excused at the request of their parents. Yet the Court held that such prayers violated the separation of church and state because they were required by the government. In a similar case, the Court barred a Pennsylvania law requiring that the Bible be read daily in the schools in that state (*School District of Abington Township* v. *Schempp*, 374 U.S. 203, 1963). Later the Court refused to permit Kentucky schools to hang a framed copy of the Ten Commandments in a classroom (*Stone* v. *Graham*, 449 U.S. 39, 1980).

There can be little doubt that in many of these cases the Court was

Should the public schools require religious observances of any kind? Who should decide?

taking the side of a small minority. Public-opinion polls have consistently shown that large majorities of the public favor school prayer. In 1962, the year that the Court ruled against school prayer, the Gallup poll found 79 percent of the public in favor of religious observances in the schools. In 1975 another Gallup poll found that 77 percent favored amending the Constitution to permit prayer in the public schools. The parents who objected (and brought the case to the courts) were a small and generally unpopular group. On the other hand, it is also clear that while many might favor the general idea of school prayers, agreement would soon evaporate over what specific language should be included.

    The Court decisions have not settled the issue. There has been a good deal of agitation for a constitutional amendment to allow prayer in the schools, though the movement has thus far not been successful. Furthermore, Supreme Court decisions are not always followed in practice. Studies have shown that many school districts have continued to allow some kind of prayer despite the Court ruling. The Court cannot monitor every district. If a school principal or a classroom teacher decides to open the day with prayer, if the school board does not object, and if no parent brings a complaint, the Court decision may be ignored.

It is generally the diversity of religious belief (and nonbelief) within a given community that makes strict separation effective. If there are only a few dissenters, no one will protect religious observances. But if, as in many American communities, there are many different religious groups, it may not be possible to agree on what kind of religious expression to have. Thus it is religious pluralism that really enforces the separation of church and state.

Government aid to religious schools   Another major controversy is government aid to private religious schools. Does it violate the separation of church and state if the government gives support to such schools? The argument in favor of such support is that these schools contribute to society by educating children. Moreover, since parents who send their children to such schools are also taxed to pay for the public school system, those who choose a religious school, which they have to support as well, are doubly burdened because of their beliefs. Opponents of aid to religious schools say that it would represent discriminatory support for particular religions.

The Supreme Court's decisions in this area have been quite mixed. In a major decision in 1947, the Court upheld a New Jersey law providing payment for bus transportation for children attending parochial schools (*Everson* v. *Board of Education,* 330 U.S. 1). The payments helped those children obtain religious training. The Court majority made a strong statement in favor of absolute separation of church and state: "The First Amendment has erected a wall between church and state. That wall must be kept high and remain impregnable. We could not approve the slightest breach." It is evidence of the uncertainty of the Court's position that this statement appears in a ruling that approved payment for busing to parochial schools.

The Court has drawn some complex boundaries. A state can provide transportation to parochial schools and pay for textbooks. It cannot pay for the maintenance or repair of such schools. On the other hand, state funds can be used for construction in church-related colleges. In 1948, the Court rejected as unconstitutional a "released-time" program allowing children to be excused from public school to attend religious training. Four years later it found a slightly different program to be acceptable. The "wall of separation" has become what Chief Justice Burger has called "a blurred, indistinct and variable barrier depending on all the circumstances of a particular relationship" (*Lemon* v. *Kurtzman,* 403 U.S. 602, 1971).

The Court insists that the government not use its funds to support the teaching of any religious tenet. On the other hand, it cannot inhibit the right of citizens to exercise their religion freely by denying them ordinary government support and protection, such as police protection, when they attempt to practice their religion. Free transportation to parochial schools was defined as a program for the welfare and safety of children, not as support for religion. Similarly, the Court allows government support for church-related schools at the college level but not at the elementary and secondary levels. The reasoning is that college training is less likely to involve actual indoctrination in a religion, while elementary and secondary education may.

In recent years the Supreme Court majority has employed a three-part test in determining whether some government programs violated the establishment of religion clauses:

1. The policy must have an obvious legitimate secular purpose (e.g., education).
2. The policy's primary effect must neither advance nor inhibit religion.
3. The policy must not foster excessive entanglement of government and religious institutions.

If a program violates any one of these three principles, it is invalid. Now all that remains is for the judges to determine what is a legitimate secular purpose, whether religion has been advanced or inhibited, and what constitutes excessive entanglement.

THE RIGHT TO PROPERTY

Throughout American history, a large share of the national wealth has been in the hands of a fairly small minority. This condition has persisted despite the principle of majoritarianism, which would seem to give the poorer majority a means of using the government to redistribute wealth. As we saw in Chapter 4, this redistribution has not taken place. We reviewed some of the reasons in that chapter. Here we wish simply to stress that the Constitution helps protect the property rights of citizens.

During the 1780s, unlike today, there was no talk of property rights versus human rights. The rights for which the Revolutionary War was fought were the rights of political liberty and property. "The true foundation of republican government," wrote Thomas Jefferson, "is the equal right of every citizen, in his person and in his property." This did *not* mean that every citizen would have equal amounts of property. The delegates to the Constitutional Convention met not to redistribute property but to protect it.

Protection of Property Rights

Protection of property rights was written into the Constitution and is established in legal precedent. For example, the Constitution prohibits any state from passing a law that would impair the obligations of contract. There is also a just-compensation clause. The nation's Founders recognized that privately owned lands might be needed for public projects, but they were concerned that the costs of such a project should be widely distributed. Thus the property owner would be fairly compensated out of the public treasury. Other clauses restrict both federal and state governments from depriving a citizen of property without *due process of law*. Stemming from these comparatively simple constitutional provisions are many laws protecting private property, and standing behind them are, of course, the police.

What is meant by *property rights?* We have in mind the basic right to own something and to prevent others from using it. So we put locks on doors. We also mean the right to sell or trade the thing we own, be it tangible property such as a car or a house or intangible property such as stocks and bonds. Furthermore, we mean the right to will property to chosen heirs. But the rights to own, sell, and give are limited. The courts and legislatures in the United States have put many restrictions on private property, restrictions that raise complicated questions about minority rights in a majoritarian democracy.

Property Rights Versus the Public Interest

Government restrictions on property often rest on the claim that the public interest overrides the rights of property. The owner of a 300-horsepower automobile cannot drive it at its highest speed, because that would threaten the public safety. The homeowner with a diseased elm tree is told to cut it down to prevent the disease from spreading. The contractor building a downtown apartment building has to include parking space in order to reduce the public nuisance of cars parked on the streets. In each of these cases, one might well ask, "Who are they to tell me what to do with my property?" "They" is the government claiming to act in the public interest.

The task of defining and then applying a concept as vague as "public interest" is very complex. The definition of public interest varies from one area to another and from one time to another. Take billboards, for instance. The right of a property owner to lease land to a billboard company was not challenged through much of our history. As a result, our public highways are flanked by private advertisements. But now, spurred by a different concept of public interest, some local and state governments are restricting this practice. In this respect, the United States is catching up with other nations. You can drive from one end of Canada to the other and never have the scenery blocked by a billboard.

Property Rights Versus Human Rights

On the 1964 ballot in California there was a proposed state constitutional amendment guaranteeing the right of all property holders in California to sell, lease, or rent the property to anyone they chose. This seems a reasonable enough proposal and certainly is in line with property rights. The proposed amendment, however, was in fact in response to an open-occupancy bill passed by the California legislature. The open-occupancy law banned racial discrimination in selling and renting property. Here is a clear case of property rights (the right to do what one wants with one's own home) versus human rights (the right of black citizens not to be discriminated against). The voters of California passed the amendment, but it was later declared unconstitutional by the state supreme court, and this ruling was upheld by the United States Supreme Court.

The open-occupancy law in California shows how legislatures and courts restrict the uses of property when those uses violate other constitutional rights—in this case, the right of equality before the law. When two constitutional rights are in conflict, it is the courts that must make a final decision. Sometimes this puts the courts on the side of the minority against the majority. Such was the case in California, when both state and federal courts overturned the clear preference of the majority. The property rights of the majority were restricted in favor of the human rights of the minority.

At other times, it is the minority whose property rights are restricted in favor of the human rights of the majority. Progressive income taxes and inheritance taxes can be looked at in this light. A portion of the wealth of the richer groups in society is taxed. This leads to some redistribution from a minority to the majority. We saw in Chapter 4 that this does not go very far; it nevertheless shows some attempt to restrict the property rights of a wealthy minority.

Despite limitations on property because of the public interest or because of competing constitutional rights, there remains firmly planted in our heritage a strong respect for the rights of private ownership. It is remarkable that the restrictions on property are so few. In this way, majoritarian democracy has been much less of a threat than many feared. John Dickinson, a delegate to the Constitutional Convention, warned that "the most dangerous influence" to public order was "those multitudes without property and without principle with which our country, like all others, will soon abound." But Dickinson was wrong because of one very important fact: The multitudes have not been without property and thus have not supported any major challenge to the rights of private ownership. Thomas Jefferson saw the importance of widespread ownership of property when he remarked that "everyone, by his property, or by his satisfactory situation, is interested in the support of law and order." The support of law and order meant in Jefferson's time, as it does today, the use of the legal and police powers of the government to protect private property.

THE RIGHT OF PRIVACY

Does the Constitution protect individual citizens from the society and the state when it comes to their private lives? This is a new and fascinating area of constitutional interpretation. Many states have laws regulating the sexual activities of citizens. At one time or another, the laws have made so-called deviant sexual behavior or the use of any birth control device illegal. In addition, most states have had laws making abortions illegal.

In recent years, a majority of the Supreme Court has seemed to uphold a citizen's right to privacy—arguing, that is, that the state has no business regulating the intimate behavior of individuals. The right of privacy is not mentioned in the Constitution. However, the Court has found that such a right is implied in other rights that are mentioned, such as the Fourth Amendment right against "unreasonable searches and seizures," the Fifth Amendment protection against "self-incrimination," and the broad but undefined "other rights" mentioned in the Ninth Amendment.

The Supreme Court cited these rights in overturning a Connecticut law that made it illegal to use any drug or device to prevent conception (*Griswold* v. *Connecticut*, 381 U.S. 479, 1965). Lower federal courts have cited the same right of privacy to challenge Virginia's sodomy statute, broadly ruling that states could not regulate the private behavior of individuals whether married or unmarried. As the court put it, the right of privacy applies to "intimate sexual relations between consenting adults, carried out under secluded conditions." A similar decision by a federal district court recently held that a school district violated the right to privacy by barring the hiring of homosexuals: "The time has now come for private, consenting, adult homosexuality to enter the sphere of constitutionally protected interests." In cases of this sort, the courts expand the range of private activities that are protected from the control of the state, even though such activities may be looked upon with disfavor by a majority of the population.

The most controversial issue involving the right of privacy is that of abortion. As we saw in Chapter 5, few Court decisions have aroused as much conflict. The Catholic Church opposes abortion, as do many other groups. The opponents of abortion claim to represent the constitutional rights of another group: unborn children. It is likely that this controversy will continue, for there are deeply felt interests on each side. Some antiabortionists are seeking an amendment to the Constitution to overrule the Supreme Court, but political disputes in America have rarely been resolved through constitutional amendment.

THE RIGHTS OF THE ACCUSED

The area of rights of those accused of crime may be the hardest one in which to balance individual freedom and majority concerns. Crime has grown to huge proportions in American society. Each year, crimes against property and violent crimes number in the millions. A large proportion of Americans have been victims of crime, and an even larger number fear crime. Many people have blamed the growth in crime on Supreme Court decisions "coddling criminals." During 1968, Richard Nixon, campaigning for the presidency, charged that the Court had put up a "barbed wire of legalisms . . . to protect a suspect from invasion of his rights [and] has effectively shielded hundreds of criminals from punishment." According to this view, if we put fewer restrictions on the police and the prosecutor, we would rid society of more criminals.

Perhaps so, but a democratic society has other values besides protection from criminals. Citizens in a free society are also to be protected from excessive and arbitrary use of police power. This raises the dilemma of buying greater security against crime at the price of greater insecurity against abuse of government power. For example, in the Drug Abuse Act of 1970, Congress authorized the use of "no-knock" search warrants by federal narcotics agents. Agents could break into homes without knocking if they could later persuade a magistrate that giving a warning would have resulted in destruction of drugs as evidence. But the result was that narcotics agents took advantage of the no-knock rule to break into homes in the middle of the night, harass innocent people, and destroy personal property—all without a warrant. Congress accordingly repealed the rule in 1974.

During the last 25 years the Supreme Court has ruled on dozens of cases involving the claim by someone convicted of a crime that he or she was not treated fairly in the way the Constitution requires. The justices have often disagreed, and as the composition of the Court has changed, the Court's majority itself has shifted direction. During the 1960s the Warren Court issued several notable opinions that expanded the protections afforded to the accused. After President Nixon appointed a new chief justice, Warren Burger, and three other members, the Court proceeded to restrict the application of these doctrines and allow somewhat more leeway to police officers and trial courts.

The focus of criminal rights   Like the rights discussed earlier, the rights of persons accused of crime are rooted in our constitutional system. Common law assumes that a person is innocent until proved guilty and that the accused has the same rights as all other citizens and is similarly protected against violation of those rights. Here the due process clause of the Fifth Amendment is basic: It affirms not only that the government itself is subject to the law but also that citizens cannot be denied legal recourse when their basic rights are violated.

But what are the particular rights at issue? It is useful to distinguish between the *substantive* and the *procedural* aspects of criminal rights. By substantive rights we mean the essence of what is protected: privacy and dignity, freedom of person and property, and protection against "cruel and unusual" punishment. Procedural rights involve the steps and standards that the government must follow before imposing punishment. These procedural rights, originally applicable only to the federal government, are guaranteed in the Bill of Rights. They have been elaborated by Supreme Court rulings and extended to the states as well. It should also be noted that each state has its own constitutional protections for people accused of crime.

The rights of people accused of crime become matters for judicial review only if they are convicted. If a person is acquitted, there can be no appeal because to do so would place that person in jeopardy twice for the same offense, and *double jeopardy* violates the Constitutional guarantees. Conviction on criminal charges may involve several areas of possible rights violation. The defendant has a right to a fair hearing at every stage of the adjudication process. If convicted, the punishment cannot be "cruel and unusual," and there must be reasonable opportunity to appeal. Also, conviction for a crime depends upon evidence introduced during the trial, and the Constitution requires that this evidence be obtained in a reasonable manner.

Search and seizure   "The right of the people," states the Fourth Amendment, "to be secure . . . against unreasonable searches and seizures, shall not be violated, and no warrants shall issue, but upon probable cause . . . and particularly describing the place to be searched, and the persons or things to be seized." The interpretation of this right is so dependent on particular circumstances that Supreme Court rulings have varied almost as widely as police practices. In general, the Court has confined the area to be searched with a warrant to the person of the suspect and to the immediate area under the suspect's control. If the authorities wish to look into a suspect's home or office, they normally must get a warrant. A police officer may carry out a search and seizure without a warrant, however, if there is probable cause to believe that a crime has been committed and there is no time to get a warrant, or if it is necessary to seize weapons or to prevent the destruction of evidence. These rules are easy enough to apply in many cases, but situations often arise in which decisions must be made on the spur of the moment and in real danger.

The Court has found it very hard to establish general principles on the application of "stop and frisk" laws used in several states. The court has approved of at least modified searches when there is enough cause to suspect criminal activity but no reasonable or probable grounds for arrest. For example, in 1968 the Court found it reasonable for a detective to question and then search three men whom he observed repeatedly casing a store. The Court then affirmed their conviction for carrying concealed weapons. On the other hand, in the same year the same justices reversed a conviction, holding that the fact that the defendant was seen talking to a number of known drug addicts did not justify his being searched and convicted for possession of heroin.

The Court has also moved to bring electronic eavesdropping within the scope of the guarantee against unreasonable search and seizure, saying that such eavesdropping is illegal without a court order. In addition, there are numerous cases involving the search of automobiles occupied by the persons arrested, of their house or apartment, and of luggage or packages they were carrying. In every case the key word is *reasonable* in the total circumstances of the situation. Still, some justices, including a majority of the Burger Court, have interpreted police actions as reasonable which the Warren Court thought were in violation of the Constitution.

To discourage unauthorized search and seizure, the Court has established exclusionary rules that ban the use in court of evidence obtained in this way. When Daniel Ellsberg was prosecuted for making public the "Pentagon Papers," revealing numerous secrets about American involvement in Vietnam, his case was dismissed when it was shown that the government had used illegal means to get evidence against him. (See Chapter 12 for more on the Pentagon Papers case.) No police officer wants a suspect to get off because the evidence is excluded; hence, the Court's rules are generally effective.

The right to a fair hearing   The conditions necessary for a "fair hearing" might be inferred from the constitutional requirement of due process. But the Constitution specifically insists on prohibitions against having to testify against oneself, unreasonable bail, and double jeopardy (a defendant can be tried only once for a single act). The Constitution also guarantees the right to a speedy and public trial, to an impartial jury, to be informed of the charges against one, to confront the witnesses against one, and to make favorable witnesses appear in one's behalf (the power of subpoena). Moreover, the Court has ruled that the police must inform the accused of their constitutional rights, including the right to free counsel, before the police can begin questioning (*Miranda* v. *Arizona*, 384 U.S. 436, 1966).

Clarence Earl Gideon studied enough law in prison to write in longhand to the Supreme Court appealing his conviction. He won, and his victory established the precedent that every person accused of crime must be provided an attorney.

By far the most important of these procedural rights is the guarantee of legal counsel (*Gideon* v. *Wainwright*, 372 U.S. 335, 1963). An able lawyer can provide the guidance necessary to insist that all the other rights are observed from the time of arrest right through to the end.

Though the Bill of Rights does not specifically mention a right to appeal, the federal government and all the states allow at least one such appeal as a matter of legal right. The appellate court examines the trial as a whole to make sure that it was fair to the accused in both substance and procedure—to ensure, for example, that the judge was unbiased, the jury was not improperly influenced, and a reasonable body of people could have concluded from the evidence that the defendant was guilty. Here, too, the Supreme Court has ruled that the government must give needy convicts free legal counsel in order to make good the right to an initial appeal. Even without professional assistance a person may appeal a conviction even to the Supreme Court, and some of the most notable victories for procedural rights have come from appeals of prisoners who believed they had been convicted unfairly.

Cruel and unusual punishment The Constitution prohibits cruel and unusual punishment. In 1791 this concept meant that such practices as the stocks, the rack, and the thumbscrew were forbidden. In more modern times "third degree" police methods of interrogation were brought under this provision, as well as the excluding of confessions that had been extracted by coercive methods. Today, the most difficult problem arising under this provision involves capital punishment. Some justices have argued that execution necessarily and by definition violates the Constitution, but the Court majority has refused to go this far. What they have insisted on is that capital punishment be used only for the most serious offenses and under the most carefully drawn standards. In some parts of the country only those who were poor or of racial minorities were ever executed. The Supreme Court has therefore required the states to eliminate discretion in sentencing offenders to death, so that everyone in similar circumstances will be treated the same.

Thus the Bill of Rights also provides a number of protections for those accused of crime. The Court has enforced the right of an accused person to have a lawyer, to have adequate warning against self-incrimination, and to be protected against having evidence seized by unfair methods.

ADJUDICATION AND CIVIL LIBERTIES: CONCLUDING THOUGHTS

If someone were to ask, "What is the policy of the American government toward civil liberties?" we would have to look at all branches of the government to find the answer. Each branch of the government is involved in acts that affect fundamental liberties such as freedom of speech or of the press. Laws of Congress, like the Smith Act or the McCarran Act, affect our freedoms. Actions by the executive branch, like President Truman's loyalty and security program or even FBI harassment of suspect mobsters, similarly affect such liberties. Bureaucratic decisions, such as those made by law-enforcement officers in investigating crime or by local officials in giving or withholding a parade permit, may have serious implications for liberties guaranteed in the Bill of Rights. But of all the institutions of government, the courts have played a central role in determining the extent of civil liberties in the United States. Note how much of what we discuss in this chapter involves decisions of the Supreme Court.

We have noted a few of the reasons why the courts are so crucial in the area of civil liberties. What are the consequences of the fact that policy toward civil liberties is more often made by the courts than it is made by Congress or the executive? To answer the question, we must look at the special way courts make policy: by a process of **adjudication.**

Policymaking Through Adjudication

Courts adjudicate; that is, they sit in judgment on specific cases and settle disputes between specific parties. In the process of settling the dispute, they may discuss general social issues or announce general social policies, but the primary purpose for which they convene is to hear a plaintiff. In many of the civil liberties cases decided by the Supreme Court, the plaintiff is a citizen or a group of citizens with a complaint against the government. The plaintiffs may argue that a government official acted in ways that deprived them of their constitutional rights. Or they may argue that a law of Congress or of a state legislature represents an unconstitutional deprivation of their freedoms. We must remember, however, that in order to make such an argument, one must have been injured by the government action; otherwise one has no "standing" in court. In most cases involving procedural rights issues the "injury" arises from the fact that the person has been convicted of a crime.

The fact that policy toward civil liberties grows out of this process of adjudication has a major impact on the nature of that policy.

Advantages   What are some of the advantages of policy made through a process of adjudication?

1. The courts take on real cases in which the claim is made that civil liberties have been violated. They do not waste their time discussing hypothetical cases.

2. To win a case before the court, you do not have to show that you have public or political support. Plaintiffs who claim that their freedom to speak has been curtailed, that the requirement that their child recite prayers in school violates the Constitution, or that they have not received a fair trial appeal to principles of law. They have to show that a claim is just under the Constitution, not that it is popular or supported by powerful political groups.

This is the most crucial aspect of the way courts deal with civil liberties. The case one has to make before the Supreme Court is very different from the case that those who want something from Congress make before that body. Lobbyists and interest groups who want something from Congress—to pass a law favorable to them or to modify some law they consider injurious—mobilize public and political forces. If they get sufficient public and political support, Congress is likely to respond. If they cannot mobilize such support, they may well be ignored.

In contrast, one does not need to bring political allies or invoke public opinion before the Supreme Court. One argues that the government, in limiting one's freedom, is violating the Constitution. Justices are aware of public opinion and political forces, and sometimes they bend their decisions accordingly. But the appeal a plaintiff makes is to rules of law.

This difference between the courts and Congress helps explain why the courts are so important in relation to civil liberties. Many of the groups and individuals who claim their freedom is threatened are minority and unpopular: small religious sects, radical political groups, and criminals. As we will see in the next chapter, the public supports the freedoms of the First Amendment in the abstract, but it has a less favorable view of the rights of unpopular minorities. If these minorities had to appeal to popular opinion to protect their freedom or had to demonstrate substantial political influence, their chances would be weak indeed. The fact that the courts will respond to their appeal to legal principles, even if not backed by much political clout, gives them a better chance to protect their freedom.

Policymaking through a process of legal adjudication means that minorities can defend their rights against a majority. Many disadvantaged groups have used the court system in this way: blacks, Hispanics, and other ethnic minorities; Jehovah's Witnesses and other minority religious groups. Sometimes the minorities involved have been anything but deprived. For many years American corporations took advantage of the process of adjudication to defend their "rights" before the government. Indeed, from the 1890s until about 1937, protection of minorities by the Supreme Court meant primarily the protection of a business elite against popular attempts to regulate the economy. The Court was defending freedom of contract and freedom to conduct one's business without government interference. Since the late 1930s, however, the courts have paid more attention to the freedoms of less advantaged minorities. They have protected such freedoms as freedom of speech, freedom of religion, and freedom from discrimination.

Disadvantages   The process of policymaking through adjudication also has some serious disadvantages. What are these?

1. The fact that decisions are made on a case by case basis makes it possible for the courts to create rules that are inconsistent with one another. Sometimes a decision in one case suggests one general rule, a decision in another case another rule, and citizens are left with a good deal of uncertainty as to what the current law is in relation to the subject matter. In many areas involving civil liberties it is unclear what the dominant court position is. New majorities may form as Court personnel changes or justices change their minds. This means that individuals who wish to say or publish something on the borderline of what the courts may accept do so at some risk.

2. Adjudication may help unpopular individuals and disadvantaged minorities who might not win their point through political influence. But those who want the help have to be able to find the resources to bring a case to court. The process of adjudication requires expert lawyers and, often, high legal fees. Access to the courts is rarely easy and never cheap. Those who would defend their rights through court action may spend their own fortunes, the fortunes of their friends, and wind up deeply in debt. Indeed, many who feel their rights have been infringed hesitate to take their case to court because of the time, effort, and financial strain involved.

Organizations like the American Civil Liberties Union try to help those people who would bring such cases to court by providing both funds and skilled lawyers. However, their help is not sufficient to cover most cases. Public defenders and legal aid services also help, but it cannot be said that all Americans have a truly equal chance at effective protection of their full Constitutional rights.

3. The fact that the Supreme Court acts slowly means that substantial limitation of free speech can take place before the Court acts to correct the situation. Consider two important First Amendment cases, *Dennis* and *Yates.* In the Dennis case, the Court took a restrictive view of free speech. The leaders of the American Communist party were sent to jail under the Smith Act because of the "bad tendency" of what they were teaching. Six years later the Court substantially modified the Dennis doctrine and decided that one could not convict people simply because they taught and advocated abstract beliefs. This made it much more difficult to convict leaders of the Communist party. Though the Supreme Court did not specifically overturn the Smith Act or reverse its Dennis decision, its interpretation in the Yates case so limited its application that it became much less of a threat to freedom of speech.

A long time elapsed between the Dennis and Yates cases. In the six years intervening there had been 145 cases brought under the Smith Act, of which 87 led to convictions. The process was slow indeed, and many individuals were punished in the meantime for exercising what eventually were held to be their First Amendment rights.

4. A Supreme Court decision does two things: It comes to a specific decision on a particular case, and it enunciates the principles behind that decision. Sometimes these two components of the decision seem to run in opposite directions.

Often in the history of our First Amendment and other civil liberties cases, the Court has announced doctrine in support of free speech while at the same time upholding the conviction of the specific defendant before it. Justice Oliver Wendell Holmes expressed his famous views about clear and present danger in the case of *Schenck* v. *the United States.* The same decision upheld the conviction of Charles Schenck for mailing out pamphlets attacking the draft in World War I. To the justices these pamphlets constituted a clear and present danger.

The case of *Gitlow* v. *New York* is famous for the fact that the Court expanded the protection of the First Amendment to actions of the state governments. In this particular case, however, that expansion did not help Gitlow much, since the Supreme Court upheld the right of the state of New York to enforce its law against "criminal anarchy" and to punish Gitlow for "utterances inimical to the public welfare." So it has gone in many cases. The Court may speak out for freedom in general, but not in the particular case at hand.

In other cases, the Court appears to do the opposite—to come to a decision supportive of free speech or the press in the specific case, but to enunciate doctrine that makes the protection of freedom somewhat less clear for future cases. In the Pentagon Papers case (*New York Times* v. *United States,* 403 U.S. 713, 1971), the Court prevented the government from imposing prior restraint on the *New York Times* and other newspapers in order to block the publication of documents dealing with the war in Vietnam. However, in the same decision the Court expressed the view that under certain circumstances prior restraint might be legitimate. This was the first time that such a possibility had been specifically acknowledged by the Court. In addition, the justices wrote so many opinions that the principles behind the specific decision remain unclear.

5. Supreme Court decisions are not automatically put into practice. The specific case is remanded to a lower court to be put into effect, and the lower court has some leeway in doing that. Implementation is even less certain in relation to other people than the specific litigants in the case the Court has decided. If the Court decides that certain police procedures violate the Bill of Rights, police forces all over the country do not automatically change their behavior. It may take quite a while before the behavior of the local police conforms.

THE SUPREME COURT: BASTION OF FREEDOM? MAYBE

Is the First Amendment and Supreme Court's enforcement of the First Amendment a "bastion of liberty" in the United States? A look at the record leads to a mixed answer. The rhetoric about how important the freedoms of the First Amendment are to American democracy has not always been matched by actions of the Court. The Court has balanced free speech and press against other values, and the freedoms have not always come out on top. Furthermore, some critics of the Supreme Court argue that it fails as a defender of freedom just when it is needed the most—at times when the national mood leans in the direction of the restriction of freedom. During the attacks on subversives in World War I and its aftermath, and when alleged subversives were again attacked at the beginning of the Cold War in the 1950s, the Supreme Court upheld the convictions of many of those accused of dangerous speech. When Japanese Americans were evacuated from the West Coast during World War II, the Supreme Court did not intervene. When we also consider the expense and difficulty of bringing one's case to the Court, we can certainly see obstacles to full reliance on the First Amendment and the Supreme Court to defend freedom of speech and the press.

Nevertheless, though freedom of speech and of the press is far from unlimited in the United States and its defense on the part of the Supreme Court far from certain, it still exists in quite a large measure. The press in the United States is free to criticize government officials, freer than the press in most other countries of the world, freer even than in a large number of other democratic countries. In few countries does the press have as much latitude to engage in investigative reporting that may challenge the authority of the state. Government officials, as each president learns, have no immunity from denunciation by public or press. The existence of the First Amendment, coupled with the ability of the Court to review legislation in the light of that amendment, is basic to the maintenance of that freedom.

Protection against overzealous police and prosecutors or careless trial judges is certainly not complete. Here too, however, the Supreme Court has importantly expanded the effectiveness of the constitutional requirements. In doing so, undoubtedly some guilty parties have escaped conviction. But when we consider how many countries utilize police-state methods with no prospect of appealing to a Supreme Court to enforce fair methods against the government itself, we must acknowledge the importance of the Court, however imperfect it may seem, to the preservation of individual liberty in America.

PROFILE ■

THOMAS JEFFERSON (1743–1826)
Third American President,
Author of the Declaration
of Independence

The extraordinary richness of Jefferson's life as statesman, diplomat, inventor, and architect provides many different themes for consideration today. He was America's most eloquent exponent of the possibilities of free democratic government, not only in the Declaration but also in public speeches and voluminous private correspondence with people throughout both Europe and America. Along with his Virginia colleague James Madison he developed much of the basic rationale for the separation of church and state, and he is still a valuable fount of eloquence regarding the importance of individual rights in a free society.

Jefferson was a politician, too. He was the first leader of the opposition to the Adams Federalists and, with Madison, put together the first real political party, with a loyal following in Congress and organized voter support throughout the nation. Indeed, Jefferson's Democratic-Republicans were so successful that the Federalist opposition rapidly withered and in a few years disappeared entirely.

As president, Jefferson, the advocate of states' rights and limited government, exercised strong leadership at home and abroad. He negotiated the Louisiana Purchase and then sent Lewis and Clark on their historic journey to discover what had been acquired. He fought the barbary pirates, and trying to stay out of the Napoleonic wars in Europe, he secured congressional approval for an embargo against both the British and the French.

Jefferson was an agrarian, suspicious of the city, and convinced that a free republic would be best served in a society dominated by yeomen farmers, among whom no extremes of wealth or poverty existed. He believed also that in a republic each person must serve the community in whatever ways were needed, and sometimes at great personal sacrifice, he himself answered every call of civic duty. He also served as governor of Virginia and was founder of the University of Virginia.

Above all, Jefferson was a supremely civilized person, knowledgeable in science, music, literature, architecture, and fine wines, to name just a few areas of his expertise. His personal library was immense and became the initial foundation of the Library of Congress. He wrote some 30,000 letters and was acquainted with most of the important writers, scientists, philosophers, and statesmen of his time. It may be hard to imagine a person like Jefferson getting along in the arena of public service today, but then he was astonishing in his own day, too.

CHAPTER HIGHLIGHTS ■

1. <u>The First Amendment protects free speech,</u> but the protection is not absolute. Free speech often comes into conflict with other values such as majority rule, national security, or the rights of other individuals.

2. The Supreme Court has used several standards to decide cases of free speech versus national security. The current doctrine is not completely clear, but it involves balancing freedom and national security.

3. The Court has not completely ruled out applying "prior restraint" to speech or publications, but it is very unlikely to allow it.

4. The Supreme Court has tried to balance free speech with other values in relation to a number of topics: campaign expenditures, obscenity, and libel.

5. <u>The First Amendment forbids the government to support any religion and also guarantees freedom of religion.</u> The Court has interpreted the First Amendment as barring prayer in the public schools, one of its most controversial positions.

6. The Constitution also protects property rights, rights to privacy, and rights to a fair trial. In each area, the Court balances these rights against other social issues.

7. The fact that the Court decides through a process of adjudication has advantages and disadvantages for protecting free speech. The advantage is that it deals with real cases and can protect unpopular people. The disadvantage is that the process is slow and the results inconsistent.

SUGGESTED READINGS ■

The problems of individual liberty are quite often philosophical, usually legal, and always political. So it is with the relevant literature.

Classic works on individual liberty and the state are: John Stuart Mill, *On Liberty* (1851); Henry David Thoreau, *On the Duty of Civil Disobedience* (1849); Zechariah Chafee, Jr., *Free Speech in the United States* (1941).

Modern commentaries on the subject include: Henry J. Abraham, *Freedom and the Court* (4th ed., 1984); Lucius J. Barker and Twiley W. Barker, Jr., *Civil Liberties and the Constitution* (5th ed., 1986); Walter Berns, *The First Amendment and the Future of American Democracy* (1976); Richard Kluger, *Simple Justice* (1977); Anthony Lewis, *Gideon's Trumpet* (1964); John Hart Ely, *Democracy and Distrust: A Theory of Judicial Review* (1980).

The 1984 Republican convention

Voting Booths

Chapter 7

POLITICAL
PARTICIPATION

P olitical participation is crucial in a democracy. It is the means by which citizens inform political leaders of their preferences and pressure the leaders to serve their needs. This chapter will describe the many ways in which citizens are active in politics. It will show that participation is unequal across groups. We will consider the important issue of which citizens are inactive, for inactive citizens are likely to have their views ignored. Also, we will consider the way in which groups that have few resources for participation can sometimes overcome that disadvantage, often by using unconventional modes of participation. The underlying question is: Is the participatory system in America biased against poorer and less educated citizens?

WHY IS PARTICIPATION IMPORTANT?

Political participation is important in a democracy for several reasons. To begin with, it is important to the individual participant for its own sake. The ability to participate in decisions that affect one's life is an important source of human dignity. In a democracy, where citizens are supposed to rule, those who do not participate are in a sense not full citizens. Certainly, they cannot be full citizens if they are not allowed to take part in political life—if, for instance, they are barred from voting by restrictive laws. Throughout the history of the United States those who have fought for the right to participate in politics—the suffragists who fought for the right of women to vote, the civil rights leaders who fought to overturn state laws that kept blacks from having free access to the polls, and others—were battling to obtain recognition for these groups as full members of American society. Political philosophers have argued the importance of political participation for the individual citizen on further grounds. The British philosopher John Stuart Mill argued that individuals learn to be responsible citizens—to care for the common good, not only for their own narrow interests—by taking part in democratic political life.[1] They also learn tolerance of alternative views, an attitude that is crucial for the give and take of democratic politics.

There is a second reason why participation is important over and above the fact that it is valued for its own sake. Through participation, citizens tell the government what it is they want, what policies they want the government to pursue, and how they want it to allocate resources. Not only do they inform the government of their desires, but they also apply pressure on the government to compel it to comply. They do this by voting for candidates who they think will satisfy their desires, by offering or withholding campaign contributions, and by strongly asserting their views to public officials, sometimes even by disrupting the government. If some citizens participate while others are passive, the government officials are likely to pay attention to the needs and desires of the active citizens and ignore

---

[1] John Stuart Mill, *On Representative Government* (New York: Liberal Arts Press, 1958).

the inactive ones. Thus, who participates determines a good deal of what the government does.

As we shall see later, participation does not always send the government a clear message. The electorate may vote one candidate out and another in, but it may be unclear exactly what the public wants the newly elected official to do. This is called **mandate uncertainty.** The election winner is put into office by the public's vote but does not have a clear directive from the public. Yet, even when participation sends no clear message, it is an important way by which citizens prevent the abuse of power by officials. These officials may not know precisely what the people want the government to do—the people themselves may not be sure—but the elected officials know that they will be *held accountable* at the next election for what they have done. Thus officials worry about satisfying the public. Officials, however, will worry more about the reaction of those citizens they think are likely to be participants—those likely to vote or to make campaign contributions. Indeed, as you will remember from our discussion of the political theory of the Constitution, this is what the Founders intended.

There is one last reason why participation is important. Through participation citizens express not only their preferences for specific policies but also their support for the democratic process. In the next chapter we will discuss the importance of *legitimacy*—that is, the belief that the government ought to be obeyed even if you, as an individual, do not agree with a specific decision. In the United States, the government ultimately achieves legitimacy on the basis of the fact that its top officials are elected by the citizenry. If only a few citizens bother to take part in that selection—if election turnout is low—the public may be expressing a lack of democratic support.

Note an important difference between these last two functions of participation, the function of influencing government policy and the function of according support and legitimacy to the government. For the former function, what counts is not so much *how many* people participate as *how representative* of the population are the participants. Even if only a minority of the public is active—40 percent, 30 percent, or less—they still can speak effectively for all citizens, active and inactive, if they accurately reflect all the differing political views in society. If the participants are an accurate replica of the population as a whole—representing in proper proportion rich and poor, black and white, men and women, pro- and antiabortion groups, pro- and antiwelfare groups, and so forth—the fact that they are only a small proportion of the population may not be important.

When it comes to citizen expression of support for the government, however, the fact that only a small proportion participates is, in and of itself, a problem even if the participants are representative of the public at large. If about one-half of the eligible voters do not vote, as has happened in recent presidential elections, democratic government will be weakened.

Is Participation Always a Good Thing?

We have just seen why citizen participation is vital in a democracy. There are, however, some scholars who take a different position; they say that *too much* participation may be unhealthy for democracy. They make several arguments. One argument is that politics and government are too complicated for the average citizen. It is better to give officials more autonomy to do what is in the best interest of the citizens, even if the citizens themselves are too shortsighted to see their own interest.[2] Another argument is that too much participation "overloads" the political system. More demands are placed on the government than it can handle. The result is that the government does nothing well, and the public is made unhappy. The last argument is that those people who are less active—as we shall see, they are people with less education—are the ones who are least committed to democracy. As we shall see in Chapter 8, inactive citizens are less supportive of free speech. If they are less committed to democracy, perhaps it is just as well that they are not active.[3]

These arguments have led to a great debate among political scientists. How much participation should there be? Some have countered the arguments of those who are skeptical about participation. The proparticipation writers agree that citizens may be shortsighted, that they may make too many selfish demands, and that they may not be as committed to democracy as are the more educated and active ones. Nevertheless, they argue, participation itself will help cure this. These writers echo the ideas of John Stuart Mill. Citizens learn about politics by taking part in government. They also learn to think beyond their own narrow interests and to have more respect for democratic values.

The debate will not be settled soon, but it does not, in any case, eliminate the importance of participation. Even those who say that *too much* participation is bad agree that *some* citizen participation is needed to prevent the abuse of power by the government.

VARIOUS MODES OF PARTICIPATION

There are many ways in which citizens can participate. Some means of participation are more widespread than others; some means are more difficult or costly than others; some means are more effective than others.

Voting

Periodic elections are crucial in a democracy. Through voting, citizens choose the nation's leaders. Because of their desire to be elected or re-elected, political leaders are sensitive to the public's needs and desires. The vote of an individual citizen is, to be sure, not a very powerful tool. A single voter is only one of many. If a voter decides to express dissatisfac-

---

[2] This argument is made by Joseph A. Schumpeter, *Capitalism, Socialism, and Democracy* (New York: Harper & Row, 1942), and by Walter Lippmann, *Public Opinion* (New York: Free Press, 1965).

[3] This argument is based on Samuel Stouffer, *Communism, Conformity and Civil Liberties* (New York: Wiley, 1966). For evidence that differences in tolerance between well- and less well-educated citizens may have been exaggerated, see John L. Sullivan, James Pierson, and George Marcus, *Political Tolerance and American Democracy* (Chicago: University of Chicago Press, 1981).

tion with an officeholder by voting for the challenger or not voting at all, that fact is hardly noticeable. Furthermore, the vote carries with it little precise information. The voter pulls a lever for one candidate or another. There is no way the voter can send a more precise message saying, "I am voting this way, because I want policy *X*"; or, "I am voting for you, because I did not like what your opponent did in relation to *Y*."

This, of course, does not stop people from reading meaning into a vote. Evidence suggests that in 1980 people voted for Ronald Reagan because they thought the previous administration was incompetent and that it was time for a change.[4] However, many people interpreted the vote as a mandate for specific policies. Many of Ronald Reagan's supporters thought the people were calling for his particular economic program. Supporters of such groups as the Moral Majority, for example, thought there was a specific mandate for their conservative moral positions. Reagan's reelection in 1984 was widely regarded as support for his actions in office, but there was still disagreement about what should be done next.

Even if the vote of a single individual carries little weight, the votes of the electorate as a whole are decisive in determining who runs the country. Even if a single vote conveys little information as to what is on the voter's mind, the overall vote distribution gives some indication of what motivated the public to vote as it did. Winners and losers in elections—aided by journalists and other analysts, as well as by public opinion polls—watch the pattern of voting and try to interpret its meaning.

Voting Turnout

Voting is the most common political activity of the American public. This is seen in Table 7.1, in which we show the proportion of Americans who engage in various acts of participation. Voting in presidential elections is the only act for which we see a majority active—and it is a bare majority at that. In recent elections the turnout in presidential elections has hovered around 50 percent. In 1980 it was 53.9 percent, and in 1984 it was nearly the same, 53.3 percent. In local elections a little less than half the eligible voters vote regularly. Note that voting is the easiest political act. It takes little time and, more importantly, little initiative. Thus it is not surprising to find the highest activity rates in voting. (Another important question about voting, to be considered in Chapter 11, is, How rationally do citizens vote?)

Though more Americans vote than engage in other more difficult and time-consuming political activities, voting turnout in the United States is not high. It has usually been well below that in most European democracies. In Europe, 85 to 95 percent of the voters usually turn out for major national elections. What accounts for the difference?

One explanation has to do with differences in the laws governing elections. In Europe, it is easier to vote: The government automatically registers all citizens. In the United States, you have to register on your own. Elections

---

[4] Everett C. Ladd, "The Brittle Mandate: Electoral Realignment and the 1980 Presidential Election," *Political Science Quarterly* 96:1–25.

TABLE 7.1

ACTIVITIES PERFORMED BY CITIZENS

Mode of Activity	% Active
A. Voting	
Voted in 1980 presidential election	54%
Voted in 1976 presidential election	54
Voted in 1978 congressional election	35
Votes regularly in local elections	47
B. Taking Part in Campaign Activities	
Persuade others how to vote	37%
Work for a party	4
Attend political rallies	6
Contribute money to a candidate	16
Member of a political club or organization	8
C. Cooperative Activities	
Worked through local group	30%
Helped form local group	14
Active member of organization engaged in community activities	32
D. Contacting Officials	
Contacted local officials on some problem	20%
Contacted extralocal officials on some problem	18
Wrote a letter to a public official	28

SOURCE: The data on cooperative activities and local voting are from Sidney Verba and Norman H. Nie, *Participation in America: Political Democracy and Social Equality* (New York: Harper & Row, 1972). The presidential and congressional voting data are from official statistics. The remaining items are from the University of Michigan, Center for Political Studies, 1976 survey of the presidential election.

abroad are often held on Sunday, making it easier for working people to get to the polls. In the United States, most elections are held on Tuesday, a working day.

If our laws made voting easier, more people would vote. In several states there was a noticeable increase in turnout when it was made easier to register, by allowing registration at the polling place rather than in advance. One team of scholars concluded that turnout would rise by about 9 percent if all states had laws as lenient as those states that make it easiest to vote.[5]

The difference in election laws is, however, not adequate to explain the low turnout in the United States. In recent years, election laws have been greatly liberalized. Federal law has done away with poll taxes, literacy tests, lengthy residency requirements, and other legal impediments to vot-

---

[5] Raymond E. Wolfinger and Stephen Rosenstone, *Who Votes?* (New Haven: Yale University Press, 1980).

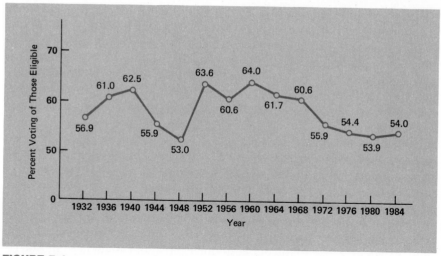

FIGURE 7.1

Voting Turnout in Presidential Elections, 1932–1984

ing. This would lead us to expect turnout to rise. In fact, it has not. Figure 7.1 shows the turnout in presidential elections since the start of the New Deal in 1932. With the exception of 1932 itself and a pair of elections toward the end of World War II, turnout used to be over 60 percent. Since 1960, however, the trend has been downward.

Despite the fact that it is now easier to vote, the decline in voting turnout appears to be linked to two changes in the electorate: a growing belief that the government is not responsive to the people and a declining commitment to the political parties. Over the past two decades, surveys show that more and more Americans have come to believe that the government is not responsive to their needs—to believe, for instance, that the government "does not care what people like me think." People who feel this way are less likely to vote, probably because they think that elections make little difference. As more people come to believe the government is not responsive, more stay home from the polls.

Another explanation has to do with the growing weakness of the American political parties, something we shall discuss at some length in Chapter 10. The higher turnout in European elections may be due to the fact that political parties are better organized there. They can get their voters to the polls. In the United States, parties have long been weaker organizations than in Europe, especially at the national level. They have been getting weaker still in recent years. Furthermore, the number of Americans who identify with one or the other of the political parties has fallen substantially. More people claim to be independent. People with no partisan affiliation are less likely to vote. These two factors—a decline in the belief in the government's responsiveness and a decline in party affiliation—go a long way toward explaining the decline in voting turnout.[6]

It should be noted, however, that nonvoters in the United States are

---

[6] See Paul R. Abramson and John H. Aldrich, "The Decline of Electoral Participation in America," *American Political Science Review* 76 (September 1982):502–521.

mostly also nonregistrants. Registered voters participate in U.S. national elections at rates that are roughly equivalent to the Europeans. Moreover, the federal system presents the American voter with many more opportunities to vote. Large numbers of state and local officials are elected and numerous issues appear on the ballot. Therefore, the total amount of electoral participation in the nation is considerable. Nevertheless, there is a sizable group of citizens who take little or no part in the democratic process.

Declining Turnout: Does It Make a Difference?

At the beginning of the chapter we indicated that participation expresses the citizenry's support for democratic government, and it expresses the preferences of the citizenry as to how the government should be run and what it ought to do. When it comes to expressing support for the government, the fact that fewer people vote is significant. Jimmy Carter, while president, spoke to the public about a "crisis of confidence" in American society, and one of the measures of that crisis was the fact that "two-thirds of our people do not even vote." That so many stay home from the polls is an indication of weakness in American democracy.

What about the other function of participation: expressing the preferences of the public? What counts here is whether the participants are representative of the public as a whole. The fact that turnout is down would not affect the outcome of a presidential election if potential Democratic voters were as likely to stay home as were potential Republican voters. The overall number of voters might be down, but the percent going to each party would remain the same.

We know, however, that nonvoters differ from voters. Nonvoters tend to be people with lower levels of education and lower-status occupations. They come from groups that ordinarily vote more heavily for Democratic candidates. This fact has led many observers to conclude that low turnouts benefit Republican candidates because their higher-status supporters are likely to be among the voters, while high turnout elections benefit Democratic candidates because the additional voters who come out to the polls come heavily from lower-status groups that lean in a Democratic direction. One close study of election turnouts shows that for most elections there is a tendency in this direction—if more people had voted, the Democratic candidate would have done better—but it is not much more than a tendency. In most elections the outcome would not have been much different if those who stayed at home had, in fact, voted. The 1980 presidential election was one in which the impact of low turnout was particularly pronounced. Citizens who supported Ronald Reagan were more likely to register and vote than were citizens who supported Jimmy Carter or John Anderson. One estimate is that if all eligible citizens had in fact voted, Reagan's margin of victory would have been reduced from 10 percent to 5 percent. That is a substantial difference, but Reagan would still have won the election.

Campaign Activity

Each citizen is limited to one vote in an election. That vote is only one of thousands or millions and can play only a small role in the results.

Citizens can increase their voting influence, however, in one perfectly legal way. They can try to influence the votes of others. One of the most common forms of political activity takes place during the course of an election campaign. Citizens ring doorbells, work at the polls, talk to their friends and neighbors to try to affect their votes, or donate money to a candidate or party. If political leaders pay attention to voters, they may pay even more attention to the citizens who supply the work and money needed to conduct a campaign.

Campaign activity takes more time, initiative, and commitment to a particular candidate or party. This is not an activity for everyone, as we can see from Table 7.1. A little over one-third of all citizens said they tried to persuade others how to vote, only 4 percent worked for a political party, and only 16 percent gave money to a candidate. (These figures apply to campaign activities during the 1976 election.)

Though voting turnout has declined, there is less evidence of a decline in campaign activity. Survey studies of the activity of Americans in election campaigns show no clear upward or downward trend in activities such as trying to persuade friends and neighbors to vote a particular way or taking part in party activities. There is some evidence that more people are contributing money to political campaigns—partly in reaction to the new campaign finance laws that make it necessary for candidates to raise money through many small contributions. (See the discussion of these laws in Chapter 11.)

Communal Activity

Elections are an important way in which citizens influence government officials, but elections have a big drawback. They are very blunt instruments of citizen control. Elections take place only at fixed intervals, every two, four, or six years, depending on the office. Then the choice is between only two or maybe three or four candidates.

Citizens, on the other hand, have many and varied interests. In fact, one can imagine each group as having a list of priorities on which it would like to see the government act. Sometimes these interests have to do with broad national policies. For example, American Jews are concerned with Middle East policy, conservationists with nuclear testing, and blacks with civil rights enforcement. Sometimes the interests are local—a group of neighbors wanting to prevent the building of a road in their section of town, a group of parents wanting to improve school facilities, or a group of high school students wanting the community to provide a recreation center.

Political interests are indeed varied. An election could not possibly offer a choice in all of these areas. Citizens often find that the issue that concerns them the most is not an election issue, for neither candidate has a position on that issue or both candidates take the same position. Furthermore, the problems and interests that citizens want the government to deal with do not arise only at election time. Thus participation in election campaigns is not enough to tell government officials what citizens want.

Other means of participation are needed to fill in the gaps left by elections—some way in which specific groups of citizens can tell their more precise concerns to the government as they arise. We call this *communal activity,* meaning the activity of groups of citizens working together to try to influence the government. They may work through informal groups, as when neighbors join to protest to city hall about some issue. They may also work through more formal organizations such as unions, PTAs, or civic associations. This kind of activity has two important features. First, citizens work together. This is important, because the government is influenced more by a group than by a single individual. Second, citizens are active on the problems that concern them most—parents will work in the PTA, welfare recipients in a welfare mothers' group, and so forth.

About one-third of U.S. citizens participate in communal activity by working with a local group on a community problem. A similar number work through formal organizations.

Communal participation is particularly well developed in the United States compared with other nations. Citizens in several countries were asked how they would go about influencing the government. In the United States, over half of those who thought they could have some influence felt that they could best do so by joining with others. In the other countries studied, citizens would be more likely to work alone or through some more formal organization, such as a political party. The willingness to work with others—friends, neighbors, and co-workers—is found in all social groups in the United States.

Data on the actual behavior of citizens show that in the United States there is much more community-oriented activity involving the cooperation of citizens—more informal groups formed to deal with some local problem and more formal organizations concerned with schools, recreation facilities, and the like (see Table 7.2). In fact, this type of behavior is not new in America. It was noted over a century ago by Alexis de Tocqueville, who commented on the zest for cooperative activity that he found in America compared with Europe.

As noted, such activity is important because it can deal with the most immediate problems of citizens. In this way, individual citizens increase their own influence on the government, because many voices generally carry more weight with government officials than few.

There are few precise measurements of the change over time in the amount of such cooperative activity, but it seems fairly clear that there has been a substantial growth in such activity in recent years. The number of interest groups active in Washington has increased dramatically. Local, state, and national officials frequently observe, and sometimes complain, that they are constantly being approached by citizen groups demanding this policy or protesting that action. We will look further at group activity in Chapter 9.

Citizen-Initiated Contacts

So far we have mentioned ways in which citizens participate along with others—as part of the voting population, in campaigns, or in cooperative groups. Some citizen activity is carried on alone, as when one writes to one's member of Congress or to a newspaper, or visits a government office to make a request or lodge a complaint. We may not think of this as political participation, for citizens may be dealing with very narrow and

TABLE 7.2

COMMUNITY ACTIVITY OF CITIZENS

	United States	Austria	India	Japan	Nether-lands
Percent who belong to an organization active in community affairs	32%	9%	7%	11%	15%
Percent who have worked with a local informal group to solve a community problem	30%	3%	18%	15%	16%

SOURCE: Based on data from Sidney Verba, Norman Nie, and Jae-On Kim, *Participation and Political Equality. A Seven Nation Comparison* (New York: Cambridge University Press, 1978).

specific problems that concern only them. They may ask their district's member in Congress to help a relative get an immigration visa, or they may complain about the condition of the sidewalk in front of their house. They may even ask, as Chrysler officials did, for a multimillion-dollar loan guarantee. This is another way in which citizens influence what the government does.

Citizen-initiated contacts are another activity engaged in by a minority of the public. Citizens often say, "I'm going to write to my congressman!" on this, that, or the other problem; but only about one American in four has ever written to any public official. Only about one in five has ever contacted a local official or an official outside the community on a problem.

Just as cooperative attempts to influence the government have increased in number, however, so have the number of contacts by individual citizens. Congressional offices report a great increase in the amount of casework done by members of Congress and their staffs. Casework refers to the handling of individual requests from constituents for help, information, or favors. In 1964, 17 percent reported in a national sample that they had written a letter to a public official. In 1976, a similar question was asked in another survey, and the percentage had risen to 28. Citizens as individuals are making their voices heard more and more.

Protests, Marches, Demonstrations

One of the most dramatic changes in American political life in recent decades has been the growth of new ways to participate—through direct action, such as protest rallies, demonstrations, and marches. More and more citizens are using direct means of showing their point of view. They may march to protest American foreign policy, and demonstrate to oppose busing for integration or to decry the lack of busing. Some of these activities are ways of showing political preferences in a more dramatic way. Some are ways of directly affecting the workings of the government, such as blocking the entrance to a post office where draft registration is taking place, preventing school buses from running, halting work in a government office to protest hiring practices, or blocking the entrance to a nuclear power plant.

Marches and demonstrations have become a familiar tactic in many political disputes.

Though the number of demonstrations has risen dramatically, it appears that only a small percentage of Americans take part in them. In 1976 slightly below 2 percent of the adult population said it had taken part in some kind of protest, sit-in, or demonstration. This is not a large proportion of the public, though it is still a substantial number of people—over 3 million—loudly expressing their views.

Protests, marches, and demonstrations have become more common in recent years, perhaps even more than other activities. The great explosion of direct action occurred during the 1960s. In each year from 1960 to 1967 there were as many protest incidents recorded as in the entire decade of the 1950s.

After the end of the war in Vietnam in the early 1970s, the size and intensity of demonstrations diminished. The use of direct action—marches, demonstrations, boycotts, sit-ins—has continued since then, however. Furthermore, even among those who have not themselves taken part in such protest activity, there has been a growing tolerance of such activities. During the 1960s the majority of Americans opposed direct, unconventional political activity. By 1972, however, over half gave at least qualified support to legal protests, demonstrations, and civil disobedience.

What about more extreme forms of political action? Even though riots and other violence may not be accepted as legitimate methods of accomplishing political purposes, protest demonstrations sometimes get out of hand and result in violent clashes, either with the police or with opposing groups of citizens. Here, too, a bare majority of the public was willing to tolerate political demonstrations even though there was reason to believe they might become violent.[7]

Increased tolerance of direct political action is an important feature of contemporary American political life. One still must ask, however, whether protests, marches or even riots are effective means of gaining the desired policy results compared with more conventional methods. The answer is certainly not clear-cut. The massive protests against the Vietnam War may have persuaded some key policymakers that the war was too costly in terms of domestic conflict to continue. It may, however, have been the mounting casualty rate from the war itself that was the factor that turned public opinion around and, in turn, convinced the administration to withdraw.

Did the urban riots of the 1960s result in more money being put into housing, social services, and other programs of assistance to impoverished city dwellers? Again the answer is perhaps. At least for a time more money was pumped into the inner cities, though it is not clear that it benefited the neediest elements there. When militant farmers drove their tractors up the steps of the Capitol in 1978, they certainly got the attention of Congress, as have other actions of distressed farmers to block or control foreclosures and sheriffs' sales of farms in the Midwest. But there is no clear causal path from those "illegitimate" acts to effective policy relief. Extralegal political action, even though viewed with more tolerance than in earlier generations, remains a risky course.

CHANGING RATES OF PARTICIPATION: WHAT DO THEY MEAN?

If we look at the variety of ways in which people participate, we see something curious. There have been recent changes in how active people are,

---

[7] Herbert McClosky and Alida Brill, *Dimensions of Tolerance: What Americans Believe About Civil Liberties* (New York: Russell Sage Foundation, 1983), p. 119.

but the changes go in opposite directions. Voting turnout has been falling slowly, perhaps reflecting growing cynicism and disenchantment with American politics; yet other forms of activity are up. Citizens are more likely to cooperate with others to deal with specific problems, to contact government on their own, and to engage in direct protest activities.

These contradictory trends may be part of a general tendency in American politics, a tendency that some have labeled *atomization*. Citizens and groups are more active, but their activity is limited to narrow and specific interests. Each individual and group pursues with great intensity its own particular concerns and needs. They seek specific benefits for themselves, or they pursue quite specific policies. The repertory of activities they use is varied and has expanded to include more direct and unconventional means. Yet when it comes to the broadest and most basic decision in which citizens can participate, an election to determine who will be elected to high public office, they take a less active role.

Some students of politics argue that this is simply rational behavior. After all, the single voter can have little effect on the outcome of an election. Perhaps it is a waste of time to vote, even more a waste of time if more and more citizens have come to see little choice between presidential candidates, which appears to be the case.

Other observers worry. Participation, especially in presidential elections, is one way by which citizens express their support for the political process. It is, as we have suggested, the way in which political leaders obtain legitimacy. If fewer and fewer citizens take part in such elections, it may mean a fundamental reduction in support by Americans for the democratic process. When a president is elected by winning just over fifty percent of the votes, but only fifty percent of the people voted, the winner has been chosen by a mere twenty-five percent of the total electorate. What kind of a mandate is that?

EQUALITY OF POLITICAL ACCESS

Compared with other nations, Americans are relatively active politically; measured against our own sense of civic obligation, we seem to fall short. But there is another standard by which we can measure political participation in the United States. Our discussion of why some groups use one means of participation rather than another brings us to the next major issue: the equality of political participation. How equally do citizens participate in America? Are all types of citizens equally active, or is participation mostly in the hands of a few? As we have pointed out, the answer is very important in understanding how participation works in America. Citizens communicate their needs and desires to government leaders through participation. They also use participation to pressure leaders to act on their needs and desires. Thus the citizen who does not participate may be ignored. The government will respond to the participant.

The issue is not whether all citizens participate but whether the citizens who do are representative of the rest. As we have seen, not all citizens are active in politics, nor is it realistic to expect them to be. However, if the activists have the same problems, needs, and preferences as the nonactivists, they may speak for those who do not take part. On the other hand, if they are different from the rest of the population—if the activists come from selected social groups, have particular problems, or want the government to do special things—then political participation may serve to reinforce other forms of priority and power.

Who Are the Participants?

Citizens from all walks of life participate in American politics. No group is totally barred, but certain kinds of citizens participate much more than others. Close studies come to the following conclusions about which citizens are likely to be active in politics:

1. *Education.* If you have a college education, you are much more likely to be politically active than if you have less education.
2. *Income.* People with higher incomes are likely to be active; people with low incomes are much less likely to.
3. *Race and ethnicity.* Black Americans are, on the average, somewhat less active than whites, but the difference is not very great for most types of activity. Puerto Ricans and Mexican Americans are, in general, less active than other Americans.
4. *Sex.* Men are somewhat more active than women, but the difference in activity between the sexes is less in America than in most other nations, and it is shrinking.
5. *Age.* Both young and old citizens tend to be somewhat less active than those in their middle years.

Of these factors, education may be the most important. One careful study of voting turnout has as its core finding, ". . . the transcendent importance of education: the personal qualities that raise the probability of voting are the skills that make learning about politics easier and more gratifying and reduce the difficulties of voting."[8] This conclusion probably applies to other political activities as well as to voting.

In sum, if you are highly educated and wealthy you are much more likely to be a political activist than if you are less well educated and poor. Being white, male, and middle-aged helps as well.

The important question is whether the differences in participation rates among these various groups make a difference in what the government is told. If voters are *demographically* unrepresentative (better educated, wealthier) than the population as a whole, are they also *attitudinally* unrepresentative as well (more conservative, less committed to social welfare)? One careful study of voting turnout found relatively little difference between the political attitudes of the voters in the 1972 election and those of nonvoters.[9]

If we look beyond voting, however, to other types of political activity

---

[8] Wolfinger and Rosenstone, *Who Votes?* p. 102.
[9] Ibid., pp. 108–110.

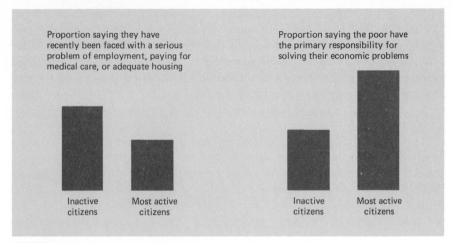

FIGURE 7.2

**Problems and Responsibilities: Differing Views of
Active and Inactive Americans**

SOURCE: Based on data from Sidney Verba and Norman H. Nie, *Participation in America: Political
Democracy and Social Inequality* (New York: Harper & Row, 1972), chap. 15.

that can be effective in communicating the needs and problems of individuals—to communal and contacting activity, for instance—we find that the inactive and active citizens differ both demographically *and* attitudinally. Those who are inactive—the poor and the less well educated—have different problems from those who are more active. Inactive citizens also have different ideas about what the government should do.

Let us compare the problems of the most active citizens with those faced by the least active (see Figure 7.2). We find that the inactive citizens are nearly twice as likely as the active ones to say that they have recently faced serious problems in paying for medical care, getting a job, or finding adequate housing. Active citizens tend to believe that the poor must solve their problems through their own effort. Those who are inactive are less likely to think this. They think the government should deal with such problems, but their views are not very well communicated. Thus the government official who learns what the public wants by considering the preferences of the active citizens will not be fully aware of how serious the economic problems of people are and will find that a majority feel that the economic problems of the poor are their own responsibility and not an area for government action.

The fact that the activists differ from the inactive citizens in their political preferences does not necessarily mean that political leaders will receive more conservative messages from political activists. Though the active citizens are more affluent and are therefore less likely to have income or job problems, on some issues they may be more liberal than the citizenry as a whole. We will see this to be the case when we consider attitudes toward freedom of speech (see Chapter 8). In addition, there has been a growing number of well-educated political activists with liberal views that can be mostly identified with the Democratic party. These activists take a more liberal position on many economic, racial, and foreign-policy matters.

The result of the increase in the number of liberal activists is that the activist population contains both more conservatives *and* more liberals than the citizenry as a whole. Inactive citizens are more likely to be middle-of-the-road on issues or to have no opinion, whereas activists take sides.

Why do those who need help least participate most? The answer is that what makes them better-off in social and economic terms also makes them better able to participate. Education and wealth provide the resources needed for participation. Wealth is the most obvious resource. Few citizens can give substantial sums to political candidates. Those who can are likely to have greater political influence. Skills are another resource, and these come largely through education. The educated are more likely to "know the ropes" of politics—whom to see and what to say.

The better educated are more active in politics for another reason. Many studies have shown that the more educated citizens are more motivated to take part in politics. Political motivation is important. It is not enough to have the necessary resources. One must be willing to use them. Education creates a set of attitudes—a belief that one can be effective in politics, that one has a responsibility to be active—that leads citizens to participate.

The situation illustrates the paradox of political equality as an ideal (reflected in "one person, one vote") in contrast with sharp social and economic inequalities. The real inequalities in social and economic terms—the fact that some citizens have substantially more education or income than others—mean that the political ideal of equality is not achieved. The wealthy and the better educated have greater resources and motivation for political activity. Though opportunities to be politically active may be legally equal for all, those who are already well-off take more advantage of these opportunities.

EQUALIZING POLITICAL PARTICIPATION

Can political participation be made more equal so that citizens who are less well-off in income or education are not the least effective participants? There are several ways to achieve greater political equality.

Placing a Ceiling on Political Activity

One way might be to limit individual political activity. The most obvious place to do this is at the polls. Each citizen, no matter how rich or well educated, is limited to one vote for each political office. If voting were the only way citizens took part in politics, the rule of "one person, one vote" would make all citizens equal politically; at least they could be equal if they all voted. As we have seen, however, there are many other forms of participation, and these are often more powerful than voting. A millionaire, like a factory worker, has one vote, but contributions to candidates could give him far more voice than a factory worker. Can one put a ceiling on campaign contributions?

In the wake of the Watergate episode in 1974, Congress amended the Federal Election Campaign Act to provide that individuals may give no more than $1000 to a candidate in any federal election. A person may give $1000 to a presidential candidate, $1000 to a Senate candidate, and so forth. The limit is $1000 in any single race. This hardly makes campaign contributions as equal as the vote. Very few citizens can give $1000. Moreover, individuals may contribute to Political Action Committees (PACs) which in turn may give up to $5000 per candidate per race. (See Chapter 9 for more discussion of PACs.) In addition, the Supreme Court has ruled that individuals and groups may pay for advertisements for candidates without spending limitations—as long as they do it on their own, outside of the candidate's campaign organization (*Buckley* v. *Valeo*, 424 U.S. 1, 1976). This allows still more political influence for those with money.

There are many kinds of political activity that cannot easily be limited without severely limiting freedom of speech. No one would want to prohibit lobbying, for instance, since the essence of democracy is that citizens be free to express their preferences to the government. Such activities depend on both motivation and resources, however, and the better-educated citizens are more likely to be motivated toward political activity and to have the necessary resources.

Mobilizing the Disadvantaged

Another way to equalize participation is to mobilize the disadvantaged. Rather than put a ceiling on the activity of the wealthy, one *raises* the level of activity of the poor. The poor obviously have an interest in common—higher income and better living conditions. Two additional ingredients are necessary to raise their activity level to that of the wealthy and better educated: awareness of their disadvantaged position, and organization. In America, the poor tend to lack these two ingredients.

Awareness   Observers of American politics, particularly those who make comparisons with politics in Europe, often comment on the absence in the United States of any strong sense of economic class. This is very noticeable among American workers. It is particularly striking, because a sense of class can be found in many other industrialized democracies. American workers sometimes think of themselves as workers and make political decisions from that point of view, but often they define their interests in terms of other aspects of their identity. They may think politically as Catholics, as suburbanites, as whites or blacks, and so forth. This separates them from other workers—from Protestants if they are Catholic, from blacks if they are white. A sense of membership in a *working class* is absent.

Organization   What about organization? Two kinds of organization might help disadvantaged citizens participate more in politics, political parties, and voluntary groups. They might help by providing channels for activity and by increasing a sense of group identity. These organizations are also settings where citizens can get "training" for political participation. Studies show that people who participate in organizations are more likely also to participate in other forms of political life.[10]

---

[10] Gabriel Almond and Sidney Verba, *The Civic Culture* (Princeton: Princeton University Press, 1963), chap. 12; Carole Pateman, *Participation and Democratic Theory* (London: Cambridge University Press, 1970).

In many countries political parties are organized along class lines. There are parties of the working class, parties of the farmers, and parties of the middle class. Parties that are limited to a particular class tend to do a better job of recruiting the members of that class. Thus socialist or workers' parties tend to mobilize working-class citizens. In contrast, the parties in the United States have no strong class bias. Democrats are more likely to receive support from workers, and Republicans from business, but both parties get support from all levels of society. The result is that citizens with a lower social status do not get as much attention from party organizations trying to bring them into politics.

The same can be said for voluntary groups, such as civic associations, fraternal groups, and church groups. These organizations might help citizens become more active, but members of these associations tend to be of higher social status already. As Table 7.3 shows, citizens with more education are more active in organizations. Only about half the citizens who have not finished high school belong to a voluntary organization; over three-fourths of those with some college training do. Only about one-fourth of those without a high school degree are active in an organization, whereas one half of the college group are. If organization is a way to make groups of citizens politically meaningful, then it is clear that this resource is also more available to upper-status citizens.

BLACK VERSUS WHITE: POLITICAL MOBILIZATION OF A DISADVANTAGED GROUP

We can illustrate how a disadvantaged group can attain **political mobilization** through organization and self-awareness. Our example is American blacks. They have a history of relatively effective organization, at least more effective than that of white Americans of similar social and economic status. There are many reasons for this, perhaps the most important being the fact of segregation and social separation. Forced to live apart from whites, blacks have been better able to organize as a separate group. Numerous black organizations, from the NAACP to more militant groups, have played an important role. In addition, the black churches have provided an important organizational base. It was the churches, especially in the

TABLE 7.3

WHICH CITIZENS BELONG TO ORGANIZATIONS?

	Among Those Without High School Education	Among Those With Some High School	Among Those With Some College
Percent who are members of an organization	49%	67%	78%
Percent who are active in an organization	27%	43%	59%

SOURCE: Based on data from Sidney Verba and Norman H. Nie, *Participation in America: Political Democracy and Social Equality* (New York: Harper & Row, 1972).

The 1965 Voting Rights Act brought the federal government into states and communities to assure the opportunity to register and vote. This picture shows the effect: large numbers of black citizens waiting to vote in Birmingham, Alabama, in 1966.

South, that were the main foundation of the civil rights movement in the 1950s and 1960s. When Jesse Jackson undertook his 1984 campaign for the Democratic presidential nomination, the black churches again served as important instruments for reaching people and mobilizing their support.

Studies show that through black self-awareness citizens who might not otherwise participate can become active in politics. Black Americans, on the average, still participate in politics somewhat less than white Americans. This is what one would expect, given the fact that blacks generally have lower incomes and less education than whites. However, among blacks who have a strong sense of group identity (who, for instance, mention problems of race when asked what are the most important problems for themselves or the nation), political activity equals that of whites. In other words, the consciousness of black identity helps overcome the disadvantage in political activity resulting from lower educational and income levels.[11]

---

[11] Sidney Verba and Norman Nie, *Participation in America: Political Democracy and Social Inequality* (New York: Harper & Row, 1972), chap. 10.

The situation can be seen more clearly if we look at the situation over time. In 1952—two years before the Supreme Court's historic school desegregation decision and three years before the first bus boycott led by Martin Luther King, Jr., in Montgomery, Alabama—black Americans were much less active in political campaigns than the average whites. The combination of the civil rights movement, Supreme Court decisions, and voting rights legislation changed both the legal setting for black political action and their sense of what might be possible through more active participation.

By the 1960s the difference between black and white rates of campaign activity had nearly vanished. More and more black candidates were running for and winning public office. By 1984 four of the five largest cities in the nation had elected black mayors. Jesse Jackson's campaign for the 1984 Democratic nomination attracted 18.6 percent of the total votes cast in the 24 contested primaries, more than 3 million votes in all.

Of course, Jackson lost the nomination. Even when blacks win office they are not easily able to use their political power to overcome the economic and educational handicaps that so many black Americans still experience. Blacks, Hispanics, and some other minority groups are still disadvantaged relative to whites in terms of political participation and impact. But the size and scope of their disadvantage is much less than it was. (See Table 7.4.)

In the 1984 campaign for the Democratic presidential nomination the Reverend Jesse Jackson was able to get large numbers of blacks to become active who would otherwise probably have remained nonvoters.

TABLE 7.4
BLACK ELECTED OFFICIALS IN THE UNITED STATES, 1985

	Total	Federal	State	Local	Legal	School
Louisiana	475	0	134	159	59	123
Mississippi	444	0	94	189	75	86
Alabama	375	0	76	212	39	48
Illinois	357	3	56	202	24	72
Georgia	340	0	85	179	17	59
Arkansas	317	0	5	169	41	102
South Carolina	310	0	80	128	3	99
Michigan	300	2	44	109	55	90
California	296	4	20	57	76	139
North Carolina	291	0	50	162	13	66
Others	2551	11	395	1332	259	554
Total	6056[a]	20	1039	2898	661	1438

[a] Up from 5700 one year before, representing 1.2 percent of all elected officials in the United States.

SOURCE: *National Journal,* June 1, 1985, p. 1324.

POLITICAL ACTIVITY OF WOMEN

Women have generally been less active in politics than men. Traditionally, they were less likely to vote, to be active during election campaigns, or to run for office. The reasons why poorer and less educated citizens are less politically active probably apply to women as well. We have seen that those with lower levels of education are more likely to feel that they have no responsibility to take part in politics, and that they have a weaker sense of their ability to influence politics. Studies of school children have shown that girls traditionally were raised to believe that politics was not for them. The result is that women felt less politically able and were therefore less active.

Though women are still less active than men, the difference between men and women in political activity is much less in the United States than in other democracies. Figure 7.3 shows the results of a comparative study of political participation in several democracies. Men and women were given scores on a political-participation scale based on how active they were. The difference between men and women was found to be much greater in the other nations than in the United States.

Furthermore, there is evidence that the somewhat lower level of activity by women was in part a function of their personal life situation. Women who work outside the home or have a college education are more active than those who work at home or have less education. As women participate in the labor force to a degree equal to men and as they move toward equality in education, both of which are happening, the remaining participation gap may be expected to close.[12]

---

[12] Kent L. Tedin, David W. Brady, and Arnold Vedlitz, "Sex Differences in Political Attitudes: The Case for Institutional Factors," *Journal of Politics* 39 (1977):448; Kristi Andersen, "Working Women and Political Participation," *American Journal of Political Science* 19 (1976):439–453.

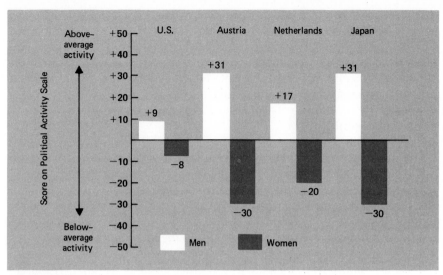

FIGURE 7.3

**Political-Activity Levels of Men and Women in the United States
and Other Democracies**

SOURCE: Adapted from Sidney Verba, Norman H. Nie, and Jae-On Kim, *Participation and Political Equality* (New York: Cambridge University Press, 1978), chap. 13.

There is an important qualification to be added before one concludes that there are or will shortly be few differences between men and women in political activity. Men and women are most similar in the United States when it comes to "low-level" political activities. Women are as likely as men to be ordinary campaign workers—to ring doorbells, send out letters, and make telephone calls soliciting votes. When it comes to "high-level" activities, however, the male-female gap widens. Whereas women are as likely as men to *work* in campaigns, they are less likely to *direct* campaigns. Women are as likely as men to work *for* a candidate, but they are less likely to *become* candidates themselves. As one moves up the ladder of politics, one finds fewer and fewer women. One study has found that responsibility for child-rearing is the major factor that inhibits women from seeking public office.[13]

This difference may take longer to overcome, since it is likely to be enforced by more direct discrimination. Yet the same forces that equalize other forms of participation may equalize political activity at higher levels as well. Geraldine Ferraro's nomination for vice-president on the Democratic ticket in 1984 was an important step. Ferraro had spent part of her life raising her children before returning to her career and eventual political success. Her example may encourage others to follow.

CHOOSING HOW TO PARTICIPATE

Why do some citizens choose to become politically active? And why do those who become active choose one means of participation rather than

---

[13] M. M. Lee, "Why So Few Women Hold Public Office," *Political Science Quarterly* 91 (1976):297–314.

another? There is no single and simple answer. People may be active in a particular way simply out of habit. Many people vote out of habit. Or they may feel they are fulfilling a civic obligation. Many people vote for that reason as well. Perhaps they are active in response to pressure from friends and neighbors. That is how many people get recruited to be active in political campaigns or in communal activities.

Using Resources

If we think of political participation as the means whereby citizens use their resources to try to get the government to respond to their preferences, we may get a better idea of what means a group of citizens is likely to choose when they participate. There are many resources a particular group may have, such as money, skills, connections, and access. Sheer numbers can also count as a resource. Groups that can deliver a large number of followers can more easily capture the attention of political leaders.

Groups choose to participate in ways that let them use their resources most effectively. Think of voting. It does not take much in the way of money, skill, or access in order to vote. Thus lots of people from all walks of life vote. For a group to be an effective voting force, however, so that candidates pay attention to it, the group needs numbers. A few voters make little difference. Vote power is, therefore, most effective when exercised by large groups, especially if they are located in key areas. In presidential elections, candidates monitor the preferences of the major religious groups, ethnic groups, workers, or farmers. They calculate how to appeal to them. A smaller group that can deliver only a few votes is more likely to be ignored.

Numbers matter less for active campaign involvement or communal activity. Smaller groups can make their voices heard, because they can express their views more forcefully. This activity requires more resources; skill, access, and money are the most useful. People who are more affluent or better educated are much more likely to be active in these ways.

Those few individuals who control massive resources, such as the top executives of corporations or labor unions, may accomplish a lot through direct contact of officials. Such leaders not only control large financial resources, they have good connections, are personally skilled, and also have professional staffs to help them. They can readily gain access to high government officials, whereas ordinary individuals might encounter less willingness to listen to their concerns.

Nevertheless, direct contacts are not limited to the very wealthy or the very powerful. Ordinary citizens can sometimes be quite effective in contacting government officials. They deal most often with lower-level officials, on the local level perhaps, and they usually don't ask for multimillion-dollar loan guarantees. Ordinary citizens typically are concerned about matters that are of great significance to themselves, such as a job, a license, or a government grant, but are an insignificant fraction of the overall programs of the government. Hence, these needs can often be accommodated more easily than the "big ticket" items sought by the larger more powerful groups.

Contacts of any kind require a certain amount of resources—skill in knowing whom to contact, what to say, and perhaps good connections. Hence, even contacting tends to be carried out by those who are better off or better educated.

What about those groups that have few members and limited financial or skill resources? Ethnic and racial minority groups are sometimes like this. Many are relatively small and therefore cannot vote people into or out of office. In addition, they do not have the financial resources nor the access to officials that more established groups have.

It is these groups that sometimes turn to protest activities. Protest is a means of overcoming the lack of other resources. Protests can be effective if they mobilize other groups in society to support the protesters. The early southern civil rights protests, led by people such as Martin Luther King, Jr., pitted southern blacks against southern white segregationists. The protests were successful because they mobilized liberal white support for the civil rights movement. Protests in places like Birmingham and Selma, Alabama, led to violent reaction on the part of some southern law-enforcement officials. The media gave the protests wide coverage. One news picture showed police dogs attacking black marchers; another showed a black woman being beaten by a white sheriff. The result was that the civil rights movement received the support of white people throughout America.

Protests, therefore, are a means of political participation likely to be favored by those who otherwise have few other resources. They are likely to be successful if they help gain new resources—by mobilizing new allies.

This 1978 "tractorcade" protest by the American Agriculture Movement was intended to dramatize the economic plight of farmers and their determination to get helpful political action.

If protesters are perceived by others as protesting for a just cause, and if they appear to be the victims of violence, they may rally support from others. This is what brought so many to support the early civil rights movement. But, of course, things do not always work that way. More often than not, the public standing on the sidelines and watching the protest sees the protesters as wrong or as the instigators of violence. Under such conditions, the reaction is negative. Instead of winning support, the protesting group loses it. Protest may substitute for other resources, but as we have noted, it is a risky business.

CONCLUDING THOUGHTS

Political participation is the means by which democracy is made vital and effective. If legal barriers prevent large groups of people from taking part—as was true in the United States so long as women and black Americans were denied the vote—the nation falls short of the democratic ideal. Today nearly all those legal barriers have been eliminated, but political participation is still very far from equal. Significant segments of the population take little or no part in the democratic process. One result is that they lose the opportunity to grow and develop their individual potentialities as citizens. Another consequence is that public officials are likely to know less about and pay less attention to their problems. When this happens, will not a sizable number of citizens begin to wonder whether American democracy is really working? Will they lose faith and trust in their government? These are some of the important issues we turn to in the next chapter.

CHAPTER HIGHLIGHTS ■

1. Participation is crucial in a democracy. It communicates citizen preferences to government officials, helps create a legitimate government, and conveys the full dignity of citizenship to the individual. The accurate communication of preferences depends on how representative the participants are of the population as a whole. The legitimacy of the government may depend upon how many citizens participate.

2. There are many ways in which citizens participate in government, including voting, campaign activity, communal activity, contacting the government, or taking part in protests.

3. Political participants are not representative of the population as a whole. They are more likely to be educated and affluent, to be white, male, and middle-aged. They are less likely to face severe economic needs.

4. Disadvantaged groups can be mobilized to political activity through consciousness and organization. Black Americans and American women have taken this route to political activism.

5. Voting is an effective activity for groups that are large in number. Campaign and communal activity is often used by the more affluent, while protests are a technique used by those who have neither numbers nor affluence.

PROFILE ■

JOHN STUART MILL (1806–1873)
English Philosopher, Economist, and Reformer

Mill's father, James, was a noted political economist, and an associate of Jeremy Bentham in the development of utilitarian thought. John Stuart Mill was subjected to rather extreme force-feeding of education by his father, studying Greek when he was 3 and mastering the bulk of Latin literature before he was 12. Mill's primary importance is not as a prodigy, however, but as a political philosopher with a strong commitment to reform.

In *On Liberty* (1859) Mill offered one of the most effective arguments for preserving individual freedom, not only because of the inherent value of each person, but also because ideas needed a free and tolerant environment in which to compete. If people were not free to think and say whatever they could, the rest of society would be denied the chance to gain the value that might have been contained in their ideas. Error and misconception would go uncorrected. The community would be the poorer.

In *Representative Government* (1861) Mill strongly defended the then-new idea of proportional representation whereby political parties or groups would gain legislative seats in approximate proportion to their share of the vote. At a more fundamental level, Mill argued that the central purpose of government was to create the conditions for and foster an active participating citizenry whose members could stand up for their rights and through civic participation enlarge their human potentialities. In his emphasis on individual liberty and self-fulfillment through active citizenship, Mill expressed some of the basic commitments of liberalism. In his active support for woman's suffrage and opposition to prohibition and much other restrictive social legislation, he exemplified a liberal spirit in the best sense of the term. He was an optimist regarding human possibilities—which perhaps is the identifying mark of a liberal.

SUGGESTED READINGS ■

Most of the careful analyses of who participates in politics and in what ways are fairly recent.

Among the valuable modern studies of political participation are: Carole Pateman, *Participation and Democratic Theory* (1970); Sidney Verba and Norman Nie, *Participation in America: Political Democracy and Social Equality* (1972); Sidney Verba, Norman Nie, and Jae-On Kim, *Participation and Political Equality: A Seven Nation Comparison* (1978); Samuel H. Barnes, Max Kaase et al., *Political Action: Mass Participation in Five Western Democracies;* Lester W. Milbrath and M. L. Goel, *Political Participation* (2d ed., 1977); Raymond E. Wolfinger and Steven J. Rosenstone, *Who Votes?* (1980); Jerome H. Skolnick, *The Politics of Protest* (1969).

Chapter **8**

The School—One Source of Political Socialization

POLITICAL BELIEFS

D emocracy works where people believe in it. If people do not hold to some fundamental democratic values, all the laws and constitutions that can be written will not serve to preserve a democratic government. This has been the sad lesson learned by many nations that have tried to establish democracy where citizens were not committed to it. This chapter will look at basic political values and commitments and try to assess the extent to which Americans truly believe in democracy. We will look at basic beliefs about the legitimacy of the government, about the kind of government we ought to have, and about such issues as equality and inequality. We also consider where these beliefs come from and how they change. To avoid the false conclusion that all Americans agree in their basic political beliefs, we will look also at some who deviate from the mainstream.

A Child's Beliefs

Several years ago, two political scientists wanted to know how young children think about politics and political leaders. They tried this out on some 11-year-old children. "One day the president was driving his car to a meeting. Since he was late, he was driving very fast. The police stopped the car. Finish the story."

Here is the response by Charles, 11 years old, the son of a white-collar worker from upstate New York.

CHARLES: Well, if I was the policeman, I would have given the president a ticket, because it doesn't make a difference who you are in this country. You still have to obey the law.

INTERVIEWER: What do you think the president would say when the policeman stopped him?

CHARLES: If he was a good president, he would congratulate the policeman for giving him a ticket and not letting him go with just a warning.

INTERVIEWER: How about the policeman? What does the policeman say when he stops this car and finds out that it is the president?

CHARLES: He'd probably be a little bit surprised to find the president, the one who was really passing all these laws about speeding, speeding himself.

INTERVIEWER: What do you think the policeman would say to him?

CHARLES: "I'm afraid I'm going to have to give you a ticket."

INTERVIEWER: Okay, then what does the president say?

CHARLES: I don't know. He's probably going to tell the policeman that he deserved it or something.[1]

Charles is only 11, but he already has some pretty basic beliefs about politics. In his description of what happens when the president is nabbed

---

[1] Fred I. Greenstein and Sidney Tarrow, *Political Orientation of Children: The Use of a Semi-Projected Technique in Three Nations,* Sage Professional Papers, Comparative Politics Series, Mo. 01–009 (Beverly Hills: Sage, 1970), p. 493. Copyright 1970 by Sage Publications, Inc. Reprinted by permission.

for speeding, he expresses two basic views. In the first place, he clearly believes that laws apply even to the president. If Charles had had some courses in political science, he might have phrased his answer in stronger rhetoric: "Ours is a government of law, not men." He clearly did not need such courses to come to that belief. Second, he sees the president as a fairly benign figure, someone who can be trusted and who tries to be helpful and supportive.

Of course, not all American children would say this. The researchers who spoke to Charles spoke to many children in the United States and in other countries. They found that in the United States, young children were much more likely to "finish the story" in ways that expressed a belief that the president is subject to the laws and that he is a trustworthy and kind person.

The views expressed by Charles may seem to be remote from the problems that concern us in this book. They are not. The beliefs that people have about politics—about what government is, how it operates, and how it ought to operate—are learned early in life (as this example shows) and have a major effect on what in fact happens in politics. That most Americans would share Charles's views about a government of laws, not men, is important. At an earlier time, most shared his view about the trustworthiness of political leaders, but the latter belief is changing as more Americans become cynical about politics. That change is important.

This chapter deals with the basic political beliefs of Americans, what they are, where they come from, why they are important.

CALCULATION VERSUS CULTURE

We can explain a person's political behavior in two different ways, as a result of rational calculation of interests or as a result of cultural commitment to values. The citizen who chooses how to take part in political life on the basis of rational calculation of interests acts like a person in a marketplace. He or she calculates the benefits of a particular political act, compares them to the costs, and chooses to do what maximizes benefit at the least cost. A person who acts on the basis of cultural commitment to values does not make such a conscious calculation in choosing how to act. He or she is guided by basic beliefs or values, often learned in early childhood. These beliefs and values are unquestioned *habits of thought* that tell the person what to do, what choice to make.

An example of a rational calculation is the purchase of a major appliance by a careful shopper. The shopper compares the various brands in terms of cost and quality and chooses that which gives the most value for the least money. An example of cultural commitment is religion. Most people do not choose their religion by calculating carefully which religion gives the most benefit for the least cost; rather, religious commitments are usually basic beliefs, in most cases acquired from one's family.

Consider two ways in which individuals can decide how to vote. Individual voters can calculate which candidate is more likely to carry out policies that are in their interest and vote accordingly. If presidential candidate *A* will do more about unemployment than candidate *B*, the voter who is unemployed or worried about unemployment and votes on the basis of calculation will be inclined to vote for candidate *A*. On the other hand, a voter might vote on the basis of habitual commitment. Many voters have long-term, habitual identifications with one or the other of the major political parties. They have always been Democrats or Republicans. Often that partisan identification is a family tradition. When it comes to a choice between candidates *A* and *B*, such voters make no calculation as to the benefits to be gained from the victory of one candidate over the other. They vote for the candidate of the party with which they are habitually affiliated. (In Chapter 11 we will discuss more fully how voters decide how to vote.)

Cultural Commitments and Democracy

The distinction between a cost-benefit calculation and cultural commitments is fundamental to one theory of how democracy works. The theory is as follows: Democracy survives if citizens act culturally when it comes to basic democratic beliefs but make rational calculations when it comes to specific issues. According to this argument, citizens must agree on some basic cultural and political beliefs, largely without questioning them. The two that are most important are belief in the **legitimacy** of the government (i.e., it deserves the support and obedience of its citizens) and belief in the **rules of the democratic game** (i.e., key democratic procedures, such as freedom of speech and free elections). If there is widespread agreement on the legitimacy of the government and on the rules of the democratic game, the nation can stand the strain of disagreement on more specific matters. For example, citizens may calculate which presidential candidate will act in their interest and be happy or sad about the election result. But they should not hesitate to accept that result as legitimate. Citizens may calculate whether placing a stiff tax on gasoline in order to encourage energy conservation is in their interest. Although some may favor such a tax, while others oppose it, citizens should not calculate whether to obey the law and pay the gasoline tax.

The point about the absence of cost-benefit calculations when it comes to the basics of democracy is extremely important. Democracy allows— indeed fosters—the free expression of political preferences. Citizens can work to get the government to carry out the policies they prefer. They do this by supporting candidates in elections or by pressuring government officials. Since citizens have different preferences, some will support one candidate and others the opponent. Some will want a particular policy, while others will oppose it. The result is that there are participants who win and others who lose. Why should the losers accept a result that is not in their immediate interest? Why should those who prefer the Republican candidate accept the election of a Democrat? One answer is that the losers accept their loss because they have a deeper commitment to the rules of procedure by which elections are held. They believe in free elections even if they sometimes lose. Furthermore, if both winners and losers agree on the rules, the losers will have another chance to win. The winning party, because it too shares the democratic commitment, will not use its position in office to abolish elections or to put its opponents in jail. Legitimacy requires sticking to the rules.

Legitimacy is an important concept in political science and deserves further discussion. When citizens consider a government to be legitimate, they consider it to be worthy of obedience even if it does not act in their immediate interests. You obey a new tax law not because a cost-benefit calculation tells you that you will gain from it, but because the law was passed by a legitimate government, and you therefore *ought* to obey. It is your moral obligation, not just to your own selfish advantage. It is easy to see why legitimacy is basic to democracy. Democracy depends on voluntary consent by citizens. If most citizens do not give such consent, the government is likely to rely more and more on force. Citizens, in turn, are likely to be attracted to political movements that are opposed to democracy.

What makes a government legitimate in the eyes of the people? For one thing, citizens may accord the government legitimacy simply out of long-term cultural habit. They may accept the government as proper, because early in life they developed a commitment to the symbols of American democracy and a basic sense of trust and confidence in the government. As long as the government follows the proper procedures—as long as elections are carried out freely and fairly and laws are passed in the way authorized by the Constitution—government will be accepted as worthy of support over and above any narrow calculation of interest. But in the long run legitimacy may also depend on success. A legitimate political system is one that works.

POLITICAL BELIEFS OF AMERICANS: THE EVIDENCE

The argument that certain basic beliefs are fundamental to democracy was developed long ago. It was uncertain, however, whether the public actually held this set of beliefs. Fortunately, in recent years, social scientists have developed such techniques as the in-depth sample survey of public attitudes. We can now look at systematically gathered data on the beliefs of the American people. As we will see, they do believe in the legitimacy of the government and in the rules of the democratic game, but such commitments are by no means unqualified.

We will look closely at these beliefs about democracy. They define what Americans mean by liberty and freedom. However, there is another set of crucial values that affect politics in America—beliefs as to what kind of society we ought to have. Americans have some distinctive views about the nature of equality and the role of the state in relation to equality. These views affect what Americans want from the government. We will look at these views as well.

Legitimacy of the Government

Are Americans committed to the American political system? Do they give it their long-term trust and loyalty? One way in which such trust and loyalty are shown is through commitment to the *symbols* of American

Trust in government plummeted during the Watergate crisis until at last Richard Nixon resigned as President.

democracy. Over the years, studies have found that Americans have, in general, a deep commitment to the symbols of the American political community. Reverence for the flag and the Constitution is taught in the schools and maintained throughout the life of the average American.

The Constitution

At many places in this book, we stress the importance of the Constitution as a guiding document for the American political system. This eighteenth-century document and its subsequent amendments still provide the basic framework for our government. They also provide a major focus for the beliefs and commitments of Americans. If something is constitutional, it is considered correct and to be obeyed; if it is unconstitutional, it is wrong and to be changed. In short, what is constitutional defines what is legitimate.

Consider an example. In 1973 Vice-President Spiro Agnew resigned in the midst of a bribery scandal. Gerald Ford, a member of the House of Representatives from Michigan, was appointed vice-president. The next year, President Richard Nixon resigned in the wake of the Watergate investigation, and Gerald Ford became president. The Watergate events and Nixon's resignation were the subject of great controversy at the time. However, no one questioned the right of President Ford to succeed Nixon in office. All Americans—the public, the media, Congress, the members of the executive branch, the Joint Chiefs of Staffs of the military forces, and the governors of the various states—accepted Ford as the new head of state.

Several European commentators at the time raised the following question: How can Americans be committed to democracy if they accept as their president someone who has never won a national election? After all, Gerald Ford had never run for national office. He had never been elected by any constituency larger than that of his congressional district in Michigan.

The answer to their question is quite simple. Gerald Ford was accepted as the legitimate occupant of the Oval Office, because he had been selected according to the rules and procedures set down in the Twenty-fifth Amendment to the Constitution. The point is so obvious to most Americans that it was hardly noticed at the time—just as fish may be the last to notice the water in which they swim. However, just as water is crucial to fish, so is this constitutional commitment crucial to American politics. The fact that Gerald Ford was selected by a procedure never used before (since there had never been another case where both the president and vice-president resigned), coupled with the tension of the Watergate crisis, might have made the peaceful succession in office more problematic. If all this had happened in some other countries, disaffected citizens might have taken to the streets to demand that the new president step down. The opposition party might have called for a special election. Some generals might have decided that this was the moment to take over.

The fact that there are established procedures set down in the Constitution and that the American public accepts those procedures as right and proper provides stability and legitimacy to the political system. Not everything is that smooth and simple. What is or is not constitutional is often controversial. The fact that almost no one questions the legitimacy of the constitutional rules does not mean that all agree on how to interpret those rules. As we have seen and will see even more clearly when we discuss the role of the Supreme Court, there are many disagreements as to the correct interpretation of the Constitution. Nevertheless, the fact that all accept the Constitution, even while debating its meaning, provides some cement to hold the American political system together.

Political Commitment and Growing Distrust

The commitment of Americans to the basic structures of politics was made clear in an early comparative study of political beliefs. This study compared the political beliefs of Americans with those of citizens in four other countries. The researchers asked citizens what they were proud of about their countries. Two results are important. For one thing, few Americans, only 4 percent, replied that there was nothing they were proud of, a response that would have showed general hostility to the political community. In the other four countries, the portions who were proud of "nothing" ranged from 10 percent to 27 percent. More interesting is what Americans *were* proud of. In comparison with the citizens of other nations, Americans showed particular pride in the governmental system of their society—the Constitution, political freedom, and democracy. Eighty-five percent of those who were interviewed in the United States, twice the percentage in the next highest country, mentioned political aspects of society.

This study was conducted, however, just before the turbulent events of the 1960s, when many groups and individuals came to challenge American politics. Is support for the American political system still as firm two

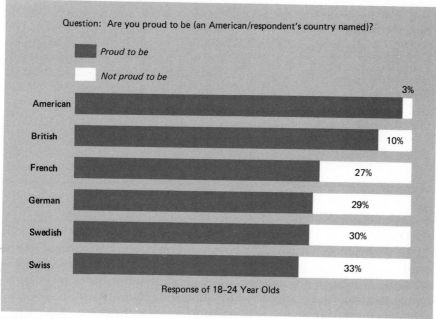

FIGURE 8.1

No Holes in Our Swiss Cheese

SOURCE: Survey by Nippon Research Center, Ltd., and Gallup International, November 25, 1977–January 6, 1978. The survey was sponsored by Youth Bureau, Prime Minister's Office, Japan. From *Public Opinion,* June–July 1981, p. 25. Reprinted by permission.

decades later? The answer is a qualified yes. In terms of the public's general views of America, pride appears to be intact. During March 1981, a sample of citizens were asked, "What are you proudest of about America?" Only 1 percent said "nothing." The most frequent answer was freedom or liberty (71 percent). Indeed, when citizens in seven nations were asked during 1978 whether they were proud of their country, 97 percent of Americans said yes—more than in any other nation (see Figure 8.1). In addition, a 1982 survey found that 71 percent of Americans were "willing to fight for their country," a higher proportion than in other western democracies.

On the other hand, there is clear evidence that the public has become less trusting of the government in recent years. Political scientists at the University of Michigan have traced the level of trust in the government over nearly three decades, asking a series of questions about whether people trust the government to do what is right, whether they think the government is run by a few big interests, and so forth. On this basis, they categorize Americans as trusting or cynical. As we can see from Table 8.1, during the late 1950s, when they started asking these questions, most Americans were in the trusting category. Only about 1 in 10 could be considered cynical. Starting with the tensions over racial issues and Vietnam in the 1960s, the number who were trusting fell and the number of cynics rose. By the time of Richard Nixon's term in office, there was an equal number of trusting and cynical citizens. After the Watergate crisis, trust plummeted further. In recent years the number of citizens cynical about the operation of the government has been almost twice as large as the number who express trust.

TABLE 8.1

INDIVIDUAL CONFIDENCE IN GOVERNMENT, 1964–1982

Question: How much of the time do you think you can trust the government in Washington to do what is right— just about always, most of the time, or only some of the time?

	1964	1966	1968	1970	1972	1974	1976	1978	1980	1982
None of the time	0%	3%	0%	0%	1%	1%	1%	4%	4%	2%
Some of the time	22	28	36	44	44	61	62	64	69	62
Most of the time	62	48	54	47	48	34	30	27	23	31
Always	14	17	7	7	5	3	3	3	2	2
Don't know	2	4	2	2	2	2	3	3	2	3

SOURCE: University of Michigan, Survey Research Center.

The decline in optimism and trust in political leaders had begun well before the **Watergate scandal.** Watergate increased public dissatisfaction, but the decline in confidence seems to have had its roots in a belief that the government could not cope with the many serious problems it faced during the late 1960s and the 1970s—racial tension, Vietnam, law and order, pollution, economic stagnation, inflation, and the energy crisis. Since 1980 the trend has changed somewhat, with trust recovering some but not all of the losses of the two previous decades.

The long-term implications of the decline in trust in government are unclear. Some believe the decline was a temporary reaction to specific policies and personalities, and hail the recent upturn as an indication that a popular president like Ronald Reagan can restore the lost confidence. Others argue that there is a deeper **alienation** in the land that could threaten democracy.

Thus far, the evidence shows that the public is dissatisfied with political leadership but has not yet lost confidence in the "form of government." Public-opinion studies continue to show that Americans still consider the political system to be basically sound. One thorough study of political alienation found that many citizens are dissatisfied with specific policies of the government or with specific people. However, there is little evidence that citizens want fundamental changes in the form of government or in our system of freedoms.[2]

The same conclusion has been reached by those who have studied the recent "taxpayers' revolt." In a number of places, citizen groups have attacked government programs and tried to limit them. The most dramatic example was the passage of Proposition 13, in California, a measure that severely limits the amount of taxes that the state and local governments could raise from citizens. What were citizens upset about? Close studies of public opinion show that it was not, as some believed, a reaction against the massive government programs that existed in California and elsewhere. The public wanted the government to be active in education, in health, and in improving the welfare of the citizens. The public was protesting

[2] Paul Sniderman, *A Question of Loyalty* (Berkeley and Los Angeles: University of California Press, 1981).

what it saw as waste and inefficiency in government programs. It was not against those programs or against government itself.[3]

The American public seems to be saying, "The system is all right; it is just working badly." A long period of dissatisfaction with the way the system works might lead to a more general loss of legitimacy for the political process as a whole. As yet, there is little evidence that this is happening. Nevertheless, the firm, almost uncritical, support for the government once found among the American people is now somewhat weaker.

Citizens' Belief in Their Political Efficacy

Another citizen attitude closely related to belief in the legitimacy of the government is **political efficacy.** This is the belief of citizens that they, themselves, have a voice in the government. Democratic government is supposed to be responsive to the people. If citizens do not believe they can influence the government, they are less likely to feel that it deserves support.

Do Americans have a strong sense of political efficacy? In general, yes; but, as with trust in the government, the number who feel this way has declined recently. Most Americans believe the vote is effective for controlling government officials, but they are considerably less confident than they were in 1960 that government officials are basically responsive to the people. Moreover, two-thirds believe that congressmen lose touch with the people. Nevertheless, if we compare Americans to citizens of other nations, we find that they are more likely than most others to think they can have some effect on a local government regulation or a law of Congress they consider unfair or unjust. About 3 out of 4 Americans say they could do something about such a regulation. The percentages are generally smaller elsewhere (see Table 8.2).

American citizens, this suggests, do not feel helpless before the government. To some extent at least, believing that they are not helpless makes them less so. Those who feel able to influence the government are more likely to try.

Periodic measures of "citizen efficacy" during the last few decades show that feelings of efficacy are lower than they once were but still quite substantial. In 1952, 69 percent of a sample agreed that people have some say about what the government does; by 1960, the figure had risen to 72 percent. By the late 1960s, however, the portion agreeing with that statement had fallen to 60 percent, and it has remained at about that level ever since.

SUPPORT FOR THE DEMOCRATIC RULES OF THE GAME

Agreement on the rules of the game means agreement on the basic procedures of democracy, such as regular elections and freedom of speech. We

---

[3] Mervin Field, "Sending a Message: Californians Strike Back," *Public Opinion* 41 (1978), p. 3.

TABLE 8.2

CAN YOU DO SOMETHING ABOUT A REGULATION YOU CONSIDER UNFAIR?

	United States	Great Britain	Germany	Nether-lands	Austria
Percentage saying yes in relation to national government	71%	64%	67%	62%	43%
Percentage saying yes in relation to local government	78%	57%	56%	43%	33%

SOURCE: Based on data from Samuel Barnes and Max Kaase, *Political Action* (Beverly Hills: Sage, 1979), p. 141.

have seen why agreement on these rules is important. Those who argue that the survival of democracy depends on the commitment of the citizens to democratic procedures stress the importance of citizen support for freedom of speech. The Bill of Rights may provide formal guarantees of freedom of speech, but unless the public supports the right of freedom of speech, the Bill of Rights will be meaningless. Democracy depends, they claim, on the willingness of the majority to tolerate unpopular political views.

If Americans agree on these basic rules, the argument goes, they will be able to disagree on other issues. Should there be federal control of the oil companies? Should there be a constitutional amendment barring abortion? Americans disagree on such matters, sometimes quite sharply. However, as long as all tolerate the right of opponents to express themselves and as long as they accept the outcome of the dispute when it is settled according to the constitutional rules of the game, democracy survives.

Do Americans in fact agree with the rules of the democratic game? In part, the answer is implied in the fact that the symbols they are committed to include the Constitution and the Bill of Rights. When they talk about the political institutions they are proud of, they mention the symbols of democracy. But we can look closer.

Commitment to Democratic Procedure—How Consistent Is It?

Several studies have shown that the American people generally agree with the principles of democratic government. By "generally," we mean that usually more than 9 out of 10 support them. They agree that the rights of minorities to freedom of speech should be protected, that public officials should be chosen by majority vote, that a person is entitled to all legal rights no matter what his or her political beliefs. For example, a recent study found that 85 percent of the people favored "free speech for all no matter what their views might be," and only 9 percent disagreed. In short, most Americans support the basic rules of the democratic game.[4]

---

[4] John L. Sullivan, James E. Pierson, and George E. Marcus, *Political Tolerance and American Democracy* (Chicago: University of Chicago Press, 1981). Similar findings are reported in Herbert McClosky and Alida Brill, *Dimensions of Tolerance* (New York: Russell Sage Foundation, 1983).

Most people support free speech in the abstract but often are less willing to defend the rights of those they dislike.

American commitment to the rules of democratic procedure may be relatively shallow, however. In theory, one should allow free speech no matter how one feels about the speaker or the content of the speech—at least if the speaker does not directly preach violence or the breaking of the law. That is what tolerance implies—willingness to allow the expression of views you do not like. In the abstract, Americans agree. When it comes to specific unpopular groups, they are less certain. When one asks whether groups with unpopular views (e.g., communists or atheists) should be allowed to make speeches, the American people are not sure speech should be that free. Indeed, a large number of Americans are opposed to letting groups of this sort make speeches in their community, and large numbers would remove their books from the local library. For example, a National Opinion Research Center survey in 1980 found that only 60 percent would allow a Communist to make a speech in their community and only 67 percent would allow someone who is "against church and religion" to do so. Similarly, the same survey that found over 9 out of 10 Americans favoring freedom of speech in general reported that 2 out of 3 favored outlawing "organizations that preach the violent overthrow of the government."[5]

Many people seem willing to allow freedom of speech for those they like but not for those they dislike. Ninety-five percent of the population said yes when asked if a group of their neighbors should be allowed to circulate petitions to ask the government to act on some issue, a clear

---

[5] Ibid.

There is one other explanation of why the less than complete support for free speech that one finds in public-opinion polls is not reflected in repression of free speech. Many of the people who answer questions in public-opinion polls are expressing views that they hold with little intensity and upon which they are unlikely to act. This is not true of all Americans, however. For some, politics is a very important activity. The people who are politically concerned and active form a minority of the population. Many studies have shown that activists are more likely to be committed to the democratic rules. Like the rest of the public, political activists agree with the general principles of democracy, but they also support those principles when they are applied to specific cases.

Thus the study that found Americans opposing freedom of speech for various unpopular groups also found that active citizens, those who participated in politics, were much more likely to support freedom of speech for such groups (see Table 8.5). As another study found, almost one-third of all Americans thought that the majority has the right to deny freedom to minorities; a much smaller percentage, 7 percent, of the nation's political leaders (in this case, delegates to the national conventions) took this undemocratic position. When political activists are asked about free speech for the group *they* like the least, they look less tolerant than when they are asked about groups the researcher thought were unpopular. Even so, activists are still substantially more tolerant than those citizens who are less active.[6]

These data suggest that democratic values may be less firmly held among most of the American people than is generally believed. They seem to be stronger, however, among those who are likely to have a greater voice in how things are in fact run—those who are active in politics and in organizations. Democracy may be based on democratic political commitments, but it may be a narrow base.

Several additional points can be made, some discouraging, some encouraging for democracy. A discouraging point is that, as we have seen, a large group in the population is not in favor of political freedom for unpopular groups; they might therefore tolerate or even actively endorse antidemocratic political leaders or movements. This discouraging thought must be measured against two others. For one thing, the general commitment to the values of democracy, vague thought it may be, counteracts the less democratic views. At least it provides a set of values one can appeal to. Further, all evidence shows that commitment to democratic values, in both the general and the concrete sense, is strongest among people with higher education. As the population becomes more and more educated, as has been happening over time, we can hope to find a larger portion of the population with political views that are consistently democratic. Indeed, there is evidence that the political tolerance level of the public has been rising. Nevertheless, Americans cannot be overconfident regarding the popular support for democracy. A dramatic political crisis might be exploited by an eloquent leader to attract those whose commit-

---

[6] See McClosky and Brill, op. cit.; Sullivan et al., op. cit.

TABLE 8.5

POLITICAL ACTIVISTS ARE MORE TOLERANT THAN ORDINARY CITIZENS OF UNPOPULAR VIEWS

	Among a Cross Section of Citizens	Among Political Activists
Percent saying they would allow an admitted communist to speak in public	58%	88%
Percent saying they would allow an atheist to speak in public	65%	95%

SOURCE: Kay Lehman Schlozman and Kristi Andersen, "Changes in the Level of Tolerance for Dissent, 1954–1974." Unpublished paper based on National Opinion Research Center data.

ment to political tolerance is shallow and vague. It was thus that the European Fascist and Nazi movements arose earlier in this century, and we cannot be certain that even in the United States something like them will not reappear.

BELIEFS ABOUT EQUALITY

We have just considered the beliefs of Americans about liberty. The other great democratic ideal at the heart of American political beliefs is equality.

Foreign observers, such as the Frenchman Alexis de Tocqueville, who visited the United States during the early decades of the Republic, were struck by the extent of equality in the United States, both as an ideal in which people believed and as a reality. There were many reasons for the special place of equality as an American value. The Puritan religious tradition was one that stressed the equality of individuals before God. America had no feudal past as the nations of Europe did; therefore, it had not experienced the rigid class system of feudalism. During the early nineteenth century most Americans were farmers who owned their own land. We did not have a large class of landless peasants. (Of course, all this can be said only if one ignores the plight of Native Americans and the system of black slavery in the South. As Tocqueville himself observed, the American tradition of equality was for the white population only.) Lastly, American equality depended on a belief in social and geographic mobility. One could always start afresh on the frontier, where all people were equal.

During the nineteenth century the United States was transformed from an agrarian nation into an industrial one. It was no longer a nation of independent farmers. It had become a nation of industrial managers and workers. Millions of immigrants poured into the country, immigrants who did not share the Puritan heritage. Most of them settled in the rapidly growing cities and went to work in shops and factories. By the end of the century, little usable land was available for new settlement, so the frontier was no longer an outlet for those who were discontented with their station in life. Yet the commitment to equality remained after the conditions that had been the foundation of that commitment disappeared. Lord Bryce, an Englishman who visited the United States near the end of the nineteenth century—50 years after Tocqueville and after the transformation of the United States into an industrial nation—still commented on the egalitarian attitude of Americans. One of the reasons that the belief in equality remained so strong was that the new population of industrial workers accepted the view that America was a land of opportunity, where individuals could improve their lives by their own efforts. Historians debate whether in fact social mobility in the United States was greater than in Europe. In any case, most agree that Americans believed, more than people in other nations, that mobility was possible.

Equality can have many meanings. As was pointed out in Chapter 5, to Americans it has almost always meant equality of opportunity, not equality of condition. Americans do not believe that everyone should have an equal income or an equal life-style. They do believe that everyone should have an equal chance to get ahead. Such a belief is a highly individualistic one. All individuals should be free to develop their talents to the utmost.

The commitment of Americans to the ideal of equality of opportunity is illustrated in a recent study of leaders in the United States.[7] Leaders from all areas of American life were asked their views on equality. Some, such as black or feminist leaders, come from the segments of society that have been challenging the status quo in America. They have been demanding more equality. Others, such as business leaders, come from more conservative segments of society. The leaders were asked whether they believe in *equality of opportunity*—giving each person an equal chance for a good education and to develop his or her ability—or *equality of results*—giving each person a relatively equal income regardless of his or her ability. The left-hand side of Table 8.6 shows the results. Equality of opportunity is indeed the dominant ideal for American leadership groups. It is not surprising to find business leaders believing in this form of equality. But more than 4 out of 5 of the leaders in each of the other groups also accept this individualistic ideal.

As we saw in relation to beliefs about freedom of speech, agreement on abstract ideals does not imply agreement on more specific matters. The fact that most leadership groups agree on an abstract ideal of equality does not mean that it is a noncontroversial matter. These same leaders differ sharply on a number of more concrete issues. They disagree on the extent to which the American system actually provides equal opportunity for all people. The same study asked these leaders whether the main cause of poverty in America was that the American system did not give all people an equal chance or was it that the poor have themselves to blame.

As we can see from the right-hand side of Table 8.6, the consensus that appears in relation to the philosophical ideal of equality disappears in relation to the question of how well the United States lives up to that

---

[7] Sidney Verba and Gary R. Orren, *Equality in America: The View From the Top* (Cambridge: Harvard University Press, 1985).

TABLE 8.6

**ATTITUDES ON EQUALITY OF OPPORTUNITY
AND RESPONSIBILITY**

Group	How Best to Deal with Inequality		Poverty in America	
	Equality of Opportunity	Equality of Result	Fault of Poor	Fault of System
Business	98	1	57	9
Labor	86	4	15	56
Farm	93	2	52	19
Intellectuals	89	3	23	44
Media	96	1	21	50
Republicans	98	0	55	13
Democrats	84	8	5	68
Blacks	86	7	5	86
Feminists	84	7	9	76
Youth	87	7	16	61

SOURCE: Sidney Verba and Gary Orren, *Equality in America: The View from the Top* (Cambridge, Mass.: Harvard University Press, 1985), pp. 72, 74.

ideal. On this issue, business leaders and leaders of the Republican party take a sharply different view from that of labor leaders, black and feminist leaders, and leaders of the Democratic party. These differences in perception are also reflected in policy differences. The same study shows large differences among these groups in their views of how active a role the government should take in reducing inequality. For instance, only 14 percent of the sample of business leaders think the government should do more to reduce the income gap between rich and poor, while 82 percent of the black leaders feel this way.

These leaders differ on whether there should be more equality in America, but they agree that some inequality is acceptable. As we saw in Chapter 4, one of the major characteristics of the American economic system is that it provides for wide differences in rewards to those in different occupations. Do Americans think such differences are justified? The same set of leaders were asked what they believe people earn in various occupations and what they *ought* to earn. The various leadership groups agreed that the top executive of a major corporation probably earns about 30 times as much as an unskilled elevator operator. When asked whether that gap is proper, business leaders say, "Yes, a reward 30 times as great is about right." Leaders of labor unions, black leaders, and leaders of feminist organizations say, "No, such an income gap is too large." Yet even they do not believe that the executive and the elevator operator ought to earn the same amount. They feel that the executive ought to earn about 11 to 15 times as much as the unskilled elevator operator. They would reduce the gap but still leave a substantial one.

These are views of the nation's elite. The public agrees. They support the private business system in America by 9 to 1 and (in 1978) they opposed the idea of setting a top limit of $100,000 on incomes by 8 to 1.

In sum, there is a broad philosophical consensus in America on the ideal of equality. Equality means the right of each individual to do the best that he or she can. This consensus fades, however, when it comes to the question of the extent to which the American system in fact lives up to this ideal and the question of how active the government should be in trying to reduce inequality. The agreement on an abstract ideal does not prevent political controversy over the extent to which that ideal is matched by reality.

We have discussed two major components of American political beliefs, legitimacy and equality. We have seen that in each case there is very broad commitment to the general value but considerable disagreement about many of the particulars. If we turn to other types of political concern, we find a very similar pattern. For example, in early 1985 more than three-fourths of the people thought the federal budget was too big and favored cutting government spending. Yet a majority of these same people opposed cuts in 8 out of 10 specific program areas.

It may seem inconsistent for people to hold such opinions simultaneously. But studies of public opinion have found that in fact most Americans quite comfortably express views that to an outside observer seem mutually contradictory. Is it consistent to urge that the American government should intervene in the Middle East but not in Central America? Or that we should ban abortion but restore capital punishment? Or increase the defense budget in order to improve the chances of obtaining international disarmament? Consistency among public policies is often a tricky matter to determine, and vigorous arguments are common.

The point to be stressed is that people can and do hold many different combinations of views. This fact takes on special importance because in the media, in the classroom, and in political campaigns we engage in a great deal of labeling. In particular, we often call both individuals and specific policy viewpoints *liberal* or *conservative.* Since the Roosevelt New Deal of the 1930s the term *liberal* has generally been used to identify programs and candidates urging greater involvement by the federal government. Conservatives, by contrast, have called for less government regulation of the economy and less federal spending. But in recent years people who call themselves conservatives have generally favored a bigger defense budget, a more interventionist foreign policy, and more active government control of what is sold in book stores or broadcast on television.

Generally, those who are politically most active do hold more consistent sets of opinions. Their views may fall short of full-blown ideologies, intricately interconnected beliefs that cohere in a broad system of thought encompassing the full range of life's problems. Nevertheless, among the activists, a category that includes political officeholders, of course, as well as commentators and critics, the broad political labels mean something, and at least in a general way their debates will reflect those ideological positions. Among the mass of voters, however, such consistency of thought is relatively rare. Many people are unable even to define liberal or conservative, and even politicians often refer to themselves as conservative on some issues, like spending, and liberal on others, such as civil rights. Much American public opinion is ad hoc, shifting with circumstances and responding to initiatives of the nation's leaders. This can often be frustrating to ideological purists, who sometimes seem to regard any political opinion that does not conform to their particular "true faith" as heretical, even sinful. But the American electorate does not generally respond favorably to, or vote for, such purists. The voters are too diverse in their views, and successful political leaders must learn to cope with that diversity.

WHERE DO POLITICAL ATTITUDES COME FROM?

Political Socialization

Basic beliefs are formed early in life. This is true for basic religious beliefs. We usually learn them in the family. It is true for basic political beliefs as well. Charles, whom we quoted at the beginning of the chapter, had some quite well-formed political beliefs at age 11. **Political socialization** is the term given to the process by which young people learn basic political beliefs. This process takes place primarily in the family and in the school.

Learning legitimacy   As we have shown, a crucial political belief is that the political system is legitimate. Such basic beliefs begin to be formed quite early in life. In elementary school, children learn to prefer the American flag over other flags. As early as kindergarten, children already show a preference for the stars and stripes. It is after symbolic attachment to the political system has been formed that children begin to give some content to their beliefs. During the elementary school years children come to identify America with the rules of the democratic game—with "freedom" or the "right to vote." At the same time, they learn what it means to be a "good citizen." They come to identify a good citizen with political responsibilities: voting, keeping informed, and the like.

The president plays an important role in the political socialization of children. Children first personalize the government; it is identified with the president. The president is, as Charles illustrated, first seen as an idealized figure. Young children think of the president as similar to their fathers, as wise and supportive. Only later do they develop a more precise and realistic understanding of what the president actually does.

The sequence by which children learn about political life is important. They are first exposed to the symbols of government—the flag, the president, and so forth. This creates a solidly supportive attitude toward the political system long before there is much understanding of how that system works and what it produces in the way of policies. This support is the kind of cultural commitment that we discussed earlier: a belief in the legitimacy of the government over and above any calculation of whether it is acting in the individual's interest.

During the Watergate crisis of the mid-1970s, children's idealized view of the presidency was somewhat tarnished. Even young children ceased to have as high a view of the office. Some observers wonder whether the Watergate generation—that is, those who were in elementary school at the time—will have a less positive and trusting view of politics throughout life. Though there is much talk about the cynicism of youth, there is, as yet, little evidence of clear generational differences in trust in the government.

Learning to participate   Children learn other political lessons early in life. In the home and at school they have their first exposure to authority, to parents and teachers. There is some evidence that they generalize from what they see in the home and school to the larger political world. Participation in high school politics and extracurricular activities is a training ground for later political activity. Those who are active in high school are likely to be active as citizens. In any case, the child's sense of political efficacy (the belief that one can influence the government) increases dramatically during the elementary school years (see Figure 8.2).

Socialization and Later Life Experiences

The fact that children learn about politics early does not mean that learning stops then. Political beliefs are affected by experiences throughout life. There is a major reason why political learning continues during adult life. As a child, one might learn general beliefs—faith in government, a sense of political efficacy, and so forth—that carry over to adulthood. But a child cannot learn specific views on specific issues of the future. For instance, one cannot learn as a child which candidate to support in an

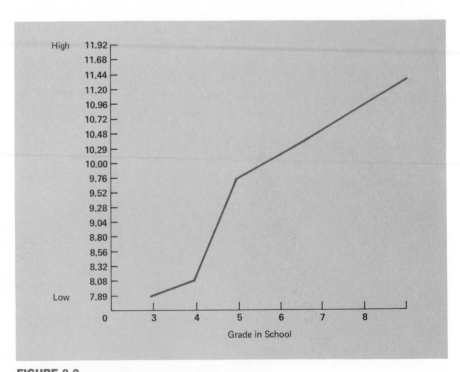

FIGURE 8.2

Average Scores on a Political Efficacy Scale

SOURCE: Robert D. Hess and Judith V. Torney, *The Development of Political Attitudes in Children* (Chicago: Aldine, 1967), p. 69.

election occurring years later or what position to take on an issue like the tax reforms debated in 1986. The candidates and issues will have changed by the time one has become an adult. Much of what one learns as a child about candidates or issues will be irrelevant.

Certain political attitudes are likely to be relatively stable, however, even while others change in the face of events. The data on distrust of government suggest that people are more likely to change their view and come to think that the government is run inefficiently or that particular political leaders are not to be trusted than they are to reject the basic rules of democracy. On some political issues, citizens have fairly firm and stable views; on others, they have uncertain or shallow opinions that can change from moment to moment. Which views are firm and stable and which are changeable, of course, varies from citizen to citizen, depending on what issues they care about. In general, however, some types of political attitudes are likely to be more strongly held than others.

Political scientists have studied the stability of political attitudes. How likely is it that an individual will take the same position on some issue if asked about it twice over a period of several years? They find that when it comes to certain moral issues—for example, abortion or the legalization of marijuana—there is a great deal of stability. In contrast, on many issues of foreign policy, people have less firm and stable views. Domestic economic issues and civil rights issues fall somewhere in between. The data suggest that the impact of early socialization in the family is likely to be stronger and more durable in relation to issues of morality than in relation to public issues such as foreign policy. Attitudes on the latter are more the result of what one sees, hears, and learns as an adult.

Other Sources of Political Attitudes

What does shape the attitudes of adults on political issues? When individuals are faced by a political issue—a policy controversy or a decision on how to vote—they are likely to seek guidance. How do we form our opinions on political issues? How do we know what is right or wrong? Citizens usually have no direct information about many issues: What is really going on in Central America? Who is to blame for inflation? When we cannot test our opinions against reality, we test them against the opinions of others. We learn from others around us.

Who are these "others" who help shape opinions? They include peers, political authorities such as the president or the Supreme Court, the political party, and the mass media.

Peers Studies have shown that groups of individuals who are in contact with one another are likely to have similar opinions. This is particularly true of what are called *primary groups*—friends, families, neighbors, and others who come into face-to-face contact. In part, the opinions of members of such groups are similar because they are in similar real circumstances. Members of primary groups tend to have similar occupations, to live near one another, and so forth. Thus they may face similar political and social problems.

In addition, individuals may change their opinions to fit those that are dominant in the groups to which they belong. This becomes a way

Many of our political beliefs are shaped in school and in conversation with our peers.

of increasing their acceptance by such groups, reduces tensions with friends and relatives, and gives them some sense that their views are right, since others agree with their opinions. When this happens, of course, the opinions that result are not based directly on consideration of the issues or on the merits of a candidate; rather, they are derived from social forces within the group and the individual's desire to be socially accepted. On the other hand, under certain circumstances, this may be a reasonable way to form a political opinion. If one cannot afford the time and effort to find out all the information on an issue, the opinions of one's associates are perhaps as good a guide as any to political beliefs.

Many groups have in them what have been labeled **opinion leaders,** who follow the news more closely, are more outspoken, and are usually better informed. Their judgments then help others to form opinions. Since members of your own face-to-face group are likely to have similar interests, one might do worse than follow opinion leaders. They may share your interests and know more about how they are best served.

Political authorities   One can also turn for guidance in political uncertainty to leading political authorities. The Supreme Court is one such authority. If it has taken a position on an issue, many Americans feel that it must be the right one. This is so for several reasons. One is that the Supreme Court has traditionally been seen as above partisan politics. Another is that the Supreme Court has the ultimate authority to interpret what is constitutional and what is not. In a nation where the Constitution is the highest political symbol, such authority gives the Court a special position.

This does not mean that the court is beyond criticism. In recent decades, the Supreme Court has been dealing with very controversial issues. Many people have denounced the Court for one decision or another. Nevertheless, it still stands as a symbol of law and the Constitution, an important guide to citizens as to what is right and what is wrong.

Another such figure is the president. The president differs from the Supreme Court as a guide for public opinion. The president expresses only one opinion and represents one political party, while the Supreme Court is a nonpartisan institution on which there may be several different opinions. The president is well covered by the news media, so that presidential views are widely known and usually respected. This is particularly true on issues that are "distant" from the average American, such as foreign policy.

During the Vietnam War, for instance, observers noticed an interesting fact. Over time, popular support for the war declined. Polls showed a steady drop in the number of people who thought the president was doing a good job with Vietnam. However, whenever the president did something dramatic—increasing the bombing or stopping the bombing, taking a new hard line or a softer line—the portion of the population who approved of his activities went up, only to fall again shortly. The increase in support for the president after making a dramatic announcement was due largely to the importance of the presidency in the public mind and the willingness of the people to be guided by the president in matters that they did not understand.

The phenomenon was not limited to Vietnam. Most presidents have seen their support go up at the time of a foreign policy crisis. Jimmy Carter's popularity fell during his term of office. Carter's popularity rose after the Camp David summit conference on the Middle East, however, and again after the seizure of American hostages in Iran during November 1979 (see Figure 8.3).

As we have seen, citizen attitudes on foreign policy are more easily changed than are those on domestic issues. Thus the president cannot sway the public as easily on matters such as civil rights, the economy, and moral issues. In addition, the Watergate scandal and the resignation of President Nixon probably made citizens less likely to defer to the president as an authority figure. However, the president will continue to hold a major role as a source of political beliefs. No other figure gets as much attention from the public.

The political party   Party identification has been a major source of political opinions. It is often transmitted from generation to generation. Children take on the partisan identification of their parents, and that identification serves as a guide to later political behavior. The importance of party identification has faded in recent years, as we will see in Chapter 11. Nevertheless, it remains an important guide on many issues. Issues are often complicated, and they change over time. Furthermore, a candidate's position on an issue may be unclear. It is therefore understandable that many citizens use their party as a guide to political opinion. The party is a handy anchor for political beliefs in a rapidly changing world.

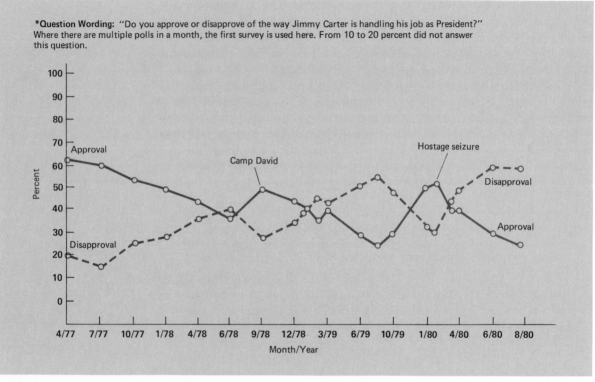

*Question Wording: "Do you approve or disapprove of the way Jimmy Carter is handling his job as President?" Where there are multiple polls in a month, the first survey is used here. From 10 to 20 percent did not answer this question.

FIGURE 8.3
The Public's Rating of President Carter
SOURCE: CBS News and CBS News/New York Times polls.

The mass media   Citizens also learn about the political world through the mass media: television, newspapers, and magazines. By far the major source of information for the average American is television news. More Americans are exposed to the political world through the evening news than through any other medium.

The news media vary in how broad a segment of American society they reach. Television reaches into almost every home. The network evening news is watched by people from all walks of life. Newspapers are read widely, but the educated and politically involved citizens are more likely to read news about national and international affairs than those who are less well educated or less politically involved. Newspapers differ from television in a crucial way. It is easier to be selective in reading the news in a newspaper than in watching the news on television. The newspaper reader who has little political interest can easily skip to the sports page with hardly a glance at the political news. In contrast, the TV viewer must sit through the political news before the sports news comes on. For this reason, television news reaches many people who were previously uninvolved in politics.

Certain key national newspapers play a special role. The *New York Times,* *Washington Post,* and *Wall Street Journal,* plus national news magazines such as *Time* and *Newsweek,* are followed closely by political leaders and others who are politically active. They have a political influence far beyond their circulation. In addition, magazines that express political opinions play an important role. Such magazines as the *New Republic* or *National Review*, as well as specialized journals such as *The Public Interest* or *Foreign Affairs*, are read by a very select audience of involved and influential people.

The fact that the various media reach different audiences means that the bulk of the American public receives a much more limited and more homogeneous set of messages than citizens who are more politically concerned. Television news offers little variety and little depth. News magazines offer greater depth and a richer variety of news.

We will examine the role of the mass media in greater depth in Chapter 12. Here we will make one other point. In recent years, investigative reporting has become a major media activity, stimulated, no doubt, by the success of Carl Bernstein and Bob Woodward in their investigation of the Watergate scandal for the *Washington Post,* later published as *All The President's Men.* [8] Such reporting has as its goal the revelation of government corruption, inefficiency, or bias. This reinforces the view among many government officials that the media are opposed to them.

The media, in turn, do not take on investigative reporting simply in order to push a particular political point of view. They do it because they feel it is their job to expose the shortcomings of government. As one reporter put it, he was a Democrat under Republican administration, and a Republican under the Democrats. Exposures are also good business. Bad news is more interesting than good news. In the competition to gain readers and viewers, the media often stress the negative. Indeed, one analyst of the media claims that a good deal of the decline in trust results from its greater exposure to politics through the medium of the evening TV news.

CURRENTS AND CROSSCURRENTS

In this chapter, we have been looking at the American public in rather broad terms, and one may get the impression that all Americans are the same. That is not the message we wish to convey. Indeed, when we look more closely at American opinion, what seems at first glance like consensus, say, on democratic values, appears on closer study to represent a much greater variety of opinion. All, or at least most, Americans agree with the general principles of democracy, but when it comes to specific cases, the portion supporting these principles falls to one-third, one-half, or two-thirds, depending on the groups we are talking about. Figures such as one-third or one-half taking a particular position indicate just the opposite of consensus. They indicate quite a bit of disagreement.

Social Bases of Political Beliefs

So far, we have not asked which groups disagree with which in American society. This is, of course, one of the main questions that may be asked about politics in any society: What groups of the population are opposed

---

[8] New York: Simon & Shuster, 1974.

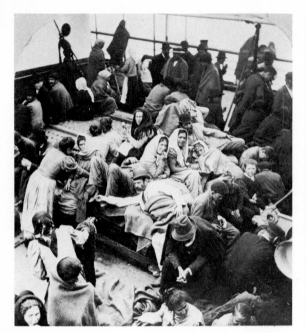

Nearly all Americans are immigrants or descended from immigrants. The ethnic diversity of the population continues to expand as Haitian refugees and other groups arrive.

to one another or, in other words, what are the social bases of conflicting political beliefs? In the United States there are many such bases. People who live in different regions, people with different occupations, and people of different races, ages, religions, or ethnic origins may well have different political views. This theme is so important that we will devote part of the next chapter to it. The struggle among opposing groups and the problem of which groups are more powerful go to the heart of American politics. Here we want to glance at some of the different viewpoints of such groups in terms of the underlying set of American political values.

There are, as we have just suggested, many ways to divide up the American population—into northerners and southerners, men and women, young and old, rich and poor, black and white—that is, by region, sex, age, income, or race, as well as many other ways. Each such division of the population would reveal some interesting differences in political beliefs that we have been discussing in this chapter—basic commitment to political freedoms, sense of ability to influence the government, basic trust in the government, and basic sense of obligation to participate in politics. Some of these divisions of the population would reveal little difference in overall attitudes, however. For example, although there are some differences, inhabitants of different regions are no longer greatly at odds with each other on most issues. Men and women do not differ very much on basic political principles, nor do young and old.

The division of the population that makes the most difference in attitude on these matters is between the better educated on the one hand and the less well educated on the other. We have already seen that commitment to democratic values is strongest among political activists and leaders of organizations. This is so, probably, because such commitment is most often found among people with more education, and such people are also likely to be the political activists and the organization leaders. As one student of political socialization has put it, "There is a mountain of evidence showing that in adult population education ordinarily bears a strong relation to . . . democratic values."[9]

The model of the democratic citizen—a person who is committed to the values of democracy, with a strong sense of obligation to participate, and with well-thought-out and consistent political views—does not fit the American population very well, but it fits the educated part best. Americans are much more likely than citizens of other countries to believe that citizens should be active in their local communities—an important part of the democratic model. Only one-third of the citizens who have a primary education feel such an obligation, however, in contrast with two-thirds of those with a college education. Similarly, with regard to the ability to influence the government, citizens were asked whether they could do anything about an unjust or corrupt public official; among those with only a grade school education, 35 percent said yes, while among the college educated, 71 percent said yes.[10]

Suppose we turn from the average white middle-class American to those who have generally been deprived of the full benefits of citizenship and of the full opportunity to participate in political life—the blacks, the Chicanos, the Appalachian poor. What are their political attitudes? Detailed data are hard to get for some deprived minority groups, but what we know confirms that they only partly share the outlook of the average white American.

In some ways, black and white Americans have similar political attitudes. When it comes to some general views about the American political system, we do not find as much difference as we might expect. Yet when asked about how the workings of the government affect them, blacks respond much more negatively than whites.

Consider the kind of treatment citizens expect from officials of the government. A study of political attitudes found that Americans were much more likely to expect equal treatment in a government office than citizens in most other nations. Table 8.7 shows how different the attitude of the average American is from that of the citizen of, say, Italy or Mexico. The American has much more trust in government agencies. Indeed, the percentages expecting equal treatment are so different that the authors of this study suggest that citizens in the United States and in Mexico live in

[9] M. Kent Jennings, "Comment on Richard Merelman's 'Democratic Politics and the Culture of American Education,' " *American Political Science Review* 74 (1980): 333.

[10] U.S. Senate Subcommittee on Intergovernmental Operations, Committee on Government Operations, *Confidence and Concern: Citizens View Their Government* (Washington: USGPO, 1973).

TABLE 8.7

ATTITUDES REGARDING EQUAL TREATMENT IN GOVERNMENT OFFICES IN FIVE NATIONS

	United States	Great Britain	Germany	Italy	Mexico
Percent saying they expect equal treatment in a government office	83%	83%	65%	53%	42%

SOURCE: Based on data from Gabriel Almond and Sidney Verba, *The Civil Culture: Political Attitudes and Democracy in Five Nations* (Princeton, N.J.: Princeton University Press, 1963). Copyright © 1963 by Princeton University Press. Reprinted by permission of Princeton University Press.

different political worlds. The vast majority of Americans expect fair treatment. Mexicans are much less likely to have such expectations.

The average black American also lives in a different world from that experienced by the average white American. Almost 90 percent of white Americans expect equal treatment from the government; a little less than half of the blacks have such expectations. These differences between blacks and whites, first noted in 1959, have appeared again and again in more recent studies. Most dramatic are the differences between the races in attitudes toward the police. Urban blacks have less confidence in the honesty of the police, less favorable expectations of fair treatment by them, and less favorable experiences in dealing with them. Furthermore, blacks are less satisfied with public services in their neighborhood. They complain more about high prices and the quality of the goods in neighborhood stores.

In sum, when it comes to their actual lives and their relations with the government, blacks differ sharply from whites in attitude. Furthermore, many of the distinctive characteristics of black attitudes appear early in life. Black school children are more likely to be skeptical about the government, less likely to see the president as a benign figure, and less likely to believe in the equality of all Americans.

Racial Hostility

Have blacks and whites become more hostile to each other over the years? Certainly someone comparing the newspapers of 1950 with those of 1985 might conclude that hostility had grown. Thirty or forty years ago, one read little about racial issues in the papers; today hardly a day goes by without some news of racial conflict. However, this is merely to say that racial differences have come into the open. It does not mean that bitter race hatred has recently developed.

Over the years white attitudes toward blacks have undergone striking, but somewhat ambivalent, changes. In general, whites have become more favorable toward blacks, more responsive to their demands. In 1949 the National Opinion Research Center asked people whether "Negroes were as intelligent as whites." At that time only 42 percent of whites thought so. By 1956 the percentage had risen to 78, where it has stabilized. In 1942 only 30 percent of white Americans said that white and black children should go to the same schools. By 1956 (shortly after the Supreme Court decision in *Brown* v. *Board of Education*) the percentage had risen to 48 percent, and by 1968 to 60 percent. By 1984, 90 percent of white Americans favored desegregated schools. The same is true of attitudes toward integration of housing. From 1942 to 1976 the percentage of whites who would not object to integration of housing rose from 35 percent to over 80 percent. The era of more open racial conflict was also one in which white attitudes toward blacks improved a lot.

There are several qualifications to this generalization. For one thing, as the data indicate, a considerable number of whites still oppose integration. Furthermore, white support for the goals of blacks has been accompanied by a general and growing rejection of militant tactics. Whites have generally rejected direct action by black groups, even when it is peaceful and fully within the law. Thus the Harris poll found that 80 percent of black Americans favored Martin Luther King's 1963 Poor People's March on Washington—a massive, peaceful rally at the Lincoln Memorial—whereas only 29 percent of whites did. Since about 1972 the liberalizing trend of white attitudes has slowed down, and there is even some evidence of a reversal. Whites seem to have accepted the goals of blacks, but many feel that perhaps blacks are "pushing too hard."

The data on political differences between blacks and whites suggest both the basis for continuing conflict and some hope for cooperative progress. The progress could be based on the general commitment of the two groups to the democratic process. It could also be based on the reduction in overt racial antagonism between blacks and whites and on greater acceptance by whites of black goals.

The danger of continuing conflict lies in the greater differences between the races when one gets down to specifics. Blacks may trust the system in general, but they have less confidence in government officials. Whites may accept black goals, but are more hesitant about specific aspects of those goals, are opposed to pressure from blacks to achieve those goals, and have begun to feel that "things are moving too fast."[11]

What about extremist political beliefs that there is a need for fundamental change in the American system? We must distinguish two types of extremism. One type is that associated with particular issues. Groups may take extremist positions—radically to the left or radically to the right—on specific subjects. An extremist position would be one that few other Americans share. An extreme left economic position might be in favor of nationalizing all industry; an extreme right economic position might be the abolition of the income tax.

There are many extremist groups in America who argue for this, that, or the other fundamental change. Historically, they have had little success, and most are quite small. This is not because such views are suppressed, even though those who hold them often risk social ostracism and, at times, political repression; rather, there are tendencies in American politics that

---

[11] John G. Condran, "Changes in White Attitudes Toward Blacks: 1963–1977," *Public Opinion Quarterly* 43 (1979), pp. 463–476.

take away many of the issues around which radical politics might be organized. If an issue begins to attract substantial public support, one of the two major political parties is likely to "steal the thunder" of such groups by adopting this position.

There is a second type of extremism: groups with extremist attitudes toward the democratic process itself, who think decisions should be made by some other rules. Such attitudes can be held by those at either end of the political spectrum. Democratic procedures may be rejected by those who see them as blocking rapid social change. They might argue, "Problems such as war, pollution, the cities, poverty, racism are too great to be dealt with through the 'system.'" Or the rules of democracy may be rejected by those who see such rules as the cause of violence and decay in our society. "We have too much freedom of speech," they might say. "We cannot tolerate the political views of those who would destroy the system and challenge the American way of life."

In fact, few groups take such a position. As we have seen, the commitment to the rules of democratic procedure (at least on the general level) is so widespread that it is embraced even by those who are deeply dissatisfied with the operation of that system. For a time young voters were considerably more critical of political institutions in America than was the population as a whole. A 1972 poll asked young adults about American democracy. About 6 out of 10 thought the country was democratic in name only and was run by special interests. Yet even then, in the aftermath of Watergate, Vietnam, riots, and assassinations, only 18 percent thought the system was inflexible and needed radical change. Sixty-two percent thought political parties needed major change, but only 12 percent thought the Constitution did.[12] Only by the 1980s young Americans had returned to a more fully supportive position, holding much the same views as other age groups.

Many of the more radical criticisms of American politics come not from people who would prefer other rules but from people who see the rules working poorly and would prefer to see more effective democracy in the United States. These would include those who want more real participation in the political process or greater power in the hands of local government. Direct criticism of the rules—for instance, rejection of elections or free speech—comes less from the belief that such rules are bad per se than from the belief that these rules have resulted in a poor performance on some issue.

DOES PUBLIC OPINION MAKE A DIFFERENCE?

We have looked at American attitudes toward government in general and toward some specific issues, such as race, but a major question has not yet been answered. What difference, if any, does public opinion make? Does it shape government programs, or do officials pay it lip service and largely ignore it?

---

[12] Daniel Yankelovich, *The New Morality: A Profile of American Youth in the 1970s* (New York: McGraw-Hill, 1973), p. 116.

When the **public-opinion poll** was originated in the 1930s, some thought it would be a great thing for democracy. Officials in Washington could now get an accurate idea of the feelings of the American people on the important issues of the day. Policy could really follow the views of citizens. An accurate poll could tell what the American people thought of unemployment insurance, defense spending, or farm supports. At the same time, other observers expressed concern. Polls would cause trouble. The public was too ill-informed, too fickle, and too irrational to guide public policy. Good policy requires careful study and thought, which is possible only if officials are protected from the day-to-day opinions of the majority. Actually, the public-opinion poll has never been used to set government policy, as the optimists hoped and the pessimists feared. Polling and pollsters have become important features of our political system, however, and public opinion has its effects largely through the reports the polls provide.

Two somewhat contradictory points can be made about the impact of public opinion on government leaders. One is that most officials, especially elected ones, pay great attention to the public-opinion polls, mail, and all sorts of indicators of public opinion. Not only do politicians follow Gallup, Harris, and other national polls, they also have special polls taken for themselves to find out public opinion on a particular issue. Furthermore, political leaders believe that public opinion is important and should be followed—at least up to a point. On the other hand, policy is rarely made directly on the basis of what the polls say. Why is this the case?

Public Opinion Does Not Always Become Public Policy

One might imagine that if the polls showed that the majority favored a particular position, that position would sooner or later become law, but it often does not. In 1972, for example, the Harris poll asked a sample of Americans whether there should be a strict federal law requiring that handguns be registered. Seventy percent said yes, but no such law has been passed. One might answer that such things take time. If the public continues to feel that way, a law is likely to be passed. However, in one of the earliest public-opinion polls, conducted in 1940, the Gallup poll asked an almost identical question. At that time, 79 percent favored a gun-control law.

How can the public overwhelmingly favor a particular piece of legislation for over 45 years and yet have no response from Congress? The answer is simply that most people in the large majority that favors gun control do not feel very strongly about it, while the minority that opposes gun control does feel strongly on the matter and, reinforced by the vigorous efforts of the National Rifle Association, is active in support of their position.

The example of gun control teaches an important lesson. A small, intense minority is often more effective than a large majority that is not as concerned with the problem. This fact is so central to American politics that it will be a theme of the next chapter. When we vote for candidates in an election, each vote counts the same no matter how strong or indifferent the voter's views. On policy questions, however, the level and quality of one's opinion as well as the intensity of feeling and the resources one is prepared to invest in trying to influence the policy result all make a difference. Until all of these factors can be taken adequately into account, it will be difficult to predict when an opinion poll result will be reflected in a policy decision.

Public Opinion Tends to React to, Not Guide, Current Policy

The public official who is trying to choose a policy does worry about the public and usually tries to keep informed about its attitudes. On many issues, however, the public is ill-informed, and its policy preferences are often unclear. We have seen evidence of this. Officials also know that if they do badly, the public may react negatively. They worry much about how the public will react to policy failure. Public reactions and public-opinion polls tell them much less about what policy to pursue in the future. They do often learn what troubles they are likely to face at the next election if they do not deal with certain problems. The public will not tell a political leader how to deal with inflation but will let the leader know if prices are too high.

The history of public attitudes toward the Vietnam War illustrates this point. No war has ever aroused as much public concern and disapproval. From the time the war first became a leading public issue, around 1964 and 1965, the portion of the American people who were satisfied with government policy went steadily downward. The low point was reached around the time of President Johnson's March 1968 decision not to run for office again. Public unhappiness with the war certainly had much to do with that decision.

Public opinion was a far from adequate guide for specific policy, however. When pollsters asked citizens for their preference on the war—Should we escalate to win, deescalate and get out, or keep up our present policy?—they typically found the public divided among the three positions. How could a president follow that lead? Furthermore, the public seemed to be pleased whenever the president did anything—increased our military commitment or decreased it—as long as something different was done. The pleasure ended as soon as it became clear that the new move was not going to end the war. The conclusion was obvious. The public was unhappy and wanted results. Political leaders had to pay attention to that unhappiness or they would lose in the next election, as the Democratic party learned in 1968. What the public wanted done was less clear. The administrations involved, the Johnson and Nixon administrations, were under public pressure to do something, but there was not public consensus regarding the specific actions to take.

Limits to Public Tolerance

There is another way of looking at the role of public opinion in the policy process. This involves recognizing that public opinion sets certain limits to acceptable policy. There are some things the public will not stand for. Yet, even when tolerance sets some outer boundaries to what is acceptable policy, the guidance is seldom clear. One reason is that one can never tell what those boundaries are from the answers to the questions asked in public-opinion polls. Political leaders do not know the limits to public tolerance in advance; they may have to test the public to find out.

An example will make the point and teach us some important lessons about public opinion. For many years, observers claimed that the American public set definite limits to foreign policy. The public, we were told, would not tolerate an administration that recognized the People's Republic of China or allowed it to join the United Nations. Students of foreign policy often complained that this public stand kept American political leaders from establishing better relations with China. Indeed, public-opinion polls over the years showed that a large majority of the American public was against recognition of China.

When President Nixon made his historic trip to China during 1972, however, the Harris poll found that 73 percent of the people approved. The notion that public opinion stood in the way of better relations with China was probably a myth. Government policy toward China did not reflect public attitudes; rather, public attitudes reflected government policy. Change the policy, and the attitudes change. Political leadership plays a major role in shaping public opinion.

The case of China may exaggerate the changeability of public opinion and the real flexibility it gives to leaders. Such flexibility is probably greater in foreign affairs, about which most citizens do not have firmly fixed opinions. On issues closer to home, the limits set by public opinion may be more rigid. Attitudes on racial matters are less easily manipulated, and the threat of electoral punishment by an unhappy public on such an issue may be more real to an elected offical than the supposed threat of public disapproval of a new China policy. Public attitudes on such matters may have a strong effect on leadership. Even in these areas, however, where public opinion seems firmer, one can never be sure how much it might be altered by strong opinion leaders. As we have seen, public support for integrated schools showed a large increase after the Supreme Court declared segregated schools unconstitutional.

A Nation of Many Publics

We can end our discussion of the impact of the public on government policy by making one major point: In most cases, one should not think of the public as a single entity. There are many publics. There are the citizens who are inactive in politics, and those who are active. There are those who are uninterested in political matters, and a smaller number who are interested. There are, above all, differences in what it is that interests citizens. Different citizens are concerned about and active on different sets of problems. This is important in understanding how the attitudes of the public affect government policy. Political leaders are likely to be responsive to certain parts of the public, especially those that are active on a particular issue. Rather than asking about the impact of public opinion as a whole, therefore, we have to ask about the impact of the special publics involved. We turn to this topic in the next chapter.

PUBLIC OPINION: HOW DO WE FIND OUT ABOUT IT?

Throughout this book we present information about the attitudes and behavior of the American people. We look at their political beliefs, the ways

POLLING PLACE
選舉站
LUGAR DE VOTACION

PRECINCT
選舉區
PRECINTO   *6697*

 Electioneering is Not
Permitted Within 100
Feet of Voting Place

嚴禁在選舉站一
百英呎之內進行拉票活動。

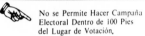 No se Permite Hacer Campaña
Electoral Dentro de 100 Pies
del Lugar de Votación.

America is a multicultural society, and some groups do not speak much English. In order for them to exercise their rights as citizens, official documents must sometimes employ several languages.

they act politically, how they vote, and how they decide to vote the way they do. How do we find out about the American public?

Each of us may often think we know how the American public feels about things. In a sense we have a right to think so. For one thing, each of us is a member of the American public, so our own views are part of public opinion. For another, we talk to many other people who are also members of the public; we read newspapers, where we see reports of public attitudes or letters to the editor; and we watch television. But for several reasons such information—based on observation of the world around us—can often be wrong, sometimes seriously wrong.

First of all, we often look at our own views and assume that other people share them. This is not a safe assumption. People have widely differing views on political issues and react to political events in varied ways.

Sometimes we feel that we learn more about public opinion by talking to our friends, neighbors, or fellow workers. Such conversations are likely to give us distorted views of public opinion, since most of us meet only certain kinds of people.

An example is the college campus. During the late 1960s students on some campuses, noticing that there was a great deal of activity against the Vietnam War, began to think that everybody under 30 was against the war and to talk of a "generation gap" between their generation, which seemed to be solidly opposed to the war, and the older generation, which was in favor of the war. If, however, one looked at the entire younger generation—students on all college and university campuses plus those who did not go to college—one found a much wider range of opinions and

How does the public-opinion pollster deal with these issues?

1. *An adequate number.* A good survery researcher will not be satisfied by talking to one, two, or a few dozen citizens. Even if they are chosen at random, they will be too few to tell us much about the general population. There is too much chance that one will accidentally find people who are very different from the rest of the public. Most good national public-opinion polls interview about 1500 people.

2. *A wide geographic spread.* It is important that the people interviewed come from a wide range of places, not just the pollster's hometown. Survey organizations conduct interviews all over the country to get a good geographic spread. A national survey will not contain a representative sample of any particular state or city. That would require a separate survey, randomly choosing people within that area.

3. *A wide range of types.* The most important thing about a sample is that it allows all types of citizens an equal chance to be interviewed. If the selection process is biased so that one type of person is eliminated, the resulting sample will not represent the population as a whole. In former years, many surveys were taken of people who happened to pass by in public places such as railroad stations. It is not difficult to see why such surveys were often inaccurate. People were omitted who did not happen to commute by railroad—homemakers, college students, elderly pensioners, automobile riders, and so on. Certain groups, such as office workers, were overrepresented, and other groups were not represented at all.

4. *A random selection.* The pollster selects; he or she does not let the respondent self-select. An important aspect of a good sample is that a pollster chooses, on the basis of statistics, who is to be interviewed. The pollster does not wait for people to volunteer. This point is important, and it is this that makes the sample survey different from the ways of finding out public opinion that are used in everyday politics.

The members of Congress who judge public opinion on the basis of letters from constituents are assuming that the opinions of those who voluntarily write are representative of the opinions of their constituents as a whole or of the public as a whole. This is probably an incorrect assumption, for letter writers usually differ in important ways from those who do not write.

The fact that the pollster talks to all kinds of people—those who do not volunteer their opinions as well as those who do—is the greatest strength as well as the greatest weakness of the public-opinion poll. The great strength of the poll is that it gets at the opinions of all citizens, whether or not they have chosen to volunteer their views. In this sense, a good survey represents all citizens—the articulate few who volunteer their views as well as the "silent majority."

This can be a source of weakness as well, however, because the pollster records the opinions of many citizens who basically have no opinions.

Often a person has not thought about a particular problem until a public-opinion pollster appears to ask about it. Rather than admitting that he or she has no opinion or does not know anything about the issue, the uninterested or uninformed person will usually give an offhand answer. Such a response is highly changeable; if the pollster returned the following day, a different answer might be given. Every sample survey contains such answers by respondents who don't really know or care about the issue. This must be borne in mind when interpreting sample survey data.

The questions used   Sometimes two different polls will come up with what seem to be different or contradictory results. When this happens, it is usually because the two polls have asked different questions. This, then, is another general principle of survey technique: the answers you get depend on the questions you ask.

Those who have worked professionally with sample surveys know how even small changes in the wording of questions can change the results. People respond to the symbols contained in questions. If you ask a question about Russia, people will respond one way. If you ask a question about Communist Russia, people will respond more negatively, simply because you have added the negative symbol "Communist." Similarly, if you asked about aid to families with dependent children, you would get a different set of answers than if you had asked about welfare or government giveaway programs.

Thus polls are quite accurate in telling you how Americans responded to a particular question. But the wording of the question always has an effect on the response. Public-opinion polls provide very useful information about the American public, but the information is valuable only if it is used carefully.

CHAPTER HIGHLIGHTS ■

1.   Americans have a fundamental commitment to the symbols of American democracy, especially the Constitution, thought their trust and confidence in specific individuals running the government have gone down.

2.   Citizens support democratic rules in the abstract, but they are less convinced that such rules as free speech should be applied to unpopular groups.

3.   Americans agree on an ideal of equality of opportunity; they disagree on how close we have come to that ideal.

4.   People learn political beliefs in school and in the family as children. Such learning goes on throughout life when beliefs are influenced by friends, neighbors, and workmates as well as by political authorities such as the president and the Supreme Court. The mass media also play an important role.

5.   Officials pay a lot of attention to public opinion, but the opinion of a small, intense minority is likely to carry more weight than a less intense majority opinion. Public opinion reacts to what officials do even more than officials react to public opinion.

PROFILE ■

ALEXIS DE TOCQUEVILLE (1805-1859)
Writer-Traveler and
Commentator on American Life

Tocqueville visited the United states for several months in 1831–1832, ostensibly to study the American prison system, at that time regarded as a model of enlightened incarceration. Tocqueville, an aristocrat, came partly to avoid trouble from France's new regime led by Louis Phillipe, but mainly to observe the American people in order to understand what he thought was likely to become the dominant force in Europe as well: egalitarian democracy. The two volumes of his *Democracy in America* were published in 1835 and 1840. The first volume concentrates on description of how American government and society function, while the second is more reflective and analytic, focusing on the impact of individualism, liberty, and equality on literature, the family, politics, and many other aspects of life.

Tocqueville was an extraordinarily acute observer. With his friend Beaumont he traveled through much of the country as far as the Mississippi River. His critique of slavery and his forecast of probable disaster resulting from the race problem were astonishingly accurate. He grasped the essentials of capitalism and the alienating effects of factory specialization on the workers before Marx had written about them. He constructed an amazingly well-balanced and complex portrait of America, "warts and all," that continues to merit a close reading.

For Tocqueville the essential features of American society were: first, equality of economic status, with some people getting rich, the rich going broke, and no fortunes accumulating to build lasting inequity; and, second, fierce individualism "rightly understood" whereby Americans staunchly defended their right to act as they pleased but in actual practice cooperated extensively to accomplish common purposes.

Tocqueville returned to France and played a significant role in public life, as well as writing a second important book on the French political experience. His grasp of what was distinctive about the United States and of both the promise and the problems of democratic societies everywhere has rarely if ever been matched. And he was only 25 years old when he was here.

SUGGESTED READINGS ■

Classic studies of American political beliefs are: Alexis de Tocqueville, *Democracy in America*, 2 vols. (1835–1840); James Bryce, *The American Commonwealth* (1893); Gunnar Myrdal, *The American Dilemma* (1943); Walter Lippman, *Public Opinion* (1922).

Modern commentaries on the subject include: Gabriel Almond and Sidney

Verba, *The Civic Culture: Political Attitudes and Democracy in Five Countries* (1963); *The Civil Culture Revisited* (1980); Robert E. Lane, *Political Ideology* (1962); Richard Dawson, Kenneth Prewitt, and Karen Dawson, *Political Socialization* (1977); Paul R. Abramson, *Political Attitudes in America* (1983); Angus Campbell et al., *The American Voter* (1960).

Survey research has enabled investigators to study public opinion in great detail.

National headquarters of the Chamber of Commerce, Washington, D.C.

Chapter **9**

INTEREST GROUPS AND POLITICAL CONFLICT

P olitics involves conflict. If everyone agreed on what government should do, there would be no need for a political process. Public officials would simply carry out the popular consensus. But people do not agree. They seek diverse and often conflicting policy goals, and they do so not simply as separate and distinct individuals but in conjunction with others who share their objectives.

There are several different organizational forms of this collaborative activity. A particularly important form in democratic systems is the political party, and we will examine American political parties in some detail in the next chapter. Labor unions and business corporations are organizations created primarily for economic purposes, but it is obvious to all that they sometimes become important political actors as well. So, too, do professional associations, religious organizations, ethnic and fraternal associations, and a host of others.

Ever since its beginning the United States has had a reputation as a nation of joiners, where it was common for specifically political purposes to be achieved by means of group organization and pressure. This long-standing American reputation for interest group politics leads us to ask a number of important questions. To what extent is America really a nation of joiners? Are interest-group politics a route of political action that is truly open to everyone? Are some potential groups left out or disadvantaged? What kinds of public policy result from a system dominated by interest groups? Are there feasible alternatives compatible with the maintenance of democratic freedoms? In this chapter we address these questions, but as we do so, we also present a considerable amount of information about contemporary patterns of group activity in American politics.

THE ASSUMPTIONS OF PLURALISM

The key word in discussions of the role of interest groups in American political life is **pluralism.** There is argument over what the word means, as well as whether, in fact, we have a pluralistic system and whether, if we do, it is adequate to our needs. These latter issues will be discussed later; first, let us identify some of the elements of a pluralistic political order.

1. Pluralism refers to a society that is heterogeneous, with many different groups divided along many different lines.
2. People with common interests are free to form organized groups to express those interests and, in fact, most politically relevant interests are expressed in this way.
3. The most appropriate way to express dissatisfaction with any aspect of the existing system is to organize a new group for that purpose.
4. Government officials will be responsive to group demands.
5. The diversity of interests in the society makes bargaining, compromise, and mutual toleration essential among the competing groups lest the process degenerate into nastier forms of politics.

Our next question is: To what extent does the United States actually meet these pluralistic conditions?

Homogeneity and Diversity in America

In Northern Ireland the religious conflict between Catholics and Protestants dominates all other differences. In South Africa the struggle between blacks and whites over *apartheid* leaves little room for any other issue. In several Western European societies class conflict between bourgeois property owners and workers has been a fundamental basis of political dispute and party formation. Ethnic minorities have been the principal building blocks of politics in many countries, from Switzerland and Belgium to India and Malaysia. All these types of conflicts are present in the United States, but no one of them dominates the others. We will look briefly at religious, race, ethnicity, and social class differences in the United States and at how these are expressed in the form of interest group organizations.

Religion   Americans are among the most religiously devout people in the world. In contrast to countries like Sweden or Britain where one denomination receives tax support but relatively few people attend church, American churches have been kept quite strictly separate from public support, but have drawn undiminished commitment from the people. Church attendance is high, and support for the central tenets of Judeo-Christian doctrine is nearly universal. At the same time there is a bewildering variety of religious sects and denominations, as Table 9.1 indicates.

Religious diversity is important politically because of two factors. First, many religious groups have had their own specific public-policy concerns. At one time, for instance, Mormons sought to defend polygamy. Catholics and some other groups have long sought public support for religious schools. Jews have urged strong U.S. support for Israel. Second, and far more significant, religious groups have been the driving forces behind many policy efforts of broader application. The campaign for national prohibition was led by Protestant church groups; so was the pre-Civil War campaign to abolish slavery. More recently, church-related groups have been major actors in conflicts as diverse as U.S. policy toward China, South Africa, and Central America; abortion, sex education, and rock music; and farm-worker organization, capital punishment, and the basic fairness of modern capitalism.

The most dramatic recent trend in religious interest group activity has been the rise to prominence of what is generally called the *religious right*. Religious fundamentalism is not new in the United States, but in recent years fundamentalist churches and ministers have made especially effective use of television and developed a large and intensely committed following. Polls have shown that only about 6 percent of the voters consider themselves part of the religious right. Nevertheless, as part of a broader resurgence of political conservatism, such "televangelists" as Jerry Falwell and Pat Robertson have become significant figures.

Church-based groups are active on the political left as well (see Table 9.2). Much of the lobbying to block American military involvement in Central America, for instance, has been done by church-related groups.

TABLE 9.1
CHURCH MEMBERSHIP IN THE UNITED STATES, 1979

Denomination	Membership
American Lutheran Church	2,362,695
Assemblies of God	958,418
Baptist General Conference	126,800
Christian and Missionary Alliance	173,986
Christian Church (Disciples of Christ)	1,213,061
Church of God (Anderson, Ind.)	175,113
Church of God (Cleveland, Tenn.)	411,385
Church of Jesus Christ of Latter-day Saints	2,706,000
Church of the Brethren	172,115
Church of the Nazarene	474,820
Cumberland Presbyterian Church	94,574
Episcopal Church	2,841,350
Evangelical Covenant Church of America	76,092
Free Methodist Church of North America	67,394
Jehovah's Witnesses	526,961
Lutheran Church in America	2,921,398
Lutheran Church—Missouri Synod	2,623,181
Mennonite Church	98,027
North American Baptist Conference	42,779
Presbyterian Church in the U.S.[a]	852,711
Reformed Church in America	348,417
Reorganized Church of Jesus Christ of Latter-Day Saints	188,580
Roman Catholic Church	49,812,178
Salvation Army	414,659
Seventh-day Adventists	553,089
Southern Baptist Convention	13,372,757
United Church of Christ	1,745,533
United Methodist Church	9,653,711
United Presbyterian Church in the U.S.A.[a]	2,477,364
Wisconsin Evangelical Lutheran Synod	404,564

[a] Now merged into one denomination.
SOURCE: Jacquet, Jr., Constant H., ed. *Yearbook of American and Canadian Churches* (Nashville: Abingdon Press, 1983).

Support for beleaguered farmers in the Midwest and efforts to enlarge public-policy support for them has also rested heavily on liberal church groups, as has much of the civil rights movement, past and present. Jesse Jackson's 1984 campaign for the Democratic presidential nomination drew on black churches as his main organizational base of support.

American churches are organizations with financial resources and personnel that can be and often are devoted to advancing public policy causes as well as those more directly a part of their religious faith. Moreover,

Founder of Moral Majority and Liberty Forum, the Reverend Jerry Falwell has sought to mobilize his fundamentalist followers for political action.

they provide opportunities to advocate causes of political action, sometimes from the pulpit itself, and so to mobilize their followers. Their enormous variety has always meant that they do not speak with a single voice, but in some parts of the country a single denomination may dominate and then the political impact of "the" church may be very substantial. In any case, American churches are active participants in the total political process.

Race America has always been a multiracial society. From the beginning there were Native Americans and blacks as well as white Europeans. Later, substantial numbers of Asians added further variety. This much is evident. Familiar, also, is the fact that for all racial groups *except* white Europeans discrimination and inequality have been massive.

Has interest-group formation and action been an effective means of achieving corrective public policy? There has been no lack of effort by racial minorities to move in exactly this way. Particularly among black Americans the use of organized interest groups to raise resources and mobilize support and to develop and pursue strategies of political action has won important victories. The civil rights movement of the 1950s and 1960s had many successes in breaking down barriers of segregation. But the

TABLE 9.2

**CHURCH-BASED GROUPS THAT GENERALLY TAKE
LIBERAL POSITIONS ON POLITICAL ISSUES**

American Baptist Churches, USA
American Ethical Union
American Friends Service Committee
American Jewish Committee
American Jewish Congress
Baptist Joint Committee on Public Affairs
B'nai B'rith International Council
B'nai B'rith Women
Christian Church (Disciples of Christ)
Christian Science Committee on Publications
Church of the Brethren
Church Women United
Church World Service and Lutheran World Relief
Episcopal Church
Friends Committee on National Legislation
Impact
Interfaith Action for Economic Justice
Jesuit Social Ministries
Lutheran Council in the USA
Maryknoll Fathers and Brothers
Mennonite Central Committee
Mennonite Immigration and Refugee Service
National Assembly of Religious Women
National Association of Evangelicals
National Conference of Catholic Charities
National Conference on Ministry to the Armed Services
National Council of the Churches of Christ in the U.S.A.
National Interreligious Board for Conscientious Objectors
Network
Presbyterian Church (U.S.A.)
Salvation Army
Seventh Day Adventist Church General Conference
Synagogue Council of America
Union of American Hebrew Congregations
Unitarian Universalist Association
United Church of Christ
United Methodist Church
United Methodist Church, National Office
United Methodist Church, Women's Division
United States Catholic Conference
Universal Fellowship of Metropolitan Community Churches
Washington Office on Africa
Washington Office on Haiti
Washington Office on Latin America

SOURCE: *National Journal,* September 14, 1985, p. 2081.

inequalities of income and opportunity that blacks and other racial minorities have suffered proved much more resistant to the strategies of group politics. Asian-Americans have made relatively little use of interest groups to secure favorable policy, and the efforts of Native Americans to follow a group-politics course of action have generally ended in disaster. The United States is certainly pluralistic in terms of race, but it does not follow that each racial group may confidently seek equal status by means of interest group organization and action.

Ethnicity   America is an extraordinarily polyglot society in terms of the ethnic origins of its people. Not only are nearly all Americans immigrants or the descendants of immigrants, but their origins lie in every part of the world. Most of the early settlers, of course, come from Great Britain and Africa, but great waves of Germans and Irish entered in the first half of the nineteenth century, to be followed by large numbers of Scandinavians, Italians, Poles, and Russians (many of whom were Jewish). More recently, the influx of Spanish-speaking people from Puerto Rico, Cuba, Mexico, and Central America has transformed the social composition of several large cities and of substantial sections of the Southwest. Hundreds of thousands of Asians have added still further variety to the mixture that is the American people.

Just exactly what constitutes an **ethnic group** is a matter of some argument. A common language is obviously one element, but as the cultural diversity among Hispanics indicates, national origin and a common culture are also important. The *political* importance of this ethnic variety shows up in several ways. First, ethnic groups constitute potential voting blocks to which political candidates may make special appeals, emphasizing their devotion to the cause of Irish independence from Britain, for example, or their support for German-language instruction in the schools. Indeed, some issues appear on the political agenda primarily because of the effort to attract ethnic group voting support. Second, political parties often try to attract ethnic group support by slating candidates with clearly recognizable ethnic identity. Polish names abound on the ballot in Chicago, for example, and an Irish moniker is still an advantage in Boston.

A third feature of ethnic politics is the periodic pressure from organized ethnic groups regarding what American foreign policy should be. What, for instance, should the United States do with respect to the island of Cyprus? A dispute over Cyprus between Greece and Turkey has raged for years. Greece and Turkey are both part of NATO, so the United States does not want to alienate either country. But there is a rather small but well-organized Greek-American community in this country and very few Turks, and so American policy tilts toward Greece more than it otherwise would. Many Americans from Eastern Europe are ardently opposed to any accommodation with the Soviet Union, feeling that to relax America's Cold War posture would be a betrayal of the hopes of Hungary, Poland, Estonia, and other so-called captive nations. The pressure of the American Jewish community for aid to Israel is of obvious importance in shaping

Successful candidates for political office must recognize the extraordinary diversity in the ethnic backgrounds of American voters.

our foreign policy. The Arab-American community cannot hope to muster comparable strength. American foreign policy is affected by many factors, of course, but ethnic group politics plays a significant part and has done so for much of our history.

Social class   Compared with citizens in most western democracies, Americans do not think of themselves as firmly and permanently located in a particular class. They do not define their social world or their political values in terms of whether they are in the working class or the middle class. Income level and type of job have some effect on how we vote, of course, but for many Americans they are not the dominant basis of attitudes and behavior, and so social-class factors have not been the dominant basis of political conflict either.

Are there interests in common among the working class, those who are wage earners or have low incomes as compared with the salaried and better-off middle class? Full-employment policies, more extensive public education, welfare, and services, and laws facilitating labor organization and bargaining power might be among the goals widely shared among the working class. But despite the persistence of poverty, many American workers enjoy a decent standard of living. Moreover, they believe that opportunities exist for better income and upward social mobility for themselves and their children. They can do it as individuals, they feel, so they do not need to work through a broad class movement.

To say that the working class has generally accepted the American dream of individualistic success is to say that they lack **class consciousness.** That is, they do not assume that the interests of workers and managers or owners are fundamentally opposed and that therefore the only way for workers to better their lot is to stick together.

Class consciousness has been weakened by a number of special characteristics of American history. The United States does not have a feudal past. We have never had the rigid social structure of Europe, where people were born into a particular social class, clearly distinct in its way of life from other classes, and were destined to remain there for life. Social boundaries were always more fluid in America. The exception is black Americans, but for them race is more important politically than class. Workers did not see the middle class as occupying an unassailable enemy territory; rather, they saw it as a group that they could aspire to join.

The class consciousness of American workers was weakened further by the existence of other identifications that divide the working class. American workers come from different ethnic backgrounds. Some are black, and some are white. They live in different settings, and they have different religious faiths. These characteristics have often been more important to them than their class identification.

A further reason class consciousness has not dominated American politics is that our organizational systems have not been class-based. The most important organizations for class politics are political parties and labor unions. In Europe, socialist unions support the political activities of socialist parties. In the United States, the major political parties have not depended on one class for support; they have been multiclass parties. The fact that the American parties antedate the growth of the American working class is important. When America industrialized during the nineteenth century, there already existed a political-party structure—particularly the Democratic party in the major industrial cities—that was anxious to obtain the support of the working class. There was no need for workers to form their own party; instead, they were welcomed into the existing parties. This provided an organization for the American working class, but not one that was exclusively theirs. Workers were not isolated from other groups.

Furthermore, for many years unions in America did not concentrate their efforts on political activity. Rather, under the leadership of Samuel Gompers, head of the American Federation of Labor (AFL) from 1886 to 1924, they focused on improving the economic condition of American workers, particularly skilled craft workers. Unions in America never fostered a sense of class consciousness among American workers. The result is that workers are diverse in their political values and loyalties, and this fact, in turn, helps reinforce the pluralism of American politics.

A Nation of Joiners?

There is no doubt that the United States is a land of organizational abundance. The telephone book lists an enormous number and variety of groups we can join, and almost any newspaper account of a political, social, economic, or professional controversy will mention the involvement of organized groups. Nevertheless, there are several serious questions that must be asked regarding this "interest-group universe." Do all Americans belong to organizations? Is organized cooperation the best way to affect public policy? Is it a feasible strategy for everyone? Or does the interest group system give consistent political advantage to some interests and disadvantage others?

Lane Kirkland (left) became president of the AFL-CIO in 1979, taking the gavel from George Meany, who had presided over the Federation since its formation in 1955.

How many belong?   When we compare the United States with other nations, we find that a larger percentage of Americans are members of voluntary associations of one kind or another than elsewhere. Current figures indicate that about 6 out of 10 adult Americans belong, while in Germany or England a little less than half participate in organized groups. Nevertheless, 4 out of 10 Americans do *not* belong, so it can hardly be said that *all* Americans pursue their interests through voluntary association membership.

People of higher socioeconomic status are considerably more likely to join than those lower on the social scale. The neediest segments of the population are the least likely to participate in interest groups, just as they are less likely to vote (see Chapter 7). Many of the organizations in Table 9.3 were formed for purposes having nothing to do with politics, of course; they relate to all kinds of recreational, educational, and economic concerns. Yet all of these types of groups *may* become politically active if and when they are affected by government policy, actual or prospective. Church groups, for example, are not usually formed for political purposes, but, as we have seen, they get involved in all sorts of public-policy issues. So it is also with most farm organizations, nationality groups, and professional associations. They are not formed initially or primarily to lobby for or against government programs, but many come to do so.

Why is it that some interests seem to have great difficulty in organizing? Why, for example, do most women *not* belong to groups advocating women's rights? We are all consumers; why are consumer groups so small? The answer is in three parts; self-awareness, leadership, and the free-rider problem.

TABLE 9.3

TYPES OF ORGANIZATIONS TO WHICH INDIVIDUALS BELONG

Type of Organization	% of Population Reporting Membership
Political groups such as Democratic or Republican clubs: political-action groups such as voters' leagues	8%
School service groups such as PTA or school alumni groups	17
Service clubs such as Lions, Rotary, Zonta, Junior Chamber of Commerce	6
Youth groups such as Boy Scouts, Girl Scouts	7
Veterans' groups such as American Legion	7
Farm organizations such as Farmer's Union, Farm Bureau, Grange	4
Nationality groups such as Sons of Norway, Hibernian Society	2
Church-related groups such as Bible Study Group, Holy Name Society	6
Fraternal groups such as Elks, Eagles, Masons, and their women's auxiliaries	15
Professional or academic societies such as American Dental Association, Phi Beta Kappa	7
Trade unions	17
School fraternities and sororities	3
Literary, art, discussion, or study clubs such as book review clubs, theater groups	4
Hobby or garden clubs such as stamp or coin clubs, flower clubs, pet clubs	5
Sports clubs, bowling leagues, etc.	12

SOURCE: Based on data from Sidney Verba and Norman H. Nie, *Participation in America: Political Democracy and Social Equality* (New York: Harper & Row, 1972).

It may well be true that all Americans have an important stake in reducing automobile fumes, but most do not seem to care very much. Many women seem not to be very concerned about unequal treatment. Many poor people appear to be resigned to their lot. Consciousness of common class interests is not widespread in the United States, as we have seen, and to a large extent consciousness is also lacking regarding other broad interests that perhaps exist "objectively" but not in the subjective awareness that might lead people to join together.

Organizations do not automatically spring into existence just because there are people with a common interest. They must be organized, put together in viable form by a leader. Once the group is in operation, moreover, the skills of the leadership continue to have an important impact on what the group is able to accomplish. From the late 1950s until 1968 the Southern Christian Leadership Conference owed most of its effectiveness to the leadership of Martin Luther King, Jr., as did the whole civil rights movement. John Gardner created Common Cause; without him it probably would not exist. Ralph Nader's entrepreneurial skill continues to be decisive to the success of his consumer-oriented lobbying efforts.

A former cabinet member under President Johnson, John Gardner founded Common Cause in 1970 to lobby in behalf of reforms for "good government."

Successful interest groups, like other organizations, are usually able to establish orderly procedures of leadership succession. The AFL-CIO did not collapse when its president, George Meany, gave way in 1979, after 30 years, to Lane Kirkland. Common Cause has flourished long after the withdrawal of John Gardner. Nevertheless, it cannot be assumed that an interest group will always have equally effective leaders, and a group's impact on public policy will often depend on how skillful politically its leaders are.

The third factor we must consider in accounting for group success grows out of the "free-rider problem." The idea of a free-rider is simple. Why should a doctor join the American Medical Association (AMA) to help lobby for higher Medicare fees? If the AMA succeeds, the doctor will get the benefit anyway. Why help bear the costs of a lobbying struggle? Why should blacks join the National Association for the Advancement of Colored People (NAACP) to help support litigation to break down racial barriers? A favorable court decision will benefit nonmembers just as much as members. On nearly every public policy issue it can be shown that it is "rational" for an individual to avoid the costs of contributing to a lobbying effort, especially when the potential group is large and individuals cannot expect their personal contributions to make a significant difference to the outcome. It is this logic that helps us understand why such large, diverse "groups" as women, consumers, or poor people are so difficult to recruit into organizations strong enough to have real lobbying impact.

On the other hand, there *are* thousands of groups in action. They have been organized, recruited members, and tried to secure public-policy objectives, in some cases over many decades. How are their free-rider problems overcome? A large part of the answer is found in **selective benefits** available to members only. In addition to whatever collective benefits may accrue from effective lobbying efforts, many groups offer insurance, publications, technical assistance, cheap charter flights, and the pleasures of social interaction with others like oneself. These benefits are made available to members only; if you don't join, you don't enjoy the fruits of belonging.

Many Americans belong to a lobbying organization because they believe in the organization's cause and think they ought to help. This motive for group membership is in effect a form of philanthropy by which, as in United Way campaigns, people contribute to public-policy campaigns they think are important. Those who belong to the Sierra Club or the Wilderness Society do so not just to get handsome calendars and books at reduced rates; they are devoted to the principle of preserving the undamaged fragments of the natural environment. The American Civil Liberties Union is supported by people who are committed to defending the First Amendment freedoms; they do so not for their own immediate needs, since they themselves are seldom arrested, but for those others who do hold truly unpopular beliefs.

An important point about interest groups in American life follows from what we have said. People who join interest groups because they believe in the cause must be able to afford the dues, the time, and whatever other resources are required for effective membership. Poor people typically cannot afford to join many groups, however helpful to their long-run interests membership might be. Consequently, organizations representing the interests of poor people are very difficult to create or maintain, except insofar as the traditional charitable groups, notably the churches, try to speak to these concerns.

Our discussion up to now has centered entirely on the dynamics of voluntary membership associations. Some of the most prominent parts of the interest group world are composed of this kind of organization, and to understand their problems, such as "free-riderism," helps us understand why certain groups are strong and others are not. A large fraction of the "interested" activity designed to influence public policy, however, is undertaken by institutional actors, not voluntary associations.

Business corporations are especially prominent. Chrysler and Lockheed gained notoriety when large federal loans and guarantees enabled those firms to weather financial storms. Many other companies have established Washington offices where their government-affairs staff can monitor government programs and the development of policy, alerting the firm when its corporate interests may be affected and, when necessary, lobbying, alone or in concert with likeminded firms, to secure favorable policy (see Table 9.4). Universities likewise are active in trying to affect federal policy decisions. So are the representatives of state and local governments. These institutional actors have come to recognize how much effect federal actions have on their situation and what a large difference it can make to their well-being to keep alert to the possibilities and to intervene (i.e., lobby) when appropriate. This representation of institutions adds considerably

TABLE 9.4

BUSINESS VIEWS OF THE TAX-OVERHAUL BILL, DECEMBER 1985

For[a]	Against[b]
American Apparel Manufacturers Association	American Bankers Association
American Electronics Association	American Insurance Association
American Trucking Associations	American Mining Congress
Food Marketing Institute	American Petroleum Institute
Grocery Manufacturers of America	Business Roundtable
National Association of Wholesaler-Distributors	National Association of Home Builders
National Federation of Independent Business	National Association of Manufacturers
National Retail Merchants Association	National Machine Tool Builders Association
Allied-Signal	U.S. Chamber of Commerce
Beatrice	Aluminum Co. of America
Dart & Kraft	AT&T
Digital Equipment	Bank of America
Federated Department Stores	Caterpillar Tractor
General Mills	Chase Manhattan
General Motors	Dow Chemical
IBM	Duke Power
Levi Strauss	DuPont
PepsiCo	Exxon
Philip Morris	Ford Motor
Procter & Gamble	GTE
R. J. Reynolds Industries	Inland Steel
Sara Lee	Mobil
3M	Rockwell International
	Texas Instruments
	Weyerhaeuser

[a] All members of the Tax Reform Action Coalition and the CEO Tax Group, two lobbying groups formed to support tax reform.
[b] Signers of a petition sponsored by the U.S. Chamber of Commerce, asking the president to set aside tax reform.
SOURCE: *Wall Street Journal,* December 5, 1985.

to the disproportionate lobbying presence of corporate business, since corporations can generally afford the costs of Washington representation more easily than nonprofit institutions like universities, hospitals or museums.

THE MODERN LOBBY SYSTEM

In many respects the "modern" system of interest-group activity in Washington can be said to begin in 1946. In that year the current Regulation of Lobbying Act was passed; it and the 1938 Foreign Agents Registration Act are still the main (and very weak) instruments of federal regulation. They require **lobbyists** to register and file quarterly reports of expenditures. The 1946 Act touches only congressional lobbying, however, and only some forms of that. Moreover, it assumes that somehow the mere prospect of registration and possible publicity will keep lobbying pressure within reasonable bounds. Efforts to strengthen the law have run into two barriers.

One is the First Amendment and its protection of the right to speak and petition. The second is the fact that so many groups are now active on the Washington scene, and having adjusted to this situation, Congress is uneasy about changing it. No one thinks the present law is much good, but no alternative has yet attracted enough support to become law.

A second feature of the post-1946 world is that ever since then, in both domestic and foreign policy, there have been both extensive commitment to an active federal role and substantial continuity in the general shape and direction of federal effort. A safety net of domestic welfare programs, a large defense budget, a network of international commitments for alliance and aid, and an ongoing investment of great magnitude in domestic facilities, such as highways and hospitals, scientific research, and cultural institutions—all these have been more or less in continuous operation during the post-World War II era. Furthermore, it may be said that the effort devoted to interest group lobbying is in rough proportion to the size and scope of the impact of federal policy on the lives of people and the fortunes of institutions.

Third, many of the most active and prominent interest-group actors on the federal scene have been in place since 1946 and in some cases much longer. It is true that many consumer and public-interest groups, like Common Cause and the Nader groups, have been established since 1960. It is also true that many other groups and institutions have become more active politically as the scope of governmental programs has grown. The size of the Washington lobby has grown substantially, but its general character and contours are much as they were 40 years ago.

Finally, throughout this period the basic assumptions regarding what it takes to lobby effectively, what tactics are most likely to work, and where the limits of legitimate action life have remained rather consistent. (1) Lobbying is seen primarily as a communications process, not a pressuring effort; (2) the lobbyist must gain and keep access to key decision makers so as to present the group's case, and (3) credible information relevant to the policy issue is the most valuable way to achieve access and maintain communication.

In this "modern" system of interest-group action not only are most of the major private organizations veteran participants, but so also are many of the individuals who occupy the key roles. As we will see in Chapter 14, most members of Congress have rather long careers in that august body. Their staff aides often do not stay as long, but many of them are also old hands in Washington. So are most bureaucrats in the executive branch, though the top appointees tend to have much briefer tenures. Major Washington lobbyists likewise have generally been plying their trade, pursuing the same general group interests and working in behalf of the same organizations, for many years. One study found that among more than 800 Washington representatives in 1983 the average length of service with their present organization was 12 years.[1] In short, despite its expansion

---

[1] Robert L. Nelson, John P. Heinz, Edward O. Laumann, and Robert H. Salisbury, "Washington Representatives and National Policy Making," mimeographed, 1986.

Nearly 2000 trade associations and hundreds of other organizations maintain lobbying staffs in Washington. Many are located along K Street, N.W., the so-called "K Street Corridor."

in overall size, this is a system that is quite stable in its structure. Therefore, as we turn to an overview of the major groups, we can be confident that most of them will be around for years to come.

The Size of the Universe

How many politically active interest groups are there? No one knows for sure. The most extensive annual effort to count the full list, published under the title *Washington Representatives*,[2] lists more than 10,000 institutions and organizations that retain someone to look after their federal policy interests. More than 7,200 individuals registered in 1985 as lobbyists under the 1946 Act, more than twice the number of 10 years earlier. Some 850 registered as agents of foreign governments. Nearly 2,000 trade and professional associations, employing a total of some 50,000 people, now have their headquarters in Washington. This is about 30 percent of the national total, an increase from less than 20 percent located there in the 1960s. Lawyers have long been regarded as prominent among the "heavy hitter" lobbyists; their number grew from less than 11,000 in 1973 to more than 37,000 in 1983. By any standard there are a great many people involved in lobbying and associated activity.

---

[2] Edited by Arthur Close (Washington, D.C.: Columbia Books, 1985).

THE ORGANIZATIONAL PARTICIPANTS

The Business Community

Individual firms   More than 500 individual firms are represented by company officials located in Washington. For example:

General Motors, in 1983, listed 41 public-affairs personnel, 11 of whom were registered as lobbyists in Congress; in addition, in 1985 six different Washington law firms were of counsel to GM and one public-relations firm had been retained.

The Monsanto Company had 35 people in public affairs in 1983, 4 registered as lobbyists, but retained no outside lawyers or public-relations consultants.

Mobil Oil listed 15 people, including 4 registered lobbyists, 5 Washington law firms and 2 consulting lobbying firms.

Trade associations   Approximately 1,800 trade associations keep representatives permanently stationed in Washington. Some trade associations have large memberships and budgets; others are quite small. Some, though small, enroll an entire industry and have great impact when lobbying for that industry's concerns. Some examples are the following:

The American Petroleum Institute, established in 1919, is the chief lobbying arm for some 350 corporations and several thousand individuals in all phases of the oil and gas business, with some 300 people in Washington and others located elsewhere in the country.

The Grocery Manufacturers Association represents some 150 firms, such as General Mills and Pepsico, that manufacture soft drinks and all kinds of food and paper products.

The Pharmaceutical Manufacturers Association, representing some 130 firms making biological, pharmaceutical, and medical diagnostic products and devices, has a staff of about 100, and a budget of well over $1 million.

Peak associations   Organizations that try to represent or speak for the entire business community include the following:

The National Association of Manufacturers, organized in 1895 to promote international trade, soon began to emphasize opposition to labor unions and developed a reputation for resisting government intervention into economy. It lost membership after the early 1950s, but has remained active on a wide spectrum of policy issues. With a membership of about 12,000 business firms, it is still quite conservative.

The U.S. Chamber of Commerce, formed in 1912 with encouragement from President Taft, has some 200,000 members—corporate, individual, and state and local chambers. Sometimes more moderate politically than the NAM, it is active on nearly every issue and very effective at mobilizing grass-roots support for its views.

The Business Roundtable, formed in 1973, is composed of some 200 chief executive officers of major U.S. corporations. Involved in those issues of special importance to large corporate business, it is very effective since its lobbying is actually done by its members, not by "hired guns."

The National Federation of Independent Business, the largest (ca. 600,000 members) of several groups seeking to be the "voice" of small business.

Labor

Individual unions.   Some are large (the Teamsters, ca. 2 million members, and the United Auto Workers, ca. 1.15 million), some medium-sized (the Lady Garment Workers, ca. 265,000, and Hotel and Restaurant Workers, ca. 400,000), and some quite small (Air Line Pilots, ca. 34,000, and the Newspaper Guild, ca. 32,000).

Community and state labor councils.   These cooperative organizations frequently serve to coordinate labor's lobbying and election activity at local and state levels.

AFL-CIO.   Formed in 1955 through the merger of the American Federation of Labor and the Congress of Industrial Organizations, it is the "peak association" of American labor, composed of 106 constituent unions—*not* including the Teamsters, the United Mine Workers, and some others. About 15 million of the nation's 18 million union members are affiliated with the AFL-CIO.

Only about 18 percent of wage and salary employees in the United States belong to labor unions, down from about 28 percent in the mid-1950s. White-collar workers are less likely to join, as are women and workers located in the South and in hi-tech industries, like computers.

Agriculture

General farm organizations.   The American Farm Bureau Federation (AFBF) is much the largest organization of individual farmers and others closely connected to agriculture. Strong in the Midwest, this organization of over 3 million members has traditionally taken a relatively conservative position on farm policy, opposing high price supports and working cordially with Republican administrations. The farm crisis of the 1980s, however, has pushed the AFBF into urging more substantial federal help for farmers.

The AFBF is joined by the National Farmers Union, a smaller but more militant group with strength in the wheat belt and with close ties to labor; the National Grange, the oldest national farm organization but no longer much of a force politically; and the American Agriculture Movement, a militantly demonstrative group formed in the 1970s to try to force more federal assistance for farmers.

Commodity organizations. In recent years these organizations have increased in both number and influence over policy. The National Milk Producers Federation is an example of a particularly effective lobbying group, favoring price supports for dairy products and contributing substantial amounts of money to congressional campaigns. Nearly every agricultural commodity has its own association, from the National Association of Wheat Growers (90,000) to the American Honey Producers Association (600) and the American Bee Keeping Federation.

Agribusiness firms and associations. The food industry is large and complex. Land O'Lakes is a butter cooperative, for instance. Campbell Soup is both a producer and consumer of large amounts of agricultural commodities. Coca-Cola uses enormous amounts of sugar, and actively lobbies on legislation affecting sugar prices. The National Soft Drink Association represents the full soft drink industry and also participates on sugar issues. The list of interested groups active in agriculture issues is very long.

Professional associations

Broad membership associations. Potentially enrolling all members of the profession (American Medical Association, American Bar Association, American Dental Association, American Institute of Architects, and so on), these groups have encountered difficulty in recent years in attracting young professionals to membership. Partly for this reason these associations have become more flexible on policy issues, accepting more government intervention in their fields than they once found tolerable.

Specialty practice associations. Trial Lawyers Association, Patent Attorneys, American Psychiatric Association, American College of Surgeons, and many others.

Academic professionals. Professions located primarily in university settings: American Chemical Society, American Economics Association, and the like.

Nonprofit institution associations

American Council of Education, Association of American Universities, National Council of Churches, American Symphony Orchestra League, National Guard Association of the United States, and others.

"Public interest" organizations

Liberal. Common Cause, League of Women Voters, assorted components of Nader-organized groups, Consumer Federation of America.

Conservative. Eagle Forum, American Security Council, Heritage Foundation, Moral Majority.

Single-issue groups

National Rifle Association, Nuclear Freeze Movement, Women's Christian Temperance Union, Right-to-life Movement.

Other beneficiary groups.   American Association of Retired Persons, Veterans of Foreign Wars and American Legion.

Civil rights   National Association for the Advancement of Colored People.

Civil liberties   American Civil Liberties Union.

Environmental   Sierra Club, Wilderness Society, Audubon Society.

Nationality   Sons of Italy, National Association of Arab-Americans.

LOBBYING STRATEGIES AND TACTICS

When lobbyists go into action, their choices of how to proceed are governed by several factors. First, and most important, is the question of institutional arena. American government, as we know, is split into a great many parts: three branches of the national government; numerous departments, agencies, committees, and other subunits; and 50 states and thousands of local governments, each with its subdivisions. An interest group surveying this array must decide where to focus its resources. There is little point in lobbying the state legislature if the crucial decisions are to be made by Congress. Congress, in turn, may be a relatively unimportant arena for determining such matters as who gets the contract to build a new bomber, in which case it is better to aim one's lobbying energies at the Defense Department.

A second consideration, however, involves the group's own resources. Where can it be most effective, given what it has to work with? For example, for many years civil rights groups were completely unable to influence state and local governments in the South and not much more effective with Congress. They lacked important resources for impact in these arenas. They could not vote in southern constituencies, and they had no money for election campaign contributions; therefore, instead the NAACP concentrated its efforts in the judicial arena, where votes didn't matter.

When students began protesting against the Vietnam War in the mid-1960s, they focused on such targets as the universities themselves, not because those target institutions had the authority to stop the war, but because that was the only setting in which the students had any ability to have a real impact. They could not force a change in the Pentagon, but they hoped that by shutting down the universities they would impress key decision makers with how deeply committed they were to American withdrawal from Vietnam. In fact, there is evidence that some major public officials did indeed conclude that the war was not worth the cost in domestic upheaval and conflict.

Protests and demonstrations are one way to arouse public opinion and, perhaps, influence policy.

A third factor affecting a group's course of action, in addition to relevant institutional authority and group resources, is how a particular issue fits into the larger array of matters that concern the group. An organization like the National Rifle Association is concerned only with gun control. It forms alliances and enters other policy disputes, if at all, in terms of how those actions might affect its lobbying strength on gun control. By contrast, the U.S. Chamber of Commerce, the AFL-CIO, and some of the other "peak associations," have long lists of issues that concern them at any one time.

Many of these questions, including gun control as well as a host of economic and social disputes, are more or less permanent items on the national political agenda; in one form or another they come up nearly every year. Interest groups that anticipate such continuing need for effective lobbying cannot afford to act in a manner that alienates or offends important decision makers. They must keep the channels of communication open and maintain their access to those in authority. This usually leads them to a certain amount of restraint in what they do and say. Most interest groups avoid direct personal attacks on incumbent members of Congress, for instance, and are wary of seeming to threaten electoral reprisals against those who fail to endorse their policy goals.

Some organizations, however, are more intensely committed to a point of view and refuse to compromise or moderate their position. Right-to-life advocates have tended to operate this way on the abortion issue, as

Charls Walker, one of the more influential Washington lobbyists, has a doctorate in economics and specializes in the complex issues of tax legislation.

have numerous conservative organizations. On several consumer and environmental issues, the groups associated with Ralph Nader have been similarly loath to compromise. The lobbying system operates mainly to encourage compromise and bargaining, but that system also contains some of the most deeply committed, often highly moralistic, elements of the American culture. In other words, the interest-group universe reflects the nation itself.

The variety of possible techniques employed by lobbyists is great, as Table 9.5 indicates. Keeping in mind that the choice of tactics will reflect both the group's resources and the particular institutional configuration that will determine an issue result, we can make three general observations about what interest organizations do to influence policy. In the first place, they convey information. Several of the most heavily used techniques in Table 9.5 involve the presentation to officials of information about the issue, the interests involved and how they will be affected, what alternatives there may be, and the like. Indeed, interest groups are a major source of information for decision makers; without interest groups policymakers would have to find alternative sources.

A second technique of importance to many groups is the mobilization of grass-roots supports. Politicians live and die at the ballot box, and constituent pressure is nearly always the most effective kind. An important part of the lobbyist's job is to alert the constituents, members of his organization or officials of his company, to contact members of Congress or the executive branch. Not all groups have much grass-roots support, of course, and in any case it is less relevant regarding the finer details of policy. But it should be emphasized that even when grass-roots mobilization is not attempted, the lobbyists spend much of their time keeping watch, monitoring the policy process to detect anything that might affect the interests of the organization or its members.

Finally, there is the matter of money. One way to try to influence public policy is by making material contributions to officials. Bribery, of course, is illegal and, happily, it is rare these days. A hot tip on the stock market or an opportunity for the official to buy in on the ground floor of a promising new venture is generally legal and not uncommon. Sometimes public officials leave government and take jobs with private firms or as-

TABLE 9.5

PERCENTAGE OF ORGANIZATIONS USING
EACH TECHNIQUE OF EXERCISING INFLUENCE

1. Testifying at hearings	99%
2. Contacting government officials directly to present your point of view	98
3. Engaging in informal contacts with officials—at conventions, over lunch, and so on	95
4. Presenting research results or technical information	92
5. Sending letters to members of your organization to inform them about your activities	92
6. Entering into coalitions with other organizations	90
7. Attempting to shape the implementation of policies	89
8. Talking with people from the press and the media	86
9. Consulting with government officials to plan legislative strategy	85
10. Helping to draft legislation	85
11. Inspiring letter writing or telegram campaigns	84
12. Shaping the government's agenda by raising new issues and calling attention to previously ignored problems	84
13. Mounting grass-roots lobbying efforts	80
14. Having influential constituents contact their congressional representative's office	80
15. Helping draft regulations, rules, or guidelines	78
16. Serving on advisory commissions and boards	76
17. Alerting congressional representatives to the effects of a bill on their districts	75
18. Filing suit or otherwise engaging in litigation	72
19. Making financial contributions to electoral campaigns	58
20. Doing favors for officials who need assistance	56
21. Attempting to influence appointments to public office	53
22. Publicizing candidates' voting records	44
23. Engaging in direct-mail fund raising for your organization	44
24. Running advertisements in the media about your position on issues	31
25. Contributing work or personnel to electoral campaigns	24
26. Making public endorsements of candidates for office	22
27. Engaging in protests or demonstrations	20

SOURCE: Kay Schlozman and John Tierney, *Organized Interests and American Democracy* (New York: Harper & Row, 1985), p. 150.

sociations for whom they may have done favors while in office. The most widely discussed form of money connected to the policymaking process, however, is the political action committee (**PAC**) campaign contribution.

Political action committees have been around, used especially by labor unions, for several decades. Since the 1940s union members would contribute money to a fund that was distributed among candidates favored by the union leadership. A few other groups had also created PAC mechanisms. In 1974, however, legislation was passed that made it entirely legal for a corporation, trade association, professional organization, or any other group to establish a PAC, solicit individual contributions to it, and distribute the money to candidates for political office. At the same time, public financing for presidential elections was introduced, and stricter limitations were imposed on how much an individual person could give to a candidate. As a result of these changes, PACs were created in large numbers and swiftly came to be important factors in financing congressional political campaigns and in the planning of interest groups' strategies.

Many labor unions already had PACs, but they were soon surpassed in number and size by corporations and business trade associations. More than half the interest groups studied by Schlozman and Tierney made campaign contributions through PACs. Labor PACs give nearly all their money to Democrats; business groups are somewhat more bipartisan, supporting some Democratic incumbents, but predominantly favoring political conservatives, most of whom are Republican. In addition to these economic interests, PACs have been created by more ideologically based groups. The National Conservative Political Action Committee (NCPAC) is one of the largest and best known, but there are others on both the right and left of the political spectrum.

The Supreme Court has ruled in *Buckley* v. *Valeo* that independent PACs can spend any amount they want on a campaign as long as they do not coordinate their plans with the candidate. Accordingly, in the last several elections NCPAC has targeted senators who are regarded as too liberal and has spent very large sums trying to defeat them. In 1980 and 1982 NCPAC had considerable success, but it had less in 1984. The prospect of a wealthy interest group coming from outside the state to campaign against an incumbent senator has raised a number of worrisome questions, but as the Court itself said, how, under the First Amendment, can a group be prevented from speaking out whenever and at whatever cost it chooses?

PACs may spend what they like on an independent campaign, but they cannot contribute more than $5,000 per candidate per race. For any single group, therefore, the ability to be a decisive force in bringing about defeat or victory would seem remote. Moreover, candidates themselves can and do exploit the PACs. Important senators and representatives hold fund-raisers and pointedly remind the PAC that they will be very disappointed if the PAC does not come through with a few hundred dollars. Several congressional leaders, who in fact faced no opposition for their own reelection, have raised hundreds of thousands of PAC dollars to use in helping to elect *their* supporters.

This discussion of PACs serves to highlight several of the most basic questions about the role of organized interests in American political life.

First, and most obvious, is that PACs in particular and interest groups in general require money. Those interests in society which can most readily command financial support will, in general, be the most active in pushing their electoral and policy objectives. At least they are likely to spend the most, and since most business firms are wealthier than welfare recipients or conservationists, they can afford to be more vigorous on behalf of their policy interests.

Studies of PACs thus far are inconclusive, however, as to whether interest-group spending translates very directly into influence over policy decisions. It is easy to find cases of lavish group expenditure that failed totally to bring about intended goals. Many close observers have pointed out that, after all, hardly any congressman will be influenced by a mere $5,000 contribution when the election campaign costs a million dollars. Moreover, senators who are not personally wealthy may find PAC contributions their only hope to compete against rivals with their own fortunes to spend. In Minnesota in 1982, for instance, Mark Dayton was reported to have spent some $7 million of his own dollars trying to defeat incumbent Republican Senator David Durenberger, who has, in turn, defended PACs as a necessary balancing factor.

It is true that a single PAC can give only $5,000 to a given candidate in a given race. But if each of the PACs in, let us say, the life insurance industry gives $5,000 to a candidate in each of the thirty-odd Senate races of a given election, the total impact of that investment could be truly massive. As Table 9.6 indicates, there has been some very heavy spending by industry groupings in recent years, even though individual PACs are limited.

Three other points must be added. One is that total PAC spending only amounts to about one-fourth of the staggering amount of money spent by congressional candidates in the last several elections. That means that three times the PAC spending is provided from individual contributions (plus the candidate's own funds), and these, by law, may not be greater

TABLE 9.6
POLITICAL ACTION COMMITTEES IN ACTION, 1982

Committee Type	Number Contributing	Contributions (millions)
Labor	293	$20.9
Corporation	1317	29.4
Nonconnected (usually ideological)	407	11.0
Trade association/ membership/health	524	22.9
Cooperatives	11	2.2
Corporations without stock	22	1.1
Total	2665[a]	87.6[a]

[a] In 1978 there were only 1474 PACs with total contributions of 35.2 million dollars.

SOURCE: Norman Ornstein et al., *Vital Statistics on Congress, 1984–1985 Edition* (Washington, D.C.: American Enterprise Institute, 1984), p. 91.

than $1,000 per candidate per race. In fact, a much larger number of *small* contributions are given to candidates today than in the past, so that the story of money in politics is not entirely one of victory for the biggest spenders.

A second consideration to be kept in mind is that not all the PACs push in the same direction. Labor and business operate in opposite ways, as we have seen. But even within business there is often disagreement. Many industry and trade association PACs, especially those that are controlled by their Washington-based staffs—the actual lobbyists who are sensitive to the best ways to play the political game—are quite pragmatic, contributing to party leaders and influential members of both parties in order to maintain access and good relations no matter who wins. For them lobbying depends on communication. It is a two-way process that continues year after year to involve negotiation and compromise far more than speechmaking and table pounding.

The third point, which sometimes gets lost from view among all the dazzle, is that other factors besides money affect policy decisions. The deep beliefs and principles of public officials are not lightly tossed aside in return for a check or a promise of a future job with the group. Good arguments and persuasive evidence of need will sway public officials, and it is no accident that Table 9.4 lists these kinds of group tactics at the top, as being far more frequently employed than giving money or otherwise trying to influence election outcomes.

CONCLUDING THOUGHTS

What conclusions can we reach regarding the power of interest groups in American public life? Are they major forces that affect who gets what from policy decisions? Absolutely. Do these organized groups represent more or less faithfully every sector of American life? Certainly not. Are economically and socially disadvantaged Americans and such diffuse and difficult-to-organize groups as consumers least well represented? Yes. Could these underrepresented groups rectify this imbalance by "getting their act together" and forming effective lobbies of their own? Probably not, although here and there effective exceptions have emerged—among them, Common Cause, Ralph Nader, the NAACP for some of its history, the ACLU, the Moral Majority, and environmentalists during the late 1960s and early 1970s.

Is American public policy too much the product of organized group pressure and not enough the reflection of broader conceptions of the public interest? This is what once, before inflation set in, was called the $64 question. There is no easy answer. Should veterans get extensive medical benefits? Your reaction may depend on whether you are a veteran. Are student loans unnecessary subsidies to people who do not need government help? Is a big defense budget a boondoggle for generals and airplane manufacturers? Almost any imaginable version of the public interest would

There are more and more elderly people in the country, and they have gained considerable political influence. In this picture Maggie Kuhn, a founder of the Gray Panthers, confers with Claude Pepper, long-time Representative from Florida and leading advocate of senior citizens' interests.

benefit some interests more than others, and it could and probably would be attacked as one more instance of special-interest legislation.

What is certain is that organized interest groups play a very large role in our political system. There are more of them than ever before. They are more active, on a wider array of issues, spending more money and operating with greater sophistication than ever before. Restricting them or trying by law to reduce the scope of their activities would run into severe problems with the First Amendment's protection of free speech and petition, and it also might block the formation of new groups expressing new concerns and articulating new issues arising in a dynamic society.

Publicity through registration and reporting is today the main method of regulating interest groups. Publicity is not an automatic cure for abuses, of course. If interest groups are kept out in the open, however, with regular reporting of their spending and vigorous media coverage of their actions, then each of us may be able to spot what we and our group regard as danger signs and mobilize ourselves for corrective effort.

A pluralistic democracy cannot guarantee policy results that please everyone or satisfy every need. It can offer those who want to change the status quo the opportunity to organize and act. It is not an opportunity every group can make much use of, however, and that is why American pluralism falls short of its own ideal.

CHAPTER HIGHLIGHTS ■

1.   America is pluralistic in that it is made up of many groups, all of which are free to express their views. Not all groups are equally effective in political action, however, and the government is not equally responsive to all of them.

2.   There is no single basis for group conflict in America. Social class has not been as important a basis as in other nations, whereas race, ethnicity, and religion have been very significant.

3.   Americans have a high rate of group participation, but many do not participate in the vast array of organized groups that are often the most effective means of bringing citizen interests to bear on public decisions.

4.   In recent years there has been a greater presence of "public interest" groups, but there are still much larger numbers of "self-interested" organizations at work on behalf of economic interests.

5.   Interest-group activity in Washington has increased in response to the increased scope of the federal government's programs. Much group activity consists of monitoring what government officials do.

6.   Groups employ many tactics of influence, but for the most part they seek to keep communications open and maintain access to public officials. This often leads them to moderate their positions and to avoid alienating other groups.

SUGGESTED READINGS ■

The daily newspapers are rich in specific illustrations of interest-group activity and the efforts of lobbyists to influence government.

Classic studies of interest-group activities and influence are: David B. Truman, *The Government Process* (1951); E. E. Schattschneider, *The Semi-Sovereign People* (1960); Theodore J. Lowi, *The End of Liberalism* (1969); Mancur Olson, *The Logic of Collective Action* (1965).

Other modern commentaries are: James Q. Wilson, *Political Organizations* (1973); Lester Milbrath, *The Washington Lobbyists* (1963); Jeffrey Berry, *Lobbying for the People* (1977) and *The Interest Group Society* (1984); Andrew McFarland, *Common Cause* (1985); Kay Schlozman and John Tierney, *Organized Interests and American Democracy* (1985).

Tammany Hall—Legendary headquarters of New York City Democrats

POLITICAL PARTIES

P olitical parties play a central role in all democracies. They are mechanisms that link the citizenry with the government through the electoral process. They also build linkages among different groups in society enabling majorities to form and making democratic government possible. The American party system was the first true party system. Though it has gone through many transformations, it preserves some of the main features it had in the early days of the Republic. American parties have some distinctive characteristics, the understanding of which is the subject of this chapter.

RUNNING AGAINST THE PARTY SYSTEM

At the beginning of each presidential election year, numerous candidates campaign for the presidential nomination of one of the two major political parties. Only one person makes it in each party. Sometimes a defeated rival for the nomination is chosen as the vice-presidential running mate, as George Bush was selected by Ronald Reagan in 1980. The rest of the contenders for the nomination usually express regret that they lost, but they wind up supporting their party's nominee, although sometimes grudgingly.

In 1980, one of the defeated contenders for the Republican nomination decided to try a different approach. John Anderson decided to run as an independent for the presidency.

Anderson's campaign began with high hopes. Public-opinion polls in the spring of 1980 showed almost one-quarter of the electorate ready to vote for him, a remarkably high figure for an independent. Furthermore, the public seemed quite unhappy with the choices that the Democrats and Republicans were offering. Anderson communicated an image of trustworthiness, honesty, and competence. He was not one of those candidates who appealed to only a fringe group; and as Anderson himself put it, he was there for one purpose only—to win.

Anderson hired a top campaign manager, New York political consultant David Garth. He raised substantial money. He was invited to debate the other two candidates on national television. (He actually debated Ronald Reagan, whereas Jimmy Carter refused a three-way debate.)

The high hopes of the spring were dashed in November. Anderson ended up with less than 7 percent of the popular vote. There were many reasons, but the main one was simply that although the public had earlier admired someone who ran against the party system, most voters ultimately could not accept a candidate who was neither a Democrat nor a Republican as a serious contender in the election. Such is the dominance of the two American parties. As Anderson himself noted: "To break with the established party system is not easy."

There is no mention of **political parties** in the U.S. Constitution, nor was there discussion of them at the Constitutional Convention. The silence on the issue is not really remarkable, because the organizations that mobilize voters on behalf of particular candidates, which we call political parties, had not yet been invented. Nevertheless, they soon emerged as significant parts of the American political process and have remained so ever since.

It would be difficult to imagine national elections in the United States in the absence of political parties. The two main political parties, the Democrats and the Republicans, are visible nearly everywhere. All presidents, almost all members of the Senate and House of Representatives, almost all governors, and the overwhelming majority of other elected officials have been elected under one of those two political party labels. Many smaller parties have contested in these elections as well, but rarely do they offer serious competition. From time to time a candidate may run for a major office without any party affiliation, as John Anderson did, but such candidacies are rare, and like the candidacies of those who run under minor party labels, they rarely present a serious challenge to the two major political parties.

In this chapter and the next we will look closely at the American political parties to see what role they play in the governing of America.

Political parties are organizations whose main purpose is to contest and win elections. Parties nominate candidates for public office and organize campaigns for those candidates. To do this, political parties organize the public. They have local organizations in communities and neighborhoods. They have campaign workers. They hold rallies, distribute literature, and ring doorbells. Sometimes they even recruit people to run for office. If a political party then wins an election, it attempts to organize and control the government. If one party has a majority, its members (or most of them) work together in the legislature to try to pass laws reflecting the principles on which the party's candidates have run. In a system such as that of the United States, where a president and a Congress are elected separately, the bond of party makes it easier for the two branches to work together in order to govern effectively—at least when the president and the majority in Congress are from the same party. In short, political parties try to organize the public to elect their candidates and, if elected, try to organize the government.

At the same time, the parties provide many Americans with important cues as to which candidate to prefer and what issue positions to take. When, for example, a Republican president espouses a new program, millions of people who identify with the Republican party are quickly persuaded to believe in it also. In recent years, as political parties have grown weaker, they have performed these roles less effectively. Even though the American parties have been far from perfect, however, citizens and their government are much more effectively linked than they would be in the absence of parties. If the American political parties were to disappear, they would be greatly missed.

WHY DID POLITICAL PARTIES DEVELOP?

The writers of the Constitution did not think well of political parties. To James Madison, the "spirit of party" was dangerous. The possibility that the nation might divide into two large factions or political parties seemed very threatening. Washington joined him in this view. In his Farewell Address of 1796, Washington condemned the "harmful effects of the spirit of party."

It would be unfair to condemn the Founders of the Republic for their lack of foresight. Nor should we criticize Madison for inconsistency when, a decade after the writing of the Constitution, he joined Thomas Jefferson in a vigorous attempt to create a political party. The framers of the Constitution were setting out on uncharted seas. No government had ever been founded with as firm a constitutional provision for the popular election of governing officials. The Founders of the Republic thought that political parties would work against the common good, that parties would represent specific and partial interests rather than the general welfare. They realized that people had competing interests—indeed, Madison had based his entire theory of the Constitution on that insight—but the Founders hoped that citizens would come together in temporary factions only to express those interests. Sometimes a person would join one faction based on an interest, and another time the same person would join a different faction based on a different interest. Moreover, the factions would be many and small. They felt that the division of society into a few permanent competing parties would lead to intense conflict. Moreover, the Founders hoped that public officials would be able to rise above factional pressures and act for the broader public good. Parties might dominate the government and thus damage the spirit of representative democracy. What they did not realize was that the system they created, a system in which governing officials achieve office by popular election, required some mechanism to organize the public to take part in those elections. That institution was to be the political party.

Though the Constitution did not mention them, it created a framework for political parties. The First Amendment to the Constitution guaranteed the citizenry the right to speak out on political matters and "peaceably to assemble" to take part in political life. Thus the Constitution provided the freedom for people to organize into political parties. The Constitution, in addition, created the necessity for political parties by mandating the election—either directly as in the House of Representatives or indirectly as with the Senate and the presidency—of the major national governing officials.

Political parties of a sort had existed in England before the founding of the American Republic. The English parties had been *legislative* parties, however; that is, they existed only in Parliament and were organizations of the members of Parliament into competing groups, the Whigs and the Tories.

Parties began in the United States in a similar manner; they were groupings of like-minded legislators. These groups appeared in the decade after the writing of the Constitution as the members of Congress organized to support or to oppose Alexander Hamilton's economic policies. The Federalists (as the supporters of Hamilton called themselves) and the Democratic-Republicans (as his opponents led by Jefferson and Madison called themselves) soon became cohesive groups in Congress.

The parties in America, however, soon took on a much broader meaning than they had in England. They expanded their activities beyond Congress. Elections took place in the states and communities as well as for national office. It soon became clear that if all these elections were to be contested effectively, organizations were needed to gain the support of voters. During the first few decades of American history the parties converted themselves into institutions with mass followings organized to contest elections. The parties were a new type of institution, organized in the government as a faction of members of Congress and organized as well in the public as a means of gaining the support of voters. They represented a major political "invention," first created in the United States, that has become a basic instrument of democracy here and abroad.

PARTY SYSTEMS IN AMERICAN HISTORY

The current American party system dominated by the Democratic and Republican parties is the latest stage in a long evolution. There have been a number of party systems in American history, within which different coalitions faced each other and competed for electoral victory. The names of the political parties confronting each other have seldom changed. Since the rise of the Republican party shortly before the Civil War, almost all party confrontations have been between the Republicans and the Democrats. Yet these two parties have represented quite different coalitions of interests and voters in different periods. The shifting nature of the party coalitions reflects the changing nature of the groups and values that have been significant in our history.

The Founding: The First Party System

The first of the American party systems took shape during the closing years of the eighteenth century, under John Adams's presidency. He had been elected in 1796 to replace the retiring George Washington. The parties that appeared under John Adams had their origin during Washington's administration, as disputes emerged between the supporters of Alexander Hamilton and those of Thomas Jefferson. Under Jefferson's leadership, an organization called the Republican party was formed. Its purpose was to endorse candidates for Congress who would be sympathetic to the Jeffersonian point of view and to endorse presidential electors with similar sympathies. The great institutional innovation of that time was the development of a system of committees in the various states whose job it was to bring out the vote for the party's candidates. The committees were linked together through active correspondence and a general acceptance of Jefferson as the "party" leader. The Federalists responded by forming their own party organizations. The new Republican party organizations were instrumental in Jefferson's election in 1800.

The election of 1800 is a landmark in the history of the United States and, indeed, in the history of democracy. For the first time, the candidate of an opposition party defeated the incumbent head of state and without riots or assassinations took over the reins of government. The peaceful change of leaders through popular elections—a process we now see as routine—was at that time a major innovation, and one that set a precedent for America's future.

Issues in the first party system   The various party systems in American history have been characterized by distinct coalitions of interest, clashing over a particular set of issues important to that period. In the first party system, the clash was between a Federalist coalition made up of the wealthier and more established sectors of American society—on the one hand, bankers, merchants, manufacturers, and large landowners, and on the other hand, the Republican party of Jefferson and Madison, representing primarily the smaller farmers, laborers, and debtors.

What issues divided them? The Federalists represented the "money" interests. They spoke for a strong central government and a strong presidency, which they felt would further these interests. Hamilton and the Federalists waged for the development of manufacturing protected by tariffs. Their rivals opposed a strong federal government and emphasized agrarian values, not industrial development. The Republicans also favored a more democratic government based on popular participation, while the Federalists were much more inclined to limit citizen participation.

These issues—between those who favored a strong central government and those who did not, between those who favored the money interests and those who spoke for less affluent members of society, and between those who spoke for more popular participation in government and those who wanted less—are issues that, in one form or another, have remained on the political agenda in the United States until the present day.

The Second Party System: Jacksonian Democracy

Beginning in the mid-1820s and very much aided by the election of Andrew Jackson to the presidency in 1828, political parties began to take on a character that is familiar today. During the first three decades of the nineteenth century, American elections became much more democratic. Presidential electors came to be chosen in popular elections rather than by state legislators. Jackson was the first presidential candidate to be nominated by a party convention rather than by a relatively closed caucus of party notables. Also, the franchise was extended in most states to include all white adult males rather than being limited to property holders. The new parties that emerged in the second party system reflected these democratizing changes. The political parties more and more came to be mass-based organizations, organized so as to mobilize a mass electorate on the national, state, and local levels. The development had begun in the first party system, but mass-based party organizations and mass election campaigns were carried much further during the Jacksonian era.

Issues in the second party system   The second party system saw a clash between Andrew Jackson's Democratic party, a direct descendant of Jefferson's Republicans, and the Whig party, which replaced the disappearing Federalist party and took up many of its positions. Whigs drew more support from merchants and businessmen and spoke, as did the Federalists before them, for national power. Like Federalists they tended to represent the more affluent members of society. The Jacksonian Democrats represented the less affluent farmers and workers. They were strong in the Trans-Appalachian West, which had brought Jackson to national prominence. They also began to receive support from new immigrant groups, often Catholic, that began to arrive during the 1830s.

The issues that divided the parties during the second party system were to some extent a continuation of those of the first party system. The Democrats did not greatly favor using the central government to promote the economic development of business, and they were more open to popular participation. The Whigs stood for a more active central government and were somewhat more conservative on participation. In neither party, however, was there a rigid commitment to one side or the other. In addition, with the arrival of many new immigrants from the Catholic parts of Europe, there began to emerge a new issue that would play a major role in future party competition. This was the issue of "nativism" or anti-Catholic sentiment. Numerous Protestant groups argued against immigration and wanted a limitation on it. The Democratic party tended to oppose these restrictions and to be more welcoming to the new Catholic Americans, giving them positions within the party. The Whigs, though less supportive of the new Catholic immigrants, were not bitterly opposed to them. Much of the nativist opposition to Catholics moved into a third party, the Know-Nothings.

There was, in addition, a more explosive issue waiting in the wings: the issue of slavery. This issue set northern business interests against southern plantation interests, split the Protestant denominations, and eventually split the Democrats and destroyed the Whigs. The forces of free labor versus those of slave labor generated a conflict that could not be managed by the political parties. The result was a Civil War and a new party alignment.

The Third Party System:
The Civil War and Its Aftermath

The third party system extends from the mid-1850s to the end of the nineteenth century. The parties we know today as Republican and Democratic can be traced back to this period. The Republican party was the party of the North. It replaced the Whigs, which had foundered on the issues of the Civil War. The Republicans were opposed to slavery and represented the interests of a commercial class based on free labor. They also drew strong support from midwestern farming areas. The Democratic party had been strongest in the South, but it had attracted support from every region. The 1860 election badly fractured the Democrats, but they quickly regained some strength in northern cities. Once the southern states were allowed once again to participate fully in national politics, the parties were very evenly matched. Most of the presidential elections between 1876 and 1896 were very close, and in Congress the parties were also very evenly matched.

The basic party structures remained the same. The system of mass-based political parties that nominated candidates at party conventions had been firmly established during the Jacksonian era and remained the dominant pattern well into the twentieth century. Some important developments did, however, take place during this period. For one thing, the passage of the Fifteenth Amendment after the Civil War gave blacks the right to vote. This might have been a major change and a major extension of

Posters, parades, and campaign hoopla are traditional features of American party politics, as this 1860 poster illustrates.

democratic participation, but it turned out not to be. After the end of Reconstruction in 1877, southern states began to enact various kinds of restrictions on blacks. After 1890 Jim Crow laws effectively denied blacks the vote. The poll tax and literacy tests were used to prevent black voting. In addition, the emergence of the all-white primary in southern states where only the Democratic party was an effective force meant that blacks could not take part in the only election that counted—the Democratic primary.

Another institutional development during the third party system was the growth of the big-city machine. These organizations provided a political home for many of the new immigrants. They represented an extension of the mass-based political parties developed during the Jacksonian era. Many of them also came to be instruments of corruption and misrule, and before long reformers began to campaign against party government as it operated at the local level.

Issues in the third party system   During the period from the Civil War to the end of the nineteenth century, the Democrats established firm support in the South, while the Republican party found its strength in the North and West. The Democratic party appealed to a combination of rural interests, and big-city immigrants, while the Republicans appealed to farmers and to business and the rising industrial interests. Most Republicans supported tariffs to protect American industry. Most Democrats opposed the tariffs that made it more difficult to export southern cotton. Neither party, however, was completely committed to either side. Each party had both rural and urban wings. During this period the Democrats continued to attract the ethnic and Catholic groups in the northern cities.

The parties had been divided over the issue of Reconstruction. The Democrats spoke for the South, whose leaders aimed to reestablish the position of that region in the Union under white supremacy. The Republicans initially took a strong position in favor of civil rights for the newly freed blacks, but after 1876 the Republicans compromised with the South in favor of a more lenient position toward the former rebels. Nevertheless, both parties waved the "bloody shirt" and evoked all the symbols and sentiment attached to the Civil War. As the issues (though not the symbols) of the Civil War era faded from the national agenda, economic ones replaced them. The Democrats tended to favor agrarian interests; the Republicans tended to favor industrial interests.

The Fourth Party System: 1896–1932

In 1896 the Democratic party nominated William Jennings Bryan for president. Bryan spoke for the rural wing of the Democratic party. The groups that supported Bryan represented one major pole of the Democratic party and one major force in American politics: agrarian groups, located in the South and the West, largely fundamentalist Protestant in beliefs. They were deeply antagonistic toward the industrializing Northeast with its large corporations and its growing ethnic working class. In part, because of the nature of his opposition, the Republican candidate, William McKinley, was able to unite behind him the industrial Northeast. This included the industrialists themselves as well as the new immigrant workers in the big cities, who found their interests and way of life challenged and despised by fundamentalist Protestant Americans. The linking of workers and capitalists within the Republican party in response to the agrarian challenge from Bryan and the Democrats gave the Republican party a dominant position in American politics for an extended period. From 1896 until 1932, Republicans dominated the White House, with the only victorious Democrat, Woodrow Wilson, winning when the Republicans were split.

The dominant cleavage that divided McKinley from Bryan was one that we have seen earlier in the conflict between the Catholic immigrants in the cities and the Protestant farmers during the Jacksonian era. The conflict was cultural and religious as well as partisan. It involved such issues as prohibition, which was firmly supported by Protestant rural America against the "wet" views of the cities.

During the fourth party system there were a number of important developments in the structure of American electoral politics. In response to reform-minded Progressives several major changes in party politics were adopted. Political corruption was widespread. The purchase of votes, the abuse of political patronage, and profiteering from public contracts were common. To clean up politics, the reformers introduced such measures as voter registration, secret ballots, and civil-service reform. The direct primary was widely adopted in an effort to reduce the control of party bosses over nominations. At the local level, where corruption was the most massive, nonpartisan elections and new forms of city government were established. The purpose was reform, but one of the major consequences

Socialist Eugene Debs ran for president several times—once from a jail cell. In 1912 he received 1 million votes, and while he never came close to winning office, he and his party did contribute ideas that later were widely accepted.

was the weakening of political parties as mass-based organizations. By reducing the resources and incentives of party leaders the reforms made it harder for parties to organize support among the voters.

Some interpretations of this period of American history suggest that the target of most of the political reforms was the growing number of industrial workers living in the cities. The industrial elite feared the radicalism of these urban voters. The elite, it is said, weakened the parties so as to reduce the chance that popular majorities would be mobilized against the interests of the business and commercial class. But the conflict was also cultural: middle-class Protestants largely of British origin against working-class Catholics from Ireland, Italy, and Poland. Also, it should not be forgotten that there was indeed massive corruption. In any case, the reforms tended to neutralize the great bulk of immigrant urban dwellers and prevented them from having as much influence on elections as their numbers might have warranted.

The Fifth Party System:
The New Deal Coalition, 1932 to . . . ?

In the fourth party system the major strength of the Democratic party had been in the South and the West. The Democrats also had support from northern ethnic workers, mobilized by some of the big-city machines, and this support gradually increased in size and strength. The two wings of the Democratic party engaged in furious battles during the first three decades of the twentieth century. In 1924 they fought it out over the presidential nomination at the Democratic convention. There was a record 103-ballot stalemate between Senator William McAdoo of California, a representative of the fundamentalist agrarian wing of the party, and Al Smith, the governor of New York, who stood for the Catholic and urban wing of the party. The party could not decide between the two and finally nominated a compromise candidate. In 1928, however, Al Smith won the nomination and ran as the first Catholic candidate for president. This drew still more urban ethnic workers of the northern cities to the Democratic party.

The Great Depression that began in 1929 provided the major shock that completed the transformation from the fourth party system to the fifth party system—the New Deal system. In response to the depression, Franklin Delano Roosevelt was elected president. He led the Democratic party in the direction of massive economic reform, which he labeled the New Deal. These reforms put the Democratic party on the side of the working class. The Democrats stood for greater government intervention into the economy, commitment to government welfare programs, such as social security and unemployment insurance, and support for labor unions in their struggle to organize. The Republican party, on the other hand, maintained its commitment to the business community and to a less active government.

Out of this struggle grew the **New Deal coalition** that made the Democratic party the larger of the two parties and the dominant force in American elections for more than two decades after 1932. The keystone of the Democratic coalition was the blue-collar workers in northern cities. These workers were often Catholic and of immigrant stock. The coalition was based on both cultural and economic issues. Al Smith had spoken for the northern urban way of life with its opposition to fundamentalist Protestantism and prohibition. Franklin Delano Roosevelt added to this a commitment to economic reform. Both the cultural and the economic positions appealed to the urban workers, who became the central group in the New Deal coalition.

The Democratic party was a broad coalition, however, with overwhelming support in the South. The southern branch of the party was very different in its composition and political ideology. Southern Democrats were committed above all to white supremacy, and most took conservative positions on social and economic issues. The Republicans became the party of middle-class and Protestant America, with heavy support in non-southern farm districts as well.

The New Deal coalition dominated electoral politics for a number of years. The Great Depression ended with the advent of World War II, which was followed by an extended period of relative prosperity. Despite the fading of the issues on which the New Deal coalition had been formed—that is, the issue of recovery from the Depression—the Democratic party remained the majority party. Many more Americans considered themselves Democrats than Republicans. The Republicans could elect a president when the president was a personally popular war hero like Dwight D. Eisenhower (elected in 1952 and reelected in 1956), but the public remained heavily Democratic. Democratic majorities in Congress remained firm through the 1960s and 1970s even though the coalition showed signs of weakening.

The Post–New Deal Party System: Is There One?

Each of the party systems emerged from a "realigning election." In such an election, groups in the population switch their allegiance from one party to another or groups that were previously inactive as voters join the electoral process and choose one of the parties to support. Realigning elections usually create a new majority coalition that tends to dominate elections for years afterward. Thus, after 1896 the Republican party became dominant on the basis of its strength in the industrial North and East. During the 1930s the Democratic New Deal coalition emerged, to be dominant for decades afterward.

Beginning in the middle of the 1960s and accelerating through the 1970s, the New Deal coalition began to weaken and fall apart. In the South, Republican presidential candidates began to prosper as early as 1952 and gradually more and more, mainly white, southerners abandoned their Civil War-based loyalty and supported Republicans for office. Among such groups as Catholics, blue-collar workers, and various ethnic groups, Democratic support was no longer as firm or reliable as it had been. Political observers have been waiting for the new alignment and the resulting new party system. Thus far it has not happened. As the New Deal coalition has weakened, no clear coalition has emerged to replace it. Rather, more Americans are taking part in the electoral contest as independents. Millions of others, retaining a party identification, are likely to split their votes between the various candidates on a ballot and to switch back and forth from one election to the next. Moreover, both parties have become weaker as organizations and are less effective in mobilizing voters.

This had made the future of the American party system somewhat uncertain. We will return to this theme and look more closely at the decline of the New Deal party system, as well as parties more generally, in the next chapter. Now let us look at how the American parties are organized and operate.

PARTIES: THEIR MAIN CHARACTERISTICS

Strong Parties: European Examples

Observers from some European countries often comment on how "weak" the American political parties are in comparison with the "strong" political parties they know in their own countries. What do they mean by this? We can answer the question by looking at some features of the strong parties of Europe.

Organization   European parties are often strong, centrally run organizations. They have a large central office, a big bureaucracy, with separate departments to deal with research, communications, and other business matters. Most important, the central organization dominates the local branches of the party. Nominations for office, particularly nominations for candidates to run for the legislature, are determined in the central office. Campaign finance and campaign organization are controlled centrally, not by individual candidates.

Program and ideology   European parties usually have well-developed programs and ideologies. These programs are recorded in the official publications of each party and make clear how each party differs from the others.

Clearly defined social support   In the European countries, each of the major parties is likely to appeal to a clearly defined social group. Socialist or labor parties receive their support from industrial workers but little support from any other economic groups; Catholic parties get the votes of Catholics but not of non-Catholics; agrarian parties get farmer support but no support in cities. Each party has a group of supporters who stick to that particular party.

Control of the government   The parties organize and control the government if they are elected. In a parliamentary system, if a party wins a majority of the seats in a legislature, it takes over the reins of government, controlling both the legislature and the executive branch. If no party wins a majority, a group of parties may form a coalition to do the same thing.

Weak Parties: The United States
In each of the following respects, the American parties are different:

1. They are decentralized and weak organizations rather than strong and centralized ones.
2. They are likely to have fuzzy positions on issues rather than clearly defined ideologies and programs. Many issue positions of the two parties are very similar.
3. Each party receives support from a variety of social groups rather than from a specific, clearly defined group.
4. Lastly, the winning party does not necessarily dominate the whole government once it is elected.

Each of these characteristics is crucial in determining how the political parties operate in America. Let us look at each more closely.

Organizational weakness   Both the Democratic party and the Republican party have national committees in Washington, chaired by a leading member of the party supported by a staff and assistants (see Table 10.1).

TABLE 10.1

COMPOSITION AND EXPENDITURES OF THE NATIONAL COMMITTEES OF THE TWO MAJOR PARTIES, 1982

	Republican	Democratic
Composition	54 men, one from each state and territory	200 persons, at least two per state, plus others from strong Democratic states
	54 women, one from each state and territory	104 persons, chairperson of each state party plus counterpart of opposite sex
	54 party chairpersons of each state and territory	33 persons chosen from governors, mayors, and other group and official leaders
		Up to 25 others to balance ethnic and racial bloc strength
Total members	162	362
Expenditures	$85,113,252	$16,547,601

SOURCE: Robert J. Huckshorn, *Political Parties in America,* 2d ed. (Monterey, California: Brooks/Cole, 1984); Michael Malbin, ed., *Money and Politics in the United States* (Chatham, N.J.: Chatham House, 1984).

However, the national committees in no way resemble the strong and tight central bureaucracies that dominate parties elsewhere. The national party headquarters has little control over what is done in the party's name at the state or local level. There are, in fact, 51 separate and largely independent Republican parties and 51 Democratic parties, one in each of the states and the District of Columbia. There are even more party organizations if we include some of the strong and nearly independent organizations at the county or city level. These state and local parties are loosely linked together by the national committee. However, organization charts that show lines of communication from national headquarters down to state parties and from there to county or district or ward parties are misleading if they suggest that these are chains of command.

The active units of the party—where there are active units—are mainly at the local level. This contributes to variety. The Democratic party of Biloxi, Mississippi, is a different political animal from the Democratic party of Palo Alto, California; each, in turn, is quite different from the Democratic party in Chicago. On most major decisions each unit of the party goes its own way, not worrying about what another county or state party might be doing. For example, the nomination of candidates for state and local office is under the control of the local party and the local voters if nominations are made in a primary. The nomination of candidates for federal office—for the House of Representatives and the Senate—is also controlled locally, and it is seldom even influenced by the national committee in Washington. There is no effective chain of command with instructions and policies formulated at the top and passed down the line. Fund raising has traditionally been a largely local affair. The national committees of the parties can offer advice to local candidates but relatively little money.

There is only one task that the two political parties have to carry out as nationwide units: the nomination and election of presidential and vice-presidential candidates. In the next chapter we will deal with the process of nomination and election of a president, but we should point out that even in connection with this task, which puts pressure on each of the parties to speak with a single unified voice, the political parties do not act as strong centralized organizations. The struggle for the nomination of the president takes place within the individual states, where convention delegates are selected by primaries or party caucuses. In past years the party conventions—where delegates come together from all parts of the country to choose a presidential candidate—were often the crucial setting when the decision on the presidential candidate was made. However, even when presidential nominations were effectively decided at the national party convention, the convention was actually a meeting of delegates from independent state and local organizations. These delegations would negotiate and compromise at the convention, but they did not give up their autonomy to a central party organization. Today, as we shall see in the next chapter, the convention has been weakened by the importance of primaries in the individual states.

Nor do the national party organizations gain much strength and vigor during the presidential campaign. Presidential campaigns tend to be run by personal organizations of each of the two major candidates. The political parties are most important as symbols under which the two major candidates run. Those symbols are important, however, since only a candidate who has the Democratic or Republican symbol by his or her name is likely to be a serious contender for the election, as Independent John Anderson learned during 1980.

There have been periodic attempts to strengthen the central organs of the political parties, usually by giving a stronger role to the national committee. In recent years, both parties have attempted this. The Republicans have been somewhat more successful. The Republican National Committee has used computer technology or organized mass mailings to Republicans, it has raised and disbursed funds to candidates for Congress, and it has organized campaign schools for candidates. These services do not convert the party's Washington office into a command post dominating state and local parties, but they do give the national organization a greater role than it previously had.

Variations among local parties   The fact that party organization tends to be most solid on the state and local level does not mean that all state and local organizations are strong within their own areas. Some local or state party organizations have a strong and tightly knit organization. They control nominations, organize public debate, get out the vote at election time, and dominate the government of their local area if they are elected. Over time such well-organized political parties have become fewer and fewer. Examples of such strong organizations could sometimes be found in the urban machines that existed in cities like Chicago. During the last few decades most of these machines have grown weaker. Even the famous Chicago Democratic party has lost much of its organizational vigor in recent years.

Part of the traditional basis of party organization strength lay in its control over the "spoils" of office. If the party that won the election was cohesive and well led, it could determine who would fill the various jobs in government, who would get the contracts to pave the streets or build the new court house, and so on. The reforms of the Progressive era mentioned earlier in this chapter gradually undermined many of these practices. Civil-service systems replaced job patronage. Competitive sealed bidding did away with much of the favoritism in awarding contracts. Loyal support of the political party was no longer such an appealing route to these rewards. Deprived of many of its "perquisites," the party was not able to attract and hold the devoted service of workers.

In many local areas, party organization resembles that of the weak national parties. The state or county party committee may, like the national committee, have little real influence. Local committees are often challenged by a rival party group interested in political reform or in pushing an alternative political position. State and local elections may resemble those on the national level. Most candidates are nominated through a direct primary, with or without the support of the local party committee. They then run their campaign with a personal organization, just the way presidential election campaigns are run.

In summary, the party system in America is weak because the national party does not control the local units, and because most of the local units themselves share the disorganization and weakness of the national parties.

PROGRAM AND IDEOLOGY: ARE THE PARTIES DIFFERENT?

Parties link citizens with government by offering the electorate a choice in an election. The voters express their preferences by choosing one side or the other. In some countries the political parties offer the electorate a clear and sharp choice. Each party has a program, party programs differ from each other, and each program is presented clearly to the voters. In the United States the two main political parties do not offer the public that sharp a choice. There are three points to note:

1. Democrats and Republicans agree on some basic characteristics of American government and American society. In this, they share a general consensus in the American public.
2. On many of those issues on which Americans disagree—on which there is no overriding national consensus—the two political parties cannot present clear-cut positions because each is divided internally. Indeed, on some issues there is almost as much division within each of the parties as there is between the two parties. Points 1 and 2 show why the parties are similar.
3. However, we must add a third point: Despite the consensus *between* the parties on some basic issues and the differences *within* the parties

on other issues, the two political parties do differ from each other on many matters. They are not identical twins.

Let us look more closely at each of these three points.

Consensus Between the Parties

The major political parties agree on the basic characteristics of American government and society. Each of the parties supports the Constitution and the structure of democratic government created by it. Neither party would change such features of the Constitution as the separation of powers, federalism, or the Bill of Rights. Both parties support the system of elections in America, and they try to gain office through the electoral route. In some other countries, parties that do not succeed in winning an election may be tempted to turn to other means. They may try to use force to gain office. Neither American party would consider this.

Each of the major political parties, furthermore, is committed to a capitalist economic system based on private ownership. The Democrats and Republicans share in the general consensus that exists on this matter in the United States, as we have shown in Chapter 4.

This is not to say that there are no differences on such matters in the American public nor that such differences are not sometimes reflected in differences between the two political parties. However, these differences are within a relatively narrow range: which way to tilt the balance between the federal government and the states under federalism, how much weight to give to the rights of the accused under the Bill of Rights, and how free of governmental interference the free-enterprise system should be. On such matters the parties do differ. But they do not differ on their commitment to federalism, the Bill of Rights, or an economic system based on private ownership of business. In many European countries, the political parties present the electorate with sharply different portraits of the government and society they favor. The portraits presented by the two American political parties differ in detail and shading, but both paint similar basic pictures of how American life is and should be.

Divisions Within the Parties

The fact that there is basic consensus in America on certain matters ought not to obscure the fact that Americans have many differences of opinion on other things. They differ on economics: How much control should the government have over the economy? How much should the government do to provide social welfare and benefits for the citizens? They differ on racial matters: Should the government push hard for racial integration? Should it support programs of affirmative action? They differ on social issues: Should the government limit the right of abortion, the rights of homosexuals, and so forth? From the point of view of understanding political parties, the important point is that these differences of opinion are found within each of the political parties. Neither represents a closed and cohesive group of like-minded individuals; rather, each party is like a large umbrella under which one finds many different people with varied views.

The Democrats The Democratic party has always been a large and heterogeneous party. For most of this century the Democratic party contained both a conservative southern wing committed to white supremacy and opposed to social and economic reform and a more liberal northern wing supported by unions, blue-collar workers, and racial and ethnic minorities. In recent years the division between these two groups has been blurred as the South has undergone massive change. The solid Democratic control of the South has been broken. Many southern conservatives have moved across to the Republican party, and many blacks now vote in the South, overwhelmingly supporting Democrats.

There are still many conservative southern Democrats, however. For instance, in 1981 Ronald Reagan was able to push through major budget and tax legislation despite the fact that the Democratic party had a majority in the House of Representatives. One reason he was able to do this was the strong support he received from about 35 Democratic members of Congress from the South. They were elected as Democrats from districts where most voters consider themselves Democrats. But they were closer in policy position—conservative on economic matters, in favor of military spending—to Ronald Reagan than to most northern Democrats (see Table 10.2).

The Democratic party remains divided into many groups and factions. In addition to the southerners, there are what are sometimes called old-style New Deal Democrats committed to the Democratic party's liberal position on economic matters. They support government programs to reduce unemployment, to enhance social-welfare programs such as Social Security and Medicare, and to strengthen the position of trade unions in relation to business. This wing of the party receives its support from labor unions, from white blue-collar workers, and from ethnic groups. It is they who have most eagerly sought help for the declining industrial areas of the country. They are quite different in style and concerns from the "new Democrats." This wing of the party supports many of the same economic positions supported by the old-style Democrats, but it is also deeply committed to social change on a variety of issues such as relations between the races or the sexes. This group tends to be supported by liberal more affluent professionals and other middle-class voters. Blacks and other ethnic minorites share some of the new-style Democratic values, but they also are strongly committed to the economic "bread-and-butter" goals of the New Deal faction.

In 1984 the contest for the Democratic presidential nomination reflected rather clearly this three-way division. Walter Mondale, with early labor support, was primarily a traditional Democratic candidate, representing the old New Deal coalition; Gary Hart was mainly backed by the new-style Democrats; and Jesse Jackson received most of his support from blacks and minorities.

The Republicans The Republican party has a somewhat smaller and more homogeneous following, with a decided tilt in the conservative direction. For much of this century the main division within the Republican party was between "Wall Street" and "Main Street." The Wall Street wing of the party represented northern and eastern industrial interests. Though

TABLE 10.2

PARTY SUPPORT AND UNITY IN CONGRESSIONAL VOTING, 1954–1983[a]

Year	House			Senate		
	All Demo-crats	Southern Demo-crats	Repub-licans	All Demo-crats	Southern Demo-crats	Repub-licans
1954	80	n.a.	84	77	n.a.	89
1955	84	68	78	82	78	82
1956	80	79	78	80	75	80
1957	79	71	75	79	81	81
1958	77	67	73	82	76	74
1959	85	77	85	76	63	80
1960	75	62	77	73	60	74
1961	n.a.	n.a.	n.a.	n.a.	n.a.	n.a.
1962	81	n.a.	80	80	n.a.	81
1963	85	n.a.	84	79	n.a.	79
1964	82	n.a.	81	73	n.a.	75
1965	80	55	81	75	55	78
1966	78	55	82	73	52	78
1967	77	53	82	75	59	73
1968	73	48	76	71	57	74
1969	71	47	71	74	53	72
1970	71	52	72	71	49	71
1971	72	48	76	74	56	75
1972	70	44	76	72	43	73
1973	75	55	74	79	52	74
1974	72	51	71	72	41	68
1975	75	53	78	76	48	71
1976	75	52	75	74	46	72
1977	74	55	77	72	48	75
1978	71	53	77	75	54	66
1979	75	60	79	76	62	73
1980	78	64	79	76	64	74
1981	75	57	80	77	64	85
1982	77	62	76	76	62	80
1983	82	67	80	76	70	79

[a] Figures show percent of party members voting with their party on all roll calls in which a majority of one party opposed a majority of the other.

SOURCE: Norman Ornstein et al., *Vital Statistics on Congress, 1984–1985 Edition* (Washington, D.C.: American Enterprise Institute, 1984), p. 183.

this group was conservative compared with much of the Democratic party, it tended to represent an "enlightened conservatism." It supported some social-welfare programs and took an internationalist position in foreign policy. The Main Street wing of the Republican party was centered in the Midwest and spoke for small businesspeople, farmers, and small-town and rural America. As conservatives, they were opposed to the big labor unions, but they also opposed big business and what they saw as the eastern establishment. In foreign policy they were more isolationist.

This division has remained within the Republican party. During recent years, however, it has taken a somewhat different form. The more conservative wing of the Republican party still has roots in the Main Streets of American small towns and cities, but its center of gravity has moved farther west and south toward the Sun Belt. This branch of the Republican party supported the nomination of Senator Barry Goldwater for president in 1964 and was the driving force behind the nomination and successful election campaign of Ronald Reagan in 1980.

Republicans have attracted increasing support from middle-class white southerners and from younger voters everywhere. As the Depression and the New Deal fade from memory, many have been attracted by the Reagan emphasis on strong defense and on promoting economic growth through reduced taxes and government regulation.

The Parties Are Not Identical

Many critics have come to the conclusion that, as George Wallace put it during his third party campaign in 1968, "there's not a dime's worth of difference" between the two parties. This is an exaggeration. The parties may share certain basic values, and they may be divided internally on other matters, but there are still significant differences between them. The Democratic party tends to be more liberal on economic matters, providing more support for social-welfare programs, for programs that reduce unemployment, and for government regulation of the economy. Republicans lay more stress on an unregulated economy and on reducing most government spending, even if that involves curbing social programs. On social issues, such as women's rights, racial equality, and the like, Democrats are likely to be more liberal as well. These differences are expressed in a number of settings.

Platforms   The **party platforms** that are adopted at the national conventions are broad and general. They try to satisfy many groups. Nevertheless, those scholars who have looked closely at the platforms of the two parties find that there are clear differences between them. The Democratic party spends more time in its platform talking about the ravages of unemployment or the problems of poverty, while the Republicans emphasize inflation and the dangers of a powerful government. The Democratic platform is likely to talk about the expansion of governmental programs in health, occupational safety, or the improvement of the environment. The Republican platform is more likely to stress the reduction of governmental involvement in these matters.

Party leaders   The same differences can be seen in the attitudes of the people who are active in the two political parties. A study of the political opinions of delegates to the presidential nominating conventions in 1956 concluded that the Democratic party "is marked by a strong belief in the power of collective action to promote social justice, equality, humanitarianism, and economic planning, while preserving freedom," while the Republican side "is distinguished by faith in the wisdom of the natural competitive process and in the supreme virtue of individuals, 'character,' self-reliance, frugality, and independence from government." Although this fit is not

George Wallace, long-time governor of Alabama, ran for president as a third party candidate in 1968, carrying five states and drawing nearly 14 percent of the vote, much of it in the South. Wallace began to campaign again in 1972, but his prospects were cut short by an assassination attempt that left him permanently paralyzed.

perfect, "the American parties do tend to embody these competing points of view and to serve as reference groups for those who hold them."[1]

Research done two decades later, in 1976, found the same pattern, only perhaps more pronounced. Members of the national and state party committees and county party chairpersons were surveyed. Democrats differed from Republicans along the same philosophical lines found earlier. "Who," they were asked, "is to blame for poverty in America? Is it that the system does not give everyone an equal break or are the poor themselves largely to blame?" Democratic party leaders blamed the system by 5 to 1. Republican leaders blamed the poor by 4 to 1. "Should the government guarantee a job for all Americans who are able to work?" By 6 to 1, Democratic leaders said yes; by 10 to 1, Republican leaders said no.[2] The leaders of the two parties also differed on the importance of national goals. Democrats were most interested in reducing unemployment, and they believed that reducing the role of government was the least important of 10 goals about which they were asked. The Republicans were more interested in reducing the role of government (ranking this goal second in importance after curbing inflation), and they ranked the reduction of unemployment quite low (see Table 10.3).

---

[1] Herbert McClosky et al., "Issue Conflict and Consensus Among Party Leaders and Followers," *American Political Science Review* 54 (1960): 406–427.

[2] See Sidney Verba and Gary R. Orren, *Equality in America: the View from the Top* (Cambridge: Harvard University Press, 1985).

TABLE 10.3

HOW PARTY OFFICIALS VIEW THE IMPORTANCE OF 10 NATIONAL GOALS

Party officials were asked to rank, in order of importance, solutions to 10 major problems.

Republicans	Democrats
1. Curbing inflation	1. Reducing unemployment
2. Reducing role of government	2. Curbing inflation
3. Maintaining a strong military defense	3. Protecting freedom of speech
4. Developing energy sources	4. Developing energy sources
5. Reducing crime	5. Achieving equality for blacks
6. Reducing unemployment	6. Reducing crime
7. Protecting freedom of speech	7. Giving people more say in government decisions
8. Giving people more say in government decisions	8. Achieving equality for women
9. Achieving equality for blacks	9. Maintaining a strong military defense
10. Achieving equality for women	10. Reducing the role of government

SOURCE: Based on a 1977 survey by the *Washington Post* and the Harvard University Center for International Affairs.

The differences are striking. They suggest an important point about American elections. Some critics of the American party system have claimed that elections make little difference in America. The parties sometimes seem to sound as different as possible during elections, but their candidates do not differ when they take office. These critics may have the situation reversed. Evidence suggests that the parties usually try to sound the same when campaigning for office, since they both want the support of the undecided voters who are likely to be middle-of-the-roaders. In office, however, they may behave quite differently. When a Democratic president succeeds a Republican, as in 1977, or when a Republican succeeds a Democrat, as in 1981, a new crew of top and middle management is brought along—the more than 2000 appointees who run the departments and agencies of the federal government. Democratic presidents draw their appointees largely from Democratic ranks, and vice versa for Republican presidents. The people they choose tend to represent quite different viewpoints as to the proper role of government. In 1981, Ronald Reagan began a massive attempt to redirect the government from its path of the past 45 years. To do so, he appointed officials who shared his philosophy of limited government. It made a difference.

Do Democratic and Republican Members of Congress Differ?

When it comes to votes in Congress, neither party can enforce strict party loyalty. The president and the leaders of the president's party in Congress can put pressure on fellow party members, but they can go only so far. Republicans and Democrats in Congress are relatively independent of their parties. The reason is that the party leadership in Congress has very few sanctions to keep the member of Congress in line. The leadership cannot deny a member of Congress renomination for office at the next election, as party leaders can in a nation with strong political parties. Nor does the member need the support of the national party to win reelection. How well the members have built local support in their respective districts is much more important. Members of Congress are likely to be more responsive to voters back home and to those who provide financial support at election time than they are to party leaders. (See Chapter 14 for a full discussion of the ties of members of Congress to their constituencies.) They also follow their own philosophies when deciding how to vote.

This does not mean that Democrats do not, on average, vote differently from Republicans in Congress. Political scientists who have studied congressional votes have reached two conclusions: (1) There is much cohesion within each party, and there are major policy differences between the parties, and (2) deviations from these patterns are due almost entirely to the influence of constituents. Thus if a Democrat votes differently in Congress from fellow Democrats, as some of the southern Democrats do, it is usually because of pressure from the voters back home or from an important interest group in the home district.

Differences in voting records between the two parties may be seen in roll call votes in the House of Representatives. Table 10.4 lists votes on selected legislative proposals over the past quarter century; the striking contrast between Republicans and Democrats is evidence that there are differences between the parties. The Republican party delegation in Congress has opposed government regulation of the economy, income equalization, and social-welfare programs, and has favored policies that create jobs and economic growth through free enterprise and private initiative. The Democrats introduced Keynesian economics, with its emphasis on greater government intervention in the economy; they have tried to reduce income differences through tax reform; and they have favored social-welfare programs. In addition, they are more concerned about unemployment.

Why do Democrats differ from Republicans in congressional voting if the party leadership has so little power to get members of Congress to vote as a group? In substantial part the answer is that Democrats come from different kinds of constituencies than Republicans do. They represent districts or states with somewhat different problems. In addition, however, the members of Congress have philosophies of their own. As political activists they identify with their party more strongly than most of us and do not need to be persuaded to vote with the majority of their party. Of course, they sometimes deviate from their personal views if there appears to be strong voter pressure from their district, but usually this is not the case. Democrats and Republicans, in general, have differing philosophies of government, and these are revealed in many of the actions Congress takes.

WHO SUPPORTS THE PARTIES?

Political parties differ in the extent to which they represent distinctive social groups. In some European countries, as we have pointed out, each political party draws its support from a limited and quite specific part of

TABLE 10.4

PARTY DIFFERENCES IN THE HOUSE OF REPRESENTATIVES, 1945–1984

Year	Selected Legislation	Democrats in Favor	Republicans in Favor
1945	Full Employment Act	90%	36%
1947	Maintain Individual Income Tax Rates	62	1
1954	Increase Unemployment Compensation	54	9
1961	Emergency Education Act	67	4
1964	Antipoverty Program	84	13
1969	Tax Reform	86	22
1971	Hospital Construction	99	41
1973	Increase Minimum Wage	88	27
1974	Federal Aid to City Transit Systems	81	23
1975	Emergency Jobs for the Unemployed	92	13
1976	Block Deregulation of National Gas	70	10
1978	Full Employment and Balanced Growth Act	85	18
1981	Reduce the Federal Budget	12	99
1982	Require American-Built Content in All Cars	74	25
1983	Prohibit Covert Aid to Nicaragua	81	11
1984	Budget Resolution	89	13

SOURCES: Based on data from Robert A. Dahl, "Key Votes, 1945–1964," *Pluralist Democracy in the United States* (Chicago: Rand McNally, 1967), pp. 238–242; *Labor Looks at the 91st Congress,* an AFL-CIO Legislative Report, 1971; *Labor Looks at Congress 1973,* an AFL-CIO Legislative Report, 1974; *Labor Looks at the 93rd Congress,* an AFL-CIO Legislative Report, 1975; *Labor Looks at the 94th Congress,* an AFL-CIO Legislative Report, 1977; *Congressional Quarterly Almanac,* vols. 29–34 (Washington, D.C.: Congressional Quarterly); and *Congress and the Nation,* vol. 6 (Washington, D.C.: Congressional Quarterly, 1985).

the population. Catholic parties will get their support from Catholics and number among their supporters almost no one from other religions. Agrarian parties will have farmers as supporters but no urban dwellers. Socialist or labor parties will get their support from industrial workers. The American political parties are not like this. The two American parties are *catchall parties;* that is, each seeks and receives support from a wide range of groups. They cast their nets wide in appealing to voters as they try to to get all sorts of voters on their side.

The parties do not receive support from identical groups, however. Since the development of the New Deal party system, each party has drawn its support from a somewhat different party of the population. The Democratic party has been the party of blacks, immigrant workers, the poor, and the unemployed. The Republican party has been the party of business and commerical interests and more affluent voters. There are also religious differences between the parties: Catholics and Jews are more likely to be Democrats, and northern white Protestants are more likely to be Republicans. This distinctiveness in where the parties draw their suppport should not be overlooked.

The important point, however, is that in most cases, a particular group *tends* to support one party or the other. It does not give all support to a particular party. Catholics lean in a Democratic direction. Does this mean that all Catholics are Democrats? No. About 40 percent of the Catholics consider themselves Democrats, 25 percent consider themselves Republicans, and the rest consider themselves independents. This represents a decided tilt in the Democratic direction, but hardly unanimity in Democratic support. (We are talking here of the party with which they identify, not necessarily how they vote. We will return to this distinction in the next chapter.) The same can be said for northern white Protestants, who lean in a Republican direction. Nearly half are Republicans, perhaps one-fourth are Democrats, and the rest independents. Black Americans are an exception to the tendency of most American groups to divide their party support. Blacks are the most distinctively Democratic group, giving 80 or 90 percent of their support to that political party.

Note one additional fact about party support. Even when a group gives its support overwhelmingly to one or the other of the political parties—as American blacks do to the Democratic party—that does not mean that the political party represents only that group. For example, in 1984 over 90 percent of black Americans who voted did so for the Democratic candidate. Only about 10 percent of the total votes for the Democratic candidate came from blacks, however. We can see how this can happen if we remember that blacks are now about 12 percent of the population and that their turnout rate is not very high. Though they all vote Democratic, they still make up only a small portion of the Democratic coalition. On the other hand, in that same year, about 44 percent of Catholics voted for the Democratic candidate, but they constituted 26 percent of the total Democratic vote.

In sum, most groups in the population divide their party loyalties even if they tilt one way, and neither party depends on one limited social group for the bulk of its support. The consequence of this for the American political parties is great. Since both parties need support from a wide range of social groups, neither can pitch its case to a limited segment of the population. Each must present positions that have a broad appeal to a range of social groups. Each of the major political parties must, to some extent, be a party of compromise, a party whose programs can satisfy a wide range of groups.

THE PARTIES IN GOVERNMENT

In parliamentary systems, when a political party wins a majority of the vote, it "organizes" the government. The leader of the winning political party becomes the prime minister and therefore the chief executive. The prime minister can count on the support of the legislative branch, within which the members of the prime minister's party will always vote for the government's policy.

In America, a winning political party does not take control of the government in the same way. For one thing, the president and Congress are elected separately and sometimes represent different political parties. Presidents Nixon and Ford, for instance, were Republican presidents faced with Democratic majorities in both houses of Congress. President Reagan entered office with a majority in the Senate in the hands of his Republican party but with a Democratic majority in the House of Representatives.

Even when the president and both houses of Congress come from the same political party, as was the case under President Carter, this does not mean tight party control. The president does not control the votes of the members of Congress who come from the same party. The president can only negotiate with them, try to cajole them into voting the way he wants, and maintain close ties with the party leadership in each of the houses. Members of the House and Senate feel free and are free, however, to go their own way if they wish to vote against the program of the president. The party leaders in Congress—the majority leader and the minority leader in each house of Congress—do not control the votes of their party delegations either.

Nevertheless, party leadership is not completely ineffective. The party leaders in Congress cannot give orders to the members, but they do have some sanctions and can often be persuasive in holding a large part of the party delegation together on a particular vote. Similarly, though a president cannot control the members of Congress who come from the same party, the president can often secure the support of most members of his own party.

We will return to this subject in our chapters on the presidency and Congress. It is enough to say here that we do not have *party government* in America; that is, the government is not entirely dominated by one political party even if that party controls the White House and has a majority in each of the houses of Congress. On the other hand, party ties do help to hold the government together. They play an important role in congressional voting, and they facilitate cooperation between the president and Congress.

THE TWO-PARTY SYSTEM

One of the most important facts about American party life is that there are only two major parties. For over a century almost all members of Congress have been either Democrats or Republicans. Every president has represented one or the other party. There have been third parties in American politics, but they rarely have been powerful. George Wallace's American Independence party received 13 percent of the vote in 1968, and Robert La Follette's Progressive party received 16 percent in 1924. These are the only two third parties to receive over 10 percent of the presidential vote. Theodore Roosevelt's Bull Moose party received 27 percent of the vote in 1912, but it was really a part of the Republican party that had split off and adopted a new name for that election.

When we talk about two parties in America, however, we must be very clear about what we mean. We mean that in most elections—for the presidency, for governorships, for seats in the Senate and the House of Representatives—the contest is between two candidates, one from each of the major parties. If we were not looking at a particular electoral contest but considering, instead, the organized structure of parties in America, we might count more than two. As we suggested earlier, there may be 100 parties in America—a Republican and a Democratic organization in each of the states. One can even think of there being more parties than that if one looks at organizations on county and local levels. To say there is a two-party system is to say that most campaigns are between a Democrat and a Republican. It is not to say there are only two party organizations in America.

Third Parties in American History

The American party system is basically two-party. Third parties have been remarkably unsuccessful in winning major state or national offices. From another perspective, however, third parties have played an important role in our political history. If they have not been successful at winning office, they have often been quite successful in other ways. They have brought new ideas into American political life, and sometimes, they have seen those ideas incorporated into the programs of the major parties. Third parties have served as critics of the two major parties. They have also provided an electoral outlet for those who could find no satisfactory home in either major party.

Third parties often emerge when a segment of the population feels its interests are being ignored by the two political parties. During 1968, for instance, Governor George C. Wallace of Alabama ran under the banner of the American Independence party. He appealed to dissatisfied conservative voters and, in particular, to many white voters who felt that racial integration was moving too fast and too far. Neither party, Wallace claimed, was taking a strong stand on this issue and offering the voters an effective choice. In 1980, Congressman John Anderson ran as an independent, refusing to set up a party organization. His issues were quite different from those of George Wallace. He appealed to middle-class, well-educated voters who were concerned with problems of the environment and with competence in government. Anderson was like Wallace, however, in arguing that the two political parties offered no real choice.

Third-party candidates like Wallace and Anderson do not have to win in order to have some impact on American politics. The very fact that millions of people vote for a third-party candidate—usually in the knowledge that their candidate has no chance—expresses to the two major parties the fact that many voters are unhappy with both. It is not an accident that George Wallace adopted the slogan "Send them a message" for his campaign during 1968. A vote for Wallace, like a vote for Anderson in 1980, was a message to the two political parties that some voters did not see a satisfactory alternative. Furthermore, third-party candidates can influence the outcome of an election by taking votes away from one of the two major party candidates, thereby aiding the other. In 1980 many observers thought that John Anderson's candidacy would hurt Jimmy Carter more than Ronald Reagan, because both Carter and Anderson would appeal to the same moderate and liberal voters. In fact, however, the best evidence suggests Anderson's vote did not much affect the outcome.

Third parties also have an impact by raising new problems and new issues with which the established parties are not yet ready to deal. Examples include the Populist party of the 1890s. The Populist party was founded by farmer groups in the Midwest and West who were upset by the corporate monopolies and trusts that developed during the latter years of the nineteenth century. They agitated for a variety of reforms to protect the interests of the farmer. They ran their own candidate in 1892 without great success, getting only 9 percent of the vote. But they had shown enough strength to pull the Democrats in their direction, and when the Democrats nominated Bryan and adopted much of the Populist platform in 1896, the Populist party endorsed the Democratic nominee and soon disappeared as a separate organization.

Third parties sometimes fade, not because their ideas are rejected, but because their programs are absorbed by the major parties. They lose their reason for existence. When the established parties "steal their thunder," the third parties may disappear. The Populist party disappeared after 1896. Norman Thomas, the perennial Socialist presidential candidate, said that he finally quit running for office because the New Deal had adopted most of the Socialist party's program.

Third parties also face formidable obstacles because of the laws surrounding elections. In many states it is difficult for third-party candidates to get on the ballot. In 1980 John Anderson had to spend a good deal of time and a substantial portion of his campaign funds fighting legal battles to get his name on the presidential ballot in each of the states. In addition, the Federal Election Campaign Act provides millions of dollars in public funds to the Republican and Democratic nominees for the presidency but nothing to third-party candidates. A third-party candidate must win more than 5 percent of the popular vote for the presidency before he can receive federal support. John Anderson managed to borrow money against the hope that he would get more than 5 percent of the vote and be able to pay back these loans. He did achieve his goal, receiving almost 7 percent, and obtained over $4 million in federal support. The support came only after the election, however, and not, as for the two major parties, during the election campaign itself.

Splinter parties   Third parties sometimes break off from one of the major parties when compromise fails to hold together the main factions that make up any large party. Theodore Roosevelt's Bull Moose party of 1912 was a *splinter party* resulting from a split in the national leadership of the Republican party. Roosevelt won the largest third-party vote ever for a presidential candidate, 27 percent, and actually came out 4 percentage points ahead of the Republican candidate, William Howard Taft; however, they both lost to Woodrow Wilson, the Democratic candidate, and this vividly illustrates why party leaders try to avoid a split during an election.

John Anderson's independent 1980 campaign for the presidency looked as if it might have a major impact on the race and the nation, but Anderson received only 7 percent of the vote and carried no states at all.

Roosevelt's large vote should perhaps be counted not as a major third-party success but as a vote for one of two Republican candidates. Similarly, the Dixiecrat party of 1948 and George Wallace's American Independence party can both be thought of as predominantly southern conservative splinters from the Democratic party. The Conservative party of New York is an example of a state-level party that had its origin as a splinter of the Republican party.

Minor parties Some third parties are major national forces. Even though the candidates may have little chance to win, they may have become much discussed national figures during the presidential election. There are, however, a large number of additional parties that appear on the presidential ballots in one or more states. These parties usually stand for some particular policy or some special ideology. Some, such as the Socialist Labor party, the Socialist Workers' party, and the American Communist party, stand for leftist ideologies. Others, such as the Libertarian party and the Independent Conservative party, stand for conservative ideologies. Some parties focus on a particular issue—the Prohibition party, the Right-to-Life party (opposed to abortion), and La Raza Unida (speaking for the interest of Hispanic citizens).

These parties do not really expect to gain national political office. They use the election process as a way to publicize their views. By running candidates they get press coverage and citizen attention. In some cases, when a large enough segment of the population shares their views, these parties can play a significant role in the contest between the two major political parties. La Raza Unida is a significant factor in many local elections in the Southwest. By throwing their support to one or another of the major candidates, they may deliver a crucial bloc of votes in a close race.

The Right-to-Life party attempted to play such a role during the 1980 election, putting its support behind a number of congressional candidates who took antiabortion positions. A party of this sort may not have very many supporters—certainly not enough to make it a serious contender for electoral victory—but its supporters care intensely about the issue. They are willing to vote on that issue and that issue alone, and they are dedicated enough to give time and effort to election campaigns. Such a party can, if the time is right, have some electoral clout.

WHY IS THE PARTY SYSTEM THE WAY IT IS?

There are four factors that help explain why the political party system takes the shape it does: federalism, the separation of powers, our winner-takes-all electoral system, and the historical evolution of group conflict in America.

Federalism

The federal structure of American government places a distinctive stamp on the party system. Most American elections are on the state and local level. We elect only two people nationwide, the president and vice-president, but we elect 50 governors, 100 senators, 435 representatives, and tens of thousands of state legislators, mayors, local council members, county commissioners, school board members, and the like. Most of the political action in the United States occurs on the state and local level, which is where the political party organizations have grown up and been strongest. Even those political leaders who wind up in Washington—in the Senate, in the House of Representatives, and sometimes even in the White House—have their political roots in the states and localities. The fact that the nomination for these offices is dominated by local party groups and organizations reinforces local control.

Federalism reinforces the decentralization of American parties in another way. Most of the laws controlling nominations and elections are state laws. This gives local parties a major stake in maintaining their local independence.

The Separation of Powers

The constitutional separation between the president and Congress also affects the nature of the party system. Unlike parliamentary systems, where the prime minister is elected by the legislature, the U.S. system is one of independent elections for the president and the members of the House and Senate. Their terms of office differ. The president is elected every four years and the House every two years, while the Senate is only partially replaced every two years. In addition, the two branches are given different powers and mutual checks on each other.

All this has impeded the development of a unified national party system. The president and the leaders of the president's party in Congress are often rivals. They can and do act independently of each other. Any attempt to create a united and strong party founders on this basic division between the branches.

Winner-takes-all Elections

Elections in America are contests in **single-member districts** in which the winner takes all. Only one member of Congress is elected from each district; the candidate with the most votes wins the election. Senate elections are conducted on the same basis. In most election years only one senator is elected from any state, and the candidate with the most votes wins. The presidential elections are run on a winner-takes-all basis as well. In each state, all the electoral votes go to the candidate with the largest popular vote. Of course, the presidential election, as seen from the point of view of the whole nation, represents one large winner-takes-all election to provide us with the chief executive.

This differs substantially from a system of **proportional representation,** in which legislative seats are allocated to parties in proportion to the number of votes they win in the nation as a whole or in large regions of the nation. Under proportional representation, a party that got 10 percent of the vote would get 10 percent of the seats in the legislature. In such a system of elections, smaller parties can gain a share of the seats in the legislature. In a winner-takes-all system, all the representation goes to the largest party in the district.

Winner-takes-all elections have four main consequences. In the first place, they make local and state party organizations more important. If only one person from a certain area can be elected, then the national party is dependent on the local party organization to nominate the right person and to get out the vote in that district.

In the second place, parties tend to be large and heterogeneous. In order to win any representation at all, a party must be the largest in the district. It therefore must win support from a wide variety of groups. If it appeals only to a narrow group of like-minded citizens, it will remain permanently out of power. This applies all the way up the line. Candidates for the House of Representatives must have broad appeal in their districts, because only one candidate, the one with the largest vote, will be elected to Congress. Senatorial candidates must appeal across an entire state, as must those who would be elected governor. It applies most dramatically to presidential candidates. A presidential candidate who appeals only to one particular group—blacks, Catholics, born-again Christians, industrial workers, farmers, or whomever—does not have much chance of being elected. Putting together enough votes to be the leading vote-getter in a presidential election requires that the candidate make a broad appeal to a variety of groups.

The third consequence of a winner-takes-all system is a two-party system. How does this happen? Most voters want to vote for a candidate who has a chance of winning. Smaller parties have no chance. Therefore, voters are unlikely to "waste" their votes on a sure loser. The result is that they support one or the other of the large parties that have a chance of winning. Furthermore, the two major parties are constantly on the lookout for new sources of support, since they have to be bigger than the opposition to win. If a significant third party appears, one or the other of the major parties is likely to try to capture its voters by appealing to whatever interests the third party represents.

Last, a winner-takes-all system usually gives an extra bonus of congressional seats or electoral votes to the party that comes out ahead in the popular vote. Much depends on how the vote is distributed across the many districts, but in general a small lead in the popular votes translates into a larger lead in terms of who is elected. A simple and extreme example will make this clear. Suppose the Democratic popular vote for the House of Representatives was 51 percent nationwide during a particular year, while the Republican vote was 49 percent. In a system of proportional representation, approximately 51 percent of the members of the House would be Democrats, and 49 percent would be Republicans—a narrow Democratic margin. But suppose we have a winner-takes-all system, and the 51 to 49 percent split occurs in each one of the individual districts. Under the circumstance the Democrats would control every seat in the House of Representatives, even though they just squeezed by in the popular vote. The same would happen if the Democrats carried every state in the presidential election by a similar narrow margin. The Democratic candidate would get 100 percent of the Electoral College vote.

Things do not happen quite as dramatically in real life, but there is a clear bonus to the party that is ahead. In 1976, for instance, Jimmy Carter won a narrow victory over President Gerald Ford, winning 50.1 percent of the vote. That translated into 55.2 percent of the votes of the Electoral College. The bonus to the party that is ahead can boost a presidential candidate who receives only a minority of the vote into a strong majority in the Electoral College provided that the candidate is the leading vote-getter. As another example, in 1968 Richard Nixon won the election with only 43.4 percent of the vote. Though not a majority, it was the largest vote total received by any candidate, as just 42.7 percent went to Hubert Humphrey and 13.5 percent to the third-party challenger, George Wallace. Nixon's minority popular vote converted into a clear 55.9 percent majority of the electoral votes. Consider 1980. Ronald Reagan won 50.9 percent of the popular vote. He led Jimmy Carter, who won 41.2 percent of the vote, by about 9.7 percent. In the Electoral College, Reagan won 89.9 percent of the vote and led Carter (who received the rest of the electoral votes) by 80.8 percent. In 1984 Reagan's 59.2 percent victory over Walter Mondale yielded him 97.6 percent of the electoral votes.

The system reinforces the tendency toward two parties because it has a particularly harsh impact on third parties. Unless their vote is heavily concentrated in one state or district where they can manage to be the largest party, third parties can gain a substantial number of votes but receive almost no payoff in terms of electoral success. In 1980, for instance, John Anderson won 7 percent of the popular vote but no Electoral College representation. This also explains why, though there have been many and varied third parties in American history, almost all members of the House of Representatives and the Senate come from either the Democratic or the Republican party.

Suppose We Had Proportional Representation: How Many Parties?

It is interesting to speculate how many parties we would have in America if we had a system of proportional representation. With such a system, a

party could be successful if it made a narrow appeal to a particular group
in society. A party that appealed only to American blacks would have no
chance of national success in our winner-takes-all system. But in a proportional representation system such a party might elect a number of members
of Congress. It could elect about 12 percent of the members of Congress
if it gained the support of all the blacks, who number about 12 percent
of the population.

How many parties might we have? We do not know for sure, of course,
but it is quite likely that there would be a party representing American
blacks. They would not necessarily get all the black votes and might not
achieve a full 12 percent in congressional representation, but they would
win some seats. There might be parties representing other ethnic groups.
Religious groups such as the Fundamentalists might form their own party.
There would also probably be several parties representing the different
ideological branches of the Democratic party and several reflecting the
ideological splits within the Republican party. The various groups that
now work together in uneasy coalition within each of the parties might
find themselves divorced and living in much narrower and more homogeneous parties. Proportional representation would result in a very different
electoral system.

Parties and Group Conflict

There is one last reason we should mention why the American political
parties have traditionally been broadly based parties that appeal to a large
number of social groups. Such an appeal fits nicely with the nature of
group conflict in America. Conflict in America tends to occur among many
diverse and overlapping interests. The United States is not divided into
a small number of antagonistic groups—workers versus the middle class,
Protestants versus Catholics, or blacks versus whites.

If there were one overriding conflict in American politics, our political
parties could make narrower and more specific appeals to particular groups.
If, for instance, class conflict based on economic position were *the* crucial
conflict in America, we might expect to find a labor party representing
industrial workers and a more conservative party representing business
interests and the middle class. If the overriding conflict in America were
a religious one, say, between Catholics and Protestants, and if no other
issue really made a difference to people, we would expect a Catholic party
to be opposed by a Protestant party and likewise for other deeply felt
conflicts based on race or region. In such a situation each political party
would find that its best strategy would be to appeal specifically to one
group. The labor party would appeal to the industrial workers and not
attempt to balance its programs by policies that would satisfy the middle
class; the middle-class party would do the opposite. The Catholic party
would appeal to Catholics and make no attempt to get support from among
the Protestants; the Protestant party would write off the Catholic vote and
aim its appeal at its own specific group.

Such a strategy cannot work in America because, as we have emphasized
in previous chapters, there is no single overriding issue or group conflict
in American politics. If a party wants to win an election, it must put together
a diverse coalition of supporters.

PROFILE ■

"THAT'S WHAT'S THE MATTER."

Boss Tweed. "As long as I count the Votes, what are you going to do about it? say?"

WILLIAM MARCY TWEED (1823–1878)
New York City
Political Leader

In the years just after the Civil War, Tweed held various public offices, but his main power came from the fact that he was Grand Sachem of the Tammany Society (Tammany Hall), which meant he ran the New York City Democratic party. The Tweed Ring, comprised of Tweed and numerous business and political associates, engaged in extensive New York real estate speculation and development and used their political influence, at both local and state levels to create "opportunities" for profit. In 1871, however, the complicated structure of Tweed's financial manipulations came tumbling down, and Tweed himself went to jail. He had been the first urban political leader in America to see and seize the possibilities of great profit in local politics. He would not be the last.

CHAPTER HIGHLIGHTS ■

1. Parties are not mentioned in the Constitution, but they are crucial institutions for American democracy because of their central role in elections.

2. There have been many different party systems in American history in which one interest or group was pitted against others. Many of the same conflicts—on social, cultural, and economic grounds—have persisted for a long time.

3. American parties are weak organizations; there is little control by the national party over state and local parties.

4. The American parties agree with each other on many fundamental issues of economics and politics.

5. They also differ on many social and economic issues, with Democrats likely to be more liberal and Republicans more conservative.

6. However, the parties are themselves internally divided, with each containing a more liberal and a more conservative wing.

7. The parties seek support from a wide range of groups. Each represents a broad coalition. Nevertheless, they differ in which groups tend to lean toward them.

8. The parties are weak organizations when it comes to running the government. The presidential and congressional parties may be divided from each other, and the congressional party itself is not under the tight control of the party's leadership.

PROFILE ■

MARK HANNA (1837–1904)
Politician and Promoter
of Business Interests in Government

A Cleveland businessman with extensive interests in coal, iron, street railways, and other Ohio enterprises, Hanna became active in local and state politics. After successfully supporting Congressman William McKinley twice for the Ohio governorship, he then devoted full time to securing for McKinley the 1896 Republican presidential nomination. Hanna's success led to his being chosen chairman of the Republican National Committee. He secured funds from business interests everywhere and raised the unprecedented sum of $3.5 million for the 1896 campaign. Hanna also helped design a strategy that attracted many industrial workers to the Republican ticket.

In 1897 he was elected to the U.S. Senate, and until his death he continued to promote industrial growth but, unlike many of his contemporaries, without alienating labor. His greatest distinction, however, was as the first strong national party chairman who raised the first truly impressive national campaign fund.

9. The fact that there are only two parties is crucial for how the party system works. Third parties are not unimportant, but they have little chance of winning office.

10. The party system takes the shape it does because of federalism, the separation of powers, the winner-takes-all election system, and the absence of a single dominant basis of conflict in America.

SUGGESTED READINGS ■

Not only are there important studies of the unique system of political parties in America, there is also a rich literature dealing with specific state and local parties. Classic studies of the organization and workings of American political parties are: William Riordan, *Plunkitt of Tammany Hall* (1948); Pendleton Herring, *The Politics of Democracy* (1940); E. E. Schattschneider, *Party Government* (1942); V. O. Key, Jr., *Southern Politics* (1949).

Modern commentaries on the American party system include: Frank Sorauf, *Party Politics in America* (5th ed., 1984); Xandra Kayden and Eddie Mahe, Jr., *The Party Goes On* (1985); Nelson Polsby, *The Consequences of Party Reform* (1983); Byron Shafer, *Quiet Revolution: The Struggle for the Democratic Party* (1983); Steven Rosenstone et al., *Third Parties in America* (1984).

PROFILE ■

RICHARD J. DALEY (1902–1976)
Mayor of Chicago

Often referred to as the last of the city bosses, Daley was a classic example of an urban political leader who combined a strong "deliverable" base of working-class voting support with vigorous pro-downtown business development policies to create a powerful regime that dominated Chicago from 1955 to 1976. Chicago had had strong political leaders before. Anton Cermak and Ed Kelly had from the 1920s to the 1940s combined the mayor's chair with leadership of the Democratic party to form a strong coalition from the diverse ethnic groups that make up Chicago's population.

Daley, who was already chairman of the Cook County Democratic party when he took office as mayor, carried the coalition to peak performance. Political power—or clout as it is called in Chicago—was centered in the mayor's office where city policies were developed and implemented and slates of Democratic candidates for local and state office were constructed. Daley's party machine dominated most of the city's 50 wards and could deliver the votes needed to nominate Democratic candidates. Patronage in Chicago politics was massive and used to keep the machine in good working order. Chicago citizens had long since learned that the best way to get a sidewalk fixed or a rundown building condemned was to work through the Democratic party.

Where Daley differed from many traditional city bosses, however, was, first, in his personal integrity and modest life-style—he never left the Irish neighborhood of Bridgeport where he was born—and, second, in his view that "good government is good politics." He brought in noted professional experts to run the police and administer the budget. Above all, he worked closely with business to redevelop the city's core and to encourage the glittering construction that characterizes so much of Chicago today. He did not solve the problems of race or poverty or education—but what city mayors have? As long as Daley was mayor Chicago was known as "the city that works." Soon after he died, the machine began to crumble. Antimachine candidates won the mayoralty contests in 1979 and 1983. When winter blizzards hit, the city no longer worked. Daley probably could not have prevented the fragmentation of his city or the weakening of his clout, but in his time he was the most effective city mayor in the nation.

The 1984 Democratic Convention

Chapter 11

ELECTIONS

very four years in America a major event is the presidential election. Everyone's attention is focused on it. It represents one of the major ways the public exercises control over the government—by voting into office the administration it wants. To become president, an individual must clear two very high hurdles: the party nomination and the popular election. Political parties play a crucial role in the electoral process. They select the candidates to run for office, they organize the election campaign, and they provide the American public with a choice between alternatives. At least that is what parties traditionally did in the United States. In recent years the role of the parties in the electoral process has declined somewhat. An increasingly important role has been played by the mass media, by candidates acting independently of the political parties, and by voters who vote independently of the parties.

There are two steps to the White House, each one long and difficult. First a candidate has to achieve the nomination of one of the parties. It is not impossible for a candidate from a third party to win, but it is highly unlikely—so unlikely that it has never happened since the party system was established. The person who would be president must win the Democratic or Republican nomination. The next step is, of course, winning the election. The road to the nomination and the road from the nomination to the election are somewhat different. We will consider the nomination process first, then the election.

NOMINATING THE PRESIDENT

In a strong centralized party system, the national party would control all nominations for office: for the presidency, for Congress, and for local offices. This has never been the way things worked in the United States. The national parties do not control local nominations. In fact, they do not even control the nomination for the presidency. The choice of the party's candidate for president has always involved bargaining in which state and local party organizations take a major part. This is an important point to remember. It affects the nature and the strategy of presidential elections. In order to achieve the nomination, a potential candidate has to find support in many individual states. He or she can become a national candidate only by obtaining grass-roots support in many parts of the country.

In earlier years those people who sought their party's nomination for president sought support from the powerful state and local party organizations that existed in many parts of the country. In particular, they would look to those organizations that controlled a large bloc of delegates: the party machines in the big urban centers, and the strong state organizations that existed in many of the bigger states. In recent years the power of these organizations has weakened. Potential nominees have a more complex task in gaining state and local support. In many states they have to win primary elections in order to gain the support that once came from party organization. This is in some ways a more difficult task. They have to convince a large number of primary voters to support them rather than convince a few party leaders.

The nomination process has gone through a long evolution since 1800. It was not always as it is today. We will describe that evolution briefly before turning to a discussion of how candidates are nominated today.

King Caucus

The earliest political parties were composed of small groups of men working together across the several states on behalf of candidates and policies. The key units of action were the party **caucuses** that brought together party members in each of the legislatures around the country. State legislative caucuses would choose the party nominees for governor and other state offices. Congressional caucuses nominated the presidential candidates, who then took their case to the voters. This system was termed *King Caucus.*

Conventions

King Caucus did not last long, but it was the first step in the process leading to party domination over access to public office. The second step came with Jacksonian democracy, a political movement of the early nineteenth century named after Andrew Jackson, the seventh president. Jacksonian democracy attempted to broaden participation in American politics. One of its notable successes was the replacement of the caucus system of party nominations with **national conventions.** Conventions were made up of delegates selected by state and local party organizations; thus they were expected to be more broadly representative than caucuses.

Primary Elections

Party conventions were supposed to be more democratic than caucuses because they brought in many more people and were not as easily controlled by a small group of party leaders. Nevertheless, as state and city party machines grew stronger, conventions came under attack. By the end of the century, various reform groups were anxious because party conventions had come under the control of political bosses and their "handpicked" candidates were too often controlled by special interests. The reformers felt that a larger dose of democracy would cure this ill, and they turned to primary elections.

Primary elections are a means of involving party members in the nomination process. From among the numerous possible candidates in a party, the supporters of that party choose the person they consider best qualified to run in the general election—at least this is the theory. Some form of primary election has now been adopted in every state for the governorship and other state offices, for state legislatures, and for Congress. Candidates for many local offices are also nominated in **direct primaries.** In addition, the primary as a means of selecting delegates to the presidential nominating conventions has become much more common. The increased role of primaries in the presidential nomination process is one of the most significant changes in that process in recent years.

Presidential Primaries Versus Nominating Conventions

Primary elections have been part of the presidential selection process for a long time. In earlier years a presidential hopeful might pick up some delegates by winning the primary in those few states that had them. More important, he might have gained important recognition early in the election year by winning a primary or two and showing he was a "serious" candidate. The famous New Hampshire primary comes early in the election year, and candidates can make a name for themselves by winning there. Not many delegates are involved, but the media and the nation pay a lot of attention because there is so little other campaign action that early in an election year. Indeed, a candidate might do well even by losing in New Hampshire. In 1968 Eugene McCarthy challenged President Johnson for the Democratic nomination. McCarthy lost to Johnson in New Hampshire, but he did so well that he immediately became a national figure and a serious contender. A primary election played a decisive role in John Kennedy's quest for the presidential election in 1960. His victory in the West Virginia primary was a major boost to his candidacy, proving that a Catholic could win in a heavily Protestant state. A candidate could also lose credibility by failing to show strength in early primaries. Wendell Wilkie was knocked out of the 1944 Republican race by losing the Wisconsin primary to Thomas Dewey. In 1984 John Glenn was the most prominent of several candidates to pull out of the Democratic party contest after failing to do well in the primaries.

Though primaries were important, until recently they were never conclusive. Most delegates to the national convention were selected by conventions or by caucuses in their individual states, not by primaries. Such delegates were much more under the control of local party leaders. A candidate might do well in the primaries but would not win the nomination without support from these other delegates. Furthermore, even the delegates won in a primary might be lost at the convention. The laws of many states allowed delegates who were elected to support one candidate to switch their allegiance to another one. As recently as 1968, only 17 states had presidential primaries. Hubert Humphrey won the 1968 Democratic nomination without entering any of them.

Primaries have grown in importance in two ways. First, the number of states holding primary elections jumped dramatically (see Table 11.1). Second, most state primary laws were changed so that the delegates elected in the primaries were pledged to a particular candidate. They could not switch their votes at the convention. The result is that the national party conventions have played a smaller role. The nominations have tended to be decided before the conventions even met. By 1976 the number of states holding primary elections had grown to 30. On the Democratic side, Jimmy Carter was so successful in the primaries that the delegates he won in that way gave him nearly enough convention votes for the nomination. Carter was so far ahead of his competitors that the party unified around him the week before the convention. On the Republican side, the expanded 1976 primaries gave Ronald Reagan the opportunity to mount a serious and sustained challenge to the incumbent president, Gerald Ford. In this case the primaries did not settle the nomination. The two ended in a virtual tie. What the primaries did was to allow the challenger to take his case directly to the party's rank and file.

The 1980 election demonstrated more strongly the importance of pri-

TABLE 11.1

CONVENTION DELEGATE SELECTION BY PRESIDENTIAL PRIMARIES, 1948–1984

Year	Number of Primaries		Voters (millions)		Proportion of Delegates Selected	
	Dem.	Rep.	Dem.	Rep.	Dem.	Rep.
1948	13	12	2.1	2.6	36.3%	36.0%
1952	15	13	4.9	7.8	38.7	39.0
1956	19	19	5.8	5.8	42.7	44.8
1960	16	15	5.7	5.5	38.3	38.6
1964	16	16	6.2	5.9	45.7	45.6
1968	15	15	7.5	4.5	37.5	34.3
1972	21	20	16.0	6.2	60.5	52.7
1976[a]	15	27	16.0	10.4	72.6	67.9
1980[a]	34	34	19.5	12.8	74.7	74.3
1984	30	24	17.9	6.5	67.1	—

[a] Excludes Vermont (1976, 1980, 1984) and Texas (1980, 1984), which held nonbinding primaries in which delegates were not selected.

SOURCES: For 1948–1972, *Guide to U.S. Elections* (Washington: Congressional Quarterly, Inc., 1976), pp. 342–349, and Austin Ranney, *Participation in American Presidential Nominations, 1976* (Washington American Enterprise Institute, 1977), Table 1, p. 16; for 1976, Ranney, ibid., and *Guide to 1976 Elections* (Washington: Congressional Quarterly, Inc., 1977), pp. 26–30; for 1980, *Congressional Quarterly Weekly Report* 38 (July 25, 1980), 1870–1871; for 1984, *Congressional Quarterly Weekly Report,* 42 (February 11, 1984): 252, and ibid. (July 7, 1984): 1620.

maries. There were even more primaries: 36 for the Republicans and 34 for the Democrats. It was in the primaries that Ronald Reagan and Jimmy Carter sewed up the nominations. Nominating conventions had once been exciting events. Their outcome was often uncertain, and major political bargains were struck behind the scenes by party leaders. In 1980 the Republican convention merely endorsed a decision that had already been made by Republican primary voters who had presented Ronald Reagan with an overwhelming majority of the delegates.

On the Democratic side, there was somewhat more controversy. Even though he was the incumbent president, Jimmy Carter came into the convention with only 60 percent of the delegates pledged to him, largely on the basis of primary victories. Supporters of Senator Edward Kennedy attempted unsuccessfully to change the convention rules so that delegates pledged to Carter could vote for another candidate. The Kennedy forces pushed this point of view, because it favored their candidate who would otherwise automatically lose to Carter. There was, however, a more general issue behind the argument. Would the national convention become a mere rubber stamp for whichever candidate managed to do well in the primaries or would it become again what it once was—the place where the real decision as to the party presidential candidate was made? In 1980 the conventions were relatively unimportant compared to the primaries.

The Democrats started out with an abundance of candidates for the 1984 presidential nomination, but primary results soon narrowed the field to three: Walter Mondale, Gary Hart, and Jesse Jackson.

Once more in 1984 the conventions merely ratified what the primary voters had already decided. President Reagan had no opposition, of course, but Walter Mondale's success in the primary contests against Gary Hart, Jesse Jackson, and others had clinched his nomination well before the Democratic convention began.

Presidential Primaries: Strengths and Weaknesses

Since primary elections are now the major road to the presidential nomination, it is useful to look carefully at what effects they have.

Are primary elections more democratic? Primaries were introduced in order to make the presidential selection process more democratic. They take power out of the hands of party professionals and put it in the hands of the ordinary members of the party. Many more people participate in the primary process than participated in the old style of candidate selection. Studies show, however, that those who participate in the primaries are still only a small fraction of the supporters of either of the political parties, and not a very representative fraction at that. The primaries do expand popular participation, but participation rates remain low.

How representative are the primaries? Primaries are supposed to allow a more accurate reading of the preferences of rank-and-file Democrats or rank-and-file Republicans. But they give disporportionate weight to the preferences of Democratic and Republicans in a few key but unrepresentative states. Early primaries determine a lot; many would say too much. The results of a primary election in a small atypical state such as New Hampshire—the state that traditionally has the first primary—can create a front-running candidate. In 1980 Ronald Reagan's strong showing in New Hampshire gave him decisive momentum. Other top candidates did less well in New Hampshire, and most withdrew shortly thereafter. The importance of the New Hampshire primary gives one pause about the representativeness of the primary system. New Hampshire is a small state— it has less than 1 million population—and is quite atypical of the nation as a whole. It is only one of over 30 primaries, yet its influence can be overwhelming.

What effect do primaries have on political parties?   Primaries tend to weaken the political parties. The primary system allows the emergence of candidates who are not tied to regular party organizations. Jimmy Carter had no strong party organization behind him. He owed his success in 1976 to his victories in a number of early primaries.

Primaries reduce the power of party organizations in another way. They undercut the power of the **party regulars,** members of state and local parties who are committed to the party as an organization. They want to see the party win. What the candidate stands for may matter less than the candidate's chance of winning. Why do they care so much for victory and so little for what the candidate proposes to do? Often it is because they are officeholders whose jobs depend on their party's being in power. The Democratic machine in Chicago and most other machines were based on such support.

Party regulars usually have the dominant voice in local party conventions and caucuses. Primaries provide a voice for a different kind of political activist: the amateur politician, or *political purist.* They are also interested in finding a winning candidate, but amateur activists are generally committed to finding a candidate with whose program they can agree. The conservative Republicans who nominated Barry Goldwater in 1964 had strong commitments to his program. The supporters of Eugene McCarthy in 1968 or of George McGovern in 1972 were of this sort. They supported their candidate because they believed deeply in the importance of the policies the candidate stood for: commitment to free enterprise in the case of Goldwater, and opposition to the Vietnam War in the cases of McCarthy and McGovern.

Party regulars play a much more important role in conventions. The primaries have been the usual road for amateurs. The existence of such a large number of primaries increases the political importance of the latter. The Democrats adopted new rules for 1984, seeking to bring more elected officeholders and party officials to the nominating convention in an attempt to reverse this tendency and give party regulars a bigger role.

What effect do primaries have on the quality of presidential candidates?   This is, of course, the most crucial question. How adequate are the procedures we now have for providing us with the leadership we need?

Although primaries are widely used to select convention delegates, caucuses—mass meetings of local party supporters—are employed in some states and provide an example of direct democracy.

The answer is somewhat uncertain. Primaries open the presidential nomination process in many states to almost anyone who can put together an organization in order to run. This may allow good candidates to come forward who would not otherwise be successful because they do not have strong ties with one of the political parties. On the other hand, many have suggested that such an open process of seeking the nomination for president may provide us with people who are not really competent to hold the office if elected.

One reason they suggest this is the time and effort that must go into the process of seeking the nomination through the primary route. Presidential campaigns now begin long before the election and become a full-time job for those who seek the nomination. Candidates cannot prepare to be president because they are too busy running for the office. Furthermore, the selection of candidates without strong party ties means that we may have more presidents who have little experience with the party system and less ability to work effectively with Congress and state leaders. A primary campaign with heavy media coverage is not a good setting in which to practice the arts of bargaining and compromise, which may be the most important requirements for an effective president. In the absence of a major role for political parties in the nomination process, the media, particularly television, become very important. Television stresses personality over substance, giving us candidates who look good on the television screen but may be less competent in fact. Finally, the lengthy sequence of primary campaigns is enormously expensive. As we will see, the costs of running for the presidential nomination are large, and primary contests for other public offices are also very expensive. The candidates must raise money and assemble a media-oriented campaign organization, but that is not necessarily the best preparation for the highest office in the land.

THE PRESIDENTIAL CAMPAIGN

Two major presidential candidates and their vice-presidential running mates will be left in the race at the end of the nomination process. Now starts the great democratic ritual of American politics, the presidential campaign.

Appealing to the Voters

Political campaigns, it is often argued, should give the public a choice and also educate the public. Candidates should present their positions clearly, spelling out why they differ from those of the opponent. They should offer the public a choice between two clearly delineated positions and explain to the public why their position is better. In fact, however, campaigns do not work that way. In every campaign we hear complaints about the low level of the debate, the lack of clarity of issues, and the lack of a true choice. Why is this the case?

Candidates have to decide how to appeal to the voters. It is this set of decisions that sometimes results in a campaign that is less edifying than many people would like. Candidates can appeal to voters on the basis of party affiliation, personal characteristics, or positions on political issues.

Party affiliation As we will see when we look more closely at the American voter, many citizens have long-term party identifications. They consider themselves Democrats or Republicans and often have felt that way for their entire adult lives. Candidates can appeal to voters on this basis—the Democratic candidate asking for votes from Democratic supporters and the Republican candidate asking for the votes of Republicans. This tactic is more likely to be used by a Democratic candidate, because in recent decades there have been more Democrats than Republicans; therefore, a Democrat gains more if voters choose on the basis of party.

In many nations, elections are run largely on this basis. People vote for the candidates of the party they have always supported. The candidates try to win the votes of those who are committed to their party and to increase their turnout. They do not appeal to the voters who support opposing parties. In the United States, on the other hand, candidates do not appeal only to the supporters of their own party. They make a broader appeal. For one thing, a crucial bloc of voters are **independent voters.** Nearly 40 percent of the public has no party identification. Furthermore, many voters who identify with one party do so only locally and can often be lured over to vote for the presidential candidate of the opposing party. Since the New Deal, Republican candidates, because of their status as the candidate of the smaller party, are under particular pressure to make a nonpartisan appeal. Millions of Democrats crossed party lines to give presidential victories to the Republican candidate in 1952 and 1956 (Eisenhower), 1968 and 1972 (Nixon), and 1980 and 1984 (Reagan).

In addition, the growing importance of the mass media, particularly television, reduces the extent to which candidates will use partisan appeals. When campaigns were conducted through personal appearances, candidates knew that they were usually addressing voters who supported their own party. Democrats came out to see the Democratic candidate, Republicans to see the Republican candidate. The candidate could safely appeal to partisan loyalties. When facing a national television audience on prime time, however, candidates know that the audience includes supporters of their own party, supporters of the opposing party, and millions of independents; thus they are likely to downplay partisanship.

Personality   Candidates also present themselves to voters as personally appealing. They try to paint themselves as trustworthy, competent, and fully capable of running the government. In the wake of the Watergate scandal, for example, both President Ford and Jimmy Carter tried to stress their personal honesty. In 1980 Ronald Reagan stressed his competence as a potential president compared with Jimmy Carter. Candidates who appeal on the basis of personality do not ask for public support as Democrats or Republicans or because of their position on the issues. They ask for support not for what they will *do* but for what they *are* as individual persons. Perhaps as important as the candidates' attempt to project an image as trustworthy or competent is the attempt to characterize their opponents as irresponsible or incompetent. In 1964 the Johnson campaign used some incautious statements by Senator Barry Goldwater on nuclear weapons to label him irresponsible in such matters. In 1972 the Nixon campaign labeled Senator George McGovern an incompetent, using some evidence of his indecision (in his choice of a vice-presidential candidate and in his plan for a tax rebate for poor people) as the reason. In 1984 Ronald Reagan spoke disparagingly of the lack of experience of his opponent, Walter Mondale. Even though Mondale had been vice-president and a senator, he had never been president and Reagan had. In each case, the effort appears to have had some success.

When campaigns depend as heavily on mass media exposure as they do today, there is a tendency to emphasize even more strongly such superficial considerations as hair color, speech mannerisms, or accent. Yet close media scrutiny over many months of campaigning may also reveal important aspects of a candidate's ability to cope with the crises of office. It is often said that people are irrational if they vote for a candidate on the basis of personal characteristics. This is probably true if the choice is really made on the basis of the candidate's smile, but it certainly is not irrational to choose a candidate who gives evidence of trustworthiness or ability. Such characteristics may be hard to judge, but a long campaign often reveals them, and they are far from irrelevant.

Issues

Candidates also appeal to the public by taking positions on political issues. There are many kinds of issues on which they can take positions.

Consensual issues   On some issues there is little disagreement among the public as to what the goal for America should be. All Americans want peace. They all want prosperity. On issues of this sort candidates will not differ from one another. No candidate is going to come out for war or recession. They debate such issues in terms of which candidate can do a better job in solving a particular problem. An example of such an issue is governmental corruption, which was a major topic in 1976. Both presidential candidates agreed that government power had been abused in previous administrations; each claimed that he would do a better job of cleaning things up than his opponent.

Intense issues   Another type of issue is that on which there is a special, intensely concerned public. One pattern of issue conflict involves a relatively small group of citizens deeply concerned about a particular issue, while the rest of the public is only moderately concerned. There are many such issues. Gun control is an example. A small group of Americans is strongly opposed to any gun-control legislation. Most Americans take the opposite position, but they do so with little intensity. Abortion is a similar issue, with a small, intense minority arguing for measures prohibiting abortion, despite the fact that many people favor permitting it.

How do candidates handle such an issue? Often they try to avoid taking a stand on it. If candidates take a stand in opposition to the intense minority, they lose votes. The intense group will vote against those candidates no matter what their positions are on other issues. For this intense group, only one issue counts. If the group is large enough and located in the right states, it can be a potent voting bloc. Even if not large, the group can be potent beyond its numbers because it is willing to put time and money into campaigning against the candidate it opposes. If an intense group is opposed by a moderately concerned majority, the candidate will worry about the intense minority. The less involved majority will not vote on the basis of the candidate's position on that issue. The 1980 election saw an explosion of groups with intense issue commitment. The most effective were conservative groups, such as the Moral Majority and the National Conservative Political Action Committee (NCPAC).

Issue alternatives   A third type of issue is one on which there are alternate positions and the public is divided. In some cases, most of the public takes a relatively moderate position on one side or the other. In other cases, there are intense publics on either side. There are many such issues on which the public is divided. How much commitment should the government make to welfare spending? Should farmers be protected against adverse market conditions? Should children be bused to foster integration of the public schools? These are the issues on which one expects political candidates to stake out clear positions and give the public a real choice. But that often does not happen. An analysis of election strategies in a two-party system will explain why.

Strategy on Issues

Imagine an issue scale on which citizens can take positions to the left, the right, or in the middle. Assume also that citizens will vote for the candidate whose position is closest to their own. Where will the candidates

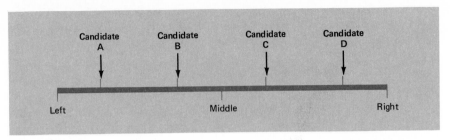

FIGURE 11.1
Issue Scale

who want to win the most votes position themselves? The answer is that candidates who want to maximize the chance of winning will take a position as close to the middle of the road as possible.

Why? The answer lies in our system of elections. As we saw in the previous chapter, we have a winner-takes-all system. In presidential races, the candidate with the most votes wins (subject to some strange things that can happen in the Electoral College, to be discussed shortly). The same is true in races for Congress. The candidate with the highest vote wins the seat. Those who come in second get nothing. This, as we have shown, differs from the system of proportional representation used in many nations with parliamentary systems, where the number of seats won by any party is proportional to the party's share of the electoral vote.

If a party that receives, say, 20 percent of the vote can get some share of government power by winning seats in the parliament, it may choose to direct its appeal to a small proportion of the public. It can take a position on the left or on the right, receive the votes of the minority that shares its views, and elect some members of parliament. But if only one candidate can win, the winning election strategy must try to attract the largest number of voters. This means that a candidate will move toward a compromise, middle-of-the-road position.

This situation is illustrated in Figure 11.1. Imagine an issue (e.g., welfare spending) on which one can take a left, center, or right position; that is, one can favor spending a lot, a moderate amount, or nothing. The voting public is spread out along the scale—some citizens are on the left, some in the middle, and some on the right. If a candidate takes a position on the far left (candidate A) and runs against a candidate only slightly to the right of center (candidate C), it is clear that there are more voters close to C than to A. Similarly, if a right-wing candidate (candidate D) runs against a candidate slightly to the left of center (candidate B), B will get more votes. If the Democratic candidate (who is usually to the left) wants to maximize votes, and the Republican candidate (who is usually to the right) wants to do the same, both will probably wind up close to the center, near the positions of candidates B and C. The farther either candidate moves from the center, the more that candidate risks losing votes to the opponent.

Usually, therefore, candidates who want to maximize their vote stick close to the middle. In some elections, however, a political party has nominated a candidate who is farther from the middle of the road. In 1964 the Republicans nominated Barry Goldwater, a self-styled conservative. He was opposed by Lyndon Johnson, who took a position closer to the center. Goldwater suffered a resounding defeat as many Republicans deserted him to choose the more moderate Johnson. In 1972 a similar thing happened on the other end of the political spectrum. The Democrats nominated George McGovern, who took a position toward the left end of the political scale. He, too, went down to crushing defeat as Democrats crossed over to vote for Nixon. In each case the losing candidate was the one who presented the clearest electoral alternative. Goldwater's campaign slogan during 1964 was to give the American people "a choice, not an echo." He did, and the American public demonstrated that, given a choice, it preferred the echo.

Ronald Reagan, whom the Republicans nominated in 1980, came from the same conservative wing of the Republican party as did Barry Goldwater. Nevertheless, he won the 1980 election. He did so, however, by deliberately trying to demonstrate that he was a moderate and not a conservative like Goldwater. Goldwater had stressed his conservative views. Reagan's contrasting approach was described by one news magazine: "His battle plan is direct and simple. Reagan will seek to capture the middle ground, aiming his message more at wayward Democrats than at the conservative faithful."[1] He chose a vice-presidential candidate from the more moderate wing of the Republican party. In addition to underplaying conservative issue positions, he stressed his own *personal* attractiveness compared with his opponent. Here is how Ronald Reagan's pollster described the themes his campaign staff tried to get across: "We wanted first to establish that in addition to the fact that Ronald Reagan is a strong, decisive individual that he also is compassionate, has a very broad point of view in terms of the values of the family, neighborhood, work place, peace and freedom."[2]

In his attempt to project a personally attractive image, Reagan was aided by the remarkably negative image that Jimmy Carter had in the eyes of the public. Jimmy Carter was a candidate of the middle of the road, which should have given him an advantage in his quest for reelection. But the public turned against him, not because of his specific position on one issue or another, but because they felt that he had managed the economy and the nation poorly. Once again, in 1984, Reagan was very successful in occupying the political center. Although his opponent, Walter Mondale, tried hard to present himself as a moderate Democrat, President Reagan was able to attract a large number of moderate Democratic voters, while at the same time he was acclaimed by conservatives as one of their own.

The Special Position of Party Activists

The preceding discussion suggests that candidates who want to win should take a middle-of-the-road position on most issues. But the situation is often more complicated for the candidate. As we saw in the previous chapter, each of the political parties is divided internally, with the party

---

[1] *Newsweek*, July 28, 1980, p. 32.
[2] *Public Opinion* 4(1981): 2.

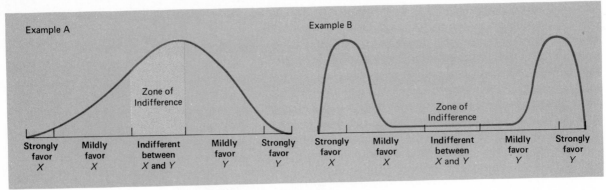

FIGURE 11.2
Two Hypothetical Distributions of Voter Opinions.
What positions do competing candidates take?

activists likely to take positions farther from the center of the political spectrum than do most of the ordinary party supporters. Democratic activists are more liberal than rank-and-file Democrats; Republican activists are more conservative than rank-and-file Republicans. The candidate who moves to the middle of the road to maximize votes may alienate some of the most active supporters—the people who contribute time or money to a campaign.

Furthermore, party activists are most important in the nomination process. They are more likely to vote in primaries and to wind up as convention delegates. Therefore, in order to win the nomination, candidates may have to take a strong liberal or conservative position. To win an election, however, they may have to take a more moderate one (see Figure 11.2 and Table 11.2).

The complexity of this situation puts great pressure on the candidate to find a position that will gain the support of party activists and at the same time maximize the appeal to the public at large. The difficulty of this balancing act was seen during the 1976 election. President Ford chose Senator Robert Dole of Kansas as his vice-presidential candidate. He did

TABLE 11.2
POLITICAL POSITIONS OF CONVENTION DELEGATES,
RANK-AND-FILE PARTY SUPPORTERS, AND THE GENERAL ELECTORATE

	1976		1980		1984	
	Liberal	Conservative	Liberal	Conservative	Liberal	Conservative
Republican convention delegates	3%	48%	2%	58%	1%	60%
Republican voters	—	—	8	41	—	—
General public	20	28	17	28	16	32
Democratic voters	—	—	21	21	—	—
Democratic convention delegates	40	8	46	6	50	5

SOURCE: New York Times–CBS polls.

Political conventions are not totally occasions of cheering and celebration, as these Republican delegates of 1984 make clear.

this in order to maintain the support of the large number of conservative Republicans who had supported Ronald Reagan, approved of Dole, and were very active in the Republican party. Some observers felt that Ford should have chosen a more liberal running mate in order to compete better with Jimmy Carter in the general election. They felt that the choice of Dole as a running mate made Ford less attractive to the electorate. In trying to satisfy conservative activists in his party (whose support he needed), he may have lost some votes in the general public (which he also needed). Interestingly, Dole himself began to take more moderate positions as he unsuccessfully sought the presidential nomination in 1980, and in 1985 he became Republican majority leader in the Senate.

In 1980 Ronald Reagan had the opposite problem from that of Gerald Ford in 1976. Reagan had the support of the party's conservatives and chose a moderate, George Bush, as his running mate in order to hold on to the more moderate and liberal sections of the Republican party. This turned out to be a wise election strategy and helped establish Ronald Reagan as a sufficiently middle-of-the-road candidate in the eyes of many Americans. Reagan, however, risked alienating some of his conservative supporters. There was grumbling from many of them at the convention and during the campaign, but most of them stuck with Reagan. One of the reasons they did was that they "had no other place to go." If Reagan was not conservative enough for them, the other two candidates in the election race—Carter and Anderson—were even less so.

The dual goals that a candidate is called upon to pursue sometimes lead to inconsistencies during a campaign. Often the activists who work for the nomination of a candidate are disappointed by the candidate's campaign. The candidate does not sound as committed to a policy position that they like (a liberal or conservative one) as before the nomination. The reason is that the candidate is modifying the issue stand in order to appeal to as wide a range of voters as possible.

Staying in the Middle

There are a number of strategies that a candidate can use in trying to maximize votes in a situation in which the middle position is the winning one. The one that we have already discussed is to take a moderate position on the issue. Another strategy is to try to make the public think the opposing candidate is far from the middle of the road, that the opponent is on the extreme left or right. As Figure 11.1 shows, it is to a candidate's advantage to make the public think the opponent is at the end of the issue spectrum. In 1964 Johnson characterized Goldwater as an extreme conservative, and during the 1972 campaign Nixon characterized McGovern as a leftist. In 1980 Carter tried to characterize Reagan as a right-winger but had less success in getting this message across to the American public. In part this was because Carter's standing with the public was so low, and in part it was because Reagan so effectively presented himself as a moderate.

Another possible approach is deliberate ambiguity. Candidates can take a middle position by being deliberately unclear on where they stand. An example of ambiguity is found in Richard Nixon's 1968 campaign. Vietnam was a major issue. The public was unhappy and tired of the war but divided on what it wanted done. Nixon wanted to exploit the unhappiness, much of which was directed at the incumbent Democratic administration, without alienating either those voters who wanted to escalate to win the war or those who wanted to withdraw our troops. His solution was to announce that he had a plan but could not reveal it.

One other point should be made. Candidates will seek the middle ground *if* that is the way to capture the largest vote. But what happens when voter opinion itself is concentrated at one end of the spectrum, or divided sharply into two competing camps? Figure 11.2 illustrates the situation. In the left-hand example both candidates will have to move to the right, but with the Democrat likely to be less strenuously conservative than his rival. The example on the right presents an interesting case, rather rare in American political experience, where the best strategy for both candidates may be to be avowedly liberal or conservative and try to get the largest possible turnout of their supporters. Such a campaign would be a very lively one with sharp disagreements and vigorous debate.

CAMPAIGN FINANCE

During the late 1960s and early 1970s, primarily due to rising media costs, political campaigns grew more and more expensive. Candidates were dependent on large campaign contributions, and elections sometimes seemed to be for sale. The 1972 campaign for the presidency cost the candidates and the parties more than $100 million. Senate and House races had soared in cost as well. Naturally the candidates needed all the money they could get. The Watergate scandal revealed widespread abuses in campaign contributions. Direct contributions from corporate funds, unlawful since 1907, were among the abuses discovered in the Watergate investigations.

Campaign Funding Reform

The abuses revealed by the Watergate investigations led to major legislation in 1974 and 1976 that tried to control campaign funding. There are three main parts to the legislation: (1) limits on the amount of money an individual or an organization can give, (2) limits on how much candidates for various national offices can spend, and (3) provision for public funding of presidential elections (see Table 11.3). Under the law, individuals may contribute no more than $1,000 to any one candidate per election and no more than $25,000 to all candidates in any single year. The massive individual contributions of 1972 and earlier are no longer permissible.

The campaign funding law provides matching funds for presidential candidates who qualify by demonstrating fairly widespread support—the ability to raise $5,000 in small contributions in each of 20 states. If they pass that hurdle, candidates receive a big boost from the public funding to which they become entitled. This boost may be particularly useful to candidates without regular party support. It is generally agreed that public funding helped Jimmy Carter, an outsider with little party support, to win the Democratic nomination in 1976, and it has helped other candidates

TABLE 11.3

FEDERAL CAMPAIGN FINANCE RULES

Contribution Limits

$1,000 per individual for each primary, runoff, and general election, and an aggregate contribution of $25,000 for all federal candidates annually; $5,000 per organization, political committee, and state party organization for each election.

Candidate and family's contributions: $50,000 for President; $35,000 for Senate; $25,000 for House.

Individual unsolicited expenditures on behalf of a candidate limited to $1,000 a year.

Cash contributions of over $100 and foreign contributions barred.

Spending Limits

Presidential primaries: $10 million total per candidate for all primaries.

Presidential general election: $20 million.

Presidential nominating conventions: $2 million each major political party, lesser amounts for minor parties.

Senate primaries: $100,000 or eight cents per eligible voter, whichever was greater.

Senate general elections: $150,000 or 12 cents per eligible voter, whichever was greater.

House primaries: $70,000.

House general elections: $70,000.

to remain viable during the long and expensive series of primary contests. In 1984 candidates who qualified received roughly $10 million each.

In addition, the law imposes a spending ceiling on each of the candidates as a condition for acceptance of the public funds. This ceiling is a good deal less than had been spent before the law was passed. The result has been a cutback in the activities traditionally organized by political parties. There are fewer bumper stickers, buttons, billboards, and posters. There are fewer storefront campaign headquarters. And because part of the money to finance the campaign comes from the public treasury, there is less need for the fundraising dinners and picnics that political parties used to organize. All in all, there are fewer reasons for the local Democratic or Republican organization to be active.

The campaign finance law reduces the organizational role of the local parties. At the same time it encourages other organizations to take greater part in the election. The campaign law protects the right of labor unions to communicate with their members in the interest of a political candidate by mail, telephone, and door-to-door canvassing. It is almost always the Democratic candidates who benefit from this type of campaigning by unions. The law gives corporations parallel authority for partisan campaigning among their executives and stockholders. The law also has increased the role of political action committees (PACs), as we saw in Chapter 9. In addition, since a group or PAC can spend any amount it pleases on an election so long as the effort is not coordinated with the candidate, further fracturing of the party organization is encouraged.

Once the party nominees have been chosen they receive federal funding for their campaigns and may not then accept any other money. In 1980 the major candidates each got $29.4 million, while John Anderson, running as an independent, had to wait until after the election to qualify for federal support. He did so (but got only $4.2 million) because he received more than the maximum required, 5 percent of the votes. In 1984 Reagan and Mondale each received just over $40 million. The national parties have also benefited somewhat from the 1974 legislation, because it allows individuals to give up to $20,000 a year to a national party committee. The Republicans have made especially good use of this, raising over $500 million in 1983–1984, compared with the Democrats' $100 million. These funds enable the national parties to play a somewhat larger role than they could in the past.

Public financing of elections makes it possible for relatively unknown candidates, like Carter in 1976, to gain national attention quickly by means of heavy media use. On the other hand, incumbents get as much money as challengers, which, given the head start that their "name recognition" factor usually confers, makes them even more difficult to defeat.

Money and the Campaign Finance Laws

Sometimes policies are *intended* to accomplish one goal but actually have other *unintended* effects. Whatever their effects have been on the parties, campaign finance laws have not had their intended effect of reducing the importance of money in political campaigns; rather, they have changed the way in which money is raised and the kind of influence that the individuals and groups who provide the money can have in an election.

One thing that the finance laws have done is to reduce the role of individual large contributors in helping a candidate win an election. Before the new laws, a few very wealthy contributors could play a very important role in supporting presidential candidates. According to the Citizens' Research Foundation, which monitors campaign giving, W. Clement Stone, a multimillionaire Chicagoan, gave over $2 million to Nixon's reelection campaign during 1972, and Nixon's top 10 contributors during 1972 gave a total of $5.6 million, or almost 10 percent of the money he raised. Liberal candidates such as Eugene McCarthy and George McGovern were also helped by large contributions from a few very wealthy individuals. Stewart Mott, heir to the General Motors fortune, has been a generous contributor to liberal candidates. There are many more conservative multimillionaires than liberal ones, however, and the bulk of such money traditionally went to Republican candidates.

The new campaign finance laws limit individual contributions to $1000 during presidential primaries and forbid them during the general election campaign. This may reduce the importance of some rich individuals but not of money. Why not? For one thing, the campaign finance laws are much more stringent in relation to presidential campaigns than in relation to campaigns for Congress. For the latter campaigns, individuals can give money both during the primaries and during the general election, and the amount of money they can contribute is substantially larger. Individuals can give up to $1000 in each primary and general election as long as they give no more than $25,000 for all federal candidates annually. Thus an individual can give up to $2000 to a candidate for the Senate or Congress (by supporting the same person in the primary and general election) and can do that in a number of races before reaching the $25,000 limit.

Second, as we saw in Chapter 9, the campaign finance law allows corporations, labor unions, or other groups to organize political action committees (PACs). These committees can raise money from a large number of people and then allocate those funds (up to $5000 per candidate per race) to the candidate they want to support. These organizations are beginning to play the role that rich individuals once played.

Last, the Supreme Court has ruled that organizations and individuals may spend money directly for a candidate, and there is no limit to what they can spend. A person or organization cannot give money to a presidential candidate during the general election, but they can, if able to afford it, take out a full-page advertisement in a newspaper *on their own initiative* to support that candidate. In 1980 over $16 million was spent by independent organizations and individuals to support the candidates of their choice. Most of the money was spent in the presidential election, and the bulk of that went to support the Republican candidacy of Ronald Reagan. His supporters spent $10,601,864 to back him; Carter's supporters spent $27,773.

CAMPAIGN STRATEGY AND THE ELECTORAL COLLEGE

A candidate for the presidency must decide where to put campaign time and effort. Should the candidate campaign in every state, concentrate on the most populous states, or concentrate on states where the election is going to be close? These are the kinds of questions that must be answered by the campaign strategy. To some extent the answers are shaped by the Electoral College.

The writers of the Constitution intended the **Electoral College** to serve as a method of choosing a president and vice-president using a small group of respected citizens. Alexander Hamilton states the case in *The Federalist* (*No. 68*). The choice of a president "should be made by men most capable of analyzing the qualities adapted to the station. . . . A small number of persons, selected by their fellow citizens from the general mass, will be most likely to possess the information and discernment requisite to such complicated investigations." This small number of persons, the Electoral College, was to be chosen by the state legislators.

This ancient institution still plays a major role in presidential selection, though not the role the Founders intended. It has become an institution of popular democratic control. Each state has a number of electoral votes equal to the size of its congressional delegation. This number ranges from 47 (California) to 3: six small states and the District of Columbia have only 3 votes each. Electoral votes are bound by the unit rule; that is, all of the electoral votes of a state go to the presidential candidate who wins a plurality of the votes in that state. This rule makes the largest states— the urban, industrial states—most important politically. For instance, the candidate who can win the two largest states (California and New York) has 83 of the 268 electoral votes needed to win the presidency.

This situation has a major impact on campaign strategy, as both parties concentrate on winning the large states. For the Democrats this means making a special appeal to party supporters in the large cities in these states, especially the ethnic groups and minorities. If the appeal succeeds and the Democrats win, the new Democratic president, mindful of the importance of these groups to the election victories, will be anxious to represent their interests in the shaping of national government policy. For the Republicans, who have a different national constituency, the political effects of the Electoral College system are less pronounced, but they too must pay special heed to the big states.

The unit rule of the Electoral College affects how candidates allocate their time. They spend less time in areas where they cannot win, as well as in areas where they cannot lose. If a candidate is sure of victory in a particular state, nothing more is gained from increasing the popular vote there; the candidate will get all those electoral votes anyway. Similarly, if the candidate is a sure loser in another state, nothing will be gained by increasing the share of the vote if the candidate still comes in second. Therefore, candidates give their greatest efforts to states where the outcome is uncertain, especially the large states.

The Electoral College makes it possible for the candidate with the most votes to lose the presidential election. This has happened three times: John Quincy Adams in 1824, Rutherford B. Hayes in 1876, and Benjamin Harrison in 1888 entered the White House despite the fact that they ran second in the popular vote. The possibility that the candidate with the largest popular vote will lose the presidential election is the most serious criticism of the Electoral College. There are other objections. These include the winner-takes-all system, whereby a candidate who carries a state, even by the narrowest of margins, gets all of that state's electoral votes. Many people feel that this disenfranchises those who vote for other candidates. These voters elect no members of the Electoral College. Furthermore, the electors are legally free to vote for whomever they want. Though electors are pledged to vote for a particular candidate, technically an elector can violate that pledge and vote for someone else. Occasionally, this has happened.

The last important objection is to the provision that if no candidate receives a majority of the electoral vote, then the members of the House of Representatives choose among the three top candidates. Each delegation casts one vote, and a majority of the states is needed for election. (This happened once, in 1824.) A House that is controlled by one party could conceivably overthrow a popular preference for the candidate of the other party. The provision also makes it possible for a third-party candidate to get enough electoral votes to prevent either major-party candidate from winning in the Electoral College; in turn, a third-party candidate can play a crucial role in determining who wins in the House by giving support to one of the major-party candidates. Many observers thought that George Wallace might play such a role in 1968, but despite receiving 46 electoral votes, he fell considerably short. (See Table 11.4.)

Reforming the Electoral College

There have been various attempts to reform the Electoral College. One proposed amendment would provide for direct popular election of the president. This would eliminate many of the problems associated with the Electoral College. Under the amendment the presidential candidate with the largest popular vote would be elected. If no candidate won 40 percent of the vote, however, the decision would pass to a joint session of Congress, with each member having one vote.

Though the plan eliminates many of the failings of the Electoral College, it is opposed by many people who prefer the present system. They argue that we should not exchange a system that has worked quite well for a new one that may have unanticipated problems. Representatives of important voting blocs in some large states also oppose the change. It would deprive them of the special position they enjoy when they can swing a state and all its electoral votes in one direction or another.

Leaders of some small states fear that they will lose the slight additional power they receive under the Electoral College system. Under the present system each state receives a number of electors equal to the number of its senators and representatives. Small states such as Alaska, Vermont, Nevada, and Delaware get a bonus because each has two senators. They would lose strength if their vote were only proportional to their population. Lastly, many argue that the Electoral College strengthens the two main parties by making it more difficult for a third-party candidate. Such a candidate has to carry an entire state to register any votes in the Electoral College. This concern for defending what is left of the major parties and resist further tendencies to fragment the American body politic has thus far helped prevent any change in the Electoral College system from being adopted.

TABLE 11.4
PRESIDENTIAL ELECTIONS, 1789–1984[a]

Year	Candidates	Party	Popular Vote	Electoral Vote
1789	**George Washington**			**69**
	John Adams			34
	Others			35
1792	**George Washington**			**132**
	John Adams			77
	George Clinton			50
	Others			5
1796	**John Adams**	**Federalist**		**71**
	Thomas Jefferson	Democratic-Republican		68
	Thomas Pinckney	Federalist		59
	Aaron Burr	Democratic-Republican		30
	Others			48
1800	**Thomas Jefferson**	**Democratic-Republican**		**73**
	Aaron Burr	Democratic-Republican		73
	John Adams	Federalist		65
	Charles C. Pinckney	Federalist		64
1804	**Thomas Jefferson**	**Democratic-Republican**		**162**
	Charles C. Pinckney	Federalist		14
1808	**James Madison**	**Democratic-Republican**		**122**
	Charles C. Pinckney	Federalist		47
	George Clinton	Independent-Republican		6
1812	**James Madison**	**Democratic-Republican**		**128**
	DeWitt Clinton	Federalist		89
1816	**James Monroe**	**Democratic-Republican**		**183**
	Rufus King	Federalist		34
1820	**James Monroe**	**Democratic-Republican**		**231**
	John Quincy Adams	Independent-Republican		1
1824	**John Quincy Adams**	**Democratic-Republican**	108,740 (30.5%)	**84**
	Andrew Jackson	Democratic-Republican	153,544 (43.1%)	99
	Henry Clay	Democratic-Republican	47,136 (13.2%)	37
	William H. Crawford	Democratic-Republican	46,618 (13.1%)	41
1828	**Andrew Jackson**	**Democratic**	647,231 (56.0%)	**178**
	John Quincy Adams	National Republican	509,097 (44.0%)	83
1832	**Andrew Jackson**	**Democratic**	687,502 (55.0%)	**219**
	Henry Clay	National Republican	530,189 (42.4%)	49
	William Wirt	Anti-Masonic		7
	John Floyd	National Republican	33,108 (2.6%)	11
1836	**Martin Van Buren**	**Democratic**	761,549 (50.9%)	**170**
	William H. Harrison	Whig	549,567 (36.7%)	73
	Hugh L. White	Whig	145,396 (9.7%)	26
	Daniel Webster	Whig	41,287 (2.7%)	14
1840	**William H. Harrison** (John Tyler, 1841)	**Whig**	1,275,017 (53.1%)	**234**
	Martin Van Buren	Democratic	1,128,702 (46.9%)	60
1844	**James K. Polk**	**Democratic**	1,337,243 (49.6%)	**170**
	Henry Clay	Whig	1,299,068 (48.1%)	105
	James G. Birney	Liberty	62,300 (2.3%)	
1848	**Zachary Taylor** (Millard Fillmore, 1850)	**Whig**	1,360,101 (47.4%)	**163**
	Lewis Cass	Democratic	1,220,544 (42.5%)	127
	Martin Van Buren	Free Soil	291,263 (10.1%)	
1852	**Franklin Pierce**	**Democratic**	1,601,474 (50.9%)	**254**
	Winfield Scott	Whig	1,386,578 (44.1%)	42
1856	**James Buchanan**	**Democratic**	1,838,169 (45.4%)	**174**
	John C. Fremont	Republican	1,335,264 (33.0%)	114
	Millard Fillmore	American	874,534 (21.6%)	8
1860	**Abraham Lincoln**	**Republican**	1,865,593 (39.8%)	**180**
	Stephen A. Douglas	Democratic	1,382,713 (29.5%)	12
	John C. Breckinridge	Democratic	848,356 (18.1%)	72
	John Bell	Constitutional Union	592,906 (12.6%)	39
1864	**Abraham Lincoln** (Andrew Johnson, 1865)	**Republican**	2,206,938 (55.0%)	**212**
	George B. McClellan	Democratic	1,803,787 (45.0%)	21
1868	**Ulysses S. Grant**	**Republican**	3,013,421 (52.7%)	**214**
	Horatio Seymour	Democratic	2,706,829 (47.3%)	80
1872	**Ulysses S. Grant**	**Republican**	3,596,745 (55.6%)	**286**
	Horace Greeley	Democratic	2,843,446 (43.9%)	66
1876	**Rutherford B. Hayes**	**Republican**	4,036,572 (48.0%)	**185**
	Samuel J. Tilden	Democratic	4,284,020 (51.0%)	184
1880	**James A. Garfield** (Chester A. Arthur, 1881)	**Republican**	4,449,053 (48.3%)	**214**
	Winfield S. Hancock	Democratic	4,442,035 (48.2%)	155
	James B. Weaver	Greenback-Labor	308,578 (3.4%)	

(continued)

TABLE 11.4 (*Continued*)

Year	Candidates	Party	Popular Vote	Electoral Vote
1884	**Grover Cleveland**	**Democratic**	**4,874,986 (48.5%)**	**219**
	James G. Blaine	Republican	4,851,981 (48.2%)	182
	Benjamin F. Butler	Greenback-Labor	175,370 (1.8%)	
1888	**Benjamin Harrison**	**Republican**	**5,444,337 (47.8%)**	**233**
	Grover Cleveland	Democratic	5,540,050 (48.6%)	168
1892	**Grover Cleveland**	**Democratic**	**5,554,414 (46.0%)**	**277**
	Benjamin Harrison	Republican	5,190,802 (43.0%)	145
	James B. Weaver	People's	1,027,329 (8.5%)	22
1896	**William McKinley**	**Republican**	**7,035,638 (50.8%)**	**271**
	William J. Bryan	Democratic. Populist	6,467,946 (46.7%)	176
1900	**William McKinley**	**Republican**	**7,219,530 (51.7%)**	**292**
	(Theodore Roosevelt, 1901)			
	William J. Bryan	Democratic. Populist	6,356,734 (45.5%)	155
1904	**Theodore Roosevelt**	**Republican**	**7,628,834 (56.4%)**	**336**
	Alton B. Parker	Democratic	5,084,401 (37.6%)	140
	Eugene V. Debs	Socialist	402,460 (3.0%)	
1908	**William H. Taft**	**Republican**	**7,679,006 (51.6%)**	**321**
	William J. Bryan	Democratic	6,409,106 (43.1%)	162
	Eugene V. Debs	Socialist	420,820 (2.8%)	
1912	**Woodrow Wilson**	**Democratic**	**6,286,820 (41.8%)**	**430**
	Theodore Roosevelt	Progressive	4,126,020 (27.4%)	88
	William H. Taft	Republican	3,483,922 (23.2%)	8
	Eugene V. Debs	Socialist	897,011 (6.0%)	
1916	**Woodrow Wilson**	**Democratic**	**9,129,606 (49.3%)**	**277**
	Charles E. Hughes	Republican	8,538,221 (46.1%)	254
1920	**Warren G. Harding**	**Republican**	**16,152,200 (61.0%)**	**404**
	(Calvin Coolidge, 1923)			
	James M. Cox	Democratic	9,147,353 (34.6%)	127
	Eugene V. Debs	Socialist	919,799 (3.5%)	
1924	**Calvin Coolidge**	**Republican**	**15,725,016 (54.1%)**	**382**
	John W. Davis	Democratic	8,385,586 (28.8%)	136
	Robert M. La Follette	Progressive	4,822,856 (16.6%)	13
1928	**Herbert C. Hoover**	**Republican**	**21,392,190 (58.2%)**	**444**
	Alfred E. Smith	Democratic	15,016,443 (40.8%)	87
1932	**Franklin D. Roosevelt**	**Democratic**	**22,809,638 (57.3%)**	**472**
	Herbert C. Hoover	Republican	15,758,901 (39.6%)	59
	Norman Thomas	Socialist	881,951 (2.2%)	
1936	**Franklin D. Roosevelt**	**Democratic**	**27,751,612 (60.7%)**	**523**
	Alfred M. Landon	Republican	16,681,913 (36.4%)	8
	William Lemke	Union	891,858 (1.9%)	
1940	**Franklin D. Roosevelt**	**Democratic**	**27,243,466 (54.7%)**	**449**
	Wendell L. Willkie	Republican	22,304,755 (44.8%)	82
1944	**Franklin D. Roosevelt**	**Democratic**	**25,602,505 (52.8%)**	**432**
	(Harry S. Truman, 1945)			
	Thomas E. Dewey	Republican	22,006,278 (44.5%)	99
1948	**Harry S. Truman**	**Democratic**	**24,105,812 (49.5%)**	**303**
	Thomas E. Dewey	Republican	21,970,065 (45.1%)	189
	J. Strom Thurmond	States' Rights	1,169,063 (2.4%)	39
	Henry A. Wallace	Progressive	1,157,172 (2.4%)	
1952	**Dwight D. Eisenhower**	**Republican**	**33,936,234 (55.2%)**	**442**
	Adlai E. Stevenson	Democratic	27,314,992 (44.5%)	89
1956	**Dwight D. Eisenhower**	**Republican**	**35,590,472 (57.4%)**	**457**
	Adlai E. Stevenson	Democratic	26,022,752 (42.0%)	73
1960	**John F. Kennedy**	**Democratic**	**34,227,096 (49.9%)**	**303**
	(Lyndon B. Johnson, 1963)			
	Richard M. Nixon	Republican	34,108,546 (49.6%)	219
1964	**Lyndon B. Johnson**	**Democratic**	**43,126,233 (61.1%)**	**486**
	Barry M. Goldwater	Republican	27,174,989 (38.5%)	52
1968	**Richard M. Nixon**	**Republican**	**31,783,783 (43.4%)**	**301**
	Hubert H. Humphrey	Democratic	31,271,839 (42.7%)	191
	George C. Wallace	American Independent	9,899,557 (13.5%)	46
1972	**Richard M. Nixon**	**Republican**	**46,631,189 (61.3%)**	**521**
	(Gerald Ford, 1974)			
	George McGovern	Democratic	28,422,015 (37.3%)	17
1976	**James E. Carter**	**Democratic**	**40,828,587 (50.1%)**	**297**
	Gerald Ford	Republican	39,147,613 (48%)	240
	Eugene McCarthy	Independent	700,000 (0.9%)	
1980	**Ronald Reagan**	**Republican**	**43,899,248 (51.6%)**	**489**
	James E. Carter	Democratic	35,481,435 (41.7%)	49
	John B. Anderson	Independent	5,719,437 (6.7%)	
1984	**Ronald Reagan**	**Republican**	**52,609,787 (59.7%)**	**525**
	Walter Mondale	Democratic	35,450,613 (40.3%)	13

a Because only the leading candidates are listed, popular-vote percentages do not always total 100. The elections of 1800 and 1824, in which no candidate received an electoral-vote majority, were decided in the House of Representatives.

MOUNTING A CAMPAIGN

Planning a campaign, whether it is for the presidency, a Senate seat, or any other office, requires the candidate to make some important choices. One is *theme*. What theme, or core issue, will be at the center of the campaign. In 1960 John Kennedy emphasized the need to "Get this country moving again." In 1976 Jimmy Carter, building on the distaste created by Watergate, insisted that the voters would always be able to trust him. Closely associated with this substantive theme is the personal *image* the candidate hopes to project. A youthful John Kennedy stressed a dynamic approach, while Richard Nixon, then Vice-president, emphasized the importance of executive branch experience. Jimmy Carter was aided by numerous comedians in attaching to Gerald Ford an image of ineptitude, amiable enough but rather bumbling.

Concepts such as theme and image suggest that political campaigns are rather like advertising campaigns, intended to "market" the candidate by means of artful packaging and careful staging, as indeed they are. Like the marketing of detergent or long-distance telephone service, political campaigns hope to attract support by means of attractive and persuasive presentation, helped along by celebrity endorsements and, if possible, some reports of past successes.

Like other marketing efforts, in order to put together an effective campaign, the candidate must assemble a team of skilled advisers and technicians who will design, write, film, and polish the material. Given the decay of local party organizations, to which we have so often referred, candidates have increasingly relied on their own initiative in putting a campaign team together. Other factors have promoted this individualized approach to campaign organization as well. For many voters party attachment has weakened, and their susceptibility to campaign persuasion may therefore be greater. Television has become the prime medium of the campaign effort. No longer do candidates invest heavily in the time-consuming whistlestop railroad tour. Motorcades through the streets, with the candidate waving to the crowds from an open car, are rare. Now candidates travel by jet, and the emphasis is on reaching the mass audience through the mass media.

In order to mount a modern media-centered campaign, the candidate must not only have large amounts of money but must recruit sophisticated pollsters to assess public wants and reactions, researchers to gather information on public issues and problems, skilled writers to assemble the necessary rhetoric, media experts to create appealing TV spots and other program material, and strategists to assess the political implications of each move. One important development of recent years has been the emergence of a fairly large group of political consultants of various kinds to do those jobs for candidates.

Some of these people may have worked with a candidate for years. Others, especially in a presidential campaign, must be brought in to manage the vast assortment of tasks that have to be done and done quickly in the heat of a national election contest. Building a campaign organization must be done by each candidate and in most instances early enough to begin the campaign well before primary season. Therefore, by the time

The technology of campaigning for the White House has changed dramatically, from the front porch speech of William McKinley to the Truman whistle stop to the Kennedy Motorcade to the nationally televised debates of recent years.

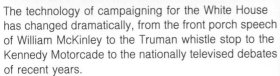

Modern campaigns are aided by sophisticated use of computerized mailings to raise money and distribute literature and of polling to determine trends in public opinion. A new breed of campaign technicians has emerged to operate the new apparatus.

the general election comes around, the campaign team has been at it for at least a year and perhaps much longer. Not surprisingly, the winner often takes some members of the team along to assist him in office as they did during the campaign.

THE AMERICAN VOTER

We have discussed how candidates present themselves to the voters. How do voters respond? The voting behavior of the American public has been closely studied by political scientists for many years. Detailed survey studies of the American electorate began during the 1950s. The scholars found that the American voter was quite different from the **rational voter** of democratic theory. The rational voter is one who has clear views on the issues of the day, knows where the candidates stand, and votes for the one who stands for policies that the voter wants. If voters behaved in this way, elections would function well as a means by which the public controls elected officials. Voters would choose the candidate who would do what the public wanted.

In fact, the American electorate of the 1950s was not like this. For one thing, the public was relatively poorly informed on political matters. It often lacked the information about the positions of candidates that would be needed in deciding which candidate to support. Even more striking was the fact that citizens did not appear to have opinions on a large number of public issues. The average American held relatively few clearly defined political views.

TABLE 11.6 (*Continued*)

Characteristic	1984			1980		
	Reagan	Mondale	Advantage[a]	Reagan	Carter	Advantage[a]
Increasing respect for the United States overseas	48	34	R 14	42	31	R 11
Dealing with Russia	48	34	R 14	37	40	C 3
Building trust in government	41	36	R 5	37	32	R 5
Reducing unemployment	45	41	R 4	41	32	R 9
Spending taxpayers' money wisely	38	37	R 1	42	29	R 13
Keeping the United States out of war	35	47	M 12	25	50	C 25
Improving the environment and dealing with environmental issues	31	47	M 16	32	37	C 5
Improving things for minorities, including blacks and Hispanics	25	54	M 29	22	49	C 27
Helping the poor and needy	25	60	M 35	24	49	C 25
Improving women's rights	20	63	M 43	23	48	C 25

[a] Percentage points.
SOURCES: CBS News/*New York Times* poll; Gallup Poll.

complex, and candidates do not help clarify things. As we have seen, they often modify their positions to reduce the sharpness of their differences with their opponent. If voters are no longer "mindless" party voters, they are not yet decisive "rational" voters.

How then do voters keep control over the officials they elect? To answer this, let us introduce a new distinction—between prospective and retrospective voting.

Prospective Versus Retrospective Voting

When voters decide how to vote in a presidential election, should they look forward or should they look backward? The answer that comes to mind when one thinks of the rational voter is that they should look forward. The voters should ask, "What kind of a future do I want for myself and my country, and which presidential candidate is more likely to create that future?" Forward-looking voters would decide what are the important issues facing the country, which candidate takes a stand on those issues that are closer to their own, and vote accordingly. If the voter thinks that the threat of nuclear war is the biggest problem facing the nation and that we need more arms control, he or she will then vote for the candidate who is more in favor of limiting nuclear arms. If a voter believes that reducing the federal deficit is the biggest issue, he or she will find out which candidate has the best program to cut the deficit and vote for that candidate. Voting of this sort is *prospective,* that is, forward-looking.

Voting this way appears to be fairly rare. It is not easy for a voter to be a prospective voter. For one thing, the voter may not know what issues are going to be most important for the nation over the next four years. Will it be the domestic economy, international tension, or what? Furthermore, the voter may not be certain what policy is best for the nation. If we are to avoid war, should we work to limit nuclear arms, or should we build up our nuclear forces? How do we curb inflation? Do we raise taxes or lower them? And, as we have seen, the candidates are not likely to make it easy for the voter. Candidates take ambiguous positions. Often they do not differ much from each other. Under such circumstances, prospective voting is not easy.

Another way to vote, however, is retrospectively, to look back. The voter may look at the way in which the country has been run for the last four years and ask: Have those who have been running the country been doing a good job or a bad job? Do they deserve to be kept in office or be thrown out? Voting retrospectively is easier than voting prospectively. We may not know what is going to come in the next four years. We have a clearer view of what has happened in the past four years.

Retrospective voting would seem to be a weaker means by which voters exercise control over elected officials. In prospective voting, voters make it clear to the officials where they want the country to go. In retrospective voting, they merely indicate whether they like how things have been going in the past. Nevertheless, retrospective voting can be an effective way of maintaining control over elected officials. The latter know that they will be punished at the polls for failure. Also, it may be a quite rational way to vote. If voters make their election judgment on the basis of how things have been going during the past four years, elected officials must constantly stay on their toes in order to perform well enough to be reelected at the next election.

Retrospective voting may not tell a president exactly what the public wants. It does tell a president that the public will reward good performance and punish bad performance. Retrospective voting has two advantages over prospective voting. It is more consistent with the level of information and understanding one can expect from citizens. Retrospective voting also gives officials some flexibility in choosing policies for the nation. The public cannot prescribe an economic policy for America. Such prescriptions require too much technical expertise. The government officials who can mobilize such expertise can choose a specific set of economic policies. But they are motivated to find a policy that will satisfy the public. The threat of the next election always looms large.

Retrospective voting has played an important role in recent American elections. The clearest example is the 1980 election, when the American public overwhelmingly indicated that it thought the country had been badly run under Jimmy Carter and it was time for a change. Public-opinion polls indicate that the public did not much favor the specific policies Reagan stood for over those of Carter. What the public wanted was a new administration in office, an administration that would do better. Over three times as many of Ronald Reagan's supporters said that their reason for voting for Reagan was that it was "time for a change" as said that they voted for him because he was a "real conservative." By the same token, in 1984 a solid majority felt that they were better off than four years earlier and that America had been heading in the right direction. So they rewarded President Reagan with reelection.

Retrospective Voting and the Decline of the Political Parties

Retrospective voting is an excellent way for a public that is only partially informed about the issues to keep control over elected officials. But retrospective voting can become very difficult if political parties continue to lose their significance in American elections. It is important to see why this is the case.

In order to vote retrospectively, voters have to be able to reward the incumbent administration for good performance and punish it for bad performance. When an incumbent runs for reelection—as did Ford in 1976, Carter in 1980, and Reagan in 1984—the public can clearly identify who it is they should reward or punish. But suppose the specific incumbent is not running for reelection. How do you know whom to reward and whom to punish? The answer ordinarily would be that you reward or punish the party that was in power. If a Democratic administration was in power and did badly, you punish it; if it did well, you reward it.

Suppose, however, that party means less and less. Suppose each of the two candidates, though they run under party labels, do not present themselves as representatives of their parties. If the party was in office and has done badly, the new party candidate says, in effect: "Don't blame me. I may have the same party label, but I am fundamentally different." (This would have been the case had Edward Kennedy won the Democratic nomination in 1980. He would have disassociated himself from the record of the Carter administration.) Under such circumstances the voter cannot vote retrospectively because no candidate accepts responsibility for the record of the previous administration. This means that, as parties grow weaker and weaker, one of the fundamental ways in which voters can control elected officials also becomes weaker.

PARTY REALIGNMENT

In the previous chapter we talked about the many "party systems" that have existed through the course of American political history. In each of the party systems, a fairly stable coalition of voters was identified with one of the parties and a different coalition with the other party. The two parties were divided on a particular set of issues. Such party systems can last for a number of years. The same issues appear election after election. The same groups vote for the parties to which they are attached. Party systems change in periods of **realignment.** Realignments take place at times of great stress, when the existing party sytem does not seem able to deal with the problems the nation faces. Is America due for a realignment in the 1980s?

Maintaining and Deviating Elections

Most elections in the past reaffirmed the pattern of support that the public gives to the major parties. These are called **maintaining elections,** because they maintain the existing party system. Voters choose largely on the basis of party affiliation, and the distribution of party support determines the outcome. In other elections, sometimes called **deviating elections,** voters temporarily abandon their party to vote for a popular candidate or for one whose issue position they prefer. Many Democrats voted for Eisenhower in 1952 and 1956, but they remained Democrats. They were drawn by a great war hero to defect temporarily from their Democratic allegiance, but they returned to vote Democratic in 1960. Maintaining and deviating elections leave a party system unchanged, because the basic distribution of party loyalties remains the same.

Realigning Elections

From time to time in American history there have been major shifts in voting patterns and in long-term party loyalty. New issues emerge that divide the population differently, and groups change their party allegiance. Voters forge new party ties, and a different, revitalized party system emerges. Realignment, some scholars argue, is the way in which the party system adapts to social change.

Realignments do not burst on the scene unannounced. Often there have been vigorous third-party campaigns and other signs of social tension that the established parties have trouble resolving. The realignment itself often takes place over two presidential elections. In the first one, the old pattern begins to fall apart as voters shift their allegiance. In the second, the shift becomes greater and the new pattern is stabilized. It is not merely that voters change their vote. They did that in 1952 and 1956, but the party system remained the same. They have to change their basic party identification. Just before the beginning of the twentieth century there was a major party realignment in the elections of 1892 and 1896, a realignment that created a Republican majority that dominated the country until the Great Depression of the 1930s.

The New Deal realignment　The last major realignment in this country took place during the Great Depression. Herbert Hoover was decisively defeated in 1932, ending a long era of Republican dominance in presidential politics. A new political coalition formed around the New Deal. It was based, as we have seen, on the urban workers in the North, many with immigrant backgrounds. The movement to the Democratic party had actually begun in 1928, when the Democrats ran Governor Al Smith of New York for the presidency. He was the first Catholic chosen to run for the presidency, and he greatly enhanced the appeal of the Democratic party to Catholics—mostly urban workers in the North—who permanently attached themselves to the Democratic party during the 1930s.

At the same time, the Democratic coalition kept control of the solid South. The South was a strange partner in the Democratic coalition. The northern Democrats were liberal, aligned with labor unions and interested in reform of the economic system. Many of the southern Democrats were conservative, with views on social and economic issues that were closer to those of the Republican party. Northern blacks supported the Democratic party, because it stood for social and economic reform. In the South, the

Democratic party's main goal was to maintain white supremacy and keep blacks from participating in the electoral process. The southern Democrats were an important part of the Democratic party, because without their support the party could not as easily have dominated the presidency as it did for two decades after 1932. But the southern Democrats were never fully sympathetic to the New Deal, and quite often they voted with the Republicans in Congress.

What causes a realignment?   The New Deal coalition in the North joined together industrial workers, immigrants, labor unions, and the urban political machines in a powerful political force. Recent research shows that the realignment that created the New Deal in 1932 and 1936 depended on two factors: new issues and new voters. The new issues were those of economic reform. The Democratic party stood for more active government involvement in regulating the economy and providing social welfare. But the new issues were not enough to create a new Democratic majority. What was also needed was a large group of voters who were not yet attached to a political party, voters who could be mobilized to support the Democratic party. These voters were found among the many young voters, often the children of immigrants who entered the electorate during the 1930s, as well as among many citizens, especially women, who had come of age during the 1920s but had not previously voted. It was not so much that many people abandoned the Republican party to become Democrats; rather, there were unattached voters ready to be tied to the Democratic party because of the new policies of the Roosevelt administration.

Realignment Today: Is it Likely?

Today the party system in America is in crisis. Many writers expect a major realignment that will reshuffle voters into new political coalitions.

If the realignment in the New Deal era depended upon new issues and new voters, we would appear to be ready for another realignment. Since the New Deal party system was established, many new issues have come onto the political agenda. During the late 1960s and early 1970s there was the burning issue of Vietnam, which sharply divided the nation. New issues of racial equality, gender equality, and energy and the environment have exploded on the national scene. In addition, many of the groups and individuals who had been committed to the New Deal approach of a big government role in solving social and economic problems have become disillusioned and seem ready to join with others who have long opposed big government. Tax reform and deficit reduction have been decisive. Certainly there are plenty of issues to generate party realignment.

Furthermore, there are new voters. A large portion of the electorate, especially the young, has no strong party ties and is available to attach itself to a new party coalition. Can these new issues and new voters be molded into a new party system?

The decline of the New Deal system   Political observers have been predicting a major party realignment for years. The New Deal party system consisted of a Democratic majority built out of the white South, Catholics (through big city organizations), blacks, Jews, and union members. It was opposed by a smaller Republican coalition supported by northern white Protestants, business executives, and people with high-status occupations.

These coalitions remained solid through the 1950s and into the early 1960s. Since the early 1960s, however, the alignment has grown weaker. American blacks and, to a lesser extent, Jews have remained loyal to the Democratic party, but other groups have been slipping. The strong Democratic support found among Catholics and union members has weakened as many have become more affluent and more conservative in their politics. The South, which used to be Democratic and conservative, is no longer as solidly Democratic. It remains a relatively conservative section of the country but has been showing a greater inclination to vote for Republican candidates (See Table 11.7.)

In 1980 Jimmy Carter carried only one of the 12 southern states—his own state of Georgia—and in 1984 Walter Mondale fared no better in the South than elsewhere in the country, getting only about 40 percent of the vote. On the other side of the fence, the Republican coalition has been losing its distinctiveness as well. Groups that were solidly Republican are becoming more divided. The Democratic party has been receiving more support from well-educated northern Protestants, formerly a solid Republican bloc. These were once a highly conservative group, but in recent years the young college-educated voters among them have been more liberal and more Democratic.

Some political commentators see the basis for a new political alignment in these changes. On the one side would be a new conservative Republican majority based on the white middle class but including affluent union members and Catholics as well. These are the groups that are well established and successful in American society. Forty years ago urban Catholic workers would not have been thought of as falling in that category. Today many do and might support such a conservative coalition. The opposition would be a new liberal coalition made up of the disadvantaged groups in American society—blacks, other minority groups, and the poor—as well as a group of well-educated and affluent liberals. This would be a collection of groups who have done less well in America, joined by liberal intellectuals and some of the young urban professionals who endorse a liberal life style. The new coalitions would also have a regional characteristic. The conservative coalition would be supported in the Sun Belt, made up of the old conservative South and the new economically expanding areas of the Southwest. The more liberal coalition would find stronger support in the older areas of the country, the upper Midwest and the Northeast.

The 1980 Election: Realignment or Dealignment?

The 1980 election resembled in many ways the beginning of a major realignment. The voters gave strong support to Ronald Reagan, a relatively conservative Republican. Moreover, much of his support came from traditionally Democratic groups. He received more of the Catholic vote than Jimmy Carter did. Reagan and Carter each received identical percentages of the vote from union members. (This even split of the union vote may not seem like a great victory for Reagan, but remember that union members

TABLE 11.7

CHANGES IN PARTY IDENTIFICATION, 1952–1984

For most of this period, party identification has been declining and identification as an independent has been increasing. Note, however, the recent rise in the percentage of people who say they are Republicans.

Category	1952	1956	1960	1964	1968	1972	1976	1980	1984
Strong Democrat	22%	21%	21%	26%	20%	15%	15%	18%	17%
Weak Democrat	25	23	25	25	25	25	25	23	20
Independent-Leaning Democrat	10	7	8	9	10	11	12	11	11
Independent	5	9	8	8	11	13	14	13	11
Independent-Leaning Republican	7	8	7	6	9	11	10	10	12
Weak Republican	14	14	13	13	14	13	14	14	15
Strong Republican	13	15	14	11	10	10	9	9	12
Apolitical	4	3	4	2	1	2	1	2	2

SOURCE: SRC/CPS National Election Surveys.

have traditionally voted overwhelmingly for the Democratic candidate. The fact that a conservative Republican does *as well as* a Democrat in union families shows a strong shift by that group.) Reagan also did well in the South and Southwest. These successes were all repeated in 1984.

Has Ronald Reagan forged a new conservative coalition that will dominate American politics for several decades to come? Or have the recent elections been more ad hoc reactions to specific candidates and policies with uncertain meaning for the future. Political observers are divided.

As we have seen, the political parties have been weakening. More and more people consider themselves Independents; fewer and fewer people vote along party lines. Party *realignment* would represent a break in this pattern. It would mean that new party coalitions would be formed and that voters would rebuild their ties to the political parties. The conservative groups would rally around the Republican party, the more liberal ones around the Democratic, and the parties would become strong again. Party **dealignment** would represent a continuation of the decline of the importance of parties. If the 1980 election was one in favor of Ronald Reagan, in favor of his conservative policies, and in favor of the Republican party, it would suggest we are moving toward realignment. If 1980 was an election against Jimmy Carter, against his handling of the presidency, and against political parties in general, it would suggest we are moving toward dealignment.

Signs that point to a realignment in the making are substantial. Whereas in 1980 the Democrats held on to a substantial lead in party identification, by 1984 that margin had nearly vanished. Independents had not increased appreciably, but Democrats had dropped 8 or 10 percent, and Republicans had grown by a comparable amount. Republican gains in party identification were especially impressive in the South, where by 1985 the Republicans had just about equaled the Democrats in party identifiers and had shown much increased strength in Congressional and state-level elections. In addition, among young voters, attachment to the Republican party has grown impressively, from 27 percent in 1980 to 40 percent in 1984.

The Democratic party in 1984 often seemed badly split among its several factions and unable to mobilize a very energetic campaign. Jesse Jackson's candidacy generated some excitement during the presidential primaries, and Geraldine Ferraro's nomination as Mondale's running mate produced more enthusiasm than vice-presidential choices usually do. But through much of the campaign there was a widespread sense not only that Mondale would lose but that the Democratic party as a whole was in deep, long-term trouble. They are no longer a really dominant party in terms of voter attachment, and they have lost four of the last five presidential elections.

On the other hand, the Democrats kept their control of the U.S. House of Representative in 1984, losing only 15 seats in the face of a Reagan landslide. Despite Republican gains in the South, the Democrats entered 1986 with control of every southern state legislature and all but three southern governorships. Republicans have dominated the western states in national elections, but there, too, Democrats hold many of the important state offices. The proportion of American voters who split their tickets between Republicans and Democrats—about 60 percent—has remained very steady for nearly 20 years.

These contradictory tendencies are difficult to sort out, and it may be impossible to predict very far in advance how they are likely to express themselves in future elections. There is no question that many American voters have changed their commitments and loyalties in recent years, but it also seems to be the case that many others have adopted a kind of wait-and-see position, evaluating each candidate in the context of America's recent political history, with the potential for considerable volatility from one election to the next. In the past, American elections generally displayed a more stable structure than they seem to do today.

It is interesting to note that other political democracies in the world have also begun to show great volatility in the patterns of party support and election results. Perhaps, therefore, the present American realignment (or dealignment) is a feature of advanced industrial societies in the late twentieth century. In any case, the very uncertainty that incumbent elected officials must feel in the fact of this volatility among voters may enhance their responsiveness to popular needs and concerns. Incumbents cannot be sure of their support from one election to the next, so they must make an effective record. That is how democracy is supposed to work.

INSTITUTIONS IN ACTION ■

THE DEMOCRATS NOMINATE A PRESIDENTIAL CANDIDATE, 1984

The Democratic Party approached the 1984 election campaign under a sizable handicap. To be sure, all the polls showed that Americans still were more likely to think of themselves as Democrats than as Republicans. Moreover, the Democrats continued to have success in electing members to Congress and to state and local office throughout the country. Nevertheless, it was clear that President Ronald Reagan was popular with the electorate, and that unless some substantial turnaround occurred, Reagan's margin over Carter in 1980, 51 to 41 percent (the rest went to John Anderson and minor candidates), was likely to increase. At the same time, and despite those pessimistic prospects, there were several Democrats who hoped to win their party's 1984 nomination. Best known was Walter Mondale, elected vice-president with Jimmy Carter in 1976 and veteran senator from Minnesota. Mondale had been actively seeking support for the nomination since 1980, and when Senator Edward Kennedy of Massachusetts took himself out of the race in late 1982, Mondale become the clear front-runner.

Front-runners had not fared very well in recent Democratic contests, however. Senator Edward Muskie of Maine was the early leader in 1972, but he faded rather quickly. Once Ted Kennedy had withdrawn in 1974 there really was no clear betting favorite for 1976 until after several of the primaries were over and Jimmy Carter had built a lead. In any case, front-runners can become targets for their opponents and see their support slip away during the several months of primary campaigning. Against Mondale were ranged several other Democrats. Four were members of the Senate: Ernest Hollings of South Carolina, Alan Cranston of California, John Glenn of Ohio, and Gary Hart of Colorado. George McGovern, Democratic nominee in 1972 and former senator from South Dakota, and Governor Rubin Askew of Florida put their hats in the ring, as belatedly did Reverend Jesse Jackson.

Unlike many previous Democratic nomination contests, the 1984 struggle contained no one who was politically conservative, though Glenn, Hollings, and Askew were more moderate in their views than the others. All, however, could claim direct descent from the New Deal, and all could appeal to the main body of traditional Democrats. But few observers thought that such an appeal would be enough to defeat Ronald Reagan, so one major dimension of the nomination struggle involved the candidates' efforts to articulate something "new," some sort of appeal that would add important strength to the Democratic ticket. A second element that was always near the surface in 1984 was the contest that would come in 1988. Even if Reagan could not be defeated, there would be another presidential election four years later without Reagan on the ticket. A Democrat who ran impressively in 1984 might use that persuasively in 1988.

Campaigning for the presidential nomination costs large amounts of money, but the prospect of getting matching funds from public financing for money raised in small sums across several states gives candidates hope that they can make a creditable showing without going totally broke. In 1984 a big reason that money was so important was the necessity for each candidate to build a campaign organization, including media experts, pollsters, political consultants, and teams of workers. The successful candidate is often the one who is the best and earliest organized and in the right states—that is, those states where primaries and caucuses are held early, so that important signals are given to the nation by the way they come out. In this regard, in 1984, the general consensus was that Mondale, who had been busily at work since 1980, would have the advantage of an early display of strength.

One other factor had shaped the contest in a way that departed somewhat from previous Democratic contests. A party commission headed by Governor James Hunt of North Carolina had recommended, and the party had adopted, several changes in the way delegates were to be chosen.

One change was to reserve some 14 percent of the total number of delegates to be chosen by party leaders and elected officials. These "super delegates" were to give the mainstream officeholders a larger voice and reduce the weight of amateur activists. The change meant that a mainstream candidate with long and faithful service was likely to have a better chance than an "outsider" such as Carter in 1976. Other changes strengthened somewhat the position of the major candidates and made long-shot candidacies less likely to succeed even with public financial help.

Mondale's long campaign, combined with the extra importance that under Hunt Commission rules would go to the candidates having early successes, led to one very important decision. The AFL-CIO decided to depart from their past practice of avoiding any candidate endorsement before the party conventions and to take an active role within the Democratic party. Before the primary season began the AFL-CIO, joined by the National Education Association (NEA), endorsed Mondale. Labor support meant money, workers, and a big chunk of voters, but it also made Mondale vulnerable to his rivals, who could and did claim that the Minnesotan was the candidate of the "special interests."

And so the race began. The first stage took place in Iowa, where caucuses met to choose delegates. Mondale did very well, getting nearly half the total. Glenn, on the other hand, did poorly. Expected to be a strong centrist challenger, building on his fame as an astronaut and capitalizing on the recent feature film, *The Right Stuff,* Glenn finished sixth in Iowa, behind "uncommitted." Gary Hart, however, did better than expected, and began to attract substantial media attention. The next step, one week later, was New Hampshire. To everyone's surprise, Hart won a plurality of votes and delegates. Suddenly he had become a serious challenger, and as Askew, Cranston, and Hollings bowed out, the race took on an unexpected shape.

The next important date was two weeks later on Super Tuesday, so called because five states held primaries that day and five others held caucuses and conventions. This was the first southern test of strength with primaries in Alabama, Florida, and Georgia. If Senator Glenn was ever to show that he had special strength among moderate and conservative Democrats, this was his chance. He failed, and soon after, deeply in debt, the former astronaut withdrew, and so did McGovern. This left three candidates in the race: Mondale, Hart, and Jackson.

Jesse Jackson was beginning to show significant strength. He got sizable blocs of delegates not only in the southern primaries but elsewhere, too, as blacks flocked to the polls to vote in unprecedented numbers. He actually won in the District of Columbia (easily) and Louisiana, and by May, Jackson had accumulated a solid 20 percent of the delegates. Jackson's campaign was projected as a "Rainbow Coalition," appealing not only to blacks but also to Hispanics and whites who believed in substantial redistribution of wealth and power in favor of the underclasses in America. In fact, Jackson's support came overwhelmingly from blacks. Jackson had never before run for political office and had no base of party organizational support. However, he utilized with great skill the organizations of the black community, especially the churches, and wherever there were sizable numbers of black citizens his candidacy attracted impresssively large turnouts in primaries and caucus gatherings. Some white liberals supported Jackson also, especially in New York and California, but some ill-chosen remarks about Jews and support from aggressively anti-Semitic Louis Farrakhan cost Jackson dearly among the liberal white Democrats. Still, even though no one supposed he could win, Jackson remained a force to be reckoned with. He controlled a sizable bloc of delegate votes, and more important, he had shown that a charismatic black candidate could attract a large number of voters to the polls who would normally have been expected to remain apathetically on the sidelines. To keep this newly aroused black vote active in the Democratic cause was a more promising challenge than had ever before been appreciated.

Gary Hart turned out to be a more complete challenge to Mondale than any of the other entrants in the race. Throughout the campaign he stressed that he was a "new" candidate with new ideas. Mondale challenged Hart, asking "Where's the beef?"—that is, what actually were Hart's proposals and what was new about them. Hart was accused of stressing image and style rather than substance. Mondale, on the other hand, was portrayed as the captive of labor and other group interests within the Democratic party, unable to break out of the commitments of the New Deal coalition and move on to new conceptions of the political agenda. Hart was portrayed as the "Yuppie" candidate, appealing to the young urban professionals with liberal life-style values but relatively conservative on such traditional Democratic issues as federal aid for the disadvantaged and vigorous regulation of business.

As these charges were hurled and rebutted Mondale recovered his momentum and rebuilt his campaign themes with considerable success in the eastern half of the nation. In the later primaries the former vice-president won big victories in Michigan, Pennsylvania, New York, New Jersey, and Maryland. He did well in much of the South where Hart did not get very far. In virtually every state beyond the Midwest, however, Hart outpaced Mondale. He carried California, and even though it had become apparent by late May that he had no real chance for the nomination he continued to attract nearly as many actual primary votes as Mondale.

In the end, Hart had received 35.6 percent of the total votes cast in Democratic primaries, Mondale had gotten 38.7 percent, and Jackson 19.5 percent. Mondale had far more delegates, however. He had by this time secured the vast majority of the officeholder and party official "super delegates," and he had maintained a comfortable 3 to 2 lead over Hart in primary-chosen delegate support. Despite the insurmountable Mondale lead, however, both Hart and Jackson stayed in the race until the end. At the convention each was able to claim a share of prime time television coverage and to remind the nation what strong candidates they had been.

The Democratic struggle demonstrated quite convincingly that Walter Mondale, with all his experience, careful preparation, organizational strength, financial support, and group endorsements, was not a particularly impressive candidate. Gary Hart had shown Mondale to be vulnerable and had forced him into positions that caused him some grief during the later campaign against Reagan. Hart and Mondale had relatively few real policy differences, and at the convention they made their peace easily. So did Jackson. Yet they had campaigned against each other so vigorously that the stresses and tensions within the Democratic Party were brought into full view, to the considerable advantage of the Republicans who could go before the electorate more unified than they had been for generations.

We should remember that not all the nominating process took place in primaries. Not only were the "super delegates" important, but there were caucuses and conventions in 27 states, seven more than in 1980. Yet it was the primaries, where the voters themselves directly registered their preferences, that drew by far the greatest share of media attention and provided the most significant evidence regarding who was ahead of whom and by how much. This "horse race" conception of the nominating process is much emphasized by the media, abetted by the numerous public-opinion polls appearing in the newspapers and on television. The sequence of primaries, spread over three or four months, lends itself to this kind of emphasis, too. From the candidate's perspective the process is a grueling test of endurance and financial backing, of organizational skills and personal charisma, of composure under tension and sometimes even of ideas. One must wonder why anyone would voluntarily undergo such an ordeal; yet every four years there is a considerable line of willing participants. Indeed, the continued vitality of democracy depends on that fact.

CHAPTER HIGHLIGHTS ■

1.   Primaries have replaced party conventions as the main path to the presidential nominations. The primary system weakens the political parties. It is uncertain whether it produces better candidates.

2.   Candidates for the presidential election can appeal to the voters on the basis of party affiliation, personality, or issues. In recent years, appeals on the basis of party have diminished in importance.

3.   When candidates appeal on the issues, they will often seek to take a middle-of-the-road position in order to maximize the number of votes they get.

4.   Compaign finance laws have reduced the role of "fat cats" but not the role of money in elections. They have had the unintended consequence of reducing the role of political parties.

5.   The rising importance of the mass media, especially television, has also reduced the role of parties. The media focus attention on personality rather than issues.

6.   The American voter is less tied to one of the political parties than was the case earlier. More are independent. They make up their minds as to how to vote on the basis of the personal appeal of the candidate, his or her issue positions, and their party identification (if they have one). Which criterion is most important may vary from election to election.

7.   Retrospective voting is a good way for citizens to keep control over elected officials, but it is more difficult if the political parties are weak.

8.   It is unclear whether we are about to experience a realignment. Many believe there will be a continuing dealignment, that is, a continuing weakening of the political parties.

SUGGESTED READINGS ■

Modern survey research and computer technology have enabled us to study voting and elections with far greater precision and accuracy than ever before.

A classic study of the electorate is: Angus Campbell et al., *The American Voter* (1960). Other modern commentaries on American elections include: Walter Dean Burnham, *Critical Elections and the Mainsprings of American Democracy* (1970); Norman Nie, Sidney Verba, and John Petrocik, *The Changing American Voter* (1979); Paul Abramson, John Aldrich, and David Rohde, *Change and Continuity in the 1984 Elections* (1986); Morris Fiorina, *Retrospective Voting in American National Elections* (1981); James Sundquist, *Dynamics of the Party System* (rev. ed., 1983); Michael Malbin, ed., *Money and Politics in the United States* (1984).

CBS Building, New York

THE MEDIA IN
AMERICAN POLITICS

In the American political system the mass communications media play a prominent role, or more accurately several roles. They report what happens in government, what public officials do (or neglect to do), and what factors influence policy outcomes. They inform us about events, great and small, that carry implications regarding what government will do. It is obvious that none of us, from our own direct experience, can aquire the information and understanding necessary to make sense of the world around us. We are dependent on what we can learn from secondary sources, and the mass media are the most visible of these sources of information and interpretation.

Having said that, however, what else can we say about the place of the media in our political life? Do they so dominate our thinking as to make us virtually their "intellectual prisoners," manipulated in our thinking and steered toward political goals selected by the media elites rather than by a truly informed public? Some people have thought so. Some political conservatives have charged that the media are dominated by liberals. Radicals have tended to see the media as instruments of capitalism and conservative in their effects. Some critics have contended that the media operate like a vast advertising agency, "selling" candidates for public office and public policies as though they were one more brand of detergent.

Many journalists and political commentators deny that the media are so powerfully manipulative; rather, they emphasize the essentially adversarial watchdog role of the media vis-à-vis government. The prime responsibility of the media, in this view, is to keep a close and suspicious eye on public officials, ferreting out wrongdoing and providing a mechanism for revealing to the public whatever information and interpretations are needed to reach reasonable democratic decisions.

These two conceptions of the place of the media in American political life—the manipulative instrument of elite domination versus the watchdog of the public interest—are in a sense caricatures of a more complex reality, but they will serve to define many of the issues that arise in the contemporary United States regarding the mass media and how these instruments of mass communication affect our politics. Some of these issues are constitutional. How much freedom should newspapers and television reporters have to write or speak? How much privacy should the rest of us have? And where are the appropriate limits, if any, on the Constitution's guarantee of freedom of the press? Some of the issues are economic. How much of a threat to effective media functioning is posed by the decline in newspaper competition and the increased importance of multimedia ownership combinations? Does the adversarial watchdog role require competition among news media to be effective, and if so, how much competition is enough?

In addition to the concerns over constitutional/legal issues and the patterns of media ownership and control, there are questions of competence. Are the reporters and commentators who tell us each day what is happening in the world adequately trained and motivated to do the job in the best interests of the public? Do they know anything much about Central America, inflation, or the arms race? Apart from their substantive competence are the media structured in a fashion that makes an informed public even possible? Can the 30-second TV story, even with pictures, ever be an adequate foundation for effective citizenship? None of these is an easy question, obviously. In this chapter, even though we fall short of definitive solutions, we will try to improve our grasp of how the mass media should function in a democratic society.

THE EVOLUTION OF THE MEDIA: FROM PARTISAN ADVOCATES TO INDEPENDENT PROFESSIONALS

When the First Amendment was written, there was only one mass medium of communication: the newspaper. Every newspaper of that day was small in size and circulation, usually appearing once or twice a week, and in most cases quite frankly partisan. Political parties, factions, and even individual political leaders had their own newspaper outlets to tell their side of current events and denounce their rivals.

When Alexis de Tocqueville toured America in 1830–1831 he was greatly impressed by the large number of papers—some 1200 were in existence by the mid-1830s—and their great importance as mechanisms for expressing political party and group positions and for linking together the people who were sympathetic toward a particular party or group. He was also impressed by how decentralized the American press was. In contrast to England or France, where the major papers were (and still are) concentrated in the capital city, American newspapers were highly localized, scattered all over the country, and none dominated the news communication process.

Tocqueville believed that this decentralization of the press was a direct reflection of the decentralization of political power in the United States, and that it contributed to keeping power also decentralized and fragmented. If each political group or faction at each level of government had its own paper and no paper could dominate the others, then it would always be difficult for a common political perspective or nationwide point of view to emerge. Our politics and our mass media would reinforce each other and in doing so preserve the localism and fragmentation of power that were such basic characteristics of American civil society.

By the end of the nineteenth century more than 12,000 newspapers were being published, each continuing to serve a largely local market and many of them still highly partisan in both news and editorial content. Important changes were underway, however. For one thing the enormous growth of the major cities meant that even though their newspapers were local in ownership and coverage there was a huge potential for any paper that could tap the truly mass markets of New York, Chicago, and other metropolitan areas. Newspaper publishers began to compare the circulation and advertising revenues that could be generated by the "yellow" journalism of scandal mongering, gossip, illustration, comics, and athletics, and they gradually moved away from the older patterns of party and group sponsorship and became independent. They also grew substantially in size and complexity and became intensely competitive with one another within each community.

BORN TO COMMAND.

OF VETO MEMORY.

HAD I BEEN CONSULTED.

KING ANDREW THE FIRST.

Political campaigning in the early days of American democracy was intensely partisan and often viciously personal. This well-known cartoon of Andrew Jackson was a relatively mild expression.

An independent press was to play a very different role in American political life than the partisan press had done. The latter served the interests of their sponsoring group, and for them freedom of the press meant that government should not be allowed to censor or prohibit any party's or group's publication. The independent press that took shape at the end of the nineteenth century came to see itself as a distinct social force, an "estate of the realm" that required protection against governmental restraint so that it, the press, could fearlessly pursue wrongdoing and corruption in government. The targets of the press came to be government as a whole, not just particular parties or politicians. Newspapers were still localized in circulation, however, and many of their targets were likewise local political figures. Attacks on urban political bosses and "the shame of cities" were staples of turn-of-the-century American journalism.

An independent press had important effects on how journalists were trained. The traditional partisan paper had often been a kind of sideline venture of someone like Benjamin Franklin, whose real trade was that of printer. But the comparatively vast size and cost of the mass-circulation press required substantial investment and energetic guidance from newspaper entrepreneurs, and a new generation of "press lords" such as Joseph Pulitzer and William Randolph Hearst came to prominence. At the "working press" end of things the move from partisanship to independence meant that reporters and editors began to see themselves quite differently, too. They began to develop a sense of journalism as a profession with its own norms and standards and even its own academic foundations. Journalism programs and schools were created at Illinois in 1904 and Missouri in 1908. The concept that journalists should be objective in their reporting and "tell it like it is," without fear or favor or partisan bias, came to dominate the new professional orientation among journalists.

THE MULTIPLICATION OF THE MEDIA

Magazine Journalism

One important development of the latter half of the nineteenth century was the rise to prominence of weekly and monthly magazines. Unlike newspapers these journals circulated throughout the whole country, and although they rarely sold as many copies as the daily press, magazines emerged after the Civil War as influential vehicles for reporting and commenting on political issues at home and abroad. Such journals as *The Nation*, *Harpers*, and *Atlantic Monthly* appealed primarily to the growing audience of middle-class readers, and the magazines tended to emphasize theories of social and political reform that many newspapers, aiming at the much larger audience of urban workers, disregarded in favor of sensationalism. The magazines of opinion were sometimes highly influential. *McClure's* and *Collier's* in the early 1900s were major **"muckraking"** reformers central to the progressive movement. The *New Republic* under Herbert Croly and Walter Lippmann held a significant place during the Woodrow Wilson presidency. Magazines could not report daily events, however; their function was more that of extended investigation of particular topics set in a context of commentary and interpretation.

Electronic Media

The electronic media added enormously to the number and variety of outlets for conveying information and opinion about public affairs to mass audiences. First radio and then television transformed many aspects of our lives. Most important for our purposes is their impact on how Americans learn about and react to political matters. As Figure 12.1 makes plain, we have come increasingly to depend on the electronic media for our news and to regard television as the most trustworthy source of information. Yet radio and television present the news quite differently from the print media, and the shift from print to electronic sources has significant implications regarding what and how much the public is likely to know.

The electronic media are not nearly as localized in their news coverage as the print media traditionally were. Today, most radio stations and many

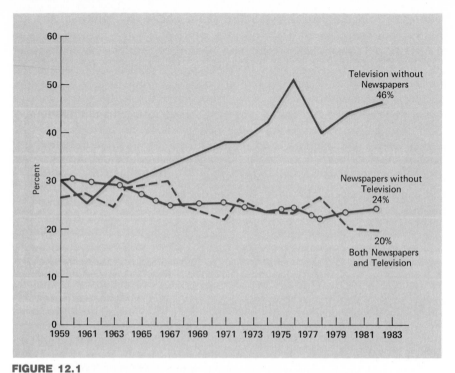

FIGURE 12.1

Where We Get Our News. Question: Where do you usually get most of your news about what's going on in the world today—from the newspapers or radio or television or magazines?

SOURCE: Surveys by the Roper Organization, as reported in "Trends in Attitudes Toward Television and Other Media: A Twenty-Four-Year Review" (Television Information Office occasional publication, 1983).

television stations remain under local ownership, but they depend heavily on the networks and wire services for their news material and offer relatively little variety in coverage or interpretation. Newspapers today also draw upon wire-service news reports and make extensive use of syndicated columnists and features, so that they, too, despite the continued localization of their markets, present rather uniform news coverage across much of the country.

In the United States there remain a very large number of mass media outlets of all kinds. As Table 12.1 shows, magazines and newspapers have decreased somewhat in number in recent years, and the number of cities in which there are competing newspapers has dropped dramatically. Nevertheless, if all the media outlets available to a typical American citizen are taken into account, there is no doubt that the quantity is large, far larger than in Europe where most newspapers are national and most electronic outlets are state controlled. The structure of media ownership and control has been changing swiftly, however, and we may note several recent trends of potential importance.

Concentration of ownership is at the center of several problems. We have noted the sharp decline in head-to-head newspaper competition, and this has given rise to the fear that without competitive media voices the

TABLE 12.1
MAJOR MEDIA OUTLETS
IN THE UNITED STATES

Newspapers	
Daily	1,687
Semiweekly	600
Weekly	6,798
Less frequent	66
Total	9,151
Periodicals	
Daily	182
Semiweekly	94
Weekly	1,376
Semimonthly	658
Monthly	4,096
Bimonthly	1,348
Quarterly	1,711
Other	1,344
Total	10,809
Radio stations	
Commercial AM	4,726
Commercial FM	3,490
Noncommercial FM	1,104
Total	9,320
Television stations	
Commercial VHF	536
Commercial UHF	334
Noncommercial VHF	107
Noncommercial UHF	172
Total	1,149
Cable television systems	5,800

SOURCES: *IMS Ayer Directory of Publications* (Fort Washington, Pa.: IMS Press, 1984) p. viii; *Broadcasting-Cablecasting Yearbook* (Washington, D.C.: Broadcasting Publishing, Inc., 1984), pp. A-2, D-3.

public will be more and more vulnerable to bias and manipulation on the part of media elites. The electronic media are alternatives to the print media, but they, too, are more and more concentrated in their patterns of control. Moreover, there has been a considerable growth in cross-media ownership concentration with newspaper firms like the Chicago *Tribune* owning television stations. Large communication conglomerates like CBS or Capital Cities often combine chains of newspapers and broadcasting activities with book publishing, movie production, and other ventures. Communication megacorporations are feared by some who feel that the media will be dominated by a single perspective on public affairs, that of big business, with no room for dissent or alternative points of view. A further concern is that as the media are taken over by chains and conglomerates they will cut back news and public-affairs coverage and concentrate on the surefire, commercially successful elements of mass communications.

William Allen White (1868–1944), the "Sage of Emporia," was widely respected and influential editor of the *Emporia* (Kansas) *Gazette.* White was one of the last to exercise significant influence through a small-town newspaper.

Sitcoms, soap operas, and cartoons might push more weighty but low-rated programs and stories into the Sunday morning hours.

These concerns are real, and few Americans can be completely happy with the amount and quality of public-affairs coverage provided by the mass media. At the same time, however, we must note that by the mid-1980s it had become possible for people in many parts of the country to receive home delivery of some of the nation's most prestigious newspapers, such as the *New York Times,* the *Wall Street Journal,* and the weekend edition of the *Washington Post.* Cable television has considerably increased the number of electronic media sources for news and commentary available in any given community. The growth of public radio and television service, supported jointly by local communities and federal appropriations through the Public Broadcasting System (PBS), has added depth to the electronic media presentation of news and public issues.

The mass media today undoubtedly provide Americans with far more information and analysis than most of us have any desire to use. Also, despite the well-founded worry over whether there is not excessive ownership concentration and inadequate variety of perspective, diversity has not disappeared. Nevertheless, most mass media firms (except for PBS) are large business corporations seeking to make money in the marketplace. For the most part it is entertainment, not public-affairs analysis, that draws readers or viewers. News coverage that involves scandal or is centered around colorful personalities will win higher ratings and thus make more money than more abstract assessments of world conditions. Insofar as we are dependent on the mass media for what we know about public issues, we are depending on organizations for which the first priority must be market success, not comprehensiveness or balance or sophistication of coverage. There is therefore a basic tension in the role of the American mass media between doing the best job they can of public-affairs reporting and assessment and of earning the largest profits possible. There have certainly been numerous situations in which the media have done a superb job of informing the American public in a comprehensive and responsible manner. Television coverage of the Watergate hearings in 1974 is one example. In 1985 the treatment given the hijacked hostages in Beirut was exemplary. Counter examples are not hard to find either, however, and we should not really expect the tension to disappear. It is a basic part of the American political system.

PUBLIC CONTROL AND THE MASS MEDIA

Mass-media organizations such as newspapers and television networks are vital mechanisms for keeping a sharply critical eye on public officials and informing the people about what government is doing. In this way the media are essential for public control of the political process, essential for democracy. At the same time, however, the media themselves constitute instrumentalities of power. There are numerous economic giants among media corporations, as we have seen. Beyond that, and because they are such important instruments of communication and information, they have great political power over what Americans know and think. Like all other power wielders in society the media may abuse it.

The possibility of abuse of power by the media calls for a measure of popular control over the way they conduct themselves, and this leads to a measure of government regulation. But regulation can quickly become censorship and repression, and this possibility requires some carefully constructed rules to limit how far government authority may go to restrict the media. Let us look at several aspects of this difficult problem of balancing competing values.

"Congress shall make no law . . ."

The First Amendment's absolutist language specifically includes the press. Congress (or any other federal government official) may not abridge the freedom of the press; nor (because the First Amendment's protections have been incorporated into the Fourteenth Amendment) can state or local officials. Yet there are laws that do limit what the press may say. For example, libel laws make it a civil offense to publish or broadcast defamatory material about someone, and in recent years some noteworthy efforts have been made to fight back against politically damaging commentary in the media by suing for libel and asking large sums of money as punishment. For example, General William Westmoreland sued CBS over what had been said about his conduct in command of American troops during the

Vietnam War. Had he won his case in 1985 (as he did not) it might have had a significant "chilling effect" on the willingness of reporters and commentators to criticize public officials. In general, the libel laws have not protected people who are in the public eye from any comments or reports that can be backed up by evidence of their truth. In recent years, however, judges and juries have been somewhat more sympathetic to public figures and skeptical of media claims to immunity.

Libel laws operate only after material has been published or broadcast. A different problem arises when government officials try in advance to prevent something from appearing. This is censorship, and the Supreme Court has been quite strict in protecting the press against any form of **prior restraint;** that is, restraint imposed before publication.

The Pentagon Papers   One of the most dramatic Supreme Court decisions on matters of freedom of speech grew out of the publication of the Pentagon Papers. The case pitted two of the best-known newspapers in the country, the *New York Times* and the *Washington Post,* against the executive branch of the government. It arose when the government tried to block publication of the Pentagon Papers, documents that contained top-secret information on the Vietnam War, in which the nation was still involved at the time.

The government was attempting prior restraint. It claimed that publication of the papers would do "grave and irreparable" damage to the national interest. This national-security interest was placed against the First Amendment guarantee of a free press. In previous cases the Supreme Court had struck down attempts at prior restraint, and in the Pentagon Papers case, it reaffirmed that rule (*New York Times* v. *United States,* 403 U.S. 713, 1971). The newspapers were freed from restraint and continued to publish the papers. The papers revealed that the Kennedy and Johnson administrations had been involved in Vietnam long before the public or Congress knew what was going on.

This Supreme Court decision was hailed as a victory for freedom of speech over national security. But such victories are rarely clear-cut. The newspapers were able to continue publishing the Pentagon Papers and the prohibition against prior restraint was upheld. But the nine justices wrote nine separate opinions in the case—six in favor of the newspapers' position and three in favor of the government's. This shows how uncertain the law is on this subject. Most of the justices said that there could be cases in which prior restraint would be allowed if publication of some national-security material would "result in direct, immediate, and irreparable damage to our nation or its people." In this case they ruled that no such damage was likely, but the possibility of prior restraint in the future was not removed.

Furthermore, the Court left open the possibility that the newspapers might be prosecuted *after* publication for harm done to the national interest. In fact, the newspapers were not brought to trial for this, though Daniel Ellsberg, who had leaked the papers to the press, was prosecuted for violations of national security. (His case, in turn, was dismissed when it was shown that the government had used illegal means to get evidence against him.)

The Progressive **and the hydrogen bomb**   The awesome choices that courts sometimes have to make on issues of free press versus national security can be seen in the case of *The Progressive,* a liberal magazine critical of American weapons policy which had obtained technical material on the making of a hydrogen bomb. The government tried to bar the magazine from publishing such material. This was also a clear case of prior restraint. The Court had not allowed prior restraint in the Pentagon Papers case but had said there might be instances where it was justified. Was not this such a case? The authors of the article said no. There was no security threat. They claimed they were merely pulling together material readily available elsewhere. The material they intended to publish could have been obtained by anyone from the Los Alamos public library.

The federal government asked the U.S. district court to issue an order barring publication of the article. The government admitted that the magazine was not publishing a "do-it-yourself kit" for hydrogen bombs, but claimed that the proposed article did contain material that would make it easier for a nation that did not already have such a bomb to make one.

In the district court the judge ruled for the government and issued an injunction that made publication illegal. He thus instituted the first prior restraint on publication in American history. The judge was by no means unaware that this represented a major challenge to the free press and the First Amendment, but he felt the balance should tip toward national security in this case. As the judge put it: "A mistake in ruling against *The Progressive* will curtail the defendant's First Amendment rights in a drastic and substantial fashion. But a mistake in ruling against the United States could pave the way for thermonuclear annihilation of all of us. In that event, the right to life is extinguished and the right to publish is moot." The judge argued that, given the risks involved, he had to rule against the magazine and allow prior restraint of publication.

This instance of prior restraint did not last very long. The district court's decision was reversed in the U.S. Court of Appeals which accepted the argument by the editors of *The Progressive* that the material they intended to publish would not damage national security, because much had already been published elsewhere.

The case never made it to the Supreme Court. A newspaper in Berkeley, California, had already published the article, so that any damage was already done. There did not seem to be much purpose in pursuing the case further. The U.S. government decided to drop it.

Though the case never received a final decision by the Supreme Court, we can learn from it. As the district court judge expressed it so eloquently, decisions in the area of free speech sometimes involve awesome choices of a most difficult kind. Furthermore, the fact that the U.S. Court of Appeals reversed the district court and allowed the publication of the article illustrates how seriously the courts take the First Amendment's free press provisions, especially when prior restraint is involved. Prior restraint of publication will certainly be rare.

Licensing

A key feature of the First Amendment protection of a free press is that no license or permit can be required in order to publish. Anyone with a printing press can speak out. Printing presses are more expensive nowadays than in 1789, but it is still generally true that there is easy access to the print media. Newspapers, magazines, and leaflets are relatively cheap to produce and distribute. Electronic media present a different situation, however. Radio and television stations cannot go on the air without approval from the Federal Communications Commission, and the FCC operates within a framework of legislation enacted by Congress. Licensing is necessary because the airwaves are in relatively short supply. Too many stations would quickly crowd one another out, and without strict adherence to frequency or channel assignments there would be noisy chaos—as indeed there was in radio before federal regulation went into effect in 1927.

If some form of licensing is necessary for radio and television, then it is an easy step to attach conditions to the license. A television or radio license is usually very valuable and much sought after. Nevertheless, the Federal Communications Commission (FCC) has governed with a very light hand. A radio or television station must, under the law, "serve the public interest, convenience and necessity." In granting a new license the FCC had tried to insure that community needs and groups outside the mainstream will be served. Rarely, however, has the FCC examined very closely how well a station has fulfilled its promises. There have been only a few cases of rejection when a license came up for renewal. The Commission has been reluctant to define more rigorously what constitutes the "public interest" in broadcasting. To do so would embroil them in heated political disputes over what the public interest actually means, and neither the FCC nor Congress has been willing to tackle the problem.

Public service, equal time, and fair treatment   The FCC has stipulated a few requirements for radio and television stations. One is that they must offer at least a minimum amount of news, public-affairs, and local community material. A second rule provides that if one candidate for public office is given or sold air time, all other candidates for that office must be afforded equal time on the same terms. A third requirement is that when broadcasters present material on controversial public issues, they must provide reasonable opportunities also to those with opposing viewpoints. Each of these rules is subject to disagreement in its application to specific situations, and several cases have gone to the courts in recent years. The FCC has taken the position that too much governmental restriction of a station's judgment about what to broadcast would amount to a kind of censorship and perhaps would drive most public-affairs material off the air altogether. On the other hand, many groups in our society still feel that the media are biased and that their point of view has not been adequately presented. If FCC regulation does not offer them a solution to their complaint, where else can they turn?

Public Broadcasting

It may seem odd, but one potential remedy for inadequate or unfair media treatment of public affairs is for government itself to enter the field. The federal government publishes an enormous amount of material, of course, ranging from the *Congressional Record* and the *Federal Register* to the hundreds of pamphlets offering people advice and help distributed through various administrative agencies. Most of the outpouring of print is noncontroversial, having little impact on public perceptions or political evaluations. Government-sponsored radio and television is something else again.

European nations have relied primarily on government-controlled broadcasting since the advent of radio in the 1920s. In the United States, in keeping with its traditional dependence on private enterprise and hostility toward state control, private firms have been virtually the only electronic-media participants. The main criticism of private broadcasting was that in their quest for profits they gave too little attention to public affairs and community service. In contrast to the British Broadcasting Company (BBC), for instance, American radio and television offered rather skimpy political coverage and little in-depth treatment of public issues. The argument was made that a government-supported radio network and publicly owned television stations, not needing to think only of audience size and advertising revenue, could usefully supplement the commercial media coverage and serve as a kind of yardstick for evaluating their performance.

It was from this kind of thinking that public television stations got started around the country, and in 1967 the Corporation for Public Broadcasting was created to provide federal money. These ventures, along with such commercially successful public-affairs shows as *60 Minutes,* have shown that news and public affairs can appeal to large audiences while, in addition, exploring topics that might be too risky for the more audience-sensitive private broadcasters.

If the government pays for the broadcasts of public radio and television, there is the constant danger that public officials will try to control and direct what is broadcast. To reduce this danger, the Corporation for Public Broadcasting is partially insulated from direct presidential or congressional control, but each year its budget is a potential target for those who dislike the political direction they believe public broadcasting has taken. That government-sponsored broadcasting has survived into the late 1980s in the face of traditional American suspicion of any sort of public enterprise is testimony to the relatively evenhanded treatment (and perhaps the political skills) with which public broadcasting has handled controversy. Still there have been critics who contend that treatment of many issues by the media is distorted and unrepresentative.

Lobbying the Media

One method is always available for action by citizens unhappy with what the mass media provide. They can organize, agitate, seek broad public support, and in various ways try to pressure media corporations to change their ways. In recent years there have been numerous citizen campaigns aimed at alleged media abuses. Political conservatives have been especially active in trying to correct what they insist is a liberal bias. One effort in 1985 even sought to gain partial ownership of CBS. Other groups have campaigned against violence in children's programs and (successfully) cigarette advertising. It is never easy to mobilize mass opinion to force change in media policy, however, because the media themselves are so vital to

TABLE 12.2

**VIEWS OF THE MEDIA AND MEDIA VIEWS: POLITICAL ATTITUDES OF
JOURNALISTS AND THE GENERAL PUBLIC**

	View of Self			View of Newspaper	
	Public	Journalists	College-Educated Professionals	Public	Journalists
Consider self/ newspaper					
Liberal	23%	55%	38%	25%	28%
Conservative	29	17	30	24	42
President Reagan					
Favor	56	30	57	29	48
Oppose	27	60	33	9	23
Economic issues					
Sympathize with					
Business	33	27	52	12	42
Labor	32	31	27	8	8
Government regulation of business					
Favor	22	49	26	9	19
Oppose	50	41	57	11	45
Government aid to those unable to support themselves					
Favor	83	95	81	38	69
Oppose	11	3	12	6	8
Government should reduce income inequality					
Favor	55	50	56	16	25
Oppose	23	39	24	4	23
Foreign affairs					
U.S. withdraw investments from South Africa					
Favor	31	62	48	13	22
Oppose	27	29	27	4	18
Verifiable nuclear freeze					
Favor	66	84	79	26	40
Oppose	22	13	17	7	23
CIA aid to Nicaraguan contras					
Favor	19	17	27	7	22
Oppose	44	76	53	14	39

(continued)

TABLE 12.2 (*Continued*)

	View of Self			View of Newspaper	
	Public	Journalists	College-Educated Professionals	Public	Journalists
Increase defense budget					
Favor	38	15	32	15	34
Oppose	51	80	63	19	38
Social issues					
Allowing women to have abortions					
Favor	49	82	68	11	43
Oppose	44	14	28	17	13
Prayer in public schools					
Favor	74	25	58	28	23
Oppose	19	67	36	11	42
Affirmative action					
Favor	56	81	67	27	58
Oppose	21	14	20	3	12
Death penalty for murder					
Favor	75	47	67	23	49
Oppose	17	47	26	6	28
Hiring homosexuals					
Favor	55	89	68	13	39
Oppose	31	7	24	7	7
Stricter handgun controls					
Favor	50	78	63	26	47
Oppose	41	19	34	12	22

SOURCE: *Public Opinion*, August/September, 1985, p. 7.

the process of mobilizing opinion. Nevertheless, public protest remains a significant instrument for limiting the power of the mass media.

THE MEDIA IN ACTION

The impact of the media in American public life is a kind of joint product of the people who gather and report the news and write the columns and editorials and the way they structure their work. We cannot disregard the personal characteristics of the newspeople. It is important to know that they are generally from middle-class backgrounds, well educated, and like other elites in the United States predominantly white and Protestant. Perhaps more important is the fact that, as Table 12.2 shows, they are substantially more liberal in their personal political views than the rest of the country.

It does not necessarily follow that these personal preferences intrude upon the reports and analyses of journalists, however. There is sharp disagreement on the point, but the most careful and responsible studies of media bias find little evidence of partisan or ideological distortion in the news. In the nation as a whole it is not true that conservative points of view are ignored or that election contests are reported in ways that make liberal candidates and causes look more attractive.

In the 1940s and 1950s it was often charged that the news media were biased toward conservative, probusiness positions because that point of view was adopted by a large share of the newspaper publishers of the country and reflected in their editorials and endorsements. Even though newspaper endorsements do count for something in election contests, however, it is rare indeed for them to have a decisive effect on the outcome.

A more subtle source of influence and possible bias lies in the way that news is reported. Most news organizations assign reporters primarily on the basis of "beats." On the national scene the most prominent beat is the White House. Others include the diplomatic establishment, the Supreme Court, and Congress, though the latter is so large and complex as to defy easy coverage. Relatively little regular "beat" attention is given to administrative and regulatory agencies. As a consequence, our information about presidential policy *proposals* is far more thorough and detailed than our knowledge of how a policy is implemented by the bureaucracy. Washington journalists report in detail what happens within the confines of particular institutions of government, but amidst all that detail on what the President had for breakfast there may be little help for the citizen who wonders what the larger political picture is like.

American journalists combine this pattern of beat coverage with a commitment to the interview as the chief technique for discovering facts. Reporters try to get officials to talk, on or off the record, and they build their stories about what has happened from the statements they can extract. There is nothing necessarily wrong with this. For one thing it protects the reporter from charges of bias, since it is the interviewee, not the reporter, who makes the quoted statements. Interview-based journalism obviously personalizes the news, giving large events and social conditions a human dimension that undoubtedly attracts readers and viewers who might otherwise ignore the issue.

Personification of the news may often obscure the more impersonal social forces at work, however, and present the world more as a melodrama with heroes and villains than as a set of complicated problems to be solved through hard work and serious citizen concern. Moreover, the reliance on interviews for information encourages reporters to avoid stories and even whole governmental beats where interviews are less useful. It is rarely possible for reporters to get Supreme Court justices to explain their decisions, for example. To cover the Court effectively requires, instead, a reporter to study legal briefs and opinions, and relatively few journalists make the intellectual commitment necessary to perform that job well.

Another problem that grows out of the structure of journalistic coverage of public affairs involves the preoccupation with investigative reporting.

The classic example of successful investigative reporting was provided by Bob Woodward and Carl Bernstein. Their long investigation into the Watergate break-in of 1972 led ultimately to the resignation from office of President Nixon and won fame and fortune for the two reporters. Every ambitious and talented reporter can entertain fantasies of following a similar path and look for the "big story" that will make their reputation. Many of the most serious issues of public policy, however, do not lend themselves to this approach. The problems of inflation and unemployment, for example, are not separate and distinct episodes but ongoing conditions. They are brought about and solved not by any specific person or decision but by a long and complex chain of factors that are hard to convert into the dramatic terms that make headlines and win Pulitzer prizes.

Television news coverage makes it even more difficult to provide the public an adequate understanding of public affairs. In addition to the stress on the dramatic investigation, the emphasis on interviews and personalities, and the reliance on institutional beats, all of which are common to all the media, television news coverage presents nearly all of its stories in capsule form. Thirty seconds of words and pictures can convey powerful impressions to an audience, of course, but a genuine grasp of the problem will require more depth and detail.

The American mass media have given rise to a role that is not matched in other democracies but has come to be of considerable importance in the United States. This is the role of "pundit," the commentator who in newspaper columns or on television interprets the news and offers judgments and recommendations about the events of the day. Newspapers have long published editorials, of course, and these do much the same job. But editorials are rarely signed and seldom have the impact as opinion leaders that prominent columnists have had.

One of the first pundits and perhaps the most influential ever was Walter Lippmann. Today, conservative columnists like William F. Buckley and Phyllis Schlafly vie with the more liberal David Broder and James Reston to set the intellectual terms in which contemporary developments will be debated. We should not overlook the political cartoonists either, for they perform much the same function as the columnists and editorial writers; that is, they try to get their readers to see a political issue or personality in a particular way, so that when the same matter appears thereafter, a similar reaction—positive or negative as the case might be—will be aroused.

Media and Government

In the previous section we noted that media coverage of politics is generally organized according to institution-centered beats. Let us now look more closely at some of the most important of these, to see how the relationship between reporters and officials or candidates takes shape.

Some 2000 reporters are accredited to the House or Senate press galleries, and about 400 of them spend all of their time on Capital Hill. By contrast, the White House press corps consists of about 70 regulars, though the presidency generates more headlines and television stories per day than Congress and nearly as many newspaper stories. This is partly because the White House beat focuses on a single individual, the president, whereas in Congress the power structure is far more diffuse. The president's press

The press conferences of Franklin Roosevelt were relatively intimate and quite informal, but as a rule the President's remarks could not be quoted verbatim.

secretary can and does provide daily briefings and handouts that are easily converted into stories with nationwide appeal. Individual senators and representatives may also hold press conferences and give out news releases, but most of them cannot command wide attention.

In the modern era, beginning with Franklin Roosevelt, presidents have made more extensive and systematic use of the press. Roosevelt held frequent press conferences, though they were usually quite informal and often "off the record." President Eisenhower began the practice of periodic televised press conferences. Recent presidents have varied a good deal in the frequency of their press conferences, as Table 12.3 shows. In any case, such public events rarely afford any serious opportunity for reporters to challenge presidential assertions or force justifications of policy.

Press coverage of the White House can often be sharply critical, however, and antagonism between prominent TV reporters and incumbent chief executives has sometimes been severe. President Nixon was reported to have been very upset with Dan Rather's reports on CBS. The Reagan White House was said to dislike Sam Donaldson's coverage for ABC. Critics of the Kennedy administration, on the other hand, charged that because several of the leading reporters were friends of the President and liked him personally they downplayed the negative features of his policies. It would take a remarkably thick-skinned chief executive not to get irritated at press criticism, but modern presidents may take some comfort from the fact that in Abraham Lincoln's day and earlier it was much worse.

TABLE 12.3
PRESIDENTIAL PRESS CONFERENCES

President	Number	Years in Office	Average per Year
Roosevelt	998	12	83
Truman	322	8	40
Eisenhower	193	8	24
Kennedy	64	3	21
Johnson	126	5	25
Nixon	37	5½	7
Ford	39	2½	16
Carter	59	4	15
Reagan	26[a]	4	7

[a] Through 1984.

Press coverage of Congress is diffuse and difficult to summarize. In part this is because there is such decentralization of power on the Hill. Each of the two chambers has its party leaders plus scores of committee and subcommittee chairs. In addition, there are local, state, and regional angles to so much of what goes on in Congress. A Chicago reporter may not want the same story as one from Phoenix.

The expansion of the Washington Press Corps and the fully public character of modern press conferences mean that the sessions are relatively formal and often, perhaps, less revealing than those of an earlier era.

Congress is an exceedingly open institution, far more accessible to an enterprising reporter than the executive branch. Administration officials regularly try to prevent leaks of information regarding their policy deliberations and plans, and while they do not always succeed, press relations are typically rather formal and structured through well-established channels, such as the presidential press conference. In Congress, however, leaks are constant and secrets are rarely kept for long. Even stories about the White House often come from congressional sources that include the several thousand staff aides as well as the members themselves. As Stephen Hess says, *"Washington news is funneled through Capital Hill."*[1]

One difficult area of media-government relations involves the handling of crises. When a flood or earthquake strikes, the mass media are an indispensable means for informing the public of what is happening and, when necessary, how to deal with the situation. An international political crisis presents a somewhat different problem. When, in 1985, Shiite Moslem extremists hijacked an American plane and took it to Beirut, the media provided virtual blanket coverage. During the 17-day crisis the three main television networks together ran nearly 300 special reports and assigned some 200 reporters and staff to the story. Some government officials complained that the terrorists used the media to gain sympathy for their cause. More serious was the charge that by staking out American military installations to watch for developments reporters might find out about and perhaps report any military undertaking before it went into effect. Media officials denied any breach of military security or undue publicity for the Shiite cause, but some critics felt it was another example of arrogance on the part of the press.

Somewhat the same dilemma emerged over the much longer crisis period of the Vietnam War. The stories and pictures American reporters sent back informed the public, sometimes in ways that contradicted official government policy, and undoubtedly contributed to a growing public disapproval of the war. A free press may often say things that officials would prefer not to hear, though sometimes those reports may be inaccurate or biased or irresponsible. The extraordinary technical skills and vast resources available to the modern media giants make them a more formidable adversary of governmental authority than was possible in earlier times. International crises themselves are more dangerous than they were in the prenuclear age. This means that we confront a most difficult problem of sustaining a free and critical press while keeping its power and impact within the limits required in a democratic society.

Media Impact

The mass communications media, print and electronic, are all around us. We watch nearly 30 hours of television a week, and three-fourths of us read a daily newspaper. Much of our information about the world and our images of the personalities and events of political life are drawn from

---

[1] *The Washington Reporters* (Washington: The Brookings Institution, 1981), p. 99. (Italics in original.)

what is presented to us by the media. Does that mean they control what we think? The answer is certainly no, and in assessing the impact they *do* have, we must also ask why that impact is not much greater than it is.

The most important limitation on the power of the media to shape our thinking involves selective perception. Most of us watch televised debates between presidential candidates, for instance, with our minds already made up as to which one we prefer. In a sense we "see" the debate through glasses that have been tinted by our party or candidate preference. Typically, we conclude that our candidate did better than the opponent. In the same way, we are not blank tablets when we read the newspapers. We bring the values and orientations we have learned at home or at school to bear on the material that the media give us, and most of the time we interpret that material to fit our already established point of view rather than allow the news to change our minds.

A dramatic example of selective perception occurred at the Democratic National Convention of 1968. The Convention took place in Chicago during the height of the protests from young Americans against the Vietnam War. Several thousand protesters converged on Chicago and with extensive television coverage engaged in some violent altercations with the Chicago police. Elsewhere in the country millions of people watched the struggle on television. Those viewers who themselves were against the war "saw" an unprovoked and vicious assault by the police against defenseless young people, while those who supported the war "saw" the police bravely upholding social order against a radical mob.

Although the media may not have much effect on the political values people hold or the basic orientations they bring to public affairs, they do have a substantial impact on what people regard as politically important. For example, news coverage of Congress gives much attention to roll call votes on the House or Senate floor. The reports are cast in terms of which side won or lost. Much less is said about what happened to the bill in committee, where, as students of Congress know, most of the important decisions and compromises will have been made. The media picture is a two-horse contest rather than a multifaceted, ongoing process.

Media emphasis on personalities can hardly help having its effect on what people believe to be important politically. One study found that three-fourths of the newspaper comments about presidential candidates referred to personal characteristics such as compassion or trustworthiness and only one-fourth to matters of philosophy or competence.[2] Moreover, as candidates for office have come to recognize more clearly the way the media operate, they have also adapted their behavior and thereby reinforced the emphasis on personality. Indeed, the direct impact of the media may be less on what voters think than on what campaign managers do.

Schedules are arranged, meetings organized, statements made, and interviews granted—all with an eye to the way in which they will be covered on the TV evening news or in the next morning's newspaper. Presidential

---

[2] Doris Graber, *Mass Media and American Politics* (Washington: Congressional Quarterly Press, 1980), p. 170.

candidates need wide media exposure and arrange their schedules with that in mind. Campaign managers organize "media events," campaign activities staged expressly for the media. They will make sure that television reporters have sufficient "photo opportunities" during the day, so that they can have interesting film to send back to their networks. The better "visuals" the candidates can provide, the more likely it is they will get substantial coverage on the evening news. Television highlights the personal characteristics and quirks of the candidates: the nervous gesture, the winning smile, the smooth reply to questions, and so forth. It is less effective in getting across the substance (or lack thereof) of their policy positions.

By choosing what and whom to cover, the media become an important force. They can help or hurt candidates a lot by the amount of coverage they give. This gives the mass media a more powerful voice at certain stages of the election campaign than at others. After the presidential conventions have selected the candidates for the two major parties, television and the newspapers have little choice but to cover those candidates extensively. That is where the big news is, and they will assign large crews of reporters to follow the major candidates around. But at other stages of an election campaign, reporters and editors have much more choice of whom or what they should cover. Early in an election year there may be many candidates competing for the nomination; at some stage, over a dozen people in each party may have thrown their hats into the ring. Press and television cannot cover all these candidates and must make a choice. The choice they make is often crucial in determining who winds up being a successful candidate. If they ignore a candidate, he or she may disappear; if they choose to follow a candidate closely, he or she may emerge a front-runner. By declaring a candidate the front-runner, however, the media may place a heavy burden of expectation on that person, so that a slight loss of momentum is read as a fatal weakness.

How do reporters and editors decide who is a good story? Certain candidates may be intrinsically more interesting than others; they have attractive television personalities, interesting backgrounds, or something else that captures the public's attention. It did not hurt Jimmy Carter in 1976 to be an obscure peanut farmer and former governor of Georgia. That made him an interesting story, and the press latched onto it. Ronald Reagan's ease and charm on television have certainly helped him. Jesse Jackson's passion and eloquence in 1984 made him a much more appealing media candidate than, say, Senator John Glenn of Ohio, whose speeches were dry and heavy with factual detail. One thing that makes a candidate interesting is, of course, the likelihood of emerging as the victor at the end of the campaign trail. The media look around to see who is doing well and give that candidate more coverage. "Reporters are notoriously fickle," one campaign manager has said. "They join up en masse while a candidate is doing well, then they drop him when he is down."[3]

The increasing importance of the media, particularly television, in elec-

---

[3] *The National Journal,* April 5, 1980, p. 561.

News coverage of most political events is extremely dense, resembling a ravenous pack, and sometimes it makes a public official's life rather uncomfortable. Here U.S. Senator Paul Tsongas (D.–Mass.) is being interviewed during his reelection campaign.

tion campaigns has several significant consequences. One consequence is that the role of party organizations diminishes even further. In the old days, a strong party organization was necessary to a presidential candidate to win an election. Party organization provided the people who rang doorbells for candidates, printed party literature, put up posters, and organized meetings and rallies for the candidate. Today, candidates appeal directly to the voters through television. They do not need party organizations. They do need money, however, and in enormous amounts. A media-centered campaign is vastly expensive and the problems of campaign finance, discussed in Chapter 11 are thus linked to the role of the media in our politics.

Second, the mass media turn campaign attention away from the issues in the campaign to the personal style of the candidate. A slip of the tongue in a presidential debate, an unguarded remark to a reporter, and a haggard look before the television camera are all in themselves very trivial, but they become magnified in importance under the daily scrutiny of the mass media. The views the candidates have on political issues—more important, but less visually interesting—may be ignored.

The television networks have defended themselves against such accusations. They claim that they try to report on the issue positions of candidates, but the public is not interested. Further, they argue, the candidates themselves are more interested in having a good "visual" on TV than in getting their argument across. The television executives may be correct in their criticism of the public and the candidates, since television cannot easily report what the public does not want to hear and the candidates do not want to say. Nevertheless, the fact remains that the very nature of television as a medium tends to personalize politics. The "unblinking eye" of the TV camera is very effective in capturing personal style and less so in reporting substance.

The presidential debates   The media have affected political practice as well, notably in the emergence of TV debates between presidential candidates. The first of these was held in 1960, when John Kennedy and Richard Nixon squared off. The debate format was revived in 1976, when Gerald Ford and Jimmy Carter participated in three debates viewed by a vast television audience. In 1980 a debate between Ronald Reagan and Jimmy Carter seemed uncertain for a while because of controversy as to whether the independent candidate, John Anderson, should be included. Reagan debated Anderson early in the campaign and then met one-on-one with Carter shortly before the election. In 1984 two debates between Reagan and Walter Mondale and one between vice-presidential candidates George Bush and Geraldine Ferraro were highlights of a rather uneventful campaign.

The debates are great media events. The candidates prepare carefully. Much time is spent negotiating with the networks about lighting, question format, and the like. The debates are important to the candidates. They are seen face-to-face by a very large proportion of the public that will vote on election day.

The debates illustrate clearly the special nature of television campaigning. The candidates present their positions on a variety of issues. Sometimes they talk in vague generalities, but sometimes they take positions clearly different from each other. The public and the press, however, appear to respond much more to the style than to the substance of the debate: which candidate appeared to be more at ease, which more sincere, and which more competent and "presidential" in his appearance.

The debates convert relatively few voters; rather, they tend to reinforce the positions that people have. Those who favor a particular candidate are likely to think that candidate did better in the debate. Some voters switch their voting intention from one candidate to another after a debate, and others who were previously undecided may come to a decision based on the debates. The grounds are more likely to be the impression that the candidate made, however, than the position the candidate took on some issue. During 1980, for instance, the presidential debates were particularly useful to Ronald Reagan. The Carter campaign had tried to picture Reagan as a dangerous hard-liner likely to risk war, whereas Reagan came across as a sincere and competent candidate who could be trusted. In 1984 Walter Mondale hoped that he would be able during his debates with Reagan to demonstrate that the President was not really on top of the facts and issues vital to the country. Mondale failed, but at least the debates had offered him the chance.

Some observers of the recent American political scene have suggested that the increasing dependence of Americans on television as a source of information has meant also an increased emphasis on personality in politics and a retreat by large segments of the public from a more complex understanding of issues. Yet, opinion survey evidence suggests that most voters have only a rudimentary grasp of issues anyway. The very substantial decline in the trust and confidence that Americans have in the institutions of authority matches quite closely the increased reliance on television. Whether there is any causal link, however, remains a speculation, as does the frequently alleged connection between violence on television and violent behavior in children. To these we must say, "Not proved."

CONCLUDING THOUGHTS

The mass media do personalize the news and often trivialize the processes of election and policymaking. They may foster cynicism and worsen social conflict. At the same time, however, they provide a rich diet of politically relevant information and interpretation. The interested citizen has ready access to a huge amount of material. The energetic candidate or public official has multiple channels of communication to get across a message. Also, the media themselves remain more competitive with each other and less restricted by government than anywhere else in the world.

A fair way to summarize the impact the mass media have on American political life might be as follows: the media *permit* a reasonably full and rich democratic political process to flourish, but they certainly *do not assure* it. Americans can become well informed about public affairs, but too often they are not. Media scrutiny may sometimes expose political wrongdoing and keep officials to a high standard of performance, but they certainly do not do so in every case.

In a sense that is the sort of "bottom line" evaluation we have reached with regard to the other components of citizen action and input to the political system discussed in the last several chapters. Political participation, individually and through organized groups, and political parties can be very effective in conveying demands to officials and pressuring them to take appropriate action. Elections can turn rascals out of office and send clear signals as to what policies the voters want adopted. But, as we have seen, these mechanisms never function automatically. Citizens are often indifferent or inattentive, their views are vague, and their messages to government are permissive rather than precise or strictly binding.

If this, in brief, is the way the mechanisms of democratic input to government officials operate, it leaves those officials with very considerable discretion to make the choices and fashion the policies that will govern the country. That discretion and their specific choices will seldom be unaffected by broader public concerns. Certainly they are rarely free from media scrutiny or interest-group attention, and elections are always just around the corner.

Nevertheless, in the American system of democracy, public officials have important areas in which they must choose among policy alternatives. Among the important factors that influence those choices are the structures and processes of the policymaking institutions of government. In other words, part of what determines what Congress does, is the way Congress

PROFILE ■

WALTER LIPPMANN (1889–1974)
Journalist, Writer, and Commentator

Lippmann was the most influential pundit of his time and, in most respects, the original model for

columnists on current public affairs ever since. As a student at Harvard, Lippmann was associated with a brilliant group of political activists, who were critical of pre-World War I American society and hoped to use the press as an instrument of social change. Lippmann joined the newly founded *New Republic* in 1914 and later became editor of the *New York World.* In 1931 he began his column "Today and Tomorrow," which he wrote until 1967. At its peak the column appeared in over 200 newspapers and was read with care by virtually every significant public figure in this country and by many elsewhere in the world. Lippmann was personally close to many political leaders as well. Though as a young man he had been a socialist of sorts, his mature point of view was seldom far from the political center. Indeed, he often seemed in his columns to *define* the center, especially on issues of foreign policy, where, he seemed to suggest, all reasonable people of good will and sound analysis would inevitably meet. Lippmann wrote books as well as newspaper columns, and several were of lasting importance; among them are *Drift and Mastery* (1914), *Public Opinion* (1922), and *The Public Philosophy* (1955).

is set up, the rules by which it operates, and those by which the other branches operate. To understand how the total system functions and to explain why public policies take the shape they do, we need to know about both the inputs from the citizenry and the institutions and processes of policy decision making. Therefore, in the next section we turn to an examination of those policymaking institutions.

CHAPTER HIGHLIGHTS ■

1.   The mass media have changed over the course of our history from small, localized, and highly partisan newspapers to larger, national instruments in both print and electronic forms.
2.   The media are more concentrated in ownership than ever before, and there is greater uniformity in what is available throughout the country. Nevertheless, there remain many different sources of news and information.
3.   The Constitution sharply restricts government at every level from censoring what the media present. There are several kinds of pressures that help limit abuses of freedom of the press.

4.   Government officials and the media coexist in an uneasy equilibrium. Each depends upon the other to do the job expected. Each tends to be critical of the other and often to feel unfairly treated.

5.   In many ways the mass media sensationalize and personalize the news, and politics sometimes threatens to turn into one long sequence of "media events." Nevertheless, the mass media continue to play a vital role in keeping public officials accountable to the voters.

SUGGESTED READINGS ■

Careful analysis of the role of the mass media in American political life is generally of quite recent vintage, and there is much we do not know.

Modern commentaries on the influences of the mass media on American politics include: Doris Graber, *Mass Media and American Politics* (2d ed., 1984); Austin Ranney, *Channels of Power* (1983); Michael B. Grossman and Martha Joynt Kumar, *Portraying the President: The White House and the News Media* (1981); Michael Robinson and Martin Sheehan, *Over the Wire and On TV* (1983); Timothy Crouse, *The Boys on the Bus* (1973); Stephen Hess, *The Washington Reporters* (1981); Edward Diamond and Stephen Bates, *The Spot: The Rise of Political Advertising on Television* (1984); John Tebbel and Sarah Miles Watts, *The Press and the Presidency: From George Washington to Ronald Reagan* (1985).

Joint session of Congress being addressed by President Reagan

Washington, D.C.

Chapter 13

THE POLICY
PROCESS

What government does is make public policy. Put the other way, public policy is composed of what government does. The votes in Congress, the decisions in the White House, the regulations issued by the bureaucracy, and the judgments of the Supreme Court are all part of the policymaking process. In the succeeding chapters we will go on to examine those institutions and their practices. As we do, we must constantly ask how our governmental institutions affect policy, for it is public policy that impinges on the lives of all Americans and, indeed, on people everywhere.

We will not get very far unless we break down the sum total of what government does into more readily understood component parts. We need to become familiar with the vocabulary of policy formation, the terms that are used to describe what government does. We need also to see that policymaking is a complicated and often drawn-out process that usually involves several stages and institutions. It does not have a well-defined beginning, middle, and end, but in most cases is ongoing with revisions and reformulations more or less continuously being proposed and debated.

One of our concerns will be the policy agenda. How do policy ideas originate? When we speak of "an idea whose time has come," what do we mean? What are the "real" issues? What policy proposals make up the political agenda at any one time, and how do we know? It has been said that if you can control what gets on the **agenda** of politics, you can pretty well control the result. Is this true, and what does it mean in American politics?

Policymaking in American politics is not an impersonal process. Ideas are proposed, programs are undertaken, and decisions are made by people, some of whom are brilliantly creative and some who are not. We will look at some of the policy actors.

At the end of the chapter we will focus at some length on a subject that in recent years has come to dominate the policy agenda, at least for domestic policy. This is the budget process and the recent additional process of deficit reduction. Part of this process has been operative since 1974, and its impact on the way Americans think and talk about government has been profound. Part of it was enacted in 1985, and its effects are not yet clear. In any case, it requires our particular attention. But first we need to clarify some terms.

ISSUES AND PROBLEMS, PROPOSALS AND DECISIONS, PROGRAMS AND POLICIES

There are several words used to identify politically interesting topics, and there is considerable disagreement about what precisely they mean. We introduce the terms here, and we will assign each a specific meaning. Our purpose, however, is not so much to tie down the words or restrict their uses as to make some distinctions in what goes on in the policymaking world. We hope that by giving each part of that activity a different name we will be able to improve our grasp of how that world functions.

Let us begin with the term *issue.* What is an issue? The simplest answer is to say that any matter bearing on what government does that is widely argued is an issue. Some issues are highly salient. Inflation and unemployment, for example, are prominent domestic issues. Central America and Lebanon, Libya, and the Philippines are the geographic focal points of widely debated foreign-policy issues. But what about soil conservation? In the Dust Bowl days of the early 1930s soil conservation was a very visible concern and enough of an issue to give rise to the creation of a Soil Conservation Service in the Department of Agriculture. By the mid-1980s, however, we listened in vain for similar expressions of concern about this problem. It was no longer an issue.

Divorce among political leaders was an issue when Adlai Stevenson ran for president in 1952; it was no longer so when Ronald Reagan ran in 1980. Prohibition of alcoholic beverages was highly controversial and salient until the repeal of the Eighteenth Amendment in 1933. Thereafter, prohibition was not a politically meaningful issue, though drinking and its control sometimes has been. Abortion, on the other hand, had long been a fact of American life, but it was one of those facts that few people ever talked about in public. It was not an issue. It became one after it was made legal in New York in 1970 and given constitutional protection by the Supreme Court in *Roe* v. *Wade* in 1973. Then and since, argument, protest, and political action concerning abortion have become loud and insistent.

Issues, then, are the topics of political argument. They differ from problems. The term *problem* refers to a condition or a situation that is either uncertain or unsatisfactory. A problem in arithmetic presents the student with a situation that is uncertain until the correct answer is reached. The problem of what to do to stop crime in the streets probably baffles most of us, though a few might contend they have the right solution. The poverty problem or the prenatal-care problem are primarily problems of inadequacy. But both dimensions are present in most problem situations. We might not be at all sure how to solve the crime problem, for instance, but in our uncertainty still favor more cops on the street, stiffer sentences, better housing, or more jobs. For a problem condition to become politically relevant it must be converted into an issue; that is, people must begin to argue about what causes the problem and what should be done about it. Many problems do not become issues because hardly anyone has an idea of what to do. The weather is perhaps as good an example as any of a (mostly) nonpolitical problem, since, as Mark Twain once said, everyone complains about it but no one does anything to fix it.

Now we come to another pair of terms, *proposals* and *decisions*. These are considerably more precise in their meaning, because most of the time both proposals and decisions are quite specific events or documented facts. A policy proposal is a design put forward to help solve problems. A legislative proposal will be in the form of a bill or an amendment that is written out and formally introduced. Similarly, one nation's proposal in a diplomatic negotiation will be offered in official form. The president's budget proposals come as an enormous 1200-page document submitted to Congress. Less formal proposals may be made in speeches and other public utterances, but even these are clearly distinguishable from ideas that may

How can lower-status citizens get their issues on the political agenda?

be bandied about in the neighborhood bar. However creative the latter might be, we would not call them policy proposals.

Decisions are even more explicit, formal, and official. Congressional members vote on a bill and collectively either pass the bill or defeat it. Both the collective action and the individual choices that make it up are decisions. So is the choice made by the President to sign or veto the bill, to appoint a new attorney general, to hold a summit meeting with the Soviet Union, or to call a press conference. Major public officials make large numbers of official decisions every year. Congress has several hundred roll call votes. The Supreme Court reports about 150 full decisions annually. Some of these choice-making decisions may by themselves be relatively trivial, but some are clearly of enormous importance. Many times these specific decisions are part of a series or set of choices that constitute a policy or program. Let us see what those terms mean.

By **policy** we generally mean continuing commitment to a pattern of specific decisions or activity. For example, from 1949 until 1971 the United States had a policy toward the People's Republic of China (PRC) of non-recognition, hostility toward economic or cultural ties, and support for the Chinese Nationalist regime in Taiwan. Then in 1971 President Nixon made the decision to reverse this policy. Since then U.S. policy has been one of encouraging normalization of relations with the PRC. By the same token, the United States has had a policy since the 1930s of supporting the market prices of certain agricultural commodities through a program of loans whenever the price fell below a stipulated level. If within a year the market price rose above the loan figure, the farmer sold the commodity and paid off the loan. If the price stayed down, the government kept the crop and the farmer kept the loan money. There have been changes over the years in the level at which prices would be supported and in numerous other specifics. Despite much criticism of the basic design of U.S. agricultural policy and many proposals to change it, it has remained largely intact when, every few years, Congress has reauthorized the program.

Some policies remain untested, as in the case of U.S. policy in the event of a nuclear attack. What will the government do? We hope we do not find out. Other policies are changed when a new party is elected to office. Still others remain largely of symbolic significance, reassuring perhaps but basically without much effect on anyone.

The impact of policies comes primarily through the medium of *programs.* Typically, when Congress passes a bill into law, it creates or modifies an administrative agency and gives it the authority to enact regulations or spend money in certain ways and for certain purposes. Thus there is a program of grants and loans for college students, authorized by Congress and administered by the Department of Education. There are numerous programs of assistance for veterans, providing health care, educational benefits, and other types of aid, all authorized and funded by Congress and implemented by the Veterans Administration. There are literally hundreds of different programs administered by agencies of the federal government. Some of these, as we saw in Chapter 3, are implemented primarily by state or local officials, with federal bureaucrats providing the money and a certain amount of supervision and control. In other cases the actual implementation may be done largely by private contractors who negotiate terms with federal bureaucrats, all within the authorizing and funding authority provided by Congressional action. This is how we procure weapons and most other material for the Defense Department, for example.

Within any broad policy commitment there is usually much room for disagreement over the specifics of program design. A policy of assisting the elderly, for instance, leaves many options open regarding the best forms or mix of assistance: pensions, health care, housing, senior citizen centers, hot meals, nursing homes, and so on. To endorse a policy of strengthened defense does not necessarily mean that one must endorse a particular program of more land-based missiles or refitting battleships. It is important politically, as well as analytically, therefore, to make these distinctions between policies and programs, and to see also how specific decisions fit into or depart from existing patterns, either of broad policy commitment or of operating programs.

As we make these distinctions we are reminded of the fact that in the American policymaking process there are several quite distinct institutional arenas of action. To follow a policy from its gestation as an idea through its formulation as a proposal, the official decisions that put it into action, and the evolution of a program of implementation requires us to follow a complicated path, often starting among interested people and groups outside government and then going from one institution to another, involving Congress, the president, the bureaucracy, and often the courts. In each arena there will be rules, both formal and informal; different individuals and mixes of points of view; and different susceptibilities to outside pressures of various kinds. The substance of the decisions made at each stage of the process will reflect those differences.

This complexity means that there are numerous opportunities to get involved in the process, whether for organized interest groups or concerned individuals. It also means that it is often extremely difficult to mount a campaign to change things or alter the direction of public policy commitment. There are too many points at which the policy status quo can be defended. One result is that in public-policy analysis the single best predictor of what the government's action will be tomorrow is the action taken today, just as today's action was forecast quite successfully by yesterday's. Change is possible, of course, but major policy change is very difficult to accomplish in a system as complex as ours.

THE POLICY ACTORS

We can be brief in identifying the chief actors in the processes of American policymaking. Most of the main players in the drama are discussed at some length in other chapters. We have said already that the several institutions of the system participate, and it is their policymaking actions that provide us the observable material with which to build our understanding and evaluation of those institutions; that is, we determine whether the president or Congress or the Supreme Court are doing a good job by examining their decisions. It is not how these institutions and officials look or whether they smile nicely that finally counts, after all, but what they do.

In addition to this official policy*making,* however, there is a vast amount of policy proposing, issue arguing, problem identifying, and related activity going on in the political milieu surrounding the key institutions. We have seen how candidates for office put forward proposed policies, endorse or oppose programs, and condemn or acclaim particular decisions. Interest groups do the same, as do party organizations in their platforms. Indeed, for third parties, such as the Socialists in the early twentieth century or the Libertarians more recently, it is largely the opportunity to put policy ideas more effectively before the public that persuades people with no realistic hope of winning to make the effort to run.

In a sense there is a tremendous amount of verbal "noise" in the political world, much of it repetitive, some of it rather silly. Vast amounts of papers are used up in the outpouring of words. To sort out the significant substance is not an easy task. One way to frame the effort is to try to define the agendas of public policy, asking where issues come from, who formulates the proposals for action, and how they get on the lists of things to be done by the various official actors in the process.

THE AGENDAS OF AMERICAN POLITICS

In early July of 1985 the advisers of President Reagan breathed a sigh of relief when 39 American hostages in Lebanon were released. The 17-day crisis "pushed everything literally to the back burner." Now attention could once more be devoted to tax reform and the budget deficit, items that the president himself, not Moslem terrorists, had framed and placed in the nation's political agenda. And as a White House aide put it, "When we control the agenda, we tend to do pretty well."[1]

It is clear that agenda control is a powerful weapon in any political situation. But that principle must be put into practice, and the actual process of agenda definition and control in the United States is very complex. First of all, which agendas are we going to examine? The president has one, and he tries through his messages to Congress and appeals through the mass media to persuade the rest of the country to accept his conception of what the "real" issues are and how they should be dealt with. Congressional leaders, however, especially those from the rival political party, will put forward a somewhat different list of items they think should receive top priority. The Supreme Court has its own quite specialized agenda. Presidential candidates, interest-group leaders, media columnists and pundits, academics and intellectuals—all are potential sources of ideas and proposals and may contribute to the definition of a particular political agenda.

We can distinguish between the relatively broad stream of policy ideas that in diverse ways are put forward and argued about by some of the various political actors referred to above and the more limited institutional agendas that confront the Supreme Court, particular committees of Congress, and so on. Items move from the broad stream to the institutional dockets, of course, and also from one institution's agenda to another. However, our main questions here involve how ideas get worked into the main currents of the policy stream and then onto the list of official business from which eventually an authoritative decision can begin a new policy or program.

It is sometimes said that there are no new ideas under the sun, but the public-policy agenda certainly is not static. Free coinage of silver was William Jennings Bryan's big issue when he ran for president in 1896, but we rarely mention it today. The various proposals of the civil rights movement that gained momentum in the late 1950s and early 1960s had been given only rather peripheral attention on the national political scene until the Supreme Court's desegregation decisions in the early 1950s. The 1955–1956 bus boycott in Montgomery, Alabama, that brought Dr. Martin Luther King to prominence, the sit-ins by black college students, and the marches for equal rights—all raised the nation's consciousness and aroused its conscience. Twenty years later, however, those concerns had faded, and despite Jesse Jackson's vigorous campaign for the 1984 Democratic presidential nomination, the national political agenda seemed largely to have consigned civil rights to the margin.

Somewhat the same course can be observed with regard to consumer issues. Brought to prominence in the early 1960s, especially through the vigorous advocacy of Ralph Nader, abetted by some effective work of key senators and their staffs, the consumer agenda led to the enactment of

---

[1] *Wall Street Journal,* July 2, 1985.

several statutes providing consumers additional information and protecting them against unsafe products. Two decades later, however, though Nader remained active and the legislation of the 1960s was still on the books, consumerism no longer carried much political excitement.

In 1981 the "hot" items politically were tax cuts and deregulation of business. Strongly supported by the Reagan administration and its congressional supporters, these issues dominated the national agenda and to a substantial extent were enacted. As Reagan's second term began, however, much of the enthusiasm for deregulation had faded, and it was not at all clear that the quite extensive business regulation that remained would be reduced in the foreseeable future. The 1981 tax cuts had been accompanied by the prediction that they would stimulate such strong economic growth that the revenue loss would be more than compensated. Growth did occur in due course, but the budget deficit also got bigger, and by 1986 the agenda centerpieces were tax reform and deficit reduction.

What factors account for these agenda changes? Are they more or less accidental, chance results of unpredictable happenings? Do they reveal a cyclical pattern, following a pendulumlike swing of public opinion seeking liberal, expansive government action for a time and then turning back toward an equilibrium by embracing more conservative, restrictive policies. There is probably a grain or two of truth in both those views, but neither gets us very close to a satisfactory understanding. Let us try to identify some key factors that contribute to this agenda-shaping process, whether it be the broad agenda of national political concerns or the narrower agendas of particular governmental institutions. We will not be able to construct a full-blown theory of agenda formation, but perhaps we can make a start.

Routines and Crises

Two kinds of agenda-setting stimuli can be dealt with rather quickly. One involves the routines that are constructed by the political rules of the game and that force certain choices to be made whether anyone otherwise would want to or not. For example: our rules require that appropriations be made annually; House members must be elected every other year; and presidential elections must be held every four years. Those and countless other items must be dealt with, not so much because of any inherent need to act, but because the rules say we must. As we will see later in this chapter, the rules now require Congress to pass a budget resolution containing a "bottom line" figure which, however unpalatable, they must vote for or against. If the rules did not require it, as they did not before 1974, few members of Congress would willingly declare themselves in favor of a multibillion-dollar deficit.

The routine decision category is enlarged by Congress's rather common practice of enacting programs for a limited number of years. In 1985, for example, the basic enabling legislation authorizing the program of subsidies to farmers had to be placed on the action agenda, not just because many farmers were experiencing desperate economic reverses, but because the basic program of price supports would expire in 1986 unless renewed. Similarly, the Clean Air Act needed Congressional action lest it too expire. Each year there are major programs that must receive attention or disappear, and as there are likely to be significant interests dependent on or strongly favoring those programs, there are powerful reasons not to allow them to die. Many programs are authorized for three or four years and thus require renewal, and when the renewals are added to the annual struggles over the budget and the appropriations bills, not a great deal of time or energy remains for new policy initiatives.

Crisis items come to the agenda from many sources. Most prominent surely are those generated by international tensions. A hostage kidnapping here, a crop failure there, or an unanticipated regime change somewhere else can require immediate official responses, usually from the president or his representatives. The 1962 Cuban missile crisis, for example, was surely the tensest 13 days of the Kennedy administration, and during that period the top administration leaders understandably had little time for anything else. Cuba *was* the nation's agenda.

In domestic affairs, crises are usually somewhat less dominating when they occur, but an event such as the accident at the Three-Mile Island nuclear plant in 1979 required a swift response from public officials. It could not "get in line" behind other issues and wait its turn for attention. The sometimes rocky road to school desegregation after the 1954 Supreme Court decision holding segregated schools in violation of the Fourteenth Amendment produced several tense crises. At Little Rock, Arkansas, in 1957, for example, President Eisenhower sent in U.S. marshalls to resolve a potentially nasty school dispute. In a very different vein, the crisis surrounding the 1972 Watergate break-in and, more importantly, the later

The Cuban Missile Crisis of October 1962 presented an extremely difficult situation for the Kennedy administration.

Economist Milton Friedman is generally regarded as the intellectual father of monetarist theory, the view that the supply of money, largely controlled by the Federal Reserve Board, is the key factor determining economic growth.

revelations regarding the involvement of the Nixon White House in the break-in and the subsequent effort to cover it up dominated the nation's political agenda during most of the summer of 1974.

Policy Entrepreneurs

The political world does not lack policy proposals. They are constantly being written down, published, promoted, tried out on audiences, urged on officials, and in every way possible pushed toward what political scientist John Kingdon calls the "windows of opportunity."[2] Who are these policy entrepreneurs?

Prominent among the tax-cut advocates of 1981 were economist Arthur Laffer and writer Jude Wanniski. Nobel Prize economist Milton Friedman has been the best-known advocate of carefully controlling the supply of money in order to reduce inflation. A generation earlier the British economist John Maynard Keynes advanced the idea that the government could help end economic recessions by engaging in deficit spending. These and a good many other economists have been prominent policy entrepreneurs, writing and teaching about their ideas and in some cases also taking positions in the government itself, on the President's Council of Economic

---

[2] *Agendas, Alternatives and Public Policies* (Boston: Little, Brown, 1984).

Economist John Kenneth Galbraith has been a major advocate of the view that the great power of large corporations should be controlled by active government intervention.

Advisors or in the Treasury Department, where their advice can be fed directly into the president's agenda.

Economists are not the only sources of ideas. Ralph Nader is a notable entrepreneur of policy proposals in the consumer field. Jeane Kirkpatrick was a political science professor at Georgetown when she published an article urging that American foreign policy be more tolerant of what she called "authoritarian" dictators, saving our real hostility for "totalitarian" regimes. Her argument appealed to Mr. Reagan, and in 1981 he named her ambassador to the United Nations. A generation earlier the scholarly George Kennan, then a member of the State Department's Policy Planning board, wrote a famous article (under the name X) in which he set forth the broad logic of containment, explaining how the United States could use it as its basic policy toward the Soviet Union.

Organizations generate many of the proposals on the political agenda. There are interest groups in the usual sense: the AFL-CIO, assorted business associations, the American Bar Association, Common Cause, and the like. In recent years a number of influential "think tanks" have come to prominence, sponsoring seminars and forums and publishing much policy-related material. They range from the very conservative Heritage Foundation through the moderately conservative American Enterprise Institute to the more liberal Brookings Institution and the still more liberal Institute for Policy Analysis. Along with numerous others, these organizations have had a considerable impact on the recent agendas of national political life.

The point is that every policy idea comes from someplace. It has an

Political Scientist Jeanne Kirkpatrick was appointed by President Reagan to be Ambassador to the United Nations after she had written articles urging the U.S. to differentiate between totalitarian regimes, such as the Soviet Union, and authoritarian countries, such as El Salvador. The latter, she said, we might not like but could still cooperate with to further our larger strategic interests.

Historian and diplomat George Kennan formulated the original doctrine of containment that has more or less guided U.S. policy toward the Soviet Union since World War II.

intellectual source to which political energy is added, and "when the time is ripe," it gets through the window of opportunity. Today policy ideas are often put into proposal form by the much enlarged staffs that serve members of Congress. Many of the consumer protection proposals mentioned earlier, for example, were promoted by staffers of Senator Warren Magnuson (D-Washington), who chaired the Senate Commerce Committee in those years. Many other staffers are engaged in designing bills or amendments that can be used by members to gain attention and perhaps legislative success.

Some of these proposals may be in incubation for years before finally attracting enough support or at least interest to get serious consideration. Health insurance proposals were offered regularly for 15 years with little hope of enactment until the Johnson landslide of 1964 changed the congressional voting lineup drastically, preparing the way for the passage of Medicare in 1965. The window of opportunity had opened. Some ideas never do come to fruition, of course, though even these may have their eternally hopeful advocates.

Precipitating Events

One source of "window opening" that lets new policy options get onto the agenda is the event that precipitates, dramatizes, or in some other way tilts the political process in a new direction. In 1974 the oil-producing states of the Middle East, supported by a few others, formed OPEC and began to increase the price of oil rapidly. That event or sequence, in turn, precipitated several policy thrusts in the United States, leading to the 55-mph speed limit, the creation of a strategic oil reserve, the Alaskan pipeline, the creation of the Department of Energy, the synthetic fuels program, and others. Perhaps some of those developments would have occurred anyway, but not as rapidly or in the particular form they took. Another example is the Supreme Court's 1973 decision in *Roe* v. *Wade,* guaranteeing women the right to choose abortion, at least during the first three months of pregnancy. That decision precipitated a long series of efforts to limit or reverse its impact through legislation or constitutional amendment. Prior to the decision these proposals were not on any active political agenda. Other Court decisions, notably those involving prayer in the schools, have had similar precipitating effects.

The Impact of Elections

Crises at home and abroad, significant events, and policy entrepreneurs are all important in agenda formation, but they should not block from our view one other factor that in a democracy is supposed to be a major force: popular elections. When a new president comes into office, bringing along a new set of advisors and administrative officials, it makes a difference.

In a government of "separated institutions sharing powers" the president and the leaders of both parties in Congress must negotiate frequently if any programs are to be adopted.

Ronald Reagan's agenda was hardly a carbon copy of Jimmy Carter's, nor was Carter's a mere extension of Gerald Ford's. Each had a distinct set of priorities. While there was much policy continuity and most programs remained in operation, there were also important changes in scope and direction. The same is true when party control of Congress changes. New legislative possibilities emerge, sometimes because the voting balance has been altered, and sometimes simply because a particularly stubborn committee chairperson has been retired from office.

It may not always be possible to tell with any precision what new policy directions will follow an electoral change. Franklin Roosevelt was elected in 1932 on a pledge to reduce federal spending and balance the budget. Only when he took office did the substance of the New Deal agenda take shape. Much the same was true of Lyndon Johnson's Great Society programs of 1965–1966, most of which were developed after his landslide victory over Goldwater in 1964. Richard Nixon's rapprochement with China was likewise developed after he was elected. The election changed the political possibilities in each case. It opened the window of opportunity. What proposals went through the window and onto the agenda of national political action depended on a combination of personalities, fortuitous circumstances, precipitating events, and a crisis or two. Only in retrospect, four years later, would the voters have an opportunity to say whether they approved of those agenda items and of the actions taken.

THE FORMS OF POLICY COMMITMENTS

Earlier we said that public policy consists of the patterns of governmental commitment. Many of these patterns are revealed in ongoing programs of spending, regulating, or other forms of action. Others show up more episodically. From time to time, for example, the President invokes the Monroe Doctrine, first enunciated by President James Monroe in 1823, to warn a European nation to stop intruding in Latin American affairs. That policy has been in continuous operation ever since 1823, but the specific decision to apply its terms occurs only now and then. It may be helpful to review some of the different categories into which public policies can be divided, partly to illustrate further their great variety and partly to show how the different types of policy commitment are arrived at by quite diverse paths of political action.

First, there are what we call *nominal* categories. These classify policies according to the names applied in ordinary discussion. We give labels to policies, such as agricultural, education, military, fiscal, transportation, and environmental. These labels serve several purposes. Many of them identify the main organizational units involved in making the decisions and implementing the programs in the domain. Agricultural policy, for example, is largely framed by the agriculture committees of Congress and implemented by the Department of Agriculture. Moreover, the people primarily affected by agricultural policy are farmers, food processors, farm equipment manufacturers and dealers, and other interests closely tied to agriculture.

We can say much the same thing for other broad policy domains in which there are congressional committees and administrative departments or agencies with reasonably well-defined jurisdiction. Defense, education, housing and urban development, even foreign policy—all present patterns of action that are substantially distinct from one another. If we were to stop now and say those are the principal varieties of American public policy, we would not lead the reader too far astray. In many respects it is true that in order to understand a particular policy area you must grasp the substantive details of political action located within the domain in question.

There are good reasons, however, for thinking about policy categories in some other ways, too. One is that the boundaries of the policy domains do not always match the names we use. Consider the food-stamp program, for instance. Is that part of agricultural policy or welfare? Large numbers of food-stamp recipients are urban poor; yet the program is authorized by legislation drafted in the agriculture committees of Congress and is administered by the U.S. Department of Agriculture. On a larger scale, the defense budget can be understood in terms of the pressures from the different services for better weapons, reinforced by the corporations that make them, but it can also be assessed as an instrumentality of American foreign policy. Quite clearly it is both at the same time. Politically you win votes for the defense budget by urging its importance for foreign policy, just as you win votes for food-stamp welfare by presenting the program as a subsidy for farmers. The labels we use to designate policy domains carry political messages at the same time that they identify the main political actors involved in making the decisions.

A second reason for looking at some other ways of categorizing public policy is that there are so many nominal categories that after a while they seem to turn into a vast laundry list of public programs. If we are to develop more powerful theories to explain why policies take the shape they do, we need to fashion a smaller number of broad categories and give them more generic names. These analytic categories grow out of common features shared across several different programs and policy domains. Political scientists have experimented with different formulations of this type without reaching much agreement on which is best. We offer some of these more to illustrate their purpose and possible usefulness than to insist on their validity.

One broad distinction we can make is between policies that confer benefits more or less directly on people and those that do not. For instance, under Social Security and Medicare, eligible recipients receive checks. The National Park Service provides recreational benefits that people enjoy on the spot. Defense contracts mean jobs for workers and profits for employers. Urban development grants go to redevelopers. Revenue-sharing money goes just as directly to state and local governments. On the other hand, the tax collection activities of the Internal Revenue Service, perhaps of very general benefit to everyone, have the immediate effects of taking our money and regulating our behavior. When it determines the supply of money available the Federal Reserve Board affects the behavior of thousands of banks and business firms and ultimately all of us, but these are the indirect consequences of its decisions. A warning that smoking is dangerous to health has rather distant effects on its presumed beneficiaries, but it regulates very immediately the manufacturers who must put the warning on every pack.

The distinction between policies that distribute benefits directly and those that regulate directly and benefit only indirectly has important political implications. In the first case the beneficiaries are likely to mobilize their political energies to protect their benefits. Senior citizens have been very successful in preventing any adverse modification of Social Security programs, for example, and so have numerous other groups. In the same, way, groups that would be regulated by government action—gun owners and dealers, for instance, or used-car dealers—have with equal success fought off regulatory proposals whenever the beneficiaries of regulation were less clearly identified and less easily organized for political action. In the case of smoking, regulation became possible when the medical profession finally agreed that smoking was a health hazard. In the case of gun control there has been no comparable proregulation group to urge its adoption.

The policy process is not simply a mechanical balancing of pro and anti forces, a testing of which side has the best-organized lobbies. Nevertheless, it is generally true that distributive subsidy programs are easier to enact and harder to limit than regulatory programs. This is quite disturbing to many observers who feel that these tendencies reflect the power of organized groups, special interests, while the rest of the country, "the public interest," is often unable to achieve broadly beneficial policies because no comparable organized groups push for them.

Economists employ a variation on this idea when they talk of "public goods," which are policies that cannot readily be divided up among recipients and once provided cannot be denied or withdrawn. National defense is a common example. Defense cannot be divided so that each of us gets a piece of it, and if you get all the defense against invasion that you want, you cannot keep me from enjoying it, too. It is often argued that public goods of this kind should be provided by government because otherwise the individual citizen can be a "free rider." Without the coercive power of government, you may be unable to persuade me to pay my share of the cost, yet you cannot prevent me from benefiting.

Even when the government provides the good, however, we must still decide what share of the cost should be borne by different groups in society. Moreover, most public goods have either special-interest beneficiaries or equally special opponents. National defense enjoys the support of the armed forces lobbies, the defense industries, and many members of Congress in whose districts defense moneys are spent. Clean air is a public good, but the polluting industries, their employees, and their elected representatives often manage to moderate the regulatory programs that would maximize air quality. Are the jobs of auto workers or shoemakers or steelworkers to be jeopardized because in the long run the economy will be more productive if international trade is free to Japanese or Korean imports? The public interest is rarely a completely clear-cut standard in politics.

A fairly large category of public-policy issues involves the design of governmental institutions and processes. What should be the number and jurisdiction of congressional committees and subcommittees? Should the President have the authority to veto specific items in a bill or only, as at present, the entire bill? Should a new court be created just below the Supreme Court to screen the appeals and reduce the Court's workload? Should we continue to have a Department of Education? Should the Director of the Office of Management and Budget have to be confirmed by the Senate? None of these policy issues involves directly the distribution of benefits in the society. None directly regulates behavior. Rather, each of them entails the structures of governmental authority. They are politically controversial—that is, they are issues—because they probably *would* have consequences as to which groups would get what benefits from the policy process; thus interest groups line up pro and con these structural issues just as they do on the allocative and regulatory disputes.

Some groups, such as Common Cause, spend most of their effort on this type of issue. Common Cause is an organization of some 250,000 people, mostly well educated and middle class in background, that was established in 1970 by John Gardner to mobilize public support for "public interest" legislation. Common Cause thinks of itself as a reform group, and the very word "reform" emphasizes the intent to change the form of governmental action. Common Cause focuses heavily on such matters as election processes, especially campaign finance, and it operates within a long tradition of institution and process reform in America that was especially prominent during the Progressive era, roughly 1900–1914, when the direct primary, direct election of Senators, and extensive city government reforms were adopted. Institutional reforms are especially prominent on the American political agenda because our institutional arrangements for making public policy are so complex that they offer many targets to the reformer. Our point here is that those reform proposals themselves provide a sizable portion of the material of American political debate.

Let us go back for another quick look at allocative policies. The political heart of these issues is how to divide the benefits and costs. Each policy presents its own constellation of contenders, but we can make some general observations regarding the patterns that tend to dominate policy outcomes in America politics. First, as we have already observed, a program of subsidies, once enacted, tends to remain in place. In part this is because the beneficiaries, including both the recipients of the subsidies and the bureaucrats who administer them, impress the legislators with both the program's value and the recipients' voting power. One method of insuring subsidy programs against political opposition is to enact them in the form of *entitlements*, saying in effect that these constitute continuing commitments of the federal government unless or until the law is changed. Social Security benefits, military pensions, interest payments, and a good many other benefit programs are insulated in this way against reduction through the annual appropriations process. (See Table 13.1.)

Second, American subsidy programs overall are of benefit to a wide range of social groups. We subsidize farmers, including some very wealthy ones; home owners, most of them middle class; airline passengers; barge-line operators; real estate developers; oil and gas exploration firms; and countless others. There are many programs of aid for the poor, to be

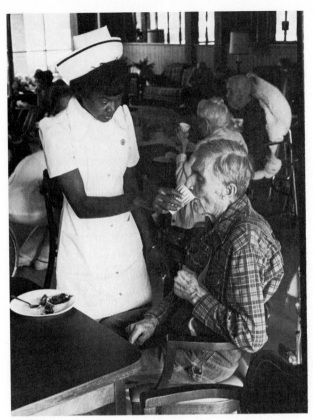

Medicare is an excellent example of an *entitlement* program. If you are over 65, you are entitled to coverage.

sure, but as we saw in Chapter 5, taking them all together, American public policies have little effect on the overall distribution of income among social classes.

The third general point, however, is that there are important redistributive elements among states and regions of the country. Think how many of our major governmental programs have quite well-defined geographic dimensions. Agriculture is an obvious example. Tobacco subsidies go to North Carolina and Kentucky. Corn prices are mainly of concern to Indiana, Illinois, Iowa, Nebraska, South Dakota, and to some extent the neighboring states. Defense programs also have geographically defined constituencies. Airplanes are manufactured primarily in Washington, California, Texas, and Missouri, while naval vessels are constructed and serviced in a very different group of states. Some programs are less obvious but still important in their differential effects. For instance, medical research money does not go to every congressional district, because there are no significant medical research facilities in many parts of the country. Such spending is concentrated in the northeastern and north-central cities and on the West Coast. Space research is heavily funded in Houston, where NASA headquarters are located, a policy result not entirely unrelated to the fact that Lyndon Johnson was vice-president when the space center was established.

TABLE 13.1

FEDERAL ENTITLEMENT PROGRAMS

Program	Fiscal 1984 Outlays (Millions of Dollars)	Estimated Changes in Fiscal 1985 Outlays as Result of 1981–1984 Legislative Action (Percent)
Social Security and Related Programs		
Social security (including disability)	178,695	−4.5
Federal Employee Retirement		
Veterans compensation	9,916	−0.9
Public Assistance		
Supplemental security income	8,498	9.0
Aid to families with dependent children	8,346	−10.5
Food stamps	11,561	−13.8
Earned income tax credit	1,193	0.1
Veterans' pensions	3,874	−2.6
Special supplemental feeding program for women, infants, and children (WIC)	1,367	9.1
Health		
Medicare hospital insurance	41,663	−6.3
Medicare supplementary health insurance	19,475	−9.3
Medicaid	18,992	−2.8
Unemployment Compensation		
Unemployment insurance	23,728	2.4
Trade adjustment assistance	35	−90.0
Other		
Guaranteed student loans	3,245	−39.0
Child nutrition	3,536	−28.0

SOURCE: R. Kent Weaver, "Controlling Entitlements," in John E. Chubb and Paul E. Peterson, eds., *The New Direction in American Politics* (Washington, D.C.: Brookings Institution, 1985), p. 325.

The point is that programs are enacted by Congress, and the members of Congress are elected from specific states and districts. These programs are implemented under the general direction of the president, and he too is chosen from a combination of particular states and districts. Successful participants in this process try to make sure that their areas are well and fairly treated in the sum total of public-policy actions. Some will seek to alter what they see as an unfavorable drift of policy, as when the Northeast-Midwest Coalition formed in Congress to promote the **Snowbelt** against the **Sunbelt.** The West wants water-resource projects. The Great Lakes area wants protection against imports of Japanese steel and automobiles. The overall result is that policies are enacted very largely in terms of their effects on different areas of the country rather than in terms of their impact on social groups or classes.

Moreover, in order to gain political support for the program needs of one area its representative in Congress will very often promise to support comparable concerns elsewhere in the country. This pattern of mutual support can often lead to broad coalitions in favor of a wide range of governmental actions that taken all together distribute funds to most parts of the nation. Critics of this tendency contend that this is an inefficient way to allocate resources. They claim that the overall economy would be better off with less regionally protective governmental allocation and more private market determination of who is to get what. Other critics say that regionally targeted programs often fail to serve the neediest people in those areas. But the American political system continues to encourage policy decisions that distribute benefits across a wide spectrum of geographically defined constituencies.

THE BUDGET PROCESS AND COMPREHENSIVE POLICYMAKING

In many ways the most important decisions of any organization involve its budget. How much money will it receive and how will it be spent? Certainly, these are major questions of federal policy, and they come up every year. They are crucial to everything that government does, and the budget process involves some of the most important interactions between the president and Congress. This process has changed quite dramatically in recent years, and as the process has changed so has the way Americans think and argue about public policy. In this section we will review how the budget process has evolved and assess its impact on policy outcomes.

The Old System

Prior to 1974 the budget-making process went like this. In May or June federal agencies would be directed by the Office of Management and Budget (OMB) to prepare their budget requests for the fiscal year that would begin the following July 1. During the next six months there would be negotiations back and forth within the executive branch, with OMB serving as the president's main coordinating mechanism to bring about a satisfactory balance of program needs and expected revenue. Then in January the president would present Congress a **budget** consisting of proposed expenditures for each part of the executive branch. In his accompanying message the president might make reference to expected revenues and even make suggestions for changes in tax rates, but the actual budget dealt only with expenditures.

Congress then took the budget and broke it into some 13 separate appropriations bills, each dealing with one or a few executive departments, and proceeded to act on each quite separately. At no time was an overall balance sheet of appropriations officially assembled, nor was any connection made by Congress between tax legislation and spending. Authorizing committees, too, went their own way without any regular coordination with the appropriations committees. Decisions in one policy area were reached without much attention to their implications for other programs, and it was often very difficult even to discover during the course of a budget year the sum total of moneys that had been spent or obligated. Whether and by how much federal spending exceeded federal income could seldom be known until well after the fact. Certainly, no vote was ever taken in Congress approving a total budget or a specific deficit position either. Then came the Budget and Impoundment Act of 1974.

The New System

The 1974 legislation sprang from two related sources. One was the very specific resentment felt by many members of Congress toward President Nixon. Of course, 1974, was the year when the Watergate scandal forced Nixon's resignation, but in addition hostilities had been building over his refusal to spend moneys appropriated by Congress. Some of these efforts to impound funds were ruled illegal by the courts, but how much discretion the president had in this area remained unclear. More generally, many in Congress were concerned that as an institution the national legislature was incapable of dealing coherently or comprehensively with the vital matters of taxing and spending. Priorities could not be established in such a fragmented process. Only the president ever put together a complete spending budget, and even that was only a proposal. Thus the authority of Congress vis-à-vis the president and the coherence of American public policy was in grave danger.

The legislation passed in 1974 dealt with impoundment this way. If the president wishes to *defer* an expenditure that Congress has appropriated, he must notify Congress of his intention and it will stand unless either house overrules the action. If, however, the president wishes to *rescind* an expenditure, he must get Congress explicitly to cancel its original decision. Rescissions have rarely been approved, but after a year or two of testing, this aspect of executive-legislative relations has settled back into the realm of routine. Impoundment is no longer an issue. The budget is.

Under the new legislation, when Congress receives the president's budget in January, it is referred to the Budget Committee created in each house to take charge of the process. They review the proposed spending levels, not agency by agency as the appropriations committees do, but in terms of broad functional categories: defense, education, welfare, and so on. They also consider questions involving probable tax revenues. In their final package they must present recommendations both on the revenue side and on expenditures. In each house the Budget Committee brings to the floor a budget resolution that combines all these factors into a single comprehensive package, and after debate, possible amendment, and usually a great deal of conflict and maneuver, it is passed. Differences between the House and Senate versions must be worked out in a conference committee, and the final product is supposed to pass both houses by May 15 of each year.

During the rest of the summer other committees of Congress are supposed to observe the limits set forth in this first resolution. By September 15 a second budget resolution, taking account of economic and political developments in the interim, is due. This one is binding on the other committees. If their decisions exceed the budget resolution totals, they can be compelled to adjust them downward through a *reconciliation* process or, alternatively, a new and more permissive budget resolution must be enacted. All this is to be completed by the new starting date of the fiscal year, October 1.

In some years since 1974 the deadlines set forth in the legislation have been met reasonably well. In others, including most recent years, the process has been considerably rockier. In 1981 the Reagan administration was successful in mobilizing congressional support for a reconciliation process that forced the spending committees to cut some $36 billion from their original recommendations. By 1985, on the other hand, the struggle over the budget had reached such proportions that even the first resolution could not be passed until August.

The most important consequence of the new budget process is probably not the specific content of one resolution or another, however, but the dramatic effect it has had on the structure of national policy debate. Before 1974 it was often true that the federal government spent more than it took in—that is there was a deficit. But this was the result of a whole series of separate decisions on annual spending levels combined with the consequences of whatever tax laws were in operation. In many years there were few, if any, changes in the tax laws themselves, but the revenue they raised would still vary considerably, depending on how well or badly the economy functioned that year. Moreover, there were changes made from time to time in the way the books were kept. For many years the Social Security programs were treated separately, for example, rather than counted along with other government programs.

Beginning in 1975 each budget resolution that comes to the floor of the House and the Senate has a "bottom line" figure, and throughout this period that figure has always been a deficit. The president's budget, which also must estimate revenues as well as proposing expenditures, presents his proposed deficit figure. Each member of Congress must vote, not once but at least twice each year, on a deficit figure. Obviously, the United States has had a budget deficit for much of its recent history, but the 1974 Act has pushed that concept into the very center of public debate. The budget deficit has become the major domestic issue of our time. (See Figure 13.1.)

It is not surprising, perhaps, that once there was a process in place that required an explicit decision about the bottom line, an enormous amount of time and political energy would go into that process. A specific deficit number has great publicity value. It fits easily into headlines, and it serves nicely as a concentration point for a long list of policy disputes. Should defense spending be cut, or food stamps, or student aid, or urban development, or medicare? These are no longer separate and distinct issues. A decision on any one of them must be weighed against all the alternative possibilities. This is also true of taxes. A deficit can be reduced by cutting spending or by raising taxes or both, and in each category there are dozens of alternative possibilities.

There is still a third area of choice required in the budget process. This has to do with the assumptions regarding the probable course of the economy during the next fiscal year. If strong economic growth is

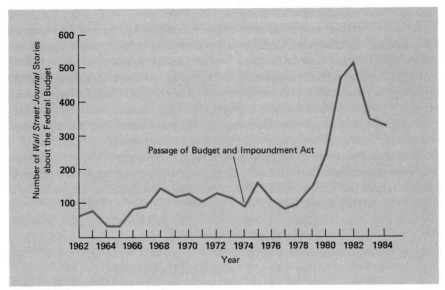

FIGURE 13.1

The Federal Budget Becomes Big News

anticipated, a given level of taxes will yield more revenue and some of the "safety net" expenditures like food stamps or unemployment compensation will be lower. If the economic projections are more pessimistic, the same policy decisions will lead to a larger deficit. In truth, the number of possible combinations of spending, taxing, and forecasting decisions that can go to make up a final budget resolution is staggeringly large. No wonder it takes Congress nearly an entire year of struggle to try to work it out. No wonder, too, that the budget has come to be the context in which nearly every other issue of public policy is debated.

Not only domestic issues are involved. Defense is the largest spending category, and its implications for our foreign policy are obvious; so too are decisions about spending on foreign aid. Also, it is not realistic to divorce assumptions about the likely course of the American economy from decisions about tariffs and international trade or the probable price of oil.

Some analysts of policymaking have argued that by forcing policymakers to confront these choices they will at last establish priorities and measure the trade-offs among the many diverse objectives they have been trying to serve. The result, it is hoped, will be a more rational overall policy that is better calculated to achieve consistent results. In turn, the voters will be able to see more clearly how previously uncoordinated and disconnected bits of decision fit together, and they will be able to come to a reasoned evaluation, pro or con, of the comprehensive policy package contained in each year's budget resolution.

A contrary reading of this process is more pessimistic. Comprehensive policymaking and evaluation of the kind envisioned is simply not possible, this view would argue. There are too many choices for any person or any institution to handle, even with the aid of modern computer technology. Congress, the pessimists say, cannot cope with the problem of comparing the relative desirability of each program with every other program and doing it every year; neither can OMB or the president. Most of the choices must inevitably be left as they have been, and only at the margin will real alternatives be considered.

This is partly a result of intellectual limitations. No one can grasp all at once the vast scope of federal policy. It is also partly a political result. Existing policies have support constituencies. They were not enacted in a vacuum. Changing them will arouse opposition, and in most cases those groups trying to preserve their favored policies are firmly convinced that their view of the public interest is the proper one.

There are other objections to trying to make policy on such a comprehensive "rational" basis. The decision-making process in a system like ours, characterized by separated institutions and decentralized power, is ill-equipped to cope with the responsibilities imposed by the budget process. With weak political parties, highly fragmented congressional decision making, an enormously diverse array of bureaucratic interests, and a highly pluralistic society, it may be too much to expect agreement on a single bottom line expressing the sum total of all the current policy commitments of the federal government. If the budget process is to be followed seriously, it invites a breakdown of the system.

An alternative argument is just as disturbing. It suggests that at least until 1986 most of the uproar over the budget and the deficit was "sound and fury," and really meant very little in actual substance. When Congress enacted a budget resolution carrying a particular deficit figure, it did not affect a single program. It raised no tax and cut no spending. It made a statement, partly of intention and partly of hope or prediction; so, for that matter, did the president when he presented his budget. Throughout the long process of argument and negotiation, within Congress and between the two ends of Pennsylvania Avenue, the statements and counterstatements were symbolic contests. They might have very real political impact, of course, because voters would often applaud one set of symbols and contest another. But the budget deficit itself was a symbol that distilled the substance of many decisions, and it might often misrepresent or at least obscure the tangible benefits and costs of these specific programs to wrap them all up in a single budget resolution package. Public attention had undoubtedly been focused in a particular way, but the budget process may not have been giving the voters a very clear view of what their elected officials have actually accomplished.

GRAMM-RUDMAN-HOLLINGS AND THE POLITICS OF DEFICIT REDUCTION

In late 1985 Congress enacted a bill, sponsored by Senators Phil Gramm (R–Tex), Warren Rudman (R–NH), and Ernest F. Hollings (D–SC), but generally referred to as the Gramm-Rudman law. This law proposed to attack the deficit in a very real way. Its objective was to insure that by 1991 the deficit of nearly $200 billion a year would be eliminated entirely. If that could not be done by means of the ordinary processes of taxing and spending, it would be done by a series of automatic spending cuts.

The Gramm-Rudman process would work this way. Each year the Office of Management and Budget (OMB), an arm of the presidency, and the Congressional Budget Office (CBO), an agent of Congress, would estimate the probable deficit, and report those estimates along with a uniform percentage reduction in spending necessary to reach deficit targets to the General Accounting Office (GAO). GAO, in turn, would transmit the report to the president and, unless Congress itself had reduced spending or raised taxes enough to meet the deficit targets established in the law, automatic cuts would be made in spending for most federal programs. Some exceptions were provided—social security, for example; but most things, including most aspects of the defense budget, were to be subject to the Gramm-Rudman ax.

In March 1986 the first automatic cuts were made, totaling $11.6 billion. In July 1986, however, the Supreme Court ruled 7–2 that a key portion of the law was unconstitutional. Congress could not give the authority to establish the deficit figures to GAO, said Chief Justice Burger for the majority, because that agency was headed by the comptroller general, who can be removed from office only by Congress. Because Congress might seem, in this way, to control the comptroller general, it would be like a congressional veto and thus violate the principle of separation of powers. Congress would be intruding on the "execution of the laws," and that authority is granted by the Constitution to the executive.

Deficit-reduction politics does not stop with the Court's decision, of course. Congress was given 60 days to reenact the March spending cuts and would soon thereafter face the challenge of finding still more politically acceptable reductions if the Gramm-Rudman deficit-reduction goals were to be met. President Reagan hoped to preserve his defense program, while many in Congress insisted that defense spending had to be reduced if a balanced budget was ever to be achieved. Without the automatic features of Gramm-Rudman, whereby the cuts themselves required no additional action from Congress or the president, the members of both branches would be forced to make the specific choices, and that continues to be a politically painful process.

CHAPTER HIGHLIGHTS ■

1. The actions of government come in many different forms. Statutes enacted by Congress, decisions of the Supreme Court, rulings by administrative agencies, and proclamations by the president are all policy decisions.
2. The agenda of political concerns—the issues and proposals actually under consideration at any one time—is of crucial significance. No idea, however good, can be enacted until it is on the active agenda.
3. Politicians and intellectuals contribute items to the agenda of American politics, as do interest groups. Outside events and crises also play an important part.
4. Much of American public policy provides benefits for particular social groups or economic interests, but when they are all put together, these programs directly benefit a large portion of American society. Their costs also tend to be widely distributed.

5. The budget process in operation from 1974 until 1986 provided a sharp focus on the relationship between total federal spending and income—that is, the deficit. Policy debate has centered on issues related to the deficit as never before.

6. The enactment of the so-called Gramm-Rudman-Hollings Bill in 1985 has added a further dimension to public-policy debate. Gramm-Rudman-Hollings requires automatic across-the-board reductions in most federal programs until the deficit is eliminated.

SUGGESTED READINGS ■

Public policy includes everything that government does, so there is a vast literature, including studies of specific policy areas and more general surveys.

Modern commentaries on the American policy process include: James Q. Wilson, ed., *The Politics of Regulation* (1980); John W. Kingdon, *Agendas, Alternatives and Public Policies* (1984); John M. Quigley and Daniel L. Rubinfeld, *American Domestic Priorities* (1985); Allen Schick, *Congressional Money;* Allen Schick, ed., *Crisis in the Budget Process* (1986); Graham Allison, *Essence of Decision* (1971); James E. Anderson et. al., *Public Policy and Politics in America* (2d ed., 1984); John L. Gaddis, *Strategies of Containment: A Critical Appraisal of Postwar America's National Security Policy* (1982); I. M. Destler et al., *Our Own Worst Enemy* (1984).

U.S. Capitol and Congressional Office Buildings

CONGRESS

All legislative powers herein granted shall be vested in a Congress of the United States, which shall consist of a Senate and a House of Representatives.

The United States Constitution; Article 1, Section 1

■ With that expansive language the Constitution announces, as its first consideration, that there shall be a legislative assembly, called Congress, made up of two houses and possessing all the legislative authority delegated by other parts of the Constitution. In Chapter 2 we saw that although the Founding Fathers intended to establish an effective executive and an independent judiciary, it was the legislature, the body that most directly represented the people, that was at the core of republican principles. It was the legislature that was to have primary possession of most of the powers necessary to govern effectively. Consequently, they are spelled out in much greater detail than are those of the other branches. In Section 8 of Article 1 are most of the pieces of authority from which the federal government derives its legitimate power to do what it does. Let us look briefly at some of the most important language in Article 1, Section 8, and see what it has come to mean.

THE POWERS OF CONGRESS

Taxing and Spending

The very first power set forth in the section is the power to "lay and collect Taxes, Duties, Imports and Excises." Taxes may be as certain as death, as the adage has it, but their amount, variety, and impact are subject to enormous dispute and conflict. They are necessary for any active government, and the inability to impose taxes directly on the people was a fatal weakness of the Articles of Confederation. What this language did, therefore, was to assure that the new government could finance itself and, at the same time, that a large share of the political struggles ever after would focus on issues of taxation.

That has never been more clear than during the 1980s. In 1981 President Reagan successfully pressed Congress to enact a substantial tax cut in order to stimulate the economy. In 1985 he proposed a major simplification and restructuring of the very complex tax code in order not only to stimulate further economic expansion but to enhance in both image and reality the fairness of the tax system. Throughout 1985 and 1986 the Reagan administration and the leaders of Congress, both Democratic and Republican, jockeyed and maneuvered to design and pass a satisfactory bill.

Taxes are important not only for the revenue they raise but for their effects, often profound, on what individuals and groups can afford or be tempted to undertake. The government may seek to discourage some activity, such as gun ownership or alcohol consumption, by imposing a tax on it. Or it may offer incentives of encouragement, say, to oil exploration or charitable contributions by providing deductions or exemptions from taxes. This latter kind of provision is sometimes called a *tax expenditure* because, in effect, the government is subsidizing the activity by granting the tax deduction or exemption. No tax is neutral in its effects and every loophole has its defenders who argue the larger social usefulness that is linked to their particular advantage. Thus tax policy offers a broad array of complicated and controversial political issues.

The other half of the tax clause of Article 1, Section 8, is equally important. The Constitution says that Congress may lay and collect taxes "to pay the Debts and provide for the Common Defence and general Welfare of the United States. . . ." In short, Congress may *spend* money for whatever purposes are deemed to fall within the limits of defense and the general welfare. People will disagree fiercely about where those limits are, of course, but there is no effective constitutional barrier erected by those words to constrain Congress's spending power. This has been important in our political history. The Supreme Court has often held that other constitutional grants to Congress contain only limited amounts of power (see the following discussion of the commerce clause), but they have permitted the spending power to be essentially unlimited. If Congress can pass it, in effect, Congress may spend it.

The Commerce Clause

One of the most far-reaching powers granted to Congress by the Constitution appears in the seemingly simple sentence that Congress shall have power to "regulate Commerce with foreign Nations, and among the several States, and with the Indian Tribes." From this sentence has come much of the very considerable power that Congress has exercised over the economic life of the nation. The writers of the Constitution looked with disfavor on the economic chaos caused by individual states trying to impose economic rules and regulations—and taxes—which would benefit one state and hurt others. To help create a single, national economy, the Constitution said that Congress should be able to regulate interstate commerce, that is, economic activities that cross state lines.

But what is interstate commerce and what is not? For many years the Supreme Court held that manufacturing was *intra*state only; so was farming; as a field of wheat could not move from Kansas to Missouri. But in time the Court accepted the view that both manufacturing and labor were part of a "stream of commerce" and that farm products also were transported and sold in interstate commerce. Thus, Congress could constitutionally regulate economic life, and in many ways, of course, it does.

The **commerce clause** has gradually been broadened by congressional action and judicial interpretation. It has allowed Congress to ban segregated racial seating on buses and many other forms of discrimination on the basis of sex or race. It has provided the legal foundation to break up corporate monopolies, to regulate wages and working conditions of most workers, and to protect consumers from unsafe or unhealthy commercial products. In short, under the commerce clause, the Congress has the constitutional authority to enact practically any regulatory law for which there is enough political support to get it passed.

Foreign Policy Powers

We usually think of foreign-policy authority as belonging largely to the President, and, as we will see in the next chapter, this is largely true. Nevertheless, Congress is not without influence in such matters. For one thing, foreign and military policy usually costs money, and Congress must provide it. Congress has the authority to establish tariffs (duties, imports, and excises), and even though this authority may largely be delegated to the executive, a Congress unhappy with the president's policy—Reagan's reluctance to curb Japanese imports, for example—could quickly recapture its constitutional prerogative by rescinding the existing law and passing a new one.

Only Congress can declare war. There has been prolonged controversy over the extent to which this authority restricts the president who under Article 2 of the Constitution is named the commander-in-chief of the armed forces and who pursuant to that authority obviously can commit American troops to battle and has quite often done so. The conflicts in Korea from 1950 to 1953 and in Vietnam from at least 1965 until 1972 looked and "smelled" very much like wars, but they were never declared to be such by Congress. Distress over the Vietnam War was particularly deep, and especially after the invasion of Cambodia, there was also sharp conflict between a Republican president, Nixon, and a Democratic Congress. Finally, in 1973 Congress passed the War Powers Act over Nixon's veto. The act limits to 60 days the amount of time a president can commit American troops in overseas combat before securing the permission of Congress to continue the involvement. The president is also required to inform Congress within 48 hours of any engagement of American troops in combat, anywhere in the world. The act has not yet really been tested since presidents using armed forces in limited military engagements have chosen either to get congressional approval, as Reagan did regarding the 1982–1983 involvement in Lebanon, or get out in less than 60 days, as he did in Grenada in 1984.

One other major area of congressional involvement in foreign affairs arises from the treaty power of the Senate. Only the President can negotiate a treaty. In order for it to be legally binding, however, it must secure the consent of two-thirds of the senators voting on the issue. Originally, this provision was intended to encourage the president to discuss in advance possible treaty provisions with the Senate and work the issues out cooperatively. President Washington found very quickly that the Senate wished to remain apart from the process of treaty negotiation and exercise its authority only after the administration presented a completed draft with preliminary agreement from the nations involved. What this has meant in practice is that as presidents negotiate with foreign governments they must be very conscious of what senators are willing to accept. This may mean making concessions or adopting positions that would not otherwise occur, and it may mean giving especially solicitous attention to the needs, personal and political, of well-placed senators. In any case it means that the making of foreign policy in the United States is a process that very much involves both president and Congress and, accordingly, is often very complex.

Confirmation and Impeachment

Much of the conduct of government is determined by the kind of people who serve at its higher levels and their willingness to adhere to both the spirit and the letter of the law. Recognizing this, the Constitution gives to the Senate the right to confirm or reject a president's nominations to the highest appointive offices in the government. During an average year the president forwards more than 130,000 names to the Senate for confirmation of appointment. Most of these are military promotions, which are approved in lots. The Senate must also approve appointments to the cabinet and subcabinet positions, all federal judgeships, including the Supreme Court, and ambassadorships. Usually the nominations by presidents meet little or no resistance from the Congress, which routinely approves them. Since 1789 the Senate has rejected only eight nominations for Cabinet officers.

During the 1960s, however, the Senate did begin to examine presidential nominations much more critically, especially for the Supreme Court. In 1968 the Senate forced President Johnson to withdraw his nomination of Associate Justice Abe Fortas to become chief justice of the United States, because Fortas was accused of unethical business dealings. Fortas later resigned his position on the bench. Two of Nixon's Supreme Court nominees were accused of insensitivity to the civil rights of blacks, and financial conflict-of-interest problems. Both nominations were rejected. Even when the appointee is confirmed, the process often affords opposing political groups a chance to attack the administration and appeal to public opinion. It also means that presidents must take Sentate interests into account in making appointments.

Nixon encountered the greatest power that Congress has over the president and other high officials—the power to impeach, to try and remove from office any official found guilty of "treason, bribery, or other high crimes and Misdemeanors." Under the Constitution such a move must begin in the House, which votes articles of **impeachment** (a form of indictment) specifying the violations of law that are suspected. The Senate then holds the trial of the president (or other official), and must convict by a vote of two-thirds on any of the articles of impeachment.

In Nixon's case, the House Judiciary Committee recommended that three articles of impeachment be adopted by the House. Before the case could be acted on further by either the whole House or the Senate, Nixon resigned, the first president to do so in American history. Nixon had been told by friendly senators that he was sure to be impeached by the House, then convicted and removed from office by the Senate.

Prior to the Nixon case, the most famous in the nation's history, was the impeachment by the House of President Andrew Johnson in 1869. Johnson's case went to the Senate, where he was tried and acquitted by a single vote. Historians consider Johnson's impeachment to have been the consequence of vindictive partisan politics, rather than based on substantial evidence of high crimes and misdeameanors, but it did illustrate a major potential check Congress has on the president.

The power of impeachment has been used very sparingly by the Congress. Since 1789, proceedings have been initiated about 60 times in the

House, but only 13 officials have been impeached: President Johnson, 1 Cabinet member, 1 senator, and 10 federal judges; only 6 of these officials were convicted.

DIFFERENCES BETWEEN THE HOUSE AND THE SENATE

We must always be aware that Congress is a *bicameral* legislature, and that the two houses are quite different in many respects. Though they share many of the powers delegated by the Constitution, only the Senate participates, as we have seen, in treaty making. Only the Senate confirms appointments. The House impeaches, and the Senate tries and convicts. Revenue measures must originate in the House. These and other differences in formal authority are important, not just as such but because they contribute to another, even greater difference.

The Senate is referred to as the upper body, possessing greater prestige to go with its greater authority. The U.S. Senate evolved from the executive councils used by many royal governors. Senators, until 1913 elected by the state legislatures rather than directly by the voters, were expected generally to be older, wiser, and less vulnerable to public pressure than House members because of their longer term of office. Also, there are only 100 Senators—originally there were only 26—so that the body's prestige is shared among fewer hands than in the House with its 435 members. All these factors have made of the Senate a kind of exclusive club whose members enjoy very high political status and share a kind of common culture that tends to blur the lines of conflict growing out of party, region, and ideology. The House is not totally different, but it is a more abrasive place with less sharing of norms, more overt hostilities among various individual members and groups, and much more detailed rules and constitutional structure.

The rules of the two bodies are rather different, as we will see. The House is so much larger that it cannot tolerate the amount of relaxed individualism the Senate displays. House debate is strictly controlled; Senate floor discussion is not. The House has fewer "characters" and much less grandiloquent oratory than the Senate, though in a television age of well-coifed hairstyles and well-modulated speech that difference has diminished. In recent years numerous presidential hopefuls have been found in both houses of Congress, but more senators than representatives cast ambitious eyes toward the White House. Finally, perhaps the most significant difference between the two bodies is in their political composition. At any one time the balance of partisan and group forces in one chamber almost always will be different from the other. When the Republicans captured control of the Senate following the 1980 elections while the Democrats held the House, this difference became highly visible. Even when both houses are in the same party hands, however, as they have been for most of the century, they present quite different configurations of liberals and conservatives, southerners and northerners, pro- and antilabor members, hawks and doves, and so on. The political challenge of trying to pass (or block) legislation always differs somewhat from one body of Con-

The U.S. House of Representatives begins again every second year.

gress to the other, but it can never be forgotten that regardless of their differences in rules or political makeup both House and Senate must agree before any bills can become law.

THE CONGRESSIONAL AGENDA

What does Congress do with its constitutional authority? Obviously it passes (or, more often, fails to pass) laws, but that hardly describes its agenda in any useful way. What are the proposals that Congress considers? Where do they come from? What forms do they take? The first point is that in order for any legislation to pass, it must be introduced in each house of Congress by a member of that body. No recommendation from the president can be enacted into law until a member introduces a bill. Any member may introduce any bill or resolution at any time, and as Table 14.1 shows, an enormous number of items are in fact put into the legislative hopper each year.

Many of these are purely symbolic gestures—"Today, I introduced a bill that would guarantee . . ."; "Mr. Speaker, I have the honor to introduce Joint Resolution #——that recognizes the valiant service to this nation of the widget manufacturers of North Outer Westovia in my district. . . ."

TABLE 14.1

THE VOLUME OF CONGRESSIONAL WORK

Congress	Bills Introduced[a]	Average No. of Bills Introduced per Member	Bills Passed	Ratio of Bills Passed to Bills Introduced
Senate				
94th (1975–1976)	16,982	39.0	968	0.057
95th (1977–1978)	15,587	35.8	1,027	0.066
96th (1979–1980)	9,103	20.9	929	0.102
97th (1981–1982)	8,094	18.6	704	0.087
98th 1st session (1983)	5,020	11.5	399	0.079
House				
94th (1975–1976)	4,114	41.1	1,038	0.252
95th (1977–1978)	3,800	38.0	1,070	0.282
96th (1979–1980)	3,480	34.8	977	0.281
97th (1981–1982)	3,396	34.0	803	0.236
98th 1st session (1983)	2,407	24.0	390	0.162

[a] All bills and joint resolutions introduced.

SOURCE: Norman Ornstein et al., *Vital Statistics in Congress, 1984–1985 Edition* (Washington, D.C.: American Enterprise Institute, 1984), pp. 144–146.

At the other end of the spectrum of importance are the bills embodying the president's legislative program. These are the matters referred to in the State of the Union Message and in the several more specialized messages the president presents to Congress each year. Much of this program actually emanates from the various administrative agencies and departments in the executive branch, but their proposals for new legislation are subjected to review and approval from the White House before being sent to Capitol Hill.

As we approach the end of the twentieth century a great deal of federal program activity is already in place. We do not begin each two-year congressional cycle with a blank slate. New legislation is not required in many areas. Legislative proposals are therefore often really proposed modifications, often quite minor, of existing practice. Of the bills that become law in any given session of Congress only a few really involve new programs or new policy directions.

The legislative process is very much a continuing story, punctuated by biennial elections that change some of the faces and may alter quite considerably the balance of forces in one or both chambers. The Senate, indeed, regards itself as a continuing body, never ceasing to exist, and so does not need to readopt its rules each two years. The House does, but it too works on an agenda with more continuity than novelty in its composition. On that agenda, besides the trivia and symbolic gestures and in addition to the budget we described in the last chapter, there are three important categories of legislative activity.

One consists of the **appropriations** bills. Some federal expenditures, such as interest on the national debt or Social Security payments, do not require annual appropriations bills. They are funded by what is called a continuing appropriation, which gives the particular function whatever money is needed, unless or until a ceiling or cap is imposed by congressional action. Other expenditures, however, including all the money to pay federal employees, must be provided for by specific legislation each year, and there are some 13 annual appropriations bills covering various groups of agencies and functions.

What if, as frequently happens, an appropriations bill does not get passed by the end of the fiscal year, September 30? The usual procedure has been for Congress to enact a "continuing resolution" that permits the agencies in question to continue to spend money at the same rate as the previous year. But what happens if no such resolution is passed? This actually occurred for a day or two in 1984 and 1985, and the answer is simple: the government shuts down—no money, no work, and no service. Members of Congress quickly hear from angry constituents and the stalemates have been brief, but this kind of crisis is always possible.

The so-called Gramm-Rudman Act, passed at the end of 1985, changes both the budget-making and appropriations processes in important ways. Under its terms the appropriation bills are all to be finished by June 30, several months earlier than in the past. If it is determined that the aggregate amount of money appropriated exceeds a stated deficit target for the coming fiscal year, percentage cuts are to be made in most, though not all, categories of federal spending. How and whether this procedure works and what the political reactions and program effects may be are yet to be seen.

Appropriations provide the actual money for government functions, but they cannot legally be made (with rare exceptions) without first having been *authorized*. That is, Congress must state that it is legitimate to spend up to a certain amount for a particular program before it can actually appropriate the funds. Often the amount appropriated will be less, sometimes much less, than the amount authorized. The appropriations process works through a wholly separate set of committees than the authorizing process, and the political balance is frequently quite different. Then the **authorization** and appropriation must be reconciled in terms of overall total money with the goals stated in the budget resolution, as we saw in Chapter 13. In any case, because very few programs are not highly dependent on money to put them into operation, the processes of authorization and appropriations are both of enormous importance to the outcomes of the policy process.

We noted that some programs require no regular renewal of their authority to spend. They continue to operate until they are stopped. Many, however, must receive not only a specific appropriation annually but periodically have their authorization, their very existence, renewed. The foreign aid program, for example, must be authorized afresh every year before any appropriation of actual money can be made. Our basic farm legislation, authorizing price supports for farm commodities, has never been authorized for more than three or four years at a time. The National Endowments for the Arts and the Humanities must be renewed every few years, and so must student loans, urban development grants, and many other programs that provide funds for all sorts of purposes. The political effects of this practice are plain. It gives Congress, and especially the program's opponents in Congress, another opportunity for critical review and keeps the program's administrators, knowing they will come up again for review, ever alert to congressional desires. Program renewal also renews the opportunity for members of Congress to claim credit with constituents for their accomplishments.

A third category of legislative business consists of those bills, great and small, for which money is usually incidental, but which regulate (or deregulate) behavior. A comprehensive revision of the federal criminal code (which failed in the Senate in 1983), a massive reworking of the immigration laws (failed in the House in 1984), and a new formulation of the copyright laws (passed in 1976) are among the types of bills, each very lengthy and complex, which require prolonged deliberation, thousands of hours of committee discussion, and extended floor debate. If, in the end, the bill is not passed during the two years of a Congress's life, the process must begin again with the introduction of a new bill.

As Table 14.1 shows rather dramatically, only a small fraction of the bills introduced ever passes. This was especially true during the period of intense activism in the late 1960s and 1970s, when new federal programs were proposed at an even greater rate than enacted. President Reagan's deemphasis on the federal role has helped bring down the rate of bill introduction, but it remains much higher than it was 30 years ago, while the number of bills passed is considerably lower. Each piece of legislation tends to be longer, however, with more amendments and more complex provisions than in earlier, simpler times.

As a concluding observation about the Congressional agenda, let us consider the information conveyed in Table 14.2. Congress today is in session substantially more than it was during the 1950s. In addition, there are far more meetings of committees and subcommittees. The number of roll call votes, which require the members to be physically present in the chamber if they are to be counted, has escalated. The sheer physical wear and tear of legislative service has obviously increased, without taking into account the time and energy members spend back home in their states or districts, which with jet planes and increased travel allowances has also gone up considerably. Small wonder that in a 1977 survey of House members they reported having less than 12 minutes of each long working day to read. Small wonder, too, that in each election year quite a few members decide not to run again, often saying, "It's not much fun anymore."

THE STRUCTURES OF CONGRESSIONAL ACTION

The Members

A fundamental fact about the United States Congress is that all 535 members (100 in the Senate and 435 in the House) are chosen separately

TABLE 14.2

CONGRESS AT WORK

Congress	Recorded Votes	Time in Session		Hours per Day in Session	Committee, Subcommittee Meetings
		Days	Hours		
Senate					
94th (1975–1976)	1,273	311	1,788	5.7	6,975
95th (1977–1978)	1,540	323	1,898	5.9	6,771
96th (1979–1980)	1,276	326	1,876	5.8	7,022
97th (1981–1982)	812	303	1,420	4.7	6,179
98th 1st session (1983)	498	146	852	5.8	2,638
House					
94th (1975–1976)	1,290	320	2,210	6.9	4,265
95th (1977–1978)	1,151	337	2,510	7.4	3,960
96th (1979–1980)	1,028	333	2,324	7.0	3,790
97th (1981–1982)	952	312	2,158	6.9	3,236
98th 1st session (1983)	381	150	1,007	6.7	1,566

SOURCE: Norman Ornstein et al., *Vital Statistics in Congress, 1984–1985 Edition* (Washington, D.C.: American Enterprise Institute, 1984), pp. 144–146.

and independently from their states or districts. No party leader in Congress and no president can control the outcome of any member's election, and each member therefore has a great deal of autonomy to decide when to cooperate with the leadership and how to play the role of senator or representative. Each member must determine what kind of image to present to the voters back home, what kind of a record to offer as a basis for reelection. Presidential candidates may affect the voters' preferences for Congress, and so may economic conditions or world tensions over which the congressional candidates have little control. Despite these factors, members of Congress have a great deal of leeway to choose what they will do, not only with regard to voting on the great policy questions, but also in working day after day with their colleagues, their party leaders, their staffs, interest-group representatives, and the many other active participants in the policymaking community.

As we try to understand how and why the individual members of Congress operate as they do, one working assumption that is useful to make is that they are ambitious. We will assume that the incumbent members generally want to be reelected or, if not, that they hope for some other preferment: a House member wanting to go to the Senate, for example, or a senator wanting to be president. If the members did not care about reelection, it might be very difficult to figure out what motivated them to do what they did, and indeed the terms of democratic theory might be hard to sustain. But most of the time it is clear that they do want to gain and hold the good opinion of their constituents, and they act accordingly. As political scientist Richard Fenno has pointed out, there are two other types of ambition that may motivate members of Congress.[1] One is the desire to enact what they believe to be sound public policy, policy that will really solve pressing societal problems whether or not there is any discernible "payoff" in terms of reelection or career enhancement. For example, a senator from Michigan once undertook a prolonged effort to improve the planning of Washington, D.C., and later a Missouri senator pushed hard for home rule for the District of Columbia, even though their own constituents were not affected. Individual members quite often take on personal policy causes, not because of the possible votes, but because personally they care deeply about the issue.

A third form of ambition is career advancement and increased influence within the House or Senate. Reelection must always come first, but once that requirement is met, members may seek a more prestigious committee assignment, campaign for a position in the leadership structure, or cultivate the good opinion and respect of their peers. Leadership ambition is not necessarily in conflict with policy commitments, of course, but generally the members who aspire to broad influence will learn to be adept at negotiating agreements and compromises rather than leading crusades. They will follow the advice of the legendary Speaker of the House Sam Rayburn (D–Tex, 1913–1961), "To get along, go along."

Rayburn's wisdom reminds us that although each house of Congress is composed of politically autonomous individuals, each is also a kind of society in itself, a political system in microcosm, with its own rules and structures of leadership and its own culture and folkways. To a considerable extent, members must adapt to those rules and expectations or be branded "outsiders," mavericks who cannot be trusted to cooperate. Both the formal rules and the informal norms make a great deal of difference to how things are done and, indeed, to whether it will be possible for things to be done at all. For this is another fundamental fact about Congress: although each member depends for election solely on his or her own constituents, no member can accomplish much of anything at all in Congress without the cooperation of other members. No individual member can produce a committee report or pass a bill unless other members go along. Individual senators have sometimes exercised great power, especially negative power, using their committee position or exploiting the rules permitting prolonged floor debate to block legislative action. In every case, however, unless a significant number of other senators is willing to cooperate with the obstructionist, the effort finally cannot succeed. Every member knows this—that cooperation among members is necessary to action and that allies must always be found. It is the complex interactions of 535 politically autonomous individual members of Congress as they confront, adapt to, and sometimes change the formal and informal structures of cooperative action that makes Congress at once mystifying to the outside observer, including the citizenry, and fascinating.

---

[1] *Congressmen in Committees* (Boston: Little, Brown, 1973).

Congressional staffs, working for committees and individual members, do a wide variety of jobs.

The Member as Enterprise

Capitol Hill is the locale of 535 members of Congress, but it is also the place of business for nearly 25,000 professional and support staff who assist the members in one capacity or another. Each House member receives a sum of money ($366,648 in 1983) to hire up to 22 staff aids. Senators' personal staffs vary in size depending on the population of their state (their budgets ranged from about $850,000 to $1.5 million in 1983), but in 1983 they averaged more than 40 per senator. In addition, most senators and many House members have effective control over one or more of the staff serving the committees or subcommittees on which the members serve. Influential senators in the majority party may command the loyal attention of well over a hundred staff people to help formulate legislation, advise on strategy, keep track of what is happening around Washington, deal with constituents, and assist in whatever other tasks the member needs done. Each member of Congress thus has come to be head of a rather good-sized enterprise (see Table 14.3).

It was not always like this. During the quieter days before World War I, House members got along with no personal staffs and senators had only one or two assistants (so, for that matter, did presidents). Total committee staff for both houses was 103 in 1891 and only about 300 in 1914. Moreover, committee staffs displayed no growth as late as 1935, in the midst of Roosevelt's New Deal, though personal staffs had increased somewhat. Even after World War II congressional committee staffs totaled only 483, and personal staffs numbered 2030, less than four per member. Since then both categories have multiplied by more than five times. Why?

TABLE 14.3

CONGRESSIONAL ALLOWANCES, 1984

	House	Senate
Salary	$72,600[a]	$72,600[a]
Washington office		
Staff	$379,480	$668,504–1,343,218[b]
Committee legislative assistants	[c]	$207,342
Interns	$1,840	—
General office expenses	$47,300	$36,000–156,000[b]
Telephone/telegraph	15,000 long-distance minutes to district	[d]
Stationery	[d]	1.4–25 million pieces
Office space	2–3-room suites	5–8-room suites
Furnishings	[d]	[d]
Equipment	Provided	Provided
District/state offices		
Rental	2,500 sq. ft.	4,800–8,000 sq. ft.
Furnishings/equipment	$35,000	$22,500–31,350
Mobile office	—	One
Communications		Provided by Senate Computer Center
Automated correspondence	[d]	
Audio/video recordings; photography	[d]	[d]
Travel	Formula (min. $6,200; max. approx. $67,200)	[d]

[a] Salary established January 1, 1984; leaders' salaries are higher.

[b] Senators are allowed expenses based on a sliding scale linked to the state's population.

[c] Provided for members of Appropriations, Budget, and Rules Committees.

[d] Expenses are covered through the general office expenses line item. In most cases supplies and equipment are charged at rates well below retail levels.

SOURCE: Committee on House Administration; Senate Committee on Rules and Administration.

One obvious answer can be found in the enormous growth of government activity beginning in the 1930s and continuing into the 1980s. The rising curve of congressional staff growth quite closely matches that of the federal budget and in the size of the Federal Register, where the rules and regulations issued by executive agencies are published. As government grew in scope and complexity, Congress members needed help, more and more of it, to maintain any degree of capability to review and guide policy development. As the executive branch grew, Congress had to enlarge its personnel resources or face an ever more severe information gap that would put them at a great disadvantage in trying to monitor what the bureaucracy was doing and critically review policy implementation. Thus part of the dramatic staff growth in Congress has been a reaction to the growth of governmental program activity generally and to the expansion of the executive branch in particular.

Growth of congressional staff has another side to it, however. Between 1970 and 1980 the volume of mail received by members of Congress tripled. And between 1954 and 1983 the amount of mail sent by Congress multiplied tenfold. Neither of these developments could have occurred without massive staff help, and a large share of the members' personal staff resources is devoted to dealing with the mail. But more than just exchanges of opinion, complaints, or information are involved. Many constituents bring very tangible problems to their senator or representative. Where is last month's social security check? Why can't I get into the local Veterans Administration hospital? How can my student resolve her visa problem? Can the Small Business Administration assist the local fast-food franchise? What about an appointment to West Point? This vast array of individual constituent problems and concerns, mostly growing out of the ways that some aspect of public policy affects them, is called *casework*, and Congressional staffs devote much effort to handling casework problems.

We shall return to the importance of casework in the job of Congress members. For now let us simply present a puzzle: Which caused what? Did the enormous growth of casework during recent decades result from the increased scope and impact of the federal government on people's lives, leading them to go to their representatives in Congress for help and thus requiring the members to add staff in order to respond effectively? Or did clever members of Congress, seeing an opportunity to build constituent support by doing favors and solving problems for people, expand their enterprises so that they could insulate themselves from shifts in political fortunes and public opinion and, by helping enough constituents, win repeated reelection? Probably it was some of each. In any case, Congressional staff, like the federal government generally, has grown only modestly since 1981, and it seems unlikely that the staff inflation of the 1970s will soon return.

Not all the staff of Congress works directly for either the members personally or the committees. Several specialized support agencies work for and answer to Congress.

The Congressional Budget Office   With a staff of more than 200 economists, political scientists, statisticians, and other researchers, it provides Congress the expertise needed to evaluate critically the president's budget and the financial predictions that are prepared in the executive branch by the Office of Management and Budget (see Chapter 15). There can be no serious checks and balances between the executive and legislative branches unless each has resources roughly equivalent to the other. It makes for expensive government, but it also assures the mutual checking that was intended by the framers of the Constitution when they invented a government with "separation of powers."

Office of Technology Assessment   The Office of Technology Assessment was established by Congress in 1972 to evaluate the technological impact of proposed legislation. About half the bills introduced in Congress are somehow related to science and technology—energy, environment, defense, and health. Few members of Congress are trained to understand the technological complexities of nuclear power plants, water and air pollution regulations, advanced weapon systems, or biomedical research. The Office of Technology Assessment is where they and their staff turn for advice and explanation.

Congressional Research Service The Congressional Research Service, technically a part of the Library of Congress, was established in 1914, and it is the oldest special support agency that helps Congress. The Congressional Research Service is supposed to answer whatever a member of Congress might ask of it. For example, one member was asked in a letter from a voter back home to provide a recipe for fig cookies. The request was forwarded to the Research Service, and a recipe was provided. Most requests are not so frivolous. A staff of nearly 1000 professionals at the Congressional Research Service provides factual answers to a quarter of a million questions every year: What is the size of different scientific disciplines in the United States? How many school children attend parochial schools? What do scientists say about the risks of a particular fertilizer? How do property taxes differ in towns and cities around the country? The Congressional Research Service assists individual members of Congress (and their staffs) and also works with some of the committees and subcommittees. In addition, the Congressional Research Service publishes reports on a variety of subjects of general interest to Congress. For example, it provides updated analyses of the world energy situation. Using a computerized tracking system of all bills before Congress and computer terminals now installed in most congressional offices, the staff can find out instantly what the status of a bill is (in which committee or subcommittee it is or when it is expected to reach the floor) and what its major provisions are.

General Accounting Office This agency, set up in 1921, conducts audits of government agencies and programs, often at the specific direction of congressional committees. Indeed, some of the nearly 5000 employees

Congressional leaders have relatively few real sanctions that can force members to conform, but they are often persuasive and have considerable impact on policy outcomes.

at the General Accounting Office (GAO) are permanently assigned to congressional committees. If Congress wants to know why there was a cost overrun on the building of nuclear submarines, it will ask the GAO to conduct an audit. Or Congress might have authorized several million dollars for a large survey of the health of the American population. It wants to find out if the survey contractor conducted an honest and complete study. The GAO is highly regarded in Congress. It has sometimes exposed corruption, which has led to changes in how an executive agency is organized. The head of the GAO is appointed by the president and confirmed by the Senate for a 15-year term. This protects the agency from political pressures, as does the fact that its employees—expert in everything from missile telemetry to psychology—are covered by civil-service status.

The status of GAO is a bit odd as it is responsible to Congress but its director is appointed by the president. When Congress enacted the Gramm-Rudman Act in an effort to bring automatic deficit-reduction procedures into effect (see Chapter 13), it designated GAO, along with the fully executive-branch agency OMB, to make the determination as to whether appropriations would exceed the deficit target and, if so, by how much. The Supreme Court ruled, however, that GAO was an arm of Congress and could not, under the separation of power, be given this essentially executive/administrative task.

All of this vast array of congressional activity requires a very substantial amount of both money and space. In addition to the imposing Capitol itself, which contains numerous offices and meeting rooms as well as the actual legislative chambers for the two houses of Congress, there are six very large marble structures, three for the Senate and three for the House, to provide office and meeting space for the members and staff. Even these are not enough, and many staff are housed in old apartment buildings and hotels in the general vicinity. The dollar cost of all the functions budgeted to the legislative branch (which includes some other rather expensive items, such as the Government Printing Office) was nearly $1.5 billion in 1984, an increase of more than 400 percent since 1946 (while the Consumer Price Index went up only 300 percent). Clearly, the Congressional enterprise has become large and expensive.

THE ELECTIVE LEADERSHIP

The leaders of the House and the Senate are political party officials. They are chosen by their respective party caucuses, and although each party welcomes support from members of the other side, most of the time the congressional leaders operate as partisans. Each party chooses its own set of leaders and, with minor changes in terminology, each house of Congress has similar leadership structures. These are diagrammed in Table 14.4.

The power of the leadership in each chamber depends in part on the composition of the party. A badly split party may give its leadership grave problems, while a cohesive party group is easy to lead. The role of the congressional leaders is greatly affected by who occupies the White House,

TABLE 14.4
CONGRESSIONAL LEADERS, 1985

House	Senate
Majority Party: (*Democrats*)	*Majority Party:* (*Republicans*)
Speaker: Thomas P. O'Neill (Massachusetts)	
Floor Leader: Jim Wright (Texas)	Floor Leader: Robert Dole (Kansas)
Whip (Assistant Leader): Tom Foley (Washington)	Whip: Alan Simpson (Wyoming)
Caucus Chair: Richard Gephardt (Missouri)	President Pro Tempore: Strom Thurmond (South Carolina, senior in point of service)
Minority Party: (*Republicans*)	*Minority Party:* (*Democrats*)
Floor Leader: Robert Michel (Illinois)	Floor Leader: Robert Byrd (West Virginia)
Whip: Trent Lott (Mississippi)	Whip: Alan Cranston (California)
Conference Chair: Jack Kemp (New York)	

too. If the **Speaker of the House** and the president are from the same party then much of the Speaker's job is to help enact the president's program. If they are on opposite sides, the Speaker, as Tip O'Neill (D–Mass) did from 1981 to 1987, may serve as a major representative of the president's opposition. The effectiveness of congressional leaders depends a good deal on their personal skills as well. During the 1950s, for instance, Sam Rayburn, (D–Tex) as Speaker, and Lyndon Johnson (D–Tex) as majority leader of the Senate were especially crafty, and despite having very narrow margins of voting support, they were able to win numerous legislative victories.

However skillful they may be, the ability of the elected leadership to gain and keep effective control of the congressional party is limited by the authority the offices possess. From the mid-1890s until 1910 the House Speaker had enormous power. He determined who could be on what committees. He himself chaired the powerful **Rules Committee,** which gave him the power to control what bills would come up for floor action and under what conditions, and he wielded an often arbitrary gavel to dominate floor debates and votes. These House Speakers, Thomas Reed of Maine and Joseph Cannon of Illinois, were conservative Republicans, and they used their power to advance their policy objectives. In 1910, however, a coalition of Democrats and progressive Republicans managed to strip the Speaker of most of his authority. Since then, Speakers have been largely dependent on their ability to maneuver behind the scenes, to persuade and cajole, and to build support through the judicious use of the small bits of authority they still possess. In neither the House nor the Senate is the elected leadership really powerful, but despite very considerable differences in the rules by which the two bodies operate, the end result is very similar; shrewd leaders can do a good deal to keep their party working harmoniously, while abrasive or unduly aggressive leaders may lose more than they win.

The Rules Committee and House Leadership

The most distinctive feature of the House rules is that most legislative proposals are brought to the House floor under the terms of a special rule that states how long debate will last, whether amendments will be permitted, and other important conditions. Each special rule must be reported by the House Rules Committee and approved by the whole House before the bill can be taken up on the floor. Thus, the House Rules Committee is the key to scheduling the legislative agenda, and the particulars of the special rule may have much impact on the final fate of a bill. If, as was true from 1910 to 1975, the Rules Committee is largely autonomous, no more subject to the control of the elected leaders than any other committee, it can become an enormous road block to legislation, and that is exactly what happened from the late 1940s until the 1960s. In 1975, however, the Speaker was given the power to designate the Rules Committee members and to name its chair, and since then it has served as an instrument of the elected party leadership rather than as an independent political force.

Senate Rules of Debate

Debate in the House is quite strictly controlled, and individual members have little chance to play a major role in blocking legislation or converting opponents with oratorical fireworks. The Senate is very different. There the membership is much smaller, and there are powerful traditions supporting the right of all Senators to hold forth on whatever topics they choose and for as long as they are able. The rule granting unlimited debate has meant that the elected leadership in the Senate have only limited ability to schedule bills for consideration, because it is often difficult to tell when the members will finally stop talking and vote. In the extreme case, one or a few Senators might try to prevent a vote from ever being taken. These **filibusters** might go on for weeks, and during the 1940s, for example, they were used several times by southern senators to block civil rights bills from floor consideration. A procedure known as *cloture* has been available to the Senate under slightly varying terms since 1917. Under this rule, if 60 senators vote to shut off debate, they can break a filibuster and proceed. But 60 votes are often difficult to obtain and smart senators have figured out other ways to block action, so prolonged debate remains a prominent feature of Senate procedure.

Thus the rules permit each Senator to talk pretty much without limit, and there are few real sanctions whereby the elected party leaders can impose their will on their colleagues (though the leaders do have a predominant voice in making committee assignments). Nevertheless, the Senate does much of its business with a surprising degree of harmony and mutual agreement. Rather than utilize special formal rules to schedule bills and establish the terms of debate, as the House does, the Senate relies largely on agreements negotiated between the majority and minority leaders and actually does much of its business under unaminous consent; that is, the members waive their individual rights in the interest of moving things along. In concluding this discussion of congressional leadership let us try to understand how, with so little formal authority, and facing independent and sometimes obstreperous members even in their own party, the leaders can so often achieve cohesive action and even unanimity.

The Folkways of Congress

In an important study of the U.S. Senate, political scientist Donald Matthews argued that among the major factors that brought senators together and enabled them to overcome their particularistic interests and partisan conflicts enough to work together and pass legislation was a set of informal norms or folkways that were widely accepted as guides to behavior.[2] A senator was expected to serve an *apprenticeship,* learning the ropes and the rules and keeping a low profile until experience had been gained. The new member should be a "workhorse and not a showhorse," devoting energy and time to the unglamorous and grubby work of legislative detail and disdaining those senators who were constantly appearing on television. The new senator was encouraged to *specialize* in some particular legislative subject matter, almost always related to the committee assignments received. In turn, each senator was expected to defer to other senators on questions within their areas of expertise, observing a norm of *reciprocity.*

Among the topics on which reciprocal deference to expertise was expected were all those issues of partisan appointments and "pork barrel" expenditures that involved only one state. The senators of that state, especially the senior senator, were to be given great deference by the rest in determining who should be a federal district judge, for example, or whether a particular dam was desirable. A special term, *senatorial courtesy,* developed to express the practice whereby other senators deferred to the one whose state was involved in presidential appointments, refusing to confirm nominees of whom the senior senator of the president's party disapproved.

Senatorial courtesy as a norm goes beyond appointment and project reciprocity, however. Matthews found that senators believed very strongly in the importance of treating one another with personal courtesy and friendship regardless of political differences. The most bitter partisan opponents could thus remain on good personal terms, and the result was a degree of trust and a muting of antagonisms that was sometimes hard for outside observers to grasp. The Senate could function more smoothly and avoid tendencies of the kind that occurred in the years just before the Civil War, when the intense political conflicts burst into personal physical battles on the very floor of the Senate and national unity was irretrievably shattered.

Senators are expected to be *institutional patriots,* loyal to the Senate as against "the other body," the House of Representatives, and loyal to the Congress as against the president, the bureaucracy, and the Supreme Court. They jealously guard the prerogatives of the body as set forth in

---

[2] *U.S. Senators and Their Political World* (Chapel Hill, N.C.: University of North Carolina Press, 1960).

the Constitution and seek to enhance its capacity to function effectively—through more and better staff, for instance—while preserving its traditions. On occasion they have voted to censure a member who, like Joseph R. McCarthy (R–Wis) in the 1950s (see Chapter 6), was deemed to have brought the Senate into disrepute by his actions.

The House has developed a somewhat similar set of folkways. They, too, are institutional patriots and are often elaborately courteous in their treatment of colleagues. They, too, value their "workhorses." In the House, even more than in the Senate, specialization is a necessity and reciprocal deference among specialists is standard practice. The House is simply too large and too decentralized to function in any other way. In both chambers it is widely believed that some of the norms have weakened their hold, that members are not nearly as likely today to conform to a single model of the "good" senator or representative, and that as a result the bodies are less cohesive and more unmanageable than they were, say, in the 1950s. The greatest breakdown is thought to be with regard to the apprenticeship norm, and an important factor contributing to the breakdown is staff growth.

Newly elected senators usually acquire part of their staff from those who helped in their campaigns, and the experience of the staff in working together gives them a running start. Additional staff are hired from among the large number of experienced hands in Washington. Very soon this new enterprise is ready to go, familiar with issues and anxious to make a mark. They will not wait cheerfully for two or three years before giving a speech on the Senate floor or introducing an amendment to a bill; nor will they limit themselves to a narrow specialty as once they did. Nearly every senator, regardless of committee assignments, has a staff person who concentrates on the budget and one who deals with foreign-policy issues. These matters are too weighty to leave to a few specialists. Just about every senator wants to contribute, and with staff assistance it is possible to do so. But if every senator wishes to speak and to offer amendments the legislative process can bog down very badly. We will come back to this problem at the end of the chapter.

LEGISLATION BY COMMITTEE

In 1885 a young scholar wrote in his doctoral dissertation that "Congress in session (i.e., floor debate) is Congress on public exhibition, whilst Congress in its Committee-rooms is Congress at work."[3]

Woodrow Wilson went on eventually to become president, but his fundamental judgment regarding how Congress does its business remains sound over a century later. Congress works through committees, each with a reasonably clear jurisdiction over particular policy issues, and committee members tend to dominate the determination of policy in their respective spheres. It is obviously impossible for 435 Representatives or 100 Senators

---

[3] Woodrow Wilson, *Congressional Government* (Boston: Houghton, Mifflin, 1885), p. 79.

to come together to consider each of the scores of issues Congress must address each year. Even if all their other commitments (running errands for constituents, fulfilling ceremonial functions, meeting with organization leaders, electioneering, raising campaign money) allowed enough time for the legislators to meet and discuss each bill, none of them could be even moderately well informed about the enormous variety of issues in the congressional agenda.

The necessity to divide the legislative labor and have small groups of members concentrate on each major policy area has given rise to a committee system, a system adhered to by virtually every American legislative body. If one is to understand how Congress works, one must begin, as Wilson did, with the committee system.

The Standing Committees

In each house of Congress there are **standing committees** that constitute the primary working groups for their areas of policy jurisdiction. Members from each party are appointed to these committees in rough proportion to their party's strength in the entire chamber—3 to 2, 5 to 4, or whatever it might be. Almost every standing committee, in turn, has several **subcommittees** on which still smaller groups of its members serve, and as we shall see, it is the subcommittees that in many areas have come to exercise the greatest influence over legislative outcomes. In addition to the standing committees and their subcommittees there are a few groups called *select* or *special* committees, mostly dealing with rather narrow topics that nevertheless have significant political appeal (aging, for example) or special political sensitivity (intelligence, for instance, which provides review of American efforts to gather information, much of it secret, around the world.)

All of these committees, listed in Table 14.5, are continuing. They operate from one Congress to the next, with many of the same members continuing to serve, build experience in the subject matter, and gain **seniority** within the committee. Occasionally, other special or select committees may be established to deal with specific issues that do not really fit into the jurisdiction of any existing committee. In 1977, for example, Speaker of the House "Tip" O'Neill created a special committee to consider some of President Carter's legislative proposals to deal with the energy crisis. In addition there are a few continuing *joint committees,* such as the Joint Economic Committee and the Joint Committee on the Library, but these groups are for study and discussion only and have no authority to review or make recommendations regarding actual legislation. Most items on the legislative agenda fall fairly naturally within the jurisdictional boundaries of existing committees, and the latter are understandably anxious to retain their chunk of authority over Congress's business. Thus the committee structure remains relatively stable, resisting periodic efforts to reshape it.

Committee assignments   In the House of Representatives, each member is normally assigned to one or two standing committees, though he or she may serve on several subcommittees. Senators, in contrast, usually have three or four committee assignments and perhaps ten or more subcommittee assignments.

TABLE 14.5
MAJOR COMMITTEES OF THE CONGRESS, 1984[a]

Standing Committees of the Senate	Standing Committees of the House of Representatives
Agriculture, Nutrition, and Forestry (6)	Agriculture (8)
Appropriations (13)	Appropriations (13)
Armed Services (6)	Armed Services (7)
Banking, Housing, and Urban Affairs (5)	Banking, Finance, and Urban Affairs (8)
Budget (0)	Budget (8 Task Forces)
Commerce, Science, and Transportation (8)	District of Columbia (3)
Energy and Natural Resources (5)	Education and Labor (8)
Environment and Public Works (6)	Energy and Commerce (6)
Finance (8)	Foreign Affairs (8)
Foreign Relations (6)	Government Operations (7)
Governmental Affairs (6)	House Administration (6)
Judiciary (8)	Interior and Insular Affairs (6)
Labor and Human Resources (6)	Judiciary (7)
Rules and Administration (0)	Merchant Marine and Fisheries (6)
Small Business (7)	Post Office and Civil Service (7)
Veterans' Affairs (0)	Public Works and Transportation (6)
	Rules (2)
Select and Special Committees of the Senate	Science and Technology (7)
Aging (0)	Small Business (6)
Ethics (0)	Standards of Official Conduct (0)
Indian Affairs (0)	Veterans' Affairs (5)
Intelligence (0)	Ways and Means (6)
	Select Committees of the House of Representatives
	Aging (4)
	Children, Youth, and Families (3)[b]
	Hunger (2)[b]
	Intelligence (3)
	Narcotics Abuse and Control (0)

[a] Number of subcommittees given in parentheses. [b] Known as task forces.

Assignment to the standing committees of the House and Senate are made by special party committees, which reflect the regional and ideological distribution of the congressional delegation. The party leaders exercise considerable influence on these decisions.

Each new member of Congress seeks a committee that will contribute benefits to constituents. Thus a member of Congress from a rural area where farming is the major economic activity may try to get a seat on the House or Senate Agriculture Committee. Someone from an urban area might be interested in committees with jurisdiction over social-welfare programs. Westerners often try to get on the Interior Committee. Tax-writing committees (Senate Finance Committee and House Ways and Means Committee) are attractive to nearly everyone because their subject matter is so vital to every economic interest. Constituency service is not the only factor to consider, however. Senators who hope to be considered prospects for presidential nomination, for instance, may decide that service on the Foreign Relations Committee is necessary to give them an image of statesmanship.

The number of seats on any given committee is limited, and generally members retain their assignments from one Congress to the next. New members may find no vacancies on their preferred committees and have to accept service on some of the less attractive "duty" committees such as Post Office and Civil Service or House Administration until a more attractive vacancy opens.

Assignments are made in each house by panels of party leaders who try as well as they can to fit together the requests of returning members for transfers, of new members for appointments that will help them back home, of endorsements of senior sponsoring members and of outside interest groups, of needs of the party leaders to have dependable support in the most important committees, and of the need to fill out the ranks of the less popular committees. This process, occurring after every biennial election, has been called a "giant jigsaw puzzle,"[4] and in recent years the pieces have been fitted together fairly smoothly with most members receiving at least part of what they want. In any case, however, the committee assignment process has enormously important consequences, because as members work their way up the seniority ladder they come to acquire a central component of power in Congress: the power of the chair.

Designating committee leaders   As long as it is true that many of the really important decisions on legislative matters are made in committees or subcommittees, then the power to designate the chairpersons of those working bodies will be of vital significance. In the 1890s and early 1900s the Speaker of the House controlled the selections on House committees and made sure that members favorably disposed to him and his views were placed in these positions. These and other powers of the Speaker were stripped away in the so-called Revolution of 1910–1911, and eventually a system evolved that operated almost automatically to bestow the chair upon that member of the majority party in the House or Senate who had the longest continuous service on the committee in question. A member who changed committees started over at the bottom of the seniority ladder, as did anyone who interrupted congressional service to run for another office, to serve in the executive branch, or because of an election mishap. Seniority favored those members who returned to the House or Senate year after year, and they, in turn, were generally those members from constituencies that experienced little partisan competition.

From the 1930s through the 1960s the Democrats controlled Congress nearly the entire time, and the main effect of this seniority rule was to elevate southern Democrats, who seldom had much election opposition, to the chairs of many of the crucial committees. Many of these committee

---

[4] The title of a study of the committee assignment process by Kenneth Shepsle (Chicago: University of Chicago Press, 1978).

leaders were hostile to the mainstream legislative agenda of the Democrats, and they used their positions to block or slow down civil rights legislation, aid to education, food stamps, and much else. Toward the end of the period some big-city Democrats began to accumulate substantial seniority, too, and in other ways the power of the seniority leaders was somewhat modified. But there remained a persistent tension between newer, younger members in both parties and their more senior colleagues.

Reforming the committee system For years there had been complaints by junior members against the nearly dictatorial power of committee chairs, and gradually modifications began to be made. Some committees adopted rules that limited the prerogatives of the chair to control the committee's agenda, its staff, and its procedure. In the House, these reforms led in 1973 to the adoption of the so-called Subcommittee Bill of Rights, whereby those subgroups of each committee attained largely autonomous status with their own jurisdiction, staff, and prerogatives no longer subject to the direction of the full committee chair. Granting such authority to 130 subcommittee chairpersons, rather than keeping it in the hands of 22 standing committee leaders, greatly dispersed the resources of influence in the House, of course, and has accentuated the fragmentation of power, a point we return to later. It also undercut the importance of seniority, for it took much less time to reach the top of your party's four-member subcommittee group than to the top of a 27-member delegation on the full committee.

Two years later, in 1975, the House Democratic Caucus, the full party membership in the House of Representatives, carried the revolt against seniority an additional step. Abandoning the traditional practice of automatic approval of seniority leaders as chairpersons, three committee chairs were deposed, including one with 46 years service in Congress. The Caucus repeated this action against one chairperson in 1985 and has clearly demonstrated that the seniority tradition will not be followed when it threatens to put party mavericks or petty despots or senile veterans in committee chairs.

The Senate also reformed its committee rules in somewhat the same fashion, making it easier for junior members to oust unpopular committee chairs and giving committee staff aid to all members. In the Senate as in the House the main effect of the reforms has been to fragment and disperse power. Each individual member has a greater degree of autonomy, and each party's leadership has less power to discipline its members. As a result the Congress is more attractive to the relatively young or newly elected members, but offers less scope to the veteran legislator.

The sources of committee and subcommittee power Why are the committees and subcommittees so important? Part of the reason we have already noted, the inevitability of dividing the immense agenda Congress faces each year. Beyond that is the fact that with very rare exceptions every bill introduced in either house of Congress is referred to a committee and, in time, to a subcommittee (and occasionally in the House to more than one) for preliminary consideration. Thereafter the bill's fate is very largely in the committee's or subcommittee's hands. Is a hearing to be held? Are witnesses to be asked to testify? The committee decides whether and who. Before the proposed legislation is brought to the floor it is the subcommittee members who do the first "mark up," refining its provisions line by line. It is they who must vote to bring the bill to the full committee, and the latter, in turn, must vote to bring it to the floor. Floor debate will largely be dominated by committee members, and when it comes time to vote, many other senators or representatives will look for guidance to those most intimately acquainted with the issues, the committee or subcommittee leaders. If the two houses pass the bill, but in different forms, it will be sent to a **conference committee,** nearly always composed of the active leaders from each party that considered the bill in committee. Thus committee and subcommittee leaders are strategically placed at each step of the legislative process.

In addition to the authority and prestige of their positions, however, committee leaders have other important resources. In many cases they know more about the issues before them than anyone else. After all, it is they who have sat through the hearings and heard the testimony, not only this year but often over many years in the past. They are familiar with the issue's history and with the problems that have cropped up in trying to deal with it. They have—very often, at least—substantive expertise that no members not on the committee cannot match. As we saw earlier, it has long been the advice of senior members of Congress to their junior colleagues that they should specialize, develop some area of policy expertise so fully that their colleagues will come to look to them with deference and accept their guidance. The committees and subcommittees are the organizational contexts in which this expertise develops.

The personal specialized knowledge of the members is fortified by their committee and subcommittee staffs who serve primarily the needs of the committee members and especially those of the chair (or ranking minority member) who appoints them. Expertise is thus institutionalized in a well-staffed committee or subcommittee. A further dimension of specialized support comes to the committee leaders when, as often happens, they develop close rapport with organized interest groups and agencies of the executive branch. The dairy subcommittee of the Agriculture Committee of each house is generally on good terms with the National Milk Producers Federation; the Armed Services Committee of each house works closely with the Pentagon.

Some committee leaders in the past achieved near-legendary reputations for their command of the arcane legislative business within their jurisdiction. Wilbur Mills (D–Ark, 1939–1976) was for 17 years the very influential chair of the House Ways and Means Committee, dominating his colleagues on the committee, refusing to permit subcommittees to function, and seldom allowing a bill out of his committee until he was sure it would pass. Mills was said to know more about tax policy than anyone else in Washington, and at least part of his power rested upon this reputation for expertise.

Not all committee chairs are so well respected, however. Some may be too friendly to organized constituencies or rubber stamps for executive agencies or simply out of step with their colleagues' views. What then? Before the 1970s, although it was possible through a discharge petition for a determined majority of the House or Senate to force a bill out of committee over the objections of a stubborn chairperson, it rarely happened. Today, the several reforms that have weakened seniority leaders have made it far less likely that they will try to prevent legislation that most members truly support from coming up for a floor vote. This is not to say that a subcommittee chair cannot still bottle up a bill. For several years in the late 1970s and early 1980s, for example, Don Edwards (D–Cal), chair of the House Judiciary Committee's Subcommittee on Constitutional Rights effectively thwarted any effort to bring to the House floor proposed constitutional amendments on school prayer or abortion. Equally clear was the fact that many members of the House, perhaps a majority, were happy to have Edwards do just that, so that they would not have to commit themselves on such controversial issues.

One final point should be made regarding the 1970s reforms of congressional committees that helped weaken the power of seniority leaders and disperse influence and power more widely. Until the early 1970s somewhat more than one-third of all the committee and subcommittee meetings held were closed to the public. Reporters had to wait outside, and interested citizens could learn only afterwards, if at all, what compromises had been made. Today closed committee meetings have virtually been eliminated, save for those involving national security questions. Anyone can watch and negotiations are out in the open. In such an atmosphere the arbitrary or heavy-handed authority of many old-time congressional leaders does not survive long. Broader participation among members and more widely dispersed influence are the result.

CONGRESS IN ACTION

As we have seen, Congress meets virtually all year long, and the individual members are involved in a hectic pace of committee meetings, floor proceedings, discussions with staff, encounters with constituents and lobbyists, frequent trips back to the states or districts, and running for reelection. In this section we will present an overview of three broad areas into which these busy congressional lives fall; the actual legislative process, investigation and oversight, and constituent service.

How a Bill Becomes Law

In earlier parts of this chapter we touched on several of the key factors that affect the complicated, often tortuous, path a bill must follow before it can become law. Here we offer only a summary of the main steps in the sequence they ordinarily follow. (See Figure 14.1.) It should always be remembered, however, that at each of these steps there are likely to be subtle maneuvers, parliamentary tricks, negotiations among the players, and often appeals to the larger public as the contending groups jockey for advantage. The legislative process has numerous steps in which a bill must move from one arena—say, a subcommittee—to another—the full committee—and then on to still another—the whole House or Senate.

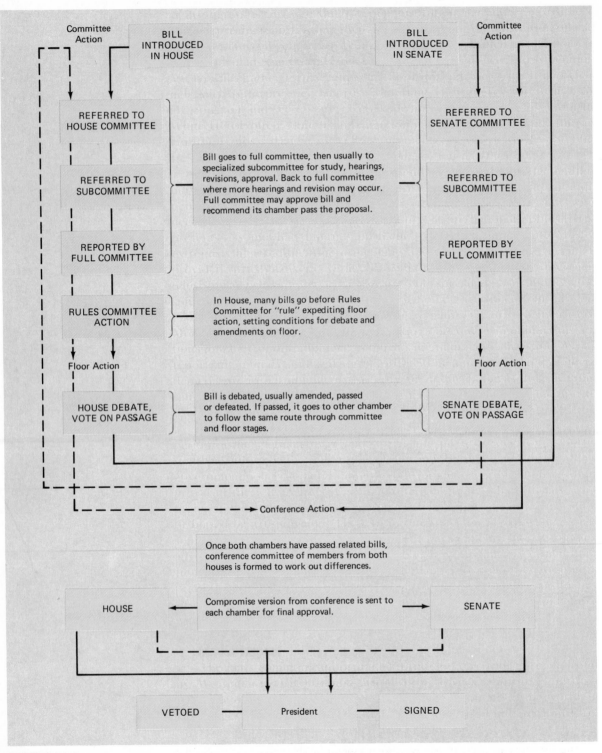

FIGURE 14.1

How a Bill Becomes a Law

SOURCE: "Congressional Quarterly Guide to Current American Government," Fall 1983
(Washington, D.C.: Congressional Quarterly, Inc.), p. 145

Each of these moves brings the bill, which by now has been steered successfully through one stage, into a setting where the political balance is somewhat different. Building a strong support coalition in committee by no means guarantees support on the floor or in the other body.

Thus the legislative process offers many opportunities for groups to block a bill or force changes in it as the price of acceptance. Compromise is usually essential. Trade-offs among diverse interests are required. The legislation that comes out at the end of this long bargaining process, if indeed any does finally emerge, may bear only a faint resemblance to the bill that was introduced. But the process of bargaining and compromise is necessary because members of Congress represent diverse interests and values, and they are all independently elected and cannot be forced by the leadership or the president to conform.

The patient willingness to compromise, adjust, and adapt is the hallmark of legislative skill, and with that skill a piece of legislation can be revised and refined until it becomes acceptable to a reasonably broad majority of the nation's political groups. Sharpness of focus may be lost; ideological coherence may be compromised away. But a bill that can pass is one that much of the country is likely to accept, and in a nation as large and diverse as the United States, for such a result to emerge from the democratic bargaining process is not a trivial achievement.

Investigation and Oversight

If Congress is to act with intelligence and understanding, there must be the authority to investigate, and Congress may therefore look into any issues on which it might conceivably wish to legislate. The organizational context for investigations is the committee system. Committees and subcommittees hold hearings and question witnesses and through this process develop a record regarding the existence and severity of a problem, evaluating alternative methods for dealing with the problem, assessing the record of administrative implementation of programs in the problem area, and so on. Not all investigations are intended to result in recommendations for legislation, but to be legitimate they must bear some relationship to possible legislative purposes. Since the legislative authority is so broad, however, this still permits the investigation of virtually anything a particular subcommittee chair might like to look into.

Witnesses before congressional committees are often representatives of organized interest groups with some concern in the problem area. Or they may be experts in the area, often from universities, who offer their best scholarly judgment. Many of those who testify are executive-branch officials, from secretaries of departments down to much lesser figures. These officials invariably testify whenever there are legislative proposals from the president, and they are often summoned by various committees to speak also about other issues in their general jurisdiction. The most prominent department heads, the secretary of state or secretary of the treasury, might spend 100 hours a year presenting testimony to Congress.

One other type of witness is quite popular with many congressional committee investigations. Prominent celebrities may be asked to give their views or tell about their experiences. Sometimes these help the members understand a problem better. More often the payoff comes from the publicity value of the witness. A famous baseball player may not add much new information to an investigation of gambling or drugs, but his appearance is sure to attract a horde of cameras and reporters. To put a well-known racketeer before the committee, even though he refuses to answer any questions, dramatizes the issue of racketeering and assures publicity for the investigating committee members.

Congressional investigations can become publicity circuses, serving mainly to advance the investigators' political careers or to damage the standing of those summoned to testify. Witnesses must answer questions essentially as they would in a regular court or be subject to a citation for contempt, which, if they are convicted, could lead to jail. A witness may have a lawyer present and may refuse to answer on the Fifth Amendment ground that the answer might tend to incriminate the witness—that is, be used as evidence against the witness in a later court proceeding. Taking the Fifth Amendment can be nearly as damaging to one's reputation as answering, of course. At various times and in various political circumstances, racketeers, labor leaders, business executives, bankers, and alleged Communists have been among those suffering from the hostile exposure of a public hearing by an unfriendly congressional committee.

The power of Congress to investigate is both necessary and broad, but in a system of separate and coequal branches how far can Congress go to compel members of the executive branch to answer questions? This issue was brought into sharp focus during the Watergate hearings in 1974. During this dramatic inquiry into the alleged violations of campaign laws (and many others) by members of the Nixon administration, with extensive live television coverage and exceptional public attention, some witnesses tried to claim "executive privilege." They contended, as many previous administrations had done, that Congress could not *compel* members of the White House staff to testify about discussions within the executive branch. As things developed, the claim of executive privilege was not tested against congressional authority but against the courts. The Supreme Court held in *U.S.* v. *Nixon* (418 U.S. 683, 1974) that while executive officials could withhold information on matters involving national security, they had no general immunity if, as in this case, the evidence was important in a criminal trial.

When the Supreme Court ruled against him and President Nixon agreed to turn over the Watergate tapes and soon thereafter resigned, a serious constitutional crisis was resolved. But the whole sorry episode illustrated the pervasive and continuing tensions that inevitably characterize the relationships among Congress, president, and Court as separated institutions sharing powers. Each branch guards its prerogatives and defends its jurisdiction, not just out of pride or institutional patriotism, but also because of concern that policies be developed and implemented in ways that those in dominant positions within each institution consider sound.

A good illustration of this is provided by what is known as the *legislative veto*. The legislative veto is a provision in a law delegating authority to the executive branch to implement a program which requires the executive agency to inform Congress in advance of action regarding rules and regula-

The investigations of Watergate by congressional committees in both the House and the Senate proved to be powerful instruments of political action—enough to force President Nixon to resign.

tions it proposes to issue. Then, though there are several variations in the way legislative vetoes work, Congress may have to approve the specifics before they can be put into effect. In some versions the executive action may be valid unless Congress *dis*approves. Depending on the program, the veto may be exercised by one house or both and even in some cases by committees. The point of this procedure, of course, is to give the interests in Congress an additional method of controlling the decisions of executive agencies. The method is of recent origin. Until the late 1950s only a few acts of Congress included legislative veto provisions, but from 1970 to 1975, generally a period of great tension between Congress and the president, nearly a hundred such provisions were enacted.

In 1983 the Supreme Court held that at least some legislative veto provisions were unconstitutional, on the grounds that under the Constitution Congress must act first and then present its action to the president for his signature or approval. (*Immigration and Naturalization Service* v. *Chadha* 462 U.S. 919, 1983). This decision and the 1986 controversy over the Gramm-Rudman deficit-reduction procedure (see Chapter 13) have revived the constitutional debate over just exactly what the separation of powers means. That debate, in turn, reflects the ongoing struggle for authority and policy influence among all three branches of the national government.

Serving Constituents

Earlier in this chapter we saw that the members of Congress, bolstered by their substantial staff resources, spend much time and energy trying to help individuals and groups of constituents with their problems. A 1976 study found that 15 percent of all adults remembered having someone in their family ask their representative in Congress for help. Hundreds of letters every week plus personal visits and phone calls bring to the members an immense array of problems, sometimes very personal and often trivial in themselves.[5] One study found that government jobs, help with Social Security and unemployment assistance, hardship discharges from the military, appointments to the service academies, and government publications were the most commonly requested items, but tax problems, legal difficulties, and many other matters great and small are brought to the members for their help. Moreover, generally help is provided. Seven out of ten respondents reported general satisfaction with the assistance.

The great bulk of this casework assistance involves problems of constituents in encounters with the federal bureaucracy. Congressional members serve, in effect, as troubleshooters, or to use a Swedish term for an official whose job is to intervene with the bureaucracy in behalf of citizens: *ombudsman.* In order to serve constituents more effectively by bringing the resources of congressional offices closer to the people, fully one-third of the total personal staffs of congressional members are now stationed in offices back in the states or districts. Furthermore, the members themselves go home with great frequency, many nearly every week and some who live near Washington, more often than that. By presenting themselves as often and as helpfully as possible to individuals and small groups, the members hope to build support for themselves as individuals, which can yield big reelection dividends.

Some members cultivate a "home style," in which they run for reelection by denouncing the federal government, emphasizing that they, in contrast to most ordinary "politicians," are protecting their constituents against the greedy bureaucrats of Washington. Others may stress how successful they are in using their congressional influence to secure defense contracts, post offices, public construction, mass-transit grants, bureaucratic offices, medical research funds, and even federal prisons. Either way, it is constituency service that becomes the central feature of the member's reelection appeal, while party allegiance and positions on the major policy issues, likely to offend some groups of voters no matter what positions are taken, are deemphasized. In the process, of course, the senator or representative may come to feel like a glorified "go-fer," a mere errand boy for self-seeking constituents. But perhaps that is an important part of what representative democracy is supposed to achieve.

---

[5] Cited in Roger H. Davidson and Walter J. Oleszek, *Congress and Its Members* (Washington: Congressional Quarterly Press, 1981), p. 126.

CONGRESS AND DEMOCRATIC REPRESENTATION

Electoral Accountability

As we saw in Chapter 2, the Constitution lays out a political theory of democracy which to this day continues to structure American politics. A crucial feature of that theory involved the role of elections to Congress. *The Federalist* (*No. 53*) observes that "where annual elections end, tyranny begins." Actually, the writers of the Constitution decided against annual elections for Congress, choosing instead to have members of the House of Representatives elected on a two-year cycle and senators elected on a six-year cycle. The principle of regular elections, however, was firmly established. By the device of regular elections, the Constitution intends to make public officials accountable to a broad electorate. This idea of **electoral accountability** is central to democratic theory.

The logic is worked out in *The Federalist* (*No. 57*), an essay which deals explicitly with how to obtain rulers who will pursue the common good of society and remain virtuous despite the temptations of high office. The argument proceeds in three steps:

1. Lower restrictions to the ballot box in order to have as broad a voting population as possible: "Who are to be the electors of the federal representatives? Not the rich, more than the poor; not the learned, more than the ignorant; not the haughty heirs of distinguished names, more than the humble sons of obscurity and unpropitious fortune."

2. Allowing anyone to stand for public office: "Who are the objects of popular choice? Every citizen whose merit may recommend him to the esteem and confidence of his country. No qualification of wealth, or birth, of religious faith, or of civil profession is permitted to fetter the judgment or disappoint the inclinations of the people."

3. Instituting frequent elections. Here the essay makes the subtle point that frequent elections will maintain in public leaders "an habitual recollection of their dependence on the people." In their initial election, the representatives would have been sensitive to what the voters wanted from government. But might not the exercise of power itself lead to forgetfulness? Not if officials must soon stand for reelection. Members of Congress, facing a future election, "will be compelled to anticipate the moment when their power is to cease, when their exercise of it is to be reviewed, and when they must descend to the level from which they were raised; there forever to remain unless a faithful discharge of their trust shall have established their title to a renewal of it."[6]

---

[6] It is not certain whether this *Federalist* paper was written by Alexander Hamilton or James Madison. The quotations are from Saul K. Padover, ed., *James Madison: The Forging of American Federalism* (New York: Harper & Row, 1953), pp. 228–229. The papers were first published in 1788 as a set of essays defending the new Constitution and urging its ratification.

In short, if the voters do not like the way their representatives take care of their interests, they are supposed to vote them out of office and find someone who will do a better job. In actual practice, however, the task of securing effective representation and a fully accountable Congress is full of difficulties. Let us consider some of them.

Do voters insist on accountability?   If the theory of electoral accountability is to mean very much, the voters will need to be able to exercise a meaningful choice at election time. There must be serious challengers to incumbent members of Congress, and the voters must be aware of at least the general shape of the choice before them. How well are these standards met? Not very well. As we can see in Table 14.6, a very high proportion of those members of Congress who seek reelection succeed. Moreover, most of them win by margins of better than 3 to 2. In addition, there is the appalling fact that only about half of the voters can even identify the candidates in congressional races. Voters' awareness of the candidates' records or promises is correspondingly meager, though they may still have reasonably clear impressions of how good a job the representative is doing. So the degree to which voters can hold senators and representatives accountable for their actions is quite limited. How then do the members behave? Do they fulfill their responsibilities in a responsive fashion?

Responsive Representatives
Members of Congress pretty clearly act as though they constantly need to win voter approval. They return to the state or district frequently, making

Members of Congress can seldom relax. Every two years each House member must run for reelection, and many are engaged almost continuously in campaigning in their home districts.

TABLE 14.6

INCUMBENT SUCCESS IN HOUSE ELECTIONS

Year	Retired[a]	Sought Reelection			Reelected		
		Total	Defeated in Primaries	Defeated in General Election	Total	Percentage of Those Seeking Reelection	Percentage of House Membership
1966	22	411	8	41	362	88.1	83.2
1968	23	409	4	9	396	96.8	91.0
1970	29	401	10	12	379	94.5	87.1
1972	40	390	12	13	365	93.6	83.9
1974	43	391	8	40	343	87.7	78.9
1976	47	384	3	13	368	95.8	84.6
1978	49	382	5	19	358	93.7	82.3
1980	34	398	6	31	361	90.7	83.0
1982	40	393	10	29	354	90.1	81.4

[a] Does not include persons who died or resigned from office before the election.

SOURCES: *Congressional Quarterly Weekly Report,* vol. 38 (January 12, 1980), p. 81, vol. 38 (April 5, 1980), p. 908, vol. 38 (November 8, 1980), pp. 3320–21; and *National Journal,* November 6, 1982, p. 1881.

speeches and appearances and cultivating support. They send out enormous amounts of mail (581.7 million pieces in 1982) and seek to be as helpful as possible to constituents with problems. They try to obtain for their constituents all the benefits that federal policy will yield, from dams and military contracts to post offices and symphony subsidies. They seem to believe that despite the statistical record of incumbent success, they are in fact "unsafe at any margin."

It is all very well to say that members of Congress should represent their **constituencies** and try hard to do so. But who are their constituents? Everyone in their states or districts? This answer is not very satisfactory. Not all the people who live in a congressional district or a state feel the same way about political issues or want the same things from their government. Whose political views should be represented? Those who speak out on issues? Those who voted for the representative in the last election? Those who can be most helped or harmed by the legislation in question? Also, what are senators and representatives to do when they see a conflict between what the constituents want and what they themselves believe would be in the best interests of the country? These are basic questions for anyone concerned about the meaning of representation in a democratic government. Political theory provides no certain answers and no final guidance to the elected official. The officials must, nevertheless, make decisions and hope on balance to secure constituency support. Let us look at some of the mechanisms that help guide members of Congress as they confront their representational tasks.

Descriptive representation: the composition of Congress When people talk about Congress as being representative or unrepresentative,

TABLE 14.7
THE COMPOSITION OF CONGRESS

	1965	1971	1977	1983
Mean length of service (years)				
House	11.0	12.0	9.2	9.2
Senate	11.1	11.5	10.6	9.6
Religious affiliation				
Catholic				
House	94	101	119	124
Senate	14	12	13	17
Jewish				
House	15	12	23	29
Senate	2	2	5	8
Episcopal[a]				
House	54	49	48	42
Senate	15	17	17	20
Blacks				
House	5	13	15	20
Senate	0	1	1	0
Women				
House	11	13	18	22
Senate	2	1	0	2

[a] High-status Protestant church with less than 3 percent of church numbers nationally.

they often have in mind the social and economic background of the members of Congress. Does the composition of Congress mirror the full variety of social classes, races, ethnic groups, occupations, and religious beliefs of the general population? Clearly it does not. As Table 14.7 shows, both houses of Congress are overwhelmingly white, male, and upper middle class. Barely 5 percent are black, Hispanic, or Asian. Only 24 are women. Nearly 70 percent of the House of Representatives came from business or the legal profession, and 80 percent of the senators came from those occupations. Nearly all have graduated from college, compared with only about 12 percent of the same age group in the general population. About 30 percent of the senators and 10 percent of the House members are millionaires.

During the past two decades, however, Congress has become more diverse in the kinds of people elected to it. There are more blacks, women, Catholics, Jews, and Hispanics in the present Congress than there were, for instance, in the 1960 Congress. Indeed, until the 1960s, Congress was essentially a white, male, Protestant institution. The political activism of the last two decades, the greater organizational strength of women, blacks, and various ethnic groups, and the more open competition for political office has led Congress to mirror more closely the population from which it is elected.

How much does it matter? Does racial, sexual, and occupational representativeness necessarily lead to greater political representativeness? Social background does not always predict political beliefs. A person who once worked in a factory does not necessarily have the interests of the working class at heart. Some men care as much or more than many women about the rights of women. White citizens, including some white members of Congress, have long been active in the civil rights movement. At the same time, it may well be that black Americans feel more fully represented by black legislators, and many other ethnic and religious groups also seek to elect "one of their own." Full representation of social groups is an important part of a truly democratic system.

But the process of political representation is more complex than descriptive representation would make it. We hope that our elected officials will not simply be "like us" but also will be persons who stand out from their fellow citizens, who are especially skilled at matters of government and have demonstrated their political wisdom and judgment. Although it does not always turn out that public officials are virtuous and wise, the intent, nevertheless, is to select as leaders those who are above average in competence, experience, and integrity.

Competent and talented individuals can come from any social background, from any racial and ethnic group, and from both sexes. The challenge is to maintain an election system sufficiently open that the most talented people of any social or economic background can reach public office. In this regard, there are still greater barriers to the poor than to the better off, to the black or Hispanic than to the white, and to the female than to the male. Eliminating these barriers is a long-term task.

Constituency consensus   We should not assume that American society is so complicated that members of Congress never know what the overwhelming majority of their constituents want. There are many issues on which the views of the folks back home are well enough known that a "wrong" vote in Congress would likely be punished at the next election. A representative from a tobacco district will vote for tobacco subsidies. A senator from a major oil-producing state will favor tax benefits for oil interests. For many years southerners in Congress voted against civil rights legislation or any other programs seeming to favor black citizens, but when southern blacks began to vote in significant numbers this behavior changed. Where there is a clear consensus of views within the district, the representative will nearly always vote accordingly, not necessarily because of any **constituency pressure,** but because anyone who can get elected from such a constituency probably shares the same widespread convictions. On many policy questions, however, the opinions of a district's voters are quite mixed. On some issues, indeed, few voters have any clear preferences at all. Where then does the representative turn for guidance? How does the representative decide whom to represent?

The importance of party   Every member of Congress today is affiliated with one of the two major parties, and with occasional exceptions this has been the pattern for most of our history. As we have seen, the leadership structures of both houses are party based, and so is the process of obtaining highly valued committee assignments. In addition, every member was elected on a party ticket and presumably drew the support of many voters because of their shared partisanship. Furthermore, the president is also a partisan, on one side or the other, and his urgings will be heard with special sympathy by his party colleagues in Congress. All this suggests that one important way members of Congress can be representative is to vote with their party. In some cases, to be sure, the bulk of the national party may represent a combination of interests quite different from those dominant in a member's district. Then the member must choose between party loyalty and a strong but conflicting constituency preference. Sometimes, too, party leaders are weak and have little to offer a member to induce support. We should not assume, however, that a member's party and constituency are always in conflict or that a faithful party supporter is not at the same time representing his or her district. There are some who feel that strengthening the role of parties in Congress would make that body more effectively representative than it is now. In any case, even now party plays a major role in shaping congressional behavior.

Representing interest groups   Although members of Congress may be uncertain about the views of the thousands and even millions of individual voters back home in the districts or states, they are less uncertain about the views of the major groups, especially those that are well organized. Much of the actual contacts the members have with their constituents takes the form of interactions with group representatives. As we saw in Chapter 9, groups with continuing interest in legislative matters often support a full-time staff in Washington to keep track of what is happening and to make sure that senators and representatives know the group's views. Where possible, of course, the groups try to influence the decisions of members of Congress by presenting persuasive arguments, providing campaign funds, and, if possible, mobilizing their supporters back in the district to vote for or against the member at the next election.

Several points regarding interest-group representation need to be made clear. First, most groups concentrate their efforts on those members of Congress who are already predisposed to be favorable to their cause. The AFL-CIO does not waste money or time on rock-ribbed free-enterprise conservatives, nor do big-city mayors, working through the U.S. Conference of Mayors, devote much effort to influencing congressmen from the rural South. Second, in many House districts and nearly every state there is considerable diversity of interests and views with no single group predominating. Members have to work out a way to represent a coalition of groups, an amalgam of interests, that will enable them to win reelection. For senators, with their larger and more heterogeneous constituencies, this problem is especially acute, and partly for this reason, senators in recent years have been more vulnerable than House members to election defeat.

From the standpoint of a particular interest group the fact that a senator has a large and diverse constituency may mean that (a) the group needs to make alliances with other groups in order to mobilize sufficiently impressive strength, and (b) most groups will not seek to *control* members' behavior but, rather, to assure reasonably friendly *access* to them. The opportunity to be heard without undue hostility is the predominant objective for most groups as they deal with Congress.

It remains true, however, that members of Congress are especially attentive to those groups with significant resources in their specific constituencies. Since congressional constituencies are based on geography it becomes very important, if we are to understand what interests are likely to be influential with which senators and representatives, to understand how the major groups are distributed across the nation. It makes a difference that doctors are high-status members of every community in the country; that unionized automobile plants are critical to Michigan but not to North Carolina; that rice is grown in Arkansas and durum wheat (used to make pasta) in North Dakota; that fighter planes are built in Missouri and Texas but not in Minnesota; and that senior citizens are numerous everywhere but especially so in Florida and Arizona.

In a sense, if members of Congress from all over the country respond to the demands of a particular group—senior citizens, for example—that is strong in nearly every state and district, then the aggregate effect of those highly particularistic pressures may be regarded as broadly representative, responsive to an interest with great national strength and relatively little explicit opposition. Party coalitions, when they are firm, can also help accomplish a considerable degree of nationwide consistency in patterns of representation, as when Democrats in Congress work closely with organized labor whether or not individual members have strong labor elements in their respective constituencies. Coalitions of interests may often cut across party lines, however. In recent years several dozen different caucuses have been organized in Congress to facilitate member cooperation in those matters which they have in common. The Congressional Black Caucus is perhaps the best known, but Table 14.8 shows that there are a great many others.

Having said all this, however, we must go on to note that a great deal of the response by members of Congress to the interests of their constituents involves not national groups or broad coalitions of interests but, rather, the highly differentiated and particularistic concerns of quite small numbers of people in the specific geographical area that elects the representative. Let us see how this works.

When Representative John Doe considers a bill to aid higher education, he might view it in the light of platform promises made by his party and its presidential candidate. Or he might examine it against the scholarly evidence of national need and arguments about resolving that need with efficiency. Or he might hark to the urgings of the National Education Association, if the NEA is strong in his district. Or he might calculate how much money would accrue to his district under the aid formula proposed (per capita income, for instance: the poorer the district, the greater the aid) and consider whether other possible formula factors (rate of population growth, say, or number of national merit scholars) would not be more beneficial for his district. Representative Rachel Roe, whose district contains a major private research university, may contend over whether and how to aid higher education with Representative Edith Brown, whose district

TABLE 14.8
INFORMAL CONGRESSIONAL GROUPS, 1984[a]

House

Democratic

Calif. Democratic Congressional
  Delegation (28)
Congressional Populist Caucus (15)
Conservative Democratic Forum ("Boll
  Weevils") (38)
Democratic Study Group (228)
House Democratic Research
  Organization (100)
Ninety-Fifth Democratic Caucus (35)
Ninety-Sixth Democratic Caucus (20)
Ninety-Seventh New Members Caucus
  (24)
Ninety-Eighth New Members Caucus
  (52)
United Democrats of Congress (125)

Republican

House Republican Study Committee
  (130)
House Wednesday Group (32)
Ninety-Fifth Republican Club (14)
Northeast-Midwest Republican Coalition
  ("Gypsy Moths")
Republican Freshman Class of the 96th
  Congress
Republican Freshman Class of the 97th
  Congress
Republican Freshman Class of the 98th
  Congress
Conservative Opportunity Society

Bipartisan

Ad Hoc Congressional Committee on
  Irish Affairs (110)
Budget Study Group (60)
Congressional Agricultural Forum
Congressional Automotive Caucus (53)
Congressional Border Caucus (12)
Congressional Coal Group (55)
Congressional Emergency Housing
  Caucus
Congressional Human Rights Caucus
  (150)
Congressional Mushroom Caucus (60)
Congressional Rural Caucus (100)
Congressional Steel Caucus (120)
Congressional Territorial Caucus (4)
Congressional Travel and Tourism
  Caucus (154)
Federal Government Service Task Force
  (38)
House Fair Employment Practices
  Committee
Local Government Caucus (22)
Northeast-Midwest Congressional
  Coalition (196)
Task Force on Devaluation of the Peso

Task Force on Industrial Innovation and
  Productivity
Conference of Great Lakes
  Congressmen (100)
Congressional Arts Caucus (186)
Congressional Black Caucus (21)
Congressional Caucus for Science and
  Technology (15)
Congressional Hispanic Caucus (11)
Congressional Metropolitan Area
  Caucus (8)
Congressional Port Caucus (150)
Congressional Space Caucus (161)
Congressional Sunbelt Council
Congressional Textile Caucus (42)
Export Task Force (102)
House Caucus on North American Trade
House Footwear Caucus
New England Congressional Caucus
  (24)
Pennsylvania Congressional Delegation
  Steering Committee (5)
Tennessee Valley Authority Caucus (23)

(continued)

TABLE 14.8 *(Continued)*

Senate

Democratic	Republican
Moderate Conservative Senate Democrats (15)	Senate Steering Committee

Bipartisan

Border Caucus	Concerned Senators for the Arts (35)
Northeast-Midwest Senate Coalition (40)	Senate Caucus on North American Trade
Senate Caucus on the Family (31)	Senate Children's Caucus (18)
Senate Coal Caucus (39)	Senate Copper Caucus (18)
Senate Drug Enforcement Caucus (44)	Senate Export Caucus
Senate Footwear Caucus	Senate Rail Caucus
Senate Steel Caucus (46)	Senate Tourism Caucus (60)
Senate Wine Caucus	Western State Coalition (30)

Bicameral

Ad Hoc Congressional Committee on the Baltic States and the Ukraine (75)	Arms Control and Foreign Policy Caucus (129)
Congressional Alcohol Fuels Caucus (90)	Coalition for Peace through Strength (232)
Congressional Clearinghouse on the Future (84)	Congressional Caucus for Women's Issues (129)
Congressional Senior Citizens Caucus	Congressional Jewelry Manufacturing Coalition
Environmental and Energy Study Conference (37)	Congressional Wood Energy Caucus
Long Island Congressional Caucus	Friends of Ireland (80)
New York State Congressional Delegation (36)	Military Reform Caucus
Pennsylvania Congressional Delegation (27)	Pacific Northwest Trade Task Force
	Pro-Life Caucus (60)
Renewable Energy Congressional Staff Group (50)	Senate/House Ad Hoc Monitoring Group on Southern Africa (53)
	Vietnam Veterans in Congress (38)

[a] Numbers of members, where available, in parentheses.
SOURCE: Sula P. Richardson, Congressional Research Service.

has only a single public junior college. They are unlikely to define either the need or the methods of assistance in the same way. When Senator Claghorn insists on a bigger budget for bombers, one may wish to look at how much defense industry his state contains. This applies to a very large share of the total volume of American public policy. Each member of Congress has a strong incentive to interpret the nation's needs in terms that will yield benefits to his or her state or district. To bring home the policy "bacon" is to represent successfully the interest of the constituents, and this is not simply a logrolling process, or (to use another common metaphor) scratching one another's back to get one's full share of the pork barrel. For if one truly represents the way one's constituents feel on an issue, it is very likely that one will see it as they do, in terms of their tangible interests.

But what then is the aggregate result in public policy? If every district insists on having its full share of the budget for scientific research, for instance, then a rather large proportion of the funds will go to places in the country that have no real research facilities. If every state must have its national parks, the parks budget will expand very rapidly. As the American system of particularistic representation has developed, this pattern of broad geographical diffusion of public money and resources has had some clearly beneficial effects: a large and efficient system of national highways, and the nationwide availability of higher education, hospitals, and post offices, as well as lots of television and radio stations, airports, and waterway improvements.

When each member insists on getting some of the action for his or her district, it is very difficult to establish priorities, to say some things are more important than others, to reduce programs selectively rather than across the board. As we saw in our discussion of policymaking in Chapter 13, this is part of the explanation for the great difficulty President Reagan had in 1985 when he tried to cut the federal budget by eliminating or drastically reducing numerous federal programs. Even though there might have been a national tide of opinion that favored the budget cuts, members of Congress defended those programs precisely because *they* were responsive to their particular district concerns. What then should be represented: the national majority, when there is one, or the interests of one's state or district? The question leads us to the next.

The Burkean controversy   Should representatives vote the interests of their district or party, or should those officials try to do what they feel is best for the entire nation—or even the world? The issue has been with us for more than two centuries. In 1774 the British political philosopher Edmund Burke told his Bristol constituents how he thought a representative should behave:

> Certainly, Gentlemen, it ought to be the happiness and glory of a representative to live in the strictest union, the closest correspondence, and the most unreserved communication with his constituents. Their wishes ought to have great weight with him; their opinions high respect; their business unremitted attention. . . . But his unbiased opinion, his mature judgement, his enlightened conscience, he ought not to sacrifice to you. . . . Your representative owes you, not his industry only but his judgement; and he betrays, instead of serving you, if he sacrifices it to your opinion. . . .
>
> Parliament is not a (collection) of ambassadors from different and hostile interests. . . . (It) is a deliberative assembly of *one* nation, with *one* interest, that of the whole—where no local purposes, no local prejudices, ought to guide, but the general good, resulting from the general reason of the whole. You choose a member, indeed; but when you have chosen him, he is not a member of Bristol, but he is a member of *Parliament.*[7]

---

[7] Ross, J. S. Hoffman, and Paul Levack, eds., *Burke's Politics* (New York: Knopf, 1949), pp. 115–116.

Could Burke be reelected in the United States after making such a speech? Americans, by a large margin, say they prefer their representatives to act as their delegates, not as trustees. As the late Senator Richard Neuberger (D–Ore, 1955–60) put it: "If there is one maxim that seems to prevail among many members of our national legislature, it is that local matters must come first and global problems a poor second—that is, if the member of Congress is to survive politically." A member of the House says: "My first duty is to get reelected. I'm here to represent my district. . . . This is part of my actual belief as to the function of congressmen . . . What is good for the majority of districts is good for the country. What snarls up the system is these so-called statesmen-congressmen who vote for what they think is the country's interest. . . . We aren't . . . paid to be statesmen."[8]

It is often said that a statesman is only a dead politician, and that the real test of democratic representation is the approval of the electorate. Reelection is the guarantor of representativeness. But now take the case of Jamie Whitten, a Democratic representative from the hill country of northern Mississippi. Through the 1980s he has been the powerful chairman of the House Appropriations Committee and of its subcommittee on agriculture. Some years ago he forced the Department of Health, Education, and Welfare (HEW) to leave Mississippi out of the National Nutrition Survey, the first effort by the federal government to investigate malnutrition in the United States. He delayed and blocked various programs that would provide surplus food to schoolchildren or other hungry citizens. He long opposed any attempt to study how technological changes in farming might affect the livelihood of farm workers or sharecroppers. It should be noted that he got major public works in his district, including the huge Tennessee-Tombigbee Waterway. But his record as an opponent of social reform measures is consistent. It might well be argued that he contributed to the massive exodus of rural poor to the cities and made the problems of blacks and whites, North and South, worse. Yet his record seems to impress his constituents, for he has been reelected continuously since 1941.

Burke held that a true representative should act as trustee of his constituents. John F. Kennedy (before he became president) wrote an influential book, *Profiles in Courage,* in which senatorial courage was held to be those acts that were unpopular, even politically suicidal, but which the senator involved nevertheless believed were right. But if everyone acted without regard for the desires of constituents, what would be left of democratic control of government? It is truly a dilemma.

Particularism and congressional elections   The patterns of particularistic representation we have been describing have important connections with the process by which members of Congress are elected. Members

[8] The Neuberger quotation appears in Samuel P. Huntington, "Congressional Responses to the Twentieth Century," in David Truman, ed., *The Congress and America's Future* (Englewood Cliffs, N.J.: Prentice-Hall, 1965), p. 15. The second quotation is from Lewis A. Dexter, "The Representative and His District," in Theodore J. Lowi, ed., *Legislative Politics U.S.A.,* 2d ed. (Boston: Little, Brown, 1965), p. 86.

seek to build electoral support, as far as they can, by attracting votes from their party's faithful adherents, but as we have seen in Chapter 11, party attachment is considerably less compelling nowadays than it was prior to the 1960s. Moreover, party organization, especially local party organization, has all but disappeared in many parts of the country. As a result, most incumbent members and most challengers must start very nearly from scratch and build their own bases of support. For incumbents this process involves a nearly continuous effort to provide services and assistance to individual constituents and groups, an effort made possible by the large increases in staff and other resources of office described earlier in this chapter. A further part of the incumbent's effort involves bringing specific policy benefits to the state or district: a dam, an air force base, a subway system, a submarine construction contract, disaster assistance for flood victims, and so on. Accompanying this effort is what political scientist David Mayhew aptly has called "credit-claiming,"[9] whereby the incumbent proclaims through the media what splendid things have been accomplished for the "good old fourth district."

Challengers to incumbents obviously face formidable problems. They have had no opportunity to provide constituency service or to claim credit for particularistic policy benefits. Like the incumbents, they have little in the way of party organization or dependable party voters to draw upon. So they, too, must build support largely on their own. How can this be done? As Table 14.6 earlier showed, the challenger's task is often beyond the power of the most energetic campaigns, but it can be and sometimes is done successfully. What does it take? Money!

Congressional campaigns have become enormously expensive. In 1982 House campaign expenditures by each candidate averaged $228,060, while Senate campaigns averaged $1,781,815. Each was about four times the cost of campaigns in 1974. A large part of the cost reflects the increasing reliance on television. In addition, candidates are making much greater use of opinion polls and professional campaign managers and media consultants.

Why spend so much money? For incumbents the mass media are the principal way they convey to the voters what they have done and claim credit for it. For the challengers those same methods of mass appeal are almost the only way they can build enough name recognition to have a chance to defeat an incumbent. Without much party organization to help them, with larger and more diverse constituencies resulting from population growth and, from time to time, redistricting as well, and with limited time and energy for personal appearances and "pressing the flesh," the candidates must fall back on the mass media and campaign techniques appropriate to those media. We reviewed some of the issues involved in media-dominated campaigns in Chapter 12. Here we will focus on a single but vital dimension: campaign contributions.

Where does the money come from? How can such huge sums be raised for campaigns every two years, and what do those who contribute get in

---

[9] *Congress: The Electoral Connection* (New Haven: Yale University Press, 1974).

Congressional campaigns have become so tremendously expensive that fundraising events are a common feature of political life, both in Washington and "back home."

return? In 1982 House candidates in the 435 races raised (or had spent on their behalf by the parties) about $190 million. For 33 Senate races a total of $127 million was raised. About half of this money came either from the candidates themselves—Mark Dayton of Minnesota was reported to have spent nearly $8 million of his own department store fortune in an unsuccessful effort to win a Senate seat—or from individual contributions of less than $500. Another one-fourth of the Senate money and one-sixth of the House funds came from individuals giving more than $500. A significant share of the money Republican candidates had available to them came from the national party organization. Ten percent of the House money and 15 percent of the Senate funds were provided this way. The Democratic party with far less effective national party fund-raising or organizational development contributed very little to their congressional candidates.

The rest of the money (31 percent in the House, 17 percent in the Senate) came from PACs, the nonparty political action committees described in Chapter 9. There has been much recent discussion of the role of PACs, and considerable alarm has been expressed that they might exercise undue influence over the congressional members they had helped to win. Some facts may help clarify the issues. The number of PACs organized in the United States has grown rather rapidly from 600 in 1975 to six times that number in 1985. The number of labor union PACs has grown little, while the number of both corporate and trade association PACs has

PROFILE ▪

HENRY CLAY (1777–1852)
Influential pre-Civil War Political Leader

Along with John C. Calhoun, Daniel Webster, and Andrew Jackson, Clay was a major figure in the second generation of American political leadership. A Kentuckian, Clay served 14 years in the House, 11 of them as Speaker. He was the Whig nominee for president twice (1832 and 1844), secretary of state for John Quincy Adams, and then senator from Kentucky (1831–1842, 1849–1852).

Like many of his contemporaries Clay was a great orator. His speeches were often influential in defining the political agenda of the time. His "American System" included proposals for extensive internal improvement and tariff protection to encourage business growth. Clay was influential in framing the Missouri Compromise of 1820, a reasonably successful effort to defuse sectional conflict between North and South. Thirty years later he sponsored the Compromise of 1850 in an attempt to stave off the threatening disintegration of the Union.

Both abolitionists and staunch proslavery advocates denounced Clay as a "mere" politician. Nevertheless, while Clay (sometimes called the Great Pacificator) and his generation lived and looked for ways to compromise their differences, the nation remained intact. In the next generation, American leaders were neither as skillful nor as devoted to the high political arts of renegotiation and compromise.

grown a lot; so have the so-called ideological PACs, a large share of which are very conservative in their politics.

The disproportionate PAC growth among business and conservative groups triggered the fear among many liberal Democrats that a campaign fund advantage would lead to a growing vote advantage. Thus far the verdict is mixed. The actual share of total campaign money derived from PACs has gone up only moderately since 1976, and other sources, including individuals, are still more important. Moreover, each PAC is limited to contributing $5000 per candidate per race (primary plus general election), and it may well be argued that such small amounts in a huge campaign war chest cannot buy much influence. Furthermore, Democrats receive just about as much money from PACs as Republicans do. To be sure, much of the Democratic money comes from labor, while the ideological PAC funds go mostly to Republicans. Business contributions actually are quite evenly divided, however, as business firms have sought to maintain friendly access to both parties and especially to committee chairpersons, which in the House still means the Democrats.

Even though the PAC phenomenon has not been lopsidedly Republican in its effects, it is still viewed with alarm by many. It places the entire

PROFILE ■

EDMUND BURKE (1729–1797)
British Political Intellectual
and Parliamentary Leader

Burke served almost 30 years in the British House of Commons, where he usually was in opposition to the government. He sharply criticized British policy toward Ireland, India, and the American colonies. He argued that the government was unnecessarily driving the colonists toward revolution. In domestic politics Burke insisted that a member of parliament owed his constituents his best judgment in matters of public policy, not blind obedience to constituency opinion.

In later years, Burke's concern about the possible excesses of popular majorities led him to oppose the French Revolution and to predict the Reign of Terror and the depotism that, in fact, developed from it. He was attacked by many as a benighted conservative. He was not an unquestioning defender of the status quo, however. His eloquent arguments stressed, instead, the importance of preserving a sense of the past and of resisting any violent break with traditional ways. He said that each generation stood on the shoulders of all those that had preceded it and so can see a bit farther into the future. Burke himself is one of those whose ideas give us a better view of what lies ahead.

process of interest representation into a context of congressional fundraising whereby almost every interest group, law firm, and corporation seemingly must have its own PAC in order to gain a friendly hearing from Congress. The members, meanwhile, are thrust into a continuous round of fund-raisers to shake the PAC "money trees." Influential members of Congress, who may have no opposition back home and hence need little campaign money of their own, nevertheless hold receptions, collect PAC contributions, and by doling out this money to other members' campaigns build their own support bases within Congress.

The real problem is probably not so much the PACs as it is the enormous cost of campaigns. Congress attempted to ease the problem by limiting expenditures and providing public funding for presidential campaigns, but in *Buckley* v. *Valeo* (1976) the Supreme Court held that to limit people's right to contribute and spend on congressional races was an unconstitutional infringement on free speech. No successful substitute has yet been developed, and there is continuing escalation in money used to finance congressional elections.

INSTITUTIONS IN ACTION ■

CONGRESS AND FARM POLICY, 1985

American farmers are in economic trouble. Since at least the last part of the nineteenth century the growers of wheat and corn, cotton and rice, cattle, hogs, and other commodities have found themselves facing unfavorable, even disastrous conditions. Agriculture prices fluctuate widely, and farmers are unable to control them. The costs of machinery, land, fertilizer, and other factors of production, including credit, do not go down when farm prices decline, however, and periodically farmers have been caught in a squeeze, unable to obtain enough for their crops to meet their payments on loans and mortgages. It is this basic difficulty that Congress has tried over and over to resolve. In 1985, once again, an Omnibus Farm Bill was enacted to provide assistance to American agriculture.

Since 1938 the basic mechanism by which the federal government helps farmers is the *price support loan.* For example, if the market price for wheat is $3.00 a bushel but farmers, on average, need to get $4.00 a bushel to break even, a loan rate is set—in this example, $3.50. The U.S. Department of Agriculture (USDA) offers to loan the farmer $3.50 per bushel and take the wheat as collateral. If, during the next year, the market price rises about $3.50, the farmer sells the wheat and pays off the loan. If the price stays down, the farmer keeps the money and USDA has surplus wheat on its hands.

Price supports have been the center of farm-policy debates for nearly 50 years. Those debates center around (1) how high the support level should be, (2) how much discretion USDA should have in lowering the support price to meet world market conditions, (3) how many commodities should be covered and in what ways, and (4) what other provisions or "sweeteners" should be added in order to make the farm bill politically palatable to a large enough coalition in Congress so that a bill can be passed.

Agriculture policymaking has been dominated by Congress. To be sure, every administration has played an active role, making policy proposals and lobbying for or against particular provisions. Nevertheless, it is on Congress that the greatest farm group pressures are felt, and it is there where most of the programs are crafted. Members of Congress represent geographically defined constituencies, and agricultural production is also defined in terms of geography: the wheat belt, the tobacco areas, the rice-growing section, the peanut-producing region, and others where commodity interests are tied very closely and clearly to congressional districts and states. The elected representatives, whose reelection prospects and personal concerns may both be highly sensitive to the ups and down of agriculture, invest substantial effort in designing programs that will improve farm income.

Two important limitations must be observed, however, in the making of farm policy. One is financial. In 1985 the federal deficit was nearing $200 billion, and agricultural price supports for 1985 had cost almost $17 billion. No new program could pass Congress or receive President Reagan's signature if its costs were too high. The second limitation results from the declining numbers of farmers. When the 1938 legislation was enacted, 25 percent of the nation's people lived on farms, as compared with only 2.4 percent in 1982. The number of farms in 1980 was less than half what it was in 1950. Farmers are simply not as important politically as they were. If they are to succeed politically, farm groups must make up for declining members by forging effective alliances and stitching together coalitions of quite diverse interests. The 1985 bill reflected this fact.

It was absolutely essential for farm groups to enact a bill. The existing program had been passed in 1981 and was due to expire in 1985. If that happened, there would still be a farm program, the one enacted in 1938, but it would fall far short of current farm needs. Moreover, 1985 was a year of rising farm bankruptcies and other distress signals that were likely to have severe political effects in the congressional elections of 1986. In particular, an unusually large number of Senate seats held by Republicans (22) would be up for election in 1986. Many of these were in farm states, and the preception was widespread that if an adequate bill was not enacted, the Republicans would risk losing control of the Senate.

Many economists and academic commentators had been arguing that the whole structure of U.S. farm policy was wrongheaded, and that in order to sell more U.S. products abroad—nearly half our wheat and corn are marketed overseas—we needed to reduce prices and return farm production to something closer to a free market. The Reagan administration was rather sympathetic to this view and was also looking for ways to reduce federal spending. But in 1985 neither the freelance conservatives nor the Reagan administration could muster much farm or congressional support for any drastic policy departures.

The traditional ally of Republican administrations in seeking to reduce the level and cost of price supports has been the American Farm Bureau Federation (AFBF). Much the largest of the farm interest groups, the AFBF has its greatest strength in the midwestern corn belt, where recent farm distress has been great. In order to pacify its own membership the AFBF had to embrace proposals to keep farm subsidies high. In this position they were joined by other, more militant farm groups, including some farm protest organizations backed by church organizations. What this meant was that the general farm organizations were in basic agreement that the 1985 bill should not be very different from its 1981 predecessor. Even though no one regarded existing farm policy as satisfactory, new programs or policy directions were not politically feasible.

Despite this general agreement there were nearly all the specifics of the bill yet to be worked out, and a complex process of negotiation and compromise began. At one level, a fairly large number of separate commodity interests had to be accommodated. At a second level, nonfarm interests had to be brought into the picture in order to build majorities in each house of Congress. At a third level, the interests of the two political parties

had to be dealt with so as not to convert farm policy into such a bitter partisan battleground that no bill could be passed.

To take the last problem first, the key partisan issue had to do with *target prices.* Remember the role of price support loans at $3.50 a bushel for wheat. In addition to that there has been a target price system in operation, whereby a figure—let us say $4.50 a bushel—is set as the price needed to produce adequate farm income. Direct cash payments are made to farmers to cover the difference between market or loan level and target price, provided that the farmer agrees to restrict production by retiring some acres. Democrats wanted to freeze the existing target price levels, while the Reagan USDA wanted to cut both target prices (and hence cash subsidies) and loan rates. It was soon clear that many Republican senators would not accept the Reagan position, however, and a compromise was eventually reached which allowed USDA to reduce price support loan levels but at the same time retained target prices at near present levels, dropping only 10 percent during the five years of the bill's life.

Commodity interests were accommodated by introducing special programs for cotton and rice growers, by maintaining close to the existing price levels for the extensive program of federal government purchase of milk solids, and by cutting back on imported sugar, thus aiding U.S. cane and beet sugar growers. Numerous other commodity interests also got specific benefits incorporated into the bill. Sunflower producers, for example, won a program of direct payments. The aggregate effect of these pressures was to maintain a broad spectrum of legislative benefits for agricultural producers, mostly in the form of specific commodity programs.

Yet all these commodity groups might have fallen short of the votes needed to pass the bill had there not been other important allies whose interests were also taken into account. One set of interests placated by the legislation were those of the conservationists. Environmental groups had tried for years to enlarge the protection of fragile soil and wetland areas. Under the 1985 Agriculture Act, farmers will be denied benefits on crops grown on such acreage. In addition, they were given substantial incentives to take land out of production, place it in a conservation reserve, and return it to grass and trees.

The second major source of extra-agricultural support for the 1985 Act came through the inclusion of a reasonably generous food-stamp program. Ever since the adoption of food-stamp assistance in the early 1960s it has functioned politically as an adjunct of farm policy. In the beginning this relationship meant adding strength for a food-stamp welfare program by connecting it to agricultural interests, which held great power in Congress. Today, the two "partners" are more equal in strength, but it is still to the political advantage of each to support the other. Accordingly, food-stamp benefits totaling $13 billion for fiscal 1986 were included in the 1985 legislation, (a small increase over what would have been provided under current law) and eligibility requirements were somewhat relaxed.

The total cost of the five-year legislation was projected to be $169.2 billion. That was hardly a fiscal bargain, but in the end it was a figure that all the principal actors, including President Reagan, were willing to accept. The House passed the final bill 325–96. In the Senate it was somewhat closer, 55–38, with some farm state Democrats and conservative Republicans resisting to the last. It had been a long process of bargaining, adjustment, compromise, and meeting of antagonisms—all the things that Congress, as an institution, does best. It was expensive, and it may in the end have done little to solve the farm problem. No later than 1990 Congress will have to take up the challenge once again.

CHAPTER HIGHLIGHTS ▪

1. The Constitution assigns important powers to Congress. Some of its most important are:
   a. The power of the purse, which Congress exercises through its control over the taxing and spending powers of government and by attempting to monitor the federal budget.
   b. The power to regulate commerce, which has become the justification for extensive involvement of the government in the economic life of the nation.
   c. The power to declare war, which Congress has reasserted in recent times.
   d. The powers to confirm and impeach, which allows Congress to exercise some control over who will occupy senior administrative and judicial positions in the country.

2. Through these powers, the Congress attempts to establish itself as a parallel authority with the presidency and to formulate national answers to national problems. However, the centrifugal forces within Congress are strong.

3. The members of Congress are assisted by staffs and staff agencies, and each member has become a virtual enterprise composed of from 20 or so to more than 100 people.

4. The leadership of Congress has relatively little authority to control the members and must rely largely on persuasion and bargaining to gain majority support. Informal norms and mechanisms are very important in Congress.

5. The committee system is the heart of the legislative process in Congress. Legal reforms have strengthened subcommittees and individual members against committee chairs, so that power is even more decentralized than ever.

6. Members of Congress must be reelected if they are to accomplish any policy goals, and they spend much time and resources serving the needs of constituents.

7. There are difficult dilemmas regarding how members of Congress should represent constituencies and what effect constituency-orientation has on public policy.

SUGGESTED READINGS ■

In recent years there has been a huge increase in the amount and the quality of scholarly attention to Congress. Modern commentaries on the organization and workings of Congress include: Arthur Maass, *Congress and the Common Good* (1984); Lawrence Dodd and Bruce Oppenheimer, eds., *Congress Reconsidered* (3d ed., 1985); Richard Fenno, *Home Style* (1978) and *Congressmen in Committees* (1973); James Sundquist, *The Decline and Resurgence of Congress* (1981); Morris Fiorina, *Congress: Keystone of the Washington Establishment* (1977); David Mayhew, *Congress: The Electoral Connection* (1974); Steven Smith and Christopher Deering, *Committees in Congress* (1984); Michael Malbin, *Unelected Representatives* (1980).

The Oval Office in the White House

Chapter 15

THE PRESIDENT
AND THE
PRESIDENCY

The executive Power shall be vested in a President of the United States of America.

U.S. Constitution, Article 2, Section 1.

The President shall be Commander in Chief of the Army and Navy. . . . He shall have Power, by and with the Advice and Consent of the Senate, to make Treaties . . . and he shall nominate, and by and with the Advice and Consent of the Senate, shall appoint Ambassadors, . . . Ministers . . . Judges. . . .

U.S. Constitution, Article 2, Section 2.

He shall from time to time give to the Congress Information of the State of the Union, and recommend to their Consideration such Measures as he shall judge necessary and expedient. . . .

U.S. Constitution, Article 2, Section 3.

From these rather meager words has grown the awesome authority of what is, in the eyes of many, the most powerful position of political leadership on earth. When the framers of the Constitution drafted Article 2 they had no very useful models or examples to draw upon. They were familiar with kings and royal governors, but there had never been a president before—in America or anywhere else. So the words they chose to establish the office were left very general, depending for their meaning on the practices of those who actually would wield presidential authority and on the expectations Americans would come to have concerning how their president should act.

At the beginning of the Republic, the office was filled by the one man in the country who was everyone's idea of a president: George Washington. Since then, however, there has been much variation in how presidents have played their roles. When Woodrow Wilson was still a college professor, he wrote: "The President can be as big a man as he can be." Some have been vigorous and forceful, and others have been relatively quiet. Some have achieved great success, while others have failed to meet the challenges of their time.

There is an office of president as well as a person. The **presidency** is an institution, a complex set of individuals and organizations which, though possessing great power, is still limited by the Constitution and the laws, the competing pressures of Congress and sometimes the Supreme Court, and public expectations and values. As we try to understand the modern American presidency, we must examine the person *and* the office and how they interact.

When all the noise of a presidential election is over, one person, and only one, is left at the top. How this individual handles pressure, works with advisers, speaks to the public, and how clearly the president thinks about problems have a large impact on life in this and other societies. Richard Nixon had the creativity to ease tensions with China and the Soviet

Union, thereby increasing the chances of world peace. He had the arrogance to think he could fool most of the people most of the time in the Watergate incident, and thus reduced the confidence of Americans in their government and even in themselves. Lyndon Johnson had the energy and forcefulness to enact new civil rights, welfare, and medical-care programs, thereby improving the lives of some of America's poor and oppressed groups. But that same energy and forcefulness led him into the thicket of the Vietnam War, from which neither he nor American society could escape unscarred. President Reagan boldly championed a radical economic program of tax reduction that even his supporters called a "riverboat gamble." If Reagan was right, many citizens would benefit. If he was wrong, many would suffer. The stakes are always high.

The stakes are high, because the powers of the modern president are awesome. Never far from the president's side is a special military aide carrying a thick, black leather briefcase, called the "football" (because it is not to be dropped), in which there are electronic controls, and codes that can start or stop a nuclear strike with the potential of destroying large regions of the earth. The president is commander in chief of armed forces of about 2 million persons, of a nuclear-equipped navy of submarines and attack aircraft carriers, and of land-based as well as airborne nuclear missiles with nearly 10,000 independent warheads.

The modern president is more than a military leader. He is the highest official in a federal government with a current budget of close to a trillion dollars, more than 20 percent of the entire gross national product (GNP) of the nation. To manage the thousands of individual programs that this budget pays for, the president is the "boss" of nearly 3 million civilian employees who work for the federal government.

The American people expect a great deal of their presidents. The president and his advisers should protect our national security, but take care to do so in a way that does not threaten international peace. They are expected to recommend to Congress wise measures to deal with problems that develop at home and abroad, carrying out their election mandate but not so as to divide the country on partisan grounds. They should manage the economy in a manner that provides employment opportunities and healthy economic growth, but do so in a manner that does not infringe on private ownership and individual initiative. They should symbolize and preserve the democratic spirit of our political tradition, but take care that "liberty" does not become "license" to disrupt the social order.

Simply put, in the president's "in box" are all the major issues and problems worrying the nation. In the president's "out box" are political choices and suggestions, personnel appointments, organizational changes, and policy directions which add up either to wise government or fall short. The president clearly exercises a great deal of power in American society and, ultimately, in the world.

This power is not easily described or explained. Indeed, the president is probably the most difficult part of American government to understand. Isn't the president the most watched and written-about person in the United States, if not in the world? Probably so, but this fact adds to our problem, rather than solving it. We know so much about individual presidents that we think of the presidency in very personal terms. It is tempting to tell stories about the individuals who have been president—about Ronald Reagan's mastery of the media; Jimmy Carter's surprising election victory as an outsider; Richard Nixon's corrupt use of office and the Watergate scandal; John Kennedy's sudden, violent death; and so on—all the way back to Lincoln, Jackson, Jefferson, and Washington.

Stories about individual presidents do not necessarily add up to much in the way of political explanations. There is a good reason for this. While presidents interest us because they have considerable power under our form of government, their powers amount to little unless they are transformed into policies by the institutions of government. Thus, in our explanation we must go beyond the individual to the institution, beyond the president to the presidency. We must ask where the institution of the presidency fits into American politics as a whole.

THE PRESIDENTIAL TASKS

Symbolic Leader

When Queen Elizabeth II of England visits a hospital, greets a visiting dignitary, reviews the troops, or goes on a royal tour, no one mistakes her for the prime minister. The latter is the *political* leader of the British

The President performs many symbolic functions, acting in behalf of the entire nation. Throwing out the first ball at opening day of the baseball season links the leader of the nation and the national pastime.

nation, and the queen is its *symbolic* head. In many democratic nations, even those without royal families, an institutional distinction is made between the symbolic head of state and the political leader. The former may be acclaimed by all the citizens while the latter is engaged in hotly disputed tasks of policymaking.

The American president is both the symbolic head of state and the foremost political leader. It is in the symbolic role that the president receives foreign dignitaries, proclaims national thanksgiving (or distress), lights the nation's holiday tree, signs the proclamation of National Pickle Week, and speaks on behalf of the United States to the rest of the world. Yet each of these actions, often noncontroversial in themselves, may have serious political significance, attracting support to the president and his programs or alienating groups of Americans. A televised concert from the White House may seem nonpartisan, but if the viewers like Willie Nelson or Vladimir Horowitz and see them performing at the president's house, some of that approval may carry over to the next election. By the same token, in 1985 a V-E Day anniversary visit to the Bitburg cemetery in Germany, intended to symbolize the healing of German-American relations, caused President Reagan considerable political trouble at home when it was discovered that some Nazi SS troops were buried there. The tension between the president's symbolic role as a unifying force in the country and his political role, inevitably reflecting partisan and other conflicts and disagreements, is continuous and inevitable. It is built into the office.

Foreign Policymaker

Under the Constitution the president has important powers to shape our foreign policy. It is he who recognizes other nations, who directs U.S. policy in the United Nations, who appoints ambassadors and makes treaties, and who, perhaps most importantly, is commander in chief of the armed forces. Beyond these formal powers, however, the president may take many initiatives that set the tone and direction of our foreign policy. In acting as commander in chief and chief diplomat, the president cannot avoid making policy with far-reaching consequences. Nixon's dramatic visit to China in 1972 is a case in point. The visit was planned in strict secrecy, congressional approval was not necessary, and the American public was not informed until the final arrangements had been made; yet the policy significance of this visit was perhaps greater than that of any other single action by President Nixon in his first term. The visit had an immediate effect on China's admission into the United Nations, on U.S. military and technical aid policy toward India, on security pacts with Japan, and on summit talks with the Soviet Union later in the year. The visit had longer-term effects on our trade and tariff policies, our nuclear strategy, and our balance of payments.

Of course, the president does not have unlimited control over foreign policy. Congress can assert its influence by threatening to shut off funds for foreign programs of which it disapproves, and during the 1980s it actively tried in this way to alter Reagan policies in Central America. The need to obtain funding for the development and purchase of major weapon systems allows Congress to influence the nation's strategic policy. The sale of weaponry to other nations also must pass through the legislative process and can be an important source of congressional input into the making of foreign policy. The Senate refused to approve the SALT II arms control agreements in 1980, reminding us that the treaty-making process is very much subject to the checks and balances of the Constitution. Since the Vietnam War, the oversight function of Congress has been applied more aggressively to a variety of matters related to foreign policy, including the covert intelligence operations conducted by the Central Intelligence Agency (CIA). These congressional investigations usually take place after the fact, however. It is still the case that in foreign affairs Congress has rarely been able to substitute its will for that of the president.

The president has one way of getting around the power to consent to treaties granted to the Senate by the Constitution (see Table 15.1). **Executive agreements** between the United States and another nation can be formulated by the State Department and put into effect by the president. Many of those agreements do not need congressional approval, and they can deal with such major issues as the location of military bases and the types of technical and military programs undertaken by the United States. Many of these, however, must be funded, which brings Congress back into the picture.

War Powers

A vital part of foreign policy involves the use of military force, as a weapon or a bargaining tool, and the president has the primary authority to employ American military power. The president's powers as commander in chief are very much greater than they appear at first glance. The president can act militarily whether there is a declared war or not. Indeed, Congress has declared war only five times since 1789: the War of 1812, the Mexican War, the Spanish-American War, World War I, and World War II. But during the same period U.S. forces have been involved in overseas military action more than 150 times. The distinction between military action and war has been basic to the growth of presidential powers in the twentieth century. President Roosevelt drew on this doctrine in 1940, when he gave military protection and supplies to Britain in the months before the attack

TABLE 15.1

TREATIES AND EXECUTIVE AGREEMENTS, 1789–1983

Period	Treaties	Executive Agreements
1789–1839	60	27
1839–1889	215	238
1889–1939	524	917
1939–1973	364	6,395
1973–1979	102	2,233
1979–1982	55	1,063
Total	1,320	10,873

SOURCE: Congressional Research Service.

on Pearl Harbor. The United States was formally neutral at the time but was clearly aligning itself with Britain against Germany. Other cases are the military action in Korea in 1950 and the stationing of seven U.S. divisions in Germany in 1951, actions taken by President Truman without a declaration of war by Congress.

More recently we have had the Bay of Pigs invasion of Cuba (under Kennedy), the military action by U.S. marines in the Dominican Republic and the attacks on North Vietnam (under Johnson), the bombing and invasion of Cambodia and Laos (under Nixon), the attack against Cambodian forces to free the crew of the captured merchant ship *Mayaguez* (under Ford), the use of the military in the unsuccessful effort to free the hostages in Iran (under Carter), and the use of military advisers in El Salvador, the invasion of Grenada and the stationing of troops in Lebanon (under Reagan). The history of the twentieth century makes it clear that the president's power as commander in chief is in fact the power to make war, and that this power has greatly increased the role of the president in international affairs.

Most cases of presidential war-making throughout our history have had widespread popular support and at least implicit congressional approval. The Vietnam experience, however, convinced many people that checks must be placed on this potentially unlimited power. As a result, in 1973 Congress overrode a presidential veto and passed the landmark War Powers Act described in the previous chapter. The War Powers Act in effect gives Congress the right to stop a war effort if it believes that some presidential use of force is misguided, and it stands as a statement that presidents do not have unlimited power to engage in armed conflict.

Why is the president the predominant institution in foreign and military policy? The founding fathers clearly expected this to be the case. Foreign affairs were understood at that time to be part of "executive," not legislative, responsibility—the importance of money in foreign policy was not as evident then as now. The president could act swiftly and with a unity of purpose that Congress could seldom display, and the modern forces of transportation and communication and the advancing technology of weaponry and destruction have made the world smaller and more interdependent. The advantages of the presidential office have grown. What happens in one part of the world affects what happens elsewhere. The business, military, and diplomatic empire of the United States is scattered around the world. A language riot in India, a border incident in Latin America, a monetary crisis in Europe, a new security pact in the Arab world—these and thousands of other happenings affect American programs and people.

World events often have a crisis aspect to them. They require quick attention and action. The president is in a position to act. Only he is in "continuous session," and for this reason, if for no other, many foreign-policy powers are claimed by the president. The president has authority over the network of ambassadors and consulates and technical-aid offices throughout the world, is responsible for the nation's military forces, and has direct access to a huge international intelligence operation that provides the information on which foreign policy is based. The National Security Council, the Department of State, the Department of Defense, the CIA, and the Joint Chiefs of Staff of the various branches of the armed forces provide the president with a set of expert advisers that cannot be matched by even the most informed members of Congress. The insistence by many that national-security matters be kept secret has also enhanced the power of the president in foreign affairs. Decisions concerning military strategy, the development of new weaponry, intelligence operations and even some negotiations with foreign powers cannot be widely publicized without endangering the country. Speed and secrecy are often necessary, and presidents may well become frustrated by what they perceive as obstruction or ill-informed confusion and delay in Congress. In 1985 President Reagan was quoted as saying, "We have got to get to where we can run a foreign policy without a committee of 535 telling us what to do."[1] Presidents have sometimes tried to keep too much from Congress and the public. The guise of national security can be used to hide ventures in foreign policy that would be controversial or politically embarrassing to the president. Moreover, dominance in foreign affairs has been at the root of efforts to extend independent presidential authority to other spheres of policymaking. The "imperial presidency" decried by so many people during the Johnson and Nixon years was in part an extension to domestic policy of the crisis mentality that rationalized presidential power in foreign affairs.

Domestic Policy Leadership

It is often artificial to separate foreign policy from domestic affairs. As American economic life becomes more and more extensively tied into the world economy, the issues of trade negotiations with Japan become also issues of jobs and profits in Detroit: Arab oil competes with Texas oil; an embargo on grain shipments to Russia may generate a crisis in Iowa; and an increased budget for the Navy means prosperity for Norfolk, Virginia. Having said this, however, we can still separate out those bundles of policies that are primarily matters of domestic concern and look at the president's leadership role in shaping those policy domains.

Both constitutional theory and political reality require the president to seek congressional approval for most of his programs. The need for legislation authorizing specific programs and for appropriations to fund them places constraints on most of the president's domestic-policy initiatives. But the president has many tools for influencing Congress. Moreover, during the twentieth century, Congress has come to expect the president to prepare detailed legislative proposals for its consideration. The president's legislative package is put forth in a piecemeal fashion, but the most important elements are set out in his State of the Union address, his budget message, and his economic report.

The State of the Union address The annual **State of the Union address** is given at the beginning of each session of Congress. It is used most often to announce the president's policy goals in a wide range of areas. President Reagan used his initial State of the Union address to outline

---

[1] *St. Louis Post-Dispatch,* May 24, 1985.

Inauguration addresses and annual State of the Union messages give the president excellent opportunities to express a sense of national purpose and present an agenda of proposed action. Here President John F. Kennedy is seen addressing a joint session of Congress.

his economic recovery program. His program included several major proposals that subsequently required congressional action, especially his proposal to reduce personal income taxes and his proposal to reduce federal support of a large number of social-welfare programs. The State of the Union address is not limited to domestic-policy discussions. For instance, Jimmy Carter used his 1980 message to stress his intention to take a strong stance in foreign affairs. The State of the Union address and other special messages are the primary vehicles by which the president communicates his legislative proposals to Congress and the nation.

The budget message Each year in January the president sends his proposed budget to Congress. This imposing document of well over 1000 pages contains the administration's detailed recommendations for how much money each program item of the whole executive branch ought to receive. Its submission marks the first step in the long and difficult budget process described in Chapter 13. Since so much of what the government does or does not do involves money, the proposed budget is a major statement of the president's position on each spending item, and by thus defining the starting point for discussion the president seizes the **fiscal-policy** initiative.

The economic report   Since 1946 the president has presented a separate report each year on the state of the economy. These reports discuss trends and indicators involving economic growth, unemployment, inflation, and the like and provide the administration's forecasts regarding what is likely to happen in the economy and what policies the president hopes will be adopted in order to improve the economic prospects. Throughout our history the president has clearly been regarded by the American public as having the primary responsibility for American economic success or failure, reaping the political rewards of prosperity and suffering defeat in times of recession. Much of what happens in the economy is beyond presidential control, however. Monetary policy (the determination, mainly by setting interest rates, of how much money will circulate) is under the jurisdiction of the Federal Reserve Board, and this body, though appointed by the president for 14-year terms, is not subject to either presidential or congressional direction. The administration may make proposals to Congress regarding desirable spending or tax levels, but it is Congress that makes the laws. Not only may it differ with the president, but it often takes months or even years to act, by which time the economy may have entered quite a different phase. "Fine-tuning" of economic policy is extremely difficult to accomplish in the American system of separated governmental institutions and fragmented political power.

The president's program   The legislative proposals that embody the president's recommendations for action constitute what is known as the president's program. This is more than just a convenient phrase. It identifies those items on which the president has expressed a clear preference, and his relative success or failure as a policy leader can be measured, after a fashion, by examining his "batting average," as is done in Table 15.2. The numbers are sometimes misleading because they may include trivial or uncontroversial proposals, but they do reveal some important things. Presidents do much better when Congress is controlled by the president's party—which is not surprising. Also presidents are more successful in getting congressional approval on foreign-policy initiatives than on domestic issues. Finally, presidents are much more successful in getting their programs enacted when they are politically popular. Again, that is hardly surprising but it has some important implications to which we will return later in this chapter.

The president's program has a kind of official status within the executive branch itself. Whenever administrative agencies wish to recommend some new legislation they cannot simply send a letter to a senator and ask for help. First, they must obtain approval from within the larger administration. Other agencies and departments must be advised and consulted as to their views on the matter and quite often interagency disputes may arise and stop the initiative. The key coordinating mechanism in this process is the

TABLE 15.2
PRESIDENTIAL SUCCESS IN CONGRESS[a]

Eisenhower		Nixon	
1953	89.0%	1969	74.0%
1954	82.8	1970	77.0
1955	75.0	1971	75.0
1956	70.0	1972	66.0
1957	68.0	1973	50.6
1958	76.0	1974	59.6
1959	52.0		
1960	65.0	Ford	
		1974	58.2%
Kennedy		1975	61.0
		1976	53.8
1961	81.0%		
1962	85.4	Carter	
1963	87.1		
		1977	75.4%
Johnson		1978	78.3
		1979	76.8
1964	88.0%	1980	75.1
1965	93.0		
1966	79.0	Reagan	
1967	79.0		
1968	75.0	1981	82.4%
		1982	72.4
		1983	67.1
		1984	65.8

[a] The figures represent the percentage of roll call votes in both houses of Congress on which the president, having taken a clear position, was supported by a majority.
SOURCE: Congressional Quarterly, Inc., *Reagan, the Next Four Years* (Washington, D.C.: Congressional Quarterly, 1985), p. 27.

Office of Management and Budget (OMB), which looks at the possible cost implications of a proposal as well as consults other units of the executive branch, and it also examines how the idea fits in with other priorities and values of the administration. This process, referred to as *legislative clearance*, goes into operation again whenever Congress passes a bill and sends it to the White House for the president's signature. OMB canvasses the interested agencies and pulls together their views into a recommendation to the chief executive, either to sign or **veto.**

The veto power   The president's veto power is an important weapon in the arsenal of policymaking authority, not only because it can effectively block legislation that cannot muster a two-thirds vote in each house of Congress, but because the threat of a veto may force Congress to make concessions in order to get a bill into acceptable form. The veto is a blunt instrument, however. It operates against an entire bill, since the president cannot—as many state governors can—veto particular items or sections of a bill and approve the rest. President Reagan has asked several times that Congress approve an amendment to the Constitution giving the president the item veto. Congressional majorities fear that Reagan would use an item veto to eliminate funding for programs that they and their constituents desire to keep, so the request has gotten nowhere. Most American presidents have not actually employed their veto power very often (see Table 15.3), but it remains an effective tool to use in the on-going bargaining process between the president and Congress.

The administrative leader Every president of the United States achieves much of whatever his years in office accomplish through the people he appoints to key positions. His constitutional authority to name his principal administrative subordinates, most of them subject to the consent of the Senate, affords him a vital opportunity to give direction to federal programs. More than that, this appointive authority gives the president the opportunity to determine a significant share of the nation's political elite. Where he turns for key appointments—business, law firms, Congress, the universities—and the kinds of people he names—women, minorities, WASPs—say much about the representational character of any administration. At the same time, however, the presidential power of appointment is restricted. Congress creates by law nearly all of the administrative structure—departments, agencies, and so on—and specifies which portions are subject to Senate approval and which are to be filled by examination or otherwise under the merit system of civil service. The actual number of appointments a president can make without regard to civil-service restrictions is only a little over 3000, not much in an executive branch of nearly 3 million people. There are restrictions on the president's power to remove some of his appointees, such as those who serve on the regulatory commissions for a fixed term and cannot be fired until their term is up. Despite these limitations, however, it is only the president who may name people to administrative responsibility, and by choosing the key personnel the chief executive imposes a heavy imprint on what the federal government does.

TABLE 15.3
PRESIDENTIAL VETOES

President	Vetoes	Overrides	Percentage Overridden
Kennedy (1961–1963)	21	0	0%
Johnson (1963–1969)	30	0	0
Nixon (1969–1974)	43	7	16.0
Ford (1974–1977)	66	12	18.0
Carter (1977–1981)	31	2	6.5
Reagan (1981–1984)	39	4	10.0

SOURCES: *Presidential Vetoes 1789–1976*, compiled by the Senate Library (Washington, D.C.: U.S. Government Printing Office, 1978), p. ix; supplemented by data in *Congressional Quarterly Weekly Report*, November 17, 1984, pp. 2956–57.

THE INSTITUTIONAL PRESIDENCY

Our schoolbook images of the American president tend to depict the office and the person as one, with that individual sitting in the Oval Office, studying the issues and deciding what to do, agonizing over the possible costs in human suffering, and being daunted by the immense complexity of so many of the choices. This view is not entirely wrong, of course. Presidents do bear awesome responsibilities, and there are a great many matters of grave import on which they alone must decide. Nevertheless, the 39 individuals who have served as president of the United States have been very human beings, with some of the same limits of energy, intelligence, concentration, and competence as the rest of us. Most of all, they have limited time, and so the president needs help. His efforts must be supplemented by others, and it is these "others" who make up the modern institutional presidency.

Each president organizes his presidency somewhat differently, partly to deal with newly emerging needs and problems and partly to reflect the distinctive style of operation with which the incumbent is most comfortable. We can examine the changing structure of the presidency and the ways various presidents have used it by looking at its three main components: the Cabinet, the Executive Office, and the White House staff.

The Cabinet

Traditionally the Cabinet has been composed of the chief executive secretaries of the major departments in the executive branch of the government. In 1789 there were only three departments, each responsible for one of the major tasks of government. The task of national security and preparedness for war was assigned to the Department of War (now the Department of Defense); the task of coining money and providing for a means of economic exchange was assigned to the Department of the Treasury; and the task of dealing with foreign nations and taking care of important documents of the new government was assigned to the Department of State. In addition, there was an attorney general, though there was not yet a Department of Justice.

At present there are 13 departments. The original departments of State, Defense, and Treasury greatly expanded their scope of activity, and the Department of Justice, under the supervision of the attorney general, was added. New departments were formed in response to the evolution of governmental functions and the formation of groups in society whose needs had to be met.

During the nineteenth century the Department of the Interior was formed to manage the western lands, mining rights, and the like, and the Department of Agriculture was formed to deal with the needs of farmers. Shortly after the beginning of this century, the Department of Commerce and the Department of Labor were formed to deal with the relevant problems that had been created as the nation became industrialized. New social problems led to the creation of new departments. The Department of Health, Education, and Welfare (HEW) was formed out of a large number of separate agencies that provided social services to citizens. HEW was

WASHINGTON AND HIS CABINET.

The first Cabinet was created by President George Washington. Here he is shown with Secretary of War Henry Knox, Secretary of the Treasury Alexander Hamilton, Secretary of State Thomas Jefferson, and Attorney General Edmund Randolph.

reorganized as the Department of Health and Human Services when a separate Department of Education was created during the Carter administration. Other departments created since 1960 are the Department of Housing and Urban Development, the Department of Transportation, and the Department of Energy. They clearly reflect the issues and problems of modern America (see Table 15.4).

The heads of departments as well as other high officials are appointed by the president. But Cabinet appointees and many others require congressional approval. When a president fills a post in a particular department, he looks for someone who is more than an expert in that policy area; political factors are also considered. Someone who is acceptable to the groups that have an immediate interest in each department's decision will be sought. The president thus tries to build political support for himself as he chooses his Cabinet and other departmental officials. This often means that Cabinet appointees have political support independent of the president. At the same time, the president seeks appointees whose views are compatible with his interests and who will be loyal members of the presidential team. These different roles make it difficult for the president to use the Cabinet as an effective instrument of leadership.

TABLE 15.4

THE CABINET, 1986

Department	Year Established	Secretary	Goals
State	1789	George Shultz	Advises president in the formulation and execution of foreign policy
Treasury	1789	James Baker	Formulates and recommends economic, financial, tax, and fiscal policies; manufactures coins and currency
Interior	1849	Donald Hodel	Responsible for most of nation's public lands and natural resources
Justice	1870	Edwin Meese	Acts as the government's attorney
Agriculture	1889	Richard Lyng	Works to improve and maintain farm income and to develop markets for agricultural products
Commerce	1913	Malcolm Baldrige	Encourages, serves, and promotes the nation's trade, economic growth, and technical advancement
Labor	1913	William Brock	Fosters, promotes, and develops the welfare of the wage earners and tries to improve working conditions
Defense	1947	Caspar Weinberger	Provides military forces needed to deter war and protect security of nation
Health and Human Services	1953	Otis Bowen	Concerned with health and welfare of citizens
Housing and Urban Development	1965	Samuel Pierce	Concerned with housing needs, fair housing opportunities, and community development
Transportation	1966	Elizabeth Dole	Establishes nation's overall transportation policy, including highways, mass transit, railways, aviation, shipping
Energy	1977	John Harrington	Provides framework for comprehensive and balanced national energy plan
Education	1980	William Bennett	Establishes policy for, administers, and coordinates most federal assistance to schools

SOURCE: Adapted from *U.S. Government Organization Manual, 1986.*

The various Cabinet departments are responsible for gathering information, advising the president, outlining policy alternatives, negotiating with Congress, and executing laws and programs authorized by Congress. There was a time when the various officials who held Cabinet rank actually functioned as a Cabinet—that is, as a group that met with the president and reviewed various policy alternatives. Votes would be taken, with the president's vote equal to that of any other Cabinet member; but gradually the president became more powerful. This is illustrated by a story told of President Lincoln. After being outvoted by his Cabinet, Lincoln announced the vote as "seven nays and one aye—the ayes have it."

By 1985 the members and White House staff participants in Cabinet meetings were too numerous for effective policy formation.

Today, the Cabinet has virtually ceased to exist as a collective body. The diversity of backgrounds and political concerns is too great. The secretary of agriculture has little to contribute on defense policy. The secretary of state knows little about urban housing. Cabinet officials have their own administrative responsibilities and their own constituencies. The symbol of Cabinet rank is important because it signifies that a particular governmental function, such as education or transportation, has been recognized as of sufficient importance to receive departmental status. Even without a department to run, Cabinet rank is a meaningful designation, which is why the U.S. Ambassador to the United Nations carries this status. But modern presidents have found that whatever their intentions may have been when they took office, they cannot utilize the Cabinet as an effective instrument for getting advice or coordinating policies. Several recent presidents have proposed restructuring the Cabinet into three or four units of more or less related policy areas—say, natural resources or economic management—but so far these proposals have not been formally approved. Informally, however, each president has found ways to restructure things.

The Executive Office of the President

Until the late 1930s the office of the president was a haphazard array of people, with various titles and organizational locations, who worked

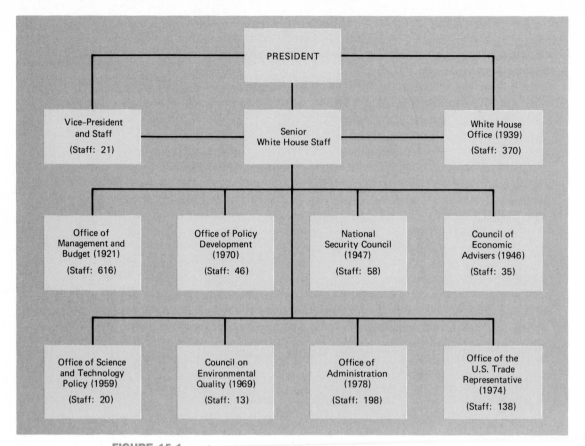

FIGURE 15.1

The Executive Office of the President

for the president but scarcely constituted an orderly administrative unit. President Franklin Roosevelt made effective use of this confusion of roles and functions, but even he finally came to support the creation of a more orderly presidential structure. In 1939 the Executive Office of the President was created. (See Figure 15.1.) The Bureau of the Budget—after 1970 the Office of Management and Budget (OMB)—became the largest and most important unit of the Executive Office, and as we have seen in our earlier discussion of the budget process and of legislative clearance, it is still central to all aspects of presidential policy leadership. The OMB attempts to supervise management efficiency within the executive branch, but its main role is to coordinate budget requests, review legislative proposals, and provide much of the staff analysis regarding the impact of various policy alternatives on the country's economy. In recent years, moreover, the director of the OMB has become a major political figure, carrying heavy responsibility for explaining and defending administration proposals before Congress and the nation. For example, David Stockman, President Reagan's OMB Director from 1981 to 1985, was a far more prominent participant in the Reagan administration than many Cabinet officials.

Henry Kissinger, as National Security Adviser to President Nixon, was generally regarded as far more influential than Secretary of State William Rogers. In 1973 Kissinger himself became secretary of state.

The National Security Council (NSC) is a second important component of the Executive Office. Created after World War II to help coordinate military and diplomatic policy, the NSC includes in its official membership the president, the vice-president, the secretary of state, and the secretary of defense. The Central Intelligence Agency (CIA) and the Joint Chiefs of Staff report to NSC and the president may invite others to its meetings. Some chief executives, notably Eisenhower and Nixon, enlarged the participation of the NSC, while others, especially John Kennedy, preferred to work with a small group. Every modern president, however, has found it essential to employ the NSC as a major planning and coordinating mechanism in the incredibly sensitive and difficult areas of foreign and military policy.

As the salience and tension surrounding NSC policy concerns have grown, so has the importance of the official who is the president's liaison with the NSC: the special assistant for national security affairs. Beginning with Kennedy's appointment of McGeorge Bundy to this position, the role has come to possess increasing weight in the making of decisions. Certainly the best known of this group of special assistants was Henry Kissinger,

THE VICE-PRESIDENCY

The original intent of the Framers of the Constitution was to have as vice-president the person receiving the second highest number of electoral votes, presumably the second most appealing political leader in the land; however, the development of political parties soon resulted in an unanticipated result. In 1800 Thomas Jefferson and Aaron Burr stood together as the Democratic-Republican candidates against Federalists John Adams and C. C. Pinckney. Jefferson and Burr each got 73 electoral votes as all the Democratic-Republican electors voted for both men. The tie was broken in the House, but only after some complex maneuvering, and soon thereafter the Constitution was amended so as to separate the elections for the two offices.

The Twelfth Admendment relegated the vice-presidency to the status John Adams gave it, "the most insignificant office that ever the invention of man contrived or his imagination conceived." From 1800 until quite recently the only importance the office seemed to have was as a place to wait in case something happened to the president. Something did happen from time to time, of course. When Harry Truman became president after Franklin D. Roose-

George Bush has been an active vice-president, assisting President Reagan and often representing him in meetings with foreign dignitaries. Here he meets with Soviet premier Gorbachev.

velt's death in April 1945, he was the seventh vice-president to move to the highest office. For a position that FDR's first vice-president, John Nance Garner, said was "not worth a pitcher of warm spit," the frequency of succession was rather high. Moreover, Truman was the third, following Theodore Roosevelt and Calvin Coolidge, who after moving up ran for reelection as president and won.

The vice-presidency in the twentieth century may still often have seemed like a political dead end, occupied by amiable figures nominated in order to give geographical or ideological balance to the ticket. Its political potential had nevertheless increased quite substantially, and today, though the office has few actual powers, it has real importance. Consider the recent vice-presidents who have become their party's nominees for president; Richard Nixon in 1960, Hubert Humphrey in 1968, and Walter Mondale in 1984. Add to those Lyndon Johnson, who became president after John Kennedy's death, and Gerald Ford, who took the highest office following Nixon's resignation. And George Bush, Reagan's vice-president is a leading contender for the 1988 Republican nomination. Since 1952 the only vice-presidents not to be nominated subsequently for president have been Spiro Agnew, who resigned from office in 1973 under a cloud of legal charges, and Nelson Rockefeller who, at the time of his appointment by President Ford in 1974, specifically disavowed any candidacy for the 1976 Republican nomination.

The only formal task of the vice-president is to preside over the Senate, where he may vote in case of a tie. Informally, however, recent vice-presidents have performed a number of roles, serving as representatives of the United States both at ceremonial occasions and sometimes in more substantive encounters with foreign statesmen. The vice-president may sometimes take on some of the more strident political tasks, as when Spiro Agnew made sharply partisan speeches for President Nixon. Other vice-presidents have taken an active role in shaping the policy of their Administration. Rockefeller and Mondale were prominent participants in domestic policy development, for example.

The vice-presidency is not exactly an apprenticeship for the presidency itself, but in the latter twentieth century it has developed into a much more consequential office than it had been. An incumbent vice-president is dependent for nomination on the president, and must be visibly loyal to administration policies. He (or perhaps, in future, she) can do only what the president allows; but no longer is this person unknown to the country. Vice-presidents get substantial media coverage. They can accurately be regarded as the heirs apparent to their party's presidential nomination, and the office is, therefore, the object of serious competition among leading figures in the party. In short, the vice-presidency may at last be turning into the kind of position the Framers originally intended, attracting the nation's second choice for political leadership of the country.

who in Nixon's second term became also secretary of state. Even when the NSC assistant is less prominent than Kissinger, however, this figure has often been a rival of the secretary of state in shaping foreign policy and, because the role is so important, a person around whom there swirls much controversy.

A third major organizational unit within the Executive office is the Council of Economic Advisors (CEA). This agency was created under the terms of the Full Employment Act of 1946 to bring into the presidential institution systematic professional analysis of economic trends and recommendations concerning how best to promote prosperity. The three appointed members of the CEA are professional economists, and they are expected, on the one hand, to give the president their best professional opinion and, on the other, to support loyally whatever decisions about economic policy the president finally makes. Sometimes this can lead to a conflict of roles and produce considerable tension, even leading to resignation if professional judgment is no longer compatible with political loyalty. As economic policies have become more prominently debated in recent years, CEA members have also found themselves very much in the public eye.

There are several other components within the Executive Office of the president, and different presidents have designed these arrangements differently. Since the 1950s, for example, there has been an Office of Science and Technology. Conditions of the 1970s led to the creation of the Council on Environmental Quality and the Office of Special Trade Representative. Each unit in the Executive Office has a reasonably well-defined jurisdiction, an area of policy in which it provides the president with staff help and advice and perhaps undertakes initiatives in the president's name to urge Congress or other parts of the executive branch to move in a particular direction.

The White House Staff

Every president has had personal advisors, people to whom he could turn for guidance with the confidence that they would not only be substantively helpful but personally loyal. Sometimes these confidantes would be Cabinet officers; sometimes they would be outside government entirely, as in the so-called Kitchen Cabinet of Andrew Jackson. What is distinctive about the modern presidency is that the coterie of intimate personal advisors has grown larger and has moved increasingly to officially appointed positions that are literally inside the White House itself. Abraham Lincoln preserved the Union with a staff of two. Since the 1950s the White House office has never had a staff of fewer than 300.

Recent presidents have organized their White House offices in several different ways, depending on how they preferred to do their work and on the personal chemistry of these close interpersonal relationships. Every president has a press secretary to deal with the media on a continuing basis, and each one has had someone in charge of legislative liaison—that is, lobbying the Congress. We have already mentioned the special assistant for national security affairs. Beyond those specifications, however, jurisdictions became blurred and responsibilities loosely defined. In President Reagan's first term a "Troika," consisting of a chief of staff, James Baker, a deputy chief of staff, Michael Deaver, and a counselor to the president, Edwin Meese, served as primary advisors. As his second term began, Baker and Meese moved to Cabinet positions and Deaver returned to private life, while Donald Regan, previously secretary of the treasury, became a "single-headed" chief of staff. It is by no means clear what the precise differences between the two systems were, but there was little doubt among observers that there was a very important difference.

Because they see the president so often and in such intimate terms the main figures of the White House staff themselves become important objects of political interest. Access to the president may require getting the nod from one of these people. It is generally assumed that the president's decisions will be greatly influenced by the views of his staff. Indeed, it was said of Eisenhower and sometimes of Reagan that they were often really the prisoners of their advisors, unable to develop their own points of view. This may well exaggerate the influence of the staff advisors, but it leads so-called White House watchers, as well as media pundits and active politicians, to spend much time and effort trying to assess the ins and outs of this American version of "Court" politics. Who has the president's ear? Throughout Reagan's first term it was said that his policies were less conservative than they would otherwise have been because the Troika consisted of political moderates who steered the president along a course of pragmatic politics. Archival sources have demonstrated that this kind of speculation about the Eisenhower administration was largely wrong, but interpreting presidential staff politics continues to be a popular sport among political commentators.

There is no doubt that the White House staff has become an important participant in any modern presidency, and that it is within the context of the White House as a political institution that most presidential policy decisions are finally determined. Earlier we noted some of the reasons that the Cabinet does not function as an effective decision-making body. For many of those same reasons the White House staff *is* effective. It is a flexible instrument, with as many perspectives present as are needed. It operates without its members being distracted by large administrative responsibilities, as Cabinet members are. Above all, the White House staff is recruited with one overriding consideration in mind, complete loyalty and subordination of self to "the Chief." For this reason White House staff members are often relatively young and drawn from among the president's long-time associates: Kennedy's so-called Irish Mafia from Massachusetts, Johnson's staff of Texans, Nixon's from southern California, Carter's from Georgia, and Reagan's from his days as governor of California. Ironically, the press seldom pays much attention to these close associates before a presidential election, but once in office they receive the closest scrutiny. Well they should, for the modern institutions of president is very much one in which the individual who takes the oath of office operates in a context of advisors and assistants who become in a real sense a part of the office itself.

PRESIDENTIAL CONSTITUENCIES

No president enters the White House with a blank slate. In order to get elected, a candidate has made promises and commitments. Party primaries have been entered and won. Convention delegates have been wooed with success. Electoral votes have been asked for and given. There is a campaign record, a successful one, and the president will not disregard it. Moreover, there is a still longer record of positions taken and values espoused in earlier phases of the president's life. These, too, become part of the president's foundation, not being blindly adhered to perhaps but helping to point the directions that policy initiatives will take. More immediately, a president surely will have gathered more support from some groups and some sections of the country than others. Appointments to major offices and legislative recommendations are likely in a rough sense to reflect those patterns of electoral support; otherwise, electoral participation would seem truly without foundation in rational self-interest.

A president starts out with an electoral base, a coalition of group support and an array of policy and personal commitments that give initial impetus, shape, and direction to the actions his administration will take. It is very likely that this foundation will be different, perhaps quite substantially so, from the political base on which the leading elements of Congress depend for support. In that case, of course, there will be conflict—often rather intense—between the president and Congress, as there was, for example, during most of the 1969–1974 period of Richard Nixon's presidency. At other times, however, a newly elected president may find that large majorities in sympathy with his views have been swept into Congress, and in the ensuing year or two be able to accomplish a great deal. Both Franklin Roosevelt in 1933 and Lyndon Johnson in 1965 enjoyed this happy experience.

The initial electoral foundation of presidential action is not permanent. Ineffectual leadership can swiftly dissipate a president's support. New conditions and crises may overtake the administration and change the terms of political conflict. The Iranian capture of American hostages in 1979, for example, and the administration's inability for so long to bring them back badly damaged President Carter's political standing. Nixon, having won a landslide election victory in 1972, was forced to leave office in disgrace less than two years later. The opposite occurred with Franklin Roosevelt. Elected by a large margin in 1932 to "do something" about the Great Depression, he undertook numerous and diverse programs of varying degrees of effectiveness, but in the process he managed to attract deep political loyalty to himself and to the Democratic party from large segments of the American electorate. After the New Deal was underway, Roosevelt's base of support was enlarged and secured well beyond the fragile foundation of the 1932 victory. In like manner, President Reagan's effort in 1985 and 1986 to revise drastically the tax code can be understood in part as an effort to deepen the Reagan voter support of 1980 and 1984 so that other Republican candidates can win in the years to come.

Within the president's broad electoral constituency another kind of constituency struggle goes on within the ranks of his advisors and others active in and around the party, the Congress, and the administration. We have already made reference to court politics, struggles over preferment within the president's staff. This is part of it. Will Reagan become too liberal? Or, to take an example from a generation ago, will President Johnson side with the Democratic hawks or the Democratic doves on Vietnam? American political parties are loose coalitions of factions and points of view, and within each there is more or less continuous jockeying for advantage. Since the presidency is the single most powerful position in our politics, it is for "the president's soul" that much of this competition is conducted, not just during election campaigns but all the time.

The president hears from another type of "constituency," sometimes with tones of such urgency, even agony, as to be impossible to resist. In the contemporary world demands for policy support come to the president from the governments and peoples of other nations, and often from dissidents as well. These will usually be accompanied by recommendations for action from agencies or officials within the administration itself. The president must heed both sources lest international disaster befall, and given his foreign-policy information advantage over Congress, it is primarily the president who is sensitive to these kinds of needs. No responsible president will ignore the pleas of allies or neglect the forecasts of his own diplomatic experts. These, too, become part of his constituency, to which the chief executive seeks to be responsive even while, oftentimes, he tries to give it a somewhat different shape.

One final point: Presidents, as we have said, are human. They have sought and won the nation's highest prize—the office of president. They are obviously ambitious, or they would never have sought the "splendid misery" of being president. Also, whatever may be their differences on matters of public policy, they share one goal: to earn the good opinion of posterity. They wish to be well regarded by history, to be thought to have done a good job. Since World War II each American president who survived has written memoirs explaining and justifying what he did in office. Libraries have been established to hold the papers and memorabilia of each administration. Nixon was so anxious to have his administration's efforts preserved for posterity that he taped White House conversations, and the tapes later became crucial evidence of administration wrongdoing. Yet even that episode illustrates that a pervasive aspiration among presidents to receive a favorable verdict from future history books may constrain them to pursue the higher values of democratic life.

THE PRESIDENTIAL AGENDA

In Chapter 13 we saw that in what political scientist John Kingdon has called the "primeval soup" of policy there are a great many ideas "floating around," defining problems and proposing solutions. Many of these never get on to any official agenda to be given serious consideration by responsible officials. The president, with all the constraints that limit his ability to act, is still by far the most influential individual in government. Therefore, it is of particular importance to ask what issues get on the president's

TABLE 15.5

PRESIDENTIAL PERFORMANCE ON CAMPAIGN PROMISES

Performance on Promises	President and Years in Office				
	Kennedy 1961–1963	Johnson 1965–1968	Nixon 1969–1972	Carter 1977–1980	Reagan 1981–1984[a]
Proposal in full or partial fulfillment of promise	68%	63%	59%	66%	53%
Little or no action taken	23	24	36	22	30
Promises turned into legislation	53	62	34	41	44

[a] Data through February, 1984.

SOURCE: Jeff Fishel, *Presidents and Promises: From Campaign Pledge to Presidential Performance* (Washington, D.C.: Congressional Quarterly Press, 1985). Recalculated from Table 2.3, p. 39, and Table 2.4, p. 42. Reprinted by permission of Congressional Quarterly, Inc.

agenda. What policy ideas does he choose to emphasize, to make his own? In 1981 Ronald Reagan gave top priority to reducing taxes. In 1985 he made tax reform the centerpiece of his program. In addition, however, there were dozens of other legislative items that the president asked Congress to enact and dozens of other matters of governmental policy that occupied his time and attention. Here we will not repeat an earlier discussion of agenda setting, but we will focus attention specifically on how the president comes to decide where to place his priorities.

First, there is the election and all that goes with it. When a president is inaugurated, much policy commitment follows. The president's party adopted a platform for the campaign, and many of its planks have been part of the party's creed for years. Cynics often dismiss the party platforms as mere campaign verbiage, but recent research has shown that a fairly large percentage of platform promises do, in fact, lead subsequently to political action.[2] (See Table 15.5.) It is also quite clear that a new administration, whatever the source of its ideas, changes the agenda of issues to be dealt with by Congress, so that in one way or another the electoral process—a very partisan process—gives shape and substance to the presidential agenda. If we wish to know what items a president will stress once in office, we should therefore listen to what is said during the campaign.

A second major source of policy ideas is the group of people who make up the institutional presidency discussed earlier in this chapter. Henry Kissinger greatly influenced the thinking of both Richard Nixon and Gerald Ford. Jeane Kirkpatrick, ambassador to the United Nations from 1981 to 1985, had considerable impact on Reagan's conception of what to do in Latin America. Stuart Eisenstadt, head of Jimmy Carter's Democratic Policy

---

[2] Gerald M. Pomper, *Elections in America* (New York: Dodd Mead, 1971).

Council, was influential in several policy areas. It should be stressed that these are presidential appointees, not bureaucrats. Bureaucrats, Kingdon reports, have a relatively minor impact on the presidential agenda. The president's close advisors were named, presumably, with some degree of confidence that their ideas were compatible with his. And the myth that crops up from time to time, in which a weak or inept president is said to be dominated by crafty and conniving advisors, is just that: a myth without much substance. What is important is that many policy ideas and proposals come from the institutional presidency and not simply from the single individual who holds the highest office.

That single individual also makes an important contribution, however, to the agenda of policy items he emphasizes. Jimmy Carter came to the White House with experience as governor of Georgia, where he had had great success in reorganizing the administrative structure to achieve greater efficiency and responsiveness from the bureaucracy. It was not surprising that he tried to achieve the same thing in Washington and finally secured passage of a Civil Service Reform Act in 1978. Ronald Reagan, after having served two terms as governor of California and having trimmed the welfare rolls there, sought to reproduce his success on the national level. President Johnson drew heavily on his early encounters with poverty in the Texas hills when he developed his "War on Poverty" as a major part of his Great Society program. Presidents emphasize not only those issues and proposals that they are persuaded to support but also those that they themselves believe in most deeply. Shortly we shall return to this very personal dimension of the presidency.

Much of what constitutes a president's agenda is not really a matter of choice. Conditions such as unemployment, inflation, budget deficits, crime, and many other problems are real and cannot be defined away by campaign speeches or ignored without grave risk of reprisal at the next election. And so policy proposals must be made. The vast bulk of what the federal government is doing will continue to be done because it is either popular or necessary, or both. Therefore, in most years the proposed budget will display only marginal changes from what went before. The urgency of political rhetoric often obscures the great continuity that characterizes most areas of public policy most of the time.

There are, however, crises. Events occur that require a presidential response: North Korea invades South Korea; OPEC sharply increases world oil prices; the Iranians seize American hostages—all these examples involve foreign policy primarily, as do most of the crises presidents confront. The domestic scene occasionally generates crises—floods and hurricanes, riots and assassinations—but in the international world of the late twentieth century such crises almost seem normal. The issues are often momentous, fraught with danger, and the crucial decisions cannot be made by anyone except the president. With the power of thermonuclear destruction literally at hand, the metaphor for presidential crises has become the button that can set off the missiles. Only the president can push it, and because the stakes of crisis decisions are often so immense, the president must devote enormous amounts of time and energy to the processes of learning, discussing, and pondering all the elements involved. The experience of recent

American presidents has been that the longer they serve in office the more of their time is taken up with the broad area of national-security policy; thus, whether intended or not, the issues of war and peace come to dominate the president's agenda.

THE TACTICS OF LEADERSHIP

In an influential study of presidential leadership, political scientist Richard Neustadt argued that the president's "task with congressmen and everybody else, *is to induce them to believe that what he wants of them is what their own appraisal of their own responsibilities requires them to do in their own interest, not his.*[3] Every president must spend much time persuading others, but they vary greatly in how adept they are in using the tools available to them. The president will attempt to establish communication with Congress on an informal as well as formal basis. He will court the leadership of the House and the Senate. The president will invite members of Congress to the White House or, for more special treatment, to Camp David, the weekend presidential retreat. In addition to the personal relations between the president and members of Congress, the administration has a full-time staff dedicated to congressional relationships.

When a specific presidential request is before Congress and is on his list of must legislation, the president may often use more pointed tactic. Bargains can be struck with individual members of Congress whose vote is particularly important. The president can help a legislator's political career. For example, a president can offer to come to the home state or district and campaign for the member of Congress in the next election. The president can use the appointment power to reward a member of Congress by appointing a federal judge or an ambassador or a top federal official who is recommended by the member. This will often strengthen the legislator's political base. Military contracts, federal grants, and backing for legislation beneficial to the member's home district can be offered by the president in exchange for a vote. The threat of withdrawing support for a legislator's pet project can also be made.

Sometimes just a phone call or an invitation to meet with the president is enough to persuade an uncertain Congress member. Here is how an influential member of the House Rules Committee commented on a telephone call from President Johnson:

> What do you say to the President of the United States? I told him I'd sleep on it. Then the next day I said to myself, "I've always been a party man, and if he really wanted me of course I'd go along even if the bill wasn't set up exactly the way I wanted it." Probably I took half a dozen guys with me. We won in the crunch by six votes. Now, I wouldn't have voted for it except for this telephone call.[4]

---

[3] *Presidential Power* (New York: Wiley, 1960), p. 35 (italics in the original).

[4] *Newsweek*, August 2, 1965, p. 22, Copyright 1965 by Newsweek, Inc. All rights reserved. Reprinted by permission.

The president can also influence Congress by getting other people, such as big campaign contributors, to make calls for him. On major issues the president can go directly to the voters and urge them to pressure their own senator or representative to support the president's program. In 1919, for example, Woodrow Wilson went on a national speaking tour to try to build support for the Versailles treaty. Franklin Roosevelt was very effective using national radio during the 1930s. More recently, television has been the favored forum. President Reagan, perhaps because he is a former actor, has been especially adept at using television to pressure Congress.

During 1981 Reagan went on national television to urge public support for his very controversial tax cut proposal then being discussed in Congress. He appealed directly to the voter:

> Now the day after tomorrow—Wednesday—the House of Representatives will begin debate on two tax bills and once again they need to hear from you. I know that doesn't give you much time, but a great deal is at stake. . . . Let me add those representatives honestly and sincerely want to know your feelings. They get plenty of input from the special-interest groups, they'd like to hear from their homefolks.

Media appeals alone are not usually sufficient to sway congressional votes. The tactic depends on the response of people in the individual member of Congress's home district. Reagan's call for support, for instance, was backed by a massive political organization left over from his campaign, which mobilized letter-writing campaigns and phone calls to key legislators. Following the speech, members of Congress were flooded with calls and mail favoring the president's position and that position won.

Presidential leadership in a system of separated institutions and fragmented power calls for continuous bargaining and the active use of the power resources available. Simply announcing one's priorities will not suffice. Presenting too large an agenda for action may be equally poor strategy. President Carter was often criticized for urging too many items upon Congress without giving enough cues as to which were most important. Reagan, in contrast, put maximum effort behind tax reduction in 1981 and much less behind the so-called social agenda items such as abortion or school prayer.

THE DILEMMAS OF DEMOCRATIC LEADERSHIP

In a democratic political system the question of how much and what kind of leadership presidents ought to exercise is not easily answered. For one thing there are conflicting theories about the nature of the office. In the past some of our chief executives have taken the view that the president should generally wait for others to take the policy initiatives, responding to them as a *chief magistrate* but not trying to dominate the policy process. Closely related to this view is the so-called *Whig theory* of the presidency, which asserts that Congress is the preeminent policymaking branch and

TABLE 15.6

JAMES DAVID BARBER'S CLASSIFICATION OF PRESIDENTS

Emotional Attitude Toward the Presidency and Being President	Energy Level on the Political Job	
	Active	Passive
Positive	Franklin Roosevelt Harry Truman John Kennedy Gerald Ford Jimmy Carter	William Howard Taft Warren Harding Ronald Reagan
Negative	Richard Nixon Lyndon Johnson Herbert Hoover Woodrow Wilson	Dwight Eisenhower Calvin Coolidge

SOURCE: James David Barber, *Presidential Character,* 3d ed. (Englewood Cliffs, N.J.: Prentice-Hall, 1985).

that the president should concentrate on carrying out congressional decisions. Theodore Roosevelt articulated the view, eventually to become the effective working theory of every president, that this office required its occupant to act as the *steward* of the nation. A conscientious steward, Roosevelt believed, should take active responsibility for identifying public problems and seeking solutions and in doing so make vigorous use of the full array of the powers granted the president.

Presidential theories, setting forth the principles that ought to guide behavior, inevitably get tangled up with the personalities of those who live at 1600 Pennsylvania Avenue. William Howard Taft, exponent of the chief magistrate theory, was a very large man and a relatively passive political personality. Teddy Roosevelt was anything but passive, and his idea that the presidency should serve as a "bully pulpit" from which the president could harangue and instruct the people fit very well his ebullient personality. Political scientist James David Barber has developed a broad typology of presidential personalities which is intriguing though widely criticized.[5] He argues that presidents may be compared along two dimensions. One involves the vigor and intensity with which they approach their tasks, the active-passive dimension; the other essentially reflects the pleasure they seem to take from their job, a positive-negative dimension (see Table 15.6). In this typology FDR and JFK were active-positive presidents. Nixon and Carter were active-negatives. From time to time historians play a presidential rating game, ranking presidents as great and not so great and attempting to explain what combination of personal and circumstantial

---

[5] James David Barber, *The Presidential Character,* 3d ed. (Englewood Cliffs, NJ: Prentice-Hall, 1985).

factors account for the rankings. Generally, the "great" presidents turn out to be among Barber's active-positive type, but that kind of analysis can easily lead us to serious misreading of what our presidents really did.

Dwight D. Eisenhower, for example, though a popular World War II general and an even more popular president, was not generally thought of as a great president by those who worry about such things. Eisenhower showed little interest in using his vast patronage powers. He did not like speechmaking and generally avoided the press. He avoided summit politics in international relations. On the latter topic, for instance, Eisenhower said: "This idea of the president of the United States going personally abroad to negotiate—it's just damn stupid." His seemingly passive character led historians and political scientists to the conclusion that he was not a very effective president. Recent study of his papers, however, has shown that this conclusion was too hasty.[6] Eisenhower was often a decisive president but preferred to keep his leadership hidden from public view. We are reminded that Eisenhower ended a war (the Korean War), kept the United States at peace for eight years, and presided over an expanding economy with very low levels of inflation and unemployment. This revision in the judgment of Eisenhower's presidency suggests just how difficult it is to explain presidential leadership.

The verdict of history is itself elusive, but there do appear to be some elements that help a president's future reputation. One is decisiveness. Consider these examples. In 1957, a federal court order directed the Little Rock, Arkansas, school system to desegregate its public schools. The white citizens of Little Rock, the school officials, and even the governor of Arkansas refused to obey. When a federal court order is disobeyed, what is the president to do? In this case the president acted as commander in chief. Eisenhower sent federal troops to Little Rock. In a radio and television address to the nation, he explained his action:

> For a few minutes this evening I want to speak to you about the serious situation that has arisen in Little Rock. . . . In that city, under the leadership of demagogic extremists, disorderly mobs have deliberately prevented the carrying out of proper orders from a federal court. . . . I have today issued an executive order directing the use of troops under Federal authority to aid in the execution of Federal law at Little Rock, Arkansas. . . . Unless the President did so, anarchy would result.

The same decisiveness was displayed five years later by President Kennedy in response to a threat from outside the nation's boundaries. In October 1962, as Kennedy was having breakfast, his chief of staff for national security affairs arrived with bad news. The CIA had evidence that the Soviet Union was arming Cuba with intermediate-range ballistic missiles that could destroy nearly any city in the United States. A week of intensive and very secret meetings between the president and his advisers resulted in the

---

[6] See Fred I. Greenstein, *The Hidden-Hand Presidency: Eisenhower as Leader* (New York: Basic Books, 1982).

Cuban blockade, a military act that prevented Soviet ships from landing and installing the missiles. The president went on national television to announce his decision:

> Now, therefore, I, John F. Kennedy, President of the United States of America, acting under and by virtue of the authority conferred upon me by the Constitution and statutes of the United States. . . . do hereby proclaim that the forces under my command are ordered . . . to interdict, subject to the instructions herein contained, the delivery of offensive weapons and associated material to Cuba.

At the time these decisions were made, there were many who criticized them as risking even worse trouble. In retrospect, however, they seem not only decisive actions but successful in accomplishing their purposes. A further example is provided by President Truman's 1950 intervention in Korea, a decision that contributed to a steep decline in his popularity in the months that followed, but which now is looked back on with widespread admiration and approval. Indeed, Truman's reputation generally has been greatly enhanced in recent years, particularly among Republicans who were then his severest critics, and the basis for this comeback is his decisiveness, his willingness to act forthrightly and accept the consequences.

Decisiveness is no help to presidential reputation, however, unless it is linked with what Neustadt has called "a purpose that moves with the grain of history, a direction consonant with coming needs."[7] Neustadt's phrase nicely captures the early years of FDR's presidency, for with a half century of hindsight it is clear that his New Deal programs did in fact move with the grain of history. But what of Lyndon Johnson's Great Society initiatives of the mid-1960s? Or Jimmy Carter's energy program of 1977? Their status is less clearly assured. History's verdict is not yet in regarding the Reagan effort to lower federal tax rates and simplify their structure. Ultimately, we regard as "great" those presidents—and other political leaders, too—who were right; who did what, looking back, we now believe they should have done and did so with courage and determination. Decisiveness joined with purposes that come to be rejected by the public does not gain applause. Presidents Johnson and Nixon both learned the hard way that presidents must have popular approval not only to gain office but also to keep it.

PRESIDENTIAL POPULARITY AND DEMOCRATIC LEADERSHIP

Presidential popularity is not the same thing as leadership, of course, but no president can lead for long if he is unpopular. Leadership, as we have seen, requires persuasion. If the president hopes to lead members of Congress, he must persuade them to do what he wants them to and to believe

---

[7] Op. cit., p. 135.

President Franklin D. Roosevelt was a master at mobilizing public support with his radio "fireside chats."

that their own interests, not just his, are advanced thereby. He may have to convince them that unless they are cooperative the members of Congress themselves will suffer at the next election. As we have seen, this means that presidents actively cultivate grass-roots support, especially through the use of radio and television. How does anyone know what policies are popular and which way the prudent politicians should move? Modern polling techniques often make this process more than just an artful game of guess and bluff. Presidential approval ratings are studied with great care and as indicators of political tides have an importance akin to the stock market or television ratings.

Table 15.7 shows the fluctuations in popularity for several recent presidents. What factors affect the public's rating of presidential performance? We first note that the popularity of most presidents declines over time. Upon entering office, the president is riding on the crest of the high expectations generated by the election victory. At this point, people generally reserve criticism until the president has had a chance to prove himself. For many presidents this "honeymoon" period is relatively brief. Jimmy Carter's drop in popularity began only a few months after he took office, and he never regained the high levels of popular approval that followed the 1976 election. Ronald Reagan experienced sharp drops in popularity in his second year in office.

The factor that has historically had the most dramatic effect on presi-

TABLE 15.7

AVERAGE APPROVAL RATINGS OF RECENT PRESIDENTS

Administration	Year 1	Year 2	Year 3	Year 4
Truman (1949–1952)	58.5	41.0	28.3	29.6
Eisenhower (1953–1956)	69.3	65.4	71.3	73.3
Eisenhower (1957–1960)	65.0	54.6	63.3	61.1
Kennedy (1961–1963)	76.0	71.6	63.5	—
Johnson (1964–1968)	66.4	51.2	44.0	41.5
Nixon (1969–1972)	61.4	56.9	49.9	56.4
Nixon (1973–1974)	41.8	25.9	—	—
Ford (1974–1976)	—	53.9	43.1	48.1
Carter (1977–1980)	62.4	45.5	38.1	39.5
Reagan (1981–1984)	57.0	43.7	44.6	54.3

SOURCE: *Gallup Report,* No. 182, October–November 1980; *Gallup Report,* No. 219, December 1983; *Gallup Report,* No. 225, June 1984. Reprinted by permission of Gallup Organization, Inc.

dential popularity has been international crisis. Whenever the public perceives a threat to the nation's security, there is a tendency to rally around the president. After the outbreak of the Korean War, President Truman's approval rating jumped 9 points within a month. The Cuban missile crisis of 1962 brought about a 15-point rise in President Kennedy's public-opinion rating. The peaks in Jimmy Carter's popularity all followed some important event in foreign affairs.

The benefit to the president does not come about only as a result of successful foreign-policy ventures. Carter's role in the Camp David peace treaty brought him popular approval, but the greatest leap in his popularity came after Iranians seized American hostages, an event over which he had little control. Likewise, John F. Kennedy's popularity rose after the disastrous invasion of Cuba at the Bay of Pigs. Nonetheless, while presidents are often adept at using such crises to accentuate their leadership abilities, not all international events enhance presidential popularity. The Vietnam War was a major factor in the downward slide of Lyndon Johnson's rating in the polls, and early in Ronald Reagan's term, the fear that the United States might intervene in El Salvador led to a drop in his public approval.

The state of the economy has an important effect on presidential popularity, although its exact impact is difficult to measure. When inflation or unemployment is high, people tend to blame the president. Anytime there is a severe recession the incumbent president, and usually his party also, can expect to suffer at the polls. The lackluster performance of Carter's economic policies no doubt contributed to the overall decline in his popular opinion rating.

Personal factors also enter into the public evaluation of the president. The antics of Jimmy Carter's brother, Billy, cost him points in the opinion polls. Ronald Reagan's coolness in the face of an assassination attempt created a great deal of public sympathy for him that carried over into approval for his policy initiatives.

Presidents try to anticipate public reactions to policy ideas, testing with "trial balloon" speeches public reaction to a new direction in foreign policy, for example. This does not mean that a president selects policies simply because a majority of the public favors them. But it may mean that the president avoids, if possible, policy issues on which the public is deeply and sharply divided. President Reagan, in trying to build consensus for his economic policies, avoided some so-called social issues, such as abortion, school prayers, and busing to integrate schools, on which there was no public consensus. His chief strategist on mobilizing public support noted that "the social issues are the ones that are divisive. Those are the issues on which (the Reagan) coalition could fracture."

The president's perception of public opinion affects not only the choice and timing of his political agenda, but it also influences the most fundamental decisions about his political career. Lyndon Johnson decided not to run for reelection in 1968 when his public-opinion rating dropped to a new low. The lack of public esteem for Richard Nixon following revelations of the Watergate scandal no doubt played a role in his decision to resign from the presidency in 1974.

Contemporary presidents, therefore, have an ambivalent relationship to public opinion. As the most prominent national leader with all the techniques of the modern media at his disposal, the president is in a unique position to be able to shape the public's political perceptions. At the same time, the president has become so much the focus of popular expectations that nearly any disappointment or inadequacy anywhere in society (or indeed in the world) may lead to a decline in presidential popularity. When popularity falls too low, whatever the reasons, effective presidential leadership is no longer possible.

INSTITUTIONS IN ACTION ■

THE FOREIGN AID PROGRAM, 1985

In early 1947 the British Government told the United States that it was no longer capable of continuing its active economic and military support of the government of Greece against insurgents aided by the Soviet Union. President Harry Truman swiftly undertook to build congressional and public support for the idea that the United States should provide assistance to both Greece and Turkey to aid them in "resisting attempted subjugation by armed minorities or by outside pressures." By May of 1947 Congress had appropriated $400 million in economic and military aid. In June the first steps were taken, leading up to the massive Marshall Plan, to provide economic assistance to Western Europe, and during the next several years military alliances were negotiated throughout much of the world, many carrying the possibility of foreign aid.

In the late 1980s it is hard to remember when the United States did not routinely dispense large sums of money to other governments in the form of economic and military aid. Throughout the 40 years of such expenditure a prime consideration, for every president from Truman to Reagan, has been to justify the aid in terms of its contribution to the struggle against communism in general and the Soviet Union in particular. Truman felt that unless Americans were truly alarmed about the Soviet threat they would not willingly spend the money on other countries. It was necessary therefore to emphasize the existence of a "Cold War" in order to persuade American voters and members of Congress to invest in economic development and military buildup abroad.

The broad policy of using American resources to support and strengthen other governments that appear threatened by Communists, either from within the country or from outside, has had some controversial consequences. One is that all sorts of political leaders can make a bid for U.S. support by asserting their unyielding hostility to Russia, and American policy has sometimes backed some rather disreputable regimes. Another consequence is that the Cold War motivational base has tended to push the emphasis in foreign aid toward more military hardware and away from economic reform and development.

A third consequence has been to draw American policy away from multilateral agencies such as the United Nations and broad programs of international collaboration and to emphasize instead much more narrowly focused military alliances and *quid pro quo* bilateral agreements. In return for the *quid* of foreign aid, the *quo* is often the right of the United States to maintain overseas military or naval bases.

Foreign aid programs must be funded by Congress; so while the President takes the lead in making proposals and negotiating terms with other nations, members of Congress can sometimes have significant effects on U.S. policy. The total dollar amount in the foreign aid bill enacted in 1985 was just over $15 billion. About 40 percent of this was for military assistance. In the three previous Reagan budgets Congress had granted an average of 20 percent more military aid each year, but in 1985 this was scaled back to a 3.9 percent growth. The scope and complexity of American commitments abroad and the frequent difficulties encountered in trying to use foreign aid as an instrument of foreign policy can be illustrated by examining some of the component parts of the 1985 legislation.

The 1985 legislation on foreign aid for fiscal year 1986 contained numerous programs as indicated in Table 15.8. Many of these programs were broken down, in turn, into country-specific aid packages. Several of these were the focus of heated debate.

The Philippines. President Reagan had asked for $100 million in military aid for this Pacific outpost of American military power, but increasing criticism of Philippine President Ferdinand Marcos had led many to urge reductions. Congress eventually approved $55 million in military assistance and $125 million in economic aid, and it was agreed that the $180 million total would constitute the U.S. commitment for the next five years. In February 1986 elections were held in the Philippines, and amid widespread charges of fraud and intimidation Marcos was once again

TABLE 15.8
FOREIGN AID PROGRAMS AND APPROPRIATIONS, FISCAL YEAR 1986

Program	Amount
Inter-American Development Bank	$ 78,000,983
Inter-American Investment Corporation	11,700,000
World Bank	109,720,549
International Development Association	700,000,000
Special Facility for Sub-Saharan Africa	75,000,000
International Finance Corporation	29,077,390
Asian Development Bank and Fund	111,909,408
African Development Fund	62,250,000
African Development Bank	16,188,910
Total callable capital for development banks	(2,884,116,052)
International Organizations and Programs	277,922,475
Subtotal (multilateral aid)	$ 1,471,769,715
Agriculture aid	699,995,900
Population aid	250,000,000
Health aid	200,824,200
Child survival fund	25,000,000
Education, human resources aid	169,949,700
Energy, selected development aid	174,358,930
Science and technology aid	10,790,000
Private sector revolving fund	(18,000,000)
American schools and hospitals abroad	35,000,000
International disaster aid	22,500,000
Sahel development	80,500,000
Foreign service retirement and disability fund	43,122,000
Rescind Syrian aid account	0
Economic Support Fund	3,700,000,000
Agency for International Development (AID) operating expenses	376,350,000
AID reappropriation	5,000,000
AID inspector general	21,050,000
Trade credit insurance program	(250,000,000)
Trade and development program	18,900,000
African Development Foundation	3,872,000
Inter-American Foundation	11,969,000
Peace Corps	130,000,000
International narcotics control	57,529,000
Migration and refugee aid	338,930,000
Anti-terrorism aid	7,420,000
Peace-keeping operations	34,000,000
Subtotal (bilateral aid)	$ 6,417,060,730

(continued)

TABLE 15.8 (Continued)

Program	Amount
Military Assistance Program grants	782,000,000
International military education and training	54,489,500
Foreign military sales, forgiven loans, and direct credits	5,190,000,000
Defense acquisition fund	(325,000,000)
Guarantee reserve fund	
Subtotal (military aid)	$ 6,026,489,500
Housing guaranty program	(152,000,000)
Overseas Private Investment Corporation	(156,750,000)
Export-Import Bank total limitation	(13,128,357,000)
Export-Import Bank direct loans	1,110,000,000
Grand Total	$15,025,319,945

SOURCE: *Congressional Quarterly Weekly Report*, December 21, 1985, p. 2692.

declared the winner. Disgust with what one influential member of Congress called "that clown in Manila," led many to question the usefulness to American interests of propping up a regime so lacking in credibility and effectiveness as Marcos's leadership offered. But the American military presence in the Far East was thought to depend on retaining the Philippine bases, so the policy dilemma was and remained severe. The use of foreign aid as a lever to affect another country was acceptable. More direct intervention was not. Persuading Marcos to step down by withholding aid was the Reagan administration's only option. Even if it worked, and Marcos left, the Philippines might be left in chaotic condition, and that would not help the American interests. Marcos did leave office late in February and fled the country. For once, U.S. pressure had worked.

The Middle East. The two largest U.S. foreign aid packages go to Israel and Egypt. In the 1985 bill, Israel got $3 billion, $1.8 billion in military assistance and $1.2 billion in economic aid. Egypt was granted $1.3 billion in military aid and $815 million in economic help, plus $220 million in food aid. Ever since the Camp David accords of 1979, when these two countries agreed to stop fighting each other, they have been popular objects of U.S. attention, and their aid packages are not subjected to much criticism in Congress. Some members of

Congress tried to limit loans and arms sales to Jordan, however, in an effort to push that country into a Middle East peace conference. Other money that in earlier years had been appropriated to aid Lebanon, but had not been spent because Lebanon was in such turmoil, was transferred in 1985 to other purposes.

Around the Mediterranean rim other countries also received American aid. Tunisia got $67 million worth of military grants and loans. Greece and Turkey, uneasy rivals of one another but both part of NATO and of America's effort to contain Soviet influence, received substantial military assistance—some $450 million for Greece and, in a long-observed ratio of 10 to 7, almost $650 million for Turkey.

Central America. Despite the many recent foreign-policy controversies involving Central America the total amount of foreign aid for the several nations in that region is comparatively small. Moreover, some of what is dispensed is covert, funneled in various ways to the Contra opponents of the Sandinista regime in Nicaragua, for instance, and these funds do not appear in the regular "books" of American policy. Even though the amounts of Central American aid are small, however, they are often the subject of dispute as congressional leaders have sought to force the Reagan administration to press more vigorously for economic reforms and respect for human rights in countries like El Salvador and Guatemala. By 1985 President Jose Duarte of El Salvador had won broad acceptance in Congress and few conditions were attached to El Salvador's money. Military aid to Guatemala, however, was made conditional on President Reagan's certification that a civilian government was in power and was making progress in establishing civil order.

In these and many other foreign aid programs the United States seeks to accomplish multiple purposes: enhancement of human rights and reduction of domestic violence and terror, establishment of responsible democratic government, economic development and (sometimes) reform, both military and social resistance to Communists from the Soviet Union, Cuba, or elsewhere. Within Congress, and often between Congress and the president, there are frequently differences of view regarding what priorities should be attached to these goals. Moreover, people disagree about how most effectively to accomplish them or, indeed, whether American money *can* achieve such an ambitious array of objectives. The foreign aid program then continues to provide an arena for many kinds of disputes and policy conflicts.

CHAPTER HIGHLIGHTS ■

1. The powers and responsibilities of the modern president are massive. They include several kinds of tasks that are often interrelated. These include symbolic leadership of the nation as well as policy leadership on domestic questions, national defense, and foreign affairs.

2. The presidency involves an institution as well as an individual. It includes the Cabinet, the Executive Office and its several component parts, and the White House staff.

3. The president represents certain constituencies growing in part out of his electoral success, in part from the demands and needs of his administration, and to some extent from elsewhere in the world.

4. Despite the great power of the presidency, the incumbent often finds it difficult to persuade Congress or even his own administration to accept fully his policy designs. Great presidents are those who most successfully master the tactics of bargaining and permission.

5. Presidential "popularity" is a vital resource of presidential leadership. If a president is to be successful in getting his policies accepted, he must maintain a reasonably high level of approval in the nation.

SUGGESTED READINGS ■

The presidential office is closely identified with the individuals who occupy the White House, and therefore much of the most interesting literature consists of memoirs and biographies as well as more analytic studies. A classic study of the presidency is Richard Neustadt's *Presidential Power* (1980).

Modern commentaries on the subject include: Benjamin Page and Mark Petracca, *The American Presidency* (1983); Thomas E. Cronin, *The State of the Presidency* (2d ed., 1980); Michael Nelson, ed., *The Presidency and the Political System* (1985); Paul Light, *The President's Agenda* (1983); Richard Nathan, *The Administrative President* (1983); Herbert Stein, *Presidential Economics* (1984); Bert Rockman, *The Leadership Question* (1984).

FBI Headquarters, Washington, D.C.

Chapter 16

THE BUREAUCRACY

The ordinary citizen sees the president on the evening television news or reads about him in the newspaper. Citizens read about their senators and representatives, and sometimes they even meet them. But the real contact that most citizens have with the government is with bureaucrats—with a clerk in the post office, with a government inspector checking whether a business meets safety standards, or with a tax examiner in the Internal Revenue Service. The person delivering the mail is a bureaucrat, as is the NASA space scientist.

Bureaucracies can be thought of as organizational machines. Just as complex machines such as jet planes, computers, or construction equipment allow societies to carry out difficult mechanical tasks that individuals and groups could not accomplish otherwise, so bureaucratic organizations allow societies to carry out social tasks that could not be accomplished by individuals or by informal groups. It takes a complex bureaucracy to deliver the mail, to provide social services, to design and produce military weapons, and to conduct foreign policy. Modern industrial societies contain a large number of big, complex organizations. Some are private organizations, such as business corporations, universities, and labor unions. But in most modern states the biggest and most complex organizations are found within the government. The army, the navy, the police, the post office, the school system, the government agencies that provide social services, the agencies that regulate the economy—all these are large, complex bureaucracies. In this chapter we will examine the characteristics of bureaucracy and see how these features are expressed in the vast bureaucratic structures of the federal government.

WHAT IS A BUREAUCRACY?

The very word **bureaucracy** conjures up images of red tape—long, complicated forms to be filled out, indifference to human needs, and waste and inefficiency. The United States has experienced repeated waves of antibureaucratic feeling. In recent years the intensity of that feeling appears to have increased. In presidential elections, candidates from both political parties take an antibureaucratic stance in their campaigns. They attack the government for interfering in the lives of citizens, for trying to regulate too many aspects of society, and for providing services that are unwanted or too expensive; yet, while politicians complain about bureaucracy, governmental programs cannot be carried out without an administrative apparatus.

Bureaucracies have a number of characteristics. Each can be thought of as something that helps a bureaucratic organization carry out its functions. At the same time, each can lead to "pathologies" that help explain why there is so much criticism of bureaucracies. What are these characteristics?

Bureaucracies are hierarchically structured organizations. They have a chain of command extending from the top officials down to subordinate offices and agencies. *Advantage:* Top officials can maintain control of subordinates and thus make sure organizational goals are carried out. In government agencies this is how the bureaucracy is controlled by the officials who have been elected by the people. The president can issue directives to the heads of the executive departments, who, in turn, can issue directives to their subordinates. *Problem:* There really are two problems here. Chains of command can be long and inefficient. Sometimes nothing gets done, because officials on the spot cannot make decisions without clearance from above. But the opposite problem appears if the chain of command is not rigidly enforced. Many organizations that appear to have a clear structure of command do not in fact work that way. Subordinate agencies often have a lot of freedom. They make and interpret policies on their own. This freedom introduces flexibility into what would otherwise be a rigid system, but it reduces control over the bureaucracy by the president and the appointed department heads. The principle of a hierarchical structure, therefore, can create two different pathologies of bureaucracy. If the hierarchy is enforced, the bureaucracy may be inflexible and inefficient. If it is not enforced, the bureaucracy may be uncontrolled.

Bureaucracies are based on specialization. They are ways of bringing together a large number of technical experts, each of whom understands some aspects of the complex problems faced by governmental organizations. For example, the Food and Drug Administration is staffed by chemists and biologists who test new drugs, by specialists in the inspection of manufacturing plants, by communications specialists, by economists, and by numerous other specialized workers. The many other agencies of the executive branch have their own specialized experts as well. *Advantage:* In this way, technical expertise is brought to bear on complex social problems. No single individual has all the knowledge that is needed to deal with most problems. Bureaucracies organize a large number of specialists so that they can work together. *Problem:* Experts are sometimes narrow; they don't see the larger problems. Moreover, those who do not have similar technical competence, such as elected officials, do not find it easy to control technical experts. This can reinforce the pathology of an uncontrolled bureaucracy.

Bureaucracies operate on the basis of impersonal rules. Bureaucrats are supposed to carry out the decisions made by policymakers in a fair and impersonal manner. They treat each citizen or group equally and impartially on the basis of rules provided by congressional or presidential policy. *Advantage:* Officials do not give better treatment to friends or to those who slip them a bribe (at least if they are honest officials, as most are). *Problem:* This also means that bureaucrats will be unsympathetic to individuals with special needs. They will "go by the book," making sure that proper procedures are followed and all necessary forms filled out, but not deviating from the rules. These very rules prevent bureaucrats from acting arbitrarily, but they also produce the red tape and rigidity about which many complain.

BUREAUCRATIC AUTHORITY

Where do bureaucrats get their authority in the United States? The Constitution barely mentions executive departments and does not even hint at the enormous impact bureaucratic activity has on the entire society. Nonetheless, the Constitution is the foundation of legitimate bureaucratic authority just as it is for the other parts of the federal government. What this means is that bureaucrats may do only those things that Congress and the president have authorized them to do. The Internal Revenue Service (IRS) writes many of the detailed tax rules, for example, but always within the legislative framework, itself very detailed, established by Congress. Furthermore, those rules are always subject to appeal to the courts to determine whether the IRS has correctly interpreted Congress's intent. Similarly, the armed forces cannot act legitimately on their own without the authority of the president as commander in chief. In actual practice, of course, bureaucrats often exercise wide discretion and sometimes seem beyond the effective control of anyone. We will examine some of these problems of bureaucratic discretion later, but first let us review briefly the growth and shape of the federal bureaucracy.

The Growth of the Federal Bureaucracy

Early in our nation's history the federal government was small. In 1802 it had only 2875 civilian employees. Only 130 of these were located in Washington. The president had one clerk. The federal government grew steadily but rather slowly through the nineteenth and the early twentieth century. New departments were added to the executive branch, and new functions were undertaken. There was rapid growth during both the Civil War and World War I, but these increases were temporary. When the wars ended, the government shrank again.

Permanent and substantial expansions of the federal government occurred during the New Deal era. At that time, the government took on important new functions: provision of social services for citizens and more extensive regulation of the economy. Until the Great Depression of the 1930s the federal government's expenditures were equal to only about one-fourth of state and local government expenditures. By 1939—after the New Deal programs had been instituted—the federal government was spending more than the states and localities. By 1949 the federal government accounted for 70 percent of all government spending. Since then state and local governments have grown faster than the federal government, tripling the number of their employees, but they derive over half their money from the federal treasury (see Table 16.1).

The number of federal employees is an indicator of the growth in the size of the federal bureaucracy (see Table 16.2). In 1802, as has been mentioned, there were 2875 federal civilian employees; in 1982 there were a thousand times as many, 2,871,000. Perhaps the best indicator of the increase in the size of federal government is not the amount of money it spends or the number of people it hires but the number of different branches and agencies that exist. There are 13 executive departments. But that is only the tip of the iceberg. Each of the departments has many subparts. The massive Department of Health and Human Services, for example, has 6 main divisions and 99 separate agencies within it. In addition to the executive departments, in 1985 there were the Executive Office of the president, with 18 separate units; 121 non-Cabinet executive agencies, such as independent regulatory commissions; and 61 advisory agencies containing a staggering 1179 committees.

TABLE 16.1

FEDERAL, STATE, AND LOCAL SPENDING, 1902–1983

Year	Total Domestic Government Spending	% Federal	% State-Local
1902	$ 106.40	28.5%	71.5%
1913	140.70	25.6	74.3
1922	214.70	34.7	65.3
1932	414.70	34.1	65.8
1940	490.50	33.9	66.1
1950	588.50	35.9	64.1
1960	759.33	34.2	65.8
1970	1215.00	37.2	62.8
1980	1661.60	46.1	53.8
1983	1653.20	48.8	51.2

SOURCE: John N. Quigley and Daniel L. Rubinfeld, *American Domestic Priorities* (Berkeley: University of California Press, 1985), p. 4.

TABLE 16.2

CIVILIAN EMPLOYEES OF THE FEDERAL GOVERNMENT, 1816–1983

Year	Total Number of Employees	Number Employed in the Washington, D.C. Area
1816	4,837	535
1821	6,914	603
1831	11,491	666
1841	18,038	1,014
1851	26,274	1,533
1861	36,672	2,199
1871	51,020	6,222
1881	100,020	13,124
1891	157,442	20,834
1901	239,476	28,044
1911	395,905	39,782
1921	561,142	82,416
1931	609,746	76,303
1941	1,437,682	190,588
1951	2,482,666	265,980
1961	2,435,804	246,266
1971	2,874,166	322,969
1981	2,858,742	350,516
1984	2,756,493	351,805

SOURCES: United States Bureau of the Census, *Historical Statistics of the United States, Colonial Times to 1970*, Bicentennial ed., Part 2, pp. 1102–03; U.S. Office of Personnel Management, Workforce Analysis and Statistics Division, monthly releases.

Herbert Kaufman, a political scientist, has written a book with the provocative title *Are Government Organizations Immortal?*[1] He found that they are not immortal but are very long-lived. Further, Kaufman found that many new agencies have been created recently, 246 in the past 50 years. Of the 27 major regulatory agencies, 21 were created since 1930, 9 of them in the past 10 years. The number of agencies is so large that a presidential assistant who was trying to plan some reorganization of the government could not find out how many there were. "We were," he wrote, "unable to obtain any single document containing a complete and current listing of government units which are part of the federal government."[2]

The number of bureaus is matched by the variety of types. Some agencies regulate things: the safety of business, the purity of drugs, or the quality of the environment. Others provide services, such as health care, educational benefits, or national defense. Others support or carry on research. The agencies of the American government are characterized by specialization. Each has a different task. In part this grows out of an Ameri-

---

[1] Washington D.C.: Brookings Institution, 1976.
[2] W. Harrison Wellford, quoted in the *Washington Post*, May 8, 1977.

The Pentagon is an architectural expression—half of it underground—of the vastness of the Defense Department bureaucracy.

can commitment to specialization as the most "scientific" way to run the government. In part it grows out of the tendency for each group in America to seek a government agency to represent its interests. In this way, such departments as Agriculture, Commerce, Labor, and Education were formed.

The Service State

The United States was late among Western nations to develop national programs of governmental service. Germany, for instance, instituted a social security program in the 1880s, whereas the United States did not enact one until 1935. Other European countries had extensive governmental health-care systems long before the United States adopted its limited Medicare and Medicaid. There was a U.S. postal system, of course, and in early years there was an extensive program for selling the public lands. Various efforts to promote and assist private business have been undertaken by the national government ever since Alexander Hamilton's famous *Report on Manufactures* issued in 1791 while he was the first secretary of the treasury. Pensions and bonuses for military veterans have been provided throughout our history, and indeed one study has found that after the Civil War pensions to Union army veterans and their families covered an astonishingly large segment of the American population.[3]

---

[3] Theda Skocpol and John Ikenberry, "The Political Formation of the American Welfare State in Historical and Comparative Perspective," in Richard F. Tomasson, ed., *Comparative Social Research: The Welfare State, 1883–1983*, (Greenwich, Conn: JAI Press, 1983), pp. 87–148.

Money subsidies, loans, and grants come in many forms and go to a great many different kinds of individuals and groups. Some transfers of funds involve relatively little bureaucratic discretion. If you meet the criteria of age or income or whatever, you get the money. Others, however, require elaborate application procedure and review, and the bureaucrats in charge may have considerable leeway in deciding whether to grant the funds or not. Many programs involve direct governmental provision of services, of course: public housing, veterans hospitals, the postal service, national parks, and so on. Direct service programs like those require larger numbers of bureaucratic personnel to administer them than do most of the programs that transfer federal funds to recipient individuals or groups. Much of the growth in federal activity since 1950, however, has been in transfer programs, and as a result, despite the vast increase in federal spending there has been only a moderate increase (about 35 percent) in the size of the federal bureaucracy.

The Regulating State

One of the main reasons for the growth and complexity of the American bureaucracy is the increased role of the government in *regulating* the activities of Americans. This is especially true for American businesses. Businesses have come under a large number of safety, environmental, and consumer product regulations. But the government regulates the lives of many citizens, especially when access to government services—welfare payments, unemployment benefits, and the like—requires that citizens conform to government regulations on eligibility. In addition, the federal government regulates state and local governments. For instance, as federal support for education has increased, so has the volume of federal regulation over school administration at the local level.

Government intervention in the economy is not new (see Chapter 4). Throughout the nineteenth century the government intervened in the economy, but the goal of its intervention was usually to protect the autonomy of business (e.g., from challenges by labor unions) and to foster its activities by providing subsidies such as grants of land to railroads.

Government regulation of the economy began during the late nineteenth century with antitrust legislation and the formation of the Interstate Commerce Commission to regulate railroad rates. During the early decades of the twentieth century the government moved against unsafe drugs and unhealthy food. During the 1930s it responded to the Great Depression with the series of social reforms associated with Franklin Roosevelt and the New Deal. The volume of regulation increased substantially. The Securities and Exchange Commission was created to regulate the securities market that had been abused in the boom of the 1920s. Banking laws were tightened. The Federal Communication Commission, the Civil Aeronautics Board, and other agencies came into being to supervise other industries. Many of these agencies were welcomed by the industries they regulated, because they protected firms from some of the uncertainties of the marketplace and sometimes also from the sharp practice of competitors. Many of these programs dealt with only one industry—airlines, radio and television stations, meat packers, and so on—and in some cases the regulators developed an excessively friendly relationship with the industry they were supposed to supervise. In any case, this array of regulating agencies, while sometimes criticized as instruments of "big government," did not impose heavy costs or detailed across-the-board requirements on most American business.

During the 1960s and 1970s the government began to intervene more directly in business practices (see Table 16.3). Protest movements had arisen across the country demanding better treatment for women and minorities, and more effective protection for the environment. The market system did not respond well to these demands, and political action followed. Numerous laws were enacted, and many of them involved regulation of the day-to-day operation of businesses. Affirmative-action programs require close regulation of hiring practices. Environmental protection requirements lead to regulation of the manufacturing process in plants. Health and safety regulations for workers involve detailed regulation of the work place. Laws requiring that manufacturers of new drugs demonstrate their effectiveness in curing what they claim to cure led to detailed requirements for drug testing by manufacturers.

New agencies were established to deal with these problems, including the Environmental Protection Agency, the Occupational Safety and Health Administration (OSHA), the Consumer Product Safety Commission, and the Equal Employment Opportunity Commission. These agencies differ from most of the earlier regulatory mechanisms in that they not only reach the fine details of what private employers do, but they include within their jurisdiction nearly all of American employers, not just those of a single industry. OSHA regulations, for example, affect universities and hospitals as well as business corporations. Thus the scope and impact of federal regulation has become very much broader.

From many sources there have been complaints about the intrusiveness of the new regulation and about its money costs. Businesses complain that they spend an inordinate amount of time and money trying to comply with goverment regulations. Controversial decisions, such as the ban on saccharin by the Food and Drug Administration (because of evidence that it could cause cancer), have led to demands for fewer regulations. On the other hand, the regulators can point to the successes of regulation, such as a cleaner environment and safer products.

When the Reagan administration took office in 1981, it sought to turn back the tide of regulation. The new president had campaigned on an antiregulation platform and brought with him to the White House a militantly antiregulation staff. Their argument was that regulation was too costly—it cost the government too much to enforce the regulations, and it cost business too much to comply. The Reagan administration announced a plan to cut about 60,000 federal employees, many from the new regulatory agencies. He also appointed people to head the regulatory agencies whose philosophy matched his own; to wit, there should be less regulation of business. The Reagan administration began to lift restrictions on business and play down the role of the government in protecting consumers, workers, and minorities. In some areas deregulation was nearly complete. Airlines, for instance, no longer need any federal approval to begin a new

TABLE 16.3

FEDERAL REGULATORY AGENCIES

Agency	Date of Establishment	Duties
Federal Communications Commission	1934	Regulates interstate and foreign communications by radio, television, wire, and cable; responsible for promoting the safety of life and property through the communications media
Federal Home Loan Bank Board	1932	Regulates savings and loan associations, which specialize in lending out money on homes and are the country's major private source of funds to pay for building and buying homes
Federal Maritime Commission	1961	Regulates the waterborne foreign and domestic offshore commerce of the United States; assures that U.S. international trade is open to all nations on fair and equitable terms
Federal Reserve System	1913	Regulates the nation's money supply by making monetary policy which influences the lending and investing activities of commercial banks and the cost and availability of money and credit
Federal Trade Commission	1914	Regulates business to prohibit unfair methods of competition and unfair or deceptive acts or practices, such as false advertising.
Interstate Commerce Commission	1887	Regulates interstate surface transportation, including trains, trucks, buses, inland waterway and coastal shipping, and freight forwarders to provide the public with rates that are fair and reasonable
National Labor Relations Board	1935	Regulates business to protect employees' rights to organize and to prevent and remedy unfair labor practices
Securities and Exchange Commission	1934	Regulates the securities and financial markets (such as the stock market) to protect the interests of the public and investors against malpractice
Consumer Product Safety Commission	1972	Regulates products produced by business to protect the public against product-related deaths, illnesses, and injuries (standards of automobile safety, for example)
Commodity Futures Trading Commission	1974	Regulates trading on the futures exchanges as well as activities of commodity exchange members, public brokerage houses, commodity salespersons, trading advisers, and pool operators to ensure fair trade practices and to protect the rights of customers and the financial integrity of the marketplace
Nuclear Regulatory Commission	1974	Regulates and licenses the uses of nuclear energy to protect the public health and safety and the environment
Federal Energy Regulatory Commission (formerly Federal Power Commission)	1977	Regulates the transportation and sale of natural gas, the transmission and sale of electricity, the licensing of hydroelectric power projects, and the transportation of oil by pipeline

SOURCE: Office of the Federal Register, National Archives and Records Service, General Services Administration, *The United States Government Manual 1981/82* (Washington, D.C.: U.S. Government Printing Office, May 1, 1981), pp. 254, 459–616.

route or cancel one, or to change their rates. The Civil Aeronautics Board has been abolished. Banks are not as restricted as they were. Neither are trucks and railroads.

Many regulations still have their sources of political support, however, and these groups have been strong enough in Congress to prevent drastic changes in many areas. The Teamsters Union, for instance, has worked hard to keep long-distance trucking under Interstate Commerce Commission (ICC) control, lest in an unregulated environment nonunion firms gain strength. The array of regulatory legislation that sets the framework of bureaucratic action has friends in the society as well as targets, and deregulation has turned out to be politically more complicated than many of its advocates had appreciated.

Organizations and Reorganizations

In Chapter 15 we noted the emergence of the 13 present executive departments. Each of these departments is itself a complex organization with numerous operating, or *line,* units and assorted *staff* units to provide various services needed to carry out the line responsibilities. Figure 16.1 illustrates the way these elements are arranged in the Department of Health and Human Services. Notice that matters of personnel, budget, planning, legal counsel, and legislation (lobbying and keeping track of action on Capitol Hill) are staff functions, and these units, all rather small, report directly to the departmental leadership. The major program activities of the Department of Health and Human Services are grouped into very distinct functional sets. At the same time, however, there are the field offices. It would be possible and perhaps equally logical to group the department's activities geographically rather than functionally: to put all the public health, Social Security, and other activities for an area of each major section of the country under a regional administrator. In effect, the State Department does just this when it groups most of its operating programs on the basis of the country and region of the world in which they occur. This is only one type of organizational dilemma that administrators and other responsible officials must try to resolve.

Many government programs are not contained within any of the thirteen departments. The Postal Service, the Tennessee Valley Administration (TVA), and the Veterans Administration (VA) are prominent domestic programs that are independent, and they are matched by the Peace Corps, the Arms Control and Disarmament Agency, and the U.S. Information Agency in the foreign-policy realm. Some independent agencies, like the TVA, operate as *government corporations,* generating their own income and setting their own policies largely outside the regular processes of congressional appropriations and control. Others, like the VA, have strong constituencies that can block any effort to subordinate them to departmental supervision; so they remain independent (see Table 16.4). From time to time, however, after several independent agencies have been established in a broad field of endeavor, they may be brought together in a new Cabinet department. This happened in 1953 when the massive Department of Health, Education, and Welfare was established and again in 1965 with the creation of the Department of Housing and Urban Development.

A third kind of organization in the bureaucracy is the **independent**

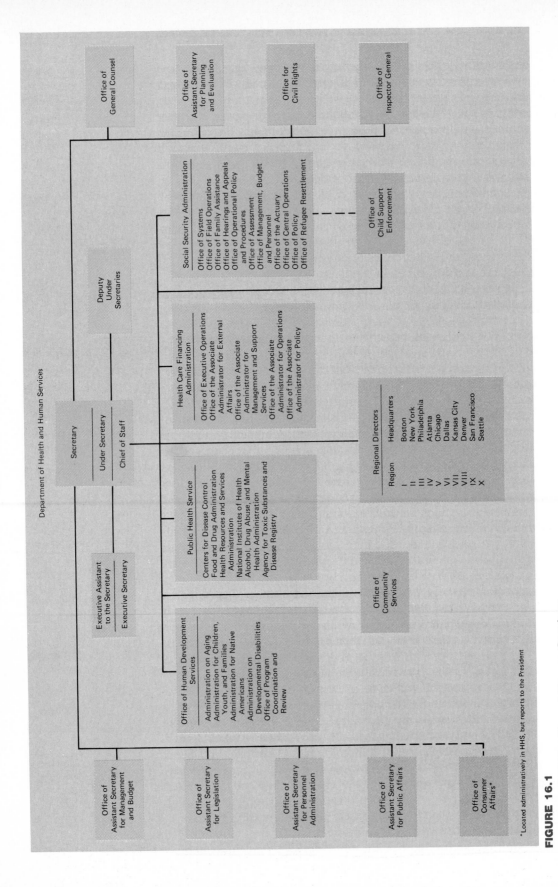

FIGURE 16.1

Department of Health and Human Services

SOURCE: *The United States Government Manual* (Washington, D.C.: U.S. Government Printing Office, 1983), p. 824.

TABLE 16.4

INDEPENDENT FEDERAL ESTABLISHMENTS AND GOVERNMENT CORPORATIONS

Administrative Conference of the U.S.	Federal Deposit Insurance Corporation	National Aeronautics and Space Administration	Pennsylvania Avenue Development Corporation
American Battle Monuments Commission	Federal Election Commission	National Capital Planning Commission	Pension Benefit Guaranty Corporation
Appalachian Regional Commission	Federal Emergency Management Agency	National Credit Union Administration	Postal Rate Commission
Board for International Broadcasting	Federal Home Loan Bank Board	National Foundation on the Arts and the Humanities	Railroad Retirement Board Securities and Exchange Commission
Central Intelligence Agency	Federal Labor Relations Authority	National Labor Relations Board	Selective Service System
Civil Aeronautics Board	Federal Maritime Commission	National Mediation Board	Small Business Administration
Commission on Civil Rights			
Commission of Fine Arts	Federal Mediation and Conciliation Service	National Science Foundation	Tennessee Valley Authority
Commodity Futures Trading Commission		National Transportation Safety Board	U.S. Arms Control and Disarmament Agency
Consumer Product Safety Commission	Federal Reserve System, Board of Governors	Nuclear Regulatory Commission	U.S. Information Agency
Environmental Protection Agency	Federal Trade Commission General Services Administration	Occupational Safety and Health Review Commission	U.S. International Development Cooperation Agency
Equal Employment Opportunity Commission	Inter-American Foundation Interstate Commerce Commission	Office of Personnel Management	U.S. International Trade Commission
Export-Import Bank of the U.S.			U.S. Postal Service
Farm Credit Administration	Merit Systems Protection Board	Panama Canal Commission	Veterans Administration
Federal Communications Commission		Peace Corps	

SOURCE: *The United States Government Manual* (Washington, D.C.: U.S. Government Printing Office, 1983), p. 810.

regulatory commission. The earliest of these bodies was the ICC, established in 1887 to regulate railroads but later taking trucking, waterways, and pipelines within its jurisdiction. The regulatory commissions are independent in the sense that their membership must be bipartisan and have fixed terms of office. Since the commissioners cannot be fired, an incumbent president cannot directly control commission decisions, though a two-term president will usually have the opportunity to remake a commission's political philosophy. Congress, too, can and does influence commission policies through appropriations and, on occasion, by changing the law creating the regulatory programs. Nevertheless, the regulatory commissions do operate with a large degree of autonomy.

The vast scope of the federal bureaucracy and the great complexity of its organizational structures make it an inviting target for proposals to make it more efficient and responsive by reorganizing it. Every modern president has made reorganization proposals, and most have succeeded in restructuring some parts of the system. In part these efforts may be motivated by a desire on the president's part to gain firmer control of the bureaucracy, to make them do his bidding rather than follow their own preferences. In part the effort may be based on the belief that the bureaucracy is inefficient and wasteful, spending large amounts of public

The government employs many trained professionals and technical experts such as this forester in Louisiana.

money on useless activity. Some reorganization proposals grow out of the belief that anything government does is inherently undesirable or ineffectual. Whatever the sources, reorganization proposals have become a part of each recent administration's effort to make a record of accomplishment. Some observers have concluded, however, that the results of reorganization are often more symbolic than real, and that usually bureaucratic life goes on pretty much as it did before the reorganization took effect.

WHO ARE THE BUREAUCRATS?

The popular image of a bureaucrat might be that of a file clerk, a bookkeeper, or a customs official with a stamp in hand, exercising the authority of government but completely anonymous and impersonal. In fact, however, there are more than 15,000 different skills represented among the nearly 3 million federal civilian employees, and they include thousands of lawyers, doctors, and scientists as well as secretaries, clerks, and inspec-

TABLE 16.5

PROFESSIONALS EMPLOYED BY THE FEDERAL GOVERNMENT

Engineers (all types)	150,504
Scientists (Biological/Physical)	95,270
Nurses/Nurses' aides	71,713
Personnel administrators	47,231
Accountants	125,795
Teachers	28,599
Forestry workers	18,847
Mathematicians/Statisticians	14,792
Attorneys	15,532
Computer operators	11,197
Doctors	8,837
Librarians	6,967
Economists	5,763
Writers/Editors	2,178
Psychologists	3,186
Photographers	2,892
Veterinarians	2,301
Pharmacists	2,158
Dentists	957
Chaplains	518

SOURCE: "Occupations of Federal White-Collar Workers" (October 31, 1978). Office of Personnel Management Work Force Analysis and Statistics Branch, 1900 E Street, NW, Washington, D.C.

tors. Indeed, more than one-third of all the professional and technical workers in the whole United States population work for government (see Table 16.5), and 7 of 8 of these bureaucrats work somewhere other than in the Washington area. They are our neighbors, and they are very diverse in religion, race, and other background factors. Skilled bureaucrats are well paid, and in recent years, despite their diversity, they have managed to organize themselves sufficiently well into unions to gain considerable bargaining power over salaries and benefits. The vast majority of federal employees operate under civil-service protection, and so they cannot be fired for political reasons.

During most of the nineteenth century, federal jobs tended to be filled under the spoils system. The main qualification was membership in the party that was in power. When a new administration came into office, it replaced government workers with its own supporters. As William Seward (later Lincoln's secretary of state) said in 1849, when Zachary Taylor took office: "The world seems almost divided into two classes; those who are going to California in search of gold, and those going to Washington in search of office." The spoils system bred corruption and inefficiency, because officials were hired for their political loyalty, not because they were qualified for the job.

In 1883 the Pendleton Act was passed. It was the first step toward replacing the spoils system with a civil-service system. The new system rested—and continues to rest—on two principles. First, selection is on the basis of merit, usually measured by performance on civil-service exams. Second, as long as there is enough money in the budget, jobs in the civil service will be secure even if the administration changes. These two principles were intended to eliminate political criteria as qualifications for office. The first two principles required a third one. The civil service was to be responsive in its actions to the political leaders of the day. It was to be neutral, with no political views of its own.

Though we have a civil service, the United States does not have a special elite corps of civil servants. This fact is very important. Throughout this book we have stressed some fundamental characteristics of American government that make the United States very different from other democratic societies. Features that make America special include constitutional provisions for the separation of powers and for federalism, the absence of sustained class conflict in America, and the special character of its political parties. The absence of an elite career civil service is another feature of American government, perhaps as important as the ones just mentioned in setting it off from governments elsewhere.

In most of the other modern democracies—in Britain, France, Germany, or Japan, for instance—the top civil servants are a very distinctive elite. In most cases they begin their careers in special selective schools that train them for high government office. They then enter government service and make it a lifelong career, moving up to occupy top governmental positions just below the level of the cabinet officials who go in and out of office with a change in the party in power. These bureaucratic officials become highly skilled and knowledgeable in what they do, and many of them wield great influence.

A permanent corps of top civil servants has a number of advantages. It puts people of great skill and experience in very high governmental positions, it gives continuity to the government as administrations change, and it helps create a strong central government. The fact that this small group of top government executives has a common background and is in office for a long time means that they know each other well and can work together. It can have disadvantages as well. The top civil servants are supposed to work for and be guided by the political appointees who come in with a new election; nevertheless, their greater expertise and continuity in office can give them the dominant role over the elected officials.

In the United States, the situation is quite different. There are many permanent civil servants—people whose life careers are spent working for the government and who are gradually promoted to important positions. Indeed, a Senior Executive Service was established in 1978 to give high rank and salary to top bureaucrats. But even these positions only go up so high in the ranks of the federal government. In the very top positions, one does not find the career executive civil servant that one finds in other countries, but rather a group of political appointees brought into office by each new administration.

Political appointees are supposed to enable the president to control the bureaucracy, but this is seldom an easy task. Political officials are usually new to the job, while the agencies they are to run are staffed by long-term career civil servants. These career employees have more subject-matter expertise and more long-term commitment to the programs and procedures of their particular agency. It is hard for political appointees to take control. Furthermore, the turnover in jobs among such appointees is fairly rapid. They average less than two years on a particular job, hardly enough time to find their way around.

During recent years, presidents have tried to increase somewhat the number of positions at the top of the government that can be filled by presidental appointees rather than by career civil servants. Their hope is to secure more complete commitment to their philosophy and avoid a situation in which an unsympathetic bureaucracy undermines the president's programs.

Though presidents may be frustrated by a bureaucracy that is not responsive to their direction, the independence of many government agencies from direct political control is important to the functioning of the government. If there is to be an effective federal program to support research on cancer, for example, it is important that decisions on what research to support are made by qualified experts who are independent of political demands that research funds be spent in one congressional district rather than another. The Bureau of Labor Statistics must be able to resist any effort by the White House to juggle the unemployment figures to serve the needs of a president running for reelection. When President Nixon tried to use the IRS to harass his political enemies, the IRS refused. Surely a bureaucracy should be under the control of elected officials when it comes to carrying out general government policy, but few want a bureaucracy that is subservient to the partisan political needs of the president.

THE POLITICS OF BUREAUCRACY

In traditonal theory, bureaucrats have no policy goals of their own. Policymakers provide a bureaucracy with goals, and the bureaucracy tries to achieve them. Congress makes the laws, and the administrative agencies implement them. Policy involves choices among competing objectives, and in a democracy only those officials who are directly responsible to the voters should make those choices. Administrators, on the other hand, should be nonpolitical in the sense that the choice-making core of the political process is not their concern. They are to carry out policy as effectively and efficiently as possible. In fact, it seldom works that way. Bureaucrats often contribute to the policymaking process. It would be strange, indeed, if, for example, the advice of expert space scientists in NASA were ignored in deciding whether to try for a mission to Mars. Furthermore, much actual policy is made after the laws are passed as the bureaucrats fill in the details. Policy and administration are not separable, and thus American bureaucracy is highly political.

Bureaucratic Discretion
The political character of bureaucracy grows out of the fact that bureaucrats possess considerable discretion in what they do. They make choices

as to which cases to pursue, which contracts to renegotiate, which research applications to fund, which new drugs to approve, and countless other specifics of government activity. Why do they have so much discretion? The short answer is that Congress has delegated much of its authority to make detailed policy to the bureaucracy. Many of the welfare and regulatory programs Congress enacted in the 1930s and in the 1960s were written in terms of very general objectives and gave the administrative agencies the authority to fill in the details. Why does Congress not write more precise laws and thereby reduce bureaucratic discretion? Congress often is not equipped with the expert and detailed knowledge needed to write precise regulatory laws. The bureaucracy has this knowledge. One of the sources of its discretionary power is its possession of expert knowledge in the area of regulation.

Few members of Congress have the training to understand the complexities of nuclear-weapons technology, drug testing, water pollution control, and so forth. Furthermore, even if they have the needed skills, they are dependent on bureaucratic agencies for technical information. Bureaucratic agencies collect the data on which policy is based—the FBI collects crime statistics; the Bureau of Labor Statistics collects data on unemployment; the Federal Aviation Administration collects information on new airplane safety devices. Regulations have to be adjusted to fit different industries. They are often complicated and require scientific and technical knowledge. The creation of such detailed regulation is left to the bureaucracy.

Furthermore, Congress often writes vague laws because it is politically incapable of agreeing on more precise regulations—regulations that may upset constituencies at home. By leaving the task of detailed regulation writing to the bureaucracy, Congress avoids the political heat that would come from an offended industry.

This approach to the writing of law is not new. One of the first regulatory acts, the law setting up the Federal Trade Commission (FTC) in 1914, said that "unfair methods of competition in commerce or unfair or deceptive acts or practices in commerce are hereby declared illegal." But what is unfair or deceptive? The answer was left to the FTC and to the courts. Or consider a more recent law, the Elementary and Secondary Education Act of 1965. It provided funds for the "special needs of educationally deprived children." But what is an educationally deprived child? And what kind of needs? The specific definitions were left to the bureaucracy. In a similar manner, recent legislation on the environment or on occupational safety mandates a general concern with the issue but leaves to the bureaucratic agency the discretion to write the precise regulations.

Congress does not always write such vague laws. In some environmental protection legislation, it has set precise criteria for acceptable pollution levels. Or take the Internal Revenue Code. Congress does not tell the IRS to "raise money by taxing income in a way that is fair." It writes a precise set of regulations specifying the exact rate at which various types of income shall be taxed. Nevertheless, the administration of the tax laws leaves a lot of discretion to the IRS, because no matter how precisely matters are spelled out, questions of application of the law to a specific case arise. Even when Congress is precise, some bureaucratic discretion remains.

Of course, there is less room for discretion if a law is precise. Social Security legislation specifies quite precisely who is eligible to receive benefits and how much they should receive. The bureaucrats administering the law have little discretion. The result is that there is little controversy or dissatisfaction over the administration of the Social Security laws.

Filling in the details of a statute and applying the law to particular situations requires the bureaucracy to make choices and thus to act politically. The writing of precise rules and regulations to carry out a broad statutory mandate illustrates the point. Once Congress had enacted the Occupational Safety and Health Act of 1970, for instance, the agency created to administer the law, a unit of the Labor Department, began to write the "rules and regs." How many toilet facilities should farm workers have? What ought to be the safety standards for ladders? And so on. Proposed rules are published in the Federal Register, so that interested groups may comment or complain. If the agency then wishes to alter its proposals, it may do so before finally promulgating the rules to be followed. Rule making is often a slow and exacting process, and it may take many months and sometimes years before a new law is implemented in detail. Bureaucrats are often criticized for being so slow, but their deliberate pace is generally a reflection of the immense amount of detail and adaptation to specific circumstances that must be incorporated into the application of the broad declarations Congress enacts.

Defending Turf and Budget

Bureaucracies have organizational goals as well as concerns with the policies that they are supposed to carry out. They seek to maintain and enhance the organization itself, and this leads them to defend their policy jurisdiction and their funds. Bureaucratic organizations are often engaged in a power struggle with other bureaucratic organizations. Many agencies try to increase their budgets, the number of people they employ, and the scope of the programs under their control. If they cannot increase budgets, personnel, and power over programs, they try at least to keep what they have. They resist budget cuts, personnel reductions, and any attempt to remove programs from their jurisdiction.

There are many reasons why bureaucrats act to protect what they have and try to get more. For one thing, their jobs depend on this effort. A budget cut may mean the loss of one's job. For another, the importance of one's job depends on it. Bureaucratic rank and prestige depend on the size of one's program. Bureaucrats try to have their programs increase in size, because their own status within the bureaucracy will rise accordingly.

Lest bureaucrats be made to sound like power-hungry officials with no interests but their own jobs and security, we must add that bureaucratic officials are usually deeply committed to the programs they administer. The officials of the agency that is assigned the task of administering the federal highway safety program, for example, are engineers who are committed to highway safety. If they struggle for increased funding for their program or for more autonomy to carry out the program, it is in large part because increased funds and increased autonomy will, they believe, allow them to do a better job and save more lives on the highways; and they believe that because they are experts, they know best how to do this.

As advocates of their own program, the bureaucrats in a particular agency often come into conflict with other bureaucrats. The Arms Control and Disarmament Agency works on problems of disarmament. Its commitment usually is to arms limitation. This often brings it into conflict with the Defense Department, whose officials are less likely to have such a commitment.

Within the Defense Department, the air force and the navy have often clashed over weapons systems. It will come as no surprise that the navy favors more funding for missile-carrying submarines and the air force more funding for supersonic bombers.

The Environmental Protection Agency comes into conflict with other government agencies when it tries to get them to live up to environmental regulations. Or it may come into conflict with agencies in the Department of Commerce that are more interested in expanding energy resources than in protecting the environment. Agency competition is a central feature of bureaucratic life.

Routines

Another important dimension of public bureaucracy involves the routines that govern its activity. Bureaucratic agencies develop **standard operating procedures (SOPs).** These are very valuable in providing routine ways of dealing with problems. It would take too much time and effort— and be too unpredictable—if officials had to decide separately how to handle each case that came before them. But standard operating procedures can create rigidity if they are applied to situations they do not fit.

During the Cuban missile crisis in 1962, President Kennedy wanted to block Russian ships from carrying missiles to Cuba. However, he also wanted to limit the confrontation with the Soviets. His plan called for a naval blockade, but one that was close enough to Cuba so that the Soviets would have time to reconsider and turn around before confronting the American naval ships. Standard operating procedure in the navy, however, was for a blockade to be set several hundred miles offshore to give ships enough room to maneuver. Kennedy had quite a struggle trying to get the navy to modify its usual way of doing things for the special circumstances of the Cuban missile emergency. We should not think this is a problem only for the American military. The Soviets had a similar problem. They wanted to get the missiles into Cuba unobserved, so they shipped them secretly. The Soviets then erected them in Cuba, using techniques that were easily observed from the air. Why? The Soviet technicians were using their standard operating procedures for erecting missiles.

At the beginning of this chapter we noted that bureaucrats often tend to "go by the book," with elaborate procedures for applications, complicated forms in triplicate, and explanations of their rules presented in almost incomprehensible language. The word *bureaucracy* is nearly synonymous in our minds with red tape and inertia. Why should bureaucrats be so dominated by procedural detail? Part of the answer is that the same paperwork that creates so much red tape also protects the administrative process from being arbitrary or corrupt. The police officer or the general who disregards "the book" may sometimes solve the case or win the battle, of course, but General George Custer, massacred by the Sioux in the Battle of the Little Big Horn, is a good example of one who ignored established procedures. Moreover, if there are good records of administrative action, it is possible for superior officials to review bureaucratic performance, for Congress to exercise effective oversight, and for the press and the public to discover what is happening in the day-to-day work of the government. Inertia and red tape are certainly real problems, but they are in a sense the price we pay for maintaining the possibility of democratic control of administrative power.

Bureaucracies and Clienteles

Bureaucrats need political support if they and their programs are to survive and flourish. They must defend themselves against bureaucratic rivals who seek to take over part of their jurisdictional turf. They must resist the budget cutters in the OMB and elsewhere in the administration. They must keep Congress convinced that they are doing a good job and a job worth doing. A politically effective bureaucracy, one with a secure jurisdiction and a growing budget, will cultivate support from among those who benefit from its programs: the program clientele. An agency's clientele can tell the administration and members of Congress that it approves of the program, wants it continued, and if necessary will use whatever political muscle it can to help elect the program's friends and defeat its enemies.

Clientele interests are often well-organized groups, and once a program is in full operation the agency, the interest groups, and the congressional committees or subcommittees with primary jurisdiction over the program

Much of what bureaucracy does is providing services to people in need. Inevitably, however, there are forms to fill out and screening procedures to prevent fraud.

may develop close relationships of mutual assistance. These three-way alliances are referred to by several names: cozy little triangles, iron triangles, whirlpools of influence, and triple alliances. Regardless of label, the situation is one that often makes the agency's program difficult to change.

Consider the program for assisting veterans. Each house of Congress has a Veterans Affairs Committee. They work closely with the large veterans' organizations such as the American Legion and the Veterans of Foreign Wars to make sure that no serious reductions are made in the budget and program of the Veterans Administration. Shipbuilding interests and the House Merchant Marine and Fisheries Committee work closely with the Federal Maritime Commission to retain subsidies for American shipping. The National Education Association, nearly 2 million strong, has close working ties with the education subcommittees in the House and Senate, and in the early 1980s they helped prevent the Reagan administration from carrying out its intention to dismantle the Department of Education. The list of such triple alliances is long.

On many issues, however, there is a much looser structure of interested participants. Rather than a narrow iron triangle there is an "issue network," a more diverse array of organized groups, knowledgeable outside observers and consultants, some congressional staffers, a few Congressional committee members with particular interest in the policy area, and perhaps several executive branch officials and agencies.

Consider, for instance, the issue area of labor policy—that is, policies dealing with employment and unemployment, job training, and the like. In Washington there are a number of specialists in that field. Some are top civil servants in the Department of Labor, while others are political appointees in that same department. Some are to be found on the staffs of the House and Senate committees that deal with labor policy; some are labor specialists employed by major interest groups concerned with these issues, groups such as the AFL-CIO and the U.S. Chamber of Commerce; some are at research centers working on labor problems; and some may be analysts and reporters who specialize in such issues for the mass media. They all form an issue network. Or if one took an area in foreign policy—our policies toward Latin America, for instance—one could locate a similar network. The members of that network would be located in the State Department, working for congressional committees, in businesses and other organizations involved with Latin America, in research organizations and universities, in the media, and in several church organizations.

People may move around within these networks, going from position to position. An assistant secretary of labor might be someone whose previous job was staff director of the House Labor and Education Committee, or who was a top union official, or perhaps a leading academician working on labor issues.

These issue networks differ from what we have called triple alliances in several ways. They are not as clearly and neatly defined. It is not always clear who is in such a network and who is outside. They are not held together by agreement on policy. The members of triple alliances usually agree on the interests and policy directions they favor. Those in an issue network are linked together by common concern with a particular policy and by their common expertise. They may disagree about policy. The network dealing with manpower policy, for instance, has both liberals and conservatives in it.

Even when network participants disagree, they know each other and tend to "speak the same language" regarding the problems and options in the policy area. At the same time, on these issues they are experts, and they may sometimes ignore the concerns of the larger but less well-informed public. The specialists might all agree that, for example, a new tank was needed for the army. Can "outsiders" turn down the request? With a defense budget of some $300 billion, this issue is of great importance, and we will come back to it in the conclusion of the chapter.

Agencies sometimes grow so dependent on the support of their clientele groups that they pretty well abandon any effort to regulate or control them. The charge has often been made that the independent regulatory commissions tended to be "captured" by the industries they were established to regulate. The ICC, for example, came to be very sympathetic toward the railroads and, after interstate trucking was brought under its jurisdiction, toward the trucking industry also. The trucking industry and the Teamsters Union have vigorously opposed any effort to deregulate trucking; likewise, the established commercial airlines opposed deregulation.

It is not surprising that regulatory agencies and regulated industries should come to share common values. They meet often. They deal with the same problems and attend the same conventions. An agency expert on the problems of a particular industry may wish to move on to another, higher-paying job with the industry that can make use of that expertise. That, of course, implies that while in office agency officials will be less demanding of the industry than if they had a truly arms-length relationship. Capture may be understandable in both human and political terms, but when it happens it does mean weaker regulation.

How serious is the capture problem? How unbreakable are the iron triangles? There is no single answer. It depends a good deal on the particular configuration of interests involved. One strategy for breaking a triangle is to reorganize the structure, either of Congress or the executive, that provides component parts. If the Veterans Affairs Committee were eliminated . . . , but, of course, the problem is exactly that the triangle's forces are strong enough to block the reorganization, at least most of the time. If, however, additional groups are brought into the picture, if the agenda is enlarged and the arena expanded, things can change. The tobacco interests began to lose their privileged position when health interests entered the contest over placing warnings on cigarette packages. The sugar producers no longer could have it all their way once the sugar consumers—primarily candy and soft drink manufacturers—became involved on the other side. Within an administration the ability of an agency to construct a cozy little triangle of support with Congress and interest groups may be greatly reduced if its program is closely reviewed by the OMB and the White House, where broader considerations are brought to bear and priorities are differently defined. The salience of the federal deficit and the problems of reducing it in recent years have challenged nearly all the cozy triangles, and some are considerably weaker today than they were once.

BUREAUCRACY IN A DEMOCRACY: ABUSES AND CONTROLS

Governing a complex modern society is clearly impossible without an extensive bureaucracy to provide the services and enforce the rules that make life possible. But bureaucracy is also a powerful instrument, and power can be abused. As we conclude our discussion of the federal bureaucracy, let us examine three types of bureaucratic abuse of power and see what, if anything, can be done to minimize their dangers.

Presidential Control

The first type of bureaucratic abuse involves the unwillingness of subordinates to carry out or comply with the directions of superior authority. In 1953 Harry Truman, who had had his full share of difficulty getting his subordinates to do what he wanted them to do, said of the man about to succeed him as president: "He'll sit there . . . he'll say, 'Do this. Do that!' And nothing will happen. Poor Ike—it won't be a bit like the army. He'll find it very frustrating."[4] Some years later, President Nixon found that there was bureaucratic resistance to some of the changes he wished to make, in part because the bureaucrats had political values that were different from the administration's. Still later, President Reagan encountered the same thing from civil servants who opposed the president's desire to cut back the role of the federal government.

The president cannot fire the civil-service bureaucrats. He cannot possibly keep track of what each administrative unit is doing or not doing. He cannot even know for sure if the information he receives from his subordinates is full and dependable. During the Vietnam War, for example, information from the field concerning the progress of the fighting was "improved" as it went "up the ladder" until, by the time President Johnson received it, things looked a lot better than they really were.

How does a president cope with these problems of administrative control? One way is to remind his subordinates that in a democracy they have a compelling obligation to follow the policy guidelines set by the elected officials. This is not mere window-dressing verbiage. Bureaucrats are citizens, too, and are likely to be at least as respectful of democratic norms as the rest of us. A second technique is to establish multiple channels of contact and communication with subordinates. A president who depends on a chief of staff to filter the information he receives may hear only a distorted version of an issue and can never learn about policy options that were not presented to him. Multiple advocacy from different agencies or departments can help enlarge the president's perspective. Franklin Roosevelt and John Kennedy were both adept at drawing upon multiple bureaucratic sources for information and advice. Closing off direct communication with all but one or two intimates, however, as Nixon did in his last months as president, makes effective leadership very difficult.

Effective use of presidental appointment power, despite the limited number of positions to be filled, can place dependable people in strategic

---

[4] Quoted in Richard Neustadt, *Presidential Power* (New York: Wiley, 1960), p. 110.

Civil Servants must be protected against politically motivated pressure, but sometimes the bureaucratic procedures seem excessively complicated. Here an official explains the steps required to fire a federal employee.

places so that they can help the chief executive run things this way. Loyalty to the president may sometimes conflict with loyalty to the agency and its traditional approach. Appointed officials, even secretaries of departments, are sometimes said to "go native," taking on the values of their program rather than those of their president. Appointed officials can be removed, however, and in order to assure the primacy of their priorities, presidents have done so. President Carter dismissed several of his Cabinet in 1978 because he felt they were not fully committed to *his* program. Even civil servants can be disciplined by denying them promotions or transferring them to unpleasant locations. But a president's agenda is typically so filled with crises from around the world that most of the details of bureaucratic supervision must fall to others, and thus the problem of bureaucratic compliance with presidental decisions remains.

Congressional Control

What happens when congressionally determined policies are ignored or subverted by bureaucrats? In Chapter 15 we looked at several mechanisms by which Congress can persuade agencies to conform. One is through legislative oversight, investigation of agency performance which may occur in conjunction with the appropriations process or may be undertaken separately. Another is through the use of the legislative veto. Beyond these formal devices, however, there is constituency casework. Most casework arises out of constituent encounters with administrative agencies, and as the congressional enterprise deals with the case, ongoing evidence is provided concerning whether and how the bureaucracies are doing their jobs.

Constituent complaints are not the only source of congressional infor-

A. Ernest Fitzgerald, a Defense Department employee, called the attention of Congress to serious cost overruns on the C-5 cargo plane. His administrative superiors were very upset, and as a result of his "whistle-blowing," Fitzgerald's career was in great jeopardy for a time.

mation about alleged snafus and other bureaucratic mishaps. Within the agencies discontented or concerned bureaucrats themselves may "blow the whistle" on situations they regard as contrary to sound public policy. Whistle blowing within the bureaucracy itself can sometimes be dangerous to the individual, who may as a "reward" be transferred to some remote outpost. A bureaucrat's discreet word to a member of Congress or staffer, however, may trigger an investigation of the alleged abuse. Thus, even if the administrative superiors ignore it, the separation of powers provides an alternative route for the conscientious bureaucrat seeking to correct a problem.

Citizen Control

If elected officials have trouble controlling the bureaucracy, can the public itself have any direct control? Americans often complain about unresponsive bureaucrats who pay little attention to the needs of citizens. One way in which citizens can keep bureaucratic officials responsive to their needs is through their member of Congress. As we have shown in the chapter on Congress, one of the main activities of representatives is individual "casework." Congressional staffs spend much of their time dealing with complaints from constituents or answering requests for special treatment.

In addition, government programs are sometimes set up so as to involve citizens in their administration. A number of Great Society antipoverty programs under President Johnson included provisions for participation by the urban poor in carrying them out. Similarly, farmers have participated in the administration of federal soil-conservation programs for many years. In general, observers have found that such participation is relatively ineffective. Few citizens take part, they are often unrepresentative of the people who are affected by the program, and they usually have little impact on the administration of the policy.

In 1976 Congress passed the "Government in the Sunshine Act." This requires that federal agencies and commissions hold their meetings and hearings in public and give adequate notice as to when and where they will be held. The purpose is to allow more citizen participation. Some agencies, such as the Environmental Protection Agency, regularly hold open hearings when they are considering certain regulations, and most invite the public to write comments on proposed regulations. Does it make much difference? In some cases, yes. The Army Corps of Engineers is one example of an agency that has become much more sensitive to public opinion than was once the case, but responsiveness can never be assumed. It must be achieved in each case by vigilant citizen concern.

Freedom of information   Public control over the bureaucracy has often been hampered by lack of information. Agencies traditionally had a good deal of discretion in withholding information. Their files were closed to the public. In 1966 Congress passed the Freedom of Information Act in an attempt to increase disclosure of information to the public. Agencies were allowed a good deal of discretion in deciding what they wanted to release. The agencies could also delay in responding to requests for information and charge high fees for the information they provided. The result was that the act was largely ineffective—a good example of how bureaucratic agencies can protect themselves from attempts to bring them under greater control.

In 1974 Congress amended the act. Agencies now have less discretion in deciding what they will release, they have to respond within a fixed time, and they have to charge reasonable fees for the material. The new law has been much more effective. Public-interest groups, academics, and citizens in general have made extensive use of the law. Their requests have focused on such agencies as the Department of Defense, the FBI, and the CIA, agencies that had rarely before been brought under public scrutiny. The requests have brought out detailed information on government spying on domestic political groups such as the Socialist Workers Party and on black and feminist groups. The FBI was discovered to have assembled damaging information on the personal lives of prominent public figures, and its longtime director J. Edgar Hoover was said to have used such information to keep himself in office and his agency free from criticism. The law brought out information from the files of the CIA on the agency's 25-year program of research on mind-control drugs. During 1976 alone, there were about 150,000 requests for information under the act.

The Freedom of Information Act was supported by public-interest groups who thought that it would enable them to oversee the activities of the bureaucracy in the name of public causes, and the press has found

J. Edgar Hoover was FBI Director from 1924 to 1972. Through careful cultivation of popular support and, it is alleged, some unsavory methods amounting almost to political blackmail, he made himself and his agency virtually invulnerable to efforts to change FBI policy direction.

it a very effective tool to assist their investigations of suspected scandals. The largest users of the law, however, have been American businesses. Corporations have been particularly active in seeking information from the Federal Trade Commission and the Food and Drug Administration. The motives behind corporate use of the Freedom of Information Act range from seeking information about competitors and trade secrets to attempting to paralyze regulatory agencies beneath an avalanche of requests.

This heavy use by business—which was not anticipated by those who originally favored the act—illustrates two points that we have made in other chapters. One is that those who have the most resources (in this case money and legal advice) can take the greatest advantage of government laws and regulations. The second is that public policies often have unanticipated consequences.

The Freedom of Information Act has given citizens some control over bureaucracies—at least in some areas. The act has been criticized as making it difficult for agencies to operate effectively. Critics complain about the burden of time and personnel needed to handle requests from citizens. Also, they claim that many requests—especially to the CIA and the Defense Department—lead to the release of information that violates national security. However one may wish to judge particular cases, there is no doubt that the people's right to know has been significantly advanced by recent policy developments. The likelihood that bureaucratic secrecy and abuses of power will do serious damage has been lessened. Nevertheless, the possibility always remains as long as bureaucrats are significant parts of the apparatus of democratic government.

CONCLUDING THOUGHTS

The dilemmas of democratic government are vividly illustrated by the problems inherent in public bureaucracies. How can the voters exercise effective control over the military establishment, for instance? Our largest and most costly bureaucracy, by far, the military is itself the source of virtually all of the specialized technical information needed to evaluate weapons, strategies, and force levels and to determine what is needed. Yet that same military bureaucracy prospers, as do its "constituents" that manufacture and supply weapons and material, with larger budgets and expanded programs. Should there be cuts? Rearrangements? Promotions? Expansions? Elected officials may do the best they can to sort out the various claims and arguments, but inevitably they are amateurs, not professionals, and their expertise is secondhand. The voters are even less able to assess the rights and wrongs of the issue and to make judgments regarding which candidates for office and what defense programs they prefer.

In Chapter 11 we discussed the question of retrospective voting, whereby, in effect, citizens express their approval or disapproval of the program of the past several years. Some issues, like inflation or unemployment, leave clear traces in our experience, so we can evaluate those. Others, like highway programs, Social Security, or national parks are tangible enough to judge whether or not we like what has been done. Most of the time military prepardness cannot be evaluated very well even in retrospect—for which, of course, we are deeply grateful. We can hardly know whether our weapons systems and personnel will perform as expected when we have had no opportunity to observe them in action. We depend, for example, on the military's own assessment of whether battleships are useful in modern warfare, as well as their judgment as to how many we need.

These are not uniquely American problems, of course. Evaluating the needs and capabilities of technically complex and costly undertakings like defense or the space programs and determining what priority to place on each is a profoundly troubling task of every modern society. The Soviet Union must struggle with the same kinds of decisions. In a democratic polity like the United States, however, the struggle has special elements. One is that, however much the bureaucratic experts may influence them, the authoritative officials must finally decide what is to be done. The president and the Congress set the budget and determine its contents for defense as for all the other activities of government. The second special element is that the voters determine who will occupy those positions of authority. Whatever collection of influences may affect this judgment, it is ultimately they who cast the votes and hence bear the responsibility for the outcome. If bureaucrats serve us badly or somehow evade our control to pursue their own private agendas of action, it is because the elected officials and, in turn, the electorate itself have not done their job.

PROFILE ■

MAX WEBER (1864–1920)
German Sociologist and Writer

Weber's prodigious output of writings provided many important foundation stones for modern social thought. Weber wrote extensively on the sociology of religion. In a work of great and lasting importance, *The Protestant Ethic and the Spirit of Capitalism,* he traced the interconnections between those two components of modern historical experience. In other works he examined religion and society in ancient China, India, and Israel. He also wrote on music, on cities, and on the economic foundations of society.

Weber only briefly held regular academic positions, but he was interested in the methodology of social science. His major contribution to that rather academic concern was his concept of *ideal type,* an abstract and general conception of a phenomenon against which real examples may be compared. Ideal types are useful means to isolate the essential features of a complicated situation, and Weber himself used this approach with lasting effect.

It was Weber who formulated the "ideal type" conception of bureaucracy that we still use. He was interested in, and worried about, the growth of state bureaucracy in the Germany of Bismarck and Kaiser Wilhelm II. In considering the problem of political power and authority he differentiated among *traditional* authority, sanctioned by long use and acceptance; *charismatic* authority, characterized by the unquestioning acceptance of the leader (e.g., Hitler) by the people; and *rational-legal* authority, in which impersonal rules and efficient implementation of explicit, consciously agreed-to policies were the operating principles. These ideal types are, of course, abstractions but they help us to sort out the elements present in the real world, whether it is Hitler's Germany or the present-day United States.

INSTITUTIONS IN ACTION ■

THE EPA AND POLLUTION CONTROL

For several years the United States has been spending more than $50 billion per year to control pollution. Governments at all levels contribute about one-third of this total, primarily to construct local treatment plants to clean up water pollution. From 1973 to 1981 nearly $33 billion was spent to clean up or improve some 20,000 sewage and waste treatment facilities. Most of the remaining expenditure, averaging about $35 billion per year, has come from the private economy, mainly from business. This is the cost of compliance with air, water, and toxic waste standards. Some of these standards have been established by Congress. Most, however, at least in their specific detail, have been formulated by the Environmental Protection Agency (EPA). The standards this agency decides to set and the vigor with which it enforces those standards have a major impact on the effectiveness of pollution control efforts.

EPA was created in 1970 as a part of the strong popular enthusiasm in those years for taking serious steps to gain control over the growing problem of pollution. Smog was all around and getting worse. Shocking events like the "death" of Lake Erie as a body of water capable of sustaining fish and the catching on fire of the Cuyahoga River near Cleveland combined with research findings about such matters as the effects of mercury and lead accumulations in the body and of permanent harm from pesticides like DDT scared Americans into supporting costly new programs. In a short space of time several major pieces of environmental legislation were enacted or greatly expanded, and a new era was underway.

The EPA was instructed under the Clean Air Act to set standards for air quality, so that pollutants would not impair health. Unfortunately, this level often could not be reached without, for example, taking all trucks, buses, and automobiles off the streets. The problem had to be redefined as a practical matter of administrative implementation. The EPA sought therefore to establish standards that were reasonable but not perfect. But what was reasonable? With regard to automobile pollution, standards were set initially that could not be met under any technology then in existence. Manufacturers were given time to improve their product and invent ways to meet the standards. Under pressure from industry, Congress allowed further delay in meeting the standards for automobiles, and EPA modified its requirements somewhat as well.

The net effect of these efforts, even with the delays, has been to lower the level of air pollution in the country by a considerable amount. For 23 metropolitan areas the number of days when the Pollution Standards Index (an EPA creation for measuring the concentration in the air of several important pollutants) goes above the primary standard, and is therefore deemed a pollution problem, dropped from 90 days in 1974 to about 40 in 1981. Some cities—such as Los Angeles, San Diego, and Denver—have gotten worse, however, despite the EPA's enforcement program and the still higher auto emission standards established by the state of California.

Control over the pollution resulting from coal-fired power plants, which many regard as the primary source of the "acid rain" that afflicts forests in the Northeast and in Canada, has been rendered ineffective because the EPA set a lax standard in order to protect jobs in the soft-coal mining industry. Thus while the air quality improvement program has had some successes, it has been rather expensive and has suffered in effectiveness because of the pressures on both Congress and the EPA to relax requirements in order to save jobs and unburden business from some of the costs of compliance.

Water pollution control programs have followed a somewhat different path but to a similar end. Most of the public spending has been undertaken by local governments to improve solid waste treatment. The huge expenditures undertaken for this purpose have had an important impact, reducing pollution from urban waste by about 50 percent. Industrial discharges also have been substantially cut as factories install equipment to clean up the effects of their manufacturing processes. There have continued to be periodic scandals of pollution—PCBs in the James River of Virginia, Love Canal near Buffalo, and others. There have also been major triumphs, however; there are once again fish in Lake Erie, for example, and in much of the Connecticut River. But the overall quality of American rivers and streams did not show appreciable improvement during the 1974–1981 period. Gains were countered by losses. A major problem was created by increasingly polluted runoff from farm lands, whose chemical fertilizers and pesticides were finding their way into the streams and underground water sources. Had EPA-administered programs not been in operation, water quality would surely have been much worse, but neither the level of spending nor the zeal of enforcement had yet conquered the pollution problem.

In 1981 the Reagan administration took office determined to reduce the magnitude and scope of federal expenditure and regulation of private business. Regulation, including pollution regulation, imposed costs on American business that were regarded as excessive, responsible for holding down economic growth and thereby reducing the jobs available. As applied to the EPA the Reagan administration's approach involved reducing the agency's budget and staff and easing up on some of the deadlines when particular industrial firms or communities were to meet EPA standards.

In addition, key Reagan appointments to the EPA badly mishandled the agency's relations with Congress and the public. EPA Administrator Ann Gorsuch Burford was cited for contempt of Congress for refusing to provide documents to House investigators and finally resigned in the face of mounting charges that she had been seeking to gut EPA's enforcement machinery. Late in the same year, 1983, the former head of EPA's toxic waste program was convicted of perjury after denying that political considerations had affected her cleanup enforcement.

Although the EPA's reputation improved under Burford's successor, William Ruckelshaus, the general assessment of the Reagan EPA was that it had made little progress in bringing about more efficient pollution control. Many economists and other policy analysts had hoped to see costs and

benefits more realistically assessed and brought into more appropriate balance, but the administration had made little effort to redirect the control programs, either by new administrative directives or by proposals for new legislation.

How much had pollution control efforts cost? We have noted that upwards of $50 billion dollars was being spent each year, but that investment itself affected the economy's performance. Would the economy have grown faster without that spending? Perhaps it would. The regulations helped spur inflation, and they also led to delays and uncertainties for firms as they planned their expansion. Some estimates place the net effect of pollution control on the growth rate at about —0.1 percent; not large, but not trivial.

How much benefit has there been? We can estimate some of the health effects: reductions in heart and lung diseases, for instance. In some instances we may have been paying a large amount to reduce disease. One study concluded that bringing carbon monoxide pollution down to the EPA's proposed standards would reduce sick days for workers at a cost of between $6000 and $250,000 per day. What's a day of sickness worth in tax dollars? How much are we willing to pay to clean up the water and air? How clean does it need to be?

The EPA is at the center of these and many other problems and conflicts. It is the main institutional home of technical experts who develop standards of air and water quality, devise methods of effective monitoring and enforcement, and carry out the rules and regulations, some designed by Congress and some by the EPA itself. At the same time the EPA is intensely and inescapably a political agency, caught up among contending interests and pressured from all sides, including Congress and other elements of the administration, to bend its policies to the needs of various groups. Sometimes it is industries that have contributed heavily to the winning candidates for office and want to be accommodated in return by being excused from meeting what they regard as unreasonable standards. Sometimes it is academic economists or liberal ecologists who fear that major social disaster awaits if the current policy direction is not changed.

The political urgency of environmental programs is not as great in the latter 1980s as it was in April 1970, when vast throngs gathered all across the nation to observe Earth Day and express their concern that public action be undertaken promptly in order to stave off environmental catastrophe. Environmental issues then ranked second only to crime control on the public agenda of important national problems. The energy crisis of the mid-1970s altered the nation's priorities. Inflation, unemployment, and the federal budget deficit largely displaced pollution as the most compelling concern. Moreover, air and water pollution were found to be more complicated, stubborn, and expensive than had at first been realized. Passing new laws and spending substantial sums was only the beginning of a solution, not the end.

And so environmental programs are continuing, long-term efforts to solve, or at least help, problems in society, problems that are also long lived and deep rooted. Like poverty, social security, medical care, military prepardness, aid to agriculture, and a host of other problems, environmental pollution has come to have a permanent place in the American political agenda.

CHAPTER HIGHLIGHTS ▪

1. Bureaucracies are inescapable features of modern life. They make possible the large-scale enterprises of private business as well as the modern state.

2. Public bureaucracy has grown in response to demands for services and the need to regulate aspects of economic and social life. In this process of growth, however, pathologies may arise and bureaucracy itself can become a serious problem.

3. Many professions and skills are represented in the federal bureaucracy. The United States does not have an elite corps of administrators as do some countries, but merit and job protection against political interference are part of the American bureaucratic system.

4. Political conflicts within and among bureaucratic groups are common. Also common is the tendency of administrative agencies to develop supporting linkages with congressional committees and with interest groups.

5. The control of bureaucracy by elected officials is essential if democratic expectations are to be met. But in American politics it is common for elected officials to disagree and, even while both attack bureaucracy in general, to use bureaucratic instruments to advance one set of values over another.

SUGGESTED READINGS ▪

The bureaucracy is generally less dramatic or colorful than Congress or the president, and the literature is not as rich. Modern commentaries on American public bureaucracy include: Anthony Downs, *Inside Bureaucracy* (1967); Harold Seidman and Robert Gilmour, *Politics, Position and Power* (4th ed., 1986); Francis E. Rourke, *Bureaucracy, Politics and Public Policy* (3d ed., 1984); Hugh Heclo, *A Government of Strangers* (1977); Graham Allison, *Essence of Decision: Explaining the Cuban Missile Crisis* (1971); Jeffrey Pressman and Aaron Wildavsky, *Implementation* (1974).

Chapter **17**

THE JUDICIARY

The Judicial Power of the United States, shall be vested in one supreme Court, and in such inferior Courts as the Congress may from time to time ordain and establish.

U.S. Constitution, Article 3, Section 1

"Scarcely any political question arises in the United States that is not resolved, sooner or later, into a judicial question." Tocqueville made this observation about America 150 years ago, but he would probably say the same thing today. The courts have always been unusually important institutions in this country. Not only have they been the chief mechanisms for determining what our property rights and personal liberties are under the law, they have also been active participants in shaping major areas of public policy. In this chapter we will examine how the judicial system is structured, how it operates, and what impact it has had.

THE FUNCTIONS OF COURTS

What does it mean to make judicial questions out of political issues? In the first place, our Constitution established a very complicated government, with three branches and two layers. Quite often, and on very serious matters, one unit of government has political differences with another unit. Such conflicts have to be settled by an umpire, and the courts play this role.

Second, Americans have a habit of taking their differences to court. This is true of everything from simple liability cases—"I'll sue you for medical costs, because I broke my leg when I slipped on the ice on your sidewalk"—to the sweeping reforms that have so transformed American society; the right of workers to form unions, of blacks to vote, of state governments to impose income taxes. The complex institutional structure of American government offers several different avenues that a given legal action can take, and we have always had an unusually large number of lawyers to guide our disputes through these avenues.

Third, there is a vast body of legislation in force, and much of it affords the right to go to court to appeal an unfavorable regulation. The government itself often goes before a judge in order to implement some program. In any case, the more statutory law there is, the more judicial action is taken. Finally, the United States probably has more "judge-made" law than any other nation in the world. In additon to the laws made by legislators—Congress, and the 50 state legislatures, as well as municipal councils—in accordance with the principle of "popular sovereignty," we tolerate judicial interpretation and even reversal of legislature-made law. The decisions judges make also become law, binding on other judges, officials, and the public at large. Moreover, in order to carry into effect what they believe the Constitution requires, judges sometimes propose and even administer specific social reforms—school-busing plans are a recent example.

545

In these four ways, then, the judiciary is very much a part of the political process in America. Umpiring disputes among different branches or layers of government, sitting in judgment on disagreements between citizens or between a citizen and the government, interpreting the meaning of a law and establishing judicial precedents—all give the courts ample opportunity to influence the social, economic, and political policies of the nation.

Settling Disputes

The basic function of the courts is to settle disputes. Citizens sue each other on all kinds of questions, great and small. In 1981, for example, a 24-year-old Colorado man sued his parents for his poor upbringing, seeking more than $250,000 for "malpractice of parenting." Students have threatened suits against professors for poor teaching, and against universities for not living up to their supposed contract to educate them. Also, citizens sue the government. A Cincinnatian filed a federal suit claiming his constitutional rights had been violated because he was not allowed to drive his Sherman tank on city streets. Fans of the Washington Redskin football team were angry about the decision of a referee on a decisive touchdown pass and asked a federal judge to overturn the referee's decision. The government also sues, of course—to condemn property, collect taxes, or most frequently to prosecute people accused of crime.

Of course, most disputes are not bizarre. They are disputes about consequential economic transactions, constitutional interpretation, interstate commerce, and civil liberties and civil rights. Some involve only the parties to the case. Some carry profoundly important implications for the entire society.

Adjudication

The technical term for what courts do when they settle disputes is **adjudication,** which is the power to interpret and apply the law in cases of legal dispute. One citizen says that a law prohibiting school segregation means that public schools cannot discriminate against racial minorities. Another citizen says that this law means that the school board must take action to bring about racial integration in the classroom. What does the law really mean? We go to court and eventually judges determine the answer. Once it is known what the law really means, then people (or school boards) who are not in compliance with the law can be punished or otherwise made to comply. Adjudication, then, not only finds out what the law means but also determines whether individual citizens or government agencies have broken the law.

The more ambiguity in a law, the greater is the likelihood that it will have to be adjudicated. In 1960 there were about 60,000 civil lawsuits filed in federal courts. By 1980 the number had almost tripled to nearly 170,000. Chief Justice Warren Burger blamed some of this sharp increase on sloppy draftsmanship of new federal laws by members of Congress. He has claimed that congressional committees sometimes refuse to deal clearly with the controversial parts of a law and seem to be saying, "Let the courts work it out."

The courts must determine what the law really says or, if there is a conflict between two laws, which one takes precedence. To understand adjudication and how the courts operate, it will help to look at the idea of judicial power, rules of court operation, and what we call the adversary process.

Judicial Power and the Types of Law

Judicial power is the authority to interpret the law—to declare what the binding rules of conduct are—with the understanding that whoever or whatever is affected by the interpretation has the legal obligation to accept the court's version of the law as final.[1] Without this understanding the act of discovering what the law means would be without consequence. It is with *the law* that the courts deal. The law is the source of the courts' power as well as a result of the exercise of that power. However, "the law" is an abstraction. There are actually several kinds of law: constitutional law, statutory law, administrative law, and common law.[2]

Constitutional law The concept of a "higher law" controlling and limiting legislation is a very old one. In the medieval period the higher law was the law of God. By the eighteenth century it had become the law of nature or of reason. What the writers of the U.S. Constitution did was to transfer this concept from the realm of theory to that of law. The Constitution was declared to be supreme law. Constitutional law is composed of the rules set forth in the Constitution proper plus the many decisions rendered by the Court when it has had to interpret the meaning of the Constitution. For example, what does it mean, as applied to some particular set of facts, when the Constitution declares that Congress has the power to regulate commerce among the several states? It is this work of interpreting constitutional provisions in relation to specific cases that constitutes the bulk of what is known as constitutional law. The most important aspect of constitutional law is that it is superior to other kinds of law. As Article 6 of the Constitution says, it is "the supreme Law of the Land."

Statutory law Statutory law is law enacted by a legislature, such as Congress. Statutes may create or revise governmental programs, or they may authorize or prohibit individual actions. They may set forth certain general rules and regulations to cover defined situations, or they may delegate rule-making authority to administrators. The principles stated in statutes are not as general as constitutional principles, but they still have to be interpreted and clarified by the courts. Thus statutory law consists of the statutes themselves plus what the courts have had to say about them.

---

[1] Another attribute of judicial power is the power of the courts to punish people who do not obey its rulings for contempt of court. This power exists in order to protect the process of the court.

[2] There is also what is known as *equity*. This is the power of the courts to prevent a person from committing an act that would obviously injure another person or damage his or her property.

Administrative law   This is a body of rules and regulations that govern the implementation of public policy. Some of these rules are contained in the statutes. Much administrative law, however, is made by administrative agencies themselves in order to carry out the objectives of legislative programs. Although these rules are not made by lawmakers, they have the effect of law. They cannot be in conflict with the statutes that authorized the legislative program involved. Examples of administrative law would be the rules made by the Federal Communications Commission governing how much TV time can be devoted to commercials.

Common law   Common law is judge-made law. It originated in England after the Norman Conquest. Judges began to resolve conflicts by basing their decisions on custom or common sense or reason in the absence of statutes or other legal codes. Early decisions served as precedents for subsequent analogous problems; that is, judges came to consider themselves bound by previous court cases in the same subject area (this is called the rule of **stare decisis**). Common law can be overridden by statutory or constitutional law, however.[3] Since common law looked so much to the past for guidelines, it could be effective only in a relatively static society. After the Industrial Revolution social change was more rapid, new problems arose, and past guidelines became less applicable. Hence the emergence of more statutory law and the rise of more dynamic and active legislatures. Common law still governs many legal relations among Americans in such areas as tort actions (in which one person sues another claiming injury or damage to property), contracts, and real property.

RULES OF OPERATION

Cases and Controversies

When confronted with a social problem, a legislature can initiate remedial action in an effort to solve it. Courts, on the other hand, must wait for someone else to bring a case or controversy to them. They cannot simply go out on their own to deal with a problem. What constitutes a case or controversy? The U.S. Supreme Court has ruled that the following characteristics must be present before a conflict or dispute will be considered to be a case of controversy that may be resolved in a court of law. First, there must be an actual conflict with two parties having adverse interests. This means that the courts will not render advisory opinions on such matters as the constitutionality of proposed laws, nor will they deal with cases in which the parties have feigned a controversy in a friendly suit. Second, one must have the **standing to sue.** Not everyone with money and an axe to grind can bring a suit before an American court. In order to be able to do that, to have standing to sue, an individual must have a sufficient interest in a controversy. Basically, he or she must prove, first, that the interest claimed is a personal one, not simply some abstract notion

---

[3] It was called common law because it applied to all of England, thus overriding local customs or rules, and it was an important early step toward the "nationalization" of government.

shared with citizens generally, and second, that the interest to be defended is a legally protected interest, or right, that is in jeopardy of real damage. Finally, the courts will not accept cases unless there is some remedy available which courts have the power to grant. If they cannot do anything about the problem, the courts will not take the case.

The Adversary Process

Unlike continental European judges, the American judge is not expected to investigate or develop evidence in a case, nor can the judge ask questions of witnesses or steer the course of the proceeding. Rather, the judge is expected to make a decision—or instruct the jury to make a decision—solely on the basis of arguments and evidence presented in the court by the opposing parties. This system is called the **adversary process.** The judge is responsible for making sure that a proper adversary proceeding is carried out: that legally correct claims and charges are entered, that each party is given a chance to present his or her case, that irrelevant testimony is kept off the record, and that illegally obtained evidence is not used.

It can be seen that the adversary process has two major stages: first, the active argument by the disputing parties' lawyers, both motivated by self-interest or the interest of their clients; and second, the disinterested evaluation of the judge, the umpire, who is not actively engaged in eliciting or bringing out the truth (as opposed to finding the truth in what has been brought out by the disputing lawyers).

It is often argued that in our adversary system, no one has the duty actively to bring out the truth and that therefore justice may often not be dispensed. The answer to this criticism is threefold: (1) Admitting that the adversary system is not flawless or perfect, neither is any alternative. If instead we had an inquisitor or judge actively intervening, what would happen if that person was oppressive, lazy, or unjust? (2) Though lawyers are expected to fight for the self-interest of their clients, they are also honor bound by certain ethical rules. They are "officers of the court" in addition to being fighters for their client's interests, and they can be punished if they misbehave. (3) Whatever their motives, lawyers' arguments must focus on the principles of justice and law, and they must persuade that their client's claim is just or is supported by the law. Lawyers are presumed to want to win for their clients, lest they be unable to attract any more clients. Thus it is in the lawyers' self-interest to do as well as possible for their clients. Assuming reasonable competence on the lawyers' part, the adversary process gives each side to a dispute an opportunity to make a case and to refute the other side. Thus each legal dispute finds competing parties, represented by lawyers arguing before a judge (and sometimes a jury). Truth and justice depend on how well this process works.

THE STRUCTURE OF THE COURT SYSTEM

American courts are organized in two distinct systems: federal and state. Each has a distinct jurisdiction, but to some extent they overlap and some kinds of cases may be brought in either state or federal courts. The vast majority of cases are disposed of in the state courts, including most criminal prosecution, divorce, and real estate cases, among others. Our attention here, however, will be focused almost entirely on the federal courts.

At the base of each system are the trial courts where a case begins. Some trials including nearly all criminal cases involve a jury as well as a judge. A trial presents issues of fact—what actually happened—and issues of law—what is the rule that should govern this case. Opposing lawyers call witnesses and ask them questions regarding the factual elements, and they present arguments about how this evidence should be interpreted and what legal rules should apply. In general, the judge decides what legal argument to accept. Then, in the light of what the judge has said about the relevant law, the jury determines what conclusion to the case is best supported by the factual evidence presented. There are some differences between state and federal courts in the way trials are conducted, and procedure differs substantially between civil and criminal trials. The basic point, however, is that factual evidence is presented only at the trial court level, whereas on appeal the only questions that can be raised involve the law to be applied to those facts.

Once a verdict is reached and a judgment rendered by the trial court, the losing party may appeal; that is, it may carry the record to a higher court. If it is a criminal case and the accused person was acquitted, however, the prosecutor may not appeal because to do so would place the defendant in jeopardy twice for the same offense, which violates the Fifth Amendment to the Constitution. There are no juries in appellate proceedings. Appeals in federal courts are heard by panels of judges, usually three for each case. To win a case on appeal, a litigant must persuade the judges that mistakes were make in the trial procedure or that legal doctrine was wrongly applied. A successful appeal will often result in the case being sent back to the trial court for further consideration or perhaps an entirely new trial.

The federal courts and most state court systems have three tiers, and the losing party in an appellate court may try once more (at least) by asking the highest court in the system to review the case. Under the Constitution the U.S. Supreme Court is at the apex of the court system. The Supreme Court has a small original jurisdiction comprising cases in which a state is a party and cases involving foreign diplomats. Those cases begin and end there. It has the **appellate power** to hear appeals from state supreme courts that involve questions of federal law and review cases from the lower federal courts. Since 1925 the Supreme Court has been able to pick and choose among the applications it receives, selecting only those cases for review which, in the judgment of at least four of the nine justices, present significant issues of judicial policy. When that happens the Court grants a writ of *certiorari* (Latin meaning "to be made more certain").

When the Supreme Court accepts a case, it usually hears oral arguments from opposing counsel as well as receiving extensive written briefs. Aided by their law clerks, recent law school graduates who assist in research and writing, the individual justices make their respective assessments and come together in weekly conferences to discuss the cases. Eventually they vote, and when they have decided where they stand, one justice is assigned,

The 1985 Supreme Court was the last headed by Chief Justice Warren Burger, who retired in 1986.

by the Chief Justice if the latter is part of the majority of the Court, to write the opinion of the Court. When that is done, it is circulated among the members. Some may wish to write concurring opinions, agreeing with the outcome but disagreeing with the reasons. Others may dissent, with or without written reasons. Finally the decision is announced, accompanied by a breakdown of the vote, the official opinion, and such other opinions as may be filed. Only the opinion of the Court majority has legal weight, but concurring or dissenting opinions are often important because they may point the way the Court might go in the future when new justices have been appointed.

Only a tiny fraction of the total number of legal disputes ever get to the top of the judicial hierarchy. For instance, in 1982 over 40,000 criminal cases and more than 200,000 civil cases were filed in federal district courts. About 28,000 were brought in that year to the federal courts of appeals (which also hear appeals from decisions of the U.S. Tax Court, the Court of Claims, and the various independent regulatory commissions). In more than 5000 cases Supreme Court review was requested, but it was granted to less than 5 percent of those. The Court actually heard oral argument in 184 cases. Even this load has been thought too heavy, and Chief Justice Burger has been active in pushing for the creation of an additional layer of judicial authority to help the Supreme Court screen the cases that come from the courts of appeals.

The increased volume and variety of cases coming before the courts has resulted in a considerable expansion in the number of judges and quasi-judicial officials to hear them. More than 1000 administrative law judges hear disputes within agencies of the executive branch. Over 200 bankruptcy judges assist federal district judges by handling the complex and often prolonged issues in bankruptcy proceedings. Several hundred U.S. magistrates also assist the district judges and even preside over certain kinds of cases. Specialized courts have been established: the Tax Court, the Court of Claims, the Court of International Trade, the Foreign Intelligence Surveillance Court, and the Court of Appeals for the Federal Circuits, which hears patents and certain other complex commercial cases. Under Article 3 of the Constitution, Congress has the authority to establish whatever "inferior courts" are thought necessary and to increase the number of judges. President Carter persuaded Congress to add 117 district judges in 1978, and a new circuit was established in 1981 to relieve the crowded court of appeals dockets. The Supreme Court still stands alone, however, at the pinnacle of this complicated and growing dispute-settlement structure, and the burden of decision on its nine members is of concern to many thoughtful observers.

Litigants, Lawyers, and Judges

The court system, like the other institutions of government, is not a legal abstraction, but a collection of people engaged in activities and reaching decisions that may involve life or death, millions of dollars, and momentous questions of public policy. The courts do not go and look for cases to decide. They function if and when litigants bring some kind of case to them, and it is important to recognize the kinds of litigants that make the most significant use of the judicial arena. Our concern here is not with most of the many thousands of cases that arise every year involving plaintiffs or prosecutors and defendants. However important most cases are to those involved, they have little significance for others in society unless they present serious questions of what the law means or what the scope of legitimate government action may be. Most cases do not involve issues of policy. Which cases do? And who is involved?

Government cases   When the Justice Department decides to go after a corporation for violating the antitrust laws, it is using the courts as a means to implement policy. A decision to prosecute is only one administrative option; other forms of action may be chosen instead—including looking the other way altogether. The point is that federal officials quite often do go to court to enforce the laws enacted by Congress, and some of those actions may result ultimately in Supreme Court review of what the law means and how it may legitimately be enforced.

Criminal prosecutions are handled in the trial court by the district attorneys of each of the 90 district courts of the country. The defense of people accused of crime may, of course, be handled by private lawyers, but public defenders are used in some districts, and indigent accused persons are assured of some form of defense counsel at public expense. The Justice Department acts as litigator in civil suits for most government agencies, and when government cases come to the Supreme Court, the solicitor general of the United States is usually the government's lawyer.

"I wuz robbed." A second source of important judicial policy cases is, in a sense, a most unlikely one. It consists of individuals who believe they have been wrongly convicted in a state criminal trial and make an argument that their rights under the federal Constitution have been violated. These people are often in prison, and most are poor and file their appeal *in forma pauperis*. A handwritten letter to a Supreme Court justice may (once in a great while) be enough to bring the case under consideration, and the costs of a formal proceeding must be paid by the government. It is in cases like these that many of the important procedural protections now guaranteed to people accused of crime were developed by the Court and imposed upon police, prosecutors and trial judges across the country. Few convicted people are successful in their appeals, of course, but, as in the case of *Gideon v. Wainwright* discussed in Chapter 6, there have been spectacular success stories, and even the slimmest hope inspires some 2500 "pauper" petitions to the Supreme Court every year.

Interest-group litigation A third source of opportunities for judicial policymaking comes from *test cases* brought by organized groups in a conscious and carefully planned effort to get the Supreme Court to shift the direction of current policy by ruling in a particular way. The NAACP is one organization that was able to mount a long-range campaign to alter national policy. Its victories in cases involving racially restrictive housing agreements and school segregation were true landmarks in American legal doctrine. To achieve those goals the organization had to raise money to finance the long process of litigation, identify individuals with standing in court (i.e., with a personal stake in the outcome) to bring the action, recruit the legal talent necessary to present the case, and develop the arguments that would persuade the Court.

More recently many different kinds of citizens groups representing many points of view, from intense liberals to extreme conservatives, have sought to use the courts as instruments to advance their policy objectives. Environmental protection and school prayer are two areas in which litigant groups have been especially active. Many organizations have tried to influence the Supreme Court by filing briefs as *amicus curiae* ("friend of the court") in cases that involve their interests. In the 1978 *Bakke* case dealing with admission quotas to medical school (see Chapter 5), 57 amicus briefs were filed by more than a hundred organizations.

Lawyers on all sides In Washington, D.C., the seat of the national government, nearly 40,000 lawyers are members of the bar and eligible to practice law, and there may be almost twice that many people there with law degrees. Lawyers are prominent in many parts of the political system, but as the courts have become increasingly prominent arenas of policymaking, lawyers have played an expanding role. On the one side there are the government lawyers, including the district attorneys and other prosecutors, the Justice Department, the many lawyers who advise executive branch officials, the legal staffs of regulatory agencies, and so on.

A second group of lawyers are also paid by public funds but, in effect, work for "the other side." We have already mentioned the public defenders who represent poor people accused of crime. In addition, there are the lawyers who work for the Legal Services Corporation, a federally funded program that President Nixon, for one, tried to eliminate, but which has survived to provide legal assistance to poor people in civil matters, such as divorce, housing disputes, and the like. We should also mention the *pro bono* bar, lawyers who donate time to help what they believe to be good legal cases for good causes. Even with such assistance, however, prolonged legal action is expensive, and groups with few financial resources are at a disadvantage in the judicial arena, as they are everywhere else.

The Selection of Judges

Federal judges are appointed for life, so that unless they are impeached—only four federal judges have ever been convicted on impeachment charges—they can be expected to serve for many years. Naturally, every president wants to be careful that each appointee is sympathetic with the general philosophy of the administration. Especially in the case of U.S. Supreme Court appointments, the past record of each nominee is closely scrutinized by every group interested in judicial policy to assess the likely policy directions the person will take once in office. Before it confirms Court appointments the Senate holds hearings at which groups may testify pro and con the nominee, and from time to time opposition to a particular individual has been great enough to block confirmation or force the nomination to be withdrawn. In the late 1960s the Senate refused to confirm three Supreme Court nominees—one of President Johnson's and two of Nixon's.

The Senate in 1970 refused to approve Nixon's appointment to the Supreme Court of Clement Haynsworth, shown here testifying before a Senate committee.

TABLE 17.1

PARTISANSHIP IN JUDICIAL APPOINTMENTS

President	Number of Appointees to District Courts and Courts of Appeals	% Democrat	% Republican
Lyndon Johnson	162	94%	6%
Richard Nixon	224	7	93
Gerald Ford	64	19	81
Jimmy Carter	258[a]	95	4
Ronald Reagan (first two years)	87	2	98

[a] Carter appointed three independents.

SOURCE: Sheldon Goldman, "Reagan's Judicial Appointments at Mid-Term: Shaping the Bench in His Own Image," *Judicature* 66 (March, 1983): 344–345.

Table 17.1 shows that presidents overwhelmingly name federal judges from their own political party. This ensures that newly appointed judges more or less reflect the current political mood, for it is that mood that has elected the president and his supporters in Congress. But judges can be appointed only as vacancies occur; thus President Carter had no opportunity to name a Supreme Court justice. Also, they often stay in office long after the president who appointed them has departed. Chief Justice Earl Warren and Justice William Brennan, Eisenhower's first two appointees to the Court, consistently voted contrary to the president's preferences—to his great irritation.

Partisanship and ideology are not the only considerations involved in naming judges. For much of our history politics was dominated by white male Protestants, and so was the Supreme Court. The first Catholic was not appointed until Andrew Jackson named Roger Taney chief justice in 1836. Woodrow Wilson appointed the first Jew, Louis Brandeis, in 1916, and the appointment was greeted with a storm of criticism, much of it thinly veiled anti-Semitism. No black was named to the Court until Lyndon Johnson appointed the noted NAACP lawyer, Thurgood Marshall, in 1967. Sandra Day O'Connor, appointed by President Reagan in 1981, is the first woman to serve on the Court.

Supreme Court appointments get massive public attention, but the lower courts handle the great bulk of the cases and appointments to those judicial positions often have a large and lasting effect on the policy impact of the federal judiciary. Even though Carter got to appoint no one to the Supreme Court, he was the beneficiary of the 1978 expansion in the number of federal judges, and as Table 17.2 shows, he used the opportunity to expand the number of women and minorities holding judgeships. Moreover, most of those appointees were relatively liberal in their policies, so that when the Reagan administration took office, they found the federal courts to be generally rather unsympathetic to their more conservative policy efforts. In 1969 President Nixon had encountered a similar situation. Ironically, Franklin Roosevelt, a liberal president, was faced and often frus-

Justice Thurgood Marshall was the first black member of the Supreme Court. Appointed in 1967 by President Johnson, Marshall had had a distinguished career as a lawyer for the NAACP and had successfully argued many of the landmark civil rights cases.

Justice Sandra Day O'Connor, formerly a state legislator and judge in Arizona, is the first woman to serve on the Supreme Court. She was appointed by President Reagan in 1981.

TABLE 17.2

PRESIDENTIAL APPOINTMENTS OF WOMEN, BLACKS, AND HISPANICS TO COURTS OF APPEAL AND DISTRICT COURTS, 1963–1982, BY PRESIDENT

President	Total Number of Appoint-ments	Women		Blacks		Hispanics	
		Number	%	Number	%	Number	%
Johnson, 1963–1969	162	3	2%	7	4%	3	2%
Nixon, 1969–1974	224	1	*a*	6	3	2	1
Ford, 1974–1977	64	1	2	3	5	1	2
Carter, 1977–1981	258	40	16	37	14	16	6
Reagan, 1981–1982	87	3	3	1	1	2	2

a Less than 0.5 percent.

SOURCE: Sheldon Goldman, ''Reagan's Judicial Appointments at Mid-Term: Shaping the Bench in His Own Image,'' *Judicature* 66 (March 1983): 339, 345.

trated by a very conservative Supreme Court during his first four years in office.

Shifts in the political makeup of one branch of government often are not matched by parallel shifts in the others. Because the judges serve for life, rather than face periodic reelection, the courts in particular tend to lag behind the changes generated by public opinion and popular election. This means that the role of the courts in the American political system is difficult to bring into harmony with our assumptions about democratic control and popular representation. We will come back to this theme after we have examined more fully the impact the Supreme Court has had on our politics during the 200 years of our history.

THE SUPREME COURT AND PUBLIC POLICY

The Supreme Court has played a significant role in many areas of public policy, defining the boundaries of legitimate government action and establishing the rights of individuals and groups. The Court's decisions grow out of particular cases, as we have seen, but they often have much broader implications and are taken as guiding precedents, not only by the lower courts but in many instances by other branches of government as well. Supreme Court decisions are themselves often the subject of continuing dispute, and it has not been uncommon to see some of the groups that have lost at the hands of the Court go on to try to reverse this result through other political channels. We will look at examples of this process as we consider four broad areas of public policy in which the Court has played an historic role of special importance.

Judicial Review

When the first Congress established the Supreme Court and several lower federal courts in the Judiciary Act of 1789, it said nothing about judicial review of congressional acts, although it did give the Supreme Court power to review state court decisions in certain types of cases. It was up to the Supreme Court itself to decide whether it was to have such power. The Court's initial history did not seem to suggest that it was going to be an agency with great power and influence. When John Marshall was appointed chief justice in 1801, there were few cases before the Court, and Marshall's Jeffersonian political enemies were capturing control of the other two branches of the national government. In fact the Court was caught up in a bitter political fight. Yet within two years Marshall cleverly managed not only to save the independence of the Court but successfully to assert the power of the Court to invalidate acts of Congress.

The Case of *Marbury* v. *Madison*

As early as the mid-1790s, two factions were trying to win the presidency. One faction, the Federalists, was led by John Adams (who became president in 1797); the other was led by Thomas Jefferson. In the election of 1800 Jefferson won a big victory. The outgoing president, Adams, appointed the outspoken Federalist John Marshall as chief justice, and in the last hours before Jefferson took over the presidency, he appointed many other Federalists to positions in the federal judiciary. Because of these so-called midnight appointments, Adams was accused of trying to entrench in the judicial branch the Federalist views that he had been unable to get accepted in the elected branches of the government.

In its last-minute haste to pack the judiciary with Federalists, the Adams administration had not been able to deliver to one William Marbury his commission as justice of the peace for the District of Columbia. President Jefferson's secretary of state, James Madison, refused to deliver the commission, and Marbury turned to the Supreme Court for a writ of mandamus compelling Madison to do so. (A writ of mandamus is an order of an official to carry out a duty which the law has placed on him or her.) Marbury based his claim for such a writ on a congressional law (the Judiciary Act of 1789) that had authorized the Supreme Court itself to issue such writs.

Marbury's suit placed the Marshall Court in an awkward position. It seemed to face two alternatives. It could order Madison to deliver the commission, but if Jefferson and Madison refused to comply with the order, as the Court suspected they would, it would advertise its own powerlessness to the world. Or it could refuse to issue the writ, which would have been to concede Madison's right to withhold the commission and again show the powerlessness of the Court. Marshall avoided this apparent dead end by creating a third alternative, an alternative that in fact gave the Court a much greater power than Marbury had asked it to exercise—namely, the power of **judicial review.**

What Marshall did was to declare unconstitutional the law on which Marbury's suit was based (1 Cranch 137, 1803). Section 13 of the Judiciary Act had given the Supreme Court the power to issue writs of mandamus in original jurisdiction. Original jurisdiction means the power to decide the case in the first instance, that is, without another court having decided the case first. But Article 3 of the Constitution provides that the Supreme Court should have original jurisdiction in only two kinds of cases: cases affecting ambassadors and consuls and cases in which a state is a party. Therefore, reasoned Marshall, Section 13 was contrary to the Constitution and was null and void. The Court had no jurisdiction and could not hear the case.

Before Marshall ruled on this jurisdictional question, he chastised President Jefferson and Secretary of State Madison. He asserted that Marbury did have a legal right to the commission, that Madison had wrongfully withheld it, and that the federal courts (though not the Supreme Court in original jurisdiction) had the power to order Madison to deliver the commission. Marshall deviated from the normal practice of ruling first on the question of whether the Court has the right to hear and decide a case. Had he followed this practice, he would not have been able to assert that the executive branch was subject to judicial control. It was precisely this part of the Court's statement that infuriated Jefferson and his followers, and it was this particular assertion that was protested and debated. The exercise of judicial review over Congress in the form of setting aside a part of a congressional law went almost unnoticed. In addition, Marshall had introduced the notion of judicial review in a case in which its exercise had made his political adversaries in the executive branch appear victorious in the particular case at hand. After all, the Court had not ordered Madison to deliver the commission.

So much for Marshall's political skills. What about his legal justification for holding that the Court had the power to invalidate congressional laws if it found them to be in violation of the Constitution? Unlike most Court opinions, the Marbury decision did not cite a single judicial precedent; and while it referred to the "original intention" of the nation's Founders, it did not attempt to document that intention by citing statements by contemporary observers who had been in the Constitutional Convention or in the ratifying state conventions. Instead, Marshall's method was an exercise in logic. "It seems only necessary to recognize certain principles," he said, "supposed to have been long and well-established, to decide it."

There are three principles that make up the basic theory of judicial review: (1) The Constitution is superior to congressional law; (2) it is the function of the Court to determine what the Constitution means; and (3) laws that conflict with the Constitution must be declared void and inoperative by the courts. Let's take each of these three principles and see how Marshall constructed and supported them.

"The people have an original right," Marshall stated, "to establish such principles of government as shall most conduce to their own happiness." This "original right" of the people to lay down a system of government for themselves and future generations echoed the so-called social-contract theory of the Englishman John Locke, which had recently been used by the American patriots to justify revolution against the British.

As for the second major principle, that the Court has the power to interpret the Constitution, Marshall held that the judicial function is not only to apply the law but also to say what the law is. He reasoned:

1. The judicial power is the power to say what the law is.
2. The Constitution is law.
3. Therefore the judiciary has the power to say what the Constitution is.

By now the groundwork had been laid for the third major principle, that laws that are contrary to the Constitution must be thrown out by the Court. Marshall was not content with simply proving that the Constitution is superior to congressional law and showing that a law that conflicts with the Constitution is void. He felt that he also had to prove that a congressional act that is in conflict with the Constitution and therefore void should not be carried out by the courts. For the courts to give effect to congressional acts that are in conflict with the Constitution would be, he said, "to overthrow in fact what was established in theory." The very concept of limited government, which is the foundation of all written constitutions, implies and dictates that laws that go beyond the limits prescribed by the Constitution shall not be permitted to become legally operative. Also, if both the Constitution and a congressional law, apply to the same case, and they are in conflict with one another, the Court must apply the superior law, namely, the Constitution.

This is how judicial review came to America. Two kinds of controversies have raged about this power ever since the Marbury case. Historians have differed concerning whether judicial review was carrying out the intention of the Founders or was a usurpation of power by the Court. There is not enough evidence to provide a clear answer.

The second controversy is even more consequential. It is about the very nature of democracy. Whatever one thinks was the true intention of the Framers of the Constitution, there can be no doubt that judicial review is now part of the political process. Though it is not used frequently— fewer than 100 Congressional statutes or parts thereof have been declared unconstitutional in the 180 years since *Marbury* v. *Madison*—judicial review has been used in some very significant cases. Often these cases have put a few Supreme Court justices, sometimes only five persons, against the clear majority preferences of Congress. What kind of democracy is it that allows as few as five unelected persons to overturn statutes passed by two houses of a popularly elected Congress and signed into a law by a nationally elected president? Political theorists have long argued whether the very idea of a judicial review is compatible with democratic government. It is an argument we will return to at the conclusion of this chapter.

McCulloch v. *Maryland:* Reviewing State Laws

The congressional chartering of the second Bank of the United States in 1816 was a widely unpopular act. Certain branches of the bank had engaged in reckless speculation and were accused of fraudulent financial practices. Many state and private banks feared competition from the national bank, and in order to protect them several states levied taxes on the operations of the Bank of the United States. Maryland was among those states. The legislature had levied a heavy tax on the bank's Baltimore branch. McCulloch, the cashier of the Baltimore branch, refused to pay the tax arguing that it was unconstitutional. When the state took legal action against McCulloch and the state courts upheld the state law, the bank appealed the decision to the Supreme Court.

The opportunity was presented in this one case to define broadly the powers of the national government and to assert the supremacy of national authority over the states. Chief Justice John Marshall took full advantage of the occasion.

National dominance Chief Justice Marshall wrote the opinion for the Court (4 Wheaton 316, 1819). While he conceded that the state's power of taxation was of vital importance, he declared that it was not unlimited. Thus the Constitution had specifically prohibited the states from laying any duties on imports or exports. Though there was no specific provision in the Constitution that prohibited the states from taxing federal agencies and instruments, such prohibition could be inferred from the nature of the system of federalism and was implied by the "national supremacy" clause. The power to tax implies the power to destroy, Marshall held, and if federal functions could be taxed by the states they would be dependent on the will of the states. This would alter the charter of the American union and would, if applied generally, make the states "capable of arresting all the measures of the government, and of prostrating it at the foot of the states." The Constitution had instead created a system in which the operation of the national government was not to depend on the goodwill of the states.

The McCulloch decision firmly established that the Supreme Court was to be the umpire that would speak with final authority in constitutional issues involving conflicts between the national and state governments. Furthermore, the Court had laid down general principles and guidelines that gave the supremacy clause some clout. No state had any power to "retard, impede, burden, or in any manner control, the operations of the constitutional laws enacted by Congress." In other words, when Congress has enacted legislation in a field where it has constitutional authority, its legislation cancels all incompatible state regulations.

The implied-powers doctrine   Did Congress have the power to charter a national bank? The counsel for the state of Maryland argued that the government of the United States was a government of delegated powers—that is, a government with only the powers specifically granted to it in the Constitution. Nowhere was there any mention of the power to charter a bank. Hence, to charter a bank was to exceed the authority granted the Congress by the Constitution. Marshall responded by referring to general principles as well as to the language of the Constitution. First, it follows from the general nature of things that a government must have all the powers it needs to carry out its responsibilities. Second, Article 1, Section 8, Paragraph 18 of the Constitution states (after having listed a series of delegated powers) that Congress shall "have the power to make all laws which shall be necessary and proper for carrying into execution the foregoing powers." The inclusion of this clause clearly indicated that the Founders intended Congress to have other powers than those that were expressly mentioned, Marshall reasoned. As Marshall put it:

> Let the end be legitimate, let it be within the scope of the Constitution, and all means which are appropriate, which are plainly adapted to that end, which are not prohibited, but consistent with the letter and spirit of the Constitution, are constitutional.

Applying this principle to the case at hand, Marshall held that in order to borrow money, raise an army, and regulate interstate commerce, all of which were expressly delegated powers, it was convenient or necessary for the national government to resort to the means of chartering a national bank. The *McCulloch* v. *Maryland* decision did not assure that every Supreme Court decision thereafter would take an equally broad view of what the national government might legitimately do. In later years the Court struck down acts of Congress on the grounds that they exceeded the constitutional grants of authority. But Marshall's interpretation of implied power eventually carried the day, and as we saw in our discussion of Congressional power in Chapter 14, the limits of constitutionality today are very broad.

Judicial Activism and the Defense of Capitalism

Through the nineteenth century the United States changed from an overwhelmingly agricultural national to an industrial power. This transformation in the character of the society inevitably led to much social tension.

The population expanded, cities grew rapidly and large factories employed veritable armies of workers, often in unhealthy circumstances. As economic power shifted from the countryside to the cities, from farmers and small business to bankers and large corporations, efforts were made, especially by state governments, to place restrictions on business. The industrial elite turned to the Supreme Court for protection, and the Court majority, committed to the ideology of economic individualism, came to the rescue.

The constitutional provisions that allowed the Court to elevate the capitalist principle of free competition into constitutional law were the "due process" clauses of the Fifth and Fourteenth amendments. The latter amendment prohibited the states from depriving "any person of life, liberty, or property without due process of law," and the former contained the same prohibition against the national government.

As a first step the Court held that a business corporation would be regarded as a "person" and thus be eligible for constitutional protection (Slaughter House Cases, 16 Wallace 36, 1873). Then the Court turned to the meaning of "due process." The due process clause can be traced to the guarantee embodied in the Magna Carta that "no freeman shall be taken or imprisoned . . . or in any manner destroyed . . . except by a legal judgment of his peers or by the law of the land." When the due process clause was included in the Bill of Rights, its meaning was clear. The government could not deprive people of their personal or property rights without following proper procedures.

In the last decade of the nineteenth century, the Court read into "due process" an altogether different meaning. The concept of **substantive due process** became a check on what the government could do instead of on the process it had to follow in order to do it, as the phrase had traditionally been defined. Any law that the Court felt was an *unreasonable* restraint on property and liberty could be declared unconstitutional. The application of such a vague judicial test turned the Court into a kind of superlegislature, which overturned laws that sought to bring under control some of the questionable practices of big business. Legislatively determined rates for public utilities and railroads, laws that provided for minimum wages, maximum hours, and price regulations were among the kinds of legislation that the Court felt constituted unreasonable interference with liberty and property.

Not all the justices of the Supreme Court adhered to the substantive due process view. One of those who did not was Justice Oliver Wendell Holmes. Dissenting in the case of *Lochner* v. *New York* (*198 U.S. 45, 1905*), in which the Court had overthrown as unconstitutional a New York law that limited hours of work in bakeries to 10 hours per day and 60 hours per week, Holmes observed:

> This case is decided upon an economic theory which a large part of the country does not entertain. If it were a question whether I agreed with that theory, I should desire to study it further and long before making up my mind. But I do not conceive that to be my duty . . . A Constitution is not intended to embody a particular economic theory, whether of paternalism . . . or of laissez faire.

The doctrine of substantive due process drew support from a majority of the justices from about 1890 until 1937. Much of this period was one of economic prosperity and business success, and the Court's position was reasonably in keeping with the views of the popular majorities that elected Harding, Coolidge, and Hoover to the presidency. But the Great Crash of 1929 and the ensuing Great Depression changed both the economic and political worlds. The idea of corporate immunity from government control was thrown on the defensive as ruined speculators, bankrupt merchants, unemployed laborers, and farmers facing foreclosure joined in the demand for sweeping government action.

As the economic crisis deepened, a governmental crisis grew. The reform administration of Franklin Roosevelt introduced laws to deal with the crisis, but these new laws repeatedly ran into the roadblock of the Supreme Court. By 1935 the Court was rejecting as unconstitutional most of the major innovations of the New Deal. Between 1935 and 1937 it set aside a total of 12 congressional statutes, nearly one-seventh of all the federal laws that had been declared unconstitutional in the Supreme Court's existence. It overturned statutes designed to bring relief to the nation's farmers, the oil industry, the coal industry, and other groups.

The Court majority reasoned that it had no choice. These laws clearly went against constitutional provisions. It appeared to believe that it should ignore the rising tide of public disapproval, congressional annoyance, and presidential frustration. The Court seemed to say that it was above politics and was merely carrying out the "automatic" task of comparing laws with the Constitution and rejecting those that did not fit its provisions. In fact, as events showed, it was wrong. It could not ignore political currents, nor were its decisions inevitable. Other justices would see things differently.

In early 1937, fresh from his landslide electoral victory of 1936, Franklin Roosevelt proposed a bill that would allow the president to add a justice to the Court, up to a total of 15, for every member over age 70. The Court's size had been changed before, but this proposal was greeted with vigorous opposition and got nowhere. In the spring of 1937, however, two members of the Court decided to oppose the New Deal no longer and voted to uphold the creation of the National Labor Relations Board. With a pro-New Deal majority in control of the Court, several of the aged members soon resigned, and FDR, who had not made any Court appointments during his first term, was now able to reshape the Court's membership.

Since 1937 there have been few *constitutional* disputes over the power of the national government to regulate economic activity—though there are certainly plenty of *political* arguments on that question. In this modern period, however, the Supreme Court has come to play an active and vital role in defining and expanding the rights of individuals in American society.

The Supreme Court and Social Citizenship

We introduced the term *social citizenship* in Chapter 5. This term describes the attempt by society to insure that certain basic social rights are available to all citizens—such as livable housing, economic security, a job, education, and even a decent diet. The Supreme Court has been involved in extending and defining social citizenship, especially in attacking various forms of discrimination.

To discuss recent trends in court-protected social citizenship, it will be convenient to discuss the Warren Court (1954–1969), so called for Chief Justice Earl Warren, separately from the Burger Court (1969–1986) named after Chief Justice Warren E. Burger.

The Warren Court was known as an activist court, implying a willingness to break with precedents and to challenge traditional interpretations of what is constitutional. The judicial activism of the Warren Court was in promoting, rather than stopping or delaying, social reform. Again and again the Warren Court took the initiative as the agent of reform when Congress, the president, and state governments were either unable or unwilling to act. This can be seen in the area of racial desegregation.

Racial Desegregation

In the southern states the law demanded segregation of the races in public schools and most other public facilities and services—libraries, parks, swimming pools, buses, and the like. This legally imposed racial segregation had been in operation since the late nineteenth century, and in 1896 (*Plessy* v. *Ferguson,* 163 U.S. 537) the Supreme Court had held that such a policy did not violate the equal protection clause of the Fourteenth Amendment to the Constitution. This clause states that "no state shall deny to any person . . . the equal protection of the law." The Court came up with the so-called separate-but-equal doctrine, holding that the principle of equality had been complied with as long as black people gained access to the same types of facilities or services that were provided for the white people.

For the next half century the law concerning racial segregation remained largely unchanged. As black Americans became better educated, and as they gained political experience and influence through the ballot box and through organization, however, they became more assertive of their right to full equality. The NAACP, convinced by experience that Congress could not be made responsive to its demands, decided to launch a series of carefully chosen suits to widen the range of constitutionally protected civil rights. One of these suits was the famous *Brown* v. *Board of Education of Topeka* (347 U.S. 483, 1954). Chief Justice Warren, speaking for a unanimous Court, ruled that "in the fields of public education the doctrine of 'separate but equal' has no place." The Court asserted that "separate educational facilities are inherently unequal."

With this decision the Supreme Court reshaped the agenda of modern American politics. Although there was considerable political resistance in some parts of the South, after 1954 racial discrimination by law could no longer be accepted as consistent with the constitutional principle of equality before the law. For the more than three decades since the *Brown* decision, the Court has remained actively involved in issues of racial discrimination, not only in schools, but elsewhere in American life, and it seems unlikely that its importance will diminish altogether as long as racism remains a part of American social practice.

One Person, One Vote

Another area in which the Warren Court broke with precedent was that of legislative apportionment. State legislatures had for a long time drawn the boundaries of congressional and state legislative districts with little regard for the number of people in a given district. A legislator elected from a rural district might represent only 25,000 voters, while one from an urban area might represent 10 times that many voters. In some states, boundaries were left unchanged for several decades, resulting in severe inequalities. For more than a generation, reformers had attempted to have the Court intervene in the area of apportionment, but it had consistently refused to do this, holding that the matter was a "political issue" and therefore should not be resolved in a court of law.

In a precedent-shattering case the Warren Court ruled that apportionment issues were justiciable after all, and it began to take jurisdiction in cases involving unfair apportionment systems. The Court's decision in *Baker* v. *Carr* (369 U.S. 186, 1962) unleashed an avalanche of apportionment litigation, along with political efforts by many state legislatures and local governments to redraw their election districts to meet the new constitutional standards. The new standards required that districts be reasonably compact—no **gerrymanders**—and that the "seats in both houses of a bicameral state legislature must be apportioned on a population basis." "Simply stated," said the Court, "an individual's right to vote for state legislators is unconstitutionally impaired when its weight is in a substantial fashion diluted when compared with votes of citizens living in other parts of the state" (*Reynolds* v. *Sims*, 377 U.S. 533, 1964). Thus the "one person, one vote" rule came to apply to both houses of state legislatures, throwing out the practice in some states of assigning seats in one house according to population and in the other using other criteria (such as counties) as bases for representation.

The political impact of the Court's intervention in the area of reapportionment, and its application of the "one person, one vote" rule, has been tremendous. It has broken the domination of many state legislatures by rural and small-town voters and increased significantly the political influence of the voters in big cities and especially suburbs at both the state and national levels.

Reforms in the Area of Law Enforcement

The egalitarian spirit embodied in the Warren Court's handling of the racial segregation and reapportionment issues was also evident in the Court's reforms in the area of law enforcement. Several major extensions of procedural rights were of particular benefit to the poor and the weak. For much of our history people accused of crimes discovered that the Bill of Rights applied only to the national government, whereas most criminal prosecutions and jail sentences were handled by the states. The Fourteenth Amendment had extended those protections against the states, but only in a general way (life or liberty could not be taken away except through due process of law). In the 1930s, as we saw in Chapter 6, the Supreme Court began to incorporate some of the procedural protections of the

Bill of Rights into the due process protection against the states. What the Warren Court did was to increase substantially the number of procedural rights that were brought under the protective umbrella of the Fourteenth Amendment against the states. To say the same thing differently, the Warren Court brought a much greater portion of state criminal procedure under federal judicial supervision.

Before the Warren Court, it was possible in some states to be sentenced to prison without benefit of counsel, and many defendants were too poor to be able to hire a lawyer. The adversary system applies to the area of criminal justice, which means that the prosecutors and defenders are the active finders and presenters of facts. The judges and jurors are not fact finders but have to select the facts from those that are brought out by the two parties to the case. Without a counsel for defense, an ordinary person would be handicapped in investigating the facts as well as in courtroom procedure, cross-examination of witnesses, and so forth. The other side (the police and the prosecutors) would have much greater resources to conduct investigations as well as expertise in courtroom procedures. The Warren Court refused to tolerate this kind of situation, and in the famous case of *Gideon* v. *Wainwright,* described in Chapter 6, it threw out Gideon's conviction, which had been procured without benefit of counsel for the defense. A counsel for the defense, said the Court, is "fundamental to a fair trial," and if need be, a state has to provide a defendant with one.

Not only did a defendant have the right to counsel at the trial; he or she should have access to counsel in the pretrial stages, such as the arraignment and preliminary hearings. As a matter of fact, in the controversial *Miranda* v. *Arizona* case the Court held that before they may even start to question a suspect in custody, the police must inform the suspect of his or her right both to have a counsel present and to remain silent. In this case the right to counsel had become a necessary means of guaranteeing the protection against self-incrimination. The Miranda decision revealed the Court's distrust of convictions based upon mere confessions. The adversary system starts with the assumption that a suspect is innocent until proved guilty, and it is the state's responsibility to prove that the accused is guilty. The protection against self-incrimination means that a defendant has no duty to help build the state's case. Without giving the "Miranda warnings" the police may too easily be tempted into tricking or coercing a suspect into incriminating statements.

The Burger Court

The Warren Court had broken with precedents and initiated reforms, and in so doing, the Court provoked a storm of criticism, protest, and even overt defiance. On two occasions the president of the United States had to call out federal troops in the South to come to the aid of the newly established law of racial desegregation in the public schools. President Nixon came into office pledged to change the direction of Supreme Court decisions. Soon Earl Warren resigned, and Nixon was able to choose a chief justice, Warren Burger, who would reflect his own political philosophy. In succeeding years Nixon made three more appointments to the

Justice William Rehnquist (right) became Chief Justice of the Supreme Court in 1986, replacing Chief Justice Warren E. Burger (left).

Court. The Burger Court did slow down the pace of change, and in some areas it weakened considerably the impact of the Warren rulings. It did not really reverse course, however. It expanded the right to counsel and drastically limited the use of capital punishment. It upheld the extensive use of busing as a tool of school desegregation. The Burger Court decisively rejected Nixon administration efforts to use wiretaps on political groups without getting a search warrant and rebuffed Nixon's claim that the Watergate tapes were protected by executive privilege. Most noteworthy among its activist decisions was the decision in *Roe* v. *Wade*, discussed in Chapter 5, that abortion was a constitutionally protected right.

The Burger Court stepped back from the Warren Court's activist posture, however. It was more sympathetic to the problems of law enforcement and avoided further extensions of the rights of the accused. In several cases involving racial bias it required specific proof of intent to discriminate before upholding a finding of unconstitutional action. It declined to rule that states must equalize fully the financial resources available to each school. In its efforts to draw appropriate lines for constitutionally protected rights, the Burger Court generally avoided sweeping assertions of doctrine and expressed its decisions in very narrow terms. In good part this may reflect the fact that the nine justices seldom agreed and many of their key decisions were almost evenly split.

The Court personnel changes, however. In 1986 Burger resigned as chief justice, and President Reagan nominated Justice William Rehnquist to succeed him. Reagan also named Antonin Scalia to the vacant seat. The new appointments were not expected to change the voting lineup on the Court since Burger, a conservative, was replaced by Scalia, also a conservative. Rehnquist and Scalia were thought likely to add greater vigor to the conservative blue, however, and if Reagan were to have the chance to name another justice, a new majority could be expected to take Supreme Court policy in quite a different direction.

THE SUPREME COURT AND POLITICAL PRUDENCE

At the beginning of this chapter we noted that the Supreme Court must wait for cases to come to it before it can affect public policy, and there are many important areas of policy—defense, for example—where the Court plays little or no role. In addition, the Court's power in the political system is limited in other ways. It has no police force of its own. It has no money of its own. It can refuse to hear cases and thus deny the judicial arena to contending parties—an effective tool against the police, for example. But in most ways the Court depends on broad public acceptance of its actions. If it is not thought to be functioning in a legitimate manner as it interprets the Constitution, it may find its membership changed, its jurisdiction narrowed, or even its constitutional decisions overturned by means of a constitutional amendment. Accordingly, the Court must guard its authority and place by exercising prudent judgment in its decisions.

For example, the Court traditionally has avoided what are called political questions. When it would be inappropriate to override congressional or presidential decisions (e.g., in the area of foreign affairs, particularly military action) or whenever there are no satisfactory *legal* criteria for a judicial determination, the controversy is said to involve a political question, and the Court will not intervene. The provision in the Constitution that the United States "shall guarantee to every state in this Union a republican form of government" will not be enforced by the Court. It has held consistently that whether a state has a republican form of government is a political question to be decided by the political branches of the government. But, of course, it is the Court itself that decides whether something is political in this sense. As we saw earlier, in the one person-one vote decisions the Court was bold enough to take on the apportionment of legislative seats, a topic that had traditionally been thought too political for Court consideration.

On a broader level, members of the Supreme Court are often involved in deciding the extent to which they will actively use their authority to limit what another branch of the government does or to restrict state or local governments. Those who believe in vigorous use of the judicial power on behalf of individual claimants are referred to as *judicial activists*. Those who argue that in a democracy the Court should defer to the popularly elected branches take a position we call *judicial self-restraint*. The Warren Court was an activist Court; the Burger majority more often chose self-restraint.

Ironically, in the 1890–1937 period, when as we have seen the Court generally supported the values of private business against government regulation, the self-restraint posture was advocated by the Court's critics. In the 1930s, in particular, political liberals denounced judicial activism as undemocratic. How in a democracy could judges, whom no one had elected to office, substitute their policy views for those of a popular president and Congress? Later, however, the Warren Court's activism in behalf of racial and other minorities, whom elected officials had failed to treat with justice or equality, was hailed by political liberals. This time it was conservatives who tried to insist on judicial self-restraint.

Judicial activism itself has taken on a new meaning in recent years as federal judges in various parts of the country have intervened to remedy inhumane prison conditions, improve state hospitals, and bring about sweeping reorganization of local schools. In each of these cases some local leaders have protested the judical action, and in 1981 Reagan's attorney general, William French Smith, denounced "unelected judges (substituting) their own policy preferences for the determinations of the public's elected representatives." He said that the courts have engaged in "some constitutionally dubious and unwise intrusions upon the legislative domain."

The humorist Finley Peter Dunne (Mr. Dooley) once wrote, in his best Irish brogue, "The Supreme Court follows th' 'illiction returns," and some political scientists have concluded that indeed the Court has seldom tried to block popular majority wishes or protect unpopular minorities for very long. At the same time, however, there have certainly been groups, whose interests had been neglected by the majoritarian institutions, which have turned to the courts for relief and been successful.

Frank Johnson, a federal district judge in Alabama who made several decisions that effectively overturned traditional patterns of administration in that state, has said: "In an ideal society [humane decisions] should be made by those to whom we have entrusted these responsibilities. But when [other] governmental institutions fail to make these judgements and decisions in a manner that comports with the Constitution, the Federal Courts have a duty to remedy the violation."[4] And Chief Justice Burger has agreed, saying, "if a State is running its prisons or its mental institutions in a way that violates the civil rights of the inmates of those institutions, then it is a judge's duty to act."[5]

---

[4] Quoted by Martin Tolchin, "Intervention by Courts Arouses Deepening Disputes," *New York Times*, April 24, 1977. Copyright 1977 by the New York Times Company. All rights reserved. Reprinted by permission.

[5] Ibid.

THE SUPREME COURT AND DEMOCRATIC POLITICS

By now it should be abundantly clear that the judiciary is fully immersed in the political process. The procedures that courts follow and the criteria of decision judges employ are not the same as those observed in Congress, the White House, or the bureaucracy. But American judges, like other officials, are fully part of the American political culture. They are sensitive to the requirements of democratic theory. They recognize that they must have broad public approval for their courses of action, because if they do not they are likely to find their authority severely undermined by popular political action. We have seen how President Roosevelt unsuccessfully sought, by temporarily enlarging the Court, to alter its policies. After the Warren Court announced the *Brown* school-desegregation decision, numerous efforts were made to reverse or limits its effects. These ranged from proposals to amend the Constitution to a noisy campaign to impeach the chief justice. More recently many attempts have been made in Congress to overturn Supreme Court decisions on school prayer, abortion, and defendants' rights. The Reagan administration endorsed constitutional amendments on both school prayer and abortion, but both were bottled up in a House subcommittee, and supporters of the Court's decisions successfully prevented the proposals from passage. Yet, even though these efforts all

The Warren Court made some politically unpopular decisions that aroused vociferous public reactions.

fell short of their policy objective, they are constant reminders that Supreme Court doctrines are not immutable.

Meanwhile, however, the Court's personnel continue to change. From 1976 to 1986 only two new members were named to the high bench, and during that time the Court was quite evenly split between liberals and conservatives. Inevitably, however, justices grow older. Even after Burger's resignation and Reagan's appointment of Antonin Scalia four others are well past 70. Insofar as these things can be predicted, their replacements, when they are named, will reflect the values of the appointing president, and so the force of public opinion will be felt in helping to shape the policies set forth in Supreme Court opinions.

PROFILE ■

**OLIVER WENDELL HOLMES, JR.
(1841–1935)
Justice of the Supreme Court**

Rivaled only by John Marshall, Holmes was the finest writer of opinions ever to sit on the Supreme Court, where he served from 1902 to 1932. His father was a Boston physician and well-known poet and essayist. Holmes, Jr., served with distinction in the Union army and then took up a career in the law, teaching at Harvard, serving on the Massachusetts Supreme Court, and finally going to Washington. He wrote an important study,

The Common Law (1881), and conducted voluminous correspondence with distinguished people in both England and the United States. It is his Supreme Court opinions, however, which have established his principal claim to our attention.

Holmes was a phrasemaker who could summarize in a sentence what less talented jurists required pages to express. In particular, he articulated some of the first and most eloquent explanations of the free speech provisions of the First Amendment. The "clear and present danger" test was his, and Holmes's opinions in several other cases involving freedom of speech, often written as dissents from the Court's majority, are also memorable.

Holmes believed that on issues involving economic regulation the Supreme Court should practice self-restraint, allowing popularly elected legislatures to work their will. In his time this was a "liberal" position to take, as was his view that the best test of truth was the power of an idea to prevail in a "marketplace" of free debate. Holmes was really more a skeptic than a liberal. He challenged the assumptions of his judicial colleagues and of society at large. He emphasized the changeable character of ideas and beliefs and the undesirability of inscribing any set of doctrines in stone or in Supreme Court opinions. Holmes's skeptical pragmatism, so stylishly expressed, makes his opinions worth reading and remembering.

INSTITUTIONS IN ACTION ■

THE SUPREME COURT AND REAPPORTIONMENT

When Earl Warren retired after 16 years as U.S. chief justice, he told an interviewer: "I think the reapportionment, not only of state legislatures, but of representative government in this country is perhaps the most important issue we have had before the Supreme Court."[1]
The Warren Court had made historic decisions on racial segregation, the rights of the accused, free speech, and school prayer, among other subjects, but the reapportionment rulings were certainly of enormous significance. Moreover, they illustrate especially well the very great impact the Supreme Court can have on the rest of the political system. As we will see, it was precisely the potential seriousness of the Court's impact that worried some of the justices, and raised in an ironic way questions about the proper role of the judicial branch of government in a democracy.

There were several rounds of reapportionment cases. The basic Supreme Court rulings occurred during the early 1960s, but state legislatures and local governments as well as state and federal courts wrestled with specific reapportionment problems for several years thereafter. Today there is little doubt as to what the constitutional requirement is. When state authorities (including local governments as well) establish districts for purposes of electing public officials, those districts must be as nearly equal in population as practicable and must not be designed so as to give marked advantage or disadvantage to any important ethnic or party group. Gerrymanders—districts designed deliberately to favor one set of interests over another—violate the Fourteenth Amendment provision that guarantees equal protection of the laws against state action. One man-one vote, the principle that every individual should have the same power to elect officials, is the constitutional requirement. That principle does

not seem particularly revolutionary in the latter 1980s; nor does it cause very serious problems when, after each national census, districts all over the nation must be reapportioned in order to adjust to shifting populations. In 1960, however, the issue was not only deeply controversial and serious, there did not seem to be any very good solution to it.

The problem of reapportionment was an old one, as old as representative government itself. If democracy rests on consent of the governed, and consent is expressed through the election by the people of representatives, what shall be the units to be represented? Are they to be pieces of territory, such as the American states? The U.S. Senate is based on such units. Or are they to be collections of individual voters, as in the U.S. House of Representatives? And if the latter, is there any justification for having some individuals or groups with more representation than others?

Specifically, because this is how it generally worked out in practice, should rural voters have more seats per capita in legislative bodies than urban voters? In England, especially before the parlimentary reform of 1832, there were numerous "rotten boroughs" that no longer contained many residents but were still entitled to seats in the House of Commons. Usually these seats were controlled by one or a few wealthy magnates who owned the borough land and dictated who would represent it. As of 1793 there were 157 members of Parliament elected by 84 voters, while entire cities such as Manchester had no seats at all.

American legislative constituencies were never as badly out of balance as that, but there were many dramatic departures from equality. In Maryland in 1960, for instance, some rural legislators represented 6500 people, while each Baltimore County representative had 82,000 constituents. In 1955, state legislative districts in Cook County, Illinois, ranged in size from 39,368 to 700,325. Some states had locked population inequality into their constitutions, giving each county at least one seat regardless of its population, for instance, or even making counties the units of representation for the state senate.

---

[1] Bernard Schwartz, *Super Chief, Earl Warren and His Supreme Court: A Judicial Biography* (New York: New York University Press, 1983), p. 410.

In other states and in most local jurisdictions, reapportionment was supposed to be done every decade, but often the requirement was ignored. For example, the Illinois legislative did not reapportion from 1901 until the 1960s despite the clear requirement in the Illinois Constitution that it should do so.

The consequences of malapportionment were generally acknowledged to be substantial. First, rural areas and interests acquired disproportionate political influence. This might sometimes be expressed by passing legislation favoring farmers and small towns, such as farm-to-market road construction, or opposing daylight savings time. In many states it meant resistance to expanded state welfare and education programs, of primary interest to urban interests. In this, however, conservative, propertied interests in the cities often collaborated with "outstate" representatives in order to keep taxes down. In the years following World War II the suburbs experienced rapid growth, and it was these areas that soon contained the most serious cases of underrepresentation.

No one doubted that by 1960 there was widespread malapportionment at every level of American government. Nor was there any question that the assumptions of democracy were seriously undermined by the practice. The question was whether, as a practical matter, anything could be done about it. In 1946 a legal challenge had been brought against the failure of Illinois to reapportion its legislature. By a 4–3 vote and with several different points of view expressed by individual justices, the Supreme Court declined, as Justice Felix Frankfurter's opinion put it, to "enter the political thicket" (*Colegrove* v. *Green,* 328 U.S. 549, 1946). Frankfurter argued that even though malapportionment was a bad thing, the courts were not the appropriate mechanisms for correcting it. This was an essentially political question that should be resolved through the usual political processes of election and legislative action. If the legislators were not doing their job, elect new ones. The problem with this approach, of course, was that new elections from the old districts were not likely to produce legislators who would wipe out the very foundation of their

election—and so a Catch-22 situation was presented. To get the legislative votes needed to redraw the districts, you needed to reapportion the legislature so as to increase the strength of the urban and suburban areas.

In 1955 a group of Tennessee plaintiffs put together a challenge to that state's failure since 1901 to reapportion the legislature. The case moved through the state courts and finally failed. The plaintiffs then went into federal courts, and eventually, in 1960, four (and only four) justices of the Supreme Court voted to hear the case. It was argued the next year, and in 1962, after considerable maneuvering among the justices regarding the various arguments, a decision was announced, with a 6–2 vote, holding that the issue of apportionment was one that could be determined by the courts (*Baker* v. *Carr,* 369 U.S. 186, 1962). That is, it did involve a matter of constitutional rights, and citizens were not compelled to await action from a reluctant legislature. The judiciary could act.

This was the first step. Justice Frankfurter was appalled. "What is actually asked of the Court," he said, "is to choose among competing bases of representation—ultimately, really, among competing theories of political philosophy—in order to establish a frame of government for the State of Tennessee and thereby for all the States of the Union." The factors involved in apportionment are political, often virulent and partisan, and not matters "for which judges are equipped to adjudicate by legal training or experience or native wit."

Having declared that apportionment was a matter on which the courts could rule, the next question the Supreme Court had to face was, what standard ought, under the Constitution, to govern apportionment? In June 1964, Chief Justice Warren gave the opinion of the Court (*Reynolds* v. *Sims,* 377 U.S. 533, 1964). "Legislators represent people, not trees or acres," he said. "Legislators are elected by voters, not farms or cities or economic interests . . . an individual's right to vote for state legislators is unconstitutionally impaired when its weight is in a substantial fashion diluted when compared to the votes of citizens living in other parts of the State." One person, one vote, and the votes should be of the same political weight and value.

Frankfurter had retired from the Court, but his dissenting colleague in the *Baker* v. *Carr* case, Justice Harlan, expressed a similar despair when he wrote that "judicial entry into this realm is profoundly ill-advised." The decision, he felt, would give further support to the view "that every major social ill in this country can find its cure in some constitutional 'principle,' and that this Court should 'take the lead' in promoting reform when other branches of government fail to act. The Constitution is not a panacea for every blot upon the public welfare, nor should the Court, ordained as a judicial body, be thought of as a general haven for reform movements."

The Supreme Court was called upon to rule in several other cases involving somewhat different combinations of factors, but its position was always the same. Legislative districts had to be substantially equal in population. No other basis of representation could meet the constitutional requirement of equal protection of the laws, and so the states redistricted. They redrew congressional district lines to make the U.S. House constituencies of the same size. City councils and county boards were reapportioned as well as, of course, the state legislatures themselves.

What was the result? It is never easy to sort out the effect of one factor from a complex political situation, but some consequences of reapportionment can be identified. First, it was the suburbs that were the big winners, because they were the largest areas of population growth.

Suburban interests generally favored spending for schools, and they now began to get it from the states. On the other hand, they were not especially interested in helping the core cities, and those areas have not fared much better from reapportioned legislatures than under the old system. At the national level, when the urban and suburban areas gained strength they were able, among other things, to insist on an expanded food-stamp program as their price for supporting continued federal subsidies for agriculture. Increased support for consumer legislation, environmental protection, and airline deregulation also seem to have followed from making congressional districts more equal in size and hence less rural and small town in substance.

Perhaps the most important effect of reapportionment, and of the Supreme Court's intervention, has been to remove the issue of constituency inequality and unfairness in representation from the American political agenda. Justice Frankfurter and Justice Harlan, dissenting sharply from their colleagues, feared that the courts would be drawn into a long series of reapportionment struggles involving many deeply felt interests and that the result would be to weaken the credibility of the judiciary to do their proper job. They were wrong. By confronting the issue squarely and setting forth a comprehensive principle, the Warren Court solved a nagging set of problems and cleared the way for representative legislatures to move ahead to other concerns.

CHAPTER HIGHLIGHTS ■

1.   The American judiciary plays an important part in the overall political system, helping to shape public policy and resolving many kinds of disputes.
2.   The court system operates through an adversary process in which contending parties present their evidence and argument in the hope that their conflict will bring out whatever is relevant and true.
3.   The selection of judges has important effects on the decisions that courts make. Since federal judges serve for life, the ability to pick members of the bench, especially of the Supreme Court, can carry with it the power to shape judicial policy for many years to come.
4.   The Supreme Court has been an active participant in many important areas of public policy, especially by means of its power of judicial review.
5.   The Supreme Court has changed its policy positions from time to time as new justices espouse different views and as new political and social forces demand to be heard.
6.   In recent decades the Supreme Court has been active in expanding the rights of minorities and of those accused of crime, and in the process it has been subject to considerable criticism.
7.   The Supreme Court is not immune to the currents of politics and public opinion but it does not always move in very close harmony with the other branches of the national government. Thus it remains the subject of considerable debate concerning the proper role of the judiciary in a democracy.

SUGGESTED READINGS ■

Scholarly examinations of courts and judges often emphasize legal doctrines and principles, but some of the most useful work places these matters in their broader political and social context. Modern commentaries on the American judicial system include: Henry J. Abraham, *The Judicial Process* (5th ed., 1984); Robert H. Carp and Ronald Stidham, *The Federal Courts* (1985); Charles A. Johnson and Bradley C. Canon, *Judicial Policies: Implementation and Impact* (1984); Lawrence Baum, *The Supreme Court* (2d ed., 1985); Donald L. Horowitz, *The Courts and Social Policy* (1977); Bob Woodward and Scott Armstrong, *The Brethren* (1979).

THE CONSTITUTION OF THE UNITED STATES

(*Preamble*)

We the people of the United States, in Order to form a more perfect Union, establish Justice, insure domestic Tranquility, provide for the common defence, promote the general Welfare, and secure the Blessings of Liberty to ourselves and our Posterity, do ordain and establish this Constitution for the United States of America.

ARTICLE 1

Section 1

(*Legislative Powers*)

All legislative Powers herein granted shall be vested in a Congress of the United States, which shall consist of a Senate and a House of Representatives.

Section 2

(*House of Representatives, How Considered, Power of Impeachment*)

The House of Representatives shall be composed of Members chosen every second Year by the People of the several States, and the Electors in each State shall have [the] Qualifications requisite for Electors of the most numerous Branch of the State Legislature.

No person shall be a Representative who shall not have attained to the Age of twenty five Years, and been Seven Years a Citizen of the United States, and who shall not when elected, be an Inhabitant of that State in which he shall be chosen.

Representatives and direct Taxes shall be apportioned among the several states which may be included within this Union, according to their respective Numbers, which shall be determined by adding to the whole Number of free Persons, including those bound to Service for a Term of Years, and excluding Indians not taxed, three fifths of all other Persons. The actual Enumeration shall be made within three years after the first Meeting of the Congress of the United States, and within every subsequent Term of ten Years, in such Manner as they shall by Law direct. The Number of Representatives shall not exceed one for every thirty Thousand, but each State shall have at least one Representative; and until such enumeration shall be made, the State of New Hampshire shall be entitled to chuse three, Massachusetts eight, Rhode-Island and Providence Plantations one, Connecticut five, New York six, New Jersey four, Pennsylvania eight, Delaware one, Maryland six, Virginia ten, North Carolina five, South Carolina five, and Georgia three.

When vacancies happen in the Representation from any State, the Executive Authority thereof shall issue Writs of Election to fill such Vacancies.

The House of Representatives shall chuse their Speaker and other Officers; and shall have the sole Power of Impeachment.

Section 3

(*The Senate, How Constituted, Impeachment Trials*)

The Senate of the United States shall be composed of Two Senators from each State, chosen by the Legislature thereof, for six Years; and each Senator shall have one Vote.

Immediately after they shall be assembled in Consequence of the first Election, they shall be divided as equally as may be into three Classes. The Seats of the Senators of the first Class shall be vacated at the Expiration of the second Year, of the second Class at the Expiration of the fourth Year, and of the third Class at the Expiration of the sixth Year, so that one third may be chosen every second Year; and if Vacancies happen by Resignation, or otherwise during the Recess of the Legislature of any State, the Executive thereof may make temporary Appointments until the next Meeting of the Legislature, which shall then fill such Vacancies.

No Person shall be a Senator who shall not have attained to the Age of thirty Years, and been nine Years a Citizen of the United States, and who shall not, when elected, be an Inhabitant of that State for which he shall be chosen.

The Vice-President of the United States shall be President of the Senate, but shall have no Vote, unless they be equally divided.

The Senate shall chuse their other Officers, and also a President pro tempore, in the Absence of the Vice-President, or when he shall exercise the Office of the President of the United States.

The Senate shall have the sole power to try all impeachments. When sitting for that Purpose, they shall be on Oath or Affirmation. When the President of the United States [is tried] the Chief Justice shall preside: And no Person shall be convicted without the Concurrence of two thirds of the Members present.

Judgment in Cases of Impeachment shall not extend further than to removal from Office, and disqualification to hold and enjoy any Office of honor, Trust or Profit under the United States: but the Party convicted shall nevertheless be liable and subject to Indictment, Trial, Judgment and Punishment, according to Law.

Section 4
(Election of Senators and Representatives)

The Times, Places and Manner of holding Elections for Senators and Representatives, shall be prescribed in each State by the Legislature thereof; but the Congress may at any time by Law make or alter such Regulations, except as to the Places of chusing Senators.

The Congress shall assemble at least once in every Year, and such Meeting shall be on the first Monday in December, unless they shall by Law appoint a different Day.

Section 5
(Quorum, Journals, Meetings, Adjournments)

Each House shall be the Judge of the Elections, Returns and Qualifications of its own Members, and a Majority of each shall constitute a Quorum to do Business; but a smaller Number may adjourn from day to day, and may be authorized to compel the Attendance of absent Members, in such Manner, and under such Penalties as each House may provide.

Each House may determine the Rules of its Proceedings, punish its Members for disorderly Behaviour, and, with the Concurrence of two thirds, expel a Member.

Each House shall keep a Journal of its Proceedings, and from time to time publish the same, excepting such Parts as may in their Judgment require Secrecy; and the Yeas and Nays of the Members of either House on any question shall, at the Desire of one fifth of those Present, be entered on the Journal.

Neither House, during the Session of Congress, shall, without the Consent of the other, adjourn for more than three days, nor to any other Place than that in which the two Houses shall be sitting.

Section 6
(Compensation, Privileges, Disabilities)

The Senators and Representatives shall receive a Compensation for their Services, to be ascertained by Law, and paid out of the Treasury of the United States. They shall in all Cases, except Treason, Felony and Breach of the Peace, be privileged from Arrest during their Attendance at the Session of their respective Houses, and in going to and returning from the same; and for any Speech or Debate in either House, they shall not be questioned in any other Place.

No Senator or Representative shall, during the Time for which he was elected, be appointed to any civil Office under the Authority of the United States, which shall have been created or the Emoluments whereof shall have been encreased during such time; and no Person holding any Office under the United States, shall be a member of either House during his Continuance in Office.

Section 7
(Procedure in Passing Bills and Resolutions)

All Bills for raising Revenue shall originate in the House of Representatives; but the Senate may propose or concur with Amendments as on other Bills.

Every Bill which shall have passed the House of Representatives and the Senate, shall, before it becomes a Law, be presented to the President of the United States; if he approves he shall sign it, but if not he shall return it, with his Objections to that House in which it shall have originated, who shall enter the Objections at large on their Journal, and proceed to reconsider it. If after such Reconsideration two thirds of that House shall agree to pass the Bill, it shall be sent, together with the Objections, to the other House, by which it shall likewise be reconsidered, and if approved by two thirds of that House, it shall become a Law. But in all such Cases the Votes of both Houses shall be determined by Yeas and Nays, and the Names of the Persons voting for and against the Bill shall be entered on the Journal of each House respectively. If any Bill shall not be returned by the President within ten Days (Sundays excepted) after it shall have been presented to him, the Same shall be a Law, in like Manner as if he had signed it, unless the Congress by their Adjournment prevent its Return, in which Case it shall not be a Law.

Every Order, Resolution, or Vote to which the Concurrence of the Senate and House of Representatives may be necessary (except on a question of Adjournment) shall be presented to the President of the United States; and before the same shall take Effect, shall be approved by him, or being disapproved by him, shall be repassed by two thirds of the Senate and House of Representatives, according to the Rules and Limitations prescribed in the Case of a Bill.

Section 8
(Powers of Congress)

The Congress shall have the Power To lay and collect Taxes, Duties, Imports and Excises, to pay the Debts and provide for the common Defence and general Welfare of the United States; but all Duties, Imposts and Excises shall be uniform throughout the United States.

To borrow Money on the credit of the United States;

To regulate Commerce with foreign Nations and among the several States, and with the Indian Tribes;

To establish an uniform Rule of Naturalization, and uniform Laws on the subject of Bankruptcies throughout the United States;

To Coin Money, regulate the Value thereof, and of foreign Coin, and fix the Standards of Weights and Measures;

To provide for the Punishment of counterfeiting the Securities and current Coin of the United States;

To establish Post Offices and post Roads;

To promote the Progress of Science and useful Arts, by securing for limited Times to Authors and Inventors the exclusive Right to their respective Writings and Discoveries;

To constitute Tribunals inferior to the supreme Court;

To define and punish Piracies and Felonies committed on the high Seas, and Offences against the Law of Nations;

To declare War, grant Letters of Marque and Reprisal, and make Rules concerning Captures on Land and Water;

To raise and support Armies, but no Appropriation of Money to that Use shall be for a longer Term than two Years;

To provide and maintain a Navy;

To make Rules for Government and Regulation of the land and naval Forces;

To provide for calling forth the Militia to execute the Laws of the Union, suppress Insurrections and repel Invasions;

To provide for organizing, arming, and disciplining the Militia, and for governing such Part of them as may be employed in the Service of the United States, reserving to the States respectively, the Appointment of the Officers, and the Authority of training the Militia according to the discipline prescribed by Congress;

To exercise exclusive Legislation in all Cases whatsoever, over such District (not exceeding ten Miles square) as may, by Cession of particular States, and the Acceptance of Congress, become the Seat of the Government of the United States, and to exercise like Authority over all Places purchased by the Consent of the Legislature of the States in which the Same shall be, for the Erection of Forts, Magazines, Arsenals, dock-Yards, and other needful Buildings—And

To make all Laws which shall be necessary and proper for carrying into Execution for foregoing Powers, and all other Powers vested by this Constitution in the Government of the United States, or in any Department or Officer thereof.

Section 9
(Limitation upon Powers of Congress)

The Migration or Importation of such Persons as any of the States now existing shall think proper to admit, shall not be prohibited by the Congress prior to the Year one thousand eight hundred and eight, but a Tax or duty may be imposed on such Importation, not exceeding ten dollars for each Person.

The Privilege of the Writ of Habeas Corpus shall not be suspended, unless when in Cases of Rebellion or Invasion the public Safety may require it.

No Bill of Attainder or ex post facto Law shall be passed.

No Capitation, or other direct, Tax shall be laid, unless in Proportion to the Census or Enumeration herein before directed to be taken.

No Tax or Duty shall be laid on Articles, exported from any State.

No Preference shall be given by any Regulation of Commerce or Revenue to the Ports of one State over those of another; nor shall Vessels bound to, or from, one State, be obliged to enter, clear, or pay Duties in another.

No Money shall be drawn from the Treasury, but in Consequence of Appropriations made by Law; and a regular Statement and Account of the Receipts and Expenditures of all public Money shall be published from time to time.

No title of Nobility shall be granted by the United States: And no Person holding any Office of Profit or Trust under them, shall, without the Consent of the Congress, accept of any present, Emolument, Office, or Title, of any kind whatever, from any King, Prince, or foreign State.

Section 10
(Restrictions upon Powers of States)

No State shall enter into any Treaty, Alliance, or Confederation; grant Letters of Marque and Reprisal; coin Money; emit Bills of Credit; make any Thing but gold and silver Coin a Tender in payment of Debts; pass any Bill of Attainder, ex post facto Law, or Law impairing the Obligation of Contracts, or grant any Title of Nobility.

No State shall, without the Consent of the Congress, lay any Imposts or Duties on Imports or Exports, except what may be absolutely necessary for executing its inspection Laws: and the net Produce of all Duties and Imposts, laid by any State on Imports or Exports, shall be for the Use of the Treasury of the United States; and all such Laws shall be subject to the Revision and Control of [the] Congress.

No State shall, without the Consent of Congress, lay any Duty of Tonnage, keep Troops, or Ships of War in time of Peace, enter into any Agreement or Compact with another State, or with a foreign Power, or engage in War, unless actually invaded, or in such imminent Danger as will not admit of delay.

ARTICLE 2

Section 1
(*Executive Power, Election, Qualifications of the President*)
The executive Power shall be vested in a President of the United States of America. He shall hold his Office during the Term of four Years, and, together with the Vice-President, chosen for the same Term, be selected as follows:

Each State shall appoint, in such Manner as the Legislature thereof may direct, a Number of Electors, equal to the whole Number of Senators and Representatives to which the State may be entitled in the Congress: but no Senator or Representative, or Person holding an Office of Trust or Profit under the United States, shall be appointed an Elector.

The Electors shall meet in their respective States, and vote by Ballot for two Persons of whom one at least shall not be an Inhabitant of the same State with themselves. And they shall make a List of all the Persons voted for, and of the Number of Votes for each; which List they shall sign and certify, and transmit sealed to the Seat of the Government of the United States, directed to the President of the Senate. The President of the Senate shall, in the Presence of the Senate and House of Representatives, open all the Certificates, and the Votes shall then be counted. The Person having the greatest Number of Votes shall be the President, if such Number be a Majority of the whole Number of Electors appointed; and if there be more than one who have such Majority, and have an equal Number of Votes, then the House of Representatives shall immediately chuse by Ballot one of them for President; and if no Person have a Majority, then from the five highest in the List the said House in like Manner chuse the President. But in chusing the President, the Votes shall be taken by States, the Representation from each State having one Vote; A quorum for this purpose shall consist of a Member or Members

from two thirds of the States, and a Majority of all the States shall be necessary to a Choice. In every Case, after the choice of the President, the Person having the greatest Number of Votes of the Electors shall be the Vice-President. But if there should remain two or more who have equal Votes, the Senate shall chuse from them by Ballot the Vice-President.

The Congress may determine the Time of chusing the Electors, and the Day on which they shall give their Votes; which Day shall be the same throughout the United States.

No person except a natural born Citizen, or a Citizen of the United States at the time of the Adoption of this Constitution, shall be eligible to the Office of President; neither shall any Person be eligible to that Office who shall not have attained to the Age of thirty five Years, and been fourteen Years a Resident within the United States.

In Case of the Removal of the President from Office, or of his Death, Resignation, or Inability to discharge the Powers and Duties of the said Office, the Same shall devolve on the Vice-President, and the Congress may by Law provide for the Case of Removal, Death, Resignation or Inability, both of the President and Vice-President, declaring what Officer shall then act as President, and such Officer shall act accordingly, until the Disability be removed, or a President shall be elected.

The President shall, at stated Times, receive for his Services, a Compensation, which shall neither be encreased nor diminished during the Period for which he shall have been elected, and he shall not receive within that Period any other Emolument from the United States, or any of them.

Before he entered on the Execution of his Office, he shall take the following Oath of Affirmation:—"I do solemnly swear (or affirm) that I will faithfully execute the Office of the President of the United States, and will to the best of my Ability, preserve, protect and defend the Constitution of the United States."

Section 2
(*Powers of the President*)
The President shall be Commander in Chief of the Army and Navy of the United States, and the Militia of the several States, when called into the actual Service of the United States; he may require the Opinion, in writing, of the principal Officer in each of the executive Departments, upon any subject relating to the Duties of their respective Offices, and he shall have Power to grant Reprieves and Pardons for Offences against the United States, except in Cases of Impeachment.

He shall have Power, by and with the Advice and Consent of the Senate, to make Treaties, provided two thirds of the Senators present concur; and he shall nominate, and by and with the Advice and Consent of the Senate, shall appoint Ambassadors, other public Ministers and Consuls, Judges of the supreme Court, and all other Officers of the United States, whose Appointments are not herein otherwise provided for, and which shall be established by Law: but the Congress may by Law vest the Appointment of such inferior Officers, as they think proper in the President alone, in the Courts of Law, or in the Heads of Departments.

The President shall have Power to fill up all Vacancies that may happen during the Recess of the Senate, by granting Commissions which shall expire at the End of their next Session.

Section 3
(Powers and Duties of the President)

He shall from time to time give to the Congress Information of the State of the Union, and recommend to their Consideration such Measures as he shall judge necessary and expedient; he may, on extraordinary Occasions, convene both Houses, or either of them, and in Case of Disagreement between them, with Respect to the Time of Adjournment, he may adjourn them to such Time as he shall think proper; he shall receive Ambassadors and other public Ministers; he shall take Care that the Laws be faithfully executed, and shall commission all the Officers of the United States.

Section 4
(Impeachment)

The President, Vice-President and all civil Officers of the United States, shall be removed from Office on Impeachment for, and Conviction of, Treason, Bribery, or other high crimes and Misdemeanors.

ARTICLE 3

Section 1
(Judicial Power, Tenure of Office)

The judicial Power of the United States, shall be vested in one supreme Court, and in such inferior Courts as the Congress may from time to time ordain and establish. The judges, both of the supreme and inferior Courts, shall hold their Offices during good Behavior, and shall, at stated Times, receive for their Services, a Compensation, which shall not be diminished during their Continuance in Office.

Section 2
(Jurisdiction)

The judicial Power shall extend to all Cases in Law and Equity, arising under this Constitution, the Laws of the United States, and Treaties made, or which shall

be made, under their Authority;—to all Cases affecting Ambassadors, other public Ministers and Consuls;—to all Cases of admiralty and maritime Jurisdiction;—to Controversies to which the United States shall be a Party;—to Controversies between two or more States;—between a State and Citizens of another State;—between Citizens of different States;—between Citizens of the same State claiming Lands under Grants of different States, and between a State, or the Citizens thereof, and foreign States, Citizens or Subjects.

In all Cases affecting Ambassadors, other public Ministers and Consuls, and those in which a State shall be Party, the supreme Court shall have original Jurisdiction. In all the other Cases before mentioned, the supreme Court shall have appellate Jurisdiction, both as to Law and Fact, with such Exceptions, and under such Regulations as the Congress shall make.

The Trial of all Crimes, except in Cases of Impeachment, shall be by Jury; and such Trial shall be held in the State where the said Crimes shall have been committed; but when not committed within any State, the Trial shall be at such Place or Places as the Congress may by Law have directed.

Section 3
(Treason, Proof and Punishment)

Treason against the United States, shall consist only in levying War against them, or in adhering to their Enemies; giving them Aid and Comfort. No Person shall be convicted of Treason unless on the Testimony of two Witnesses to the same overt Act, or on Confession in open Court.

The Congress shall have Power to declare the Punishment of Treason, but no Attainder of Treason shall work Corruption of Blood, or Forfeiture except during the Life of the Person attainted.

ARTICLE 4

Section 1
(Faith and Credit Among States)

Full Faith and Credit shall be given in each State to the public Acts, Records, and judicial Proceedings of every other State. And the Congress may by general Laws prescribe the Manner in which such Acts, Records and Proceedings shall be proved, and the Effect thereof.

Section 2
(Privileges and Immunities, Fugitives)

The citizens of each State shall be entitled to all Privileges and Immunities of Citizens in the several States.

A Person charged in any State with Treason, Felony,

or other Crime, who shall flee from Justice, and be found in another State, shall on Demand of the executive Authority of the State from which he fled, be delivered up, to be removed to the State having jurisdiction of the Crime.

No person held to Service or Labour in one State, under the Laws thereof, escaping into another, shall, in Consequence of any Law or Regulation therein, be discharged from such Service or Labour, but shall be delivered up on Claim of the Party to whom such Service or Labour may be due.

Section 3
(Admission of New States)

New States may be admitted by the Congress into this Union; but no new State shall be formed or erected within the Jurisdiction of any other State; nor any state be formed by the Junction of two or more States, or Parts of States, without the Consent of the Legislatures of the States concerned as well as of the Congress.

The Congress shall have Power to dispose of and make all needful Rules and Regulations respecting the Territory or other Property belonging to the United States; and nothing in this Constitution shall be so construed as to Prejudice any Claims of the United States, or of any particular State.

Section 4
(Guarantee of Republican Government)

The United States shall guarantee to every State in this Union a Republican Form of Government, and shall protect each of them against Invasion; and on Application of the Legislature, or of the Executive (when the Legislature cannot be convened) against domestic Violence.

ARTICLE 5

(Amendment of the Constitution)

The Congress, whenever two thirds of both Houses shall deem it necessary, shall propose Amendments to this Constitution, or, on the Application of the Legislatures of two thirds of the several States, shall call a Convention for proposing Amendments, which, in either Case, shall be valid to all Intents and Purposes, as Part of this Constitution, when ratified by the Legislatures of three fourths of the several States, or by Conventions in three fourths thereof, as the one or the other Mode of Ratification may be proposed by the Congress; Provided that no Amendment which may be made prior to the Year One Thousand eight hundred and eight shall in any Manner affect the first and fourth Clauses in the Ninth Section of the first Article, and that no state, with-

out its Consent, shall be deprived of its equal Suffrage in the Senate.

ARTICLE 6

(Debts, Supremacy, Oath)

All Debts contracted and Engagements entered into, before the Adoption of this Constitution, shall be as valid against the United States under this Constitution, as under the Confederation.

This Constitution, and the Laws of the United States which shall be made in Pursuance thereof; and all Treaties made, or which shall be made, under the Authority of the United States, shall be the supreme Law of the Land; and the Judges in every State be bound thereby, any Thing in the Constitution or Laws of any State to the Contrary notwithstanding.

The Senators and Representatives before mentioned, and the Members of the several State Legislatures, and all executive and judicial Officers, both of the United States and of the several States, shall be bound by Oath or Affirmation, to support this Constitution, but no religious Test shall ever be required as a Qualification to any Office or public Trust under the United States.

ARTICLE 7

(Ratification and Establishment)

The Ratification of the Conventions of nine States, shall be sufficient for the Establishment of this Constitution between the States so ratifying the Same. Done in Convention by the Unanimous Consent of the States present the Seventeenth Day of September in the Year of our Lord one thousand seven hundred and Eighty seven and of the Independence of the United States of America the Twelfth In witness whereof We have hereunto subscribed our Names.

Go. Washington
Presidt and deputy from Virginia

New Hampshire	John Langdon
	Nicholas Gilman
Massachusetts	Nathaniel Gorham
	Rufus King
Connecticut	Wm Saml Johnson
	Roger Sherman
New York	Alexander Hamilton

New Jersey	Wil: Livingston
	David Brearley
	Wm Paterson
	Jona: Dayton
Pennsylvania	B. Franklin
	Thomas Mifflin
	Robt. Morris
	Geo. Clymer
	Thos. FitzSimons
	Jared Ingersoll
	James Wilson
	Gouv Morris
Delaware	Geo. Read
	Gunning Bedford jun
	John Dickinson
	Richard Bassett
	Jaco: Broom
Maryland	James McHenry
	Dan of St Thos. Jenifer
	Danl Carroll
Virginia	John Blair
	James Madison Jr.
North Carolina	Wm Blount
	Richd Dobbs Spaight
	Hu Williamson
South Carolina	J. Rutledge
	Charles Cotesworth Pinckney
	Charles Pinckney
	Pierce Butler
Georgia	William Few
	Abr Baldwin

AMENDMENTS TO THE CONSTITUTION

(The first ten amendments, known as the Bill of Rights, were proposed by Congress on September 25, 1789; ratified and adoption certified on December 15, 1791.)

AMENDMENT I

(Freedom of Religion, of Speech, of the Press, and Right of Petition)

Congress shall make no law respecting an establishment of religion, or prohibiting the free exercise thereof; or abridging the freedom of speech, or of the press; or the right of the people peaceably to assemble, and to petition the Government for a redress of grievances.

AMENDMENT II

(Right to Keep and Bear Arms)

A well regulated Militia being necessary to the security of a free State, the right of the people to keep and bear Arms, shall not be infringed.

AMENDMENT III

(Quartering of Soldiers)

No Soldier shall, in time of peace be quartered in any house, without the consent of the Owner, nor in time of war, but in a manner to be prescribed by law.

AMENDMENT IV

(Security from Unwarrantable Search and Seizure)

The right of the people to be secure in their persons, houses, papers, and effects, against unreasonable searches and seizures, shall not be violated, and no Warrants shall issue, but upon probable cause, supported by Oath of affirmation, and particularly describing the place to be searched, and the persons or things to be seized.

AMENDMENT V

(Rights of Accused in Criminal Proceedings)

No person shall be held to answer for a capital, or otherwise infamous crime, unless on a presentment or indictment of a Grand Jury, except in cases arising in the land or naval forces, or in the Militia, when in actual service in time of War or public danger; nor shall any person be subjected for the same offense to be twice put in jeopardy of life or limb; nor shall be compelled in any criminal case to be a witness against himself, nor be deprived of life, liberty, or property, without due process of law; nor shall private property be taken for public use, without just compensation.

AMENDMENT VI

(Right to Speedy Trial, Witnesses, etc.)

In all criminal prosecutions, the accused shall enjoy the right to a speedy and public trial, by an impartial jury of the State and district wherein the crime shall have been committed, which district shall have been previously ascertained by law, and to be informed of the nature and cause of the accusation; to be confronted with the witnesses against him; to have compulsory process for obtaining witnesses in his favor, and to have the Assistance of Counsel for his defence.

AMENDMENT VII

(Trial by Jury in Civil Cases)

In Suits at common law, where the value in controversy shall exceed twenty dollars, the right of trial by jury shall be preserved, and no fact tried by a jury, shall be otherwise reexamined in any Court of the United States, than according to the rules of the common law.

AMENDMENT VIII

(Bails, Fines, Punishments)

Excessive bail shall not be required, nor excessive fines imposed, nor cruel and unusual punishments inflicted.

AMENDMENT IX

(Reservation of Rights of the People)

The enumeration in the Constitution, of certain rights, shall not be construed to deny or disparage others retained by the people.

AMENDMENT X

(Powers Reserved to States or People)

The powers not delegated to the United States by the Constitution, nor prohibited by it to the States, are reserved to the States respectively, or to the people.

AMENDMENT XI

(Proposed by Congress on March 4, 1793; declared ratified on January 8, 1798.)
(Restriction of Judicial Power)

The Judicial power of the United States shall not be construed to extend to any suit in law or equity, commenced or prosecuted against one of the United States by Citizens of another State, or by Citizens or Subjects of any Foreign State.

AMENDMENT XII

(Proposed by Congress on December 9, 1803; declared ratified on September 25, 1804.)
(Election of President and Vice-President)

The Electors shall meet in their respective states, and vote by ballot for President and Vice-President, one of whom, at least, shall not be an inhabitant of the same state with themselves; they shall name in their ballots the person voted for as President, and in distinct ballots the person voted for as Vice-President and they shall make distinct lists of all persons voted for as President, and of all persons voted for as Vice-President, and of the number of votes for each, which lists they shall sign and certify, and transmit sealed to the seat of the government of the United States, directed to the President of the Senate;—The President of the Senate shall, in the presence of the Senate and House of Representatives, open all the certificates and the votes shall then be counted;—The person having the greatest number of votes for President, shall be the President, if such number be a majority of the whole number of Electors appointed; and if no person have such majority, then from the persons having the highest numbers not exceeding three on the list of those voted for as President, the House of Representatives shall choose immediately, by ballot, the President. But in choosing the President, the votes shall be taken by states, the representation from each state having one vote; a quorum for this purpose shall consist of a member or members from two-thirds of the states, and a majority of all the states shall be necessary to a choice. And if the House of Representatives shall not choose a President whenever the right of choice shall devolve upon them, before the fourth day of March next following, then the Vice-President shall act as President, as in the case of the death or other constitutional disability of the President.—The person having the greatest number of votes as Vice-President, shall be the Vice-President, if such number be a majority of the whole number of Electors appointed, and if no person have a majority, then from the two highest numbers on the list, the Senate shall choose the Vice-President; a quorum for the purpose shall consist of two-thirds of the whole number of Senators, and a majority of the whole number shall be necessary to a choice. But no person constitutionally ineligible to the office of President shall be eligible to that of Vice-President of the United States.

AMENDMENT XIII

(Proposed by Congress on January 31, 1865; declared ratified on December 18, 1865.)

Section 1
(Abolition of Slavery)

Neither slavery nor involuntary servitude, except as a punishment for a crime whereof the party shall have been duly convicted, shall exist within the United States, or any place subject to their jurisdiction.

Section 2

(*Power to Enforce This Article*)

Congress shall have the power to enforce this article by appropriate legislation.

AMENDMENT XIV

(*Proposed by Congress on June 16, 1866; declared ratified on July 28, 1868.*)

Section 1

(*Citizenship Rights Not to Be Abridged by States*)

All persons born or naturalized in the United States, and subject to the jurisdiction thereof, are citizens of the United States and of the State wherein they reside. No State shall make or enforce any law which shall abridge the privileges or immunities of citizens of the United States; nor shall any State deprive any person of life, liberty, or property, without due process of law; nor deny to any person within its jurisdiction the equal protection of the laws.

Section 2

(*Appointment of Representatives in Congress*)

Representatives shall be apportioned among the several States according to their respective numbers, counting the whole number of persons in each State, excluding Indians not taxed. But when the right to vote at any election for the choice of electors for President and Vice-President of the United States, Representatives in Congress, the Executive and Judicial officers of a State, or the members of the Legislature thereof, is denied to any of the male inhabitants of such State, being twenty-one years of age, and citizens of the United States, or in any way abridged, except for participation in rebellion or other crime, the basis of representation therein shall be reduced in the proportion which the number of such male citizens shall bear to the whole number of male citizens twenty-one years of age in such State.

Section 3

(*Persons Disqualified from Holding Office*)

No person shall be a Senator or Representative in Congress, or elector of President and Vice-President, or hold any office, civil or military, under the United States, or under any State, who, having previously taken an oath, as a member of Congress, or as an officer of the United States, or as a member of any State legislature, or as an executive or judicial officer of any State, to support the Constitution of the United States, shall have engaged in insurrection or rebellion against the same, or given aid or comfort to the enemies thereof. But Congress may by a vote of two-thirds of each House, remove such disability.

Section 4

(*What Public Debts Are Valid*)

The validity of the public debt of the United States, authorized by law, including debts incurred for payment of pensions and bounties for services in suppressing insurrection or rebellion, shall not be questioned. But neither the United States nor any State shall assume or pay any debt or obligation incurred in aid of insurrection or rebellion against the United States, or any claim for the loss or emancipation of any slave; but all such debts, obligations and claims shall be held illegal and void.

Section 5

(*Power to Enforce This Article*)

The Congress shall have power to enforce, by appropriate legislation, the provisions of this article.

AMENDMENT XV

(*Proposed by Congress on February 26, 1869; declared ratified on March 30, 1870.*)

Section 1

(*Negro Suffrage*)

The right of citizens of the United States to vote shall not be denied or abridged by the United States or by any State on account of race, color, or previous condition of servitude.

Section 2

(*Power to Enforce This Article*)

The Congress shall have power to enforce this article by appropriate legislation.

AMENDMENT XVI

(*Proposed by Congress on July 12, 1909; declared ratified on February 25, 1913.*)

(*Authorizing Income Taxes*)

The Congress shall have power to lay and collect taxes on incomes, from whatever source derived, without apportionment among the several States, and without regard to any census or enumeration.

AMENDMENT XVII

(*Proposed by Congress on May 13, 1912; declared ratified on May 31, 1913.*)

(*Popular Election of Senators*)

The Senate of the United States shall be composed of two Senators from each State, elected by the people thereof, for six years; and each Senator shall have one vote. The electors in each State shall have the qualifications requisite for electors of the most numerous branch of the State legislatures.

When vacancies happen in the representation of any State in the Senate, the executive authority of such State shall issue writs of election to fill such vacancies: *Provided,* That the legislature of any State may empower the executive thereof to make temporary appointments until the people fill the vacancies by election as the legislature may direct.

This amendment shall not be so construed as to affect the election or term of any Senator chosen before it becomes valid as part of the Constitution.

AMENDMENT XVIII

(Proposed by Congress on December 18, 1917; declared ratified on January 16, 1919.)

Section 1
(National Liquor Prohibition)
After one year from the ratification of this article the manufacture, sale, or transportation of intoxicating liquors within, the importation thereof into, or the exportation thereof from the United States and all territory subject to the jurisdiction thereof for beverage purposes is hereby prohibited.

Section 2
(Power to Enforce This Article)
The Congress and the several States shall have concurrent power to enforce this article by appropriate legislation.

Section 3
(Ratification Within Seven Years)
This article shall be inoperative unless it shall have been ratified as an amendment to the Constitution by the legislatures of the several States, as provided in the Constitution, within seven years from the date of the submission hereof to the States by the Congress.

AMENDMENT XIX

(Proposed by Congress on June 4, 1919; declared ratified on August 26, 1920.)
(Woman Suffrage)
The right of citizens of the United States to vote shall not be denied or abridged by the United States or by any State on account of sex.

Congress shall have power to enforce this article by appropriate legislation.

AMENDMENT XX

(Proposed by Congress on March 2, 1932; declared ratified on February 6, 1933.)

Section 1
(Terms of Office)
The terms of the President and Vice-President shall end at noon on the 20th day of January, and the terms of Senators and Representatives at noon on the 3rd day of January, of the years in which such terms would have ended if this article had not been ratified; and the terms of their successors shall then begin.

Section 2
(Time of Convening Congress)
The Congress shall assemble at least once in every year, and such meeting shall begin at noon on the 3rd day of January, unless they shall by law appoint a different day.

Section 3
(Death of President Elect)
If, at the time fixed for the beginning of the term of the President, the President elect shall have died, the Vice-President elect shall become President. If a President shall not have been chosen before the time fixed for the beginning of his term, or if the President elect shall have failed to qualify, then the Vice-President elect shall act as President until a President shall have qualified; and the Congress may by law provide for the case wherein neither a President elect nor a Vice-President elect shall have qualified, declaring who shall then act as President, or the manner in which one who is to act shall be selected, and such person shall act accordingly until a President or Vice-President shall have qualified.

Section 4
(Election of the President)
The Congress may by law provide for the case of the death of any of the persons from whom the House of Representatives may choose a President whenever the right of choice shall have devolved upon them, and for the case of the death of any of the persons from whom the Senate may choose a Vice-President whenever the right of choice shall have devolved upon them.

Section 5
Sections 1 and 2 shall take effect on the 15th day of October following the ratification of this article.

Section 6
This article shall be inoperative unless it shall have

been ratified as an amendment to the Constitution by the legislatures of three-fourths of the several States within seven years from the date of its submission.

the legislatures of three-fourths of the several States within seven years from the date of its submission to the States by the Congress.

AMENDMENT XXI

(*Proposed by Congress on February 20, 1933; declared ratified on December 5, 1933.*)

Section 1
(*National Liquor Prohibition Repealed*)
The eighteenth article of amendment to the Constitution of the United States is hereby repealed.

Section 2
(*Transportation of Liquor into "Dry" States*)
The transportation or importation into any States, Territory, or possession of the United States for delivery or use therein of intoxicating liquors, in violation of the laws thereof, is hereby prohibited.

Section 3
This article shall be inoperative unless it shall have been ratified as an amendment to the Constitution by conventions in the several States, as provided in the Constitution, within seven years from the date of the submission hereof to the States by the Congress.

AMENDMENT XXII

(*Proposed by Congress on March 21, 1947; declared ratified on February 26, 1951.*)

Section 1
(*Tenure of President Limited*)
No person shall be elected to the office of the President more than twice, and no person who has held the office of President, or acted as President, for more than two years of a term to which some other person was elected President shall be elected to the office of the President more than once. But this Article shall not apply to any person holding the office of President when this Article was proposed by the Congress, and shall not prevent any person who may be holding the office of President, or acting as President, during the term within which this Article becomes operative from holding the office of President, or acting as President during the remainder of such term.

Section 2
This Article shall be inoperative unless it shall have been ratified as an amendment to the Constitution by

AMENDMENT XXIII

(*Proposed by Congress on June 17, 1960; declared ratified on May 29, 1961.*)

Section 1
(*District of Columbia Suffrage in Presidential Elections*)
The District constituting the seat of Government of the United States shall appoint in such manner as the Congress may direct:

A number of electors of President and Vice-President equal to the whole number of Senators and Representatives in Congress to which the District would be entitled if it were a State, but in no event more than the least populous State; they shall be in addition to those appointed by the States, but they shall be considered, for the purposes of the election of President and Vice-President, to be electors appointed by a State; and they shall meet in the District and perform such duties as provided by the twelfth article of amendment.

Section 2
The Congress shall have power to enforce this article by appropriate legislation.

AMENDMENT XXIV

(*Proposed by Congress on August 27, 1962; declared ratified on January 23, 1964.*)

Section 1
(*Bars Poll Tax in Federal Elections*)
The right of citizens of the United States to vote in any primary or other election for President or Vice-President, for electors for President or Vice-President, or for Senator or Representative in Congress, shall not be denied or abridged by the United States or any State by reason of failure to pay any poll tax or other tax.

Section 2
The Congress shall have power to enforce this article by appropriate legislation.

AMENDMENT XXV

(*Proposed by Congress on July 6, 1965; declared ratified on February 10, 1967.*)

Section 1
(*Succession of Vice-President to Presidency*)

In case of the removal of the President from office or of his death or resignation, the Vice-President shall become President.

Section 2
(*Vacancy in office of Vice-President*)

Whenever there is a vacancy in the office of the Vice-President, the President shall nominate a Vice-President who shall take office upon confirmation by a majority vote of both Houses of Congress.

Section 3
(*Vice-President as Acting President*)

Whenever the President transmits to the President pro tempore of the Senate and the Speaker of the House of Representatives his written declaration that he is unable to discharge the powers and duties of his office, and until he transmits to them a written declaration to the contrary, such powers and duties shall be discharged by the Vice-President as Acting President.

Section 4
(*Vice-President as Acting President*)

Whenever the Vice-President and a majority of either the principal officers of the executive departments or of such other body as Congress may by law provide, transmit to the President pro tempore of the Senate and the Speaker of the House of Representatives their written declaration that the President is unable to discharge the powers and duties of his office, the Vice-President shall immediately assume the powers and duties of the office as Acting President.

Thereafter, when the President transmits to the President pro tempore of the Senate and the Speaker of the House of Representatives his written declaration that no inability exists, he shall resume the powers and duties of his office unless the Vice-President and a majority of either the principal officers of the executive department or of such other body as Congress may by law provide, transmit within four days to the President pro tempore of the Senate and the Speaker of the House of Representatives their written declaration that the President is unable to discharge the powers and duties of his office. Thereupon Congress shall decide the issue, assembling within forty-eight hours for that purpose if not in session. If the Congress, within twenty-one days after receipt of the latter written declaration, or, if Congress is not in session, within twenty-one days after Congress is required to assemble, determines by two-thirds vote of both Houses that the President is unable to discharge the powers and duties of his office, the Vice-President shall continue to discharge the same as Acting President; otherwise, the President shall resume the powers and duties of his office.

AMENDMENT XXVI

(*Proposed by Congress on March 23, 1971; declared ratified on July 5, 1971.*)

Section 1
(*Lowers Voting Age to 18 Years*)

The right of citizens of the United States, who are eighteen years of age or older, to vote shall not be denied or abridged by the United States or by any State on account of age.

Section 2
The Congress shall have power to enforce this article by appropriate legislation.

adjudication This is a technical term that refers to the power to interpret and apply the law in cases of legal dispute. It is what courts do when they "judge" the application of a law in a particular case.

adversary process In the American legal system, the judge or jury makes a decision based on the arguments and evidence presented in court. The back and forth arguments—the presenting of testimony and the cross-examination of witnesses—is the adversary process.

advice and consent Senatorial power, granted in Article 2, Section 2 of the Constitution, to approve presidential treaties and certain presidential appointments such as ambassadors and justices of the Supreme Court. Treaties require a two-thirds vote of the Senate for ratification.

affirmative action The requirement that an organization such as a school or business or government agency take action to increase the number of women or blacks or other minorities in its program or members. Sometimes called *reverse discrimination*, affirmative action is an attempt to compensate for earlier periods of racial or sexual discrimination.

agenda The list of items to be considered at a meeting or legislative session; more generally, the list of politically relevant issues.

agenda setters People who bring new issues before the public and the government.

alienation A sense of hostility to the political process.

amendment An alteration or addition to a bill, motion, or constitution. Congressional bills may be amended at virtually any point before they are passed. As specified in Article 5 of the Constitution, constitutional amendments may be proposed by a two-thirds vote of both houses of Congress or by a convention assembled by Congress at the request of the legislatures of two-thirds of the states. To be ratified, a constitutional amendment must be approved by the legislatures of three-fourths of the states or by conventions called for that purpose in three-fourths of the states.

anti-Federalists Political figures who argued against the adoption of the Constitution, and subsequently argued against allowing the central government to gain powers over the states and over individual citizens (cf. Federalists).

appellate power A legal procedure in which a case is carried from a lower court to a higher court for review or reexamination. It is the power of a higher court to review decisions of a lower court.

appropriation Congressional legislation that says how much will be spent for a particular program or project. What is actually appropriated is usually less than what was initially authorized (cf. authorization).

Articles of Confederation The rules (or "constitution") under which the United States was governed in the period after independence until the Constitutional Convention and the ratification of the U.S. Constitution.

authorization Congressional legislation that says how much might be spent for a particular program or project (cf. appropriation).

bad tendency A test sometimes used by the Supreme Court to see whether an act or speech ought to be protected under the First Amendment. The test is whether the speech might in the long run have consequences that should be barred.

Bill of Rights The first 10 amendments to the U.S. Constitution, added to the Constitution very soon after the Constitution itself was adopted. The Bill of Rights includes a listing of the specific freedoms that were to be protected against government action: freedom of press, speech, assembly, petition, and religion.

block grant Grant-in-aid from the federal government to state or local government for a general purpose.

budget A statement of estimated income and expenses. The president is responsible for preparing the annual budget of the federal government.

bureaucracy An administrative organization characterized by formal structure, hierarchy, and the use of formal rules.

capitalism An economic system based on private ownership of land and natural resources and of the means of production, distribution, and exchange, in which there is a minimum of government interference in the economy.

categorical grant Grant-in-aid from federal government to state or local government for a specific purpose.

caucus Meeting of party leaders or activists; sometimes used as the means for selecting party candidates.

centralization The gravitation of political power and decision-making responsibility from units or agencies that are geographically small or functionally specific to ones that are larger or more general (cf. decentralization).

checks and balances The principle according to which various government institutions exercise certain checks on the activities of other government institutions. Examples of this system include the president's power to veto acts of Congress and the courts' power to declare legislative acts unconstitutional.

citizen-initiated contact Activity by an individual citizen to present point of view to government official; allows citizens to express individual views.

civil liberties Liberties guaranteed to the individual by the First Amendment to the Constitution: freedom of speech, press, and assembly.

class consciousness Common sense of identification of members of the same class; usually refers to the working class.

clear and present danger Test sometimes used by Supreme Court to see whether a speech or act ought to be protected under the First Amendment. The test is whether the bad effects of the speech would both be illegal and would happen before further arguments could be made.

closed primary An election in which a party's candidates are selected and in which the participants include only those who have declared themselves to be party members or supporters (cf. direct primary).

collective good A benefit available to everyone in society regardless of whether any particular individual worked toward the attainment of that benefit.

commerce clause This clause from Article 1 of the Constitution grants to Congress the authority to regulate commerce with foreign nations and among the several states. It is this clause which has allowed Congress to exercise considerable powers over the economic life of the nation.

communism The economic system in which there is communal rather than private ownership of property and the means of production.

concurrent majority The idea that a majority of the citizens of the United States cannot determine the policy followed within a particular region; a majority of the citizens of that region must concur.

confederation A government in which most powers are in the hands of states, with limited power in the hands of the central government.

conference committee A joint Senate–House committee convened to reconcile the differences between the versions of a bill passed by the Senate and the House of Representatives.

Congressional Budget Office Established in 1974, this office, staffed by professional economists and analysts, provides to Congress the means by which to evaluate its own budget proposals and those of the president.

congressional oversight Process by which Congress supervises the activities of bureaucratic agencies.

Connecticut Compromise The delegate agreement reached at the Constitutional Convention that Congress would consist of two chambers: the House of Representatives, in which the size of state delegations would be fixed according to population, and the Senate, in which each state, regardless of population, would be represented equally.

constituency The district represented by a legislator; in broader terms, the set of interests represented by a government unit such as a congressional committee or an executive agency.

constituency pressure The idea that constituents put pressure on their elected representatives to support particular legislation.

Constitutional Convention Held in Philadelphia in the summer of 1787, this was the convention of leading political figures that produced the Constitution under which the United States is still being governed.

dealignment A movement away from the political parties, where more citizens become independent voters and parties less important in elections.

decentralization The process of passing political power and decision-making responsibility from larger political units or agencies to ones that serve smaller geographic areas or narrower functional constituencies (cf. centralization).

decision The point at which a pattern of government activity changes (cf. policy).

deficit spending When the government spends more than it takes in in taxes. The economist John Maynard Keynes argued that deficit spending could stimulate employment and increase the demand for goods and services, what is sometimes called "spending your way out of a recession."

deviating election An election that temporarily changes the balance of political forces (cf. maintaining election, realignment).

direct primary An intraparty election in which the voters choose the candidates who will run on a party's ticket in the forthcoming general election (cf. closed primary).

dual federalism The doctrine that the states and the nation have separate areas of responsibility (cf. cooperative federalism).

due process of law The protection, guaranteed in the Fifth and Fourteenth Amendments to the Constitution, that acts of government that would deprive the individual of life, liberty, or property cannot be arbitrary but must be in accordance with established judicial procedures.

electoral accountability The principle according to which officials in a democracy are held responsible (accountable) for their actions by those who elected or appointed them. Competitive elections are the major means by which accountability is enforced.

Electoral College The body of electors from each state who, after a presidential election, actually choose the new president and vice-president. Each state selects a slate of electors in the November election. Normally they vote as a unit for the candidates who received a plurality of the vote in that state in the general election. The candidates who receive the majority of the electoral votes, who may or may not be the same as those who received the nationwide plurality of popular votes, become the president and vice-president.

equality of condition The idea that citizens should enjoy equal condition with respect to, say, education or health. That is, the equality of education or health care should be the same for all citizens (cf. equality of opportunity).

equality of opportunity The idea that all citizens should have an equal opportunity to compete for unequal rewards. Some education will be better than other education, some jobs better than others, etc. There should be no arbitrary barriers (such as race restrictions) between a citizen and his or her opportunity to seek the best education or the best jobs.

equal protection of the laws Phrase in the Fourteenth Amendment used recently by the Supreme Court to require states to provide equal treatment to citizens in a variety of areas.

ethnic group A group whose members share such traits as national background, religion, customs, culture, language, or historical experience. Catholic Americans of eastern or sourthern European origin are sometimes referred to as "ethnics."

executive privilege The argument that certain records or conversations within the executive branch are "privileged" and need not be shared with Congress.

Executive privilege is customarily used in matters relating to national security, but sometimes it has been broadly construed by a president, leading to an impasse between the executive and legislative branches. President Nixon, for instance, claimed executive privilege during the Watergate hearings in an attempt to keep the tape recordings of conversations in the White House from being released to congressional committees set up to investigate Watergate.

faction A term used used by Madison in *Federalist No. 10* to refer to what we might today call interest groups or pressure groups. This might also be thought of as a political party, although Madison would not have had in mind the large organized political parties we know today.

Federalist or *The Federalist Papers* A series of essays written by Alexander Hamilton, James Madison, and John Jay in defense of the newly drafted U.S. Constitution.

Federalists Defended the growth of centralized (or federal) power in the United States (cf. anti-Federalist).

federation A government in which powers are shared between a central government and state governments.

feminists Supporters of women's rights and liberation.

filibuster Obstruction of Senate action on a bill by the use of dilatory tactics. A common filibuster technique is to take advantage of the Senate's provision for unlimited debate in order to "talk a bill to death."

fiscal policy The use of economic tools to adjust taxes, increase or decrease government spending on public projects, balance the federal budget, or engage in deficit spending in order to stabilize the national economy or to spur economic growth.

floor leaders Party leaders, one from each party in each house of Congress, who are responsible for marshaling the party's forces in legislative battles.

fragmentation of powers A general term which describes how power *within* government is fragmented through the system of federalism and the system of separation of powers; that is, through dividing powers between the central government and the states and among the three branches of government.

gerrymandering Drawing the boundaries of legislative districts in an unnatural way in order to gain partisan advantage.

Great Depression The period in American history, starting with the stock market crash in 1929, when employment and business activity sharply declined and remained low. Prior to the depression the government had not tried to manage the economy, but the depression convinced many persons that the economy was not self-adjusting and some external (government) direction was necessary.

gross national product (GNP)   This is the dollar figure obtained by adding together the value of all the consumption goods, services, and investments produced by the society in a specified time period. It is the most common measure of economic activity and tells us whether the society is expanding or contracting.

impeachment   A formal accusation of a public official for misconduct in office, made by the lower house of a legislature (a necessary step before the accused can be tried by the upper house of the legislature).

implied-powers doctrine   The judicial doctrine that the government not only has the powers delegated to it by the Constitution but also the powers implied by those duties which are expressly delegated. The government has the delegated power to raise armies and navies; it therefore has the implied power to draft persons into the armed forces. In other words, specific responsibilities imply the exercise of other powers for their implementation.

incremental policymaking   A form of planning in which problems are approached one step at a time.

incumbency effect   Incumbents are persons holding an office. The chances that an incumbent member of Congress will gain reelection are much higher than the chances of a challenger unseating an incumbent.

independent regulatory commission   An agency, such as the Securities and Exchange Commission, set up outside the major executive departments and responsible for regulating a given sector of the economy. An independent regulatory commission is generally shielded from partisan politics and from presidential control.

independent voter   A voter who identifies with neither major political party and votes on a case-by-case basis according to the specific candidates or issues involved in a given race.

individualistic equality   A belief that all individuals have an opportunity to improve their station in life through their own efforts.

inequality of distance   A term that refers to the gap in income between the rich and the poor in a society.

inequality of scope   A term that refers to the ways in which the rich are better off than the poor.

inflation   An economic situation in which an increase in prices is accompanied by a loss of purchasing power.

intensity of preferences   Citizens differ in the extent to which they feel intensely about issues. Those with more intense preferences are likely to be more active.

interest group   An organized group that uses various techniques to influence government policy; also referred to as a pressure group or lobby.

Jacksonian democracy   Democratizing movement of the early nineteenth century that expanded participation.

Jim Crow law   Any of a variety of laws passed by southern states requiring segregation of blacks and whites.

judicial review   This term usually refers to the power of the courts to decide whether a legislative act is unconstitutional, and to declare it void if it is deemed unconstitutional. It is also the power of the higher courts (especially the Supreme Court) to overrule lower-court decisions.

laissez faire   The French term "let alone." Refers to the economic doctrine of keeping government intervention in economic matters to a minimum; sometimes used as a synonym for a free market economy.

legal citizenship   The idea that all citizens are equal before the law, and that all citizens should enjoy due process of law and basic civil rights.

legitimacy   When we speak of legitimate authority, we speak of authority which is generally accepted as proper and lawful and which should be accepted by the citizens over whom it is exercised.

libel and slander   Statements, either written (libel) or oral (slander), that defame the character of a person without justification.

lobbies   A term for interest groups.

lobbyist   An individual, often representing an interest group, who seeks to influence the contents of pending legislation, the outcomes of legislative votes, or the decisions of executive agencies.

maintaining election   An election that maintains the existing balance of political forces (cf. deviating election, realignment).

majority rule   The principle that the will of the greater number, a number over 50 percent, shall prevail in making political decisions and in choosing public officials (cf. plurality).

mandate uncertainty   The difficulty experienced by elected officials in determining the preferences of their constituents.

monetarism   An economic doctrine emphasizing the importance of the money supply to economic performance. Monetarists argue that instability in the money supply interferes with the ability of the economy to regulate its own prices, employment, and levels of productivity.

monopoly When a particular industrial sector—such as petroleum or computers—comes under the control of just one giant corporation. When a few giant corporations control a sector, we refer to "oligopoly."

muckraking Investigative reporting in the early part of the twentieth century that uncovered much government corruption.

national convention Large meeting of party delegates to select a presidential nominee.

national-security state In connection with the United States, usually refers to the period from the early 1950s to the present, during which much of the activity of the state, and much of the public treasury, has been directed toward security issues, especially toward the perceived threat of the Soviet Union to either U.S. territory or the American way of life.

national supremacy This refers to the supremacy clause of the Constitution (Article IV), which provides that the Constitution and laws passed by the national government under its constitutional powers, as well as all treaties, are the supreme law of the land.

necessary and proper clause Sometimes called the "elastic clause" because it can be stretched. It is the final paragraph of Article I, Section 8, of the Constitution. The clause authorizes Congress to pass all laws "necessary and proper" to carry out the congressional powers granted to Congress by the Constitution.

New Deal Coalition Political coalition of northern workers, urban ethnic groups, Catholics, Jews, blacks, and southern whites that grew out of the depression of the 1930s and supported the Democratic party.

New Federalism Program instituted under President Reagan to return responsibility for many social programs to the states.

opinion leaders More informed and active citizens whose opinions others follow.

PACs Political action committees formed by businesses and other groups to support political candidates.

party identification Identification of an individual with one or the other political parties; often a long-term commitment.

party platform Official set of positions taken by political party before an election.

party regular Party activists more interested in party success and electoral victory than in particular issues.

patronage The power to make partisan appointments or to distribute, on a partisan basis, various jobs, franchises, contracts, or favors.

pluralism A political system with many groups that are free to compete, where those groups in fact compete and receive some response from the government.

plurality The largest number of votes. When more than two strong candidates run for a given office, the winner will usually have a plurality rather than a majority (cf. majority rule).

pocket veto A presidential power that amounts to an effective veto over legislation passed at the end of a legislative session. If the president holds a piece of legislation without signing or vetoing it for ten days—and Congress adjourns during that time—then the bill does not become law.

policy A long-term commitment of the government to a pattern of activity (cf. decision).

political citizenship The idea that all citizens should have an equal right to participate in the political life of the nation, by voting or by running for office.

political economy Refers to the interaction between and intersection of the political order (government, state agencies, etc.) and the economic system (the market, private ownership, etc.).

political efficacy A citizen's belief that he or she can influence the affairs of government by his or her own actions.

political mobilization Process of arousing the political activity of formerly inactive citizens.

political participation Activities by citizens aimed at informing government leaders of the interests of citizens and pressuring them to act on those interests.

political party Organization whose purpose is to run and win elections.

political socialization The process by which young people learn basic political beliefs.

pork barrel projects These are projects of specific benefit to a particular constituency, such as a dam or military installation or government contract. Pork barrel legislation, then, is legislation that provides the benefits to the constituency of a particular member of Congress.

preferred position The doctrine that free speech deserves special protection by the Supreme Court.

presidency The term used to describe the network of persons and offices—the White House staff, the Executive Office, the National Security Council, the Council of Economic Advisers—which directly participate in making up the president's program.

president pro tempore The presiding officer of the Senate in the absence of the vice-president. The president pro tem is always from the majority party in the Senate, regardless of the party of the vice-president.

pressure group Another term for an interest group.

primary election Election in which party supporters choose their party's nominee for political office. Presidential primaries that choose convention delegates pledged to a particular candidate have become more common.

prior restraint The attempt to block publication of material (e.g., by a newspaper) in advance.

proportional representation An electoral system in which legislative seats are apportioned to parties or factions according to their approximate electoral strength.

public opinion The attitudes of the public on some issue.

public-opinion poll Systematic sample of public opinion.

pure, or direct, democracy Often used in contrast to representative democracy. In a pure democracy the citizens would vote directly on public policy questions, whereas in a representative democracy the citizens normally vote for their representatives who in turn decide the public policy questions.

rational voter Well-informed voter who decides on the basis of a calculation of which candidate will best meet his or her policy preferences.

realignment An election in which the party that had more faithful supporters than the second party loses its advantage and becomes the minority party. This happens when many new voters identify with what had previously been the minority party or when large numbers of voters change party allegiance (cf. deviating election, maintaining election).

representation, or representative democracy A system of government in which the citizens select representatives, usually through a competitive election, who in turn decide on matters of public policy.

retrospective voting Voting decisions made on the basis of an evaluation of the performance of the previous administration.

revenue sharing A program under which federal funds are distributed to state and local governments for them to use in high-priority areas such as health care or public safety.

Rules Committee The Rules Committee of the House of Representatives often attaches a "rule" to a bill reported to the Floor for debate. This rule provides special procedures on how long the debate can continue, whether amendments can be introduced, and so forth.

rules of the democratic game The key features of democracy, such as freedom of speech and free elections.

scarce resources A term often used by economists to describe something which is valued by people but which is not available in sufficient supply to satisfy the demand for it. It is a very inclusive term which can refer to anything from living space to medical care. The study of economics is sometimes described as the study of how scarce resources are allocated.

selective benefits Benefits that are received by individuals only if they take part in some organization or activity.

seniority The traditional congressional practice of awarding a committee chair to the member of the majority party with the longest uninterrupted service on that committee. A few successful challenges to this practice have occurred in recent years.

separation of powers The principle according to which government power is shared by the three branches of government—legislative, executive, and judicial.

single-member district An electoral system where one person is elected in a district, the victory going to the candidate with the most votes.

Snowbelt States of the upper Midwest and Northeast that have been declining recently in population and industry.

social citizenship The idea that citizenship includes social well-being and security against economic injustice, and thus citizens should have equal access to a job, decent housing, adequate health care, education, and so forth.

social-welfare state This general term summarizes a large number of government programs which provide such social rights as a useful job, decent housing, adequate food, educational opportunities, and security against the threat of illness, unemployment, and old age.

Speaker of the House The presiding officer and in general the most powerful member of the House of Representatives. The Speaker is elected by the entire House but is actually chosen by a caucus of the representatives from the majority party.

standard operating procedures (SOPs) Routine ways in which bureaucracies carry out functions. Provides regularity to their functions but can produce rigidity.

standing committee A permanent committee in the Senate or the House of Representatives.

standing to sue A person can go to court in the United States only with "standing to sue," that is, the ability to show that his or her interest has been harmed or is under threat.

stare decisis The principle that past decisions should be used as guidelines in ruling on similar cases.

State of the Union address An annual speech to Congress in which the president assesses the problems that face the nation and presents a legislative program to deal with them.

subcommittee The standing committees of Congress generally are so large and have such complicated agendas that the work must be further subdivided and specialized, which has led to the vast array of subcommittees of Congress, where most of the work of Congress actually takes place.

subsidy   A general term to describe government support for private enterprise or private citizens—such as tax subsidies or benefit programs or cash payments directly from the government to citizens.

substantive due process   Until the late nineteenth century the phrase "due process of law" primarily meant that government could not deprive citizens of property or personal rights without following proper procedures. Beginning in the late nineteenth century, however, the courts began to use the due process clause in connection with the substance of laws as well as the procedures they invoked. Thus the Supreme Court could declare unconstitutional any law that it considered to be an unreasonable restraint on property or personal freedom.

suffrage   The right to vote.

Sunbelt   States of the South and Southwest currently growing in population and industry.

supply-side economics   A term popularized during the 1980 presidential campaign of Ronald Reagan. Reagan's initial presidential budget (in 1981) was widely described as a supply-side budget. If government reduces taxes, citizens will invest in economic activities. This investment will lead to economic growth which in turn will produce jobs and additional resources for the society.

tariff   A tax on imports that protects domestic products from foreign competition by raising the prices of foreign products.

third party   A party that challenges the two main parties in an election.

three-fifths compromise   The agreement reached at the Constitutional Convention that slaves would be counted as three-fifths of one person in apportioning seats in the House of Representatives.

tyranny of the majority   This term points out that in a democracy the majority can hold unreasonable power over the minority. The majority of voters would be acting tyrannically, for instance, if they were to deny freedom of speech or press or assembly to those whose political views were in the minority.

unitary government   A government in which all powers lie in the central government and none in local governments.

veto   The power to deny, usually used in connection with presidential veto, which is the power of the president to reject a congressional act. A presidential veto can be overruled by a two-thirds majority of Congress.

War for Independence, or the **Revolutionary War**   The revolt of the American colonies against the political control of Great Britain. Fighting broke out in 1775; and on July 4, 1776, the Declaration of Independence was proclaimed.

Watergate scandal   The general term used to refer to the political scandals that led to the resignation of Richard Nixon from the presidency. The term comes from the Watergate complex in Washington, D.C., a complex of hotel rooms, shops, and offices. The Democratic National Committee had offices there during the 1972 election campaign; there was an attempt to wiretap this office. The persons caught in this attempt were eventually traced back to the campaign of President Nixon.

whip   An assistant floor leader, selected in a party caucus in either house of Congress, who is responsible for acting as a liaison between party leaders and party members and for making sure party members are present for crucial votes.

Photo Credits

The numbers of the pages on which the photos appear are printed in **bold.** The credits are listed in order of appearance.

Part One opener **xiv** Granger. **3** Bettmann Newsphotos. **7** © Maher, Stock, Boston. **9** Franken, Stock, Boston. **14** Richard Lawrence Stack, Black Star. **17** Franken, Stock, Boston. **21** Granger. **22** Anderson, Art Resource. **24** Bettmann Newsphotos. **42** Brown Brothers. **45** Historical Pictures Service. **47** Granger. **48** Library of Congress. **48** Boston Atheneum. **51** Bettmann Newsphotos. **65** Johnson, Southern Light. **66** (*Above and below, left*) Bettmann Newsphotos; (*below, right*) Wide World. **71** Granger. **73** Wide World. **74** Granger.

Part Two opener **80** Bettmann Archive. **83** Wide World. **92** Richard Stromberg. **93** Wolinsky, Stock, Boston. **98** Wide World. **102** Lejeune, Stock, Boston. **105** United Press International. **110, 111** Library of Congress. **113** Kroll, Taurus. **115** Wide World. **121** National Archives. **128** (*Left*) © 1976, Ellen Shub, The Picture Cube; (*right*) Antman, The Image Works. **130** Bettmann Archive. **131** Carl Iwesaki, LIFE Magazine, © Time, Inc. **132** Adelman, Magnum. **133** Wide World. **136** Franken, Stock, Boston. **151** National Archives. **156** Bettmann Newsphotos. **161** United Press International. **166** Wide World. **168** (*Left*) Richard Stromberg; (*right*) Jim Anderson, Black Star. **172** © Flynn, Stock, Boston. **180** (*Left*) Flip Schulke, LIFE Magazine, © Time, Inc. **186** Granger.

Part Three opener **188** Bettmann Archive. **191** Franken, Stock, Boston. **202** (*Above*) © 1981, Levick, Black Star; (*below*) Wide World. **210, 211** Wide World. **215** © 1979, Fishman, Woodfin Camp. **217** Granger. **218** © Mansfield, The Image Works. **223** Mark Godfrey, Archive Pictures, Inc. **229** (*Left*) Robert V. Eckert, Jr., Stock, Boston); (*right*) Danny Lyon, © 1969, Magnum. **240** © Druskis, Taurus. **244** (*Left*) Granger; (*right*) Bob East, Miami Herald. **252** © Kennard, Stock, Boston. **253** Wide World. **257** Granger. **259** © U.S. Chamber of Commerce. **263** Bettmann Newsphotos. **266** United Press International. **268** Wide World. **270** Bettmann Newsphotos. **274** George Tames, NYT Pictures. **279** © Ellen Shub. **280** Bill Snead, The Washington Post. **285** Wide World. **287** Bettmann Newsphotos. **294** Bettmann Archive. **296** Bettmann Newsphotos. **307** Wide World. **315** Bettman Newsphotos. **320** Granger. **321** Bettmann Archive. **322** Bettmann Newsphotos. **323** Franken, Stock, Boston. **328** Bettmann Newsphotos. **330** Milwaukee Journal Photo. **337** Paul Conklin. **347** (*Above, left and right*) Wide World; (*center, right*) Bettmann Newsphotos; (*below*) Sygma. **348** Evans, Sygma. **349** Collection of the Boatmen's National Bank of St. Louis. **367** Wide World. **385** Bettmann Newsphotos. **389** © 1979, Roth, The Picture Cube. **392** Wide World.

Part Four opener **394** Bettmann Newsphotos. **397** © 1985, MacLean, The Picture Cube. **400** Charles Harbutt, Archive Pictures, Inc. **405, 406** Wide World. **407** Bettmann Newsphotos. **408** (*Left and right*) Wide World. **409** Terry Arthur, The White House. **414** © Menzel, Stock, Boston. **423** © Johnson, Southern Light. **429** Bettmann Newsphotos. **435** Herwig, The Picture Cube. **438, 453** Bettmann Newsphotos. **456** © Holland, Stock, Boston. **467** © Bennett, Southern Light. **468** The New York Historical Society. **469** Brown Brothers. **474** Brack, Black Star. **477** Courtesy FDR Library. **482** Bettmann Newsphotos. **487** Library of Congress. **488** Paul Conklin. **491, 493** Bettmann Newsphotos. **505** Bettmann Archive. **512** AP Wirephoto. **517** Malloch, © Magnum. **524** © Heyman, Archive Pictures, Inc. **531** © Grace, Stock, Boston. **535** © 1978, Brack, Black Star. **536, 538** Bettmann Newsphotos. **540** Granger. **544** Wide World. **551** © Supreme Court Historical Society. **554** Wide World. **556, 567** © Supreme Court Historical Society. **570** Fred Ward, Black Star. **571** Wide World.

An attempt has been made to obtain permission from all suppliers of photographs used in this edition. Some sources have not been located, but permission will be requested from them upon notification to us of their ownership of the material.

INDEX

597